Advanced Microeconomics

Advanced Microeconomics presents microeconomic problems in an intuitive way. Using lucid narratives to build on students' initial understanding of economics and economic reality, equations and diagrams are incorporated to provide accessibility to students with a basic level of calculus to reach precise quantitative answers. It covers the standard areas of microeconomics such as consumer theory, producer theory, economics of uncertainty, general equilibrium and markets.

The book also includes new developments such as behavioural economics, prospect and regret theory, public-sector firms, bargaining, signalling games, adverse selection and moral hazard. Real-life applications are given throughout the chapters, clearly showing students how the advanced theory connects to the real world. Each chapter provides a set of exercises for independent problem-solving. Learning is also supported by lists of key terms, chapter summaries and further reading suggestions. Advanced technical materials are presented in optional appendices. Digital supplements include quiz questions, solutions to exercises and instructor materials. The flexible chapter sequencing in the book enables instructors to create their preferred syllabus.

Developing students' intuitive appreciation for the theory as well as mathematical analysis, this is the ideal textbook for microeconomics courses at master's level (MSc and MRes) and advanced undergraduate level.

Bibhas Saha is Associate Professor (Reader) in the Department of Economics, Durham University, UK.

"Ideal for one semester intensive course in microeconomics at the master's/advanced undergraduate level. It covers core topics and information economics using game theory with many applications. Exposition is well-structured, aimed at conveying basic ideas in a free-flowing intuitive style with simple maths and graphs."

Parimal Bag, *National University of Singapore, Singapore*

"An outstanding textbook for advanced undergraduate and master's economics teaching, Prof Saha has successfully covered many important topics that guide an economics student's foundational learning and bring them a step closer to the tools and ideas of modern micro-economic theory."

Jaideep Roy, *University of Bath, UK*

"Even in the somewhat crowded world of advanced textbooks in microeconomics, this book deserves a prominent niche of its own. It incorporates many recent developments typically left out in standard texts. The exposition, while formally rigorous, is lucid and reader-friendly."

Indraneel Dasgupta, *Indian Statistical Institute, Kolkata, India*

Advanced Microeconomics

Theory, Applications and New Developments

Bibhas Saha

Routledge
Taylor & Francis Group
LONDON AND NEW YORK

Designed cover image: Getty Images

First published 2025
by Routledge
4 Park Square, Milton Park, Abingdon, Oxon OX14 4RN

and by Routledge
605 Third Avenue, New York, NY 10158

Routledge is an imprint of the Taylor & Francis Group, an informa business

British Library Cataloguing-in-Publication Data
A catalogue record for this book is available from the British Library

Library of Congress Cataloging-in-Publication Data
Names: Saha, Bibhas, author.
Title: Advanced microeconomics : theory, applications and new developments / Bibhas Saha.
Description: 1 edition. | New York, NY : Routledge, 2024. | Includes bibliographical references and index.
Identifiers: LCCN 2023059331 | ISBN 9781032129532 (hardback) | ISBN 9781032129501 (paperback) | ISBN 9781003226994 (ebook)
Subjects: LCSH: Microeconomics.
Classification: LCC HB172 .S1274 2024 | DDC 338.5—dc23/eng/20240223
LC record available at https://lccn.loc.gov/2023059331

ISBN: 978-1-032-12953-2 (hbk)
ISBN: 978-1-032-12950-1 (pbk)
ISBN: 978-1-003-22699-4 (ebk)

DOI: 10.4324/9781003226994

Typeset in Times New Roman
by Apex CoVantage, LLC

Access the Support Material: www.routledge.com/9781032129501

To
Dipti and Tuli

Contents

Figures

Tables

Preface

Why write another micro book for graduate students? Aren't there many excellent textbooks around? Yes, there are. But most of them have been written for students who are either already in a doctoral programme or on their way to one. There is a vast majority of undergraduate students who are undecided about doing PhD or going into the job market. For them, a master's programme provides a window of thinking through career options while picking up new skills and knowledge. Experience has convinced me that the standard graduate textbooks tend to dissuade them from further studying economics by demanding a disproportionately serious commitment to learn technical rigours of microeconomics ahead of intuitive reasoning and finding relevance. At the master's level, students do not have much time to make such commitments.

I have written this book with these students in mind. They can benefit on two counts. First, the technical rigour of this book is a significant step-up from their undergraduate study, but by no means will it be overwhelming. The extensive use of graphs and basic calculus will make them feel comfortable. Second, topics have been introduced with a lucid narrative. Many applications and new developments have been incorporated to show how many directions are available to them. Some of these directions are household welfare, behavioural economics, competition policy, labour economics, public economics and international trade.

The book contains 15 chapters, which is just about right for a typical master's programme taught within 10 to 15 lecture weeks (roughly 20 to 30 hours in total, excluding tutorial classes). Teachers can be selective. To give an example, if one wishes to cover less of demand theory and teach more of firms and market competition, one can manage with Chapter 3 (skipping Chapters 1 and 2 if needed). In another sequence, if one is more interested in behavioural economics and decision theory, then the first five chapters and the seventh chapter are must. Chapter 6 is a stand-alone chapter. So are Chapter 12 on bargaining and Chapter 14 on the principal–agent problems. These two are extremely appealing to students.

I owe thanks to a number of organisations and people. First, I gratefully acknowledge the permissions given by various publishers to adapt materials from their publications (books and journals). I have included a separate list to provide the details of these sources. I thank Natalie Tomlinson (formerly of Routledge) for getting the project started and especially Michelle Gallagher and Chloe Herbert of Routledge, Taylor & Francis, for guiding me to its completion. I am also grateful to the anonymous reviewers for their comments and suggestions, all of which I tried to incorporate as far as possible. Of course, all errors (if any) are mine.

I had the privilege of learning economics from so many wonderful teachers. My special thanks go to Daniel F. Spulber for introducing the economics of regulation, bargaining and non-linear pricing, which shaped my research interest in my formative years. A number of teachers influenced my own teaching and interest in economic theory. They are Wayne Shafer at

University of Southern California, (late) Arup Mallick of Calcutta University and Ganapati Majumdar and Ajit Haldar of Burdwan Raj college, India. I thank them all.

My co-authors have taught me quite a few things. Parimal Bag of National University of Singapore introduced me to economics of betting, and Jaideep Roy of the University of Bath, UK got me interested in political economy. My students, especially at Indira Gandhi Institute of Development Research, India, and Durham University have always been very supportive and their enthusiasm encouraged me to experiment, the end result of which is this book.

Last, but not least, I thank my wife and my daughter for their enthusiasm and unconditional support. They will be the happiest persons to see this book in print.

Bibhas Saha
Norwich, UK
December 2023

Acknowledgements

I gratefully acknowledge permissions from the following publishers to re-use or adapt some parts of the following books and articles. Their permissions in no way imply endorsement of my reused/adapted version. The original sources have been duly acknowledged in the relevant chapters of the book.

1. W. W. Norton: for some parts of Varian, H. (1992). *Microeconomic Analysis*, 3rd ed. New York: Norton.
2. Oxford Publishing Ltd.: for some parts of Mas-Colell, A., Whinston, M. D. & Green, J. R. (1995). *Microeconomic Theory*. New York: Oxford University Press.
3. Blackwell Publishing Ltd., (Rightsholder: Oxford University Press—Journals): Fudenberg, D. & Tirole, J. (1983). Sequential bargaining with incomplete information. *The Review of Economic Studies*, 50, 221–247.
4. Blackwell Publishing Ltd., (Rightsholder: John Wiley & Sons—Books):
   (a) Crawford, V. & Sobel, J. (1982). Strategic information transmission. *Econometrica*, 50(6), 1431–1451.
   (b) Kahneman, D. & Tversky, A. (1979). Prospect theory: An analysis of risk under uncertainty. *Econometrica*, 47(2), 263–291.
5. Oxford University Press: Bag, P. K. & Saha, B. (2017b). Corrupt bookmaking in a fixed odds illegal betting market. *Economic Journal*, 127(601), 624–652.
6. John Wiley & Sons:
   (a) Bag, P. K. & Saha, B. (2017a). Match-fixing in a monopoly betting market. *Journal of Economics & Management Strategy*, 26(1), 257–289.
   (b) Chatterjee, I. & Saha, B. (2017). Bilateral delegation in duopoly wage and employment bargaining. *Managerial & Decision Economics*, 38(4), 607–621.
   (c) Pal, R. & Saha, B. (2014). Mixed duopoly and environment. *Journal of Public Economic Theory*, 16, 96–118.
   (d) Saha, B. (1995). Side choice and bargaining under asymmetric information. *Economica*, 62, 521–539.
7. Elsevier Publications:
   (a) Kumar, A. & Saha, B. (2008). Spatial competition in a mixed duopoly with one partially privatized firm. *Journal of Comparative Economics*, 36(2), 326–341.
   (b) Saha, B. (2001). Red tape, incentive bribe and the provision of subsidy. *Journal of Development Economics*, 65, 113–133.

Chapter 1

Budget set

Abstract

A consumer's capacity to buy describes her place in the market economy. The budget set generated by the consumer's income and the prices of goods shows how many goods the consumer can buy and in what quantities. The frontier of the budget set is called the budget line. It is so called because its most common representation is linear due to the assumption that prices are invariant to the volumes bought. But in the real world, prices commonly vary with the quantities bought, as seen in bulk discounts, rationing, overtime wages, unemployment allowance and so on. When such considerations are taken into account, the budget constraint becomes non-linear. Furthermore, the idea of budget can be extended to cases in which income is not given exogenously or income may not necessarily be cash in hand. We also demonstrate that the budget set for the context in which the characteristics of the goods, rather than the quantities of the goods, are what the consumer cares about.

Keywords: Rationing, Bulk discount, Endowment income, Inter-temporal budget

1.1 Introduction

Consumerism defines modern life. In our smartphones, we carry a digital wallet so that we can instantly order anything we fancy via the Amazon app. The act of buying has become many times more varied and pervasive since the days of Andy Warhol, the American artist whose iconic 1962 paintings of Campbell's soup cans and Coca-Cola bottles celebrated consumerism. Of course, at that point, in one academic discipline, the idea of a 'consumer' and her acts of making choices had already been fully formalised. In fact, the concept was developed precisely 100 years ago in the writings of William Stanley Jevons (1862) and John Stuart Mill (1863), which, in turn, were founded upon the principle of utilitarianism proposed another hundred years earlier by Jeremy Bentham and James Mill. That discipline is economics.

At the heart of economics, and especially microeconomics, remains the idea of a rational consumer who is described by two fundamentals—her capacity to purchase and her preference. The first one relates to her income, and the second one is a statement of her liking or disliking of goods over which she is going to make a choice. Her choice will be rational if she follows her preference and makes the best use of her income.

Before we examine how a choice is made, we need to study the two fundamentals separately. Our first topic is the capacity to purchase, or what we call budget set. Although the rational choice theory is applicable not only to physical goods but also to services, such as a haircut and taking piano lessons, and even to more complex decisions, such as buying a portfolio of stocks

DOI: 10.4324/9781003226994-1

and bonds or attending university, we restrict our attention to physical goods just for convenience. The basic principle that we apply to make a career choice, say, to be an economist or an opera singer, is fundamentally not different to selecting a bottle of Australian Merlot against a fine French Chardonnay.

So, we begin by assuming that there is a set of goods that defines our relevant area of decision-making. This is the set of goods that the consumer cares about. Let the set be denoted as $X \subset R_{+}^{n}$, where R_{+}^{n} is the set of all possible combinations of n goods, including some elements being zero, none being negative and all numbers being real. A typical element of X is $x = (x_1, x_2, \ldots, x_n)$, which we will call a *bundle*. In words, the relevant set of goods can be potentially large, but what is important is that (1) there are at least two goods in the bundle and (2) unless specifically mentioned no goods can be negative.[1] Furthermore, all goods must carry a strictly positive price and these prices are outside the control of the consumer. The consumer's capacity to purchase is given by her income. In the simplest case, the income is just a given amount of money m.

1.2 The budget constraint

The consumer's **budget constraint** is the collection of all bundles she can afford with her money at prices $(p_1, p_2, \ldots, p_n)$. Mathematically, we define this to be a subset B of X:

$$B = \left\{ x \mid \sum_{i}^{n} p_i x_i \leq m \right\}$$

The budget set is shown in panel (*a*) of Figure 1.1 by the triangle for the two-good case. The bundles that cost exactly m, that is, $p_1 x_1 + p_2 x_2 + \ldots + p_n x_n = m$, constitute the budget line, and it is shown in panel (*b*) of Figure 1.1.

Assuming two goods we can write the budget equation as

$$x_2 = \frac{m}{p_2} - \frac{p_1}{p_2} x_1. \tag{1.1}$$

Intuitively, it should be clear that if the consumer had more money, she would be able to afford more of both goods. However, if one of the prices rises, the budget set would contract more along the axis of the good for which the price has just risen. This is illustrated in Figure 1.2.

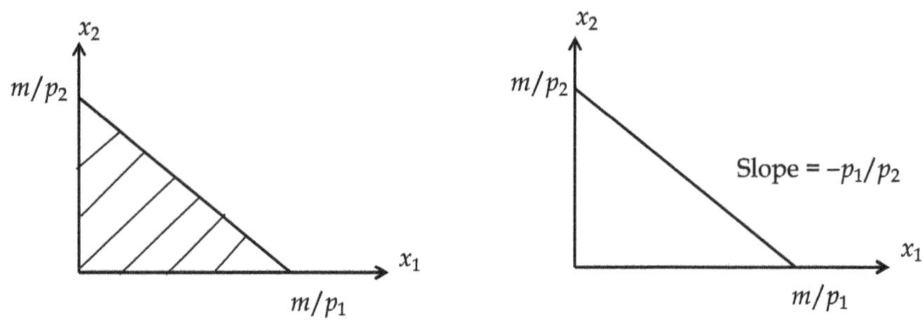

a. *Budget set*

b. *Budget line*

Figure 1.1 Budget set and budget line

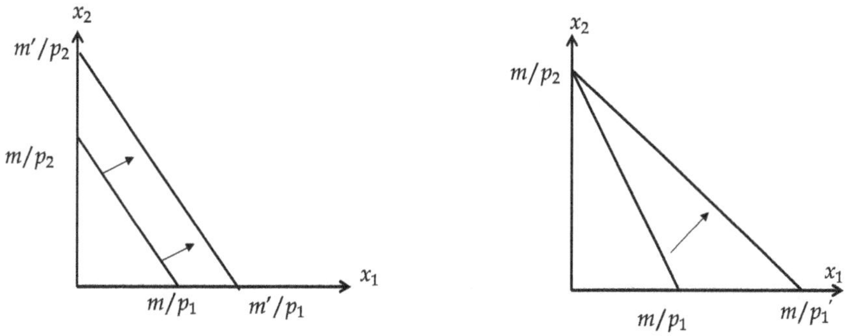

a. m *increases* b. p_1 *decreases*

Figure 1.2 Effects of income and price changes on the budget line

Panel *a* shows that if m increases, there will be a parallel shift of the budget line. The slope of the budget line is the ratio p_1/p_2. Panel *b* shows that if p_1 decreases, with p_2 remaining unchanged, the budget line shifts outward only along the x_1-axis and will have a smaller slope. Similarly, if p_2 falls, the budget line will shift outward only along the x_2-axis. It is also noteworthy that if m, p_1 and p_2 all were to rise by the *same proportion*, the budget line will not move at all. This is understandable because the consumer's extra money is wiped off by the price increases.

There are two points to note, which we are going to address subsequently:

1. The budget line is typically a straight line. But the linearity is a direct result of the assumption that price *does not change* with the quantity bought. If this assumption is relaxed, the budget line will no longer be a single straight line.
2. As said earlier, the consumer's income may not be entirely given by money. It may include, along with money, an endowment of the very goods that she is contemplating to make a choice on. In those cases (which we examine later), the budget line will look and behave differently.

1.3 When price varies with quantity

In reality, prices are not always fixed. Consumers are often showered with discount coupons and promotional vouchers. In stores, 'buy-one-get-one-free' schemes are prominently displayed in bright colours. Low-income groups receive food coupons (as in the Electronic Benefit Transfer programme of the US), free school meals (as in the UK) or subsidised food grains (as in India). Since subsidies always entail a cap on quantity; such price schemes resemble 'progressive taxation'—pay more per unit if you buy more.

The opposite scheme of taxation is bulk discounting. Supermarkets offer large discounts on bulk buying. Public transport in cities generally offers huge discounts after a minimum number of travels. If you are a tourist in Barcelona, it is a good idea to buy a 48-hour Hola Barcelona Travel Card that allows you unlimited travel for €16.30 in the city's bus and metro network. Compare this with a 10-journey ticket of €11.35. So, effectively the Hola Barcelona card makes all of your journeys free after 15 rides. Transport For London, the sole operator of the Tube and buses in London, charges a fixed bus fare of £1.75 per journey but does not take more than £5.25

in total if you make repeated journeys on the same day (provided you use the same payment method). So for Londoners, the bus fare drops to zero just after 3 journeys. These are some common examples of bulk discounts. We now examine how the budget line will change under the previously mentioned two pricing schemes.

1.3.1 *Food coupons and price subsidy*

In the US, poor people are given free (electronic) coupons that can be redeemed against the purchase of specific food and other essential items. Suppose x_1 is food and the policy of food coupons protects a certain quantity of food, say, up to k units, for a consumer with income m; assume this income level is low. If the consumer wishes to buy more food in excess of k, she can do so by spending m. The prices of x_1 and x_2 are p_1 and p_2, as before.

The budget equation is to be written as follows:

$$p_2 x_2 = m, \quad \text{for } x_1 \le k$$

$$p_1\left(x_1 - k\right) + p_2 x_2 = m, \quad \text{for } x_1 > k.$$

Equivalently,

$$x_2 = \frac{m}{p_2}, \quad \text{for } x_1 \le k$$

$$x_2 = \frac{m + p_1 k}{p_2} - \frac{p_1}{p_2} x_1, \quad \text{for } x_1 > k.$$

Combining these two segments of the budget line, it can also be written as

$$x_2 = \min\left\{\frac{m}{p_2}, \frac{m + p_1 k}{p_2} - \frac{p_1}{p_2} x_1\right\}. \tag{1.2}$$

In Figure 1.3 panel *a*, we draw the food coupon case. The consumer is assured of a bundle $\left(k, \frac{m}{p_2}\right)$, thanks to free food coupons. In the absence of the food coupons, her budget line would be given by the dotted line travelling from m / p_2 on the x_2-axis to m / p_1 on the x_1-axis. The food coupon expands her budget by an area equal to $\frac{km}{p_2}$.

Of course, it is not hard to see that the food coupon is a special case of charging a lower-than-normal price for x_1 up to the first k units and then charging the normal price for every additional unit of x_1. In India, a similar price scheme for essential goods is administered through a specialised shop network called the *public distribution system*, and eligible citizens can avail their entitlements at a predetermined subsidised price.

To describe the budget in this case, let us define p_1' as the smaller price of x_1 applicable up to the k units of x_1 and, as in the food coupon case, write our budget equation as consisting of two parts as follows:

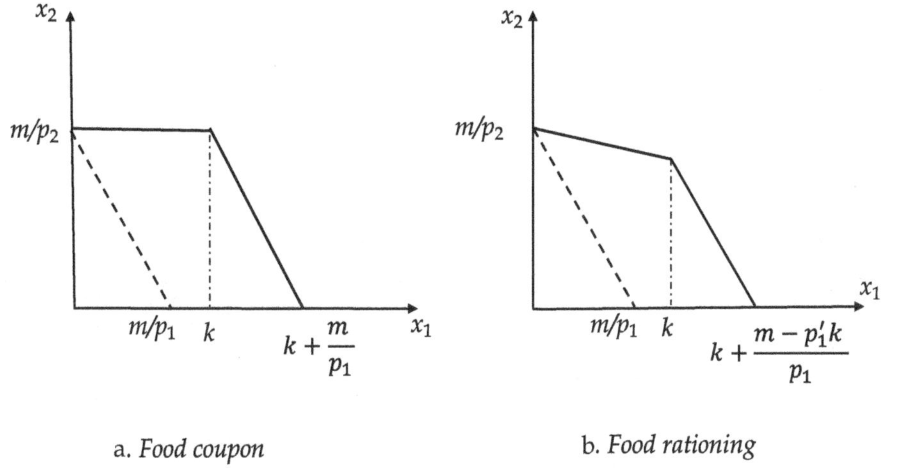

Figure 1.3 Food coupons and food rationing

$$p_1'x_1 + p_2x_2 = m, \quad \text{for } x_1 \le k$$

$$p_1'k + p_1(x_1 - k) + p_2x_2 = m, \quad \text{for } x_1 > k$$

$$\text{or,} \;\; p_1x_1 + p_2x_2 = m + (p_1 - p_1')k, \quad \text{for } x_1 > k.$$

Alternatively,

$$x_2 = \min\left\{\frac{m}{p_2} - \frac{p_1'}{p_2}x_1, \;\; \frac{m + (p_1 - p_1')k}{p_2} - \frac{p_1}{p_2}x_1\right\}. \tag{1.3}$$

In panel *b* of Figure 1.3, we draw the partial subsidy or food rationing case. The consumer's budget line has two different slopes: $-\frac{p_1'}{p_2}$ up to k units of x_1 and $-\frac{p_1}{p_2}$ thereafter. The budget line in the absence of subsidy would have been the dotted line.

A distinctive feature of the budget equations (Eqs. (1.2) and (1.3)) is that a change in the price of the good, to which the price discount applies, changes the consumer's budget in a different way. For example, if p_1 increases by Δp_1, buying x_1 beyond k units becomes more costly, but at the same time, her 'effective income' to spend on x_1 beyond k units also increases due to an increase in the *implicit subsidy* on the first k units of x_1, which is precisely $(p_1 - p_1')k$. We can see that, although there are two opposite effects, the direct effect of p_1 dominates, and the budget line contracts as shown in Figure 1.4 panel *a*. However, if the subsidised price p_1' increases by $\Delta p_1'$, the first k units of x_1 become costlier, and the 'implicit subsidy' is reduced. The budget line shifts inward, with a change in the slope in the upper part while maintaining the same slope in the lower part. This is shown in panel *b* of Figure 1.4.

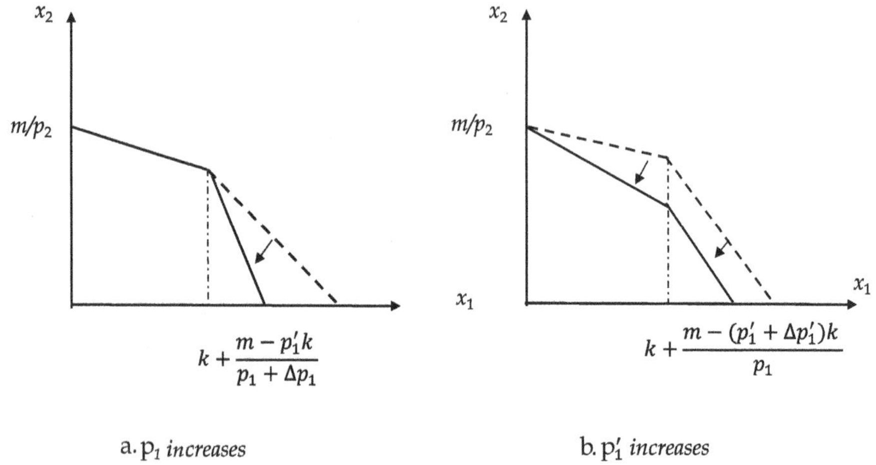

Figure 1.4 Price increase in a model of rationing

1.3.2 *Bulk discount*

While the government schemes for distributing scarce goods involve offering a subsidy with a cap on quantity (which we call rationing), private businesses tend to offer discounts on bulk purchases. That is, a subsidy is offered only after buying a minimum quantity, because selling more is often a profitable business strategy. Formally, the bulk discount case is similar to the rationing case, with p_1 and p_1' swapping places. Suppose the consumer pays p_1 per unit up to the k units of x_1 and thereafter pays a lower price p_1' for every additional unit of x_1 in excess of k. Following Eq. (1.3) but swapping the places of p_1 and p_1', the budget constraint is written as

$$x_2 = \max\left\{\frac{m}{p_2} - \frac{p_1}{p_2}x_1,\ \frac{m-(p_1 - p_1')k}{p_2} - \frac{p_1'}{p_2}x_1\right\}. \tag{1.4}$$

Note that the budget constraint now maps the maximum of the two values generated by the two lines at any given x_1. This can be easily verified by checking that when $x_1 < (>) k, \frac{m}{p_2} - \frac{p_1}{p_2}x_1 > (<) \frac{m-(p_1 - p_1')k}{p_2} - \frac{p_1'}{p_2}x_1$. The consumer is now paying an 'implicit tax' on the first k units of x_1, which reduces her 'effective income' when she buys x_1 in excess of k units.

Let us take an example, where the consumer has \$200 as her income. The price of x_1 is \$2 up to the first 60 units of x_1 and thereafter \$1 for every additional unit. The price of x_2 is \$4 all along. In panel (*a*) of Figure 1.5, we show the budget line for this example. If the consumer had faced \$1 flat for every unit of x_1, her budget line would be given by the dashed line. But she is effectively paying a tax on the first 60 units of x_1, which reduces her budget. Alternatively stated, had she faced a uniform price of \$2, the maximum amount of x_1 she could buy is only 100. But with the bulk discount, she can now buy up to 140 units of x_1. Note that the budget set has now become a non-convex set—a change that may have some implications for her choice, which we consider later.

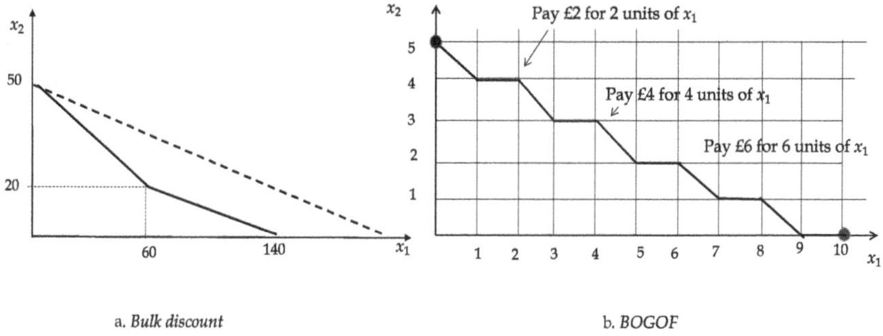

Figure 1.5 Bulk discount and buy-one-get-one-free pricing

1.3.2.1 Buy-one-get-one-free pricing

Consumers often get 'buy-one-get-one-free' deals in UK supermarkets, popularly known as BOGOF. This is a particular variety of bulk discount. Here, like any bulk discount scheme, the consumer has to buy a minimum amount to be able to get the discount, but the discount is then restricted to a limited amount. Once that limit is reached, the scheme restarts. Under BOGOF, the consumer has to buy at least one unit and then gets the second unit free. With no restriction on the total quantity one can buy, the scheme restarts at every odd-numbered unit, making the next even-numbered unit free. To illustrate what the budget constraint looks like in this case, let us take a simple example of a budget of £10 to spend on x_1 and x_2. The price of x_2 is £2 throughout. The price of x_1 is £2 with the BOGOF provision. The budget line is illustrated in panel *b* of Figure 1.5. In equation form (assuming x_1 to be available in discrete units),

$$x_2 = \begin{cases} \dfrac{m}{p_2} - \dfrac{p_1}{2p_2}x_1 & \text{if} \quad x_1 \text{ is even} \\ \dfrac{m}{p_2} - \dfrac{p_1}{2p_2}(x_1 - 1) - \dfrac{p_1}{p_2} & \text{if} \quad x_1 \text{ is odd} \end{cases}$$

1.4 Endowment budget constraint

So far, we have assumed that the consumer has a fixed amount of money to spend. But one's ability to spend depends also on other assets and total wealth in general, because such assets/wealth can be converted into money. A particularly interesting case arises if the wealth consists of a stock of the goods that the consumer is considering buying. Let us say that in addition to m, the consumer already has a bundle $\left(x_1^0, x_2^0\right)$ as an initial *endowment*. This would be the case of a farmer who grows both apricots and apples and faces a decision problem of how many apricots and apples he wants to consume. There are two selves of the farmer—producer and consumer—who need to make two separate decisions. Now her ability to purchase depends on the market value of her endowment.

Denoting her total wealth as $M = m + p_1x_1^0 + p_2x_2^0$, we write the budget equation as

$$x_2 = \frac{m + p_1x_1^0 + p_2x_2^0}{p_2} - \frac{p_1}{p_2}x_1 \equiv \frac{M}{p_2} - \frac{p_1}{p_2}x_1. \tag{1.5}$$

In Figure 1.6, we show the graph of this budget line. It must be noted that a change in price(s) will alter the value of the endowment, and thus, through an additional channel the effect of price change will be felt. When only m increases, say, to m', the budget line will show a parallel shift as before, as shown in Figure 1.7 panel (*a*). But if one of the prices changes, say, p_1 increases to $p_1{}^1$, the budget line will rotate inwardly around the point $\left(x_1^0, x_2^0 + \frac{m}{p_2}\right)$ as shown in panel (*b*) of Figure 1.7. An increase in p_1 unleashes two effects—the standard relative price effect, which makes the budget line steeper, and an increase in the value of endowments. Two effects work in opposite directions for good x_1, but the relative price effect dominates, and hence, the consumer's ability to buy x_1 falls. But for good x_2, two effects work in the same direction allowing the consumer to be able to buy more of x_2.

A special case of the endowment budget corresponds to $m = 0$ (no cash in hand). The budget line will pass through the point $\left(x_1^0, x_2^0\right)$ as shown in panel (*a*) of Figure 1.8. Later, while studying

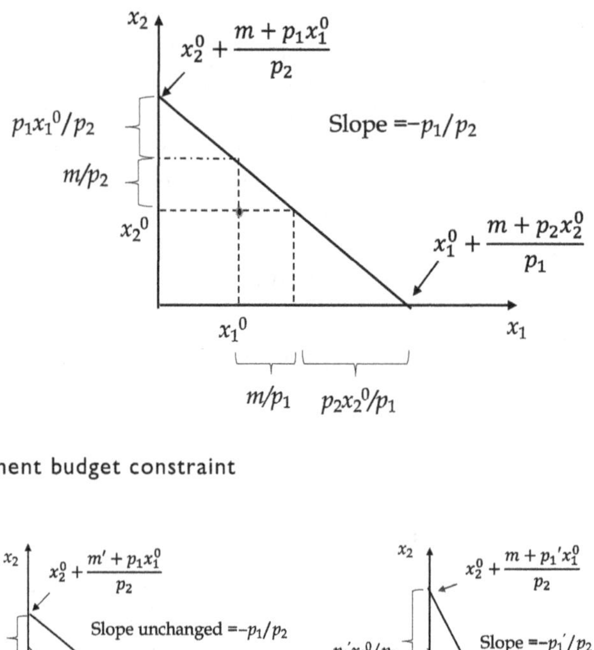

Figure 1.6 Endowment budget constraint

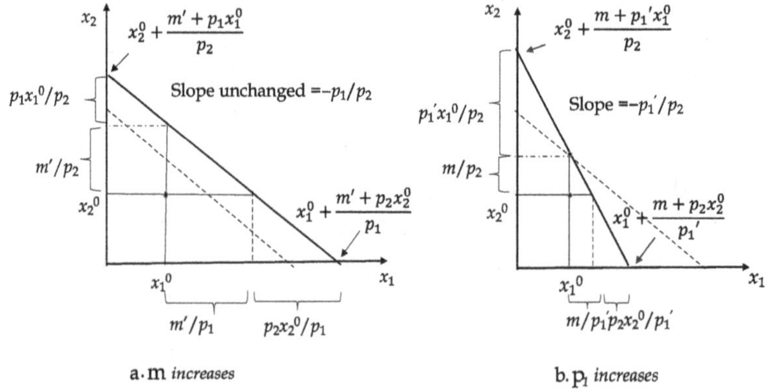

Figure 1.7 Effects of an increase in m and an increase in p_1

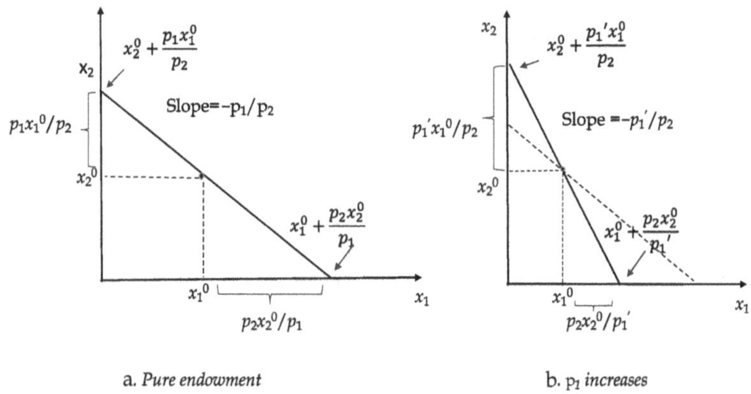

Figure 1.8 Budget lines for the pure endowment case

general equilibrium, we will see that any simultaneous acts of buying and selling of goods between different agents (as a barter trade) can be studied with this type of budget constraint. An increase in p_1 will make the budget line rotate clockwise around the point $\left(x_1^0, x_2^0\right)$. This is shown in Figure 1.8 panel *b*.

1.5 Inter-temporal budget constraint

Our idea of a bundle of goods need not be confined to the ones that are physically present side by side. It can be extended to situations in which one of the goods may be present only in future. In other words, a combination of goods from different time periods can also be regarded as a bundle. Suppose our consumer has two periods to live—present and future—and she has two pre-determined levels of income m_1 and m_2. While m_1 is available now, m_2 will arrive in the future. If we make a simplifying assumption that prices of two periods' consumption are fixed at 1 (say, inflation proof), then (m_1, m_2) is the consumer's *endowment* of consumption (c_1, c_2). That is, by default, she can always consume (m_1, m_2).

However, it can be readily seen that the consumer can expand her future income by putting some money away into a savings deposit and earning an interest rate r per dollar of savings. Potentially, she can stretch her future consumption to $m_2 + m_1(1+r)$ by putting the entire amount m_1. This is shown in panel *a* of Figure 1.9; the graph is based on the assumption that the consumer is unable to borrow for some reason. Borrowing permits the consumer to expand the present consumption.

But borrowing is not as easy as saving for a variety of reasons. First and foremost, the lender would like to be sure of the purpose of borrowing and the consumer's ability to repay. Second, the lender himself has to use someone else's savings to run his lending operations, and therefore to earn some profit, he may charge a higher interest rate than r. Suppose the borrower is charged an interest rate of ρ ($> r$). In our simple setting, the consumer's budget would look like as the one in panel *b* of Figure 1.9. Here, the maximum the consumer can borrow is $m_2/(1+\rho)$ to expand her present consumption to its maximum $m_1 + \dfrac{m_2}{1+\rho}$ and then pay back the loan in future. Note that the slope of the inter-temporal budget line is different depending on whether the consumer is saving or borrowing.

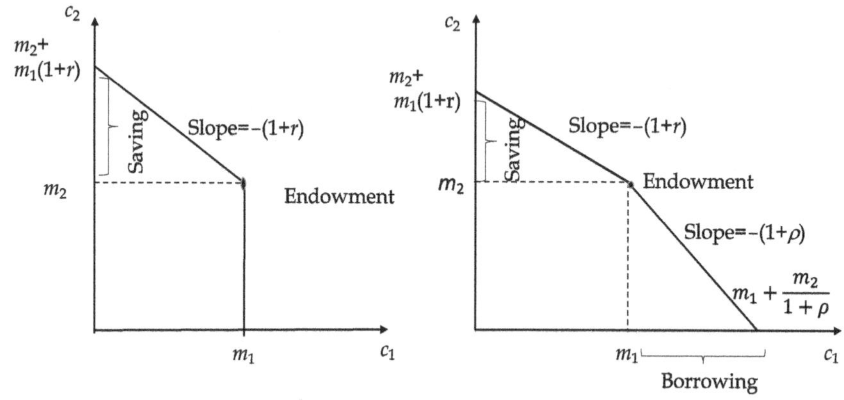

a. *No borrowing* b. *Saving and borrowing*

Figure 1.9 Budget constraint with saving and borrowing ($r < \rho$)

To arrive at the budget equation, let us define saving as $s = m_1 - c_1$ and borrowing as $b = c_1 - m_1$ (which is clearly negative of saving), and write the future consumption as

$$\begin{aligned} c_2 &= m_2 + s(1+r) && \text{for } c_1 < m_1, \\ &= m_2 + m_1(1+r) - c_1(1+r) && \text{for } c_1 < m_1, \end{aligned}$$

and

$$\begin{aligned} c_2 &= m_2 - b(1+\rho) && \text{for } c_1 \geq m_1, \\ &= m_2 + m_1(1+\rho) - c_1(1+\rho) && \text{for } c_1 \geq m_1. \end{aligned}$$

Combining the preceding two equations, we can write the budget equation as

$$c_2 = \min\{m_2 + m_1(1+r) - c_1(1+r),\quad m_2 + m_1(1+\rho) - c_1(1+\rho)\}. \tag{1.6}$$

1.6 Consumption-leisure budget

In this section, we stretch the notions of bundle and income both to a different direction. Our income comes from the number of hours we decide to work and therefore is entirely dependent on the 'bundle' we choose, which now must include time as a good. We all are endowed with 24 hours a day, and we spend certain hours of it on work that gives us our livelihoods. The remaining hours are, by default, devoted to things we love to do, such as being with family and friends or relaxing by ourselves. Time not spent in the labour market is simply our 'leisure' consumption. But consumption of other goods, such as food and clothing, has an inherent trade-off with leisure; more leisure means less money for other goods. Therefore, in this set-up, income is endogenously determined, unlike our previous examples.

To present the problem in general terms, suppose the consumer has T hours of time, which she can devote to either leisure l or work $L\ (\equiv T-l)$. The price of leisure is w, the amount of money the consumer is giving up to have 1 unit of leisure, just as p is the price of the consumption good. Starting from the income-expenditure equality $wL = pc$, we can substitute the expression for labour and rearrange the terms to derive the budget equation as

$$pc + wl = wT. \tag{1.7}$$

Despite the fact that income is dependent on the consumption of one of the goods, the budget line takes the generic form with wT, the value time endowment, taking the place of what was previously called 'income'. The budget line is shown in panel a of Figure 1.10. On the horizontal axis from the left side, we measure the hours of leisure, and from the right side (by moving leftward from point T) we measure the hours worked. Note that the intercept on the leisure axis, T, is invariant to all price changes. The consumption intercept will capture all the price changes. As shown in the graph, if the wage increases to w', the budget line shifts only along the consumption axis.

On panel a, we assume that the wage rate is constant throughout. But workers are often paid an overtime (higher) wage after k hours of work (commonly $k = 8$). Suppose the base wage is w_1 and the overtime wage is $w_2\ (> w_1)$. To derive the budget equation, let us start with the income-expenditure equality and take into account of the hours worked:

$$\begin{aligned} pc &= w_1 L && \text{if } L \le k, \\ pc &= w_1 k + w_2 (L-k) && \text{if } L > k \end{aligned}$$

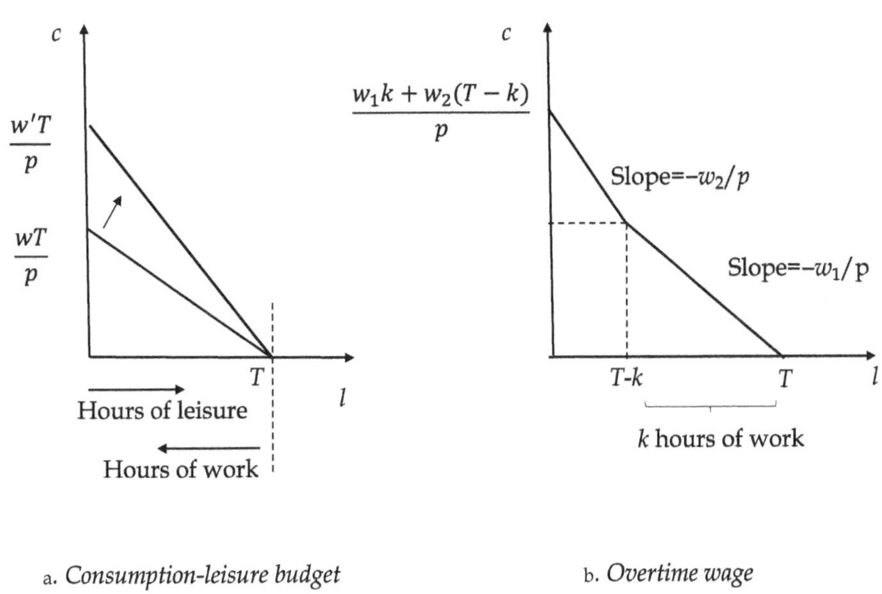

Figure 1.10 Consumption-leisure budget

The second part of the budget constraint recognises that if $L > k$, the consumer has already earned $w_1 k$ as income, and then for every additional hour, in excess of k hours, she will get the wage rate w_2. Now substituting $L = T - l$, we can rewrite the preceding as

$$\begin{aligned} pc &= w_1 T - w_1 l && \text{if } l \geq T - k, \\ pc &= w_1 k + w_2 (T - l) - w_2 k && \text{if } l < T - k. \end{aligned}$$

In other words, our overall budget equation can be written as

$$c = \max\left\{\frac{w_1}{p}(T - l),\ \frac{w_2}{p}(T - l) - \frac{(w_2 - w_1)}{p}k\right\}. \tag{1.8}$$

On panel *b* of Figure 1.10, we show the graph of this budget line. Compare this graph with the bulk discount graph on panel *a* of Figure 1.5. The shapes of the two budget lines are similar. Overtime wage is essentially a discount on having 'more leisure' beyond a threshold level. At very low levels of leisure, its price is significantly higher. Alternatively stated, at low levels of labour supply, the selling price of labour is significantly lower.

1.6.1 A technical remark

From all the examples of the budget set it should be clear to you that except for the bulk discount case and the overtime wage case, the consumer's budget set remains a **convex set**. You may read the mathematical appendix (Chapter 16) of this book to understand what a convex set is. In other words, a set is a convex set if one can travel from one point of the set to any other point of the set on a straight line without ever going outside the set. The set has no holes, bumps or dents to interrupt the shortest possible journey.

The convexity of the constraint set plays an important role in ensuring a unique solution for optimisation. While this point will be clearer when we address the problem of consumer choice, you may sense that under bulk discounting, consumers can feel indecisive about whether to buy less or to buy more. The lure of a large discount may induce them to change their purchase in a discontinuous manner.

1.7 Conclusion

We have shown a number of applications of the basic idea of a budget set. One type of budget equation we have not dealt with here is the case of price continuously changing with quantity. As this type of pricing (called smooth non-linear pricing) is not very common, we have omitted it, although we have studied some discrete versions of it. In Section 1.8, we present an interesting case in which the consumer's budget concerns calories rather than the goods from which we derive calories.

Summary

We have studied the following issues relating to the budget set:

1. The standard budget line, which is a straight line, is based on the assumption that prices of the goods don't change with the quantities bought.

2. In the real world, prices often do not remain fixed with respect to quantities bought. With bulk discount, part of the budget line shifts outward. With food coupons and price subsidies, the budget set expands, but the budget line will have two different segments.
3. In the case of a bulk discount, the budget set becomes non-convex.
4. Consumer income may have a non-cash component such as an endowment of goods. The budget line shifts here in a different way; it rotates through the endowment point.
5. Several applications, such as labour versus leisure and present versus future consumption, were also studied.
6. Finally, in Section 1.8, the budget line for Lancaster's characteristics model is considered.

1.8 Appendix

1.8.1 *Budget set on the characteristic space*

Economist Kelvin J Lancaster (1966) proposed a different approach to consumer theory. His view was that consumers derive utility not from the quantities of the goods they consume but from the characteristics or attributes the goods offer. For example, while considering which soft drink to buy, we think about the intensity of the fizz a brand might offer; when choosing how many bananas to buy, we think about how much vitamin C we need. The idea of a good as a bundle of characteristics or attributes is very general. It can be extended to any service, geographical place, and even individual. An athlete is a combination of several attributes or skills; a holiday resort should have several characteristics, such as ease of travel, natural view, good food and so on.

If we want to directly consider the characteristics as members of the consumption set, then we need to rewrite the budget set. Consider our conventional budget equation for two goods: $m = p_1x_1 + p_2x_2$. Suppose 1 unit of x_1 gives 5 units of carbohydrates, denoted c_1, and 1 unit of protein, denoted c_2, whereas 1 unit of x_2 gives 8 units of protein and 2 units of carbohydrates. Now we need to map the total affordable bundles of carbohydrates and proteins from goods space to characteristic space. The maximum numbers of x_1 and x_2 that can be bought are m / p_1 and m / p_2, respectively. That is, the two extreme bundles of goods are $(m / p_1, 0)$ and $(0, m / p_2)$; these two bundles and any linear combination of the two constitute the budget line on the goods space.

On the characteristics space, these two extreme goods bundles translate into two extreme characteristics bundles (c_1, c_2) as $(5m / p_1, m / p_1)$ and $(2m / p_2, 8m / p_2)$. Then we can take the convex combinations of these two bundles to arrive at the so-called budget line on the characteristics space. That is, the budget line is

$$B_c = \left\{ (c_1, c_2) \mid c_1 = \lambda \frac{5m}{p_1} + (1-\lambda)\frac{2m}{p_2}, \quad c_2 = \lambda \frac{m}{p_1} + (1-\lambda)\frac{8m}{p_2} \quad \forall \lambda \in [0,1] \right\}.$$

Figure 1.11 illustrates the budget set and the budget line of this example on the characteristic space. The outer line is the budget line, which consists of all the characteristics bundles generated by the convex combination of the two end-point bundles. The area encapsulated by the budget line and two rays passing through the origin constitute the budget set. Note that the budget line here will not go from one axis to the other unless one of the good is devoid of one characteristic. An increase in m will translate into an outward parallel shift of the budget line,

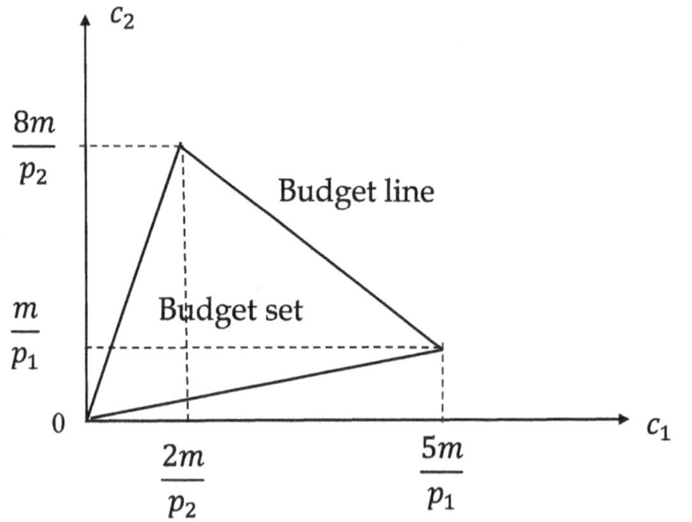

Figure 1.11 Budget set on the characteristics space

along the two rays passing through the origin. Any change in one of the prices will make the budget line shift in the usual way; however, the slope of the budget line here is not p_1 / p_2. You can quickly check that the absolute value of the slope is $\frac{8p_1 - p_2}{5p_2 - 2p_1}$. It should be noted that the straight-line budget as shown here is a result of the assumption of two goods. If we have three or more goods, the budget line may look different. But extending the model to multiple goods is straightforward.

Despite the intuitive appeal of Lancaster's characteristic-based approach, his theory did not become popular, except in one important area of microeconomics—poverty and nutrition studies. Economists who study the welfare of low-income groups quite rightly turn their attention to calorie intake rather than quantities of food, because nutrition has long-term impacts on people's human capital, labour market performance and, in some circumstances, mortality. Interested readers may look at food consumption studies by Subramanian and Deaton (1996) for India and Dubois et al. (2014) for the United States, the United Kingdom and France.

1.9 Exercises

1. Suppose Beth has received a voucher from Uber Eats for 50% discount on total spend on her next Mexican order. However, the total discount is capped at \$10. She loves to eat chicken fajitas (x_1) and chilli con carne burritos (x_2), which are priced \$2 and \$1, respectively. She wants to spend \$20. Write her budget equation. Draw it on a graph. Calculate the average price she pays for each item. Repeat your exercise for her total spend of \$30.
2. Beth's story is the same, but replace the discount of 50% by λ fraction. The cap on the total discount is \$$k$. She wants to spend m. Answer the same questions as in question 1.
3. In the example of Beth, what if the offer stipulates a minimum spend of \$$k/2$? How would the graph look like now?
4. Vicky Cristina goes to Barcelona. She has €100.30 to spend on food and travel. If she buys a Hola Barcelona 48-hour Travel Card by paying €16.30, she can travel unlimitedly,

and assume she can take at most 30 rides in 48 hours. Alternatively, she can buy a 10-ride ticket for €11.30. She must visit the famous La Sagrada Familia Cathedral and the Picasso Museum, which will cost €20 and €14, respectively. The rest is spent on food, which costs €5 per unit. Draw Vicky's budget sets for bus/metro rides and food under the two options.

5. Vicky comes to London. After setting aside the admission fee for the historic Tower of London and the cost of taking a ride on the London Eye, she is left with only £20.65, which she wants to spend on food and bus travel. Food costs £4 per unit. Bus fare for a single journey is £1.55, but after 3 consecutive journeys, her bus fare will be zero for the rest of the day if she uses the same credit/debit card for payment. Of course, she has the option of saving the bus fare fully or partly by walking from the Tower of London to the London Eye and other nearby places of interest. Draw her budget set consisting of bus rides and meals, assuming that the number of bus journeys she can make in a day is 10.
6. Consider an endowment budget with no cash income, but the selling price of good 1 is smaller than the buying price. Write the budget equation and present a graphical illustration of it.
7. Consider an inter-temporal budget problem. Suppose the consumer has endowment (m_1, m_2). Prices of present and future consumption goods are p_1 and p_2. Assume the interest rate for saving and borrowing is same. Write the budget equation and present it graphically.
8. In question 7, the inter-temporal budget problem, assume $p_2 = p_1(1+r)$. Rework your answer.
9. Emmanuel has T hours to spend on leisure (l) and work (t). He also has m amount of cash in hand, which combined with his labour income constitutes his budget. The hourly wage rate is w, and the price of the sole consumption good c is p. Write the budget equation and draw the budget line.
10. In the same set-up as question 9, what if m were negative, indicating debt? Redo the graph.
11. Furthermore, revisiting question 10, assume that Emmanuel is concerned for his ailing mother's health and spends t_0 hours caring for her. How does the graph change?
12. Consider another consumption-leisure budget problem. If the consumer does not work more than t_1 hours, he is entitled to an unemployment benefit b. If his work hours exceed t_1, the unemployment benefit is weaned off gradually. Once the work hours reach t_2, the benefit is completely taken off. Write the budget equation and draw the budget line.
13. Consider the example given in Section 1.8. Redraw the graph of Figure 1.11 for the following two cases: (a) m increases by 50%, and (b) p_1 falls.
14. Consider the same example as in Section 1.8, with the following modification: Redefine c_2 as fat instead of proteins. Suppose there is a tax on the fat content. Suppose any good having a positive fat content will be charged with a tax at the rate of $\frac{a}{a+b}$ per unit of fat when the fat-to-carbohydrate ratio is $a{:}b$. Draw the budget set before and after the tax imposition.

Note

1 In some contexts, negative variables can be meaningful such as borrowing, which is negative of savings.

Further readings

Cartwright, N. (1998). Capacities. In J. Davis, W. Hands & U. Maki (Eds.), *The Handbook of Economic Methodology*, 45–48. Cheltenham: Edward Elgar.

Dubois, P., Griffith, R. & Nevo, A. (2014). Do prices and attributes explain international differences in food purchases? *American Economic Review*, 104(3), 832–867.

Lancaster, K. J. (1966). A new approach to consumer theory. *Journal of Political Economy*, 74(2), 132–157.
Niehans, J. (1989). *A History of Economic Theory: Classic Contributions*. Baltimore, MD: Johns Hopkins University Press.
Read, D. (2004). Utility theory from Jeremy Bentham to Daniel Kahneman. Working Paper No. LSEOR 04-64. London School of Economics.
Slutsky, E. (1952 [1915]). On the theory of the budget of the consumer. In G. J. Stigler & K. E. Boulding (Eds.), *Readings in Price Theory*, 27–56. Homewood, IL: Irwin.
Stigler, G. J. (1950). The development of utility theory. I. *Journal of Political Economy*, 58(4), 307–327.
Subramanian, S. & Deaton, A. (1996). The demand for food and calories. *Journal of Political Economy*, 104(1), 133–162.

Chapter 2

Preferences

Abstract

Consumers' preferences are fundamental to demand theory. The tradition in neoclassical economics is to formalise the idea of preferences with the help of a number of axioms that provide a logical foundation to utility functions and indifference curves, which are essentially a consistent ordering of different consumption bundles that the consumer may confront at the time of making a choice. We consider a number of utility functions that are commonly used in economics and explain the connection between a utility function and its corresponding indifference curves both mathematically and graphically. The slope of an indifference curve called the *marginal rate of substitution* is derived for a variety of utility functions with special reference to homothetic preferences. It is also pointed out that while the axioms are very logical, they are not necessarily very descriptive, as some of them have been criticised to be unrealistic.

Keywords: Axioms of preferences, Convex preference, Quasi-concave utility function, Indifference curve, Marginal rate of substitution

2.1 Introduction

Imagine our consumer is spending an afternoon in a shopping mall simply for 'window shopping' with no intention of buying anything. While going through the latest designer bags, summer dresses and Belgian chocolates (and everything else there is), she knows perfectly which ones she *likes* the most and in which combinations. Will that be a bundle of two handbags and three chocolate boxes or a bundle of one summer dress and four boxes of chocolate? Her answer will be prompt and clear. She is absolutely sure about her preferences over all the bundles that are not just physically present before her but also those that are merely in the realm of possibilities. This may sound absurd, but think about a dream scenario of our consumer winning a €100 million jackpot. She will be called upon to decide which Rolls-Royce model she wants to buy, in which hotel in Monte Carlo she wants to spend her next weekend and where in Manhattan she should have a holiday apartment. We want our consumer to know it all regardless of whether she will ever face the possibility of even seeing them, let alone buying.

This is only the first step in empowering our consumer with *rationality*, a mental attribute that is pervasive in economics, and it changes meaning depending on the context. Rationality to a macroeconomist is not exactly the same thing as it is to a game theorist or microeconomist. In consumer theory, two elements are vital to rationality—first, the consumer has the full knowledge of her preferences over all existing and potential bundles, and second, the consumer cares only about her own preferences (self-interest).

DOI: 10.4324/9781003226994-2

In momentary digression, we may recall a scene from the movie *Kill Bill Volume 1* in which the Bride comes to avenge her unborn child's death at the hands of deadly Viper gang. Despite a four-year-long coma, she remembers who the killers were, and she has come prepared to engage with them one by one with a meticulous plan for every eventuality. She tells her first target Vernita Green (aka Copperhead), a young mother herself, "It's mercy, compassion and forgiveness I lack. Not rationality." She knows what she should be doing; Green agrees, being rational herself. Our consumer shares this trait of rationality: knowing in advance what to do and doing exactly that when occasion demands—no dithering, no hesitations and no emotional interference.

Returning to our consumer, not only is she rational, but her 'preferences', we fancy, must also be consistent and coherent in ways that are described by certain axioms. These axioms are so precise and watertight that not conforming to even one of them might invalidate the notion of rationality. Here, we should not confuse rational preferences with rational behaviours. While preferences concern how we *reason* in our mind to compare different bundles of goods, regardless of the price information, behaviour concerns what *decision* we make at the end, after interacting our preferences with price, our budget and other external information.

You might have already pondered a few troubling questions. First, how is preference formed? Second, do consumers know everything that they need to know? Third, are our preferences immune to price information? The first question can be set aside by saying that our preferences are formed well before we undertake the task of decision-making. Atkin (2013) studied migrant workers' food consumption patterns in India. He found that a childhood habit of consuming rice or wheat—depending on in which part of India they were born—plays a strong role in their adult lives.[1] For the second question, there is no easy answer. Not only is 'to know everything' a huge cognitive challenge, but most of us also manage to get by without knowing everything. When we go on holiday, we choose new food in unfamiliar restaurants; we ask our friends for sight-seeing tips. Most of these decisions are made without experience. The third question is about independence of preference. Although there is plenty of evidence for prices to interfere with our preference ordering, in theory, we have to maintain the independence of preferences.

Not surprisingly, the assumption of rationality that underpins our reasoning of choice or behaviours has long been a subject of debate. At least three Nobel Prize–winning economists—Herbert A. Simon (1959), Amartya K. Sen (1977) and Daniel Kahneman (Kahneman and Tversky, 1979)—have raised serious objections to the tradition of taking rationality as the bedrock of model building. Their respective criticisms were directed at boundless rationality, selfishness and the ability to decide under uncertainty. We take up these and other criticisms of the rational choice theory in a later chapter where we discuss new developments in consumer theory. At this point, we need to assure ourselves that the properties of preferences we are going to specify are *normative* (or desirable) but not necessarily *descriptive*. What we present in this chapter is a summary of over 150 years of the evolution of economic thoughts from philosophers Jeremy Bentham (1789) and William Jevons (1866) to Gerard Debreu (1954).

2.2 Axioms of preferences

Recall that our consumer has a feasible consumption set $X \subset R^n_+$, from which she can pick a bundle $x = (x_1, x_2, \ldots, x_n)$, that is, a n-tuple of real numbers. By varying the quantity of one or more goods, we can create different bundles. Thus, her feasible consumption set has infinitely many bundles. It turns out that the rational choice theory is vastly different between one good ($n = 1$) and two goods but not between two and three or more goods. So, for most of our analysis, we focus on $n = 2$. In some instances, we will comment on the case of $n > 2$.

1. **Axiom of completeness:** Given any two bundles $x, y \in X$ either $x \succeq y$, $y \succeq x$ or $x \sim y$. In words, x is either preferred or indifferent to y, y is preferred or indifferent to x or x is indifferent to y.[2]

   This is our first axiom where we insist that the consumer must have a complete ordering of each and every bundle in her feasible consumption set. Given any two bundles, the consumer must be able to say whether she is indifferent between the two or she likes one over the other. She is not allowed to say, "I do not know." That also means all bundles must be ordered in terms of the consumer's preference. Whether that is entirely realistic or not, as discussed earlier, is something we set aside for now.
2. **Axiom of transitivity:** For any three bundles $x, y, z \in X$, if $x \succeq y$ and $y \succeq z$, then we must have $x \succeq z$.

   This assumption is necessary to achieve a certain degree of consistency. Note that by the axiom of completeness, all the three bundles must be ordered (preference-wise). If it were the case that $x \succeq y$ and $y \succeq z$ but $z \succeq x$, then we have a **cycling** problem, while consistency requires an unbroken chain of ordering (of bundles) established directly or indirectly. To give a simple example, if one prefers tea over coffee and coffee over orange juice, then one must prefer tea over juice. Preferring juice over tea will be a violation of transitivity.

   However, thinking further we can see that the tea–coffee–juice example is too simplistic and potentially misleading. What we just considered is an example of three different bundles of three goods, and each bundle consisted positive amount of only one good. From the preference ordering of three extreme bundles, nothing much can be speculated about the intermediate bundles. Let us develop the argument further by taking some intermediate bundles where all goods are presented in positive quantity. Suppose these bundles are $a = (10,6,1)$, $b = (1,10,6)$ and $c = (6,1,10)$. Suppose the consumer applies a criterion of preferring one bundle over another when two of the three goods give more (or not less) in quantity. Comparing bundles a and b, we see that b gives more of x_2 and x_3. Hence, she would prefer b to a. Comparing b and c we get c is preferred to b. Therefore, by transitivity, we should expect $c \succeq a$. But by comparing a and c directly, we see that a gives more of x_1 and x_2, and hence, we have $a \succeq c$. This is a violation of transitivity. Note that if the bundle a was $(5,6,1)$, the preference ordering would have been transitive. But we should also note that the cycling problem of the preceding example is a result of the preference criterion the consumer applies (majority criterion in this case). But that is not the only criterion possible. These details are not very relevant to consumer theory; all we need is to assume that if the consumer prefers b to a and c to b, then she *must* prefer c to a.

   This example demonstrates that the axiom of transitivity is neither very intuitive nor very realistic, just as we know from our social interactions that a friend's friend is not necessarily a friend. The preceding cycling problem becomes severe when our bundles include attributes or characteristics, like features of a mobile handset. A handset can be seen as a bundle of features like memory, size, battery power, camera and so on. Even human beings can be seen as a bundle. A footballer can be seen as a bundle of several skills such as speed, accuracy of shots, stamina and more. A coach may struggle to field their best 11, because ordering players can be a nightmare, just as we find it difficult to arrange our preference for mobile handsets (perhaps except for iPhone loyalists).

   Fortunately, in our two-good environment transitivity is rarely violated.[3] As such, we will always assume transitivity. A small technical point is that a consumer's preference is said to be **rational** if it satisfies the axioms of completeness and transitivity.
3. **Axiom of reflexiveness:** A bundle is as well as (or indifferent to) itself. That is, for all $x \in X$, $x \succeq x$. In other words, the consumer must be indifferent between two identical bundles. It

may not be clear why this assumption is needed at all; this is essentially a technical assumption that is used to arrive at utility functions (to be shown later).

4. **Axiom of continuity:** Preference must be continuous. There should be no break in the ordering of goods, no matter how small the variation between two bundles may be. If between two bundles one is preferred to the other, the relationship will be carried over to small variations of the two bundles, that is, the bundles that are sufficiently close to them. The preference order should not change abruptly. Conceptually, if one prefers tea with a *little* bit of sugar over black coffee, then one should not prefer black coffee over tea with no sugar. That is to say, small variations in tea should not upset one's preference. The consumer must not be too fussy about such small variations.

   Mathematically, continuity can be defined in several ways. Suppose there are two bundles $a = (2,4)$ and $b = (4,2)$. Let us also define $a^n = \left\{\left(2+\frac{n}{n+1}, 4+\frac{n}{n+1}\right), n = 0,1,2,\ldots\infty\right\}$ to be a sequence and from b as $b^n = \left\{\left(4+\frac{n}{n+1}, 2+\frac{n}{n+1}\right), n = 0,1,2,\ldots\infty\right\}$. The limit of these two sequences are $(3, 5)$ and $(5, 3)$, respectively. From a {(2, 4), (2.5, 4.5), (2.66, 4.66), (2.75, 4.75), …} approaches (3,5). Likewise, {(4,2), (4.5, 2.5), (4.66, 2.66), (4.75, 2.75), …} is a sequence from bundle b that approaches (5,3).

   The axiom of continuity says that if every element of the sequence a^n is preferred to every element of the sequence b^n, then the limit of the sequence a^n is also preferred to the limit of the sequence b^n.

   If preference is not continuous, then we cannot talk about continuous utility functions. Discontinuous preference or equivalently discontinuous utility functions can jeopardise the idea of utility maximisation and, in turn, nullify the choice theory.

5. **Axiom of monotonicity:** This axiom concerns how preferences should behave if the quantity of one or more goods increases. It says that more should be preferred to less. But in a multi-good environment how to define 'more'? There are two ways we can compare more to less, and thus, we have two versions of this axiom. To understand this axiom, let us note that from a mathematical point of view $x = (4,2) \geq y = (4,1)$, while $x' = (5,2) > y = (4,1)$ because x' has greater amount of both goods. When $x > y$, it is natural that x should be strictly preferred to y. But if $x \geq y$, there are two possibilities of preference ordering.

   The idea of weak monotonicity entertains the possibility that the consumer can be indifferent between two bundles when one bundle gives a bit more of one good but the same of the other good(s). But strong monotonicity insists on strict preference whenever one good is slightly more even if other goods are unchanged.

   The difference between the two versions of monotonicity can be best understood with the graph of an indifference curve. An **indifference curve** is a collection of all bundles to which the consumer is indifferent. In Figure 2.1, we draw two indifference curves to illustrate the difference between weak and strong monotonicity. The left figure represents the case in which two goods are regarded 'imperfect substitutes'. The right figure shows the case of 'perfect complements' (more on these later). In the left figure, between points a and b, a gives more of x_2 but the same of x_1. Bundles a and b do not belong to the same indifference curve; a is strictly preferred to b, which means the strict monotonicity axiom is satisfied. A higher indifference curve (dashed curve) passes through point a. The right graph shows

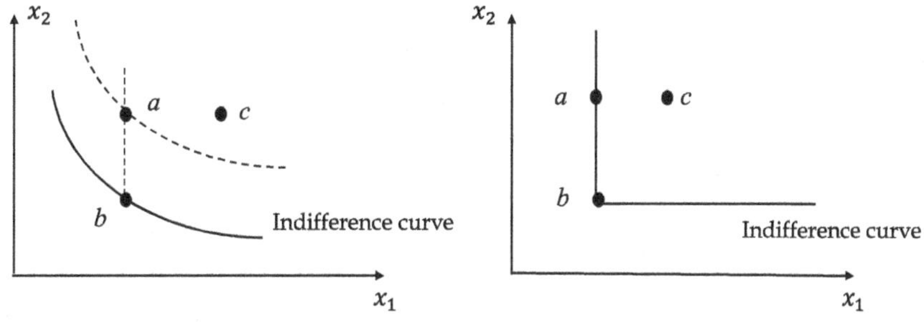

a. *Imperfect substitutes* b. *Perfect complements*

Figure 2.1 Strong versus weak monotonicity

weak monotonicity. Here, a and b are indifferent to each other. It is also clear that c is strictly preferred to a, even though c has more of x_1 but the same amount of x_2. Furthermore, c is strictly preferred to b for giving more of both goods in both graphs.

There is another version of monotonicity called the **axiom of local non-satiation**, which we discuss in Section 2.5.

a. **Weak monotonicity:** For all $x, y \in X$, if $x \geqslant y$ then $x \succeq y$, and if $x > y$ then $x \succ y$, where $\succ$ indicates strict preference.
b. **Strong monotonicity:** For all $x, y \in X$, if $x \geq y$ or $x > y$, then $x \succ y$.

6. **Axiom of convexity:** Convexity concerns the relationship between two bundles and a bundle created from a mix of the two. If we have two bundles that the consumer is indifferent to, then would she feel indifferent to a bundle that is a mix of the two or would she strictly prefer it? Two possibilities are allowed.

a. **Weak convexity:** For any two indifferent bundles $x, y \in X$, define $z = \lambda x + (1-\lambda)y$, $0 \leq \lambda \leq 1$. Then $z \succeq x$ and $z \succeq y$.
b. **Strict convexity:** For any two indifferent bundles $x, y \in X$, define $z = \lambda x + (1-\lambda)y$, $0 < \lambda < 1$. Then $z \succ x$ and $z \succ y$.

Weak convexity says that any mixed (or convex combination) bundle of two indifferent bundles should be preferred or indifferent to the two bundles. Strict convexity rules out indifference; the mixed bundle must be strictly preferred. Both axioms rule out the mixed bundle to be inferior to the two bundles.

The difference between the two versions of convexity is made clear in Figure 2.2. The left indifference curve shows that the mixed bundle c is strictly preferred to the indifferent bundles a and b. The area above the indifference curve is the strictly preferred region. The right indifference curve shows weak convexity, as the bundle c, which is a convex combination of a and b is indifferent to a and b. The convexity assumption plays a crucial role in determining the choice of the consumer (i.e., utility maximisation). Strict convexity is often used to get uniqueness of choice.[4] In any branch of economics convexity plays a crucial role, an assumption hard to dispense with.

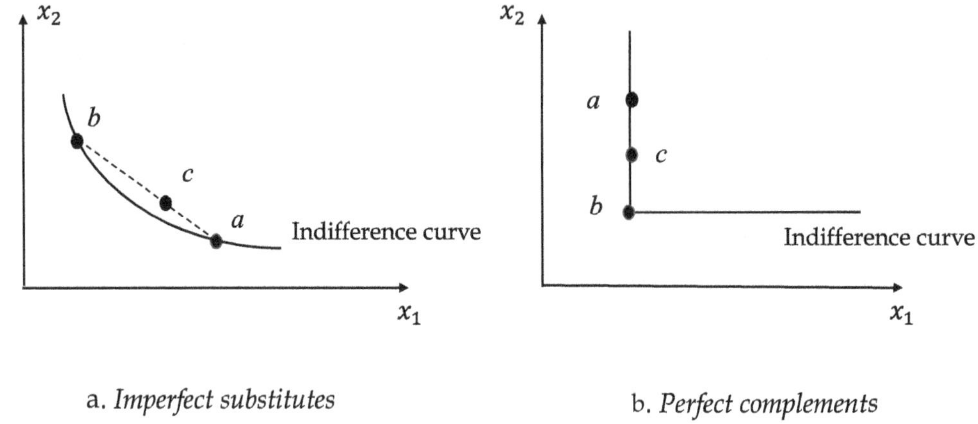

Figure 2.2 Strict versus weak convexity

2.2.1 Existence of utility function

The previously mentioned axioms provide a logical foundation for the notion of utility. In fact, given these axioms, we can be assured of the existence of a utility function so that the preference ordering of the consumer can be written by a simple function. If $x \succ y$, then $u(x) > u(y)$, and if x is indifferent to y, then $u(x) = u(y)$. Equivalently, $u(x) \geq u(y)$ implies $x \succeq y$. The formal statement of the theorem is as follows and its proof (adapted from Mas-Colell et al. (1995)) is given in Section 2.5.[5]

Theorem 1. *If the preference ordering is complete, transitive, continuous and monotonic, then there exists a continuous utility function* $u : R^n_+ \to R$ *such that* $u(x) \geq u(y)$ *if* $x \succeq y$ *and vice versa.*

One central point is that once the axioms of preferences are accepted, one can simply assume a utility function and work with it, setting aside the axioms. Moreover, utility does not have any cardinal significance; it is merely an ordering of different bundles.

2.3 Indifference curve

From this point onward, we shall assume that our representative consumer's preference ordering can be described by a continuous utility function,

$$u = u(x_1, x_2, \ldots, x_n),$$

for which the first partial derivatives $\dfrac{\partial u}{\partial x_i} \geq 0$ for all $i = 1,2,\ldots,n$ (denoted as u_i) due to monotonicity.[6] It may be instructive to present the consumer's choice with the help of an indifference curve. As already noted, it is a curve that consists of all consumption bundles that give exactly the same utility.

Let us fix a particular level of utility, say, u^0. Then our indifference curve for this level of utility is given by $I = \{x \mid u(x_1, x_2, \ldots, x_n) = u^0\}$. For the two-good case, we can write (under some condition) $u(x_1, x_2(x_1)) \equiv u^0$. Furthermore, we can draw this indifference curve by writing explicitly

$$x_2 = x_2(x_1; u^0).$$

You should be aware that writing this explicit function from $(u(x_1, x_2(x_1)) = u^0)$ is not always possible. However, by the assumption of strong monotonicity, we will have $u_1, u_2 > 0$. This permits us to use the **implicit function theorem** and assume that an explicit function of the preceding kind exists. We will see later that where only weak monotonicity holds, we have to find other ways to write the indifference curve.

We have already drawn two types of indifference curves in Figure 2.1. It should be apparent now that (1) indifference curves must be continuous, (2) indifference curves must not cross each other (to maintain transitivity) and (3) the higher the indifference curve, the higher the level of utility. The slope of the indifference curve can be found from $u(x_1, x_2(x_1)) = u^0$ as

$$u_1 + u_2 \frac{dx_2}{dx_1} = 0 \quad \Rightarrow \quad \frac{dx_2}{dx_1} = -\frac{u_1(\cdot)}{u_2(\cdot)}.$$

When $u_1, u_2 > 0$, the slope is negative. We call $\frac{u_1(\cdot)}{u_2(\cdot)}$ the **marginal rate of substitution** of good 1 for good 2, or simply MRS. The idea is easily generalisable to n goods.

Now let us turn our attention to the second-order derivative, which can be obtained by differentiating MRS in the following way:

$$\frac{d^2 x_2}{dx_1^2} = -\frac{dMRS}{dx_1}$$

$$\frac{dMRS}{dx_1} = \frac{u_2\left\{u_{11} + u_{12}\frac{dx_2}{dx_1}\right\} - u_1\left\{u_{21} + u_{22}\frac{dx_2}{dx_1}\right\}}{u_2^2(.)}.$$

Next, substituting $\frac{dx_2}{dx_1} = -\frac{u_1}{u_2}$, we obtain

$$\frac{dMRS}{dx_1} = \left[\frac{u_2^2 u_{11} - 2u_{12}u_1u_2 + u_{22}u_1^2}{u_2^3(.)}\right].$$

Although we have not yet specified the second-order derivatives of the utility function, the curvature (or the magnitude of the rate of change of the slope) of the indifference curve can be expected to vary directly with the change in MRS. In other words, if the MRS is declining, the magnitude of the slope of the indifference curve will also decline, but because the slope is a negative number, the sign-inclusive effect or the second-order derivative of the indifference curve will vary inversely with MRS. For our analysis, we are going to need **non-increasing MRS**. That is, we must have $\frac{dMRS}{dx_1} \le 0$, or equivalently, $\frac{d^2 x_2}{dx_1^2} \ge 0$.

An important question is, What sort of utility function will give rise to non-increasing MRS? We can see that non-increasing MRS requires $\left[u_2^2 u_{11} - 2u_{12}u_1u_2 + u_{22}u_1^2\right] \le 0$, or

$$\Delta u = \left[-u_2^2 u_{11} + 2u_{12}u_1u_2 - u_{22}u_1^2\right] \ge 0. \tag{2.1}$$

It can be readily checked that Δu is nothing but the determinant of the bordered Hessian matrix of the u-function. This suggests that if we require our utility function to be **quasi-concave**, then we are assured of non-increasing MRS. In particular, if the utility function is **strictly quasi-concave**, then MRS will be strictly decreasing. See Chapter 16 for a better understanding of quasi-concave functions.

2.4 Different types of utility functions

In this section, we look at some of the popular utility functions.

1. **Cobb–Douglas utility function:** The most popular of all is the Cobb–Douglas form:

   $$u = Ax_1^\alpha x_2^\beta, \quad A, \alpha, \beta > 0.$$

   Note that there is no restriction necessary on the sum of α and β. If we set $\alpha + \beta < 1$, the utility function will be strictly concave, but that is not necessary. There are many special characteristics of the Cobb–Douglas form, some of which can be easily discerned by checking its first and second derivatives. Let us have a look:

   $$u_1 = A\alpha x_1^{\alpha-1}x_2^\beta, \qquad u_2 = A\beta x_1^\alpha x_2^{\beta-1}, \qquad MRS = \frac{\alpha}{\beta}\frac{x_2}{x_1}$$

   $$u_{11} = (\alpha-1)A\alpha x_1^{\alpha-2}x_2 \quad u_{22} = (\beta-1)A\beta x_1^\alpha x_2^{\beta-2} \quad u_{12} = A\alpha\beta x_1^{\alpha-1}x_2^{\beta-1}$$

   First, marginal utilities are strictly positive (satisfying our axiom of strong monotonicity). But check from the expressions of u_{11} and u_{22} that marginal utilities need not be declining. In fact, unless $\alpha < 1$ and $\beta < 1$, they will be either constant or increasing. Regardless of the values of α and β the key condition (Eq. (2.1)) will be satisfied with strict inequality (you can check). That means the Cobb-Douglas utility function is *strictly* quasi-concave. Strict quasi-concavity tells you that goods are **imperfect substitutes**. That is, to remain indifferent, one gives up successively less of one good to consume one additional unit of another good.

   Second, the cross partial derivative u_{12} is strictly positive. This is due to the fact that utility is not separable in the two goods, a reflection of the imperfect substitutes nature of the goods.[7]

   Finally, MRS is a linear function of the ratio $\frac{x_2}{x_1}$. This is a crucial feature of the Cobb–Douglas form. If the ratio of the first derivatives of a function is a function of the ratio of the independent variables (but not of them individually), then the function is called **homothetic**. The Cobb–Douglas form is a special type of the homothetic function (for MRS being linear in x_2/x_1). We will come across a variety of homothetic functions and later examine the implications of homotheticity for consumer demand.

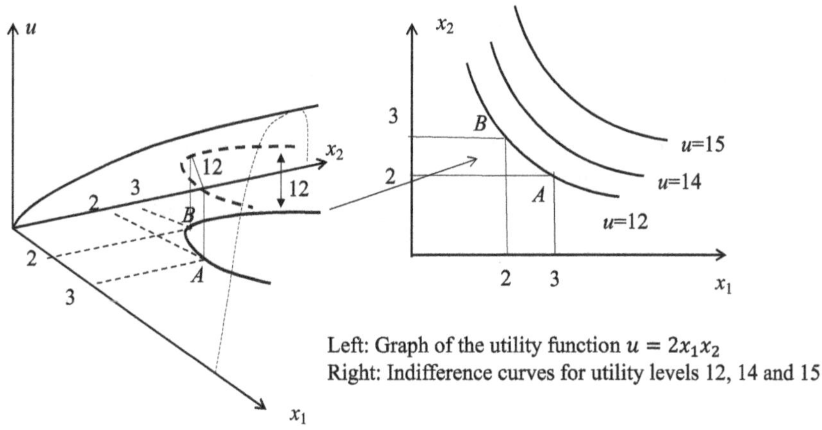

Left: Graph of the utility function $u = 2x_1x_2$
Right: Indifference curves for utility levels 12, 14 and 15

Figure 2.3 Imperfect substitutes

We graphically illustrate the Cobb–Douglas function on the left panel of Figure 2.3 assuming $A = 2$ and $\alpha = \beta = 1$. The utility graph is three-dimensional, where the x_1- and x_2-axes are like two sides of a floor and u is given by the height of the function, which is tent-shaped (rather a half-open tent). A and B are two points on the floor such that from these two points the side/roof of the tent is exactly 12 feet above. Since the height is, by definition, our utility, points A and B give exactly the same level of utility ($u = 12$), and therefore, they must be on the same indifference curve.

Given the round shape of the utility surface, we can imagine that if we were to trace all other points on the floor (which is our (x_1, x_2) plane) that also give exactly $u = 12$, the graph of these points should look like the solid curve drawn on the floor. In the right panel, we have extracted this curve; this is our indifference curve for $u = 12$. Clearly, we can go back to the left panel and map out all the points that give an exact height of 14 or 15. These curves are then shown in the right panel. As is clear by now, a family of indifference curves and their parent utility function convey the same information but in two different ways.

2. **Separable utility function:** In this case, the utility function will have its cross partial derivatives as zero but second-order derivatives strictly negative.

$$u = a\sqrt{x_1} + b\sqrt{x_2}.$$

From this utility function, we can quickly notice that

$$u_1 = \frac{a}{2\sqrt{x_1}}, \quad u_2 = \frac{b}{2\sqrt{x_2}}, \quad MRS = \frac{a}{b}\sqrt{\frac{x_2}{x_1}}.$$

I leave the second-order derivatives for you to work out and verify that the function is strictly concave. But note that the MRS here too is a function of the ratio $\frac{x_2}{x_1}$. That means, the separable concave utility function is also a homothetic function, but MRS is no longer a linear function of $\frac{x_2}{x_1}$. A word of caution here: The separable utility function will be homothetic only if x_1 and x_2 have identical power. You can check that $u = \sqrt{x_1} + x_2^{2/3}$ is not homothetic.

3. **Leontief utility function, or perfect complements:** This is also called fixed coefficient utility function. That means, utility will rise most efficiently only if the consumption of both goods is increased by maintaining a fixed proportion. The utility function given below specifies that the proportion of consumption to be $a\ /\ b$:

$$u = \min\{ax_1, bx_2\}.$$

Suppose we want to see which bundles of (x_1, x_2) will give us $u = u^0$. One bundle must be $\left(\frac{u^0}{a}, \frac{u^0}{b}\right)$ so that both numbers are exactly u^0. Now holding $x_1 = \frac{u^0}{a}$, if we keep on consuming more and more of x_2, by the utility formula, our utility will not go up at all; bx_2 will exceed $ax_1 = u^0$, but the resultant utility is still the same. Likewise, if we hold x_2 unchanged at $\frac{u^0}{b}$, any increase in x_1 will be a futile attempt to increase utility. Thus, the indifference curves for such a utility function are *L*-shaped. That two goods should be consumed in a fixed proportion is a testament to the idea of perfect complements, just like coffee and milk. Not only do they go together, but they go together in a fixed proportion.

On the right panel of Figure 2.4 two such indifference curves for $u = \min\{2x_1, 4x_2\}$ are shown. You can see points like (2,1), (3,1) and (2,3) all give utility 4. Except for (2,1), all other points on the indifference curve ($u = 4$) are 'wasteful'. The best way to increase utility is to increase the consumption of both goods maintaining the x_2 / x_1 ratio $1/2$ (or $x_1 : x_2 = 2:1$).

In the left panel of Figure 2.4, we have drawn the corresponding utility function. In a three-dimensional space, this looks like a pyramid. An indifference curve is a collection of

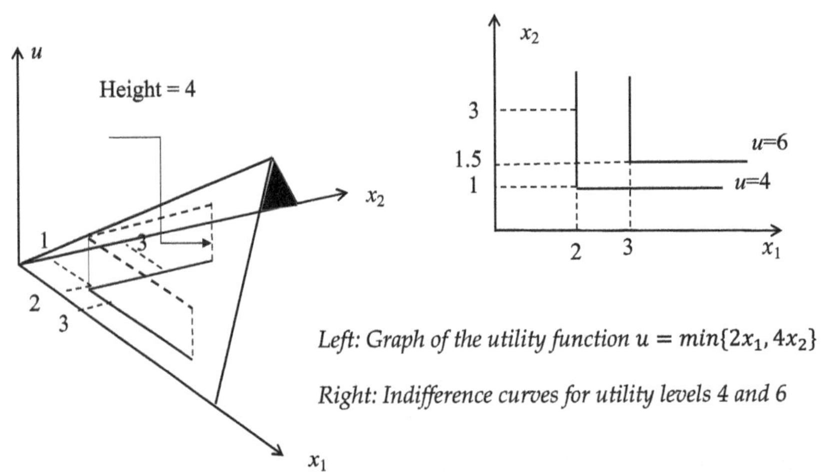

Figure 2.4 Perfect complements

all the points that will give exactly the same height (straight above) to reach the side or the ridge of the pyramid. In fact, a ridge point of the utility surface will correspond to the kink of a specific indifference curve.

An important point to note is that the Leontief utility function is not differentiable, and therefore it is inappropriate to talk about MRS.[8] The mathematical condition (2.1) is not the right condition to look at to test for quasi-concavity of the utility function. Rather, we should use the idea of the **upper contour set**, which refers to the set of all bundles that give the same or higher utility. Take $u = 4$ and consider the indifference curve and the entire north-east region to the indifference curve. This is an upper contour set, and it is evidently a convex set. This is just an alternative definition of a quasi-concave function. For more on this, see Chapter 16.

4. **Linear utility function, or perfect substitutes:** A polar opposite case of perfect complements is the case of perfect substitutes. One good can be substituted for the other without incurring any additional marginal utility loss:

$$u = ax_1 + bx_2.$$

In Figure 2.5, we have drawn this utility function and its associated indifference curves. The utility surface here is like a flat roof structure projecting forward. If one moves forward along the floor, the height to the roof will keep rising. But if one moves sideways, one will find a particular line on the floor, along which the height to the roof will be the same everywhere. We illustrate this for a utility height of 12, which is maintained by travelling from (4,0) to (0,6). In the right panel, the indifference curves are drawn. As can be seen, due to additive separability consumption of one good can go to zero and due to linearity MRS is constant. But you can check using the concept of the upper contour set that the utility function is quasi-concave.[9]

5. **Quasi-linear utility function:** This is a hybrid form of perfect substitutes and imperfect substitutes;

$$u = z(x_1) + bx_2,$$

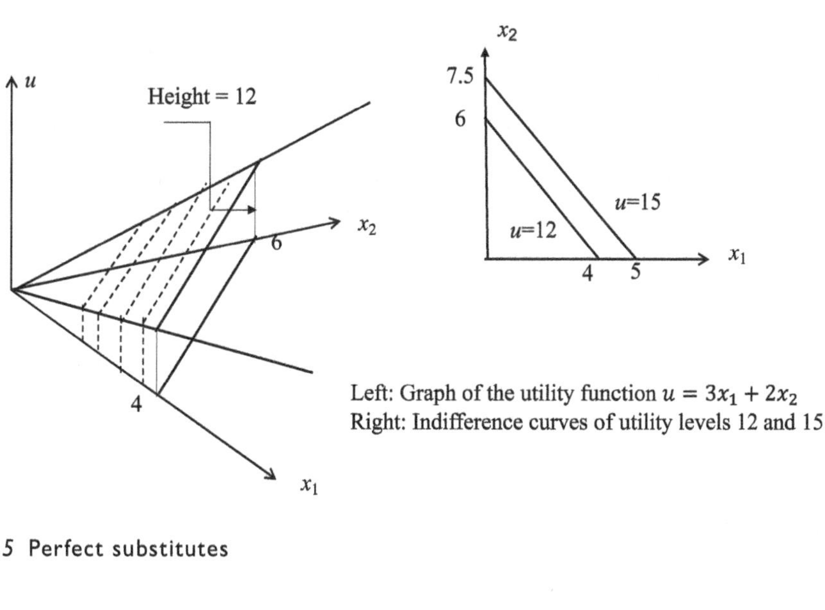

Figure 2.5 Perfect substitutes

where $z'(.) > 0, z''(.) < 0$. x_2 in this case can be substituted down to zero if needed, but the consumption of x_1 will have to be maintained at a positive level. Implicitly, x_1 is given priority over the consumption of x_2.

6. **Constant elasticity of substitution (CES) utility function:** This is a useful generalisation of some of the previous cases because each of them can be described as representing a particular value of the elasticity of substitution. We move much of the discussion of the elasticity of substitution to Section 2.5 due to the technical nature of this concept.

$$u = \left[ax_1^{\rho} + bx_2^{\rho}\right]^{\frac{1}{\rho}}.$$

We can take note of the marginal utilities and MRS as

$$u_1 = \left[ax_1^{\rho} + bx_2^{\rho}\right]^{\frac{1-\rho}{\rho}} ax_1^{\rho-1}, \quad u_2 = \left[ax_1^{\rho} + bx_2^{\rho}\right]^{\frac{1-\rho}{\rho}} bx_2^{\rho-1}, \quad MRS = \frac{a}{b}\left[\frac{x_2}{x_1}\right]^{1-\rho}.$$

Here, too, MRS is a function of the x_2 / x_1, and hence, the CES utility function is homothetic. But whether MRS will be a linear or non-linear function of x_2 / x_1 depends on the value of ρ. If $\rho = 0$, it is a linear function like the Cobb–Douglas case, and if $\rho = 1$, it is constant like the perfect substitutes case.

7. **Stone–Geary utility function:** Another utility function that is often used in many applications is the Stone–Geary utility function.

$$u = A(x_1 - \delta_1)^{\alpha}(x_2 - \delta_2)^{\beta}, \qquad \text{for } x_1 \geq \delta_1, x_2 \geq \delta_2,$$

where δ_1 and δ_2 are defined as the 'subsistence' consumption of goods 1 and 2, respectively. The consumer must consume above the subsistence levels to get positive utility.[10] You can easily derive the marginal utilities and MRS.

2.4.1 *Homothetic preference*

We have already seen that the Cobb–Douglas, the separable concave and the CES utility functions are all homothetic. That is, these functions are (at least) twice differentiable with respect to both variables, and MRS is a function of only the ratio $\frac{x_2}{x_1}$. But the Leontief function is not differentiable, the linear utility function is not twice differentiable and the quasi-linear utility function is not twice differentiable with respect to one variable. Therefore, these functions are not homothetic.

Since, in economics, homothetic functions occur more frequently and from the application point of view they assume special significance, here we present a graphical illustration of the indifference curves for these functions. In Figure 2.6, we present two contrasting cases. In the left panel, we have the case of homothetic preference. Along the line passing through the origin which consists of points *A*, *B* and *C*, the $\frac{x_2}{x_1}$ ratio is same, and the slopes of the three indifference curves are the same at points *A*, *B* and *C*. This means that the MRS along this line is constant. The MRS will change only if we move to a different $\frac{x_2}{x_1}$ ratio, such as the line passing through

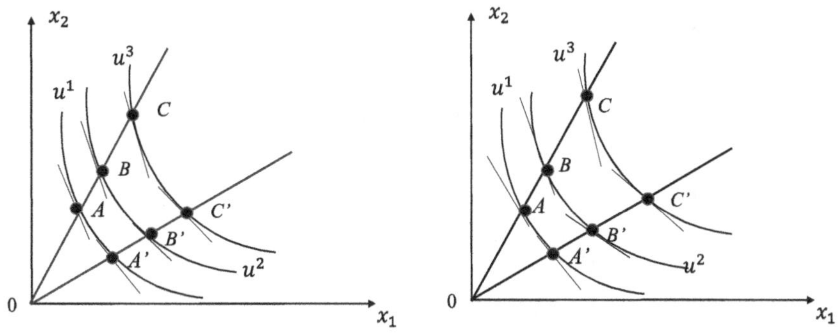

Left: Indifference curves for a homothetic utility function
Right: Indifference curves for a non-homothetic utility function

Figure 2.6 Homothetic preference

points A', B' and C'. Along the latter line, the $\frac{x_2}{x_1}$ ratio is smaller, and here, too, the MRS is the same between the three points.

In contrast, in the right panel of Figure 2.6, the slope of the indifference curve at point C is different to the slope at point B. That is, the MRS is changing despite the ratio $\frac{x_2}{x_1}$ not changing. Points C' and B' have the same problem. Thus, the preference here is not homothetic. In the next chapter, we will see that the homotheticity of a function has great implications for a consumer's choice.

2.5 Conclusion

We studied axioms of preferences that underpin the existence of utility functions, and then we considered a variety of utility functions that are consistent with these axioms. We also defined MRS and other properties of an indifference curves. Among various types of preferences, homothetic preferences deserve special attention.

Summary

1. We studied the axioms of preferences that provide the foundation of the utility function approach.
2. A variety of indifference curves/utility functions were studied. Some of them are differentiable, and some are not. But all are continuous functions.
3. We also defined concepts such as the MRS and the elasticity of substitution.
4. Differentiable indifference curves should demonstrate a non-increasing MRS.

2.6 Appendix

1. **Axiom of local non-satiation:** For any $x \in X$ and any real number $\delta > 0$, there is at least one bundle y such that $\|y - x\| < \delta$ and $y > x$.

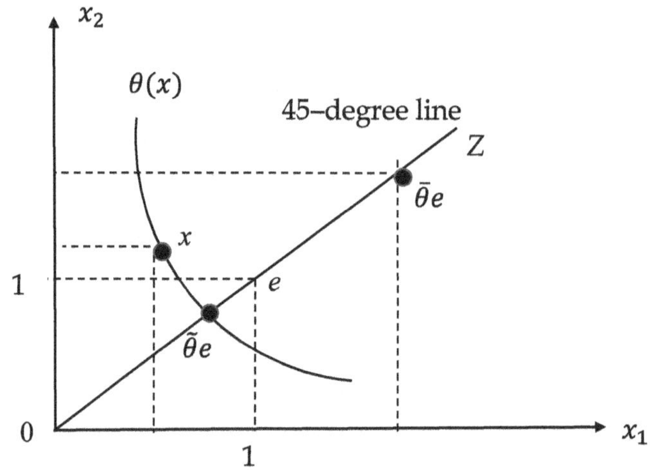

Figure 2.7 Existence of utility function

In other words, given any bundle x, we can always find a strictly preferred bundle y such that the distance (the Euclidean distance norm $\|\cdot\|$) between y and x is arbitrarily small. Note that this would be automatically true if the axiom of monotonicity (weak or strong) holds but not the other way around. If an indifference curve has an upward-rising segment, the monotonicity axiom will be violated, but the axiom of local non-satiation will hold. Likewise, if the consumer has a bliss point, meaning that at a unique bundle her utility is maximum, then monotonicity will be violated, but the axiom of local non-satiation will continue to hold except at the bliss point. This assumption can be seen as a much weaker type of monotonicity.

2. **Proof of Theorem 1:** [Adapted from Mas-Colell et al. (1995, pp. 47–48)] For ease of proof, we set $X = R^n_+$. Let $Z = \{x|(x_1 = x_2 = \ldots = x_n)\} \in X$. That is, Z is the set of all bundles that give exactly equal number of every good. On a two-dimensional graph, Z is the entire 45-degree line, as shown in Figure 2.7 by the 45-degree line. From this line, we pick our unit vector $e = (1,1,\ldots,1)$. By varying a scalar θ, we can define Z as a collection of all the following vectors: $Z = \{\theta e \mid \theta \geq 0\}$.

   Now consider an arbitrary $x \in R^n_+$, where not necessarily $x_1 = x_2 = \ldots = x_n$. By monotonicity, this bundle must satisfy $x \succeq 0$; that is, for $\theta = 0$, we have $x \succeq \theta e$. Also, we have θ, say, $\bar{\theta}$, such that $\bar{\theta}e > x$. See Figure 2.7. For instance, if $x = (1/2, 5/4)$, we have $\bar{\theta} = 2$ and $\bar{\theta}e = (2,2)$. Clearly, by the axiom of monotonicity, we have $\bar{\theta}e \succeq x$. Then it can be argued that there exists a *unique* $\theta \in [0,\bar{\theta}]$ such that $\tilde{\theta}(x)e$ is indifferent to x. The critical value $\tilde{\theta}$ will be unique, because by monotonicity (weak or strong) $\theta_2 e \succ \theta_1 e$ if $\theta_2 > \theta_1$. Hence, there is only one such scalar θ satisfying θe to be indifferent to x.

   This is not hard to see. By the axiom of completeness, for all possible values of θ (ranging from zero to infinity), the preference is (weakly) ordered. By the axiom of continuity, the upper and lower contour sets of x are closed; recall that, in any closed set, a convergent sequence will have its limit inside the set. We can define $A^+(x) = \{\theta \mid \theta e \succeq x\}$ as the upper contour set of x (i.e., the set of all preferred bundles). Similarly, define $A^-(x) = \{\theta \mid x \succeq \theta e\}$ as the lower contour set of x. By the axiom of continuity, these two sets must be closed. The intersection set of A^+ and A^- must be non-empty, and it must contain $\tilde{\theta}$ such that $\tilde{\theta}e$ must be indifferent to x.

We call $\theta(x)$ our utility function. Remember that $u(.)$ is just a mapping from R_+^n to R_{++}^1, and $\theta(x)$ is precisely that. Now as claimed in the theorem, the utility function must be continuous and must represent the preference in the sense that $u(x) \geq u(y)$ whenever $x \succeq y$ and conversely whenever $u(x) \geq u(y), x \succeq y$.

Suppose $x \succeq y$; then we know that x is indifferent to $\theta(x)e$, and y is indifferent to $\theta(y)e$. By transitivity, then $\theta(x)e \succeq \theta(y)e$. Next, by monotonicity, $\theta(x) \geq \theta(y)$, which establishes our claim that $x \succeq y$ implies $u(x) \geq u(y)$. From the other direction, assume that $u(x) \geq u(y)$. Since $u(x) = \theta(x)$ and $u(y) = \theta(y)$, we have $\theta(x) \geq \theta(y)$. Furthermore, by definition, $\theta(x)e$ is indifferent to x, and $\theta(y)e$ is indifferent to y. By monotonicity, then $\theta(x)e \succeq \theta(y)e$. Finally, by transitivity, $x \succeq y$, which completes our proof.

3. **Elasticity of substitution.** We often ask, What does a movement along the same indifference curve signify? Clearly, the MRS will change, but this will also force a change in the ratio x_2 / x_1. How proportionate is this change? How responsive is the change in $\frac{x_2}{x_1}$ to a change in the MRS? The answer is found in the elasticity of substitution.

The definition of the elasticity of substitution is $\sigma = \dfrac{d \ln \frac{x_2}{x_1}}{d \ln MRS}$. The general expression of σ for any (twice) differentiable utility function can be derived as follows:

$$d \ln \frac{x_2}{x_1} = \frac{x_1}{x_2} \left[\frac{x_1 \dfrac{dx_2}{dx_1} \cdot dx_1 - x_2 \cdot dx_1}{x_1^2} \right].$$

Substituting $\dfrac{dx_2}{dx_1} = -\dfrac{u_1}{u_2}$, we can write

$$d \ln \frac{x_2}{x_1} = -\frac{x_1 u_1 + x_2 u_2}{x_1 x_2 u_2} dx_1.$$

Next,

$$d \ln MRS = \frac{1}{MRS} \frac{-\Delta u}{u_2^3} dx_1,$$

which, after the substitution of $MRS = u_1 / u_2$, becomes

$$d \ln MRS = -\frac{\Delta u}{u_1 u_2^2} dx_1.$$

Then we arrive at

$$\sigma = \frac{u_1 u_2 \left(x_1 u_1 + x_2 u_2 \right)}{x_1 x_2 \Delta u}.$$

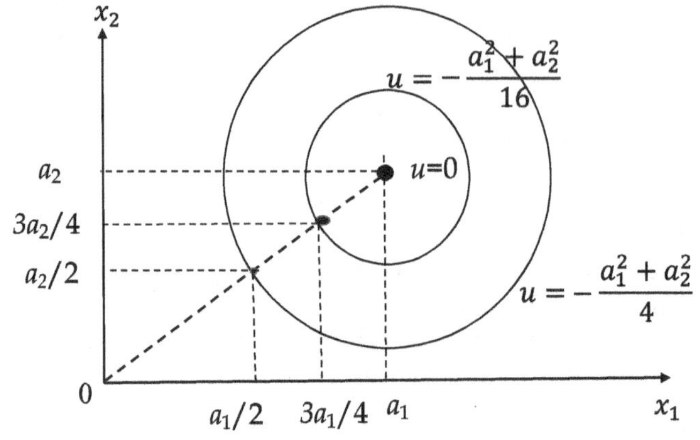

Figure 2.8 Indifference curves for bliss-point utility function

For the CES utility function, σ takes the form of

$$\sigma = \frac{1}{1-\rho}.$$

It can be shown that the CES utility function is a sort of generalisation of the other utility functions. If we set $\rho = 1$, we get the linear utility function in a straightforward manner. Similarly, if $\rho \to -\infty, \sigma \to 0$, which will correspond to the no-substitution case of the Leontief utility function. Finally, if $\rho \to 0, \sigma \to 1$, which corresponds to the case of the Cobb–Douglas utility function.

4. **Utility function with a bliss point.** In many branches of economics, such as political economy, public choice and social choice theory, one type of utility function is popular—utility function with a bliss point. For such utility functions, there is a well-defined maximum; consumption on either side of the bliss point gives a lower utility than the maximum. One obvious implication is that regardless of the price incentive, the consumer has no interest in increasing her consumption beyond the bliss-point level.

   Consider the utility function $u = -(x_1 - a_1)^2 - (x_2 - a_2)^2$. You can check that $\partial u / \partial x_1 = -2(x_1 - a_1)$, which is positive if $x_1 < a_1$ and negative if $x_1 > a_1$, and clearly $\partial u / \partial x_1 = 0$ at $x_1 = a_1$. Similarly, $\partial u / \partial x_2 = -2(x_2 - a_2)$ is positive if $x_2 < a_2$, negative if $x_2 > a_2$ and zero if $x_2 = a_2$. Thus, (a_1, a_2) is the bliss point at which the utility is maximum.

   An interesting point to note that the indifference curves for this type of utility function are circular, elliptical, oval or similarly shaped. In Figure 2.8 we draw three indifference curves for the utility function stated earlier. The point (a_1, a_2), the centre of the circles, is the bliss point, where the utility is zero. The inner circle passes through points $(3a_1/4, 3a_2/4)$; hence, the utility corresponding to this indifference curve is $u = -(a_1^2 + a_2^2)/16$. The outer circle passes through $(a_1/2, a_2/2)$, and therefore, the utility level is much lower $u = -(a_1^2 + a_2^2)/4$. Thus, as we move from left to right toward the bliss point (i.e., the innermost and the smallest circle), utility increases, and if we go further beyond the bliss point in the north-easterly direction, utility will fall. Clearly, the standard monotonicity axioms do not hold. The non-satiation axiom holds everywhere, except the bliss point.

5. **Lexicographic preference.** A special type of preference that strictly follows a hierarchical ordering is called lexicographical preference. Some of the well-known examples of lexicographical ordering are the (unofficial) Olympic medal ranking of countries, the arrangement of words in a dictionary (or lexicon, hence the word *lexicographic*) and the convention of writing one's date of birth. In the Olympic medal table, a gold medal is valued infinitely more than a silver medal, and a silver medal is valued infinitely more than a bronze medal. For example, a country with 1 gold medal and no other medals will be ranked ahead of another country if it gets no gold but 20 silver medals.

   For a consumer, this would mean that if x_1 is considered superior to x_2, bundle (2,0) is always preferred to (1,10). For a bundle to be preferred ahead of (2,0), it must have at least 2 units of x_1; for example, (2,1) should be preferred to (2,0). The main difficulty with lexicographic preference is that it is impossible to construct an indifference curve. Giving up on one good to acquire more of another good to maintain the same level of utility is ruled out here, because the goods have a hierarchy in the consumer's mind. Such preference is uncommon, although one may consider some people's absolute insistence on their favourite food more like a lexicographic preference.

   However, in many non-market provisions of social goods, lexicographic preferences are widely used. Often in non-selective government schools, several criteria are used for admission, such as duration of residency in the catchment area, distance from school and sibling preference. These criteria have a strict hierarchy; having a sibling in the same school may be given utmost priority, followed by distance from the school and then duration of residency. The school's preference here is lexicographic. Lexicographic preferences are designed to assert fairness in a strong way.

2.7 Exercises

1. a. Four footballers are given scores as high, medium or low on three skills: passing, accuracy of shots and stamina. Each footballer is seen as a bundle of skills. Footballer 1: (high, low, medium), Footballer 2: (medium, high, low), Footballer 3: (low, medium, high), Footballer 4: (high, low, low). The coach strictly prefers a player based on the strict dominance of two out of three skills. Verify if the coach's preference will be transitive.

   b. What if the coach strictly prefers one player over another only if that player weakly dominates the other player in all three skills? Can you then rank his preference over the players?
2. Draw an indifference curve of the utility function $u = \max\{x_1, x_2\}$. Is this function quasi-concave? If not, then what type of function is it?
3. Show the utility function $u = \sqrt{x_1} + \sqrt{x_2}$ is strictly concave.
4. Show that the utility function $u = -\frac{1}{x_1} - \frac{1}{x_2}$ is strictly monotonic.
5. Verify if the following utility functions are homothetic.

   a. $u = \sqrt{x_1} + x_1^{1/4} x_2^{1/4} + \sqrt{x_2}$

   b. $u = 2\sqrt{x_1} + x_2$

   c. $u = \sqrt{(x_1 - \delta_1)(x_2 - \delta_2)}$

   d. $u = \ln A + \alpha \ln x_1 + \beta \ln x_2$

6. Calculate the elasticity of substitution for $u = \sqrt{x_1} + \sqrt{x_2}$.
7. Draw an indifference map for $u = x_2 + \min\{ax_1, bx_2\}$.
8. Show that the utility function $u = x_1 + x_2 - \frac{x_1^2}{2} - \frac{x_2^2}{2} - \delta x_1 x_2$ has a bliss point.

Notes

1 Atkin (2013) also argued that at the root of habit formation lies the local abundance of a crop, wheat or paddy in this context. Thus, the physical availability and thereby the relative market price of the principal food grains play an important role in forming our habits and preferences.
2 When, $x \sim y$ both $x \succeq y$ and $y \succeq x$ hold simultaneously.
3 In one-good environments, transitivity and monotonicity imply each other.
4 Convexity axiom insists that the area above an indifference curve, which is called the upper contour set, must be a convex set.
5 Note that the theorem does not insist on reflexiveness and convexity. Reflexiveness is needed for technical convenience. Convexity is useful for choice but not necessary for utility function representation.
6 Implicitly we are assuming here differentiability. But for non-differentiable utility functions, one can simply assert that utility must be non-decreasing.
7 Many textbooks call this 'imperfect net substitutes'.
8 Marginal means tiny changes, which can be conveniently captured by calculus. But when a function is not differentiable, calculus fails to be of any use.
9 The utility function is differentiable but up to the first order. So, condition (Eq. (2.1)) is not applicable.
10 When $x_1 < \delta_1$ and $x_2 < \delta_2$, one has a choice of setting utility zero or at all x_1 and x_2 or setting $u = Ax_1^{\alpha} x_2 \beta$ or some other specification depending on the context. The key point is that this utility function is more meaningful for $x_1 > \delta_1$ and $x_2 > \delta_2$.

References and further readings

Atkin, D. (2013). Trade, tastes and nutrition in India. *American Economic Review*, 103(5), 1629–1663.

Bentham, J. (1789). *An Introduction to the Principles of Morals and Legislation*. London: T. Payne & Son.

Debreu, G. (1954). Representation of a preference ordering by a numerical function. In R. M. Thrall, C. H. Coombs & H. Raiffa (Eds.), *Decision Processes*, 159–167. New York: Wiley.

Jevons, W. S. (1866). A general mathematical theory of political economy. *The Journal of the Royal Statistical Society*, 29, 282–287.

Kahneman, D. & Tversky, A. (1979). Prospect theory: An analysis of decisions under risk. *Econometrica*, 47, 313–327.

Kahneman, D., Wakker, P. & Sarin, R. (1997). Back to Bentham? Explorations of experienced utility. *Quarterly Journal of Economics*, 112, 375–406.

Mas-Colell, A., Whinston, M. D. & Green, J. R. (1995). *Microeconomic Theory*. New York: Oxford University Press.

Read, D. (2009). *Experimental Tests of Rationality*. Oxford: Oxford University Press.

Sen, A. K. (1977). Rational fools: A critique of the behavioral foundations of economic theory. *Philosophy & Public Affairs*, 6(4), 317–344.

Simon, H. A. (1959). Theories of decision-making in economics and behavioral science. *American Economic Review*, 49, 253–283.

Stigler, G. J. (1950). The development of utility theory. II. *Journal of Political Economy*, 58(4), 307–327.

Sugden, R. (2016). Ontology, methodological individualism and the foundations of the social sciences. *Journal of Economic Literature*, 58, 373–396.

Varian, H. R. (1992). *Microeconomic Analysis*, 3rd ed. New York: Norton.

Chapter 3

Utility maximisation

Abstract

We present the utility maximisation problem where the consumer tries to achieve her highest possible indifference curve within the budget set she is endowed with. The resulting choice of the consumer gives rise to a pair of *ordinary* (or Marshallian) demand functions. We study the problem both mathematically and graphically. The graphical method is particularly useful when the utility function is not differentiable. The demand functions are then characterised, with special attention given to homothetic preferences. A number of applications, such as variable price, subsistence consumption, benefit allowance, single parent's dilemma are studied. Finally, we show how demand can be aggregated over individuals to arrive at the market demand. In Section 3.9, we briefly analyse the utility maximisation problem for Lancaster's characteristic-based preferences.

Keywords: Marshallian demand, Tangency solution, Corner solution, Homothetic demand, Gross substitutes, Price elasticity

3.1 Introduction

Near University College London, a cluster of curry houses on Drummond Street do brisk business; apart from the nearby South Asian community, university students are their regular patrons. Not far away at trendy Covent Garden, there is Dishoom, serving Indian street food with an ambience of Bollywood music and movies that reminisces Bombay before the city was renamed Mumbai. The restaurant is young professionals' favourite. But for those who do not worry about price tags, Benares is a preferred destination, a Michelin-star Indian restaurant in the upmarket Mayfair area of Central West London. As a reminder of the etiquette of fine dining, the restaurant explicitly forbids casual footwear like trainers and flip-flops.

Like these diners, our consumer is also going to get the best out of her budget. Taking quantity of goods rather than quality as our main concern, we see that the consumer's problem is to find her most preferred bundle within her budget. We know that given a set of axioms, her preferences can be described by a quasi-concave utility function. Now we state that she wishes to maximise her utility $u = u(x_1, x_2)$ subject to her budget constraint $m = p_1x_1 + p_2x_2$.

Students often feel that the 'spend it all' assumption underpinning our budget equation is unrealistic; after all, prudence requires that we do not blow our budget. True, but one simple way to restore realism is to include saving as a third good, as we discussed in Chapter 1. Another option is to assume, as indeed is the case in our static one-shot model, that there is no future. Wouldn't we blow our budget if our lives had a pre-specified expiry date? Well, maybe or maybe

DOI: 10.4324/9781003226994-3

not! But take a happier example. You have gone on holiday to Tanzania, and on the last day of your stay, you find that many Tanzanian shillings are unspent. As converting Tanzanian shillings back into dollars can be loss-making, you would perhaps blow your budget on Kilimanjaro souvenirs before catching the flight home. A similar argument applies to your living expense budget if it is borne by your parents or government; you will blow it all.

The consumer's decision problem is a constrained maximisation problem, which can be solved algebraically and/or graphically depending on the nature of the utility function as well as the dimensionality of the problem, that is, two goods or n goods. If our utility function is (at least) twice differentiable, then we can use the Lagrange method that converts a constrained optimisation problem to an unconstrained one (see Chapter 16, "Mathematical Appendix"). Otherwise, we will use the graphical approach.

3.2 Algebraic method

We consider utility functions that are at least twice differentiable. The consumer maximises the following Lagrangian function with respect to (w.r.t.) (x_1, x_2, λ), where λ is the Lagrange multiplier for the budget constraint:

$$\mathcal{L} = u(x_1, x_2) - \lambda[p_1x_1 + p_2x_2 - m].$$

Continuing with our practice of writing the first partial derivatives of the utility function as u_1 and u_2, that is, the marginal utilities of goods 1 and 2, we write the first-order conditions for utility maximisation as

$$\partial\mathcal{L} / \partial x_1 \equiv u_1(x_1, x_2) - \lambda p_1 = 0 \tag{3.1}$$

$$\partial\mathcal{L} / \partial x_2 \equiv u_2(x_1, x_2) - \lambda p_2 = 0 \tag{3.2}$$

$$\partial\mathcal{L} / \partial \lambda \equiv -[p_1x_1 + p_2x_2 - m] = 0. \tag{3.3}$$

Eqs. (3.1)–(3.3) can be implicitly solved for three variables (x_1, x_2, λ). As λ is of secondary importance, we can simply reduce the three-equation system to two equations by dividing Eq. (3.1) by Eq. (3.2) (and keeping λ out of the picture) to write

$$\frac{u_1(x_1, x_2)}{u_2(x_1, x_2)} = \frac{p_1}{p_2}. \tag{3.4}$$

Eqs. (3.4) and (3.3) can be used to solve for x_1 and x_2. The solution (x_1, x_2) will be a function of (p_1, p_2, m), and they are called Marshallian demand functions, named after the early twentieth-century economist Alfred Marshall.[1] Let us write them as

$$x_1^* = x_1(p_1, p_2, m), \text{ and } x_2^* = x_2(p_1, p_2, m). \tag{3.5}$$

Eq. (3.4) is critical to all demand functions, as it establishes equality between the marginal rate of substitution (MRS; a measure of the marginal benefit of consumption) and the price ratio (a measure of the marginal cost of consumption). In panel a of Figure 3.1, we illustrate

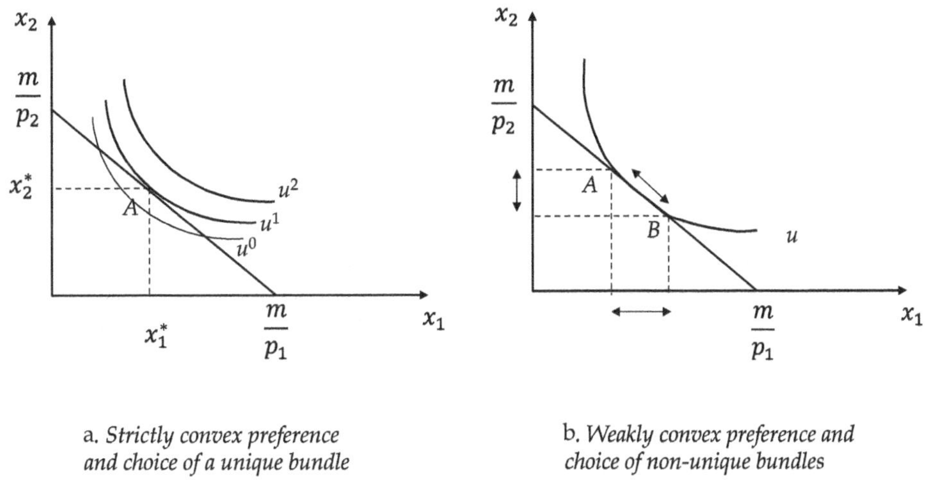

Figure 3.1 Convex preferences and choice of bundles

the utility maximisation problem. We show that the consumer has infinitely many indifference curves to choose from within her budget set but just take three of them. Of the three indifference curves representing utility levels u^0, u^1 and u^2 that we have drawn to illustrate optimality, clearly u^2 is out of reach, and u^0 is not the best. Utility level u^1 is the highest, and it is achieved via bundle A, where the marginal benefit of consumption is equal to the marginal cost of consumption. To the left of A, along the budget line, the consumer's marginal benefit exceeds the marginal cost, justifying the consumption of more of x_1 relative to x_2, and to the right of A, exactly the opposite is true. Thus, point A is the unique optimal point.

In panel b of Figure 3.1, we show that the equalisation of marginal benefit and marginal cost can occur over a range of (x_1, x_2) if the indifference curves are not strictly convex. A linear segment of the indifference curve leaves the consumer with many more bundles as utility maximising. Any bundle between points A and B will serve the consumer equally.

At this point, let us get a few technical issues out of the way. First, how do we know that a solution to our system of Eqs. (3.1)–(3.3) exists? By solution, we mean that for every given price income vector (p_1, p_2, m), there is at least one (x_1, x_2, λ) that satisfies the earlier set of equations. Second, how to ensure that the solution applies to a maximum (and not a minimum, which shares the same first-order conditions)? Third, if a solution exists will that be unique? For these questions, Figure 3.1 gives some clues.

Mathematically, the implicit equation system given by Eqs. (3.1)–(3.3) will indeed have a solution if the functions $\partial\mathcal{L}/\partial x_1$, $\partial\mathcal{L}/\partial x_2$ and $\partial\mathcal{L}/\partial\lambda$ are differentiable, and the matrix formed by their derivatives is invertible; the solution is guaranteed by the implicit function theorem. To verify that the solution indeed corresponds to a maximum, we need to check the second-order condition for maximisation. For the constrained maximisation that we are considering, the second-order condition involves the Hessian matrix of the Lagrangian, which is obtained by differentiating the first-order conditions with respect to x_1, x_2 and λ. The Hessian matrix must be negative semi-definite subject to the constraint: $dx^t D^2 u(x) dx \leq 0$ for all dx such that $p_1 dx_1 + p_2 dx_2 = 0$, where dx^t is the transpose of the vector $dx = (dx_1, dx_2)$. Verifying the second-order condition comes down to checking that the following bordered Hessian Matrix must have its (border-preserving) principal minors alternating in sign *starting from positive (or non-negative).*[2]

$$\begin{bmatrix} u_{11} & u_{12} & -p_1 \\ u_{21} & u_{22} & -p_2 \\ -p_1 & -p_2 & 0 \end{bmatrix}$$

Since utility depends only on two goods, the first border-preserving principal minor of the Hessian matrix is nothing but the determinant of the matrix itself. The determinant should be positive. To verify that substitute $p_i = \frac{u_i}{\lambda}$ and carry out the determinant, which will be positive if and only if $\frac{1}{\lambda^2}\Delta u > 0$, where (recall from Chapter 2)

$$\Delta u = \left[-u_2^2 u_{11} + 2u_{12}u_1u_2 - u_{22}u_1^2\right].$$

Since $\lambda > 0$ (because of the binding budget constraint), we must have $\Delta u \geq 0$. This is also the condition for quasi-concavity of the utility function we noted earlier in the last chapter.

Thus, ensuring a maximum more than satisfies the (sufficient) condition specified by the implicit function theorem. Furthermore, if $\Delta u > 0$, our utility function is strictly quasi-concave, and the Hessian matrix of $u(\cdot)$ will be negative definite. Alternatively stated, the consumer's preferences will be strictly convex, and the optimal bundle (x_1, x_2) will be unique as illustrated in panel *a* of Figure 3.1. In panel *b*, we have the case of a quasi-concave utility function or weakly convex preferences. In such situations, the more appropriate concept is *demand correspondence* than demand function. But the algebra for correspondences is complex. One way to get around correspondences is to assume that the consumer will pick a unique point, say, the midpoint between *A* and *B* in panel *b* of Figure 3.1. As such, the multiplicity of solutions is only temporary; with a slight price change, the problem will disappear.

To summarise our technical discussion, if the utility function is quasi-concave, then there will be a solution to the consumer's utility maximisation problem. If the utility function is also *strictly* quasi-concave, then the consumer's optimal bundle will be unique. But not having a quasi-concave utility function risks utility maximisation.[3]

3.2.1 Examples

1. **Cobb–Douglas utility function** To illustrate our algebraic method, we start with the most popular utility function—Cobb–Douglas: $u = Ax_1^{\alpha}x_2^{\beta}$. We write the consumer's problem to maximise the following Lagrangian with respect to x_1, x_2 and λ:

$$\mathcal{L} = Ax_1^{\alpha}x_2^{\beta} + \lambda\left[m - p_1x_1 - p_2x_2\right].$$

The first-order conditions Eqs. (3.1) and (3.2) take the following expressions:

$$A\alpha x_1^{\alpha-1}x_2^{\beta} - \lambda p_1 = 0 \tag{3.6}$$

$$A\beta x_1^{\alpha}x_2^{\beta-1} - \lambda p_2 = 0. \tag{3.7}$$

Dividing Eq. (3.6) by Eq. (3.7), we get $\frac{\alpha x_2}{\beta x_1} = \frac{p_1}{p_2}$, which can be rewritten as $x_2 = \frac{\beta}{\alpha}\frac{p_1}{p_2}x_1$.

Substituting this relation into Eq. (3.3), we get

$$p_1x_1 + p_2\left(\frac{\beta}{\alpha}\frac{p_1}{p_2}x_1\right) = m \quad \Rightarrow \quad p_1x_1\left(1+\frac{\beta}{\alpha}\right) = m$$

$$\text{or,} \quad x_1^* = \frac{\alpha}{(\alpha+\beta)}\frac{m}{p_1}. \tag{3.8}$$

Eq. (3.8) is the Marshallian demand function for x_1. Utilising this, we derive the Marshallian demand function for x_2 as

$$x_2^* = \frac{\beta}{\alpha}\frac{p_1}{p_2}x_1^* = \left[\frac{\beta}{\alpha}\frac{p_1}{p_2}\right]\times\left[\frac{\alpha}{(\alpha+\beta)}\frac{m}{p_1}\right]$$

$$\text{or,} \quad x_2^* = \frac{\beta}{(\alpha+\beta)}\frac{m}{p_2}. \tag{3.9}$$

The same method can be applied to any utility function that is solvable using the Lagrange method.

2. **Separable (homogeneous) utility function.** Now consider $u = a\sqrt{x_1} + b\sqrt{x_2}$. As we have seen in the last chapter, $MRS = \frac{a}{b}\frac{\sqrt{x_2}}{\sqrt{x_1}}$. Setting $MRS = \frac{p_1}{p_2}$, we substitute $x_2 = \frac{b^2p_1^2}{a^2p_2^2}x_1$ into the budget equation to arrive at the demand functions as

$$x_1^* = \frac{a^2p_2}{\left[a^2p_2 + b^2p_1\right]}\frac{m}{p_1} \quad \text{and} \quad x_2^* = \frac{b^2p_1}{\left[a^2p_2 + b^2p_1\right]}\frac{m}{p_2} \tag{3.10}$$

3. **Homothetic utility function.** For any homothetic utility function that yields an MRS of the form,

$$MRS = \frac{c_1}{c_2}\left(\frac{x_2}{x_1}\right)^{\frac{1}{\theta}},$$

where $c_1, c_2 > 0$ and $\theta \geq 1$, we derive the Marshallian demand functions as follows: First, we write $\frac{c_1}{c_2}\left(\frac{x_2}{x_1}\right)^{\frac{1}{\theta}} = \frac{p_1}{p_2}$ and obtain $\frac{c_1}{c_2}\left(\frac{x_2}{x_1}\right)^{\frac{1}{\theta}} = \frac{p_1}{p_2}$. Substituting this into the budget line and rearranging terms, we will get

$$x_1^* = \left(\frac{c_1^{\theta}p_2^{\theta-1}}{c_1^{\theta}p_2^{\theta-1} + c_2^{\theta}p_1^{\theta-1}}\right)\frac{m}{p_1} \quad \text{and} \quad x_2^* = \left(\frac{c_2^{\theta}p_1^{\theta-1}}{c_1^{\theta}p_2^{\theta-1} + c_2^{\theta}p_1^{\theta-1}}\right)\frac{m}{p_2}. \tag{3.11}$$

Now we can verify that by substituting different values of c_1, c_2 and θ, we can obtain the demand functions for various types of homothetic preferences:

a. If we set $c_1 = \alpha$, $c_2 = \beta$ and $\theta = 1$, we have the **Cobb–Douglas** demand functions as shown in Eqs. (3.8) and (3.9).
b. If we set $c_1 = a$, $c_2 = b$ and $\theta = 2$, we get the demand functions of the **separable utility function** case as obtained in Eq. (3.10).
c. For the **CES utility function** $u = \left[ax_1^{\rho} + bx_2^{\rho}\right]^{\frac{1}{\rho}}$ discussed in the last chapter, the demand curves can be derived by setting $c_1 = a$, $c_2 = b$ and $\theta = \dfrac{1}{1-\rho}$, $(0 \le \rho < 1)$.

$$x_1^* = \left(\frac{a^{\frac{1}{1-\rho}} p_2^{\frac{\rho}{1-\rho}}}{a^{\frac{1}{1-\rho}} p_2^{\frac{\rho}{1-\rho}} + b^{\frac{1}{1-\rho}} p_1^{\frac{\rho}{1-\rho}}} \right) \frac{m}{p_1} \tag{3.12}$$

$$x_2^* = \left(\frac{b^{\frac{1}{1-\rho}} p_1^{\frac{\rho}{1-\rho}}}{a^{\frac{1}{1-\rho}} p_2^{\frac{\rho}{1-\rho}} + b^{\frac{1}{1-\rho}} p_1^{\frac{\rho}{1-\rho}}} \right) \frac{m}{p_2}. \tag{3.13}$$

Note all the preceding demand functions (Eq. (3.8)–(3.13)) reflect that both goods are consumed in strictly positive quantities. That is, we always have an interior solution, and x_1^* is less than m / p_1 and x_2^* is less than m / p_2. This is true for the entire class of homothetic preferences. You can easily prove it by noting that optimal x_2 and x_1 must be consumed in a proportion that is determined by the prices of the two goods. If the consumption of one good was zero, the proportion would not be maintained, and hence, the zero consumption of that good would not be optimal.

When we step out of homothetic preferences, strictly positive consumption of all goods may not be guaranteed, as is shown by the next utility function.

4. **Quasi-linear utility function.** Suppose $u = a\sqrt{x_1} + bx_2$. Here, although the utility function is differentiable the second partial derivative with respect to x_2 is zero. This fact allows us to simplify the utility maximisation problem by substituting the budget line directly into the utility function and converting the problem into an unconstrained maximisation problem, which we write as

$$\text{Max } u = a\sqrt{x_1} + b\left[\frac{m - p_1 x_1}{p_2}\right].$$

A crucial assumption in the substitution of x_2 in the utility function is that $x_2 > 0$. So, by maximising the utility function, we can solve for optimal x_1 and then determine x_2 from the budget equation. From the first-order condition with respect to x_1, we get

$$\frac{\partial u}{\partial x_1} = \frac{a}{2\sqrt{x_1}} - b\frac{p_1}{p_2} = 0.$$

If the solution to the preceding equation is x_1^*, then $x_2^* = \dfrac{m - p_1 x_1^*}{p_2}$, provided $p_1 x_1^* < m$.

Notably, under the quasi-linear utility function, the consumer's demand for the good for which the marginal utility is decreasing (x_1 in this case) does not vary with income, when both goods are consumed in positive quantities. Her consumption of x_1 is fixed as long as prices are unchanged. Once she buys x_1 to the desired amount, not only is the leftover budget spent on x_2, but any additional income is also devoted to x_2.

If, however, the budget is not large enough to finance x_1^* or no surplus is left for x_2, the consumer will buy only x_1 as much as she can and will completely give up on x_2. Thus, her demands are summarised as

$$x_1^* = \frac{a^2}{4b^2}\frac{p_2^2}{p_1^2}, \quad x_2^* = \frac{m - p_1 x_1^*}{p_2} \quad \text{if} \quad \frac{a^2}{4b^2}\frac{p_2^2}{p_1} < m$$

$$x_1^* = \frac{m}{p_1}, \quad x_2^* = 0 \quad \text{if} \quad \frac{a^2}{4b^2}\frac{p_2^2}{p_1} \geq m.$$

With the quasi-linearity of the utility function, we are witnessing the possibility of one good's consumption going to zero, which we did not see previously. When the marginal utility of one good is constant the good is used as a left-over or 'inessential' good; it will be bought only when there is left-over money.

3.3 Graphical method

When the utility function is not differentiable, or differentiable only up to the first order, the Lagrange method is neither simple nor useful. A graphical approach is more instructive.

3.3.1 *Perfect complements*

Take the case of perfect complements or Leontief preferences from the last chapter: $u = \min\{ax_1, bx_2\}$.

This is a minimum function and should not to be confused with the instruction to minimise a function. The utility function takes a minimum of two numbers that are generated by a bundle (x_1, x_2). For instance, if $a = 1$ and $b = 2$, then for a bundle (3, 4), we have two numbers $3a = 3$ and $4b = 8$. The utility value assigned to the bundle (3, 4) is $\min\{3, 8\} = 3$. You can consider another bundle, say, (3, 5), and verify that utility still remains 3.

This type of utility function signifies the fact that certain goods need to be consumed in a fixed proportion. In this example, if we add more of x_2 to the bundle (3,4), holding x_1 unchanged, the utility does not change. So the indifference curve would be vertical in part. We can reduce x_2 from 4 up to 1.5, and the utility will still be 3. For the bundle (3,1.5), if we increase x_1, this time holding x_2 unchanged, again the utility will remain fixed at 3. Here, the indifference curve will be horizontal.

Combining the vertical and horizontal parts, we get an L-shaped indifference curve, similar to the ones illustrated in panel *a* of Figure 3.2. The key proportion at which the goods are to be combined is given by the kink of the indifference curves. All the indifference curves drawn here u^0, u^1 and u^2 share their kinks on the line $x_2 = \dfrac{ax_1}{b}$ passing through the origin. Above (or below) this line $bx_2 > (<) ax_1$, the consumer cannot efficiently change her utility.

To give an example, some of us prefer to have our coffee with a fixed amount of milk. A bit more milk does not ruin our coffee. A better example perhaps is a pair of shoes going with a pair of socks. Having 10 pairs of socks does not increase our utility until we buy at least another pair of shoes, possibly colour-coordinated with those additional pairs of socks.

Not surprisingly then, the consumer's choice will be uniquely determined by the intersection point of the budget line and the red line on the graph panel *a* of Figure 3.2 (indicating the critical proportion). Combining $p_1x_1 + p_2x_2 = m$ and $x_2 = \frac{a}{b}x_1$, we get the demand functions

$$x_1^* = \left(\frac{bp_1}{bp_1 + ap_2}\right)\frac{m}{p_1} \quad \text{and} \quad x_2^* = \left(\frac{ap_2}{bp_1 + ap_2}\right)\frac{m}{p_2}. \tag{3.14}$$

Like the homothetic preferences, perfect complements also require that both goods be consumed at all prices and income and that the choice is always unique, despite the fact that preferences here are weakly convex and weakly monotonic. In panel *a* of Figure. 3.2, if the budget line shifts, a new solution like point *A* will emerge along the line through the origin.

A word of caution: Students often mistakenly interpret point *A* as a tangency point. This indifference curve is not differentiable and therefore, it is inappropriate to think in terms of the MRS, which is meaningful only when substitution possibilities exist. The perfect complements rule out that. But regardless of substitution, it is clear that that the consumer will get her highest utility u^1 at point *A*.

3.3.2 *Perfect substitutes*

The polar opposite case of perfect complements is the case of perfect substitutes, or linear utility function, $u = ax_1 + bx_2$. Here, the utility function is differentiable and the MRS exists, but the MRS is a constant at *a/b*. Here, too, the graphical method should be relied on. In panel *b* of Figure 3.2, we have drawn a set of indifference curves for perfect substitutes. As the indifference

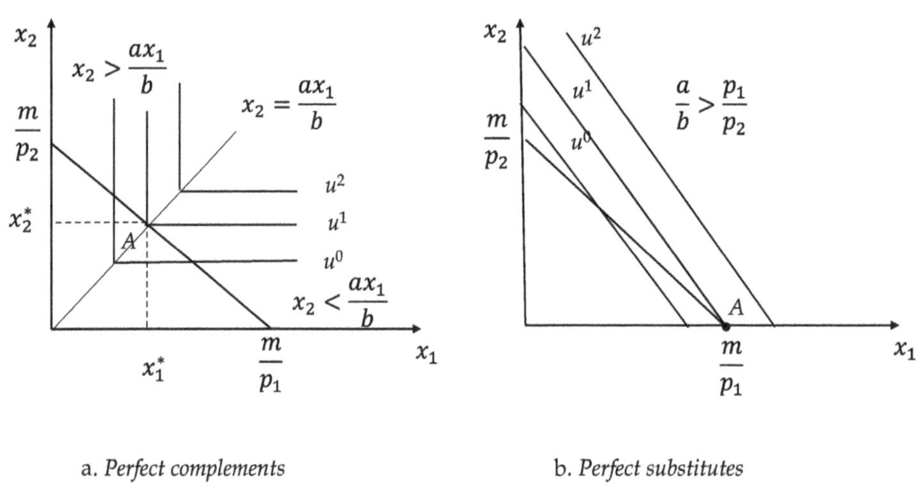

Figure 3.2 Perfect complements and perfect substitutes

curves are linear and look like the budget line, a tangency solution is meaningless.[4] But even though we do not have tangency, that is, $a/b \neq p_1/p_2$, we have a unique solution. For instance, if $\frac{a}{b} > \frac{p_1}{p_2}$, the highest indifference curve will be achieved at the right-most corner of the budget set at m/p_1 as shown in panel *b* of Figure 3.2. The consumer will buy only x_1 and no x_2. Alternatively, when $\frac{a}{b} < \frac{p_1}{p_2}$, the consumer's choice will switch to good 2, with $x_2 = \frac{m}{p_2}$ and $x_1 = 0$. The consumer here specialises in the consumption of one good alone—the good whose relative price is smaller than the MRS.

3.4 Properties and characterisation

What can we say about the Marshallian demand function? In the general case, the following can be said.

1. **Continuity** If $u(x_1, x_2)$ satisfies strict convexity of preferences, the Marshallian demand functions x_1^* and x_2^* will be continuous functions of (p_1, p_2, m).

   We have already seen that when preferences are not strictly convex, the consumer's choice may not be unique. We will then have a demand correspondence (instead of a demand function). Demand correspondences for any preference that satisfies the axioms we listed in Chapter 2 will always be continuous. But continuity of correspondence is a complex idea that we will avoid. We made a compromise by selecting a unique point from the set of choices so that we can work with demand *functions*, but then our demand function becomes discontinuous at those prices where we are selecting one out of many choices.

   But when preferences are strictly convex, such compromises are not needed. The optimal choice will be unique, and the demand functions will be continuous in (p_1, p_2, m). That is, for every possible (p_1, p_2, m), there is a unique demand pair (x_1^*, x_2^*).

   More formally for every sequence (p_1^n, p_2^n, m^n) (where $n = 1, 2, \ldots, \infty$) that converges to any price vector, say, (p_1^*, p_2^*, m^*), there is a corresponding sequence of demand functions $x_1(p_1^n, p_2^n, m^n)$ and $x_2(p_1^n, p_2^n, m^n)$ that converge to $x_1(p_1^*, p_2^*, m^*)$ and $x_2(p_1^*, p_2^*, m^*)$.
2. **Homogeneity of degree zero** Demand functions $x_1(p_1, p_2, m)$ and $x_2(p_1, p_2, m)$ are homogeneous of degree zero in (p_1, p_2, m). If all prices and income are increased by the same proportion, the budget set will remain unchanged, and therefore, the consumer's choice must not change.

It turns out that apart from the preceding two properties, nothing else can be ascertained about the demand for a general utility function. Importantly, we would like to know how the consumer's demand for a good changes if one of the prices or income changes. But there is no clear-cut answer to such questions. Of course, the ambiguity itself has profound economics behind it, and to understand it, we will characterise the demand function both in the general case and under some special cases. But first let us define the *types* of goods based on their sensitivity to singular changes in price or income.

3.4.1 *Taxonomy of goods*

Suppose $x_i(p_1, p_2, m)$ is a Marshallian demand function for good i, $i = 1, 2$. Then based on its derivative properties, x_i can be (locally) classified in the following ways:

1. If $\partial x_i / \partial p_i < 0$ the good x_i is called an **ordinary** good. The negative relationship is commonly referred to as the **law of demand.**
2. If $\partial x_i / \partial p_i > 0$ the good x_i is called a **Giffen good**, named after the Scottish statistician and economist Sir Robert Giffen, who first discovered this relationship during the Irish potato famine of mid-nineteenth century.[5]
3. When $\partial x_i / \partial p_i < 0$ we measure the extent of price sensitivity using the concept of the own price elasticity of demand, which compares the proportionate change in demand to the proportionate change in price. The measure is conveniently both scale- and unit-free, and hence, goods can be compared in terms of their price elasticity.

   The formula for own price elasticity of good i is $\varepsilon_{ii} = \frac{\partial x_i}{\partial p_i}\frac{p_i}{x_i}$. If the absolute value of the elasticity is greater than 1, the good is said to have **elastic** demand at the given value of the price where the change is measured. If the absolute value of the elasticity is less than 1, the good is said to have *inelastic* demand.

   Price elasticity gives a useful indication of how a consumer's expenditure on a good will change if the good's price changes slightly. For elastic goods, with a price rise, the expenditure will *fall*, and with a price fall, the expenditure will *rise*. For inelastic goods, the movements of price and expenditure occur in the same direction. When the elasticity is exactly 1 (called *unitary elastic* demand), any price change leaves the consumer's expenditure unaffected.
4. If $\partial x_i / \partial m > 0$ the good x_i is called a **normal** good. If $\partial x_i / \partial m < 0$, the good is an **inferior** good.
5. If the value of the income elasticity of a good, that is, $\varepsilon_{im} = \frac{\partial x_i}{\partial m}\frac{m}{x_i}$, is greater than $+1$, the good is called a **luxury** good. If the income elasticity is less than $+1$, the good is called a **necessary** good. Comparing the normal-inferior classification, it should be clear that all luxury goods are normal goods and that all inferior goods are necessary goods.
6. If $\partial x_i / \partial p_j > 0$, $i \neq j$, then good x_i is a **gross substitute** of good x_j. If $\partial x_i / \partial p_j < 0$ good x_i is a **gross complement** for good x_j. The qualifier 'gross' signifies the relationship between goods at the choice level (via price) as opposed to their relationship at the preference level.[6] Goods which are imperfect substitutes at the preference level can be gross complements at the demand level. In the case of perfect substitutes, two goods are generally unrelated at the demand level, because we have just seen that the consumer specialises in the consumption of only one good. However, goods which are perfect complements (in preference) are gross complements (in demand).

3.4.2 *Characterisation*

Having the preceding taxonomy in hand, we now proceed to characterise the Marshallian demand function. First, we show that the very fact of a consumer's budget always binds ensures certain relationships between the goods. Second, if the consumer's preference is homothetic, then quite a few more things can be said about the demand function.

1. A straightforward implication of the homogeneity of degree-zero property of demand is that for every Marshallian demand $x_i(p_1, p_2, m)$, the sum of all price and income elasticities is zero. Formally, $\varepsilon_{ii} + \varepsilon_{ij} + \varepsilon_{im} = 0$.

   To prove it, let us consider without loss of generality good 1. As $x_1(p_1, p_2, m)$ is homogeneous of degree zero in (p_1, p_2, m), we must have for any $\lambda > 0$ and for any (p_1, p_2, m)

   $$x_1(\lambda p_1, \lambda p_2, \lambda m) = x_1(p_1, p_2, m).$$

   Increasing all prices and income by the same proportion can be represented by $\lambda > 1$ and decreasing them can be represented by $\lambda < 1$. In either case, the demand remains invariant. Differentiating the above relation with respect to λ we get

   $$\frac{\partial x_1}{\partial \lambda p_1}\frac{\partial \lambda p_1}{\partial \lambda} + \frac{\partial x_1}{\partial \lambda p_2}\frac{\lambda p_2}{\partial \lambda} + \frac{\partial x_1}{\partial \lambda m}\frac{\lambda m}{\partial \lambda} = 0$$

   or $$\frac{\partial x_1}{\partial \lambda p_1} p_1 + \frac{\partial x_1}{\partial \lambda p_2} p_2 + \frac{\partial x_1}{\partial \lambda m} m = 0.$$

   Now evaluate the preceding at $\lambda = 1$ and divide both sides by x_1. Then we have

   $$\frac{\partial x_1}{\partial p_1}\frac{p_1}{x_1} + \frac{\partial x_1}{\partial p_2}\frac{p_2}{x_1} + \frac{\partial x_1}{\partial m}\frac{m}{x_1} = 0 \qquad (3.15)$$

   or, $$\varepsilon_{11} + \varepsilon_{12} + \varepsilon_{1m} = 0.$$

2. When both goods are bought, by differentiating $p_1 x_1(p_1, p_2, m) + p_2 x_2(p_1, p_2, m) \equiv m$ with respect to p_1, p_2 and m, one at a time, we get the following characterisations:

   a. If x_j is a gross substitute for x_i, then the law of demand holds for x_i. To see this, let us differentiate the above budget equation with respect to p_1:

   $$x_1 + p_1\frac{\partial x_1}{\partial p_1} + p_2\frac{\partial x_2}{\partial p_1} = 0. \qquad (3.16)$$

   If $\partial x_2 / \partial p_1 > 0$, then we must have $\partial x_1 / \partial p_1 < 0$. That is, the law of demand must hold for x_1. A similar argument can be made for x_2.

   b. If x_2 is a gross complement to x_1, the law of demand holds for x_1 if $|\varepsilon_{21}| < \frac{p_1 x_1}{p_2 x_2}$, that is, if the cross-price elasticity of good 2 is less than the ratio of expenditures of good 1 to good 2. To see this, let us rewrite Eq. (3.16) as (by multiplying and dividing the last term by $p_1 x_2$)

   $$p_1\frac{\partial x_1}{\partial p_1} + x_1\left[1 + \frac{p_2 x_2}{p_1 x_1}\left(\frac{\partial x_2}{\partial p_1}\frac{p_1}{x_2}\right)\right] = 0$$

   or, $$\frac{\partial x_1}{\partial p_1} + x_1\left[1 + \frac{p_2 x_2}{p_1 x_1}\epsilon_{21}\right] = 0.$$

When $\varepsilon_{21} < 0$ but $|\varepsilon_{21}| < \frac{p_1 x_1}{p_2 x_2}$, the term inside the bracket is strictly positive. Then for the whole expression to be equal to zero, we must have $\partial x_1 / \partial p_1 < 0$. Alternatively stated, when goods are gross complements, the elasticity restriction can be taken as a condition for the law of demand to hold.

c. If x_1 is a Giffen good, then x_2 must be a gross complement to x_1. Verify in Eq. (3.16) that if $\partial x_1 / \partial p_1 > 0$, we must have $\partial x_2 / \partial p_1 < 0$.
d. The weighted average of the income elasticity of two goods is always equal to 1, where the weights are the budget share of the goods.
Let us differentiate the budget line with respect to m:

$$p_1 \frac{\partial x_1}{\partial m} + p_2 \frac{\partial x_2}{\partial m} = 1.$$

Dividing and multiplying the first term by $x_1 m$ and the second term by $x_2 m$, write

$$\frac{p_1 x_1}{m}\left(\frac{\partial x_1}{\partial m}\frac{m}{x_1}\right) + \frac{p_2 x_2}{m}\left(\frac{\partial x_2}{\partial m}\frac{m}{x_2}\right) = 1 \tag{3.17}$$

or, $$s_1 \varepsilon_{1m} + s_2 \varepsilon_{2m} = 1,$$

where $s_i = \frac{p_i x_i}{m}$ is the budget share of good i; clearly, $s_1 + s_2 = 1$. An important observation here is that at the same time, neither will both goods be luxury, nor will both be necessary. Furthermore, if one good is a luxury, the other good must be a necessary good. Also, if the income elasticity of one good is equal to 1, the other good must also have an income elasticity equal to 1.

e. With the help of Eq. (3.17), it can also be ascertained that if the income elasticity of both goods is 1, the budget share of neither goods will change with income and the ratio of the demands for two goods x_2 / x_1 will also be invariant to income.
The first part of our claim is obvious from Eq. (3.17). For the second part, let us differentiate the ratio of optimal consumption $\frac{x_2(p_1, p_2, m)}{x_1(p_1, p_2, m)}$:

$$\frac{\partial}{\partial m}\frac{x_2(.)}{x_1(.)} = \frac{1}{x_1^2}\left[x_1 \frac{\partial x_2}{\partial m} - x_2 \frac{\partial x_1}{\partial m}\right] \tag{3.18}$$

$$= \frac{1}{x_1^2}\left[\frac{x_1 x_2}{m}\left\{\frac{\partial x_2}{\partial m}\frac{m}{x_2} - \frac{\partial x_1}{\partial m}\frac{m}{x_1}\right\}\right] \tag{3.19}$$

$$= \frac{x_2}{m x_1}\left[\varepsilon_{2m} - \varepsilon_{1m}\right] \tag{3.20}$$

Eq. (3.20) is the equation for the **income expansion path**. If the two income elasticity values are equal (which must be 1), the ratio x_2 / x_1 must remain unchanged with m. This means that, with an increase in income, the consumer is expanding her consumption of both goods in the same proportion.

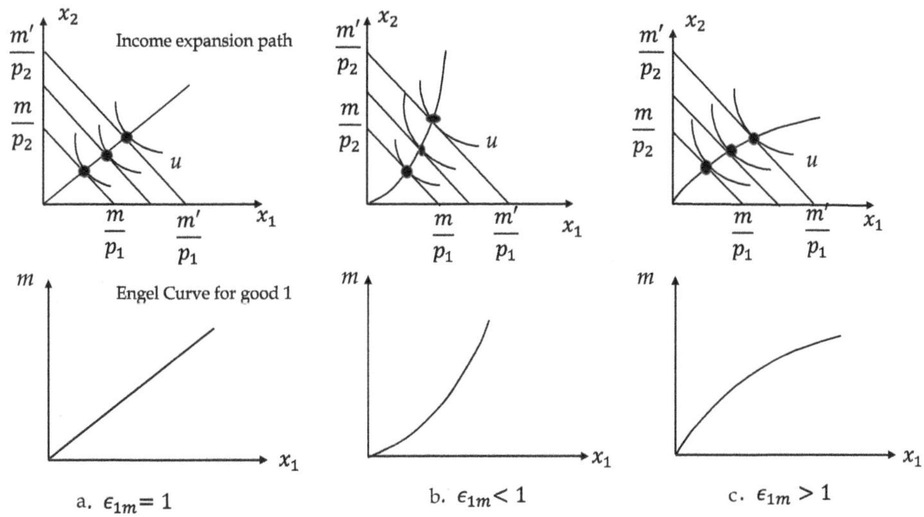

Figure 3.3 Income expansion paths and Engel curves

But if the income elasticity of good 2 is greater than the income elasticity of good 1, which also means good 2 will be regarded as luxury and good 1 as necessary, the ratio of consumption x_2 / x_1 must rise. Alternatively, if good 1 turns luxury, the ratio x_2 / x_1 must fall.

Three possible income expansion paths are shown in the upper part of Figure 3.3. Panels *a, b* and *c* demonstrate the constant, increasing and decreasing x_2 / x_1 ratios, respectively. Successive shifts of the budget lines indicate successive increases in *m*. The straight-line plots the choices when the consumer's income elasticity is 1 (for both goods) in the upper part of panel *a*. The upward-sloping convex curve represents the case where good 2 becomes a luxury good in the upper part of panel *b*. The ratio x_2 / x_1 is increasing along this curve. The concave curve represents the case where good 1 becomes a luxury good in the upper part of panel *c*. Along this curve, the ratio x_2 / x_1 is falling.

The same information is often conveyed by the **Engel curve**, which plots the relation between *m* and individual demand curves. In the bottom part of panels *a, b* and *c* of Figure 3.3, we draw the Engel curve for good 1 for the cases depicted in the upper part. One can easily draw similar Engel curves for good 2 as well.

3. For **homothetic preferences**, we can say a few more things, which we state in the form of a proposition.

Proposition 1. *If preference is homothetic then for Marshallian demand functions of all goods the following holds.*

a. *Income elasticity of each good is 1; that is,* $\varepsilon_{1m} = \varepsilon_{2m} = 1$.
b. *All goods are gross substitutes, and therefore, the law of demand holds for every good. Demands are also price elastic.*
c. *The budget share of every good,* s_i, *depends only on the price ratio* $\frac{p_1}{p_2}$, *and it is (weakly) decreasing in* p_i *but (weakly) increasing in* p_j.
d. *For the Cobb–Douglas preference, the budget share* s_i *is insensitive to* p_1, p_2 *and* m, *along with* $\varepsilon_{ij} = 0$ for $i \neq j$. *The law of demand holds.*

Proof Let us recall the homothetic demand equation (3.11). The demand functions for x_1 and x_2 are linear in m, which means the income elasticity is equal to 1. For all homothetic demand functions $\theta > 1$ (except the Cobb–Douglas case) and from Eq. (3.11), we can check that $\partial x_1^* / \partial p_2 > 0$ and $\partial x_2^* / \partial p_1 > 0$. So x_1 and x_2 are gross substitutes, which means we must have $\partial x_1^* / \partial p_1 < 0$ and $\partial x_2^* / \partial p_2 < 0$.

Gross substituteness also implies $\varepsilon_{12} > 0$ and $\varepsilon_{21} > 0$. As we already know $\varepsilon_{1m} = \varepsilon_{2m} = 1$, from Eq. (3.15), we can ascertain that $-\varepsilon_{11} = \varepsilon_{12} + \varepsilon_{1m} > 1$ and $-\varepsilon_{22} = \varepsilon_{21} + \varepsilon_{2m} > 1$. Therefore, both goods are price elastic.

We can rearrange the demand expressions in Eq. (3.11) to write the budget shares, $p_1 x_1^* / m$ and $p_2 x_2^* / m$ as

$$s_1 = \frac{c_1^\theta p_2^{\theta-1}}{c_1^\theta p_2^{\theta-1} + c_2^\theta p_1^{\theta-1}}, \qquad s_2 = \frac{c_2^\theta p_1^{\theta-1}}{c_1^\theta p_2^{\theta-1} + c_2^\theta p_1^{\theta-1}}.$$

It is straightforward to see that (given $\theta > 1$) s_1 is decreasing in p_1 and increasing in p_2. Likewise, s_2 decreases in p_2 and increases in p_1. Finally, for the Cobb–Douglas preferences from Eqs. (3.8) and (3.9), it is obvious that $s_1 = \frac{\alpha}{\alpha + \beta}$ and $s_2 = \frac{\beta}{\alpha + \beta}$ are invariant to prices and that x_1 and x_2 are unrelated in choice; that is, $\varepsilon_{12} = \varepsilon_{21} = 0$. Given $\varepsilon_{1m} = \varepsilon_{2m} = 1$, we must have $\varepsilon_{11} = \varepsilon_{22} = -1$. The law of demand evidently holds.

The Cobb–Douglas case is illustrated in Figure 3.4. On panel *a*, we show the effects of a fall in p_1 on the demands for x_1 and x_2 and on their ratio. Between points *A* and *B*, the ratio of x_2 and x_1 has fallen in line with the fall in p_1. Panel *b* of Figure 3.4 shows that the budget share of x_1 remains unchanged at $\alpha / (\alpha + \beta)$. Demand for x_2 is unaffected by changes in p_1. We add a quadrant at the bottom of the main graph, and with the help of a 45-degree line, we map $x_1^*(p_1)$ and $x_1^*(p_1')$. Then we connect these points with the budget line intercepts m / p_1 and m / p_1'. Slopes of these two lines capture the budget shares of x_1^* at two prices p_1 and p_1'. Two lines are parallel, reflecting the fact that the budget share did not change.

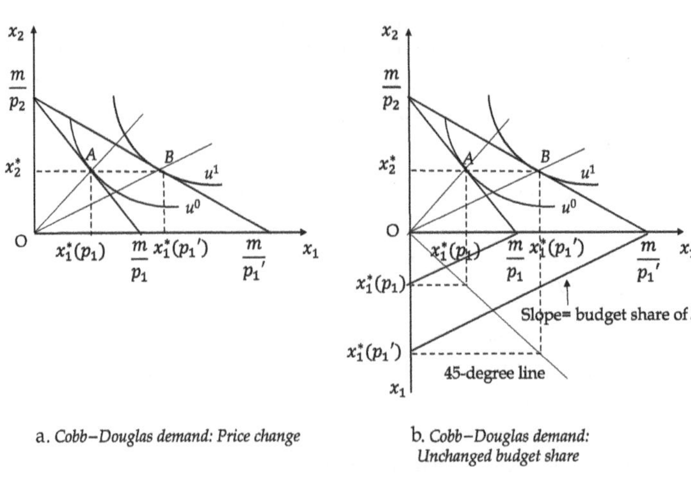

Figure 3.4 Price change: The Cobb–Douglas demand

The same method can be applied to other demand curves where the budget share does change. When the budget share of x_1 increases with a fall in p_1 (as would be the case for $\theta > 1$), we should expect the line connecting $x_1^*(p_1')$ and m/p_1' should have a greater slope than the line connecting $x_1^*(p_1)$ and m/p_1.

4. There is a wide range of preferences that generate demands linear in income and thereby render income elasticity unitary. The case of **perfect complements** also shares this feature, even if it does not belong to the family of homothetic preferences. However, it differs starkly from homothetic demands in terms of cross-price effects; goods will be gross complements, the law of demand will hold and demands will be price-inelastic. You can check these facts from Eq. (3.15). Plug in $\varepsilon_{im} = 1$ which implies $\varepsilon_{ii} + \varepsilon_{ij} = -1$ along with each term being negative. That means, $|\varepsilon_{ii}| < 1$.
5. For **quasi-linear utility functions**, income elasticity is not constant. The good for which the marginal utility falls with consumption (in our example, x_1) will have its income elasticity as either 1 or zero. It will be consumed first to achieve its desired level, provided income permits it. At this stage, the good will demonstrate unitary income elasticity. But when income is sufficiently high to support the desired level of the good, its consumption will be held fixed, and its income elasticity will be zero.[7]

To sum up, consumer theory tells us that the consumer's choice is a result of her rational pursuit of finding the best bundle her money can buy. Although the general theory is unable to guarantee the law of demand, most common preferences we work with do validate the law of demand and establish clear relationships between goods. It is also the case that in most examples, goods are unbiased in terms of income; they are neither 'luxury' nor 'necessary'. Of course, there are many potential cases where some goods may become inferior, and for them, the law of demand may not hold. We will investigate this point later.

3.5 Consumer's welfare: indirect utility function

We have argued that the consumer adjusts her choice in response to a price or income change. But can we measure her welfare in such acts of moving from one choice to another? The notion of 'indirect utility' is just one such measure. Direct utility, which is her psychological ordering of the entire feasible set of bundles, guides her to make a choice, and in the process, a connection is established between the market data, consumer's income and her utility—via the bundles she has chosen. Thus, we enter the realm of 'indirect' utility function, which describes how the consumer's welfare would change when prices or income change.

We obtain the indirect utility function by substituting the Marshallian demand functions into the utility function. From our previously discussed cases, consider the following ones:

1. First, take the Cobb–Douglas case. If we substitute Eqs. (3.8) and (3.9) into the corresponding utility function, we get the indirect utility function as

$$\begin{aligned} v(p_1, p_2, m) &= A\left[\frac{\alpha}{(\alpha+\beta)}\frac{m}{p_1}\right]^{\alpha}\left[\frac{\beta}{(\alpha+\beta)}\frac{m}{p_2}\right]^{\beta} \\ &= \left[A\frac{\alpha^{\alpha}\beta^{\beta}}{(\alpha+\beta)^{\alpha+\beta}}\right]\frac{m^{\alpha+\beta}}{p_1^{\alpha}p_2^{\beta}}. \end{aligned} \tag{3.21}$$

2. Similarly, consider the separable utility case. Substituting Eq. (3.10) into the relevant utility function, we get

$$v(p_1,p_2,m)=a\sqrt{\frac{a^2p_2}{a^2p_2+b^2p_1}\frac{m}{p_1}}+b\sqrt{\frac{b^2p_1}{a^2p_2+b^2p_1}\frac{m}{p_2}}$$
$$=\sqrt{\frac{m}{a^2p_2+b^2p_1}}\left[\frac{a^2p_2+b^2p_1}{\sqrt{p_1p_2}}\right]=\sqrt{m\left(\frac{a^2}{p_1}+\frac{b^2}{p_2}\right)}. \tag{3.22}$$

3. For the Leontief utility function, the indirect utility function becomes

$$v(p_1,p_2,m)=\frac{abm}{bp_1+ap_2}. \tag{3.23}$$

4. Finally, consider the linear utility function. Here, the consumer consumes only x_1 if $p_2>bp_1/a$ and only x_2 if $p_2<bp_1/a$. In the special case of $p_2=bp_1/a$, we assumed that she will split her budget equally between the two goods. Thus, her indirect utility is $v=am/p_1$ if $p_2>bp_1/a$ when any increase (or small decrease) in p_2 will leave her utility unaffected. Similarly, if $p_2<bp_1/a$ her indirect utility is $v=bm/p_2$, which is invariant to increases (or a small decrease) in p_1. In the special case of $p_2=bp_1/a$ her utility is $v=\frac{m}{2}\left[\frac{a}{p_1}+\frac{b}{p_2}\right]$. Evaluating it by substituting the relation between p_1 and p_2, we get $v=am/p_1=bm/p_2$. Therefore, we can combine the two linear segments of the indirect utility functions into a single function as

$$v(p_1,p_2,m)=\max\left\{\frac{am}{p_1},\frac{bm}{p_2}\right\}. \tag{3.24}$$

It may be instructive to have a quick look at Eqs. (3.21)–(3.24). One thing that is obvious is that in all these functions, if m, p_1 and p_2 were increased (or decreased) by the same proportion, the indirect utility would not change. This is homogeneity of degree zero, a property inherited from the Marshallian demand function. If demand does not change, the indirect utility should not change. This is intuitive.

Furthermore, indirect utility is decreasing in both prices and increasing in income. This is very important. Even though we have seen from the taxonomy of demand, the individual impact of income or a price on demand is ambiguous in general, but its impact on the consumer's welfare is never ambiguous. Any price rise will make the consumer worse off, and an income rise will make her better off.

This simple welfare implication is immensely useful in policy applications. If prices rise due to market conditions, the government can try to protect the consumer's welfare by providing direct cash transfers to them, and the indirect utility function tells us *precisely how much* transfer to be given. We take up this issue in the next chapter.

In Figure 3.5, we depict the indirect utility curves for three cases: Cobb–Douglas, perfect complements and perfect substitutes. As we had drawn indifference curves on (x_1,x_2)

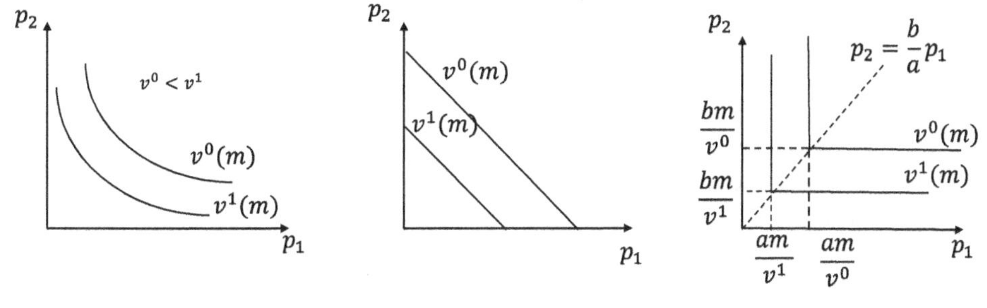

a. *Cobb–Douglas* b. *Perfect complements* c. *Perfect substitutes*

Figure 3.5 Iso-indirect utility curves

plane, we can draw **iso-indirect utility curves** or **indirect indifference curves** on (p_1, p_2). An iso-indirect utility curve gives all combinations of p_1 and p_2 that give rise to the same indirect utility level, while the consumer's income is held unchanged. The higher the curve, the lower the level of indirect utility. But the shape of the iso-indirect utility curves can be very different depending on the type of utility function we consider.

Eq. (3.21) shows that p_1 and p_2 enter the indirect utility function in the same ways as x_1 and x_2 enter the direct utility function, except for the negative sign of their exponents. This is why in panel *a* of Figure 3.5 the iso-indirect curves look exactly like the indifference curves. But the same logic does not hold for perfect complements and perfect substitutes. Eq. (3.23) shows that even though the indifference curve for perfect complements is L-shaped, and hence not differentiable, the iso-indirect utility function is a linear one and differentiable. The reason is that two goods will always be bought in a fixed proportion; with a price change, only the quantities of the goods will change but not their mix. Therefore, if one price rises, to maintain the same indirect utility, the other price must fall, and it should fall at a constant rate, as shown in Figure 3.5. On the contrary, for perfect substitutes as the consumer switches from one good to another depending on the relative price being above or below a threshold, each price will have no impact on the indirect utility over a range. Eq. (3.24) therefore gives rise to an L-shaped iso-indirect utility curve as we have depicted in panel *c* of Figure 3.5.

3.5.1 *Properties of the indirect utility function*

Although we have looked at some specific types of utility function, there are several properties all indirect utility functions share.

Proposition 2. *The indirect utility function* $v(p_1, p_2, m)$ *has the following properties:*

1. ***Homogeneity*** *It is homogeneous of degree zero in* (p_1, p_2, m).
2. ***Monotonicity*** *It is strictly increasing in m and non-increasing in* p_i, $i = 1, 2$.

3. ***Quasi-convexity*** *It is a quasi-convex function in* (p_1, p_2, m). *Its lower contour set is convex.*
4. ***Continuity*** *It is continuous in* (p_1, p_2, m).

Proof.

1. $v(p_1, p_2, m)$ is homogeneous of degree zero follows from the fact that the demand functions are homogeneous of degree zero, which, in turn, depends on the fact that the budget set does not change when p_1, p_2 and m all change by the same proportion.
2. When m rises, the budget set expands at every (p_1, p_2), which means the consumer will be able to afford a bundle that was strictly preferred but was not affordable earlier. So, $\partial v(.)/\partial m > 0$. Likewise, if p_1 or p_2 increases, the budget set contracts, and the consumer may not be able to afford the bundle that was previously optimal. So $v(.)$ may fall or remain unchanged if there is a corner solution.
3. The quasi-convexity of $v(p_1, p_2, m)$ means the lower contour set of the function $v(.,.)$ must be a convex set. From the iso-indirect utility functions drawn in Figure 3.5, it is clear that the area above any iso-indirect utility curve is the set of all (p_1, p_2) (for any given m) that gives lower utility; this is precisely our lower contour set, and it is convex. See Chapter 16 for a graphical proof.
4. The formal proof of continuity is advanced and hence omitted. However, informally we can argue that for every (p_1, p_2, m), we have an optimal (x_1, x_2). If demand is continuous, then $v(.)$ is also continuous. But even if demand is not continuous, as in the case of a linear utility function, a jump in the consumption bundle does not involve a jump in the indirect utility obtained. See Figure 3.5 panel *c*. A small change in p_1 or p_2 results in a seamless movement from one iso-indirect utility curve to another.

3.5.1.1 Roy's Identity

Because indirect utility is an optimal value function, it is possible to take a journey in reverse and retrieve the Marshallian demands. Roy's identity tells us how it can be done. Before we formally state the identity, it is important to point out that if we could empirically estimate an indirect utility function, then by studying its derivative properties, we can infer the Marshallian demands, even if these demands could not be directly estimated for lack of data.

Proposition 3. *If* $v(p_1, p_2, m)$ *is an indirect utility function the consumer's Marshallian demand function for good* i *can be derived from the indirect utility function as follows:*

$$x_i(p_1, p_2, m) = -\frac{\partial v(.)}{\partial p_i} / \frac{\partial v(.)}{\partial m}. \tag{3.25}$$

Proof. Start from the definition of the indirect utility function:

$$v(.) \equiv u(x_1(p_1, p_2, m), x_2(p_1, p_2, m)) - \lambda(p_1, p_2, m)$$
$$[p_1x_1(p_1, p_2, m) + p_2x_2(p_1, p_2, m) - m].$$

Differentiate this with respect to p_1.

$$\begin{aligned}\frac{\partial v(.)}{\partial p_1} &= u_1\frac{\partial x_1}{\partial p_1}+u_2\frac{\partial x_2}{\partial p_1}-\lambda p_1\frac{\partial x_1}{\partial p_1}-\lambda p_2\frac{\partial x_2}{\partial p_1}-\frac{\partial \lambda}{\partial p_1}[p_1x_1+p_2x_2-m]-\lambda x_1\\ &=\frac{\partial x_1}{\partial p_1}\Bigg[\underbrace{u_1-\lambda p_1}_{=0\text{ by FOC}}\Bigg]+\frac{\partial x_2}{\partial p_1}\Bigg[\underbrace{u_2-\lambda p_2}_{=0\text{ by FOC}}\Bigg]-\frac{\partial \lambda}{\partial p_1}\Bigg[\underbrace{p_1x_1+p_2x_2-m}_{=0\text{ by FOC}}\Bigg]-\lambda x_1\\ &=-\lambda x_1<0,\end{aligned}$$

where FOC refers to the first-order condition of utility maximisation. In the same way, we will get $\frac{\partial v(.)}{\partial p_2}=-\lambda x_2$.

Similarly, differentiate $v(.)$ with respect to m and write

$$\begin{aligned}\frac{\partial v(.)}{\partial m} &= u_1\frac{\partial x_1}{\partial m}+u_2\frac{\partial x_2}{\partial m}-\lambda p_1\frac{\partial x_1}{\partial m}-\lambda p_2\frac{\partial x_2}{\partial m}-\frac{\partial \lambda}{\partial m}[p_1x_1+p_2x_2-m]+\lambda\\ &=\frac{\partial x_1}{\partial m}\Bigg[\underbrace{u_1-\lambda p_1}_{=0\text{ by FOC}}\Bigg]+\frac{\partial x_2}{\partial m}\Bigg[\underbrace{u_2-\lambda p_2}_{=0\text{ by FOC}}\Bigg]-\frac{\partial \lambda}{\partial m}\Bigg[\underbrace{p_1x_1+p_2x_2-m}_{=0\text{ by FOC}}\Bigg]+\lambda\\ &=\lambda>0.\end{aligned}$$

Substitute the these expressions into Eq. (3.25) and see that both sides are exactly $x_1(p_1, p_2, m)$. In the same way, Roy's identity can be proved for x_2.

3.6 More applications

So far, we have assumed that price is fixed regardless of the quantity bought and the consumer's income is a fixed amount of cash. In this section, we consider several cases in which these assumptions are relaxed.

3.6.1 *Budget set with variable price*

The notion of fixed price is a realistic description of large markets where cutting individual deals is not possible. But, as we have discussed in Chapter 1, consumers often shop in variable-price environments. Based on our discussion in Chapter 1, we consider two cases, rationing and bulk discount.

The consumer maximises her utility maximisation subject to a variable-price budget constraint.

$$\begin{aligned}&\text{Max} \quad u=u(x_1,x_2) && \text{subject to}\\ &\qquad\ p_1'x_1+p_2x_2=m && \text{if } x_1\le k\\ &\text{and} \quad p_1x_1+p_2x_2=m+(p_1-p_1')k\,(\equiv M) && \text{if } x_1>k\end{aligned}$$

where k is the exogenously given threshold for price differential. If $p_1' < p_1$, we have the case of rationing (or price subsidy), and if $p_1' > p_1$, we have the case of bulk discount.

To solve the problem, the consumer can optimise taking one budget equation at a time and then should compare the achieved (indirect) utilities to see whether buying $x_1 > k$ or $x_1 > k$ is optimal. If the consumer's income is low enough to be content with $x_1 < k$, the demand functions will be the same as the ones discussed previously. But if buying $x_1 > k$ is optimal, the consumer's demands change to $x_i\left(p_1, p_2, M\right)$, where $M \equiv m + \left(p_1 - p_1'\right)k$ can be regarded as 'effective income'.

Let us take a graphical approach to solve the problem, assuming that our utility function is homothetic, where the MRS is constant along any ray passing through the origin. Consider panel *a* of Figure 3.6, where we draw a series of budget lines and indifference curves to represent the case of rationing. Here, the price applicable to $x_1 \leq k$ is smaller; that is, $p_1' < p_1$. Initially (up to the first two budget lines), the consumer's income is sufficiently low so that her optimal consumption of $x_1 \leq k$.

If her income increases marginally at this stage, her consumption will travel along the ray *OA*. Once *A* is reached, where buying $x_1 = k$ is optimal (by the standard tangency condition), any further small increases in *m* will leave the demand for x_1 unchanged. The entire increase in *m* will be devoted to additional consumption of x_2. The reason is that the consumer wishes to buy more of x_1 at the lower price p_1'. But the lower price p_1' is not available beyond *k*, and the consumer does her best by consuming at the kink of the budget line. This will continue until her income becomes sufficiently large so that point *B*, at which $x_1\left(=k\right)$ becomes tangent to the steeper segment of the budget line. That is, bundle *B* is optimal by the standard tangency condition with higher p_1. Beyond *B*, a further increase in *m* will translate into a greater consumption of both goods along the ray *BC*. Thus, the income expansion path here is *OABC*. Notably, the line *BC* is steeper than *OA*, indicating the fact that the consumer switches to a greater ratio of x_2 to x_1 in response to a higher price or implicit tax on x_1 for buying it in excess of *k*.

On panel *b*, we depict the case of bulk discount. The second segment of the budget line becomes flatter, reflecting the fact that beyond *k* every additional unit of x_1 is cheaper: $p_1' > p_1$. In this case, when income is low the consumer's consumption of x_1 is restricted below *k*. Her consumption will travel along the ray *OA*. But note that because the budget set is now non-convex,

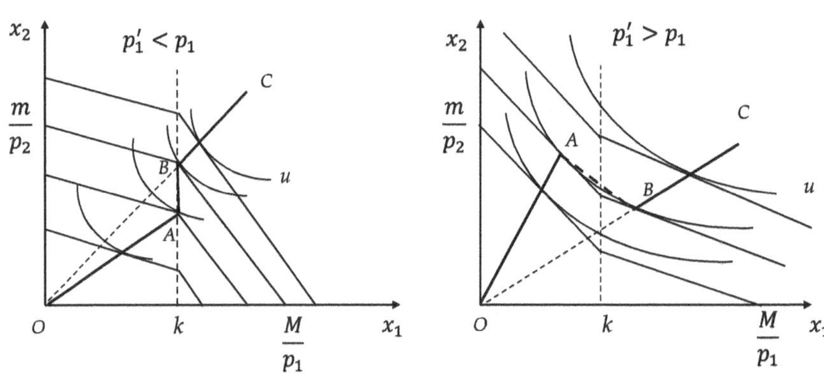

a. *Rationing* b. *Bulk discount*

Figure 3.6 Income expansion paths

there is the possibility of multiple solutions. At a moderately higher level of income, an indifference curve can be tangent to the two segments of the same budget constraint. These are precisely our points A and B. From this point onward, in response to any further increase in m, the consumer will expand her consumption along the ray BC, which is flatter than OA. As x_1 becomes cheaper (beyond k), the consumer buys x_1 proportionately more.

In either case, two important differences emerge. First, prices find an additional route to influence demand—via total income. Second, when the consumer finds it optimal to buy x_1 in excess of k, her consumption shows *income bias* despite homothetic preference. In both cases, two goods 'temporarily' behave like a luxury good—x_2 in the rationing case and x_1 in the bulk discount case. By 'temporarily' we are referring to the consumer's crossing of the threshold k of x_1. Once the threshold is crossed, the consumption ratio will again be constant.

3.6.1.1 *Properties*

We now re-examine the properties of demand when it exceeds k:

1. Marshallian demand functions are homogeneous of degree zero in (p_1', p_1, p_2, m). Note the difference in the inclusion of p_1' in the demand argument. Although it is just a different value of the same price p_1, its role is more like another element of 'income', and therefore, its change should be included to test the well-known homogeneity property. By implication, the sum of all price and income elasticity will also add up to zero provided that p_1' is included as a separate price.
2. Income now should be regarded as effective income M rather than cash in hand m. Accordingly, our taxonomy of luxury and inferior goods should also be redefined in terms of M.

   As before, for homothetic utility functions the elasticity of 'effective income' (M) is 1 for every good, but the standard income (m) elasticity will be different. This is because although a change in m causes an equal change in M (i.e., $\Delta m = \Delta M$), the proportion $\Delta m / m$ is different from $\Delta M / M$.
3. There is a close connection between the (standard) income elasticity and effective income elasticity. This is given by

$$\varepsilon_{iM} \equiv \frac{\partial x_i}{\partial M}\frac{M}{x_i} = \frac{\partial x_i}{\partial m}\frac{m}{x_i}\frac{M}{m} \equiv \varepsilon_{im}\frac{M}{m}.$$

   $\varepsilon_{iM} > \varepsilon_{im}$ if $M > m$, which occurs if $p_1 > p_1'$ (the rationing case). The opposite is true in the bulk discount case. When the effective income elasticity is 1, the standard income elasticity of both good 1 and good 2 will be less than 1 in the rationing case and greater than 1 in the bulk discount case.
4. The weighted sum of the effective income elasticity of all goods is still equal to 1 when the weights are given by effective budget shares $\tilde{s}_1 \equiv p_1 x_1 / M$ and $\tilde{s}_2 \equiv p_2 x_2 / M$, which are different from 'actual' budget shares. We can write the following:

$$\tilde{s}_1\varepsilon_{1M} + \tilde{s}_2\varepsilon_{2M} = 1$$

$$\text{or,}\quad \tilde{s}_1\left(\varepsilon_{1m}\frac{M}{m}\right) + \tilde{s}_2\left(\varepsilon_{2m}\frac{M}{m}\right) = 1$$

$$\text{or,}\quad \gamma_1 s_1 \varepsilon_{1m} + s_2\varepsilon_{2m} = 1,$$

where $\gamma_1 = \dfrac{p_1 x_1}{p_1 x_1 + (p_1' - p_1)k}$ is the valuation bias of the expenditure on good 1 and $s_1 = \dfrac{p_1 x_1 + (p_1' - p_1)k}{m}$ and $s_2 = \dfrac{p_2 x_2}{m}$ are the actual budget shares of the two goods.

5. When p_1 increases there is an additional and positive effect on x_1 occurring via M.

$$\frac{\partial x_1(.)}{\partial p_1} = \frac{\partial x_1}{\partial p_1} + \frac{\partial x_1}{\partial M} k.$$

The first term on the right-hand side is negative if the good is an ordinary good (and positive for Giffen goods). The second term is clearly positive for a normal good. Thus, we have an apparent ambiguity. In the next chapter, we will re-examine this issue and ascertain the overall sign of the derivative.

6. In the Cobb–Douglas case, where ordinarily goods are unrelated, x_2 will be a gross substitute of good 1, but good 1 will be unrelated to good 2. Thus, the relationship between the two goods becomes asymmetric.

3.6.2 *Subsistence consumption*

In the last chapter, we discussed the Stone–Geary utility function to capture the case in which the consumer has a subsistence requirement on her consumption of both goods by the amount δ_1 and δ_2, respectively. The consumer's problem is to maximise $u = (x_1 - \delta_1)^\alpha (x_2 - \delta_2)^\beta$ subject to $p_1 x_1 + p_2 x_2 = m$. Since our focus is on $x_1 > \delta_1$ and $x_2 > \delta_2$, we will assume that the consumer's income m is large enough to cover the subsistence consumption. That is, $m > p_1\delta_1 + p_2\delta_2$.

Formally, our utility maximisation problem is that of a Cobb–Douglas one with a small adjustment. Instead of posing the problem in terms of x_1 and x_2, we pose it in terms of $y_1 = x_1 - \delta_1$ and $y_2 = x_2 - \delta_2$ and accordingly rewrite the effective income as $M \equiv m - p_1\delta_1 - p_2\delta_2$.

Thus, we restate the problem as

$$\text{Max } u = y_1^\alpha y_2^\beta \quad \text{subject to } p_1 y_1 + p_2 y_2 = M$$

Applying the standard Cobb–Douglas solution rule, we get

$$x_1^* = \delta_1 + \frac{\alpha}{(\alpha+\beta)}\frac{M}{p_1}, \qquad x_2^* = \delta_2 + \frac{\beta}{(\alpha+\beta)}\frac{M}{p_2}.$$

The excess consumption of both goods (y_i) is in proportion to the net budget—the income left after meeting the subsistence needs. It is obvious that the demands in excess of the subsistence needs will remain unchanged if (m, p_1, p_2) are all changed in the same proportion; the same also holds for the total consumption of each good, x_1^* and x_2^*. Therefore, both demand functions (x_i^* or y_i^*) are homogeneous at degree zero in (m, p_1, p_2).

Considering the cross-price effects, we see that the two goods turn gross complements to each other via a reduction in the net income as the subsistence consumption becomes more costly.

Furthermore, y_i^* has an effective income elasticity of 1. But for x_1^* the effective income elasticity is strictly less than 1, because any given change in x_i is of a smaller proportion of x_i than of y_i.

For example, $\dfrac{\partial y_1}{\partial M}\dfrac{M}{y_1} = 1$, but $\dfrac{\partial x_1}{\partial M}\dfrac{M}{x_1} = \dfrac{\alpha M}{\alpha M + (\alpha+\beta)p_1\delta_1} < 1.$

It is also interesting to note that the standard income elasticity of x_1, $\epsilon_{1m} \geq 1$ if $\frac{\alpha}{\beta} \geq \frac{p_1\delta_1}{p_2\delta_2}$. If the relative utility weight of the good 1 is bigger than the relative subsistence cost of good 1, the consumer will spend proportionately more of her extra income (m) to the consumption of x_1 than to the consumption of x_2. This is easy to check.

3.6.3 *Consumption–leisure choice*

In Chapter 1, we noted that our choice of how many hours we want to work in a given week is a result of our choice between consumption and leisure. More leisure means less earnings and less consumption of food and other things, and vice versa. The wage that we earn per hour is both an element of our income and a price of leisure. If w is the hourly wage rate, p is the price of consumption good and T is the total number of hours available to work, then the consumer's budget line is $wl + pc = wT$, where l represents leisure and c represents consumption. The labour supply is $L = T - l$.

For the sake of concreteness assume that the consumer's utility function is $u = \sqrt{c} + \sqrt{l}$. Following the Eq. (3.10), where we substitute $a = b = 1$, $m = wT$, $p_1 = w$ and $p_2 = p$, we get the consumption, leisure demand and labour supply (L) as

$$c^* = \frac{w^2T}{(w+p)p}, \quad l^* = \frac{pT}{w+p}, \quad L^* = \frac{wT}{w+p}.$$

Note that here there is no exogenously given m in this model. Therefore, the homogeneity property of the demand function is to be tested against just w and p. Indeed, both c^* and l^* are homogeneous of degree zero in (w, p), and so is the labour supply function L^*.

In Figure 3.7 on panel a, we draw the consumption leisure choice for two wage rates, w and w'. From the preceding solution, we see that leisure demand is decreasing in wage and that labour supply is increasing in wage. As $w' > w$ the consumer takes less leisure (and supplies more

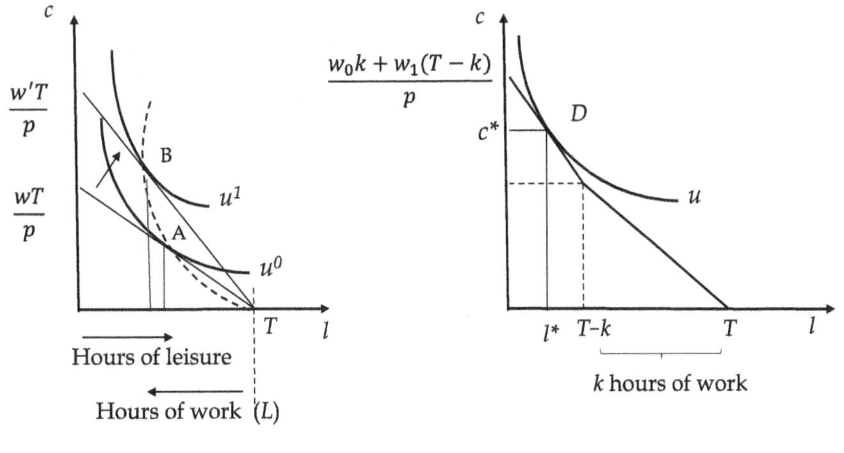

a. *Labour–leisure choice* b. *Overtime wage*

Figure 3.7 Labour supply

labour) at point B than at point A. The upward-sloping dashed curve connecting the time endowment point T with choice points A and B captures the upward-sloping labour supply curve.

We now consider several extensions of the consumption leisure choice model.

1. **Overtime wage.** Universally, someone working beyond 8 hours is entitled to overtime pay. Suppose the wage initially applies up to hours k is w_0; thereafter, the wage rate increases to w_1. To state it alternatively, the price of leisure is costly (w_1) for hours up to $T-k$; thereafter, every additional hour of leisure costs less (w_0). The budget line now has two segments (see Chapter 1 for more explanation):

$$pc + w_0 l = w_0 T \quad \text{if} \quad l \geq T-k,$$
$$\text{and} \quad pc + w_1 l = w_0 k + w_1 (T-k) \quad \text{if} \quad l < T-k.$$

If the consumer consumes more leisure (than $T-k$ hours) then her leisure demand does not involve w_1. But if she consumes less than $T-k$ hours of leisure, then her consumption (and thereby her leisure as well) will clearly depend on both w_0 and w_1. Such a situation is depicted at point D on panel b of Figure 3.7. Assuming the consumer's utility function to be $u = \sqrt{c} + \sqrt{l}$ as earlier, her choice at point D is given by

$$l^* = \frac{p\left[w_0 k + w_1 (T-k)\right]}{(w_1 + p) w_1} = \frac{pT}{p+w_1} - \frac{(w_1 - w_0) pk}{w_1 (p+w_1)}$$

$$L^* = T - \frac{p\left[w_0 k + w_1 (T-k)\right]}{(w_1 + p) w_1} = \frac{w_1 T}{p+w_1} + \frac{(w_1 - w_0) pk}{w_1 (p+w_1)}.$$

Here the homogeneity property is to be tested against (w_1, w_0, p). An interesting point to note is that labour supply decreases if the base wage w_0 increases. This is because an increase in the base wage raises the value of the consumer's first k hours of the time endowment, which, in turn, induces her to consume more leisure and work less. By comparison, an increase in w_1 induces two effects, one through the valuation of the entire time endowment T and the other directly as the price of leisure. The story here is similar, to some extent, to our earlier bulk discount case. Although the two effects of w_1 can counteract each other, the overall effect is still positive (given our utility function) as we show in the following:

$$\frac{\partial L^*}{\partial w_1} = p\left[\frac{w_1^2 (T-k) + k w_0 (p + 2w_1)}{w_1^2 (p+w_1)^2}\right] > 0, \quad \frac{\partial L^*}{\partial w_0} = -\frac{pk}{w_1 (p+w_1)} < 0.$$

This example shows that the effect of a base hourly wage rate increase may have contrasting effects on individuals' labour supply depending on the type of jobs they do and the number of hours they work. If certain jobs do not have an overtime wage, or if someone was working less than k hours, the labour supply response will be positive; people will work more if w_0 rises. But people who were working overtime will reduce their labour supply. Essentially, as

w_0 rises the gap between the base wage and the overtime wage narrows, therefore, the difference between the hours worked between two types of workers/jobs will also narrow.

2. **Decision to not work.** All of us have to work to support our livelihoods. But some people may be fortunate to escape this decision problem. If one inherits a substantial amount of wealth or wins a lottery, one may choose to not work at all. If W is the wealth inherited, the consumer's budget equation changes to $wl + pc = wT + W$. Obviously, she is guaranteed a consumption of W / p even if she spends T hours relaxing. With the utility function $u = \sqrt{c} + \sqrt{l}$, the leisure demand and labour supply functions are then modified as

$$l^* = \frac{p[wT + W]}{(w+p)w} = \frac{pT}{p+w} + \frac{pW}{w(p+w)}$$

$$L^* = \frac{w^2T - pW}{(w+p)w} = \frac{wT}{p+w} - \frac{pW}{w(p+w)}.$$

By checking the condition for $L^* > 0$, we ascertain that if $W < \frac{w^2T}{p}$, the consumer will work; otherwise, she will stop working. Of course, if wage rises, she may reexamine her decision because the threshold value of wealth will rise.

On panel a of Figure 3.8 we depict the wealth effect. The consumer's budget set has a vertical lift at $l = T$ because of the consumption level W / p she is guaranteed of. Here, initially she selects point A as her optimal bundle of leisure and consumption. At any lower level of wealth, her consumption will lie on the line OA. Clearly, she is devoting some of her time to work. If her wealth increases to W', she will choose B as the optimal bundle. Point B is the tangency point between her budget line and indifference curve; it is also the point where she

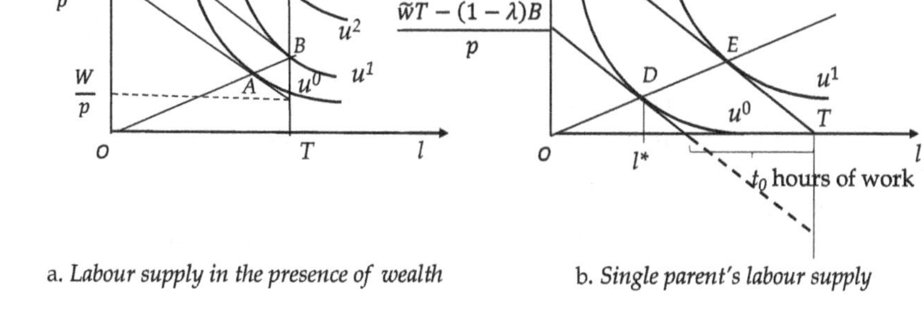

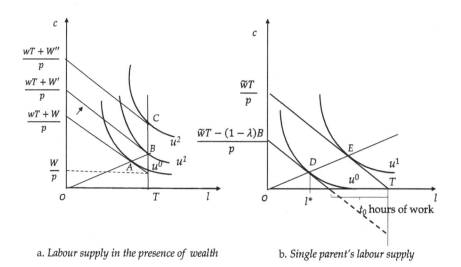

Figure 3.8 Labour supply in the presence of wealth and childcare needs

stops working. W' is the critical wealth level $\frac{w^2T}{p}$. For any further increase in W such as W'', her optimal bundles will be selected from the vertical line BC. Her consumption is financed by her wealth alone.

3. **Single parent's dilemma**. Single parents, most often women than men, face a serious dilemma in their labour leisure choice. When a child is young, the parent must work to cover the additional cost of baby care, and yet if she works away from home, she must find a babysitter. Thus, a lone mother faces problems from both sides—she must work for a minimum number of hours, and she must not also work too many hours. In developed countries, the government provides for (at least partially) the baby care costs. This helps ease the compulsion of working for a minimum number of hours.

   Suppose the cost of baby's food and other needs is B. If the government provides λB amount of it, $0 \leq \lambda \leq 1$, the consumer needs to work some minimum hours to cover $(1-\lambda)B$. But bear in mind that for every hour she works, she has to incur an additional cost of babysitting. Let the babysitter's wage rate be q. Her wage w must be greater than q; otherwise, she cannot work. Thus, if she works for L hours, she earns wL from which say pays qL to the babysitter and then spends the rest on her own consumption and baby care. That is, $pc + (1-\lambda)B = (w-q)L$. Denote $\tilde{w} = w - q$ and assume $\tilde{w} > 0$. The mother has to work a minimum number of hours, say, t_0, such that she is able to cover the cost of baby care. That is, $\tilde{w}t_0 = (1-\lambda)B$. Then using $\tilde{w}t_0 = (1-\lambda)B$ and $L = T - l$, her budget can be rewritten as

$$\tilde{w}l + pc = \tilde{w}(T - t_0).$$

Assuming her utility function is $u = \sqrt{c} + \sqrt{l}$, we derive the leisure demand and labour supply functions as

$$l^* = \frac{p(T-t_0)}{p+\tilde{w}}, \quad L^* = \frac{\tilde{w}}{\tilde{w}+p}T + \frac{p}{\tilde{w}+p}t_0.$$

Note that her labour supply is a weighted average of t_0 and T.

In panel b of Figure 3.8, there are two budget lines representing two scenarios. In the upper budget line, the government provides for the full cost of baby care (but not the babysitting fees). So the consumer's budget line is standard, except that her wage is net of the babysitting fee. Her choice is given by point E. The lower budget line represents the case where the government support is only partial. The remaining $(1-\lambda)B$ cost must be covered first by working for t_0 hours before she can even consider spending on her own consumption. At point D, she works for more hours and consumes less than that at point E. If there were no support at all for the baby care, her budget would be even smaller, and her optimal choice would lie between O and D on the line OE.

Let us now ask, How does the mother adjust her labour supply if the hourly babysitting fee q rises (but still remains below w)? This means that she is facing a fall in her net wage rate. By differentiating L^* with respect to q we get

$$\frac{\partial L^*}{\partial q} = -\frac{\partial L^*}{\partial \tilde{w}} = -p\left[\frac{(T-t_0)}{(\tilde{w}+p)^2} - \frac{(1-\lambda)B}{(\tilde{w}+p)\tilde{w}^2}\right].$$

This can be further simplified to

$$\frac{\partial L^*}{\partial q} = -p\left[\frac{T}{(p+\tilde{w})^2} - \frac{(1-\lambda)B(p+2\tilde{w})}{\tilde{w}^2(p+\tilde{w})^2}\right]$$

or, $\frac{\partial L^*}{\partial q} \geq 0$ if $\tilde{w}^2 T \leq (1-\lambda)B(p+2\tilde{w})$.

Clearly, when the baby care costs are fully covered by the government, that is, $\lambda = 1$, $\frac{\partial L^*}{\partial q}$ is clearly negative. An increase in q would encourage the mother to work less. But consider the other extreme where $\lambda = 0$. The government pays nothing to cover the baby care cost. Suppose $\tilde{w}^2 T < B(p+2\tilde{w})$. Then L^* clearly rises with an increase in q. This is akin to forced labour—forced by economic circumstances. In developing countries, young mothers from poor families (where $\lambda = 0$) do respond to the increasing cost of childcare by working longer hours, while for those from well-off families, there is plenty of support for baby care (i.e., $\lambda = 1$), and young mothers tend to take time off from the labour market when their own wage is not significantly higher than the cost of babysitting.

If the preceding scenarios hold for a given combination of (B, w, q, p), then there exists a critical λ, say, $\hat{\lambda}$, at which the consumer's labour supply response will turn from positive to negative. The critical λ is

$$\hat{\lambda} = \frac{B(p+2\tilde{w}) - \tilde{w}^2 T}{B(p+2\tilde{w})}.$$

It is important for women's welfare to provide at least this much support when they have young children to raise.

3.7 Market demand

Before the supermarkets learnt to track individual consumers through individual loyalty cards, it was the market demand that used to guide them in important decisions regarding sales, stocking and pricing—such as how much discount to give on breakfast cereals or what brands of chocolates to stock before Christmas. Theoretically, going from individual demand curves to the market or aggregate demand curve is straightforward. We need to just add up all the consumers' individual demands at a given price and then list the aggregate quantities at all possible prices. In the simplest case, if there are identical n consumers, just multiply the individual demand function by n. For example, if the individual demand for a good is given by $x = a - bp$, its market demand is simply $X = n(a - bp)$, where $X \equiv nx$ represents market demand.

Of course, rarely are people identical. Not only do we prefer things differently, but our earnings also differ. We can allow for some heterogeneity even in our simple model. Suppose there are two groups of consumers with n_1 and n_2 members. Within each group, consumers are identical (in both preferences and income), and a typical demand curve for group i is $x_i = a_i - bp$. As a first step to aggregate the demand, let us first derive the group-wise demand as $X_i = n_i(a_i - bp_i)$. Implicitly, it is assumed that in both groups, demand is positive. But this is not always going to be the case. For example, assume $a_1 < a_2$ and $n_1 a_1 < n_2 a_2$; that is, the consumers in the second

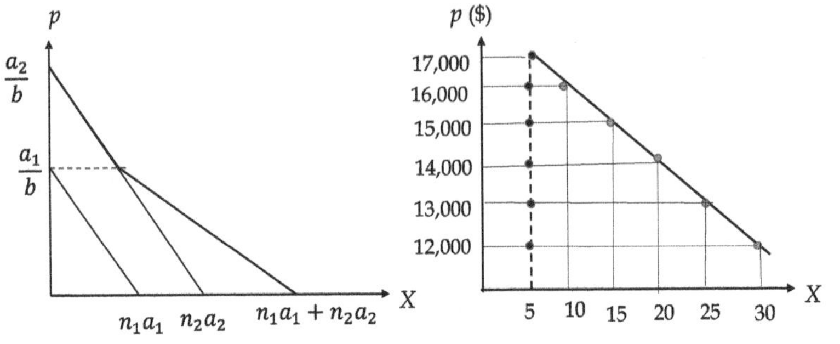

a. *Market demand from two groups*　　b. *Market demand for indivisible goods*

Figure 3.9 Market demand

group want to buy more than the first group at any given price. See panel *a* of Figure 3.9. Now if the price is too high for the first group $-\frac{a_1}{b} < p < \frac{a_2}{b}$, only group 2 consumers will buy. Group 1 consumers will start buying only after the price drops below $\frac{a_1}{b}$. Therefore, we need to write the market demand curve as

$$(X_1 + X_2 \equiv)X = \begin{cases} 0 & \text{if } p \geqslant \frac{a_2}{b} \\ n_2(a_2 - bp) & \text{if } \frac{a_1}{b} < p < \frac{a_2}{b} \\ (n_1a_1 + n_2a_2) - (n_1 + n_2)bp & \text{if } p \leqslant \frac{a_1}{b}. \end{cases}$$

Sometimes we want to know how the price elasticity of the *market* demand is related to the price elasticity of *individual demand*. If a supermarket wants to reduce the price of an Australian chardonnay by £1, say from £7, it needs to know the overall market price elasticity of chardonnay, and it would be even more helpful to know how different demographics (such as young and old, men and women) will respond to such price reduction.

Let us now try to derive the price elasticity of market demand for a general case with two groups of consumers; by 'general demand', we mean that their demand curve is not necessarily linear. Suppose $X(p) = n_1x_1(p) + n_2x_2(p)$ and assume both x_1 and x_2 are strictly positive.[8] Then

$$\begin{aligned}(\epsilon_X \equiv)\frac{\partial X}{\partial p}\frac{p}{X} &= \left[n_1\frac{\partial x_1(p)}{\partial p} + n_2\frac{\partial x_2(p)}{\partial p}\right]\frac{p}{X} \\ &= \left[n_1\frac{\partial x_1(p)}{\partial p}\frac{px_1}{x_1} + n_2\frac{\partial x_2(p)}{\partial p}\frac{px_2}{x_2}\right]\frac{1}{X} \\ &= \left(\frac{n_1x_1}{X}\right)\frac{\partial x_1(p)}{\partial p}\frac{p}{x_1} + \left(\frac{n_2x_2}{X}\right)\frac{\partial x_2(p)}{\partial p}\frac{p}{x_2} \\ &= \sigma_1\epsilon_x^1 + \sigma_2\epsilon_x^2,\end{aligned}$$

where σ_i is the market share of the ith group's purchase, and ϵ_x^i is the price elasticity of the ith group's individual demand; $\sigma_1 + \sigma_2 = 1$. The price elasticity of market demand is simply the weighted average of the individual price elasticities.

Interestingly, the market demand curve does not have many important properties, except the homogeneity (of degree-zero) property that is directly inherited from the individual demand curves. Also, when the individual demand curve is continuous, the market demand curve is also continuous.

However, the market demand curve can be a smooth curve, even if the individual demands are merely a single point. For instance, when it comes to a car, a house or a refrigerator, we buy only one unit of it. Consider a student-dominated street near a university, like West 29th Street in Los Angeles, close to the University of Southern California. Assume there are 30 international students from six countries—five students from each. They all want to buy a car for weekend leisure trips to Venice Beach, Hollywood Boulevard and China Town. Assume that the students coming from the same country are willing to pay the same price. Their willingness to pay is ordered in panel *b* of Figure 3.9. The topmost group wants to pay \$17,000 for a car, and the bottom-most group wants to pay \$12,000. Thus, for every student, we have only a point as their demand. But their aggregate demand becomes a downward-sloping continuous curve.[9] The trick of adding is to start from the highest willingness to pay. Thus, at \$17,000, our market demand is just 5 cars. Then at \$16,000, we add the next group and get the aggregate demand to be 10 cars. Proceeding in this manner, we reach 30 cars at the price of \$12,000.

3.8 Conclusion

Individual demand curves are nuanced and highly varied because of differences in individual preferences, income and exposure to different types of pricing schemes. As we have seen through many examples, individual demand curves can behave very differently and ambiguously, making them a permanent object of scholarly inquiry. However, in large markets, individual nuances get wiped out in the process of aggregation and the summary demand is more well behaved.

Which one is more important—market demand or individual demand? The answer to this question depends on the perspective and purpose. A regional car dealer would be more concerned about aggregate demand and aggregate price elasticity. But a neighbourhood car dealer would care more about individual demands around his neighbourhood. While imposing a sales tax on frozen food, a government needs to take into account its overall impact on the aggregate food demand, but at the same time, it must also consider the individual food demands of the low-income groups to protect them from the rising cost of living.

Summary

1. We learnt how to derive the Marshallian demand function.
2. We also discussed the properties of the Marshallian demand function and the indirect utility function.
3. Furthermore, we characterised the Marshallian demand curves under homothetic preference.
4. A taxonomy of goods (normal, inferior, etc.) was presented.
5. A variety of examples were studied, such as price discount, rationing and labour–leisure choice.
6. Finally, the characteristic-demand approach was presented in Section 3.9.

3.9 Appendix

3.9.1 *Lancaster's characteristics-demand model*

In the appendix to Chapter 1 (Section 1.8), we discussed what the budget set of the characteristic demand model would look like. When consumers care about the characteristics or attributes of a good, rather than the good itself, such as calories, nutrients, taste, colour and so on, as Lancaster (1966) argued, we need to think of the consumer's utility maximisation over the characteristics space. Assuming two characteristics, c_1 and c_2, we focus on a case in which two goods vary in the proportion by which they offer two characteristics. If they offered c_1 and c_2 in the same proportion, then clearly our consumer would regard them as perfect substitutes and frankly they are indistinguishable except perhaps for the cost. The utility-maximising consumer would buy only the cheaper of the two goods.

But if the two goods differ in their proportion of c_1 and c_2, then deriving the consumer's demand for characteristics and the goods is a non-trivial exercise. Let us recall the example we considered in the appendix of Chapter 1. The consumer has a conventional budget for goods as $p_1x_1 + p_2x_2 = m$. One unit of good 1 gives 5 units of c_1 and 1 unit of c_2. However, 1 unit of good 2 gives 2 units of c_1 and 8 units of c_2. On the characteristics space, spending all of m on x_1 or on x_2 will give strictly positive combinations of c_1 and c_2. In Figure 3.10, we reproduce the budget set of Chapter 1. At point E, the consumer gets the maximum amount c_1 and the minimum amount of c_2 her income can buy. From m / p_1 units of x_1, these are the appropriate amount of c_1 and c_2 she will have. Alternatively, she could spend all her money on x_2 and buy m / p_2 units of it, which will give $2m / p_2$ units of c_1 and $8m / p_2$ units of c_2. Thus, the line DE is her characteristics budget equation.

Suppose her preference is given by a Cobb–Douglas utility function as $u = \sqrt{c_1c_2}$. Then it is just our familiar constrained utility maximisation problem, except for one important difference. p_1 and p_2 are not prices of c_1 and c_2. Suppose the (effective) prices of c_1 and c_2 are q_1 and q_2. The consumer's utility maximisation exercise needs to be presented in terms of these prices, but the consumer faces in the marketplace p_1 and p_2, the prices of the goods from which the characteristics are to be obtained.

So, let us now derive the effective prices q_1 and q_2 from p_1 and p_2. On the characteristics space our budget equation is $q_1c_1 + q_2c_2 = m$. Using the information available at points D and E we write

$$q_1\frac{5m}{p_1} + q_2\frac{m}{p_1} = m, \qquad q_1\frac{2m}{p_2} + q_2\frac{8m}{p_2} = m.$$

From these two equations, we can solve for

$$q_1 = \frac{8p_1 - p_2}{38}, \quad q_2 = \frac{5p_2 - 2p_1}{38}.$$

In Figure 3.10, we have drawn the budget line with q_1 and q_2. Mind that two (dashed) segments (above D and below E) are outside the feasible set; they are drawn simply for reference. The consumer's choice must be on the DE segment. The consumer's problem is to maximise $u = \sqrt{c_1c_2}$ subject to $q_1c_1 + q_2c_2 = m$. The problem is formally identical to standard utility maximisation we have learnt. The solution is $c_1 = \dfrac{m}{2q_1}$ and $c_2 = \dfrac{m}{2q_2}$. This is shown at point A in Figure 3.10. Substituting the values of q_1 and q_2, we get

$$c_1 = \frac{19m}{8p_1 - p_2}, \quad c_2 = \frac{19m}{5p_2 - 2p_1}.$$

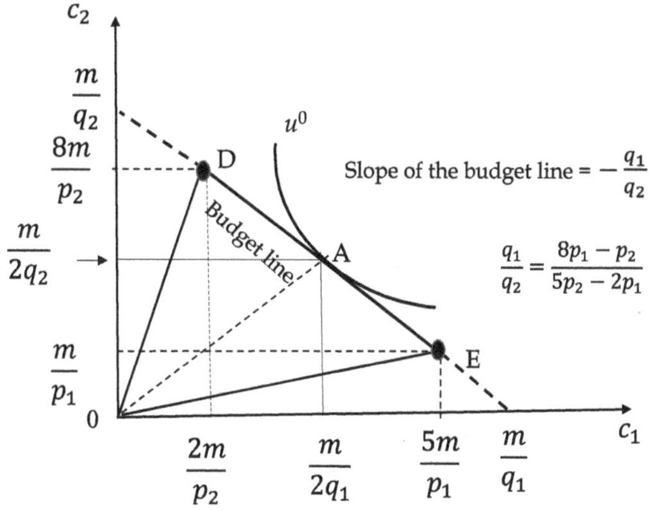

Figure 3.10 Demand for characteristics

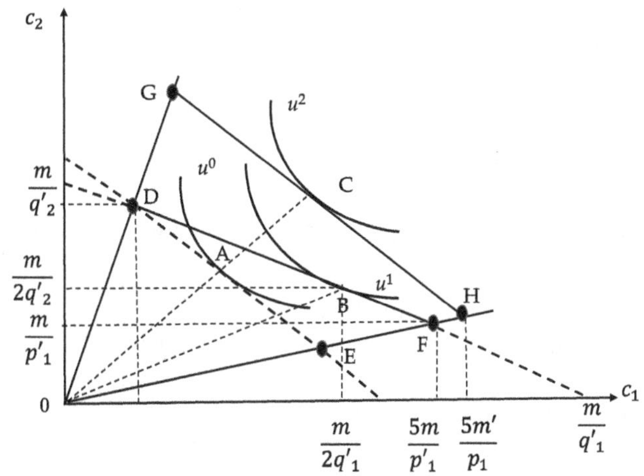

Figure 3.11 Price and income change in a characteristic demand model

We then want to see how the optimal c_1 and c_2 are related to p_1, p_2 and m. Like the goods demand characteristic demand functions are also homogeneous of degree zero in p_1, p_2 and m. Individually c_1 is inversely related to p_1 and positively related to m and p_2. But you must be careful here in the interpretation of the relationship between the characteristics and goods prices. p_1 is not the price of c_1; q_1 is. Yet c_1 is inversely related to p_1 because we have taken an example where x_1 is relatively more intensive in c_1. If we take an example where x_1 is intensive in c_2 and x_2 in c_1, then the consumer's optimal c_1 will be inversely related to p_2 and positively related to p_1. This is an important difference from standard goods demand.

A graphical representation of income and price change requires much care, as we show in Figure 3.11. First, consider a price drop for x_1; let p_1' be the new price. The budget set expands along the ray OE to OF. The consumer can buy at most m/p_1' units of x_1, which gives $5m/p_1'$

units of c_1 and m / p_1' units of c_2. But the maximum amount of x_2 she can buy has not changed. Hence point D is still the other end of the budget line. Third, DF is the new budget line in terms of p_1' and p_2, but in terms of the effective prices, the consumer is facing a new pair of prices, q_1' and q_2'. That is because, as p_1 falls q_1 falls, but q_2 rises. The new choice is at point B, which corresponds to $\left(\frac{m}{2q_1'}, \frac{m}{2q_2'}\right)$. At B the ratio of c_2 to c_1 is smaller; characteristic c_1 (and x_1 as well) is consumed more intensively, as well as in greater absolute amount, while c_2 is consumed less.

The case of income increase is shown in the parallel shift of the budget line from DE to GH. The resultant consumption point will be point C, where the consumption of both characteristics increases, but their intensity does not change. This is expected because the preference is homothetic.

Thus, we see the characteristic demand model is very similar and closely related to the goods demand model, although some differences are not to be ignored. In models of poverty and nutrition, it is quite common to work with the characteristic-demand model instead of the standard goods–demand model.

3.10 Exercises

1. Mrs Rothschild is entitled to (free) food coupons worth of \$$B$ because her income m is below poverty line $\underline{m}$. Her preferences over food x_1 and clothing x_2 are given by $u = Ax_1^{\alpha} x_2^{1-\alpha}$. Market prices of the two goods are p_1 and p_2.

   a. Derive Mrs Rothschild's demands for food and clothing.
   b. Under what condition will she buy food from the market? How will her demand for clothing depend on the price of food?
   c. Draw her Engel curves against her income m allowing the possibility that she may not remain poor in future.

2. Reconsider the question 1. Suppose Mrs Rothschild is given a benefit entitlement card which allows her to buy food at a subsidised price $\lambda p_1 (\lambda < 1)$ as much as she wants. How would her consumption change now? Would she prefer one benefit system over the other?
3. John's preference over two goods (x_1, x_2) is given by the utility function $u = a\sqrt{x_1} + b\sqrt{x_2}$. He has m amount of cash and an endowment of goods (x_1^0, x_2^0); the prices of the two goods are p_1 and p_2, respectively.

   a. Derive John's Marshallian demand functions for both goods. Determine if John's demands would exceed (x_1^0, x_2^0). Graphically present your answer.
   b. Derive John's indirect utility function. Verify Roy's identity.

4. Emmanuel has T hours to spend on leisure (l) and work (t). He also has m amount of cash in hand, which combined with his labour income constitutes his budget. The hourly wage rate is w, and the price of the sole consumption good (c) is p. His preference for leisure and consumption is given by the utility function $u = \sqrt{c} + \sqrt{l}$.

   a. Derive Emmanuel's Marshallian demand functions for both goods. Derive his labour supply function as well. Graphically present your answer.
   b. If m were negative, indicating a debt obligation, how would the labour supply have changed?

c. Next, assume that Emmanuel has a care obligation; he must spend $t_0 (< T)$ hours to care for his elderly mother. Draw Emmanuel's budget line assuming $m > 0$.

5. Vincent works in an auto garage. If he works up to k hours, he gets a base wage of w per hour. But if he works beyond k hours, then every additional hour gives an hourly wage $w + \delta$. Vincent's preferences over consumption (c) and leisure (l) are given by $u = cl$. He has T hours a day to work. The price of c is p.

   a. Derive Vincent's labour supply curve. Under what conditions will he work overtime?
   b. Show your answer graphically.
   c. Determine the critical value of k so that his indirect utility from overtime work will be greater than the indirect utility from not working overtime.

6. Answer the same question about Vincent, assuming his utility function is $u = c^{\alpha} l^{\beta}$.
7. Iris enjoys local bread (x_1) and organic fruits (x_2). Her preference over the two goods is given by the function $u = x_2 + \min[ax_1, bx_2]$. Assume that the prices of the two goods are p_1 and p_2, respectively. Her income is m. Derive her demand functions and the indirect utility function.
8. Boris enjoys two goods (x_1, x_2) and his utility function is $u = (x_1 - \delta_1)^{\alpha} (x_2 - \delta_2)^{\beta}$. Assume $\alpha, \beta < 1$ and $x_1 > \delta_1$ and $x_2 > \delta_2$. He has income m, and prices of the two goods are p_1 and p_2.

   a. Derive Boris's Marshallian demand functions.
   b. What restriction would you impose on m to ensure that his choice indeed satisfies the assumption $x_1 > \delta_1$ and $x_2 > \delta_2$?
   c. Derive $\frac{\partial x_1}{\partial p_1}$ and $\frac{\partial x_1}{\partial p_2}$.
   d. Next, assume that the price of x_1 is p_1^1 up to k. After k units of x_1, the price is $p_1^0 \left(< p_1^1\right)$ on every additional unit of x_1. Write Boris's new budget equation and present it graphically.
   e. Rewrite Boris's demand function with the discount on p_1, assuming Boris will buy more than k units of x_1. Show his new choice on your graph.

9. Suppose a consumer has m to spend on goods x_1 and x_2, prices of which are p_1 and p_2, respectively. Her preferences are given by the utility function $u = (x_1 - \delta)^{\alpha} x_2^{1-\alpha}$, where δ represents subsistence consumption of x_1.

   a. Derive the consumer's demand functions.
   b. How does the consumer's budget line change, if x_1 has two different prices, p_1 for $x_1 < k$ and a higher price p_1^1 for every additional unit of x_1 beyond k? Derive the consumer's demand functions assuming that her consumption of x_1 exceeds k.
   c. Derive the consumer's indirect utility function and verify the Roy's identity.

10. Two brothers, Ram and Rahim, have different preferences over (x_1, x_2). Ram's utility function is $u = x_1 x_2$, and Rahim's utility function is $u = \min[x_1, x_2]$. Each receives an allowance m from their mother to spend on (x_1, x_2) priced p_1 and p_2, respectively.

    a. Derive each brother's optimal (x_1, x_2) and their aggregate demand for each good.
    b. How is the price elasticity of the aggregate demand for good 1 related to the price elasticity of each brother's demand?

c. Suppose their mother does not like unequal consumption of the two goods. Hence, she decides not to give money but spend $2m$ equally on two goods and asks the boys to share equally. Will Ram and Rahim share them equally if their mother is not around? Will anyone be very unhappy with their mother's decision?
d. Derive the brothers' indirect utility under two scenarios—when they receive cash, and when they receive the goods instead and share them equally.

11. A consumer's preference is given by $u = ax_1 + b\sqrt{x_2}$, and she faces a standard budget line. Show that (a) none of the goods are inferior goods, and yet both goods will not have strictly positive income effects at the same time, and (b) when both goods are bought in positive quantities, for good 2 the own price elasticity of demand and the cross-price elasticity of demand must be equal in magnitude but opposite in sign.
12. Suppose for a consumer who buys two goods (x_1 and x_2) and has income m, you are given the following function: $\ln x_1 = a\ln p_1 + b\ln p_2 + ck$. What necessary conditions can you impose to determine that the equation relates to a Marshallian demand function?
13. Elaine's utility function is $u = \sqrt{x_1 - \delta} + \sqrt{x_2 - \delta}$, where δ refers to subsistence consumption. Her income is m, and prices of the two goods are p_1 and p_2.

    a. Derive Elaine's demand functions. What condition do you need to impose to ensure that her optimal x_1 and x_2 exceed δ?
    b. Elaine's sister Dana has the same income, but her preference is $u = \sqrt{x_1 - \gamma} + \sqrt{x_2 - \gamma}$. We do not know if $\gamma > \delta$ or $\gamma > \delta$. Compare the consumption levels of the two sisters, and determine who consumes more and under what conditions.

14. There are two groups of consumers, group A of size n_1 and group B of size n_2. Their preferences over x_1 and x_2 differ in the following way. The preference of a group A member is given by $u_A = x_1^{\alpha} x_2^{\beta}$, and the same for a group B member is $u_B = x_1^{\beta} x_2^{\alpha}$. But all consumers have the same level of income m. The prices of the two goods are p_1 and p_2, respectively.

    a. Derive the group-wise ordinary demand functions for x_1 and x_2 for each group, and then the aggregate demand functions.
    b. Derive the indirect utility function of a member of group A and show that it is homogeneous of degree zero.

15. There are two groups of consumers, group 1 and group 2. Group 1 has n_1 members, and group 2 has n_2 members; $n_1 > n_2$. Their income levels are m_1 and m_2, respectively, $m_1 < m_2$. Group 1's preference function is $u_1 = \min[ax_1, bx_2]$, and group 2's preference is $u_2 = \min[bx_1, ax_2]$. The prices of the two goods are p_1 and p_2, respectively.

    a. Derive the Marshallian demand functions for x_1 and x_2 for both groups.
    b. Graphically illustrate a consumer's choice from each group for two scenarios, $a = b$ and $a > b$, while maintaining the assumption $m_1 < m_2$. Explain how the two groups' choices would vary in the two scenarios.
    c. Derive the income elasticity of the aggregate demand (combined of the two groups) for good 1 with respect to m_1 and m_2 separately, and then derive the sum of the two. Comment on your findings.

16. Oliver's income is m, and his preference function is $u = Ax_1^{1/3}x_2^{2/3}$. Prices of the two goods are p_1 and p_2, respectively.
    a. Derive Oliver's Marshallian demand functions for the two goods.
    b. Now suppose p_1 increases to $(1+\beta)p_1$, and at the same time, Oliver receives a raise from his office, by the amount of Δm. Oliver suddenly finds that with his raise he can now just afford the bundle that he was buying before the price rise. Calculate Oliver's extra salary that he has received. Show it graphically. Explain your answer.
    c. Explain if Oliver is going to stick to his old consumption bundle or change it. Illustrate your answer graphically.

Notes

1 They are also called Walrasian demand functions, named after the nineteenth-century French economist/mathematician Leon Walras.
2 For an unconstrained maximisation problem, the second-order condition is that the Hessian matrix of the objective function must be *negative semi-definite*. In other words, the principal minors of the Hessian matrix must alternate in sign *starting from negative*.
3 Draw a concave indifference curve to represent non-convex preference and see that the consumer's choice if dictated by the first-order conditions will give minimum utility.
4 Tangency condition will lead to $a/b = p_1/p_2$, and the whole budget line will be optimal. We can get around the multiplicity of the choice (or the indeterminacy) problem by assuming that the consumer in this special case will allocate her budget equally between the two goods so that $x_1 = \frac{m}{2p_1}$ and $x_2 = \frac{m}{2p_2}$.
5 Whether Sir Giffen's discovery was truly a Giffen good has remained a subject matter of debate. More on this in Chapter 5.
6 Many authors use 'net complements' and 'net substitutes' to describe the preference-level relationship between goods.
7 For the other good, which receives the residual budget, the income elasticity will rise from zero to a greater than 1 number.
8 Demand depends on other prices and income, but we just suppress them.
9 Strictly speaking, our demand curve is actually a step function. It is continuous but full of kinks. But in a compressed scale, the kinks will disappear.

Further readings

Blundell, R., Brewer, M. & Francesconi, M. (2008). Job changes, hours changes and the path of labour supply adjustment. *Journal of Labor Economics*, 26(3), 421–453.

Blundell, R. & MaCurdy, T. (1999). Labor supply: A review of alternative approaches. In O. Ashenfelter & D. Card (Eds.), *Handbook of Labour Economics*, vol 3, 1559–1695. Amsterdam: Elsevier Science.

Deaton, A. (1997). *The Analysis of Household Surveys A Microeconometric Approach to Development Policy*. Baltimore, MD: Johns Hopkins University Press for the World Bank.

Giffen, R. (1904). *Economic Inquiries and Studies*, Vol 1. London: George Bell and Sons.

Lancaster, K. J. (1966). A new approach to consumer theory. *Journal of Political Economy*, 74(2), 132–157.

Marshall, A. (1895). *Principles of Economics*. London: Macmillan.

Roy, R. (1947). La distribution du revenu entre les divers biens. *Econometrica*, 15(3), 205–225.

Stigler, G. J. (1947). Notes on the history of the Giffen paradox. *Journal of Political Economy*, 55(2), 152–56.

Varian, H. R. (1992). *Microeconomic Analysis*, 3rd ed. New York: Norton.

Walras, L. (1877). *Elements d'Economie Politique Pure, Eng. Version: Elements of Pure Economics (1954)*, trans. William Jaffe. New York: A. M. Kelly.

Chapter 4

Expenditure minimisation and duality

Abstract

In this chapter we study expenditure minimisation where the consumer tries to achieve a given level of utility at the lowest possible cost. The resulting demand functions are called *compensated* or Hicksian demand functions, which always satisfy the law of demand. The expenditure minimisation approach is dual to the utility maximisation approach, and consequently the Hicksian and Marshallian demand functions bear close relationships. The Slutsky equation famously describes a connection between their slopes. We explore these in all settings including endowment budgets. The revealed preference theory of demand is discussed in Section 4.7.

Keywords: Hicksian demand, Expenditure function, Shephard's lemma, Duality, Substitution effect, Hicks and Slutsky income compensations, Slutsky equation, Revealed preference theory

4.1 Introduction

Unbelievable as it may sound, King Charles III of the United Kingdom, arguably the largest landowner in the world, is entitled to a hefty government allowance of £86.3 million just like his late mother Queen Elizabeth II. The allowance is called the Sovereign Grant, and it is for the purpose of maintaining the royal palaces and discharging His Majesty's royal duties, which include hosting "official receptions, investitures and garden parties".[1] The heir to the throne, Prince William, is also entitled to a generous grant. But one should not complain. Nearly one-third of the king's subjects—13 million of them being elderly—also receive government allowance.[2]

It may not be completely out of place to think that the king's Sovereign Grant and a poor man's benefit allowance have something in common; they are calculated following the same principle of meeting the recipient's needs or welfare at the lowest possible cost. In the context of our consumer, if we fix her utility at a certain level, then we can calculate the *minimum* amount of money she needs to achieve the utility level.

We should be mindful that achieving a utility level and meeting needs are not the same thing. Needs may be narrowly defined in terms of a few specific goods, whereas utility allows substitutions between many different bundles of those goods. However, we just take a given indifference curve as a target or constraint for the consumer. Then we ask, What would be the least cost bundle on that indifference curve? This is our problem of expenditure minimisation.

DOI: 10.4324/9781003226994-4

4.2 Algebraic method

The consumer's problem is to minimise expenditure $E = p_1x_1 + p_2x_2$ subject to $u(x_1,x_2) = u^0$. If $u(\cdot)$ is twice differentiable, then we can solve the optimisation problem by the Lagrange method:

$$\text{Min } F = p_1x_1 + p_2x_2 - \mu\left[u(x_1,x_2) - u^0\right],$$

where μ is the Lagrange multiplier. As in Chapter 3, here, too, we derive three first-order conditions as

$$\partial F / \partial x_1 \equiv p_1 - \mu u_1(x_1,x_2) = 0 \tag{4.1}$$

$$\partial F / \partial x_2 \equiv p_2 - \mu u_2(x_1,x_2) = 0 \tag{4.2}$$

$$\partial F / \partial \mu \equiv -\left[u(x_1,x_2) - u^0\right] = 0, \tag{4.3}$$

which can be implicitly solved for three variables (x_1, x_2, μ) But we focus mainly on (x_1, x_2) and therefore divide Eq. (4.1) by Eq. (4.2) to arrive at

$$\frac{p_1}{p_2} = \frac{u_1(x_1,x_2)}{u_2(x_1,x_2)}. \tag{4.4}$$

With the help of equations (4.4) and (4.3) we can solve for x_1 and x_2, which will now be a function of (p_1, p_2, u^0) Note that Eq. (4.4) is identical to Eq. (4) of Chapter 3, and u^0 replaces m of the Marshallian demand functions. The new functions are called **Hicksian demand functions**, named after the mid-twentieth century economist Sir John Hicks, whose contributions were critical in formalising demand theory. To differentiate between these and Marshallian demand functions we add a superscript h to x_1 and x_2 and write them as

$$x_1^h = x_1^h(p_1, p_2; u^0), \text{ and } x_2^h = x_2^h(p_1, p; u^0). \tag{4.5}$$

Since u^0 is an arbitrarily fixed level of utility, we can simplify the notation by replacing u^0 with u and write $x_i^h = x_i^h(p_1, p_2, u)(i = 1,2)$ as the Hicksian demand function for good i. These demand functions are also called **compensated** demand functions.

On panel a of Figure 4.1 we illustrate the consumer's expenditure minimisation problem. Here, the indifference curve representing the utility level u^0 is given, and the consumer is looking for the lowest iso-expenditure line, such as E_0, E_1 or E_0', to achieve u^0. Clearly, E_0 is the lowest expenditure; E_1 supports u^0, but it is not the lowest cost, and E_0' is too small to support u^0. A word of caution here. Even though the expenditure lines appear identical to the budget lines of the utility maximisation problem, they should not be called budget lines. Expenditures are a result of optimisation, whereas budgets are exogenously given. However, the consumer's choice, which occurs at point A—the point of tangency between an iso-expenditure line and the given indifference curve—involves the same ratio of x_2 and x_1 as it would under utility maximisation.

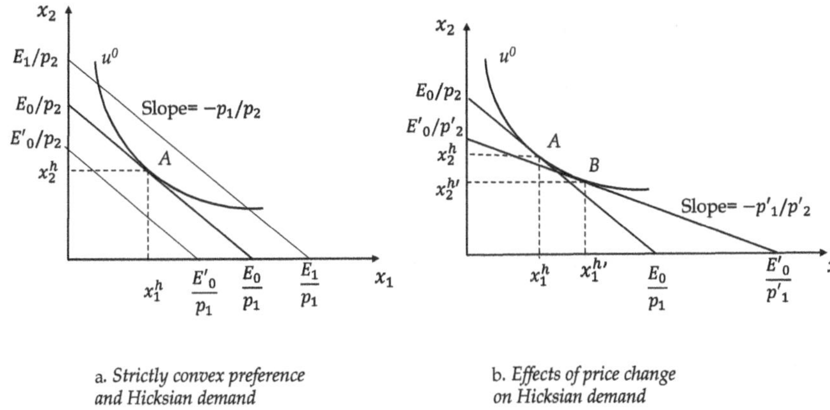

Figure 4.1 Expenditure minimisation and Hicksian or compensated demand

Once again, we need to get the technicality of the second-order condition out of the way. By differentiating Eqs. (4.1)–(4.3) with respect to x_1, x_2 and μ we get the following matrix:

$$d^2F = \begin{bmatrix} -\mu u_{11} & -\mu u_{12} & -u_1 \\ -\mu u_{21} & -\mu u_{22} & -u_2 \\ -u_1 & -u_2 & 0 \end{bmatrix}$$

Constrained minimisation requires that the determinant of d^2F must be negative.[3] After expanding the determinant, we get

$$\left|d^2F\right| = -\mu\left[-u_{11}u_2^2 + 2u_{12}u_1u_2 - u_{22}u_1^2\right] < 0.$$

Note that $\mu\left(=\frac{p_i}{u_i}\right) > 0$ by the solution to our expenditure minimisation problem, and the term inside the brackets is nothing, but Δu obtained in Eq. (2.1) of Chapter 2. By the strict quasi-concavity assumption of $u(\cdot)$, Δu is strictly positive, and thus, the condition for expenditure minimisation is easily met. In Section 4.7, we show how to do comparative statics on the first-order conditions of expenditure minimisation.

4.2.1 *Examples*

Let us now go through the commonly used utility functions and examine how the Hicksian demand functions differ from the Marshallian demand functions.

1. **Cobb–Douglas utility function.** Our first example is the Cobb-Douglas utility function: $u = Ax_1^{\alpha}x_2^{\beta}$. Noting that the $MRS = p_1 / p_2$ condition remains unchanged from our previous analysis we substitute $x_2 = \frac{\beta}{\alpha}\frac{p_1}{p_2}x_1$ into the utility function and write

$$u = Ax_1^{\alpha}\left(\frac{\beta p_1}{\alpha p_2}x_1\right)^{\beta} = Ax_1^{\alpha+\beta}\left(\frac{\beta p_1}{\alpha p_2}\right)^{\beta}$$
$$\text{or } x_1^h = \left(\frac{u}{A}\right)^{\frac{1}{\alpha+\beta}}\left(\frac{\alpha p_2}{\beta p_1}\right)^{\frac{\beta}{\alpha+\beta}}. \tag{4.6}$$

Substituting Eq. (4.6) into $x_2 = \frac{\beta}{\alpha}\frac{p_1}{p_2}x_1$, we get

$$x_2^h = \left(\frac{u}{A}\right)^{\frac{1}{\alpha+\beta}}\left(\frac{\beta p_1}{\alpha p_2}\right)^{\frac{\alpha}{\alpha+\beta}}. \tag{4.7}$$

2. **Separable utility function.** For the utility function $u = a\sqrt{x_1} + b\sqrt{x_2}$, the Hicksian demand functions are

$$x_1^h = \frac{u^2a^2p_2^2}{\left[a^2p_2 + b^2p_1\right]^2} \qquad x_2^h = \frac{u^2b^2p_1^2}{\left[a^2p_2 + b^2p_1\right]^2}. \tag{4.8}$$

3. **CES utility function.** Following the same method and denoting $\sigma \equiv \frac{1}{1-\rho}$, we can derive the Hicksian demand functions for $u = \left[ax_1^{\rho} + bx_2^{\rho}\right]^{\frac{1}{\rho}}$ as

$$x_1^h = \frac{ua^{\sigma}p_2^{\sigma}}{\left[a^{\sigma}p_2^{\sigma-1} + b^{\sigma}p_1^{\sigma-1}\right]^{\frac{\sigma}{\sigma-1}}} = \frac{ua^{\sigma}}{\left[a^{\sigma} + b^{\sigma}\left(\frac{p_1}{p_2}\right)^{\sigma-1}\right]^{\frac{\sigma}{\sigma-1}}} \tag{4.9}$$

$$x_2^h = \frac{ub^{\sigma}p_1^{\sigma}}{\left[a^{\sigma}p_2^{\sigma-1} + b^{\sigma}p_1^{\sigma-1}\right]^{\frac{\sigma}{\sigma-1}}} = \frac{ub^{\sigma}}{\left[a^{\sigma}\left(\frac{p_2}{p_1}\right)^{\sigma-1} + b^{\sigma}\right]^{\frac{\sigma}{\sigma-1}}}. \tag{4.10}$$

The effect of a price change on Hicksian demands is illustrated in panel *b* of Figure 4.1. When both goods are consumed in positive quantities, as they necessarily would be (but not exclusively) under homothetic preferences, a smaller price of p_1 (or a higher price of p_2) reduces the slope of the iso-expenditure line, and the consumer moves from point *A* to point *B*. At point *B* the consumer *must* consume more of x_1 and less of x_2. This is an inevitable consequence of the strict convexity of preferences and interior optimum. If x_i becomes relatively cheaper, its consumption *must increase*. This unambiguous relationship between the quantity demanded and its own price is one of the key features of the Hicksian demand function.

Because any price change essentially maps a substitution between x_1 and x_2 on a given indifference curve, the effect of a price change on the Hicksian demand is called the *substitution effect*. The substitution effect of own price is always negative, and the substitution effect of the other price (in a two-good setting) is always positive; the latter is called *cross-substitution effect*. However, the substitution effects get weakened—but never reversed—if some of the goods are not consumed at all or the utility function is not differentiable. Zero consumption of one good may occur when we step out of the environment of the homothetic functions, as the following case exemplifies.

4. **Quasi-linear utility function.** Recall our utility function $u = a\sqrt{x_1} + bx_2$ In order to minimise our expenditure, we recognise two possibilities: either $x_2 = 0$ or $x_2 > 0$ while always $x_1 > 0$ Assuming $x_2 > 0$, let us substitute from the utility function $x_2 = \frac{u - a\sqrt{x_1}}{b}$ into the objective function and minimise $E = p_1x_1 + p_2\frac{u - a\sqrt{x_1}}{b}$ with respect to x_1. The solution to this problem is

$$\begin{aligned} x_1^h &= \frac{a^2}{4b^2}\frac{p_2^2}{p_1^2} \quad \text{and} \quad x_2^h = \frac{1}{b}\left[u - \frac{a^2 p_2}{2bp_1}\right] \quad \text{if} \quad \frac{p_1}{p_2} > \frac{a^2}{2bu}, \\ x_1^h &= \frac{u^2}{a^2} \quad \text{and} \quad x_2^h = 0 \quad \text{if} \quad \frac{p_1}{p_2} \le \frac{a^2}{2bu}. \end{aligned} \tag{4.11}$$

Notice the difference here. When both goods are consumed the Hicksian demand function for x_1 is identical to its Marshallian counterpart (see Chapter 3). As explained earlier, under quasi-linear preferences, the consumer prioritises the consumption of one good over the other and limits the consumption of the priority good to a desired level. The desired level depends only on prices but not income or utility. If the desired level of the priority good does not yield the target utility, the consumer tops up with consumption of the second good.

4.2.2 *Graphical method*

For the two polar opposite cases of perfect complements and perfect substitutes, we need to rely on the graphical method. On panel *a* of Figure 4.2 we plot the indifference curve $u = \min[ax_1, bx_2]$, for utility level u^0. The consumer looks for the lowest iso-expenditure line that supports this utility level. If the prices are p_1 and p_2, then E_0 is the lowest expenditure to achieve u^0. The consumer chooses

$$x_1^h = \frac{u^0}{a} \text{ and } x_2^h = \frac{u^0}{b}. \tag{4.12}$$

If prices change, say, to p_1' and p_2', then the lowest expenditure also changes to E^l as shown in the graph. Two expenditure lines differ in terms of the slope, but the consumer's choice does not change; it is the same x_1^h and x_2^h that continue to be optimal even after the price change. There is no room for adjusting the mix of the goods, and therefore, the consumer's Hicksian demands are non-responsive to prices.

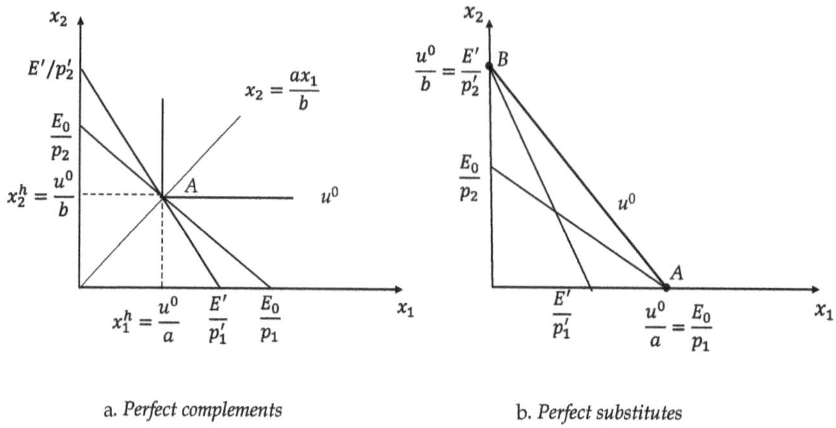

Figure 4.2 Hicksian demands for perfect complements and substitutes

A similar non-responsiveness is found for perfect substitutes as well. For utility function $u = ax_1 + bx_2$, as we demonstrate in panel b of Figure 4.2, the consumer's Hicksian demand functions are

$$\begin{aligned} &x_1^h = \frac{u^0}{a} \quad \text{and} \quad x_2^h = 0 \quad \text{if} \quad \frac{p_1}{p_2} \le \frac{a}{b} \\ &x_1^h = 0 \quad \text{and} \quad x_2^h = \frac{u^0}{b} \quad \text{if} \quad \frac{p_1}{p_2} > \frac{a}{b}. \end{aligned} \tag{4.13}$$

As before, the consumer buys only one good—the relatively cheaper one—and her demand goes through a seesaw movement. That is, if the price ratio exceeds a critical value, the consumer switches to the other good completely. Until the switch happens, demand remains non-responsive to price changes. This is equivalent to saying that demand does not respond to *small* price changes. Both perfect complements and perfect substitutes share weak convexity of preference, which induces choice at a kink or a corner and makes the Hicksian demands insensitive to prices.

4.2.3 *Properties of the Hicksian demand functions*

Let us now quickly take note of a few important properties of the Hicksian demand functions. You probably noticed that all the Hicksian demand functions we have derived as examples in Eqs. (4.6)–(4.13) are always a function of p_1 / p_2 rather than p_1 and p_2 separately. This is a very general property of the Hicksian demands to be true for any (quasi-concave) utility function. That means, if two prices are changed by an equal proportion, optimal x_1^h and x_2^h do not change. This is the first property on our list. The second and third properties, which concern own and cross-substitution effects, have been already discussed.

1. **Homogeneity** $x_i^h(p_1, p_2; u)$, $i = 1,2$, is homogeneous of degree zero in p_1 and p_2.
2. **Substitution effect** $\frac{\partial x_i^h}{\partial p_i} \le 0$. For strictly convex preferences, $\frac{\partial x_i^h}{\partial p_i} < 0$ The Hicksian demand functions obey the 'law of demand'.

3. **Cross-substitution effect** $\frac{\partial x_i^h}{\partial p_j} \geq 0(i \neq j)$ when there are only two goods. With strictly convex preference, we have $\frac{\partial x_i^h}{\partial p_j} > 0$. For $n > 2$ (n being the number of goods), $\frac{\partial x_i^h}{\partial p_j} > 0$ for at least one $j(j \neq i)$.
4. **Continuity** $x_i^h(p_1, p_2; u), i = 1, 2$ is continuous in p_1 and p_2.

While the Hicksian demand functions are conceptually attractive for their observance of the law of demand, they are less useful in empirical contexts when consumers have a fixed budget. In contrast, when consumers receive a government allowance, the law of demand helps the benefit authority to optimise the allowance to be given. Typically, the total amount of allowance will move in the direction of price change. This can be better explained by considering the *expenditure function*, which we do next.

4.2.4 Expenditure function

Once we substitute the Hicksian demand functions into the objective function, we obtain the minimum value of the expenditure or the *expenditure function*. Formally,

$$e(p_1, p_2; u) = p_1 x_1^h(p_1, p_2; u) + p_2 x_2^h(p_1, p_2; u).$$

Let us refer back to Figure 4.1 panel *b*. Initially, when prices are p_1 and p_2, the consumer minimises her expenditure at point *A*, and the resulting expenditure is E_0. Then when prices change to p_1' and p_2', her choice changes to point *B* and the resultant expenditure is E_0'. Can we determine from the graph whether E_0 is greater or smaller than E_0'? The answer is yes, and it will depend on whether both prices change or only one price changes. For instance, suppose $p_1' < p_1$ and $p_2' = p_2$ so that $\frac{p_1'}{p_2'} < \frac{p_1}{p_2}$ Then, from the vertical intercept of the graph, we can tell $E_0' < E_0$. Alternatively, if $p_2' > p_2$ and $p_1 = p_1'$ from the horizontal intercept, we can tell $E_0' > E_0$. However, if both p_1 and p_2 change in a manner that $\frac{p_1'}{p_2'} < \frac{p_1}{p_2}$, all we can say that the consumer will move to smaller x_2 / x_1 ratio (by moving from point *A* to point *B*), but we cannot compare between E_0 and E_0'. We need more information.

Let us now record the expenditure functions for our familiar examples by substituting the relevant Hicksian demand functions into $e = p_1 x_1^h + p_2 x_2^h$.

1. **Cobb-Douglas:** $e(p_1, p_2; u) = Bp_1^{\gamma} p_2^{1-\gamma}$,

$$\text{where } \gamma = \frac{\alpha}{\alpha + \beta} \text{ and } B = (\alpha + \beta)\left(\frac{u}{A\alpha^{\alpha}\beta^{\beta}}\right)^{\frac{1}{\alpha+\beta}}.$$

2. **Separable utility:** $e(p_1, p_2; u) = \frac{p_1 p_2 u^2}{a^2 p_2 + b^2 p_1}$.

3. **CES utility:** $e(p_1, p_2; u) = \frac{u p_1 p_2}{\left[a^{\sigma} p_2^{\sigma-1} + b^{\sigma} p_1^{\sigma-1}\right]^{\frac{1}{\sigma-1}}}$.

4. **Quasi-linear utility:** $e(p_1,p_2;u)=\begin{cases}\frac{up_2}{b}-\frac{a^2p_2^2}{4b^2p_1} & \text{if } \frac{p_1}{p_2}>\frac{a^2}{2bu}\\ \frac{u^2p_1}{a^2} & \text{if } \frac{p_1}{p_2}\le\frac{a^2}{2bu}\end{cases}$

5. **Leontief:** $e(p_1,p_2;u)=u\left[\frac{p_1}{a}+\frac{p_2}{b}\right].$

6. **Linear utility** $e(p_1,p_2;u)=\begin{cases}p_1\frac{u}{a} & \text{if } \frac{p_1}{p_2}\le\frac{a}{b}\\ p_2\frac{u}{b} & \text{if } \frac{p_1}{p_2}>\frac{a}{b}\end{cases}.$

In Figure 4.3, we depict the iso-expenditure curves for the Cobb–Douglas, Leontief and the linear utility functions. You might notice the remarkable similarity of the shapes of the iso-expenditure curves with that of the iso-indirect utility curves as shown in Figure 4.5 of Chapter 3. But there are some important differences too. First, the higher curves correspond to higher expenditures.

Second, from panels *b* and *c*, we can spot a very important property of the expenditure function. Consider panel *c* and consider two values of p_1 as $p_1^0=\frac{ae^0}{u}$ and $p_1^1=\frac{ae^1}{u}$. If $p_1^1=tp_1^0$ for some $t>1$, then it must be true that $e^1=te^0$ Similarly, take two values of p_2 as $p_2^0=\frac{be^0}{u}$ and $p_2^1=\frac{be^1}{u}$.

Then if $p_2^1=tp_2^0$, then we must have $e^1=te^0$ That is the new expenditure is just scaled up by a factor of *t*. In the same way, from panel *b* using the two intercepts on each of the two axes, we can conclude that if $p_1=tp_1$ and $p_2=tp_2$, then $e(tp_1,tp_2;u)=te(p_1,p_2;u)$. This property is called linear homogeneity. It turns out that linear homogeneity is fundamental

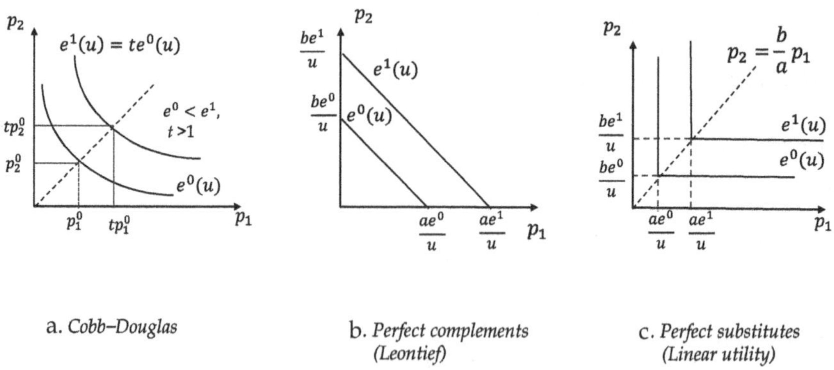

Figure 4.3 Iso-expenditure curves

to all expenditure functions. On panel *a* of Figure 4.3 we show that along any ray, which corresponds to a given price ratio, the expenditure levels would be a *scalar* expansion if we move north-east (and contraction if we move south-west). *That is, if we double all prices the expenditure will also double, but the consumer's choice of* x_1 *and* x_2 *will not change. We must note that this is true for all utility functions regardless of their differentiability or homotheticity properties.*

4.2.4.1 Properties of the expenditure function

There are a few more important properties that are not so obvious from the earlier graphs. In the following, we provide a formal proof of those properties.

1. *Continuity*. The expenditure function $e(p_1, p_2; u)$ is continuous in prices p_1 and p_2.
   Proof. Continuity of $e(p_1, p_2; u)$ follows from the continuity of the Hicksian demand functions, which is ensured by quasi-convexity of the utility function.
2. *Linear homogeneity*. The expenditure function $e(p_1, p_2; u)$ is homogeneous of degree 1 in prices p_1 and p_2.
   Proof. This is straightforward. $e(tp_1, tp_2; u) = te(p_1, p_2; u)$ for any scalar $t > 0$, because

   $$e(tp_1, tp_2; u) = \min\left[(tp_1)x_1 + (tp_2)x_2\right] = t\left[\min\{p_1x_1 + p_2x_2\}\right] = te(p_1, p_2; u).$$

3. *Monotonicity*. $e(p_1, p_2; u)$ is increasing in (p_1, p_2) That is, $\frac{\partial e}{\partial p_i} > 0$.
   Proof. Consider two price vectors $p = (p_1, p_2)$ and $p' = (p_1', p_2)$, where $p_1' > p_1$. Also assume that $x = (x_1^h, x_2^h)$ and $x' = (x_1'^h, x_2'^h)$ are the two associated Hicksian demand vectors. Then by definition, $px \le px'$ and $p'x' \le p'x$. But since $p' > p$ and $px' \le p'x'$, we get $px \le px' \le p'x'$, which says that $e(p_1, p_2; u) \le e(p_1', p_2; u)$.
4. *Concavity*. $e(p_1, p_2; u)$ is concave in (p_1, p_2).
   Proof. Let $p = (p_1, p_2)$ and $p' = (p_1', p_2')$ be two price vectors. Then concavity of $e(\cdot)$ means

   $$e(\lambda p + (1-\lambda)p'; u) \ge \lambda e(p, u) + (1-\lambda)e(p'; u), \quad \text{for } 0 \le \lambda \le 1.$$

   The proof is simple. By definition, $e(\lambda p + (1-\lambda)p'; u) =$ Min $\sum_i \{\lambda p_i + (1-\lambda)p_i'\}x_i$ $=$ Min $\{\lambda \sum_i p_i x_i + (1-\lambda)\sum_i p_i' x_i\} \ge \lambda$ Min $\{\sum_i p_i x_i\} + (1-\lambda)$ Min $\{\sum_i p_i' x_i\} = \lambda e(p, u) + (1-\lambda)$ $e(p'; u)$. This is so because the minimum of the sum of the two terms must be greater (or no less) than the sum of the minimum of the two terms.
5. *Shephard's lemma*. Whenever $e(.)$ is differentiable, $\frac{\partial e(p_1, p_2; u)}{\partial p_i} = x_i^h(p_1, p_2; u)$.
   Proof. It follows from the envelope theorem. Consider the definition of the expenditure function:

   $$e(p_1, p_2; u) = \sum_i p_i x_i^h(p_1, p_2; u) + \mu(p_1, p_2; u)\left[u - u\left(x_1^h, x_2^h\right)\right].$$

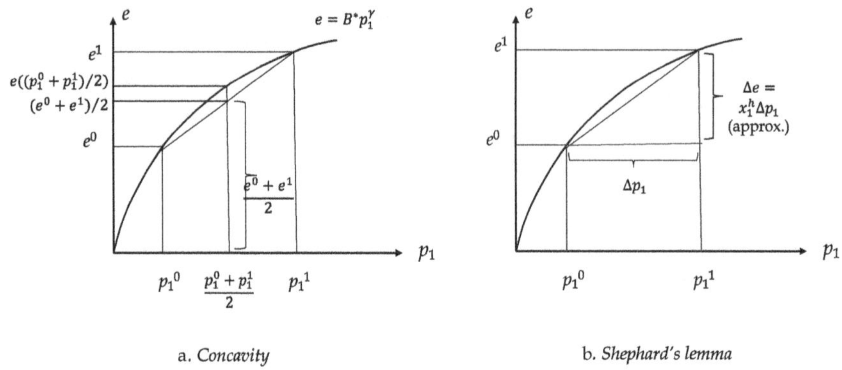

Figure 4.4 Concavity and Shephard's lemma

Differentiate the preceding with respect to p_i, and we get

$$\frac{\partial e(.)}{\partial p_i} = x_i^h + \sum_j \left\{ \left[p_j - \mu \frac{\partial u}{\partial x_j} \right] \frac{\partial x_j^h}{\partial p_i} \right\} + \left[u - u\left(x_1^h, x_2^h\right) \right] \frac{\partial \mu}{\partial p_i}.$$

But by the first-order conditions for expenditure minimisation, $\left[p_j - \mu \frac{\partial u}{\partial x_j} \right] = 0, \forall j$ and $u = u\left(x_1^h, x_2^h\right)$. Hence, we are left with $\frac{\partial e(.)}{\partial p_i} = x_i^h\left(p_1, p_2; u\right)$.

In Figure 4.4 we illustrate the concavity of the expenditure function and Shephard's lemma. Taking the Cobb–Douglas case as an example we rewrite the expenditure function as $e = B^* p_1^\gamma$, where $B^* = Bp_2^{1-\gamma}$, $\gamma < 1$ Assuming p_2 to be fixed, we plot e against p_1 on panel *a*. We take the midpoint of p_1^0 and p_1^1, and compare the midpoint value of e^0 and e^1. Since the expenditure function is clearly concave, $e\left(\frac{p_1^0 + p_1^1}{2}\right) > \frac{e^0 + e^1}{2}$ This will be true not just at the midpoint but also at any points between p_1^0 and p_1^1.

On panel *b*, we illustrate the Shephard's lemma. If we increase the price p_1 arbitrarily, say, from p_1^0 to p_1^1, then by how much does the expenditure increase? The answer is approximately by $x_1^h \Delta p_1$. This is a remarkably powerful result. If the price of a given good increases by £1, the total expenditure must increase (approximately) by the amount of the Hicksian demand for that good.[4]

Here is another *intuitive proof* of Shephard's lemma based on the graph on panel *b* of Figure 4.4. Assume p_2 is unchanged and p_1 increases from p_1^0 to p_1^1. Corresponding Hicksian demands are denoted as (x_1^0, x_2^0) and (x_1^1, x_2^1). Then we can write the following:

$$\begin{aligned}
\Delta e = e^1 - e^0 &= p_1^1 x_1^1 + p_2 x_2^1 - p_1^0 x_1^0 - p_2 x_2^0 \\
&= p_1^1 x_1^1 + p_1^1 x_1^0 - p_1^1 x_1^0 - p_1^0 x_1^0 + p_2\left(x_2^1 - x_2^0\right) \\
&= p_1^1\left(x_1^1 - x_1^0\right) + x_1^0\left(p_1^1 - p_1^0\right) + p_2 \Delta x_2 \\
&= p_1^1 \Delta x_1 + x_1^0 \Delta p_1 + p_2 \Delta x_2
\end{aligned}$$

Now rearranging terms and taking p_1^1 to be close to p_1^0 so that x_1^0 is arbitrarily close to x_1^1 (and thus ignoring the superscripts 0 and 1), we can write the previous relation (approximately) as

$$\Delta e = x_1 \Delta p_1 + \left[p_1 \frac{\Delta x_1}{\Delta p_1} + p_2 \frac{\Delta x_2}{\Delta p_1} \right] \Delta p_1. \tag{4.14}$$

Now, by definition of the Hicksian demand functions, $u(x_1(\cdot), x_2(\cdot)) = u^0$ (some constant number). Then a change in p_1 implies

$$u_1 \frac{\Delta x_1}{\Delta p_1} + u_2 \frac{\Delta x_2}{\Delta p_1} = 0.$$

Recall from the first order conditions of expenditure minimisation $u_1 = \mu p_1$ and $u_2 = \mu p_2$, and therefore, we can write the previous relation as

$$\mu \left[p_1 \frac{\Delta x_1}{\Delta p_1} + p_2 \frac{\Delta x_2}{\Delta p_1} \right] = 0.$$

Because $\mu > 0$ the bracketed term in the preceding must be zero. So, in Eq. (4.14), we have

$$\Delta e = x_1 \Delta p_1,$$

which is essentially $\frac{\partial e}{\partial p_1} = x_1^h$ when Δp_1 is arbitrarily small.

Properties 4 and 5 have important implications for the Hicksian demand functions. Property 5 tells us that even if $x_i^h(.)$ is not observable, we can derive it from the expenditure function, which can be estimated from consumption data. Property 4 says that the Hessian matrix of the $e(p,u)$ must be negative semi-definite and symmetric. This confirms two important properties of the Hicksian demand function:

- $\frac{\partial x_i^h}{\partial p_i} \leq 0; x_i^h(.)$ is non-increasing in p_i.
- $\frac{\partial x_i^h}{\partial p_j} = \frac{\partial x_j^h}{\partial p_i}$ for any i and j, $i \neq j$. The cross-price effects of the Hicksian demand functions are symmetric.

4.3 Duality and the Slutsky equation

By now it should be apparent that the *utility maximisation problem* (UMP) and the *expenditure minimisation problem* (EMP) are just two alternative ways of arriving at the consumer's choice. In UMP, the consumer's income (or wealth) is given, and we derive the Marshallian demand, from which the indirect utility can be calculated. In EMP, the journey is backward. Fixing a level of utility, we find the Hicksian demand and calculate how much expenditure is needed to support the utility. The names of these two demand functions differ entirely because of different approaches taken, but they must correspond to the same level *if* we set the level of the direct utility of EMP equal to the level of indirect utility of UMP or, conversely, *if* income in UMP is set exactly equal to the expenditure obtained from EMP. This equivalence relation is called **duality**.

Imagine your parent sends you £200 every week for your living expenses and you are happy about that. Now, if one week, your parent asks you how much money they should send, your answer should be exactly £200, and you will be buying exactly the same bundle of goods as before. This may appear trivial at first, but with introspection you should see that two approaches to demand are interconnected in a deeper way, and following the trail of these interconnections, we will be able to gain important insights into the law of demand.

But first, let us formally explore the duality relation. The equivalence of the two approaches can be seen at three levels, income and expenditure, direct and indirect utility and, of course, demand. We state the duality at the level of demand. But for a more formal and complete list of duality, see Varian (1992, p. 106).

4.3.1 Duality of demand

Marshallian demand for a given m must be equal to the Hicksian demand that takes the level of utility optimally supported by m as given, i.e., $u = v(p_1, p_2; m)$. Conversely, the Hicksian demand that takes u as given and generates expenditure $e(p_1, p_2; u)$ must be equal to the Marshallian demand when m is set such that $m = e(p_1, p_2; u)$ Formally,

$$x_i(p_1, p_2, m) \equiv x_i^h(p_1, p_2, v(p_1, p_2, m)), \text{ and } x_i^h(p_1, p_2; u) = x_i(p_1, p_2; e(p_1, p_2; u)).$$

Now we state an important relation, known as the *Slutsky equation*, between the slopes of the Marshallian and the Hicksian demand functions. Recall that the so-called *law of demand* cannot be guaranteed in the case of the Marshallian demand function. Slutsky equation helps us understand why this relationship cannot be guaranteed and under what condition we hope to get it. Essentially, the equation breaks the effect of a price change in two parts; one is a pure or direct price effect (called the **substitution effect**, *SE*), which is observed in the case of the Hicksian demand function, and the other is the indirect effect coming through a change in purchasing power, called the **income effect** (*IE*). It is the second effect, which is unpredictable and leads to ambiguity in the overall effect of a price change.

Proposition 4. *Suppose* $x_i(p_1, p_2, m)$ *and* $x_i^h(p_1, p_2; u)$ *are the Marshallian and Hicksian demand functions respectively for good* i, $i = 1, 2$ *Then the derivatives of the two demand functions with respect to* p_j *are connected by the following equation, which is called the Slutsky equation:*

$$\frac{\partial x_i(.,m)}{\partial p_j} = \frac{\partial x_i^h(.,u)}{\partial p_j} - \frac{\partial x_i(.,m)}{\partial m} x_j(.,m) \quad \text{for any } i, j = 1, 2. \tag{4.15}$$

Proof. Without loss of generality, let us consider x_1 and p_1. By duality,

$$x_1^h(p_1, p_2; u) \equiv x_1(p_1, p_2, e(p_1, p_2; u)).$$

Differentiate both sides of the preceding with respect to p_1.

$$\frac{\partial x_1^h(p_1, p_2; u)}{\partial p_1} = \frac{\partial x_1(p_1, p_2, e(.))}{\partial p_1} + \frac{\partial x_1(p_1, p_2, e(.))}{\partial e(.)} \frac{\partial e(p_1, p_2, u)}{\partial p_1}.$$

We know $e(p_1, p_2, u) = m$ Also, by Shephard's lemma, $\frac{\partial e(p_1, p_2, u)}{\partial p_1} = x_1^h(p_1, p_2; u)$, which is by duality same as the Marshallian demand. Therefore, we can write

$$\frac{\partial x_1^h(p_1, p_2; u)}{\partial p_1} = \frac{\partial x_1(p_1, p_2; m)}{\partial p_1} + \frac{\partial x_1(p_1, p_2, m)}{\partial m} x_1(p_1, p_2, m).$$

After rearranging the terms, we get Eq. (4.15) for x_1 and p_1. For any other combination of x_i and p_j, the same method can be used.

The Slutsky equation is important in many ways. First, it helps us decompose the price effect and precisely identify the role of the income effect of a price change. Second, the equation reveals how the Marshallian and the Hicksian demand functions are interrelated both at the level and in terms of their derivatives. Third, there are interesting cross-price effects between two Marshallian demand functions.

4.3.2 *Slutsky decomposition*

Let us now discuss the Slutsky decomposition in a two-good environment with the help of Figure 4.5. Suppose initially the consumer is facing prices (p_1^0, p_2) and she has income m. Her Marshallian demands for x_1 and x_2 are shown at point A in both panels of the graph. Now let p_1 rise to p_1^1 and consider panel a. With her income unchanged, the consumer moves from point A to point C on the lower budget line. Her consumption of x_1 decreases from x_1^0 to x_1^1. The total reduction in x_1 is *price effect*.

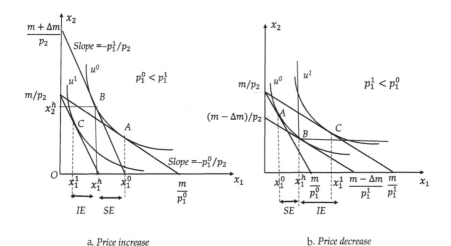

From a price increase, $\Delta p_1 = p_1^1 - p_1^0 > 0$ the change in x_1 can be decomposed as follows:

$$\Delta x_1 = (x_1^1 - x_1^0) = [x_1^h - x_1^0] + [x_1^1 - x_1^h] < 0.$$

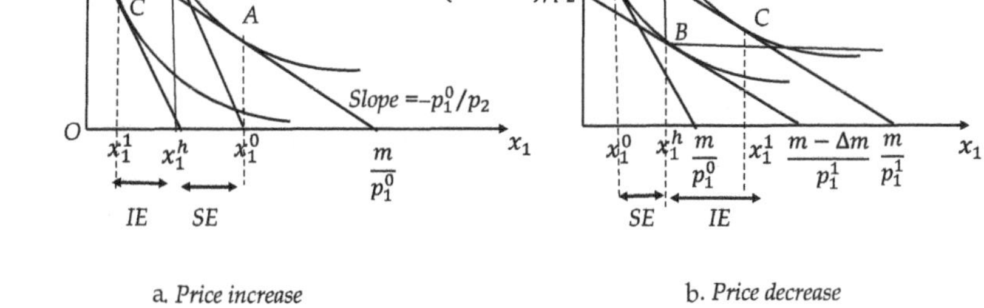

Figure 4.5 Slutsky decomposition

Dividing both sides by $\Delta p_1 > 0$, we can write

$$\frac{\Delta x_1}{\Delta p_1} = \underbrace{\frac{\left[x_1^h - x_1^0\right]}{\Delta p_1}}_{<0} + \underbrace{\frac{\left[x_1^1 - x_1^h\right]}{\Delta p_1}}_{<0} < 0,$$

$$= \frac{\Delta x_1^h}{\Delta p_1} - \frac{|\Delta x_1|}{\Delta m}\frac{\Delta e}{\Delta p_1} \quad \text{since } x_1^1 < x_1^0$$

$$= \underbrace{\frac{\Delta x_1^h}{\Delta p_1}}_{SE} \underbrace{- \frac{\Delta x_1}{\Delta m} x_1}_{IE}.$$

Please note that we have drawn Figure 4.5 with the assumption that both x_1 and x_2 are normal goods. On panel *a*, the final choice of x_1 (at point *C*) is x_1^1, which is strictly less than x_1^h. The fact that point *C* lies to the south-west of point *B* in the rectangular area $Ox_1^h Bx_2^h$ confirms that both goods are normal.[5] Conceptually, point *B* could be reached only if the consumer was given a cash transfer Δm. Then x_1^h would have been her final choice. But as that is not given, her choice must move from *B* to *C* as if she is forgoing an income loss.

In the same way, we can decompose the total price effect of a price fall, based on panel *b* of Figure 4.5, where p_1 falls from p_1^0 to p_1^1. The consumer's initial choice is point *A*, and with the price drop, she moves to point *C*. Both goods are assumed to be normal.

For a price decrease $\Delta p_1 < 0$, the total change in x_1 is

$$\Delta x_1 = \left(x_1^1 - x_1^0\right) = \left[x_1^h - x_1^0\right] + \left[x_1^1 - x_1^h\right] > 0.$$

Again, dividing both sides by $\Delta p_1 < 0$, we write

$$\frac{\Delta x_1}{\Delta p_1} = \underbrace{\frac{\left[x_1^h - x_1^0\right]}{\Delta p_1}}_{<0} + \underbrace{\frac{\left[x_1^1 - x_1^h\right]}{\Delta p_1}}_{<0} < 0,$$

$$= \frac{\Delta x_1^h}{\Delta p_1} - \frac{\Delta x_1}{\Delta m}\frac{\Delta e}{|\Delta p_1|} \quad \text{since } \Delta p_1 < 0$$

$$= \underbrace{\frac{\Delta x_1^h}{\Delta p_1}}_{SE} \underbrace{- \frac{\Delta x_1}{\Delta m} x_1}_{IE}.$$

So, regardless of price increase or decrease, the decomposition is same. In the case of a price decrease, the substitution effect captures the journey from *A* to *B*, as if the consumer has been forced to give up Δm from her budget to be able to remain on the old indifference curve at the new price ratio. But once Δm is returned to her she will add more of both x_1 and x_2 by picking a point in the north-east region of point *B* marked by two quadrant lines, which indeed houses her final choice—point *C*.

On panel *b*, if x_1 were to be inferior, x_1^1 would have been strictly less than x_1^h, and the possibility of a Giffen good could arise if $x_1^1 < x_1^0$ was the final choice.[6]

4.3.3 An illustrative example

Let us take the Marshallian demand function for x_1 from Chapter 3 (Eq. (3.8)) and derive

$$\frac{\partial x_1}{\partial p_1} = -\frac{\alpha}{\alpha+\beta}\frac{m}{p_1^2}, \quad \frac{\partial x_1}{\partial m}x_1 = \frac{\alpha^2}{(\alpha+\beta)^2}\frac{m}{p_1^2}.$$

Now from the Hicksian demand (Eq. (4.6)) we derive the substitution effect:

$$\frac{\partial x_1^h}{\partial p_1} = -\frac{\beta}{\alpha+\beta}\left(\frac{u}{A}\right)^{\frac{1}{\alpha+\beta}}\left(\frac{\alpha p_2}{\beta p_1}\right)^{\frac{\beta}{\alpha+\beta}}\frac{1}{p_1}.$$

By virtue of duality $u = v$, now substitute $v = A\frac{\alpha^\alpha \beta^\beta}{(\alpha+\beta)^{\alpha+\beta}}\frac{m^{\alpha+\beta}}{p_1^\alpha p_2^\beta}$ from Eq. (3.21) from Chapter 3 in place of u into the preceding expression of $\frac{\partial x_1^h}{\partial p_1}$ and rewrite the expression as

$$\frac{\partial x_1^h}{\partial p_1} = -\frac{m}{p_1^2}\frac{\alpha\beta}{(\alpha+\beta)^2}.$$

Finally, the left-hand side of the Slutsky equation (4.16) is

$$\frac{\partial x_1}{\partial p_1} = -\frac{\alpha}{\alpha+\beta}\frac{m}{p_1^2}.$$

The right-hand side expression of the Slutsky equation is

$$\frac{\partial x_1^h}{\partial p_1} - \frac{\partial x_1}{\partial m}x_1 = -\frac{m}{p_1^2}\frac{\alpha\beta}{(\alpha+\beta)^2} - \left(\frac{\alpha}{\alpha+\beta}\right)^2\frac{m}{p_1^2} = -\frac{\alpha}{(\alpha+\beta)}\frac{m}{p_1^2}.$$

Thus, the two sides of the Slutsky equation have been proven to be identical.

4.3.4 Discussion and observations

The Slutsky equation as presented in Eq. (4.15) is a general representation of an arbitrary price change, giving rise to two variants of it due to own price change and a cross-price change. For the benefit of discussion, let us now return to our familiar two-good setting and write the Slutsky equations for good 1 as follows:

$$\frac{\partial x_1(p_1,p_2,m)}{\partial p_1} = \frac{\partial x_1^h(p_1,p_2,u)}{\partial p_1} - \frac{\partial x_1(p_1,p_2,m)}{\partial m}x_1(p_1,p_2,m), \tag{4.16}$$

$$\frac{\partial x_1(p_1,p_2,m)}{\partial p_2} = \frac{\partial x_1^h(p_1,p_2,u)}{\partial p_2} - \frac{\partial x_1(p_1,p_2,m)}{\partial m}x_2(p_1,p_2,m). \tag{4.17}$$

Eq. (4.16) is of the own price effect, and Eq. (4.17) is of the cross-price effect. First, consider the own price effect. The equation says that the (own) price effect given by the left-hand side expression can be decomposed into two elements—substitution and income effects. Here, students often get confused by the negative sign in front of the income effect of the term. But that is because we tend to forget that the first term, $\partial x_1^h / \partial p_1$ is always negative. Therefore, when x_1 is a normal good (i.e., $\partial x_1 / \partial m > 0$) the right-hand side is truly a sum of two effects. A price increase reduces x_1 directly via the substitution effect and indirectly via a contraction of the budget. Thus, when the good is normal both substitution and income effects work in the same *direction*. Thus, for normal goods, the *law of demand* holds.

If, however, x_1 is an inferior good, the substitution and the income effects work in opposite directions. As a price increase contracts the budget the consumer is induced to buy more (because the good is inferior), counteracting the force of the substituting effect. The end result depends on which effect is stronger. If the substitution effect is stronger than the negative income effect, the law of demand will still hold; otherwise, the law of demand will fail and the good in that case becomes a Giffen good.

Now consider the equation for the cross-price effect (Eq. (4.17)). Here the substitution effect is always positive. If x_1 is an inferior good, then $\partial x_1 / \partial p_2$ is unambiguously positive. That is, in a two-good model, the inferior good will be a gross substitute for the other good. But if x_1 is a normal good, then it will be a gross complement to or gross substitute for the other good depending on the income effect is stronger or weaker than the (cross-price) substitution effect.

Proposition 5. *Suppose there are two goods* x_1 *and* x_2, *and without loss of generality consider the Marshallian demand for* x_1.

a. *If* x_1 *is normal, the law of demand must hold for* x_1; *that is,* $\partial x_1 / \partial p_1 < 0$. *Furthermore,* x_1 *is a gross complement to* x_2 *if* $\frac{\partial x_1}{\partial m} x_2 > \frac{\partial x_1^h}{\partial p_2}$; *otherwise,* x_1 *is a gross substitute.*
b. *Suppose* x_1 *is inferior. Then the law of demand holds if and only if* $\left|\frac{\partial x_1^h}{\partial p_1}\right| > \left|\frac{\partial x_1}{\partial m} x_1\right|$. *Furthermore,* x_1 *is gross substitute for* x_2.

In Figure 4.6, we draw a pair of Marshallian and Hicksian demand curves. The Hicksian demand curve is drawn for a given utility level, namely, u^0, while the Marshallian demand curve is based on a fixed level of income m^0. Two curves cross each other at price p_1^0, where

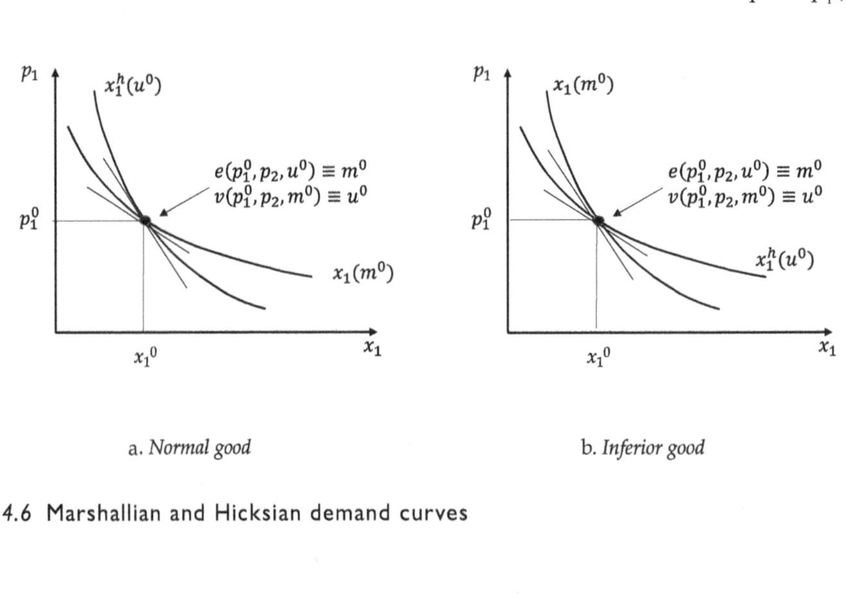

Figure 4.6 Marshallian and Hicksian demand curves

not only does the consumer buy exactly the same x_1 (and x_2, which is not shown here) but spend exactly the same amount and get the same utility. At prices below p_1^0, she will buy more of x_1 under utility maximisation than under expenditure minimisation if x_1 is a normal good (as shown in panel *a*) or less of x_1 under utility maximisation if x_1 is an inferior good (as shown in panel *b*). A lower price induces the consumer to buy more through the income effect if the good is normal. Above price p_1^0, the effects are opposite. At their point of equality, the (inverse) Hicksian demand curve is steeper than the Marshallian demand curve when the good is normal.

Utilising the Slutsky equations for cross-price effect, we can establish two more properties, one relating to the gross substituteness and complementarity of Marshallian demands and the other showing connections between the price elasticities of Hicksian demand and the Marshallian demand.

Corollary 1.

a. *Cross-price effects between any pair of Marshallian demands diverge according to the following equation:*

$$\frac{\partial x_1(p_1,p_2,m)}{\partial p_2}-\frac{\partial x_2(p_1,p_2,m)}{\partial p_1}=\frac{x_1x_2}{m}\left[\epsilon_{2m}-\epsilon_{1m}\right]. \tag{4.18}$$

For homothetic utility functions, the Marshallian demand functions will have symmetric cross-price effects.

b. *The own price elasticity of the Hicksian demand is smaller (greater) than the own price elasticity of the Marshallian demand if the good is a normal (inferior) good.*

$$\varepsilon_{ii}^h=\varepsilon_{ii}+\varepsilon_{im}s_i,\text{ for } i=1,2. \tag{4.19}$$

Proof.

a. Write $p=(p_1,p_2)$ and consider Eq. (4.15) for any $i\neq j$. By the implication of the symmetry of $\frac{\partial x_1^h(p,u)}{\partial p_2}=\frac{\partial x_2^h(p,u)}{\partial p_1}$, we must have

$$\frac{\partial x_1(p,m)}{\partial p_2}+\frac{\partial x_1(p,m)}{\partial m}x_2(p,m)=\frac{\partial x_2(p,m)}{\partial p_1}+\frac{\partial x_2(p,m)}{\partial m}x_1(p,m).$$

Or

$$\begin{aligned}\frac{\partial x_1(p,m)}{\partial p_2}-\frac{\partial x_2(p,m)}{\partial p_1}&=\frac{\partial x_2(p,m)}{\partial m}x_1(p,m)-\frac{\partial x_1(p,m)}{\partial m}x_2(p,m)\\&=\frac{x_1x_2}{m}\left[\frac{\partial x_2(p,m)}{\partial m}\frac{m}{x_2}-\frac{\partial x_1(p,m)}{\partial m}\frac{m}{x_1}\right]\\&=\frac{x_1x_2}{m}\left[\epsilon_{2m}-\epsilon_{1m}\right].\end{aligned}$$

b. From Eq. (4.15), set $i = j$ and write

$$\frac{\partial x_i^h(p,u)}{\partial p_i} = \frac{\partial x_i(p,m)}{\partial p_i} + \frac{\partial x_i(p,m)}{\partial m} x_i(p,m).$$

Multiply both sides by $\frac{p_i}{x_i^h(p,u)}$. Then, using duality $x_i^h(p,u) = x_i(p,m)$, let us write

$$\frac{\partial x_i^h(p,u)}{\partial p_i}\frac{p_i}{x_i^h(p,u)} = \frac{\partial x_i(p,m)}{\partial p_i}\frac{p_i}{x_i(p,m)} + \left[\frac{\partial x_i(p,m)}{\partial m}\frac{m}{x_i(p,m)}\right]\frac{p_i x_i(p,m)}{m}$$

$$\epsilon_{ii}^h = \epsilon_{ii} + \epsilon_{im} s_i.$$

For all goods, the left-hand side is negative. For normal goods, $\epsilon_{im} > 0$ and $\epsilon_{ii} < 0$. Hence, it must be that $|\epsilon_{ii}^h| < |\epsilon_{ii}|$. For inferior goods, $\epsilon_{im} < 0$, and clearly, $|\epsilon_{ii}^h| > |\epsilon_{ii}|$.

4.4 Welfare effects of a price change

In all major economies, governments have anti-poverty or income support programmes to protect their low-income populations. In India, poor people are entitled to cheaper food grains, such as rice and wheat; cooking gas; kerosene; sugar; and pulses. The goods are sold through specialist shops operated by franchisees under the Public Distribution System.[7] In Great Britain, low-income households are given a maximum of £20,000 a year (slightly less than 50% of the per capita income). There are additional benefits, such as child benefits and disability allowances, among others. Note that the households receive cash and therefore it can be spent on anything including tobacco, alcohol or gambling—something regarded by many as controversial.[8] The US Supplemental Nutrition Assistance Program (SNAP), previously known as Food Stamps, provides a digital card to the poor that can be used to buy only food items, such as fruits and vegetables, dairy products, breads and cereals and meat, poultry and fish.[9] For a two-person household, the SNAP benefit is US$459 a month. While anti-poverty programmes greatly vary around the world in their type, scope, and operational principles, a common objective is to address the welfare of the people.

But there are some important questions: What is the appropriate notion of welfare, and how do we measure it? Fortunately, we have a starter in the concept of indirect utility, *albeit* difficult to measure it. Setting aside the measurement issue, if we use indirect utility as a measure of welfare, how do we design compensation schemes to help people against price rises? This question is very important for practical policy reasons as well as from a theoretical point of view. Sir John Hicks (1939, 1956) proposed two alternative measures of the welfare effect of a price change. These two measures are **compensating** and **equivalent** variations in income.

4.4.1 *Compensating variation in income*

For ease of understanding, let us consider only two goods and assume that p_2 is unchanged. Suppose that initially, p_1 is p_1^0 and the consumer with her income m obtains an indirect utility of v^0. On panel *a* of Figure 4.7 this situation corresponds to point *A*. The indirect utility curve that passes through point *A* is drawn for a fixed income level m. Now p_1 increases to p_1^1. Clearly, the consumer's welfare falls, as $v(m)$ at p_1^1 gives a much lower indirect utility than v^0. But if her

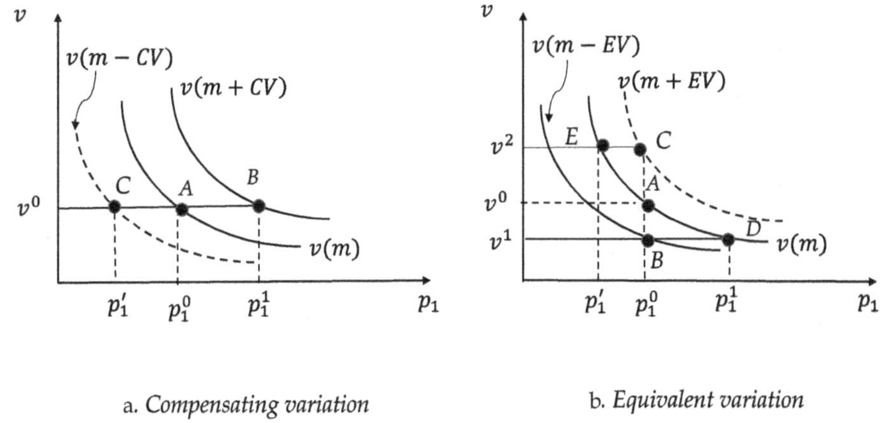

Figure 4.7 Price change and welfare effects

m is increased by, say, ΔM, such that $v\left(p_1^1, m+\Delta m\right) = v^0$, then Δm accurately compensates the consumer for her welfare loss and restores her indirect utility at the pre-price change level. Δm is also an accurate monetary measure of the welfare change. This is our compensating variation (CV) in income.

Formally, in terms of the expenditure function, we can define

$$CV = e\left(p_1 + \Delta p_1, p_2, u^0\right) - e\left(p_1, p_2, u^0\right) > 0 \text{ if } \Delta p_1 > 0,$$

where u^0 is the utility achieved before the price change. Alternatively, we can also write

$$CV \equiv \Delta m \mid v\left(p_1, p_2, m\right) = v\left(p_1 + \Delta p_1, p_2, m + \Delta m\right) \equiv u^0, \text{ where}$$
$$\Delta m > 0 \text{ if } \Delta p_1 > 0, \text{ and } \Delta m < 0 \text{ if } \Delta p_1 < 0.$$

We have depicted both $\Delta p_1 > 0$ and $\Delta p_1 < 0$ on panel *a* of Figure 4.7 by considering both price rise and price fall. When price falls the consumer's welfare improves, and the money that needs to be taken away measures how much welfare has improved. An alternative but indirect way of showing that CV has been presented on panel *a* of Figure 4.8. Here, we return to the expenditure minimisation problem and, by considering a price increase to p_1^1, show that a compensating variation of $E_1 - E_0$ is needed to protect the consumer's welfare. The amount of CV is also the income equivalent of welfare loss.

4.4.2 *Equivalent variation in income*

An alternative measure of welfare loss is to see how much income loss the consumer would need to suffer if she were to face the old price but maintain the new utility level. In other words, if p_1 rises from p_1^0 to p_1^1, the consumer's indirect utility would fall from v^0 to v^1; see panel *b* of Figure 4.7. If she is asked to maintain v^1 but is offered the old price p_1^0, then her income needs to be reduced by an amount that is called *equivalent variation*. Here, with equivalent variation, she

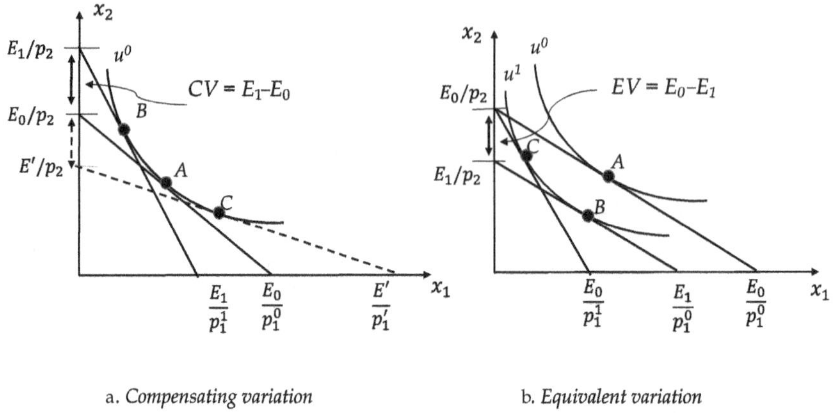

Figure 4.8 Compensating and equivalent variations of a price increase

is able to move from point D to point B. Also note that if p_1 were to fall to p_1', her utility would rise to v^2 at point E, and then the equivalent variation would be an addition to her income so that she can reach point C (panel b of Figure 4.7), where she is able to maintain her new utility v^2 at old price p_1^0. Thus, formally, we define EV as

$$EV = e\left(p_1, p_2, u^1\right) - e\left(p_1 + \Delta p_1, p_2, u^1\right) < 0 \quad \text{if } \Delta p_1 > 0,$$

where u^1 is the level of utility achieved after the price change. Equivalently,

$$EV \equiv \Delta m \mid v\left(p_1 + \Delta p_1, p_2, m\right) = v\left(p_1, p_2, m + \Delta m\right) \equiv u^1, \text{ where}$$
$$\Delta m < 0 \text{ if } \Delta p_1 > 0, \text{ and } \Delta m > 0 \text{ if } \Delta p_1 < 0.$$

Panel b of Figure 4.8 presents equivalent variation in terms of expenditure minimisation. Before the price change, the consumer is at point A enjoying utility v^0. After the price of good 1 rises the consumer reaches point C, the best she could afford with her income E_0. Her utility drops to v^1. If we move the consumer to point B by taking away an appropriate amount of expenditure, then she will have the new utility at the old price level. The expenditure taken away is a measure of welfare loss, and it is precisely the equivalent variation of a price rise.

4.4.3 *Slutsky compensation*

One obvious difficulty with CV or EV is that neither is easily measurable. This poses a problem for government agencies. Slutsky compensation scheme is a good alternative. It proposes to protect the consumer's pre-price rise consumption basket after the price change. So the government

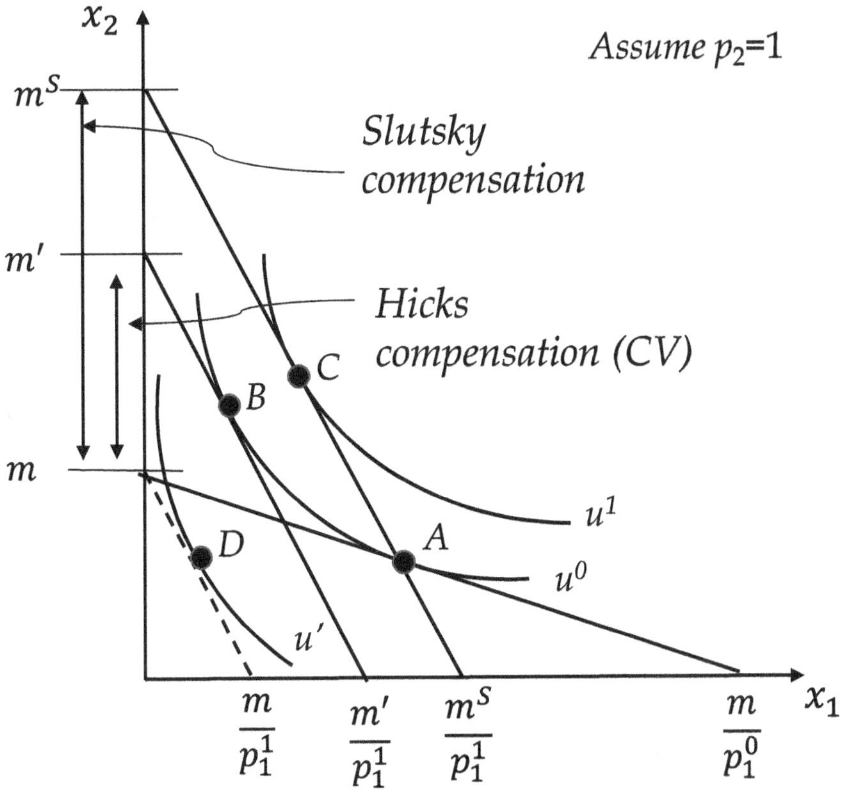

Figure 4.9 Slutsky income compensation

needs to just calculate how much money the consumer needs to be able to continue buying her pre-price rise consumption bundle at the new prices.

In Figure 4.9, we set $p_2 = 1$ for simplicity. The consumer's pre-price rise bundle is A, which costs m. If price rises to p_1^1, the consumer's moves down to the indifference curve and selects bundle D without any income support from the government. But if the government provides income support and adopts the Hicks compensation scheme, the consumer would be given $CV = m' - m$ so that her utility is maintained at u^0, but she will have to change her consumption bundle from A to B.

However, without precise information about her utility the government may simply employ the Slutsky compensation scheme, which calls for giving $m^S - m$ so that her new budget line passes through point A. That means, if she wishes she can buy her old bundle A. As a utility maximiser, she would certainly choose point C. As is obvious from the graph, the Slutsky compensation scheme is generous and thus costlier to the public exchequer, as compared to the Hicks compensation scheme. However, if the goods have little substitutability, then two schemes are approximately equal.[10]

4.4.3.1 *Illustration*

Let us take our Cobb–Douglas case and illustrate the computation of CV, EV and Slutsky compensation. For the ease of presentation let us set $\alpha + \beta = 1$ and $p_2 = 1$ We may see that our indirect utility function would then be

$$v = B\frac{m}{p_1^\alpha}, \text{ where } B = A\alpha^\alpha \beta^\beta.$$

Suppose p_1 is raised to λp_1, where $\lambda > 1$. Then CV is obtained as

$$v(p_1, m) = v(\lambda p_1, m + \Delta m) \Rightarrow B\frac{m}{p_1^\alpha} = B\frac{m + \Delta m}{\lambda^\alpha p_1^\alpha},$$

or $$\Delta m = m(\lambda^\alpha - 1) > 0.$$

Similarly, EV is computed as

$$v(\lambda p_1, m) = v(p_1, m + \Delta m) \Rightarrow B\frac{m}{\lambda^\alpha p_1^\alpha} = B\frac{m + \Delta m}{p_1^\alpha},$$

or $$\Delta m = m\left(\frac{1}{\lambda^\alpha} - 1\right) = -m\left(\frac{\lambda^\alpha - 1}{\lambda^\alpha}\right) < 0.$$

Finally, derive the **Slutsky compensation**. The consumer's old bundle is $\left(\frac{\alpha m}{p_1}, \beta m\right)$ The cost of supporting this bundle at the new price λp_1 is $m' = \lambda \alpha m + \beta m$. Therefore, $m^S = m' - m = \Delta m = (\lambda - 1)\alpha m$. It can be easily checked that $(\lambda - 1)\alpha m > m(\lambda^\alpha - 1)$ or $1 + (\lambda - 1)\alpha > \lambda^\alpha$ for every $0 < \alpha < 1$. That is, the Slutsky compensation is greater than the Hicks compensation.[11]

4.4.4 *Consumer surplus*

There is a direct (and easy-to-compute) measure of welfare called consumer surplus (*CS*), which subtracts the consumer's spending from her indirect utility. That is, $CS(p_1^0) = v(p, m) - p_1^0 x_1(p_1^0, p_2, m)$, where $p = (p_1, p_2)$ The *CS* at a given price, say p_1^0 can be easily calculated by measuring the area under the (inverse) Marshallian demand curve for x_1 above that price. However, *CS* is only an approximate measure.

The reason is simple. Let us recall the Roy's identity $x_1(p, m) \equiv -\frac{\partial v(p,m)}{\partial p_1} / \frac{\partial v(p,m)}{\partial m}$, which we can rewrite as $-\frac{\partial v(p,m)}{\partial p_1} = x_1(p,m)\frac{\partial v(p,m)}{\partial m}$ Therefore, indirect utility can be directly derived as

$$v(p, m) = -\int \frac{\partial v(p,m)}{\partial p_1} dp_1 = \int \left\{ x_1(p,m)\frac{\partial v(p,m)}{\partial m} \right\} dp_1.$$

Note that if $\partial v(p,m)/\partial m$ is constant then the area under the Marshallian demand curve gives an exact measure of utility. When the utility function is quasi-linear, $u = z(x_1) + bx_2$ with

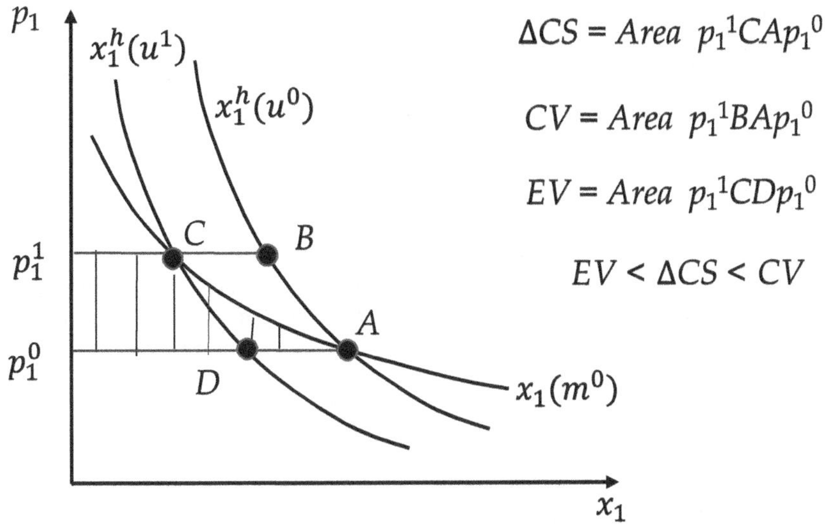

Figure 4.10 Loss in consumer surplus from a price increase

$z'(x_1) > 0, z''(x_1) < 0$, the income effect for x_1 is constant.[12] In the special case of the quasi-linear utility function, $v = \int x_1(p)\,dp_1$.

But, in general, $\partial v(p,m)/\partial m$ is not independent of prices. Therefore, the area under the Marshallian demand curve gives only an approximate measure of welfare.

It is easy to see that the welfare effect of a price change translates into a change in consumer surplus, and it will be within two bounds given by compensating and equivalent variations. See Figure 4.10, which draws a Marshallian demand curve and two Hicksian demand curves assuming that x_1 is normal. The price of good 1 rises from p_1^0 to p_1^1. The consumer surplus is reduced by the area under the Marshallian demand $x_1(m^0)$ curve between p_1^0 and p_1^1. This area is smaller than the compensating variation in income, which is given by the area under the outer Hicksian demand curve $x_1^h(u^0)$ between the same prices. Recall that by Shephard's lemma, $x_1^h = \partial e/\partial p_1$, and therefore, by integrating the Hicksian demand curve passing through point A, we get the expenditure needed to support the u^0 at a given price. The same expenditure can be estimated for the new utility level u^1 from the inner Hicksian demand curve $x_1^h(u^1)$, and the area between p_1^0 and p_1^1 gives equivalent variation. Clearly, for a normal good and a price increase, the magnitude of a change in consumer surplus is greater than EV but smaller than CV; for a price decrease, it will be the opposite. The case of an inferior good is left for you.

4.5 Endowment and the extended Slutsky equation

The Slutsky equation we derived in Eq. (4.15) represents the generic case in which the consumer's income is independent of prices. The generic case, as discussed in Chapters 1 and 3, leaves out a large number of interesting cases such as labour–leisure choice, inter-temporal consumption decisions and others. Eq. (4.15) needs to be extended to incorporate the additional effect prices have on Marshallian demand via the endowment income route.

Suppose the consumer's income is $M(p) = m + y(p)$, where m is the exogenous income and $y(p)$ is the price-sensitive income; $p = (p_1, p_2)$. The Marshallian demand in this case is written as $x_i = x_i(p, M(p))$. The total effect of a change in price p_j is

$$\frac{\partial x_i}{\partial p_j} = \frac{\partial x_i(p, M(p))}{\partial p_j} + \frac{\partial x_i(p, M(p))}{\partial M} \frac{\partial y(p)}{\partial p_j}.$$

The first term on the right-hand side is the standard (i.e., ignoring the endowment) price effect of Marshallian demand, and the second term is the endowment income effect. Slutsky equation as given in Eq. (4.15) applies to the first term of the right-hand side. Thus, we derive the **extended Slutsky equation** for any i and j as

$$\frac{\partial x_i}{\partial p_j} = \frac{\partial x_i^h(p,u)}{\partial p_j} - \frac{\partial x_i(p, M(p))}{\partial M} x_j(p, M(p)) + \frac{\partial x_i(p, M(p)}{\partial M} \frac{\partial y(p)}{\partial p_j}. \tag{4.20}$$

Note that the presence of the endowment income effect, which appears with a positive sign if $\partial y / \partial p_j > 0$ and thus counters the standard income effect and adds another layer of ambiguity. The second and the third terms on the right-hand side together determine the net income effect. If the endowment income effect is weak, then the conventional force of the normal good in ensuring the law of demand applies. But if the endowment income effect is strong, then the logic of the normal good may get turned upside down. Let us explore this issue in the next section with some interesting applications.

4.5.1 *Applications of the Slutsky equation*

In Chapters 1 and 3, we have considered several applications where the consumer's budget has a price-sensitive income component. We will see that the extended Slutsky equation will help us determine the price effects in such cases.

1. **Consumption leisure choice** Recall our consumer's problem to maximise $u = u(l, c)$ subject to $wl + pc = m + wT$ Here, the price sensitive income (i.e., y) is the value of endowment wT; clearly $y'(w) = T$.

   The extended Slutsky equation (4.20) for leisure and consumption resulting from a change in the wage rate w takes the following expressions:

$$\frac{\partial l}{\partial w} = \frac{\partial l^h}{\partial w} + \frac{\partial l}{\partial M}(T - l), \tag{4.21}$$

$$\frac{\partial c}{\partial w} = \frac{\partial c^h}{\partial w} + \frac{\partial c}{\partial M}(T - l). \tag{4.22}$$

   Note that on the right-hand side of Eq. (4.21), the income effect appears with a positive sign before it (because $T > l$), while the first term, the substitution effect, is still negative. Therefore, if leisure is a normal good, then we have ambiguity in the sign of $\frac{\partial l}{\partial w}$ in contrast to our earlier claim that for normal goods the law of demand always holds.

In fact, the law of demand is guaranteed to hold for leisure *if leisure is an inferior good.* This certainty of the inferior good effect stems from the fact that with higher wages, the consumer will reduce her leisure further in response to a budget expansion and thereby will complement the substitution effect.

By comparison, if leisure is a *strongly normal good,* then it can turn into a Giffen good. This is where we see the problem of a backward-bending labour supply curve.

For the cross-price effect on consumption, see from Eq. (4.22) if consumption is a normal good, then it must be a gross substitute for leisure, because both terms on the right-hand side are then positive. Recall that the cross-price substitution effect $\partial c^h / \partial w$ is always positive. But $\partial c / \partial w > 0$ is consistent only if $w(T-l)$ increases with w. This means that, if leisure were to rise with wage, it must not rise too much, which would force the wage earnings to fall. When wage earnings $w(T-l)$ fall following a strong decline in labour supply, consumption must fall too. Examining Eq. (4.22), we see that $\frac{\partial c}{\partial w} < 0$ is possible only if $\frac{\partial c}{\partial M} < 0$.

We summarise these important observations in the following proposition.

Proposition 6. *In a model of consumption and leisure choice, the following must hold:*

a. *If leisure is an inferior good, the law of demand must hold for leisure.*
b. *If leisure is a Giffen good, then leisure must be a normal good.*
c. *If consumption is a normal good, it must be a gross substitute for leisure.*
d. *If consumption is a gross complement to leisure, then consumption must be an inferior good.*

2. **Endowment budget** Suppose a consumer's budget equation is $p_1x_1 + p_2x_2 = p_1x_1^0 + p_2x_2^0$. A fruit grower not only consumes both apples and oranges but also grows them both. Hence, his income is sensitive to the prices of apples and oranges. A stock of apples and oranges, x_1^0 and x_2^0, respectively, is an endowment that the consumer has. Her income contains the value of this endowment as additional income, $y = p_1x_1^0 + p_2x_2^0$. If we are to consider the effect of an increase in p_1, we must take into account $y'(p_1) = x_1^0$.
The extended Slutsky equations for x_1 and x_2 with respect to p_1 are

$$\frac{\partial x_1}{\partial p_1} = \frac{\partial x_1^h}{\partial p_1} - \frac{\partial x_1}{\partial M}\left(x_1 - x_1^0\right), \tag{4.23}$$

$$\frac{\partial x_2}{\partial p_1} = \frac{\partial x_2^h}{\partial p_1} - \frac{\partial x_2}{\partial M}\left(x_1 - x_1^0\right). \tag{4.24}$$

Eq. (4.23) tells us that the income effect will work in the same or opposite direction of the substitution effect if the following two factors come together: The good must be a normal good and the consumer must be a net buyer of the good, or the good is inferior and the consumer is a net seller of it.

If demand exceeds the stock, that is, $x_1 > x_1^0$, the consumer wants to consume more x_1 than she has. When that is the case and x_1 is a normal good, the price effect of x_1 will follow the standard logic of $\frac{\partial x_1}{\partial M} > 0$. Alternatively, the consumer may be a net seller $x_1 < x_1^0$ and the good is inferior. Either way, $\frac{\partial x_1}{\partial p_1} < 0$.

However, in this set-up (with no additional cash), if she is a net buyer of x_1, then she must be a net seller of x_2, and there will be ambiguity with respect to the sign of $\frac{\partial x_2}{\partial p_2}$ (which can be analogously derived). That is to say, if both x_1 and x_2 are normal, then the law of demand cannot be taken for granted for both goods at the same time. One extreme possibility is that one good turns into a Giffen good (despite being normal) if the consumer is a net seller of that good.

Proposition 7. *Suppose the consumer's budget is solely constituted by a stock of goods. Then the following is true:*

a. *If both goods are normal, the law of demand is guaranteed for only one good.*
b. *The law of demand for a good holds if either the good is normal and the consumer is a net buyer of that good or the good is inferior and the consumer is a net seller of it.*
c. *If* x_2 *is normal and the consumer is a net seller of* x_1*, then* x_2 *must be a gross substitute for* x_1*.*

In Figure 4.11, we illustrate the price effects of an increase in p_1 or a decrease in p_2. Ω is the endowment point of the consumer, and the initial choice point is A when prices are p_1 and p_2. Now p_1 increases to p_1'. To the left of the endowment point, where the consumer is a net seller of x_1, the budget set expands, and to the right of the endowment point where the consumer is a net buyer of x_1, the budget set contracts.

On panel *a*, the consumer is choosing $x_1 < x_1^0$ and $x_2 > x_2^0$ at point A. After the price increase, by the substitution effect, the consumer moves to point B on the same indifference curve u^0. Clearly, x_1 falls and x_2 rises unambiguously. But as we try to add the income effect to point B, the direction of the final choice becomes unclear. It will depend on whether both goods are normal or not.

If both goods are normal, the final choice should be in the shaded region and on the new budget line. Point C is such an example. In the graph, we show that point C is to the north-west of point A. That means, as compared to the pre-price rise choice the post-price choice involves a slightly smaller x_1 and significantly greater x_2. It is not hard to see that the consumer can end up choosing point D (which is to the right of point A) and end up buying more of x_1, as if x_1 has become a Giffen good for her.

An even more important point is that x_1 can become a Giffen good, because of being a normal good. In fact, if it were an inferior good surely it would obey the law of demand.

Since the graph is equivalent to a decrease in p_2 and, in panel *a*, x_2 increases unambiguously, we can claim that when both goods are normal and the consumer is a net buyer of x_2, the law of demand must hold for x_2 but not necessarily for x_1.

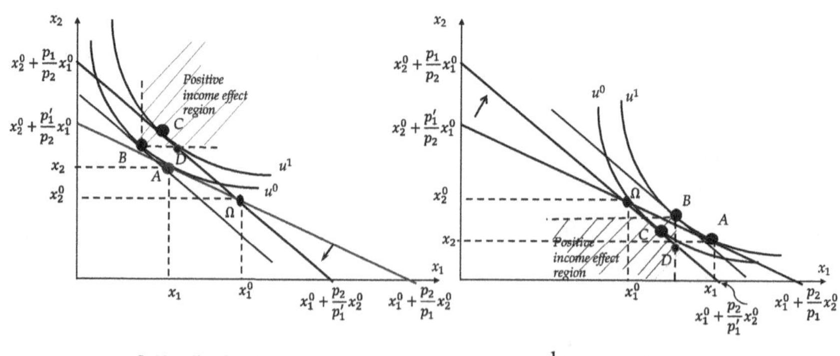

Figure 4.11 Endowment budget and the effects of a relative price change

In panel b, we depict the case of the consumer being a net buyer. Point A corresponds to $x_1 > x_1^0$ and $x_2 < x_2^0$ Here, after the price rise the consumer moves to point B through the substitution effect. Now because of the budget contraction the consumer will pick a point south-west of point B on the new budget line if both goods are normal. It is clear that in the shaded region, x_1 is smaller than the original choice (at point A). But the choice of x_2 can fall to point D, showing a Giffen good phenomenon (here, think of a fall in p_2).

In sum, the law of demand will necessarily hold for both goods if the good for which the consumer is a net buyer is a normal good and the good for which the consumer is a net seller is an inferior good.

3. **Inter-temporal consumption** Finally consider the consumption and saving decision problem. For simplicity let us set the borrowing interest rate the same as the saving interest rate r and assume the prices of consumption today and tomorrow are unchanged, which we normalise to 1. The consumer's problem is to maximise $u = u(c_1, c_2)$ subject to $c_1 + \theta c_2 = m_1 + \theta m_2$, where $\theta = 1/(1+r)$ and m_1 and m_2 are the endowment income for today and tomorrow, respectively. Of course, the consumer can augment today's budget by borrowing against her future income m_2 or augment tomorrow's budget by saving from today's income m_1. The relative price of future consumption is θ, which varies inversely with r. If the interest rate rises, the relative price of future consumption falls.

The Slutsky equation and the associated price effects are similar to the endowment budget case discussed earlier. Still, it is worthwhile to give it a separate consideration. In this model, our main interest is to see whether an interest rate rise induces the consumer to save more. But saving enters as a residual category from the first period. So a decrease in c_1 is what we would like to see. The extended Slutsky equations are

$$\frac{\partial c_1}{\partial \theta} = \frac{\partial c_1^h}{\partial \theta} - \frac{\partial c_1}{\partial M}(c_2 - m_2), \tag{4.25}$$

$$\frac{\partial c_2}{\partial \theta} = \frac{\partial c_2^h}{\partial \theta} - \frac{\partial c_2}{\partial M}(c_2 - m_2). \tag{4.26}$$

An increase in r would reduce θ, and for saving to increase, c_1 must fall. Thus, we want $\frac{\partial c_1}{\partial \theta} > 0$ in Eq. (4.25). If the consumer is already a saver $(c_2 > m_2)$ and c_1 is an inferior good, then we are assured of $\frac{\partial c_1}{\partial \theta} > 0$ and $\frac{\partial s}{\partial r} > 0$. But if c_1 is a normal good, then the sign of $\frac{\partial c_1}{\partial \theta}$ is ambiguous (mind that $\frac{\partial c_1^h}{\partial \theta} > 0$ by substitution effect). However, Eq. (4.26) confirms that regardless of saving rises or not, future consumption will unambiguously rise if c_2 is normal and if the consumer is already a saver.

Figure 4.12 illustrates the above observations. Here, initially the 'price' of c_2 is θ, and the consumer is a saver by virtue of choosing point A. Now, the interest rate rises and θ falls to θ'. The budget set expands for a saver and contracts for a borrower. By substitution effect, the consumer first moves to point B, and then if c_1 is an inferior good, she will choose a point like C, which must lie to the left of and above point B, implying that her saving will unambiguously rise and so will her future consumption. Indeed, the graph shows that c_1 will fall from c_1^0 to c_1^1 and c_2 will rise from c_2^0 to c_2^1.

By comparison, if c_1 and c_2 both were normal, the consumer's choice would lie in the shaded region, where higher consumption in the future is guaranteed but not higher savings. Future consumption can rise simply because of higher interest rate, even if saving slightly falls.

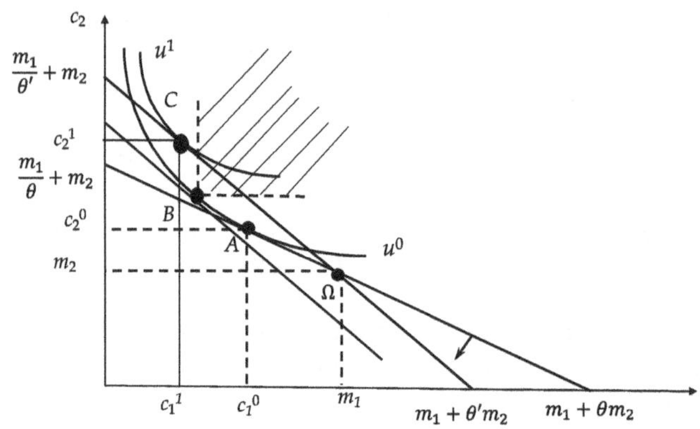

Figure 4.12 Positive relationship between saving and interest rate (c_1 is inferior)

The case of a borrower is analogous. You can do a similar graph following Figure 4.11 panel *b*. In the case of a borrower, $c_2 < m_2$, and if c_1 is normal, from Eq. (4.25) we get $\frac{\partial c_1}{\partial \theta} > 0$ without any ambiguity. But in this case, a reduction in c_1 means a decrease in borrowing and not necessarily positive saving. If the consumer's repayment amount still increases due to a higher interest rate despite a smaller borrowing, future consumption will fall. This is why there is ambiguity with respect to the sign of $\frac{\partial c_2}{\partial \theta}$.

The preceding discussion suggests that the standard Slutsky equation should be used with caution when the budget equation permits some sort of endowment income or allows prices to vary with quantities bought. Indeed, with the extended Slutsky equation, which can change considerably depending on the context, we see that the normal good logic is not sufficient to ensure the law of demand.

You should wonder where things have gone 'wrong' for our original understanding of the Slutsky equation. The answer is that in the basic model, our consumer is exclusively a consumer—a pure buyer. But in all the applications we considered here, the consumer has two roles—buyer and seller—depending on the prices and her preference over the two goods. For the labour–leisure choice model, this is very natural because leisure not chosen is labour by definition. When a price change tilts the consumer's incentive towards being a seller (of one good) the logic of a 'pure' consumer loses some of its force. This is not surprising. The challenge is to accommodate these nuances in our formal analysis in order to understand the complexities faced by real-life consumers.

We have not formally studied the price discount or taxation cases, but they will also require taking account of an 'endowment' effect at the margin. In those cases, the consumer does not drift towards a 'seller' role but still faces an impact on her disposable income once the threshold of discount or taxation is crossed. Some questions in the exercise will help you understand it better.

4.6 Conclusion

The full implication of duality in consumer theory goes beyond the Slutsky equation and the welfare analysis. One prime usefulness of the expenditure function is its amenability to empirical analysis. Various innovations have been made to make the theory applicable to consumption data that are collected in every country in the world. Empirical economists often use a softer form of homotheticity as in the Gorman form of Engel curves, Almost Ideal Demand System and many other demand equations to employ linear regression techniques or modern nonparametric methods. We clearly could not go into these fascinating topics.[13] Interested readers should read separate books for these topics.

Another issue left unaddressed, but that is conceptually important, is that duality must enable us to retrieve the utility function from a system of demand. Since the Hicksian demand functions directly depend on a given utility, by doing a reverse journey, we should be able to recover the indifference curve or the utility level that we started from. But, of course, retrieving one indifference curve is not enough. By varying the expenditure level, by holding prices unchanged, one can trace other indifference curves (both higher and lower) and potentially the whole preference set. This problem is known as the **integrability problem**. It requires a more advanced technique, and the issue is largely technical. Conceptually, it just confirms that a utility function or a preference set exists.

Summary

1. Hicksian or compensated demand functions always satisfy the law of demand. Equivalently, own substitution effect is always negative.
2. Slutsky equation shows the connection between the derivatives of the Marshallian and the Hicksian demand functions of a good.
3. The certainty of satisfying the law of demand for a normal good does not hold when the consumer's budget consists of endowment or when the budget is endogenously determined.
4. The welfare effect of a price change can be measured in several ways, such as compensating variation in income, equivalent variation in income and consumer surplus.
5. Compensating variation provides very useful guidance to protect the welfare of the poor and vulnerable people.
6. A change in the consumer surplus due to a price change is bounded by compensating and equivalent variations in income.
7. Revealed preference theory provides a simple way to test if the consumer's 'behaviour' is consistent with utility maximisation.

4.7 Appendix

4.7.1 Comparative statics

Some of the properties of the Hicksian demand functions can be directly calculated by conducting comparative statics on the Eqs. (4.1)–(4.3). Here, we show the effect of a price change on x_1^h and x_2^h.

To study the effect of a change in p_1, we completely differentiate Eqs. (4.1)–(4.3) with respect to p_1 and write the resultant three-equation system as

$$\begin{bmatrix} \mu u_{11} & \mu u_{12} & u_1 \\ \mu u_{21} & \mu u_{22} & u_2 \\ u_1 & u_2 & 0 \end{bmatrix} \begin{bmatrix} \frac{\partial x_1^h}{\partial p_1} \\ \frac{\partial x_2^h}{\partial p_1} \\ \frac{\partial \mu}{\partial p_1} \end{bmatrix} = \begin{bmatrix} 1 \\ 0 \\ 0 \end{bmatrix}.$$

Applying the Cramer's rule, we derive

$$\frac{\partial x_1^h}{\partial p_1} = \begin{vmatrix} 1 & \mu u_{12} & u_1 \\ 0 & \mu u_{22} & u_2 \\ 0 & u_2 & 0 \end{vmatrix} \times \begin{vmatrix} \mu u_{11} & \mu u_{12} & u_1 \\ \mu u_{21} & \mu u_{22} & u_2 \\ u_1 & u_2 & 0 \end{vmatrix}^{-1} = -\frac{u_2^2}{\mu \Delta u > 0} < 0,$$

and

$$\frac{\partial x_2^h}{\partial p_1} = \begin{vmatrix} \mu u_{11} & 1 & u_1 \\ \mu u_{21} & 0 & u_2 \\ u_1 & 0 & 0 \end{vmatrix} \times \begin{vmatrix} \mu u_{11} & \mu u_{12} & u_1 \\ \mu u_{21} & \mu u_{22} & u_2 \\ u_1 & u_2 & 0 \end{vmatrix}^{-1} = \frac{u_1 u_2}{\mu \Delta u > 0} > 0,$$

where $\Delta u = -u_{11}u_2^2 + 2u_{12}u_1u_2 - u_2 2u_1^2 > 0$ has been previously derived in Chapter 2 to establish quasi-concavity of the utility function. Similarly, by changing p_2, we derive

$$\frac{\partial x_2^h}{\partial p_2} = \begin{vmatrix} \mu u_{11} & 0 & u_1 \\ \mu u_{21} & 1 & u_2 \\ u_1 & 0 & 0 \end{vmatrix} \times \begin{vmatrix} \mu u_{11} & \mu u_{12} & u_1 \\ \mu u_{21} & \mu u_{22} & u_2 \\ u_1 & u_2 & 0 \end{vmatrix}^{-1} = -\frac{u_1^2}{\mu \Delta u > 0} < 0.$$

Of course, $\partial x_2^h / \partial p_1 = \partial x_1^h / \partial p_2$.

4.7.2 *Revealed preference theory*

The idea of a psychological entity like utility holding a central place in consumer theory was discomforting to many leading economists of the mid-twentieth century, at least up until Debreu's seminal work, which showed equivalence between utility and preference ordering. Samuelson (1938) proposed an alternative approach that exclusively focused on consumer behaviour. In his formulation, a consumer's behaviours would be consistent with utility maximisation if they follow certain restrictions.[14]

Suppose our consumer has £100 to spend and there are three bundles to select from $x^A = (10,20)$, $x^B = (8,18)$, $x^C = (25,12.5)$, with the prices of the two goods $(2,4)$. Suppose we observe the consumer select x^A. Clearly, she is spending all her money. We see that she could have chosen x^C, which also costs £100, or x^B, which costs £88, but she did not.

First, we need to describe her selection of x^A over the alternatives she could buy. In the terminology of the revealed preference theory this is formally written as $x^A R^D x^B$ and $x^A R^D x^C$, meaning that bundle x^A is *directly revealed preferred* to x^B and x^C. With some introspection, you can see that in principle there are infinitely many bundles costing no more than £100 (i.e., all points in her budget set) that the consumer could choose, but she directly reveals a preference for x^A over all these bundles when the price vector is $(2,4)$ and she has £100 to spare. Here, be very careful not to interpret the term *revealed preference* anything other than 'mere selection', because we have not said anything about the consumer's preference ordering or utility.[15]

Definition 1. *If x^A is chosen at price p^A, then x^A is said to be directly revealed preferred to any other $x, x^A R^D x$, if $p^A x^A \geq p^A x$.*

Note that this cost comparison is only pairwise and, hence, the word *direct*. Also, the comparison is restricted to what has been chosen and what has not been chosen but was affordable. Having observed this, we may ask, Can her selection be deemed the behaviour of a utility-maximising agent? The answer is yes if we make a simple *assumption* and an important *restriction* on her behaviour.

Assumption 1. *The consumer wants to make the most of her money, or equivalently the consumer is trying to maximise her utility.*

We do not need to define utility in a precise way as we did earlier. All that we need is that the consumer must exhaust her budget; money should not be left unspent. If we accept this assumption, then straight away, we have an explanation of the rejection of the bundle $x^B = (8,18)$; her utility is less at x^B than at x^A. However, the logic of the rejection of x^C is not obvious. There are two possible reasons for rejecting x^C: Either x^C is giving less utility than x^A or giving the same utility but the consumer randomly picked x^A. We cannot separate between the two until we get more data (which will be made clear shortly).

Now, we can impose a restriction on the consumer's selection behaviour through an axiom, called the **weak axiom of revealed preference (WARP)**, which says that if x^A is ever selected (or directly revealed preferred to) over another bundle, say, x_B, then x^B can *never* be selected over x^A when both are affordable.

Definition 2. ***WARP:*** *If* $x^A R^D x^B$ *and if* x^B *is selected at price vector* p^B*, then it must be that* $p^B x^A > p^B x^B$. *This means that* $x^B R^D x^A$ *not possible.*

WARP is asserting that if the consumer once selected x^A over x^B, then she should not ever select x^B over x^A if both are affordable; she can do that only when x^A is outside her budget set (at price p^B). Although the axiom ties the consumer's hands to stick to x^A (when both x^A and x^B are affordable) even if she was truly indifferent between x^A, the restriction generates an important pattern between price change and consumption.

In Figure 4.13 panel *a*, we consider three price-income situations as given by three budget lines BL_1, BL_2 and BL_3, which correspond to price vectors p^A, p^B and p^C, respectively. Suppose at p^A the consumer is observed to choose bundle *A*. Bundles *A*, *B* and *E* are three bundles that are affordable. But if she chooses *A*, then we describe her selection by $x^A R^D x^B$ and $x^A R^D x^E$. Next, assume that at price p^B, she selects bundle *B*. This time, *A* is not affordable, but *E* and *C* are. The consumer's choice of *B* directly reveals preference over *E*, and it

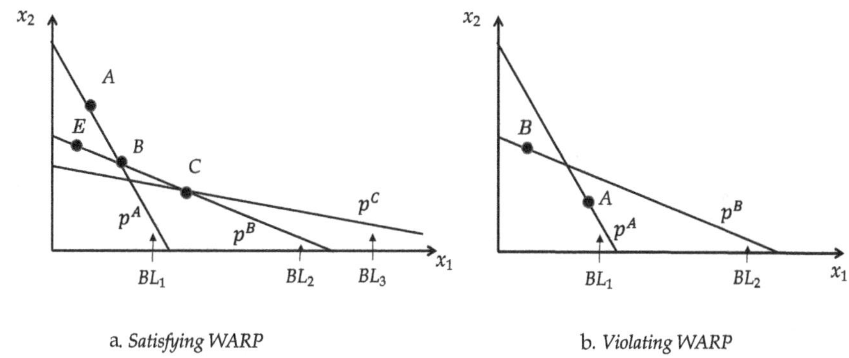

Figure 4.13 Weak axiom of revealed preference

satisfies WARP, because A is not affordable at p^B; that is, $p^B x^A > p^B x^B$. Likewise, if bundle C is chosen at p^C, then also her choice is consistent with WARP, because when C is chosen B is not available.

On panel b of Figure 4.13, we show a violation of WARP. When A is chosen at p^A, it is directly revealed preferred to B, and when the price vector is p^B, bundle B is directly revealed preferred to A. That is, when A is bought, B is available, and when B is bought, A is available. This is a clear violation of WARP.

4.7.2.1 *Law of demand*

What can we say about the law of demand, when a consumer's behaviours are consistent with WARP? Figure 4.14 presents three familiar cases of demand—Hicksian, Slutsky compensated and Marshallian or uncompensated demand. Consider panel a first. Bundle A is bought when the price is p^A (BL_1), and bundle B is bought when the price is p^B (BL_2). Suppose $p_1^B < p_1^A$ and $p_2^B = p_2^A$, where p_1^A is the initial price and p_1^B is the final price. By construction, the law of demand is observed here. Furthermore, B is not available when A is bought, and A is not available when B is bought. Therefore, WARP is not violated. Here, we satisfy the conditions

$$p^A x^A < p^A x^B \text{ or } p^A \Delta x > 0, \text{ and } p^B x^B < p^B x^A \text{ or } p^B \Delta x < 0,$$

where $\Delta x = x^B - x^A$. Then, clearly $p^B \Delta x < p^A \Delta x$ or

$$\Delta p \Delta x = \Delta p_1 \Delta x_1 < 0,$$

where $\Delta p = p^B - p^A$. This is precisely our law of demand. If $\Delta p_1 < 0$ then x_1 must be positive. Panel b is another example in which WARP is satisfied and the law of demand holds. Here we have $p^A x^A < p^A x^B$, but $p^B x^B = p^B x^A$. From these two relations, we get $p^A \Delta x > 0$ and $p^B \Delta x = 0$ Therefore, $p^B \Delta x - p^A \Delta x < 0$ or $\Delta p \Delta x < 0$. This is the case where the consumer is compensated by the Slutsky principle.

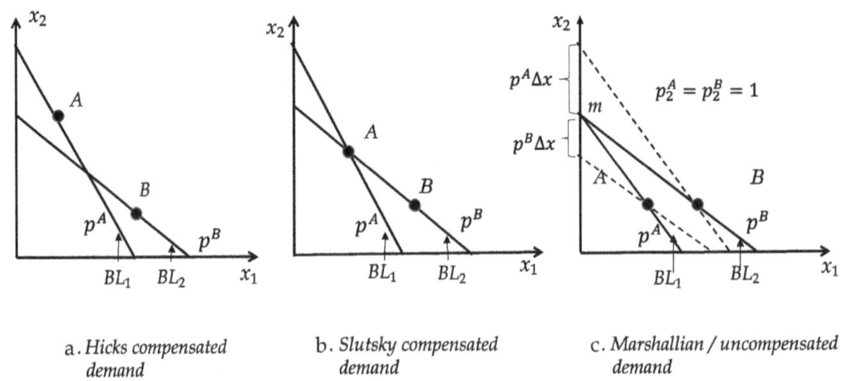

Figure 4.14 Law of demand and the weak axiom of revealed preference

But WARP does not necessarily imply the law of demand. Panel *c* shows uncompensated demand where WARP is satisfied by bundles *A* and *B* with the following inequalities:

$$p^A x^A < p^A x^B, \text{ and } p^B x^B > p^B x^A.$$

Bundle *B* is directly revealed as preferred to *A*, and when *A* is chosen, *B* is not available. Thereby, WARP is satisfied.

But here we find that both $p^A \Delta x > 0$ and $p^B \Delta x > 0$ Therefore, the law of demand is not guaranteed. However, if we impose a restriction $p^A \Delta x > p^B \Delta x$, then we get $\Delta p \Delta x < 0$. If for simplicity p_2 is set 1 and held unchanged, then graphically, this condition simply translates into a comparison of two vertical segments above and below *m*, the consumer's income. It is easy to see that if bundle *B* was close to bundle *A* or to the left of *A*, the vertical segment $p^A \Delta x$ would be smaller than the segment $p^B \Delta x$. In that case, the law of demand is violated, but WARP is still satisfied.

4.7.2.2 *Preference*

An important question in the revealed preference theory is whether the consumer's behaviour provides any clue to her preference. Alternatively stated, if a consumer is indeed a utility-maximising agent, will her behaviour satisfy WARP? To some extent, the answer is yes, as we have already seen earlier with the three demand curves generated by expenditure minimisation and utility maximisation.

Let us explore this in detail. Consider panel *a* of Figure 4.13 and bundles *A*, *B* and *E*. Bundle *A* is selected over *B* and *E* or 'is directly revealed preferred to *B* and *E*'. Our assumption of utility maximisation means that the consumer's selection of *A* must confirm the fact that she gets higher utility at *A* than at *B* or *E*. That is to say, *A* is **preferred** to *B* and *E*. However, with the knowledge of the indifference curve analysis, we can see that the consumer can be indifferent between *A* and *B*, although WARP does not allow the consumer to switch back and forth between *A* and *B* when both are available. Another issue is that WARP does not allow one to compare bundles *A* with *C*, which are never simultaneously available (as we have drawn). Therefore, we cannot say whether *A* is indifferent to *C* or preferred to *C* or otherwise. The only conclusion we can make is that the choices of *A* and *C* do not violate WARP.

An alternative axiom, the strong axiom of revealed preference (SARP), resolves this issue by invoking a transitivity argument. We see that *A* is directly revealed as preferred to *B* and *B* is directly revealed preferred to *C*. So we can say that *A* is indirectly revealed preferred to *C*. SARP says that bundle *C* cannot be directly or indirectly revealed preferred to *A*.

Definition 3. *SARP*: *If there is a sequence of choices* $\{x^A, x^B, x^C\}$ *such that* $x^A R^D x^B$ *and* $x^B R^D x^C$, *then* x^A *is indirectly revealed preferred to* x^C, *or by notation* $x^A R x^C$. *Bundle* x^C *cannot be directly or indirectly preferred to* x^A.

A more general axiom that combines both WARP and SARP is the generalised axiom of revealed preference (GARP):

Definition 4. *GARP:* *If* x^A *is directly or indirectly revealed preferred to* x^C, *that is,* $x^A R x^C$, *then* x^C *cannot be directly revealed preferred to* x^A, *that is,* $x^C R^D x^A$, *is ruled out.*

In general, GARP helps us narrow down the goods space to a region that contains the consumer's indifference curve. Therefore, the reverse journey from behaviour to preference that Samuelson originally envisaged was indeed successful.

Revealed preference theory has been extended in an important direction by departing from deterministic demand and allowing probabilistic choices (Bandyopadhyay et al., 1999, 2004). In reality, consumers often seem to be undecided and make their choice with an element of randomness. This could be because their preference is stochastic, or their demand appears to be random because they might be defining their goods as contingent goods. In either case, revealed preference theory can be applied by allowing their choice to be probabilistic. This approach is fundamentally different from choices made under uncertainty. Instead, it is a generalisation of the deterministic version of the revealed preference theory.

4.8 Exercises

1. Muchen's preference function is $u = \sqrt{(x_1 - \delta_1)(x_2 - \delta_2)}$, where δ_1 and δ_2 are the subsistence amounts of the two goods. Prices are p_1 and p_2.

   a. Derive Muchen's Hicksian demand functions.
   b. Write the expenditure function and graph it against p_1, and show how the curve shifts if p_2 increases.
   c. Suppose the price of x_1 rises to $2p_1$ and Muchen is on disability allowance. By how much should Muchen's allowance be raised if his utility were to be protected at the pre-price rise level?
   d. Discuss if the government wanted to protect his pre-price rise consumption levels instead of his utility, how would the allowance change?

2. Mrs Jennings has two periods to live. Her incomes are predetermined at m_1 and m_2 for periods 1 and 2, respectively, and her preference over consumption in two periods is given by the utility function $u = \sqrt{c_1} + \sqrt{c_2}$ The price of the consumption good is fixed at 1 in both periods. Assume that the interest rate on borrowing, r_b, is greater than the interest rate on saving, r_s.

   a. Derive Mrs Jennings' budget equation.
   b. Next, derive her Walrasian/Marshallian demand functions, assuming she is a saver. Show her choice on a graph.
   c. Now suppose her second-period income m_2 increases to m_2' such that she becomes a borrower. Write her new demand functions (without redoing the optimisation). What should be the minimum value of m_2' to turn her from a saver to a borrower? Show her changed status on the graph.
   d. Derive $\frac{\partial s}{\partial r_s}$ and $\frac{\partial s}{\partial r_b}$ when she is saving and $\frac{\partial b}{\partial r_s}$ and $\frac{\partial b}{\partial r_b}$ when she is borrowing (b denotes borrowing).
   e. Verify if the results from question 1(d) conform to the extended Slutsky equation.

3. Robert and Samantha share their joint income $2m$ equally, but their preferences are independent and quite different to each other's. While Robert's preference function is $u_R = \min[ax_1, bx_2]$, Samantha's preference is given by $u_S = x_1^2 x_2$. Prices of the two goods are p_1 and p_2.

   a. Derive the Marshallian demand functions of Robert and Samantha. Also, derive the aggregate household demand for each good.
   b. Write the indirect utility functions of both individuals and plot them against m.
   c. Imagine Robert's own income is less than Samantha's, so much so that after an α proportion increase in the price of x_1, Robert receives a government allowance that should allow

him to buy his pre-price rise x_1 and x_2. However, as Robert and Samantha always share their combined income equally, Samantha also gets to enjoy a part of this allowance.

i. Derive their new consumption levels.
ii. Discuss if both Robert's and Samantha's indirect utilities will be restored to the pre-price rise level or of only one of them. If needed, make suitable assumptions.

4. Mia's preference is given by the function $u = x_2 + \min[ax_1, bx_2], a, b > 0$. Derive her Hicksian demand functions, and then applying duality derive the Marshallian demand functions.
5. Zara must spend R as a fixed cost (for rents, utility bills and broadband charges) before she can buy food and clothing, x_1 and x_2, respectively. Her utility function is $u = \sqrt{x_1 x_2}$.

a. Derive Zara's Hicksian demand functions for a given utility level u.
b. Derive her total expenditure function. Does it satisfy all the properties of the expenditure function? Explain your answer.
c. Derive her total expenditure function. Does it satisfy all the properties of the expenditure function?
d. If she gets a flatmate, how will her Hicksian demand functions be affected? Will her Marshallian demand functions be affected?

6. There are two groups of consumers, group A and group B. Their preferences over two goods, x_1 and x_2, are $u_A = x_1^\alpha x_2^\beta$ and $u_B = x_1^\beta x_2^\alpha$. The prices of the two goods are p_1 and p_2, respectively. All consumers have the same income m.

a. First derive the Marshallian demand functions for each individual and then aggregate them for each group and finally over two groups.
b. Derive the Hicksian demand functions for x_1 for a representative individual from each group.
c. Suppose X_1 is the aggregate (over two groups) Marshallian demand for x_1. Derive $\partial X_1 / \partial p_1$ and, utilising the Slutsky equation, rewrite the price effect.
d. Repeat your exercise for the price elasticity of the aggregate demand.

7. Rohan's preference over two goods (x_1, x_2) is given by the utility function $u = a\sqrt{x_1} + b\sqrt{x_2}$. Prices of the two goods are p_1 and p_2, respectively. Rohan also has an endowment $\left(x_1^0, x_2^0\right)$.

a. Derive Rohan's Hicksian demand functions.
b. Applying duality, derive his Marshallian demand functions.
c. Determine conditions under which he is a net buyer of x_1.
d. Apply the extended Slutsky rule to derive $\frac{\partial x_1}{\partial p_1}$.

8. Derive the Hicksian demand functions from the preference $u = x_1 x_2$ and then derive the substitution effect $\frac{\partial x_1^h}{\partial p_1}$. Apply duality to derive the indirect utility function.
9. Pablo works for t hours a day out of total T hours, and $T - t$ hours are devoted to leisure, which is denoted by l. He earns a wage rate of w per hour and spends all his income on food consumption, denoted by c, which is priced at p per unit. Now assume that the consumer's preference over l and c is given by the utility function $u = \sqrt{l} + \sqrt{c}$.

a. If Pablo were to minimise his expenditure for a given utility level u^0, how much money would he need, and how many hours will he have to work?
b. Using duality, derive his Marshallian demand functions and the labour supply function.
c. Applying the extended Slutsky equation derive the slope of his labour supply curve.
d. Now assume $p = 1$ and $w = 2$ and a benefit amount b for not working (for a good reason like attending university). Assuming that university fees are zero, should Pablo stop working and go to university (ignore his future income and focus on his current wage)?

10. Newman's utility function is $u = \frac{x_1 x_2}{A}$, and he wishes to achieve a utility level u_0.
    a. Derive Newman's demand functions that would support the utility level u_0.
    b. Now suppose p_1 increases to λp_1, where $\lambda > 1$. Derive the compensation amounts that Newman may have to be given under two alternative principles of compensation—Hicks and Slutsky.
    c. Newman's identical twin brother, Jeremy, has the same utility function but gets a smaller salary than Newman so that his total expenditure was just half of Newman's expenditure before the price rise. What was Jeremy's achieved utility level in comparison to Newman's?
    d. Suppose Newman was compensated following the Hicksian principle and Jeremy was compensated following the Slutsky principle. Can you determine if Jeremy will ever be able to catch up to his brother in terms of the consumption of the two goods or utility?

11. Derive Sunil's Hicksian demand functions and the border-preserving principal minors expenditure function for his preference $u = \sqrt{x_1 x_2}$. Next, show that if p_1 rises to $4p_1$ and the government wishes to compensate Sunil by the Hicks or Slutsky principle, how much compensation should Sunil receive under each principle? Which one will Sunil prefer, and why?
12. Let $p = (p_1, p_2)$ be the prices of x_1 and x_2 and $z_j = (x_1^j, x_2^j)$ be the observed choices made by a consumer in price-income situation j. There are four such situations: $j = A, B, C, D$ Accordingly, we have the following data points.

    $$p_A = (2,4)\ p_B = (3,3)\ p_C = (4,2)\ p_D = (5,1)$$

    $$z_A = (5,10)\ z_B = (9,7)\ z_C = (4,12)\ z_D = (3,15)$$

    Verify if WARP is violated by the observed behaviour.
13. Table 4.1 describes three bundles bought at three price-income situations, A, B and C. Verify WARP and establish a preference ordering amongst the three bundles. Can you say that bundle x_B is preferred to a fourth bundle $x_D = (13,12)$? If so, which axiom does allow you to make that conclusion?

Table 4.1 Consumer's demand behaviours

Bundle (x_1, x_2)	Price (p_1, p_2)
$x_A = (15,10)$	$p_A = (3,2)$
$x_B = (20,8)$	$p_B = (2,4)$
$x_C = (10, 20)$	$p_C = (2, 3)$

Notes

1 www.gov.uk/government/publications/sovereign-grant-act-2011-guidance/sovereign-grant -act-2011-guidance, accessed on 20 October 2022.
2 The data on the elderly people are as of 2019. www.gov.uk/government/statistics/dwp-benefits -statistics-august-2019/dwp-benefits-statistical-summary-august-2019, accessed on 3rd January 2022.
3 In a more than two-good case, the border preserving principal minors of the matrix d^2F must all be negative.
4 The measure is approximate because the price increase is not sufficiently small. By taking Δp_1 arbitrarily close to zero, we will get the slope of the expenditure function, which will be exactly equal to the amount of the given good.
5 This is why in our decomposition while deriving the income effect we wrote $\Delta x_1 / \Delta m$ as $-|\Delta x_1| / \Delta m$. If x_1 was an inferior good, then x_1^1 would be greater than x_1^h, and we would have entered the income effect term with a positive sign before it. Alternatively, if x_2 were inferior it would be strictly greater than x_2^h.
6 Similarly, if x_2 were inferior, the final choice of x_2 would have been smaller than x_2^h (at point C).
7 See https://nfsa.gov.in and https://elibrary.worldbank.org/doi/10.1596/978-1-4648-1087-9.ch.
8 For more, see www.gov.uk/benefit-cap/benefit-cap-amounts.
9 www.fns.usda.gov/snap/recipient/eligibility
10 The idea of Slutsky compensation can be applied also to a price fall. Less money, then, is to be taken away from the consumer than under the Hicks compensation principle.
11 The case of a price fall is easily accommodated by assuming $\lambda < 1$. The signs of the transfers then change.
12 Recall that when both goods are consumed in positive quantity, the demand for x_1 will be independent of income. Thus, the area under the demand curve plus a constant gives the utility of the consumer. Any change in utility due to a change in p_1 is accurately captured by the change in consumer surplus.
13 The author pleads ignorance on these.
14 One should not think of the revealed preference theory as a precursor of modern-day behavioural economics, because rationality plays a very important role here, whereas a behavioural economist would constantly question the notion of rationality.
15 Samuelson himself used the term 'selected over'. But subsequent authors popularised 'directly revealed preferred to', and 'selected over' was forgotten.

References and further readings

Afriat, S. N. (1965). The equivalence in two dimensions of the strong and weak axioms of revealed preference. *Metroeconomica*, 17, 24–28.

Bandyopadhyay, T., Dasgupta, I. & Pattanaik, P. K. (1999). Stochastic revealed preference and the theory of demand. *Journal of Economic Theory*, 84(1), 95–110.

Bandyopadhyay, T., Dasgupta, I. & Pattanaik, P. K. (2004). A general revealed preference theorem for stochastic demand behavior. *Economic Theory*, 23(3), 589–599.

Bhattacharya, S., Falcao, V. L. & Puri, R. (2017). The public distribution system in India: Policy evaluation and program delivery trends. In H. Alderman, U. Gentilini & R. Yemtsov (Eds.), *1.5 Billion People Question: Food, Vouchers, or Cash Transfers?* Washington, DC: World Bank.

Blundell, R., Browning, M. & Crawford, I. (2003). Nonparametric Engel curves and revealed preference. *Econometrica*, 71(1), 205–240.

Deaton, A. (1983). Demand analysis. In Z. Griliches & M. Intrilligator (Eds.), *Handbook of Econometrics*. Greenwich, CT: JAI Press.

Hicks, J. R. (1939). *Value and Capital*. Oxford: Oxford University Press.

Hicks, J. R. (1956). *A Revision of Demand Theory*. Oxford: Clarendon Press.

Rubinstein, A. (2012). *Lecture Notes in Microeconomic Theory*, 2nd ed. Princeton, NJ: Princeton University Press.

Samuelson, P. A. (1938). A note on the pure theory of consumer's behavior. *Economica*, 5(17), 61–71.
Samuelson, P. A. (1948). Consumption theory in terms of revealed preference. *Economica*, 15(60), 243–253.
Varian, H. R. (1992). *Microeconomic Analysis*, 3rd ed. New York: Norton.
Varian, H. R. (2006). Revealed preference. In M. Szenberg, L. Ramrattan & A. A. Gottesman (Eds.), *Samuelsonian Economics and the 21st Century*. New York: Oxford University Press.

Chapter 5

Critiques of the demand theory and some new developments

Abstract

Over the last 30 years economists have questioned, verified and challenged almost every element of the rational choice theory. In this chapter, we discuss some of these developments. We begin with the household utility maximisation problem, where preference interdependence is unavoidable. Similar preference interdependence can also arise vis-à-vis outsiders, but there the main questions concern the extent of altruism in our preference. We study an array of experimental work in this regard. Then we look at the bounded rationality issue that leads to miscalculation of marginal costs. Finally, we return to two extreme goods discussed earlier—luxury goods and Giffen goods. Giffen goods are elusive. So far, there is only one evidence of it, and it is definitely not the Irish potato.

Keywords: Household preferences, Altruism, Fairness, Inequity aversion, Giffen behaviour, Bounded rationality, Veblen effects, Conspicuous consumption

5.1 Introduction

Several elements of demand theory are now subjects of scrutiny for either logical consistency or empirical validity. While some of the developments are in the spirit of extending demand theory to more complex settings—for example, household demands—most other developments are criticisms spearheaded by behavioural economists. How much of a consumer's choice is a result of rational calculation and how much is an act of *impulse* or an outcome of manipulation by marketing techniques are open questions. Such issues are essentially empirical, but there is also a methodological issue of whether we need to start from a set of axioms to conceptualise what an *ideal consumer should be* (a normative principle) or one should start from the consumer's behaviours as they are (a positive perspective), which can be a result of the interplay of many psychological traits.

Most of the new developments pursued by behavioural economists are questioning the axioms of preferences, their independence from prices, the cognitive ability of the consumers to make a rational choice and so on. One can summarise these as serious challenges to the paradigm of rational choice itself, without which the neoclassical demand theory would have no logical foundation.

In this chapter, we look at some of the new developments. In Section 5.2, we show that household preference, especially with respect to labour supply, requires a substantial modification of consumer theory. Section 5.3 addresses one fundamental assumption of rationality—self-interest. We discuss studies on altruism, fairness and inequity aversion. Sections 5.4 and 5.5 stay with the

DOI: 10.4324/9781003226994-5

assumption of self-interested individuals and discuss bounded rationality and stability of preference respectively. Section 5.6 shows how to model Veblen goods. Section 5.7 discusses empirical evidence of Giffen behaviour. Section 5.8 presents some concluding remarks to note the selective and incomplete nature of this chapter.

5.2 Household demand: who decides?

Going from one consumer to many is not a simple aggregation of demand when it comes to a household. There are two reasons to consider. First, there are dependents (children and older adults) whose needs are different and who may not have the capacity to decide what they should buy. Second, living together means pooling incomes and sharing fixed costs (such as utility bills, broadband charges, etc.). The household needs to decide how the fixed costs are to be shared. But then who in the household decides? Head of the household? Or all the adult members together? In many cultures, most important decisions are vested with the head of the household. In that case, our simple demand model can be good enough. The same can be done when all members of the household have identical preferences. This is called unitary decision-making model for households as suggested by Becker (1981). The vast empirical literature on demand and household welfare has relied, until recently, on the unitary approach; even data collection agencies interview mainly the head of the household to collect information on other members.

This approach is changing thanks to an increasing recognition that the income-earning adults of a household engage in a decision-making process that is better described by 'bargaining'. Hence, household decision-making should be described by the maximisation of a weighted sum of the utility functions of the income-earning adults.[1]

Chiappori (1988) was among the first few economists to recognise that due to the complexity of intra-household decision-making, individual labour supply decisions may not be efficient. This is a consequence of the fact, he noted, that the bargaining powers are dependent on the wage rate. But one can extend the logic and see, as we have argued earlier, that the bargaining power of a partner depends on how much time they spend in the labour market or how much they earn relative to the other adult members of the households. Basu (2006) elaborated on this theme and provided a detailed formal analysis of the problem with special attention given to the issues of female labour supply and child labour in poor families of many developing countries. You may read Duflo (2012) for a survey of the recent literature on the issue of female empowerment and their labour market participation.

Let us take a small family of a young couple—individual 1 (wife) and individual 2 (husband). Both work, pool their income and jointly decide how much each should consume. The wage rate of the wife is w_1, and that of the husband is w_2. The maximum time available for work is T_1 for the wife and T_2 for the husband. Their labour supplies are L_1 and L_2, and they enjoy leisure l_1 and l_2, respectively. There is only one consumption good, say, c, the price of which is set to 1. The household's consumption budget is $w_1L_1 + w_2L_2 = c_1 + c_2 + F$, where F is a fixed cost. If F is just the rental/mortgage cost of the house or utility bills, then the couple has clearly halved their fixed cost by living together. Similarly, F could also include the cost of raising a child.

Now let us consider the preferences of the households. There are two ways we can approach it. Individual preferences can be 'egoistic', that is, individuals care only about their own consumption and leisure, or their preferences can be 'altruistic' or 'interdependent' in the sense that one's consumption enters the utility function of the other member. This is especially true for couples, because enjoying leisure together is important to a family.

5.2.1 Egoistic preference

Suppose the wife's and husband's preferences are independent. Denoting the wife's utility as $u_1 = u_1(c_1, l_1)$ and the husband's utility $u_2 = u_2(c_2, l_2)$, we can write the household's decision problem as to choose (c_1, l_1, c_2, l_2) by solving the following:

$$\begin{aligned} \text{Max} \quad & V = \theta u_1(c_1, l_1) + (1-\theta) u_2(c_2, l_2) \\ \text{sub. to} \quad & c_1 + c_2 + F = w_1 L_1 + w_2 L_2 \\ & l_1 = T_1 - L_1, l_2 = T_2 - L_2, \end{aligned}$$

where θ is the 'bargaining power' of the wife. Although you have not been introduced to any formal notion of bargaining, it is not difficult to see that θ is just a relative weight on the wife's utility function. If θ is 0 or 1, we return to the unitary model. If $\theta = 1/2$, we have an egalitarian household.[2]

If θ were independent of c or l, then the problem is a marginal extension of our unitary model. A more interesting, and non-trivial, exercise is to allow θ to depend on the wife's contribution to the household income. Thus, we can take a particular function of θ as

$$\theta = w_1 L_1 / (w_1 L_1 + w_2 L_2).$$

Furthermore, to see how the household decisions can drastically differ from individual decisions, let us assume identical Cobb–Douglas preferences: $u_i = cl$, $i = 1, 2$. You can easily check that if these two individuals were living in two separate households, the woman would be working $T_1 / 2$ hours and the man $T_2 / 2$ hours. But when they live together their decisions change. We rewrite the household's objective function as

$$\text{Max}\, V = \theta(w_1, w_2, L_1, L_2) c_1 l_1 + (1 - \theta(w_1, w_2, L_1, L_2)) c_2 l_2.$$

Basu (2006) proposed that a solution to this problem should be obtained by first deriving optimal $(c_i, l_i)(i = 1, 2)$ for a given θ and then determining θ that is indeed given by those optimal (c_i, l_i). In other words, θ and optimal (c_i, l_i) must be mutually determining each other. Let us write the Lagrangian as

$$\mathcal{L} = \theta c_1 l_1 + (1-\theta) c_2 l_2 - \lambda [c_1 + c_2 + w_1 l_1 + w_2 l_2 + F - w_1 T_1 - w_2 T_2].$$

The first-order conditions are

$$c_1 : \theta l_1 - \lambda = 0 \tag{5.1}$$

$$c_2 : (1-\theta) l_2 - \lambda = 0 \tag{5.2}$$

$$l_1 : \theta c_1 - \lambda w_1 = 0 \tag{5.3}$$

$$l_2 : (1-\theta) c_2 - \lambda w_2 = 0 \tag{5.4}$$

$$\lambda : -[c_1 + c_2 + w_1 l_1 + w_2 l_2 + F - w_1 T_1 - w_2 T_2] = 0. \tag{5.5}$$

First, divide Eq. (5.1) by Eq. (5.3) and Eq. (5.2) by Eq. (5.4) to obtain

$$c_1 = w_1 l_1 \text{ and } c_2 = w_2 l_2$$

and substitute them into the budget equation (5.5) to obtain

$$w_1 l_1 + w_2 l_2 = \frac{w_1 T_1 - F + w_2 T_2}{2} (\equiv k, \text{ say}).$$

Next divide Eq. (5.1) by Eq. (5.2) to write $l_2 = \frac{\theta}{1-\theta} l_1$ and then substitute that into the budget equation:

$$w_1 l_1 + w_2 \frac{\theta}{1-\theta} l_1 = k.$$

From this, we derive the households' choice for a given θ as

$$l_1(\theta) = \frac{(1-\theta)k}{(1-\theta)w_1 + \theta w_2} \quad (5.6)$$

$$l_2(\theta) = \frac{\theta k}{(1-\theta)w_1 + \theta w_2} \quad (5.7)$$

$$c_1(\theta) = \frac{(1-\theta)w_1 k}{(1-\theta)w_1 + \theta w_2} \quad (5.8)$$

$$c_2(\theta) = \frac{\theta w_2 k}{(1-\theta)w_1 + \theta w_2}. \quad (5.9)$$

Now we try to find θ that are determined by $l_1(\theta)$ and $l_2(\theta)$. Thus, the equilibrium θ is implicitly solved from the following equation:

$$\theta - \frac{w_1 [T_1 - l_1(\theta)]}{w_1 [T_1 - l_1(\theta)] + w_2 [T_2 - l_2(\theta)]} = 0.$$

Because this is a non-linear equation, we provide a graphical illustration of the solution. Figure 5.1 presents one likely solution. In the right quadrant, we draw the wife's (so-called) bargaining power θ as a function of L_1 and her labour supply curve $L_1 = T_1 - l_1(\theta)$, where $l_1(\theta)$ is given by Eq. (5.6). These two curves may intersect in two places, as shown here, but only one of them can be equilibrium, as shown by the left quadrant of the figure where the labour supply curve and bargaining power of the husband are drawn. The shape of these curves suggests that they will intersect only once. Thus, our equilibrium is θ^* and (L_1^*, L_2^*). In this equilibrium, the wife works many more hours than the husband, and therefore, her bargaining power θ^* is also high. An alternative possibility is the wife working less than the husband and resulting in a low θ^*. You can check that $L_1^* = T_1/2$ and $L_2^* = T_2/2$ will not be optimal for the household.

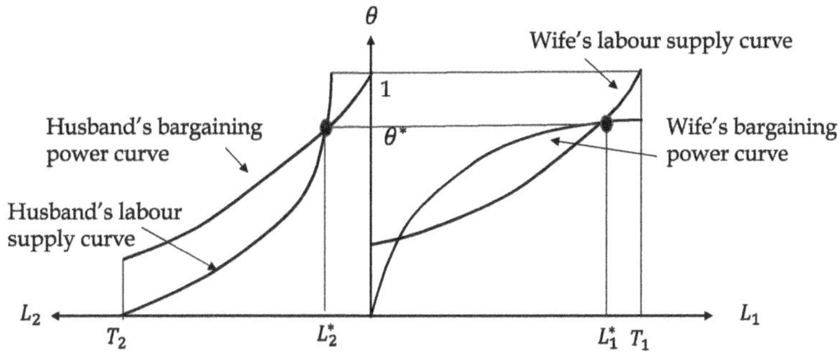

Figure 5.1 Equilibrium labour supplies and bargaining power

5.2.2 *Interdependent preference*

The following model is adapted from Basu (2006). Suppose the husband always works a fixed number of hours and his income covers the private consumption amounts of the couple, which are fixed by assumption. The husband's net contribution to the household budget is Y. The key decision concerns the wife's labour supply and the household's spending on joint consumption (public goods like TV, house decoration, etc.), which we simply denote by c for which the price is set at 1. Importantly, the husband suffers some disutility from his wife's working outside. The husband's utility function is $u_2 = c - \phi_2(L_1)$, where $\phi_2(.)$ is the husband's disutility from the wife's labour supply. The wife's utility function is $u_1 = c - \phi_1(L_1)$. We assume $\phi_i'(.) > 0, \phi_i''(.) > 0$ for $i = 1, 2$. The individual utility functions are quasi-linear for simplicity.

The household's objective function is to maximise $V = c - \theta\phi_1(L_1) - (1-\theta)\phi_2(L_1)$ subject to $\theta = \theta(w_1 L_1)$, $c = w_1 L_1 + Y$ and $L_1 \leq T_1$. The bargaining power function θ can be very general; it is just a positively sloped function of the wife's income. Substituting the consumption budget equation into the objective function we rewrite the objective function as

$$V = w_1 L_1 + Y - \theta\phi_1(L_1) - (1-\theta)\phi_2(L_1).$$

The solution to the household's problem is given by the following two equations:

$$w = \theta\phi_1'(L_1) + (1-\theta)\phi_2'(L_1) \tag{5.10}$$

$$\theta = \theta(wL_1). \tag{5.11}$$

From the first-order condition, we derive

$$\frac{\partial L_1}{\partial \theta} = \frac{\phi_2'(L_1) - \phi_1'(L_1)}{\theta\phi_1''(L_1) + (1-\theta)\phi_2''(L_1)} > 0 \text{ if } \phi_2'(L_1) > \phi_1'(L_1).$$

In some societies, women's outside work causes a greater marginal disutility to their husbands than to themselves. This could be either because of altruism or cultural restrictions on women's labour market participation as perceived by male members of that society. When this is the case, an interesting possibility emerges. The labour supply curve can cross the bargaining power curve multiple times giving rise to (at least) two equilibria, one with low labour market participation and the other with high labour market participation. An important point is that two households despite being identical in all respects can make two very different female labour supply decisions. There is no *a priori* reason why a household (and, for that matter, a society) may end up in a specific equilibrium. It just does.

5.2.3 *Parental decisions for a child's education*

In poor countries, low-income families face an awful dilemma of sending their children to work or keeping them in school. Staying in school gives a greater future income prospect for the child, but it comes with sacrificing some income opportunities at the present. Even if no consideration of child's future well-being is taken into account, parents may simply value the child's education while they face a serious difficulty of meeting the family's subsistence consumption. Thus, effectively, the choice the family makes is the one of child's premature labour market participation that has serious implications for the labour market as well.

Basu and Van (1998; henceforth BV) presented a model of child labour supply with a very simple set-up as follows: Suppose a household consists of one parent and one child, each having 1 unit of labour to supply. As the child's productivity is expected to be lower than the adult's, 1 unit of child labour is assumed to be equivalent to $\gamma(<1)$ unit of adult labour. This also means where an adult receives a wage w for 1 hour of work, the child will receive γw for working one hour. The child's time is divided between outside work e and schooling $(1-e)$. The parent inelastically supplies his labour to earn w; leisure has no utility to him. The parent must meet a subsistence consumption $\underline{c}$ before he values his child's education.[3] The subsistence consumption requirement is incorporated by assuming a Stone–Geary utility function. The child's consumption is $\beta(<1)$ units of the adult's consumption. The household's problem is then the parent's problem of maximising

$$U = \begin{cases} (c-\underline{c})(1-e) & \text{if } c \geq \underline{c}, \\ (c-\underline{c}) & \text{if } c < \underline{c}, \end{cases} \tag{5.12}$$

subject to the household budget constraint $w + e\gamma w \geq c(1+\beta)$. The solution to this problem gives the child's labour supply e^*

$$e^* = \begin{cases} 0 & \text{for } w > \dfrac{\sigma}{1-\gamma} \\ \dfrac{1}{2} + \dfrac{\sigma - w}{2\gamma w} & \text{for } w \in \left[\dfrac{\sigma}{1+\gamma}, \dfrac{\sigma}{1-\gamma}\right], \\ 1 & \text{for } w < \dfrac{\sigma}{1+\gamma} \end{cases} \tag{5.13}$$

where $\sigma \equiv \underline{c}(1+\beta)$. There are two critical values of wage, namely, $\frac{\sigma}{1+\gamma}$ and $\frac{\sigma}{1-\gamma}$, such that when the adult wage exceeds $\frac{\sigma}{1-\gamma}$, the child spends all of her time at school, and when the adult wage falls below $\frac{\sigma}{1+\gamma}$, the child works full time. At the intermediate wages, the child works partially and crucially her labour supply curve is downward-sloping, which can potentially affect the labour market equilibrium.

The main point of the BV model is that poverty, but not any exploitative attitudes of the parent, drives children to work and that local labour markets in poor societies may exhibit certain peculiarities due to the participation of the children. This argument has inspired a large empirical literature on child labour.

5.2.4 *Self-employment of parents*

When the outside labour markets offer little income, households may engage in small businesses and other self-employment activities. If such activities can be undertaken without substantial capital, then poor people can protect themselves and their children from the worst. However, self-employed households are not fully immune to children's dropping out of school. They may also be tempted to employ their children at home production. The question is, When?

To study this problem, let us consider the same set-up as before, with one important difference. The parent now works full-time at his home production; in addition, he may use outside labour (l) or his own child's labour (e). The child does not work outside; either she goes to school or works at home.[4]

Suppose the production technology of self-employment is given by a (strictly) concave function $q = \theta R(1+\gamma e+l), R'(.) > 0, R''(.) < .0$, where θ is a productivity parameter. Clearly, the household is guaranteed of a minimum income of $\theta R(1)$. The income of the household is $y = \theta R(.) - wl$. The household's objective function does not change from Eq. (5.12), only the constraint does. The new budget constraint is

$$\theta R(1+\gamma e+l) - wl \geq c(1+\beta). \tag{5.14}$$

To focus on the more interesting cases, let us make the following assumption, which says that without hiring outside labour the family can meet its subsistence consumption, but the child must be employed.

Assumption 2. *θ is such that $\theta R(1) < \sigma < \theta R(1+\gamma)$.*

Substituting the constraint (5.14) into the objective function (5.12), let us write Eq. (5.12) as $z(e,l)$, and then maximising it with respect to (e,l), we write the first-order conditions as

$$z_1 : (1-e)\theta R'(1+\gamma e+l)\gamma - [\theta R(1+\gamma e+l) - wl - \sigma] = 0 \tag{5.15}$$

$$z_2 : (1-e)\left[\theta R'(1+\gamma e+l) - w\right] = 0. \tag{5.16}$$

It will not be difficult to see that in this model, child will never work full-time, nor will the household settle for the lowest income $R(1)$. That is to say, $e = 1$ is never optimal. Equally, the family will hire either outside labour, or their own child's labour or both. In addition, if the household stops hiring outside labour, it will use only a partial amount of the child's labour.

To see these, plug $e = 1$ in the first-order conditions; the demand for outside labour will be indeterminate. Similarly, by plugging $e = l = 0$, we will violate both conditions. Suppose $l = 0$ is optimal. Then Eq. (5.16) should be violated to give $\theta R'(1+\gamma e) - w < 0$, and in Eq. (5.15), we plug $e = l = 0$ to get $\theta R'(1)\gamma - [\theta R(1) - \sigma] = 0$. But by Assumption 2, $\theta R(1) < \sigma$ and $\theta R'(1)\gamma - [\theta R(1) - \sigma] > 0$, which means $e = 0$ cannot be optimal. Next we see that when $l = 0$, Eq. (5.15) holds with equality at some e, say, $\bar{e} < 1$, which does not depend on w.

The main insight of this exercise is that if self-employment is moderately remunerative, then the household will be able to earn a decent income, but it will try to substitute child labour for outside labour when the wage rate increases. As a result of this tendency, the child's education will be inversely related to the market wage rate. This is the most important difference to the results of the BV model.

Proposition 8. *Suppose optimal* $e > 0$, $l > 0$ *resulting in* $c > \underline{c}$. *Then with an increase in the wage rate, the household's use of child labour* e *rises and the outside labour* l *falls.*

Proof of Proposition 8. From Eqs. (5.15) and (5.16), write the second-order derivatives as[5]

$$z_{11} = (1-e)\theta\gamma^2 R''(.) - 2\theta\gamma R'(.)$$

$$z_{12} = (1-e)\theta\gamma R''(.)$$

$$z_{22} = (1-e)\theta R''(.) = \gamma z_{12}.$$

By carrying out total differentiation with respect to w, we further obtain $z_{1w} = l$ and $z_{2w} = -(1-e)$. Then by applying Cramer's rule, we get

$$\frac{\partial e}{\partial w} = \frac{-z_{1w}z_{22} + z_{12}z_{2w}}{z_{11}z_{22} - z_{12}^2} = \frac{l + \gamma(1-e)}{2\theta\gamma R'(.)} > 0$$

$$\frac{\partial l}{\partial w} = \frac{-z_{11}z_{2w} + z_{21}z_{1w}}{z_{11}z_{22} - z_{12}^2} = -\frac{R''(.)(l + \gamma(1-e)) - 2R'(.)}{2\theta R'(.)R''(.)} < 0.$$

5.3 Are we always self-interested?

The notion of a rational consumer consists of several elements: (1) He is *self-interested.* (2) In pursuit of his self-interest he is *able to compute* marginal benefit and marginal cost to make a rational choice. (3) His preferences (as the internal structure of self-interest) are primitive and must be independent of prices.

All of these have been challenged. Sen (1977) criticised Edgeworth for assuming that individuals are egoist. According to Sen, Edgeworth had doubted self-interest to be a primary human trait except in war and contractual situations, yet he initiated an intellectual tradition that is premised on this fundamentally unrealistic assumption. Sen went on to further criticise the discipline for justifying the 'self-interest' assumption as being not only compatible but also essential for achieving Pareto-optimal economic allocations. To Sen, the notion of Pareto optimality as a measure of social welfare was flawed, from a philosophical point of view. Later on, we will discuss the idea of welfare proposed by Pareto.[6] At this point, we should take the core of Sen's criticism relating to the assumption of individuals maximising their own interest or utility.

Modern economics has addressed this limitation by incorporating altruism and concern for others. These are now regarded as equally important traits of an economic agent, and to distinguish them from self-interest, they are called *social preferences* or, more generally, *other-regarding preferences*. Broadly, social preference includes altruism, fairness, reciprocity, inequity aversion and the like. The main way to model social preference is to allow an agent's utility to depend on both what she gets and what others are getting, from a given economic transaction.

5.3.1 Fairness

The concept of fairness has been widely addressed in the *ultimatum game* (UG). Two randomly matched, preferably unrelated, players are given the task of sharing a sum of money (endowment), say $10. One player is the *proposer*, who has to propose a split of the endowment. The other player is the *responder*, who will then accept or reject the proposal. If he accepts, the split is executed, and if he rejects the endowment is taken off the table. The interaction is only one-shot.

Rational choice theory suggests that the responder should accept any amount of money, however small, because something is better than nothing. Realising this, the proposer should propose a split that gives maximum to himself—for instance $9.99 to himself and $0.01 to the responder. The responder should accept this proposal. But in reality, almost universally, such a proposal would be rejected; even a split of $9:$1 would be considered preposterous. The reason is the concern of *fairness* that plays an important role in our real-life interactions, but it has been ignored in the rational choice theory.

The game was introduced by Güth et al. (1982), and since then it has been reproduced innumerable times in many countries and many different settings. The key result is that the proposer offers 40 to 50 per cent of the endowment and the responder almost always accepts. If the offer falls below this level, the probability of acceptance also falls. An offer of 20% of the endowment is rejected half of the time.

These results are remarkably robust across space and time, barring some variations. It has been noted that in societies where social cooperation is highly prevalent, offers that deviate from 50:50 are rejected with high probability. Thus, what is a 'fair' split varies between cultures. The 'accepted' offer also falls with social distance between the two players (when the opponent's social identity is made known). The probability of rejection is also sensitive to the size of the endowment. With higher stakes, the offer size falls. The UG has generated great interest, and it has been applied to a variety of contexts such as bargaining, development, the evolution of fair choice and reciprocity. See the 17-author article by van Damme et al. (2014) for a comprehensive discussion of the game.

It should be apparent by now that the UG is not as simple as it appears. In deciding on the optimal offer, the proposer must take into account what the responder would consider a fair offer. This introspection is crucial at all offers except 50:50. When offering less than 50% the proposer must assess how the responder would react and decide on her reaction the responder needs to make an inference about what the proposer deems fair. These layers of introspection make pinpointing the true cause of rejection—mere unfairness or incorrect reasoning on the part of the responder—harder. Likewise, the proposer's offer is influenced by the threat of rejection from which his own sense of fairness cannot be easily distinguished. However, one thing we can be overwhelmingly certain about: that is, people are not entirely self-interested. Fairness does creep into 'rational' calculation.

5.3.2 Altruism

Taking leads from Daniel Kahneman's (Kahneman et al., 1986) earlier work to modify the UG, Forsythe et al. (1994) introduced the *dictator game*. The dictator game also has an endowment and two subjects, a dictator and a passive recipient. The dictator decides how much money from the endowment would be left for the recipient. Here, there is no question of acceptance or rejection. The dictator can give anything from nothing to everything; the rest is hers. Therefore, her offer should be taken as a measure of her *altruism* (rather than fairness).

As in the ultimatum game, most dictator game experiments consistently find that dictators, on average, allocate a non-trivial sum of money to the recipient—roughly 20–30% of the endowment. Unsurprisingly, this is slightly less than what the ultimatum game finds. Many authors have examined if 'framing' has any effect on altruism, by asking the dictator to 'take' instead of 'giving' from the endowment (Korenok et al., 2013). The change of framing here implicitly appeals to a sense of ownership or property right, which may vary from culture to culture and between genders. What you are asked to 'take' from is not yours, and what you are asked to 'give' away is deemed yours.

There are many studies that have examined the framing effects and the gender effects separately (see Eckel and Grossman, 1998). The results are mixed. Very often, the gender effects are absent or taking versus giving reveals the same level of altruism. However, one paper Chowdhury et al. (2017) has studied the two dimensions together and their results are intriguing. They find the following: (1) Males are more generous in giving games than they are in taking games. (2) Females are more generous in taking games than they are in giving games. (3) Females are more generous than males in taking games but equally generous in giving games. Furthermore, the study also finds that when the combined pool of data is analyzed (combining males and females), asymmetric giving and taking effects of the two genders cancel out each other, making the two frames equivalent. But altruism differs significantly between genders due to their difference in their psychological attitude to the property right, according to this study.

5.3.3 Reciprocity

The idea of fairness or altruism intrinsically brings the well-being of other people into consideration, and by implication a behaviour of reciprocity. Citing numerous examples of voluntary contribution to public goods, such as lifeboat services, building arts centres and so on, Sugden (1984) proposed a formal definition of *reciprocity* by introducing a moral constraint on individual self-pursuits. In his words,

> Let G be any group of people of which i is a member. Suppose that every member of G except i is making an effort of at least ξ in the production of some public good. Then let i choose the level of effort that he would most prefer that every member of G should make. If this most preferred level of effort is not less than ξ, then i is under an obligation to the members of G to make an effort of at least ξ. I shall call this the *principle of reciprocity*.
>
> (Sugden, 1984, p. 775)

In this definition, an individual faces a moral compulsion to match others' contribution, not because he would benefit from it but because he thinks others should pay at least that amount. Therefore, the act of paying less alone—an act of free riding—would be extremely *unfair*.

But reciprocity cuts both ways—paying more against more and paying less against less. Matthew Rabin (1993) writes, "If somebody is being nice to you, fairness dictates that you be nice to him. If somebody is being mean to you, fairness allows—and vindictiveness dictates—that you be mean to him" (p. 1281). Being nice to somebody means sacrificing one's own material pay-off in order to maximise the material pay-off of the other. Conversely, being mean to another means sacrificing one's own material pay-off to minimise the material pay-off of the other. Rabin called these behaviours mutual-max and mutual-min behaviours. When two (or many) people engage in these types of behaviours in a mutually consistent way, we observe fairness equilibrium. Rabin (1993) formalised his idea using game theoretic language (for the obvious reciprocal nature of emotions involved).

5.3.4 *Trust*

Berg et al. (1995) made an interesting variation of the UG, in which the proposer and responder are each given an endowment of say \$10. From her endowment, the proposer decides to transfer some or none to the responder; say, this amount is x, $(0 \le x \le 10)$, which is tripled on the way before it reaches the responder. The responder decides how much to keep from the amount received (\$$3x$) and how much to return to the proposer. In this game, when a proposer leaves a non-trivial amount for the responder, she is taking a risk, and it must be justified on the grounds of *trusting* her unknown partner. Similarly, when a responder reciprocates, she is proving that she is *trustworthy*. This is why the game is called the *trust game*. As the money sent by the proposer is tripled creating room for improving both players' final pay-off, this is also called the investment game.

The findings of the experiment were quite revealing. Of 32 proposers, only 2 sent nothing, another 2 sent just \$1 and 28 sent more than \$1, including 5 proposers who sent their entire endowment of \$10. Of the 28 responders who were sent more than \$1, 11 returned more than what their partners had sent, 15 returned less than what their partners had sent and only 2 returned zero or \$1. Thus, 11 out of 30 proposers who sent money had a positive return, ending up with more than \$10. Of course, 35.33% suffered a loss. More importantly, on average an investment of \$5 generated \$7.17, while \$10 generated a modest amount of \$10.20.[7]

Trust, as expected, depends on the cultural context and may also vary with gender. Croson and Buchan (1999) studied this dimension using previously collected data from the United States, China, Japan and Korea. They found that for the money sent by proposers, there is no significant gender effect, but for money returned by the responders there is. Women sent back 37.4% of the money as opposed to men's 28.6%. This means that women are more trustworthy than men, but when it comes to trusting others, they are essentially the same.

5.3.5 *Inequity aversion*

Another closely related idea is *inequity aversion*. People may display altruism, not necessarily to benefit others but out of a preference for an egalitarian society. They may have an aversion to inequity in the distribution of material pay-offs. Along this line, Fehr and Schmidt (1999) proposed the following utility function. Suppose that there are two individuals and that from some transaction, they get a monetary pay-off $y = (y_1, y_2)$. Their utility from the pay-off depends not only on what they get for themselves but also on the difference between the two pay-offs. More generally, if the individuals are inequity-averse, they may suffer from the pay-off difference in either direction.

For instance, if $y_1 < y_2$ individual 1 would naturally feel upset for having what the authors call *disadvantageous inequality*. Suppose θ captures the intensity of this disutility. But having an *advantageous inequality* in $y_1 > y_2$ may also cause disutility if individual 1 is inequity averse. Let γ capture the intensity of such disutility.

With the preceding conceptualisation of inequity aversion, we can write the utility functions individuals of 1 and 2 as

$$u_1(y_1, y_2) = y_1 - \theta_1 \max\{y_2 - y_1, 0\} - \gamma_1 \max\{y_1 - y_2, 0\},$$

$$u_2(y_1, y_2) = y_2 - \theta_2 \max\{y_1 - y_2, 0\} - \gamma_2 \max\{y_2 - y_1, 0\}.$$

It is natural to restrict $0 \le \gamma_i < \theta_i \ (i = 1, 2)$ as disadvantageous inequality hurts more than the advantageous one. Of course, the special case of no inequity concern is $\theta_i = \gamma_i = 0$. The idea can be extended to n individuals. There, of course, in many ways, inequality can be measured. See Fehr and Schmidt (1999) for their specific formulation.

In Figure 5.2, we show how individual 2's utility will depend on individual 1's material payoff, say, income, while individual 2's income is m. In the conventional models, the utility of individual 2 will not depend on the income of individual 1; hence, it will be a straight line at m against individual 2's income as shown in panel a. If this individual is self-interested and only averse to others having more income than hers, then her utility will fall beyond m as shown in panel b. Alternatively, if she is averse to having more than others but indifferent to having less than what others have, then her utility function would be the one depicted in panel c. The more general case of inequity aversion—suffering disutility in either direction of inequality is shown in panel d.

The Fehr and Schmidt (1999) utility function is useful for its applicability to a wider set of games and experiments, including the UG and the dictator game, with the additional power to

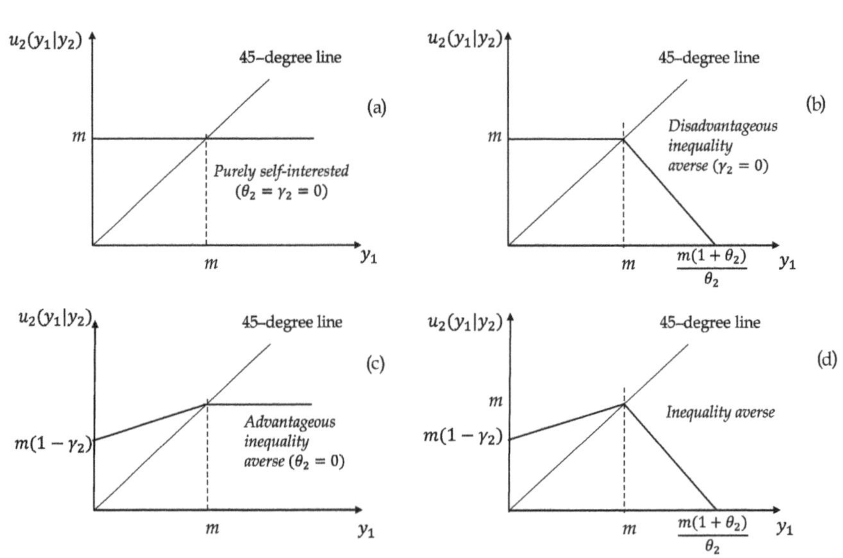

Figure 5.2 Utility function for social preference

explain many anomalies that have been observed in experiments. Their framework is also suitable for market transactions or public good contribution games.

However, the previously discussed utility function is linear in the material pay-offs. While allowing non-linearity is conceptually possible, the model loses its simplicity that is vital for commonly used laboratory experiments in which pay-offs are monetary. It is also an assumption, and for any other 'other-regarding preference' function, that the consumer must have knowledge of others' material pay-off resulting from the transaction. This is not easy to be true when many people are involved. One way to reduce this informational burden is to consider inequity only in reference to an average pay-off.

5.4 Computing marginal costs

Rationality requires the economic agents to compute the right notion of costs and benefits. As we discussed earlier, in the context of how many units of a given good to buy, the consumer should equate the marginal cost with the marginal benefit. Therefore, recognising the true marginal cost is paramount.

Many of our modern necessities come with a monthly fixed charge. Subscribing to Netflix, buying a mobile call plan and signing up for a broadband service are just a few examples. Some of these services also have a lock-in period, and often, the marginal cost of such services is zero, such as watching a movie on Netflix after paying for a subscription or free download from broadband, while the subscription charges are non-refundable.

But there are occasions where we fail to recognise that our costs have been sunk and that therefore, they should have no bearing on our subsequent choices. Consider the following scenario. Suppose a couple are to fly from London to Venice for a weekend leisure trip. They have booked their tickets from a low-cost airline, which are non-refundable, but luckily the hotel booking is refundable. On the day of their journey, they learn that unseasonal rains have badly flooded most of the city of Venice (just as happened in November 2019).

What should they do? As the airfares are sunk cost, the main elements of consideration should be the marginal benefit and marginal cost of undertaking the travel. Compared to any normal circumstances, their marginal benefits would be substantially less and the marginal costs would be significantly greater. They should not travel.

Yet it is quite probable that the couple would still travel, as many of us in dilemmas like this do. While sunk costs should not affect our future decisions from a normative point of view, in reality, they do. Psychologists Kahneman and Tversky have argued that we use some sort of mental accounting in making real-life decisions and that in the mental accounting, losses are weighted much more than gains. In the example given earlier, if the sunk costs are not small, we feel an urge to obtain some utility 'gains' to make up for the loss. Since the loss is sunk, the only way we can reduce the burden of it in our mental accounting is by undertaking the trip. In that sense, sunk costs affect our behaviours, not in spite of but *because* of being sunk.

It might very well be that after taking the troublesome journey the couple would regret their decision (and they are aware of this possibility). But by cancelling the trip, they will hold themselves responsible for incurring a loss (a mental agony). Either way, it is a dilemma. Should the airlines cancel the flight or a transport strike in London makes it impossible to travel, they will be mighty relieved. In essence, the decision to incur the loss should be taken out of their hands.

A classic experiment on sunk cost, first conducted by Richard Thaler and written about it in passing in one of his many influential articles (Thaler, 1980, p. 48, footnote 8) is an all-you-can-eat pizza experiment. At the university town of Ithaca, a pizza restaurant offers a buffet for $2.50

(that was the price back in the 1980s). One of Thaler's students disguised himself as a waiter and randomly offered half of the diners a full refund and then kept track of how many pizza slices each diner was having. Since the price paid by the group that did not get refund was sunk, the marginal cost of eating an extra slice of pizza was zero for both groups, and their average consumption should be statistically identical. But it was found that the free diners ate significantly *less*—an apparent violation of the logic of sunk costs.[8]

Having said that, it is not readily explainable why the free eaters ate *less*. One can argue that after getting the refund, the diners' mental accounting completely changed. Getting the unexpected refund, they might have felt grateful to the owner and restrained their consumption. Indeed, many experiments confirm that the presence or absence of a monetary price does alter our behaviours unexpectedly. When invited for dinner at a friend's house, we take a bottle of wine, flowers or some nice gift (in the worst case of misjudgement, nothing) but never leave cash at the end of the meal. But when we meet the same friend at a restaurant, we split the bill. From a sociological point of view, money symbolises economic transactions—a conscious calculation of parity between giving and taking. Attaching a monetary tag to social interactions demeans the emotional experience we get from social interactions.

Gneezy and Rustichini (2000) report an interesting experiment in day-care centres in the city of Haifa, Israel. The study was conducted in 1998 over a period of 20 weeks involving 10 (private) day-care centres. Parents are expected to pick up their children at four in the afternoon; however, frequently, some parents (not necessarily the same ones) tend to come late, forcing the staff at the day-care centres to stay longer than expected. In the first 4 weeks, no measures were taken to stop parents from coming late. From the fifth week, a fine was introduced in 6 out of 10 day-care centres for being more than 10 minutes late. The fine was again removed from the 17th week onwards.

In the intervening 12 weeks, to the surprise of the researchers, the number of parents coming late steadily *increased* after the fine was introduced. The order of increase was above 50%, and some weeks, it reached even 100%. When the fine was finally removed, the frequency of parents late coming did not change from the intervening weeks. In the control groups of 'no fine' day-care centres, parents' lateness remained unchanged throughout.

As economists commonly prescribe, in unison with legal, criminal and psychological studies, an increase in punishment (monetary or physical) should deter crime or unacceptable behaviours. However, in the Haifa experiment, it had the exact opposite effect. Worse, even after the removal of the fine, parents coming late became a norm in those day-care centres, at least during the study period.

Why is this so? The answer lies in the fact that the introduction of a fine changed the parents' perception and attitude. Previously, late coming was equivalent to buying an extra amount of childcare free of cost, for which parents had 'guilty feelings' and therefore kept it under moral restraint. But once the monetary fine was introduced, they began to see the fine as a market price for additional childcare. Based on their own value of time, many found the fine a bargain and responded as a rational consumer. In other words, in the absence of a fine, parents saw their relationship with the day-care centre after 4 p.m. as a social one. The introduction of a fine made this relationship flip to a market one. Furthermore, once the fine was removed, the parents could not switch back to the previous relationship; they perceived their market attitude to be socially acceptable.

In organisation studies, it has been long understood that pay raises and promotions are not everything; non-pecuniary incentives are just as good. Recognitions like 'employee of the year', 'best salesperson' and so on have strong incentive effects, especially among the less-paid workers. In an important contribution, Benabou and Tirole (2003) argued that employees have both intrinsic and extrinsic motivations. Monetary incentives work well for extrinsic motivations. But when the employee's intrinsic motivations become important, for instance when the quality of effort is important, as in an old-age care home, academic research and innovations, among others, giving too many monetary incentives undermines the employee's intrinsic motivations and ultimately reduces the productivity of the organisation. It has also been recognised that many individuals may pursue 'social objectives' alongside their monetary or career objectives. See also Besley and Ghatak (2005) and Benabou and Tirole (2006) for agents who have pro-social objectives. The key point is that wage or any monetary incentive scheme is not only a weak notion of the price of labour but can also perversely undermine the work incentive when pro-social objectives are present, just as they complicate psychological responses as seen from the Haifa experiment.

Failure to understand the appropriate costs and benefits that are required to arrive at the best decision even in market settings is broadly called *bounded rationality*. Often, these bounds are imposed on us by complex pricing schemes presented by the sellers. In the UK electricity market, a Google search reveals that tariff options offered by any energy company runs into 20s. The plans vary in terms of types of energy (gas or electricity), mode of payment, peak and off-peak pricing, types of meter (single, dual, prepaid etc.), standing charges, per unit charges, exit fees and many more. Studying the future energy cost under each option and then making a rational choice is a huge cognitive challenge. A similar problem is with the mortgage market, although admittedly mortgage is a more complex product than electricity, which is a perfectly homogeneous good.

When confronted with complex pricing schemes, a general tendency is to simplify the calculation by deriving an average cost. In fact, in the mortgage market, the average payment called annualised percentage rate (APR) is the crucial variable that borrowers rely on to make their decisions.

Ito (2014) studied the Southern California domestic electricity market. Residents here did not have a choice over their energy suppliers; instead, their zip code determined who their supplier would be. Focusing on the border area of two electricity suppliers around Orange County, Ito exploited several variations in the non-linear pricing schemes of the two companies that occurred between 1999 and 2007. As the residents lived in the border area of the two companies' service territories, this was a case of similar households facing different prices. In a non-linear price scheme, the marginal price would be very different from the average price. In fact, for electricity, the average price is smaller than the marginal price, because the marginal price of electricity is set higher on environmental grounds to discourage greater energy consumption. Ito (2014) concluded that consumers in both areas systematically made their electricity consumption decision based on a 'perceived' price that is approximated by the average price implied by the price scheme. Marginal price did not drive their choice. From an environmental policy point of view, such a misjudgement of marginal cost meant greater electricity consumption at the margin than intended.

To illustrate how the consumption bias may result from such a miscalculation of the marginal cost, let us take an example. Suppose the non-linear pricing scheme is regressive (as shown on panel *a* of Figure 5.3):

$$p = \begin{cases} p^0 & \text{for } x \le x^0 \\ p^0 - \Delta p & \text{for } x > x^0. \end{cases}$$

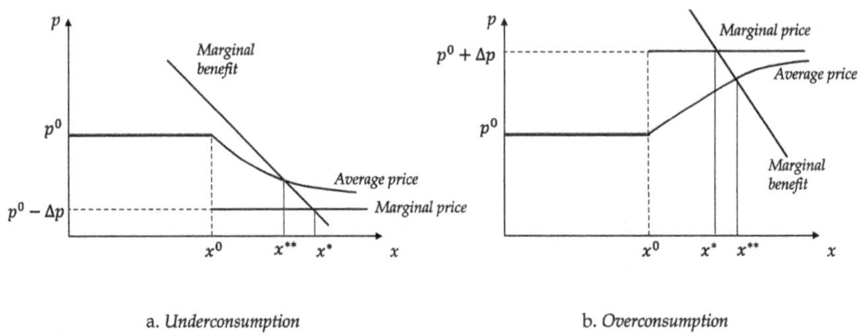

Figure 5.3 Consumption bias under non-linear pricing and bounded rationality

From this, we calculate total expenditure as

$$TE = \begin{cases} p^0 x & \text{for } x \leq x^0 \\ p^0 x^0 + \left(p^0 - \Delta p\right)\left(x - x^0\right) & \text{for } x > x^0. \end{cases}$$

and the average price as

$$AP = \begin{cases} p^0 & \text{for } x \leq x^0 \\ p^0 - \Delta p + \dfrac{x^0 \Delta p}{x} & \text{for } x > x^0. \end{cases}$$

Similarly, for a progressive non-linear price scheme, the average price is (as shown on panel *b* of Figure 5.3)

$$AP = \begin{cases} p^0 & \text{for } x \leq x^0 \\ p^0 + \Delta p - \dfrac{x^0 \Delta p}{x} & \text{for } x > x^0. \end{cases}$$

We have also drawn the marginal benefit curve of the consumer. The optimal consumption of x is given by x^*, given by the marginal benefit and the marginal price. But as the consumer is able to compute only the average price and equate *AP* with marginal benefit (as reported in Ito, 2014), the actual choice is given by x^{**}. Clearly, there is under-consumption when the non-linear price scheme is regressive and over-consumption when the non-linear price scheme is progressive.

Misreading the marginal cost can occur from inattention as well. Many stores do not include the tax in their posted price, and consumers may not realise this until they have to pay. Chetty et al. (2009) found from a grocery store experiment that when the posted price does not include tax, people buy more. Tax-inclusive posted price with tax salience reduces demand by 8%. The impact of tax salience on demand has also been studied by Finkelstein (2009). She analysed the impact of switching from cash to electronic collection of tolls. As the electronic method is less salient, consumers tend to travel more leading to an increase in the toll collection by the order of 20–40%.

5.5 Inconsistency and arbitrariness of preferences

Imagine you are trying to decide whether to buy a MacBook (costing around £1,000) or a low-end Dell (costing £500). Given the substantial price difference and your needs, the Dell seems just fine, although MacBook is attractive. Suppose you prefer the low-end Dell to MacBook and decide to go for it. At this point, the salesperson shows you a top-end model of Dell; it is more expensive than the MacBook you just decided against—clearly an irrelevant option. But due to the insistence of the salesperson, you take a closer look and find that it is pretty much same as, if not inferior to in some respects, the Mac. With this realisation, you change your mind to buy the Mac.

The example demonstrates a violation of what is called independence of irrelevant alternatives, which says that if a consumer chooses *A* over *B* and then if *C* is added to the list, where *C* is inferior to *B*, then the choice of *A* should not be affected.[9] But in real life, this is often violated. As shown in this example, when the top-end Dell is shown, choosing the MacBook gives a feeling of choosing something really superior both in price and quality (against the top-end Dell), and it confers an unambiguous sense of gains, which could not be obtained from the initial choice of the low-end Dell.

One potential criticism of this example is that it is not a fair criticism of the axioms of preferences; it is more about choice. Under the rational choice theory, we make the choice by interacting our preference with price information. Behavioural economics adds our emotions (or our psychological responses) to it. The rational choice theory says that we should not let these emotions stand in our way. Behavioural theory says that these emotions are real and that our choice theory must incorporate them.

5.5.1 *Coherent arbitrariness*

In the rational choice theory, consumer preference is fundamental, which cannot be manipulated, should not be arbitrary and should remain stable throughout the decision time. That these preferences should not be arbitrary is important for the fact that a consumer's willingness to pay (WTP) sets the upper bound on the price of a product. Clearly, for non-arbitrariness to be true, the consumer should have prior experience with the goods; for exotic and unknown goods, the consumer's WTP might change considerably before and after the experience of it.

Ariely et al. (2003) addressed this issue by conducting an experiment with MBA students of the Sloan School of Management.[10] Ordinary products like computer accessories (cordless trackball and keyboard), wine bottles (average and rare), luxury chocolates and books, which had an average retail price of \$70. But the subjects were asked whether they would buy the products (yes/no) at a price equal to the last two digits of their Social Security number and, if yes, how much they were willing to pay. Students were also told that they could actually buy one of the products at their stated price so that their WTP would be credible.

The strategy to base the 'yes/no' decision on the last two digits of their individual Social Security numbers was meant to see if their valuation of a product was subject to arbitrary influence, or what is called the *anchoring effect* (Tversky and Kahneman, 1974). The Social Security number of a student was purely random and should have no connection with the true prices of the products shown. It turned out that the students' decisions to buy and their WTP were both highly correlated with (the last two digits of) their Social Security number for every product. Subjects whose Social Security numbers were above the median stated a WTP between 57 percent and 107 percent greater than subjects whose Social Security numbers were below the median. Valuations at the upper end of the distribution (5th quintile) were typically greater by a factor of three. Such was the scale of the anchoring effect. For example, the top-quintile subjects were willing to pay \$56 on average for a cordless computer keyboard, compared to the bottom quintile's average WTP of \$16.

This is proof that our preferences suffer from arbitrariness. In the absence of prior knowledge of the true market price, consumers tend to anchor their valuation on arbitrary cues that may be presented before them by the sellers, the selling environment or a related product. This is one of the reasons sellers try to target individual consumers with personalised promotions and advertisements.

However, the preceding experiment also revealed relative valuations of the subjects over these goods. Nearly all ranked the rare wines above the average wines and a keyboard above a trackball by stating higher WTP figures. That means their relative valuations were orderly and coherent. The general conclusion of the study is that our preference suffers from arbitrariness (in line with many other psychological experiments) but, at the same time, remains stable and orderly. The positive finding on coherence corroborates one important assumption of the rational choice theory—preference ordering.

5.6 Veblen goods

In his famous 1899 book, *The Theory of the Leisure Class*, Thorstein Veblen wrote that wealthy people buy conspicuous goods mainly out of a desire to advertise their wealth, because wealth brings prestige, but wealth is not directly observable to others while conspicuous consumption is. These goods are therefore called status goods or positional goods. Veblen's view, largely accepted over a century, has led to significant research on consumers' motivation to buy luxury goods. Leibenstein (1950), among others, extended Veblen's idea to *bandwagon effect* and *snob effect*. The bandwagon effect describes a situation in which we demand a good because others are demanding it—complementarity of consumption in the social dimension. Snobbism is its opposite: I demand less of it because others demand more of it (substitutability). Then there is also the idea of 'keeping up with the Joneses'—an act of competitive consumption. All these ideas, related but distinct, can be largely grouped under Veblen goods. What is common here is the consumer's recognition of how others react to her consumption of those goods that are publicly observable.

Of course, in modern days, there are many ways that wealth information can be conveyed. There is a list of the richest 100 people. Many governments are happy to disclose the highest-income taxpayer of the year. Magazines carry pictures of celebrity weddings, holidays and parties. But for the neo-rich, there is still a problem of communicating to their 'social contacts' how much richer they have become this year. Such communication is important to them, because others knowing their income or wealth elevates their social status. In this case, conspicuous consumption is an important way to signal one's income.

Suppose in a neighbourhood, everybody knows who has the most expensive car, who has the second-most expensive car and so on. People assign social prestige exactly in the same order as the value of their cars, and everybody cares about this prestige. Then, in this neighbourhood, following Frank (1985), we can argue that people will be spending excessively on their cars, ignoring consumption of other important things, such as holidaying, dining out, healthy meals and so on. Frank (1985) assumed that the consumer's utility function in this sort of environment is

$$U = U\left(x, z, F(x)\right),$$

where x is a conspicuous consumption or status good, z is a non-observable (private) consumption good and $F(x)$ is the percentile ranking (a number between 0 and 1) of x in its distribution. Therefore, if $f(x)$ represents the density function of x, then having $x = x_1$ gives someone a rank$F(x_1) = \int_0^{x_1} f(x)\,dx$.

A consumer with a budget equation $m = z + px$, where the price of x is p and price of $z = 1$ maximises her utility by choosing x and z from the following equations:

$$\frac{U_1}{U_2} + \frac{U_3}{U_2} f(x) = p \text{ and } z + px = m.$$

Because $U_3 > 0$ the marginal benefit of conspicuous consumption exceeds the marginal rate of substitution (U_1/U_2), and therefore, the consumer buys more of x, which then reduces the consumption of z relative to the private benchmark.

Apart from the obvious distortions in consumption, a remarkable outcome of the privately optimal decisions is that the distribution of the conspicuous consumption x will exactly mirror the distribution of the consumers' income. The richest person will occupy the first rank and the poorest person will occupy the lowest rank in the distribution of x.

If the status utility depended on the ranking of income instead of conspicuous consumption, there would be no distortion in consumption. The consumer's preference then would be given by

$$U = U(x, z, G(m)),$$

where $G(m)$ is the distribution of the consumer's exogenous income. Utility maximisation in this case would result in $U_1 / U_2 = p$. Therefore, to engage in conspicuous consumption to maintain a relative position in society is collectively harmful; it reduces social welfare.[11]

Corneo and Geanne (1997) proposed a model similar to Frank (1985) with more structure to the utility component arising from social status, which they call rank utility. They also assume that conspicuous consumption does not have any intrinsic utility; it is merely used to signal wealth. Thus, they proposed a utility function for individual i: $U_i = u(z_i) + v(\delta_i)$, where δ_i is an indicator variable for buying the conspicuous consumption good (by a fixed unit of 1), $\delta = 1$ if it is bought and $\delta = 0$ if it is not bought. The consumer's budget is $y_i = p + z$.

The authors assume the following specification for $v(.) : v(\delta_i) = E(a(i) \mid \delta_i)$, where $a(i)$ is the rank utility function. Thus, the utility from conspicuous consumption is the conditional expected rank utility.

Consumer i's utility from conspicuous consumption is

$$U_i(1) = u(y_i - p) + E(a(i) \mid 1)$$

and from not buying the conspicuous consumption good is

$$U_i(0) = u(y_i) + E(a(i) \mid 0).$$

Consumer i undertakes conspicuous consumption if

$$U_i(1) - U_i(0) \geqslant 0, \text{ or } E(a(i) \mid 1) - E(a(i) \mid 0) \geqslant u(y_i) - u(y_i - p).$$

This leads to a cut-off y, say, $\tilde{y}$; only individuals with income above this level buy the conspicuous consumption good. The cut-off level is endogenously determined by the number of people who decide to buy the good, as well as the shape of the rank utility function $a(.)$. In equilibrium, conformism (or bandwagon effect) emerges if the utility from the conspicuous consumption increases as more people do the same, and alternatively, the snob effect emerges if the utility increases as fewer people consume it.

However, where maintaining social ranks is not important, conspicuous consumption serves other purposes, such as signalling wealth and gaining status, the consumer's preference needs to be modelled differently. For instance, Basu (1987) assumed that the WTP for a status good depends on the excess demand for it, which is clearly dependent on other people's demand relative to the market supply of it. However, he did not develop the preference function, because his focus was on the pricing decision of a monopolist supplier of the status good.

Ireland (1994) and Bagwell and Bernheim (1996) proposed a framework to model the signalling motive. A basic sketch of their models is as follows. Suppose a consumer's wealth/income m can be high or low, m_H or m_L. People do not know who has m_H and who has m_L, but they know their distribution in the population. Consumers spend their wealth on two types of goods, ordinary (z) and conspicuous (x). As before, people observe the consumption of the conspicuous good but not that of the ordinary good. However, from the observation of conspicuous consumption, people can infer a consumer's true income.

Ireland proposed that such a consumer's preference can be presented as

$$U_i = (1-\alpha)u_i(z,x) + \alpha u_i(s), i = H, L,$$

where s is social status and α is a measure of the consumer's preference for social status. If $\alpha = 0$, the consumer cares only about her own/private utility $u_i(z,x)$. But status is nothing but others' inference about one's income or the total utility from private consumption. In turn, their inference is generated by the conspicuous consumption the consumer chooses. Thus, if the inference can be written as a function $\rho(x)$, the consumer's utility function can be written as[12]

$$U_i = (1-\alpha)u_i(z,x) + \alpha u_i(\rho(x)), i = H, L.$$

The function $\rho(x)$ results from optimisation and the equilibrium of the whole model.

Bagwell and Bernheim (1996) added more structure to conspicuous consumption. In their view, quality is an important aspect of conspicuous consumption. People demonstrate their wealth not by buying more of the same good but by buying a much higher quality of that good, say, by adding a new BMW to their fleet of cars. To add goods of different brands/qualities to one's consumption profile they defined the conspicuous consumption good as

$$x \equiv \int_{\underline{q}}^{\overline{q}} \mu(q)x(q)dq,$$

where q represents quality, $x(q)$denotes the quantity of the conspicuous consumption of quality q and $\mu(q)$ is the weight associated with the quality q. The range of qualities available is assumed to be $[\underline{q}, \overline{q}]$. Producers set price contingent on the quality; that is, $p = p(q)$. The consumer's total expenditure on conspicuous consumption s depends on how many different brands are bought and in what quantities.

In both models, the consumer's problem is to credibly communicate or signal their wealth. For credible communication, an individual of wealth m_H must choose a sufficiently high level of x, say, x_H, that an individual of wealth m_L will not find optimal to imitate; he will choose a lower level of conspicuous consumption, x_L. Others then would be convinced about their true wealth levels. The equilibrium of this variety is called the *separating equilibrium*, because it clearly separates the types of consumer (in this case, their wealth level).

In addition, Bagwell and Bernheim argue that producers of high-quality brands must make a 'pure profit' that cannot be eroded by competition. This is what is called the Veblen effect. For the Veblen effect to be present, high-wealth individuals must pay, according to their WTP, well in excess of the marginal cost of production. This is what was argued by Basu (1987) as well, where the demand for the status good must depend on the 'excess demand' for it.

While these models have analysed the key problem of wealth signalling, the work in this area has not progressed much. One obvious limitation of these models is that conspicuous consumption is presented in terms of a single good (with different qualities permitted), but in reality, we see an array of different goods and services. Owning a new BMW is not enough; one must have a big house in an expensive location, must wear designer clothing, travel first class if a private jet has not yet been added to the shopping list and so forth. The conspicuous consumption bundle should have more than one element, each with different varieties. The range of available goods, of course, depends on society as well. In Indian towns, the rich face the problem of not finding enough goods for conspicuous consumption. Weddings then become a public spectacle of lavish spending.

5.7 Why are Giffen goods so elusive?

One of the most intriguing examples in economics is Giffen good, named after the Scottish statistician Robert Giffen, who proclaimed that consumption of the potato went up during the time of the Irish famine of 1845–47 when the potato price went up four times in absolute terms and five times relative to the prices of other staples. Alfred Marshall publicised Giffen's observation in his 1895 edition of the *Principles of Economics* and added that bread in Victorian England was another Giffen good. But both the potato in Ireland and bread in Victorian England have been discarded as Giffen goods.

Rosen (1999) studied the potato prices of nineteenth-century Ireland and concluded that the potato was an inferior good but not a Giffen good. The Irish famine was one of the worst catastrophes of modern history, killing 12 percent of the population and displacing another 6–8 percent. But the problem started with a crop failure of potato in 1845 due to a previously unknown fungal infection that remained and substantially reduced potato productivity for the next 35 years. Rosen argued that in 1845, after the crop failed, people mistakenly thought the crop failure was temporary and saved a much larger proportion of the potato stock for the next year. They actually consumed less, and the price was raised to reduce the consumption as well, in order to set aside the seed potato. Therefore, it was incorrect to assume that the potato was a Giffen good. Furthermore, Rosen (1999) explained that by raising the price of potatoes to save excessively for future seeds made the famine catastrophic, as switching to other crops was delayed.

The main difficulty of identifying the Giffen good lies in separating the substitution and income effects of a price change and then showing that a negative income effect overturned the substitution effect. From the early work of Marshall to modern studies, it is well accepted that if a Giffen good is found it should be a necessary good, such as rice or wheat, and the consumers must be low-income earners for whom the subsistence consumption constraint is real.[13] Unfortunately, consumption data group various necessary foods under one heading, and thus, identification becomes problematic. It is also the case that the government often controls the price of the staple, or free trade makes price variations insignificant to allow for useful econometric studies.

Jensen and Miller (2008, p. 1557) proposed an indifference map that includes three different types of indifference curves in the presence of a minimum calorie requirement. Figure 5.4 depicts their argument. Suppose x_1 is a staple like wheat, rice or bread and x_2 is a 'fancy' good, like meat or milk, that is consumed more for taste and enjoyment. There is a minimum calorie requirement given by the thick line, which gives all the possible combinations of the two goods that give the same number of calories. Above the minimum calorie curve, the goods plane has two regions—the subsistence zone and the standard zone. In the subsistence zone, the calorie intake is low but not very alarming.[14]

In the standard zone, where the consumer is considering both goods in abundance and, thereby, plenty of calories, which is possible only at a sufficiently high-income level, the indifference curves are of a standard shape, with a continuously changing marginal rate of substitution (MRS). On the other extreme, below the minimum calorie curve, the indifference curves are linear, as if the consumer is trying to substitute as much of x_2 as possible for x_1. Note that the intercept on the x_2 is much higher, suggesting that for the same number of calories, the consumer needs to buy a lot more of the fancy good. In the intermediate subsistence zone, preference is somewhat mixed. The indifference curves are elbow-shaped. There is a bias towards the staple good, but the fancy good is no longer a perfect substitute everywhere.

A consumer's choice in this case demonstrates Giffen behaviour. A pair of budget lines is drawn for each region. We see that both in the standard and the calorie-deprived zones, demand

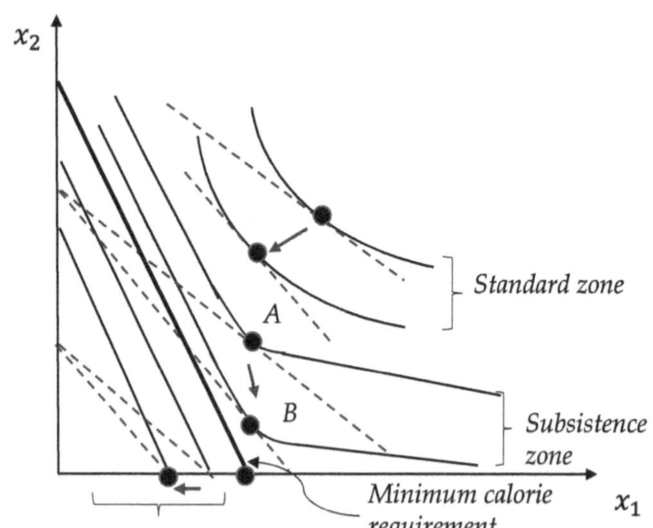

Figure 5.4 Giffen behaviour

Source: Jensen and Miller (2008, p. 1557)

for x_1 falls with an increase in its price. But in the subsistence zone, the effect is the opposite. The choice here is mainly around the elbow point. With an increase in p_1, the consumer moves from point A to point B. This is exactly what a Giffen good is.[15]

Jensen and Miller tested their theory in 2006 by conducting field experiments in China involving 1300 households with 3661 individuals who were officially classified as 'urban poor' in two provinces, Hunan and Gansu. Households were randomly assigned to one control group and three treatment groups. The three treatments differed in receiving price subsidies for rice and wheat. The authors found that in Hunan, a 1 percent increase in the price of rice caused a 0.22 percent increase in rice consumption—confirmation of the Giffen behaviour (see pp. 1565–66, and Tables 3 and 4).

So far, to the best of our knowledge, this is the only evidence of a Giffen good found by economists. Previous claims have been proven to be factually incorrect or methodologically unreliable. Thus, we can say that Giffen goods are definitely out there, but they are elusive, like dark matter to physicists.

5.8 Conclusion

In this chapter, we discussed several directions modern research has extended the theory of consumer behaviour and rational choice from its neoclassical version that every student of economics is familiar with. By no means the discussion presented here is complete. Much more could be written for new developments in revealed preference theory, particularly new work that attempts to incorporate normal and inferior goods (Cherchye et al., 2018).

Summary

1. Within a household many decisions, such as a wife's labour market participation and, in poor societies, children's work, are outcomes of negotiations or interplay of complex factors. Preferences can also be interdependent.
2. We are not as self-interested as the rational choice theory assumes. We summarised evidence of altruistic behaviours, fairness, reciprocity and inequity aversion.
3. Bounded rationality is a factor that interferes with our marginal cost computations. The implications of this type of error are significant.
4. We reported studies that have found that our preferences are vulnerable to arbitrary influences. But they are also order-preserving.
5. Modelling Veblen effects is challenging. Preferences in these cases should take into account 'rank utility' via other people's judgement. These models are complex.
6. Finally, Giffen goods are elusive. So far, there is evidence of only one.

Notes

1 The model can be easily extended to allow older members to also have a say.
2 Egalitarianism does not have to be equal consumption and equal work.
3 BV called this luxury axiom, which has been an important object of empirical investigation.
4 See another formulation of parental self-employment and child labour in Saha (2019).
5 We assume that the second-order conditions are satisfied: $z_{11} < 0, z_{22} < 0$ and $z_{11}z_{22} - z_{12}^2 > 0$.
6 Sen (1977) ominously said, "It is very much an open question as to whether these behavioral characteristics can be at all captured within the formal limits of consistent choice on which the welfare-maximisation approach depends" (p. 324).

7 We report mainly from the 'no history' experiment. The authors subsequently conducted another experiment in which the results of the first round of experiments were told to the subjects in order to convey a norm of trust. This experiment shows a much higher level of trustworthiness.
8 The experiment has been repeated many times since then, and many of them compared buffet versus *à la carte* pricing.
9 In spirit, this is also like the weak axiom of revealed preference of the revealed preference theory.
10 Some of the experimental research conducted by Dan Ariely has been found to be in violation of ethics and data integrity. The article discussed here is not one of them.
11 When income is not exogenous, the competition would move to the labour market. Robert Frank discusses the role of unions in curbing such collectively harmful competition.
12 Ireland (1994) presented the problem as the spectator's inference about the consumer's private consumption of the ordinary good z. But essentially, it is the same.
13 Jensen and Miller (2008) argue that consumers should not be too poor to have only one survival good in their basket; they should also have another good that they consider a 'fancy' good.
14 The subsistence zone can gradually fade into the standard zone.
15 A similar argument has been made, but without any reference to subsistence requirement, in Moffatt (2002). He provides some specifications of the indifference curve that would generate backward bending offer curves, which is both necessary and sufficient for Giffen behaviours.

References

Ariely, D., Loewenstein, G. & Prelec, D. (2003). "Coherent arbitrariness": Stable demand curves without stable preferences. *The Quarterly Journal of Economics*, 118(1), 73–105.

Bagwell, L. S. & Bernheim, D. B. (1996). Veblen effects in a theory of conspicuous consumption. *American Economic Review*, 86(3), 349–373.

Basu, K. (1987) Monopoly, quality uncertainty and 'status' goods. *International Journal of Industrial Organization*, 5(4), 435–446.

Basu, K. (2006). Gender and say: A model of household behaviour with endogenously determined balance of power. *The Economic Journal*, 116, 558–580.

Basu, K. & Van, P. H. (1998). The economics of child labor. *American Economic Review*, 88, 412–427.

Becker, G. S. (1981). *A Treatise on the Family*. Cambridge, MA: Harvard University Press.

Benabou, R. & Tirole, J. (2003). Intrinsic and extrinsic motivation. *Review of Economic Studies*, 70(3), 489–520.

Benabou, R. & Tirole, J. (2006). Incentives and prosocial behavior. *American Economic Review*, 96(5), 1652–1678.

Berg, S., Dickhaut, J. & McCabe, K. (1995). Trust, reciprocity and social history. *Games and Economic Behavior*, 10, 122–145.

Besley, T. & Ghatak, M. (2005). Competition and incentives with motivated agents. *American Economic Review*, 95(3), 616–636.

Cherchye, L., Demuynck, T. & de Rock, B. (2018). Normality of demand in a two-goods setting. *Journal of Economic Theory*, 173, 361–382.

Chetty, R., Looney, A. & Kroft, K. (2009). Salience and taxation: Theory and evidence. *American Economic Review*, 99(4), 1145–1177.

Chiappori, P. (1988). Rational household labor supply. *Econometrica*, 56(1), 63–90.

Chowdhury, S. M., Jeon, J. & Saha, B. (2017). Gender differences in the giving and taking variants of the dictator game. *Southern Economic Journal*, 84(2), 474–483.

Corneo, G. & Geanne, O. (1997). Conspicuous consumption, snobbism and conformism. *Journal of Public Economics*, 66, 55–71.

Croson, R. & Buchan, N. (1999). Gender and culture: International experimental evidence from trust games. *The American Economic Review, Papers and Proceedings*, 89(2), 386–391.

Duflo, E. (2012). Women empowerment and economic development. *Journal of Economic Literature*, 50(4), 1051–1079.

Eckel, C. C. & Grossman, P. J. (1998). Are women less selfish than men? Evidence from dictator experiments. *Economic Journal*, 108, 726–735.
Fehr, E. & Schmidt, K. M. (1999). A theory of fairness, competition and cooperation. *Quarterly Journal of Economics*, 114(3), 817–868.
Finkelstein, A. (2009). E-ZTax: Tax salience and tax rates. *Quarterly Journal of Economics*, 124(3), 969–1010.
Forsythe, R., Horowitz, J. L., Savin, N. E. & Sefton, M. (1994). Fairness in simple bargaining experiments. *Games and Economic Behavior*, 6(3), 347–369.
Frank, R. H. (1985). The demand for unobservable and other nonpositional goods. *American Economic Review*, 75(1), 101–116.
Gneezy, U. & Rustichini, A. (2000). A fine is a price. *Journal of Legal Studies*, 29, 1–17.
Güth, W., Schmittberger, R. & Schwarze, B. (1982). An experimental analysis of ultimatum bargaining. *Journal of Economic Behavior & Organization*, 3(4), 367–388.
Ireland, N. J. (1994). On limiting the market for status signals. *Journal of Public Economics*, 53, 91–110.
Ito, K. (2014). Do consumers respond to marginal or average price? Evidence from nonlinear electricity pricing. *American Economic Review*, 104(2), 537–563.
Jensen, R. T. & Miller, N. H. (2008). Giffen behavior and subsistence consumption. *American Economic Review*, 98(4), 1553–1577.
Kahneman, D., Knetsch, J. & Thaler, R. (1986). Fairness as a constraint on profit seeking: Entitlements in the market. *American Economic Review*, 76, 728–741.
Korenok, O., Millner, E. L. & Razzolini, L. (2013). Taking, giving, and impure altruism in dictator games. *Experimental Economics*, 16, 1–13.
Leibenstein, H. (1950). Bandwagon, snob, and Veblen effects in the theory of consumers' demand. *Quarterly Journal of Economics*, 64, 183–207.
Moffatt, P. G. (2002). Is Giffen behaviour compatible with the axioms of consumer theory? *Journal of Mathematical Economics*, 37, 259–267.
Rabin, M. (1993). Incorporating fairness into game theory and economics. *American Economic Review*, 83(5), 1281–1302.
Rosen, S. (1999). Potato paradoxes. *Journal of Political Economy*, 107(6), S294–S313.
Saha, B. (2019). Household self-employment eliminates child labour. In S. Bandyopadhyay & M. Dutta (Eds.), *Opportunities and Challenges in Development: Essays for Sarmila Banerjee*, 357–366. New Delhi: Springer Verlag. DOI: 10.1007/978-981-13-9981-7.
Sen, A. K. (1977). Rational fools: A critique of the behavioral foundations of economic theory. *Philosophy & Public Affairs*, 6(4), 317–344.
Sugden, R. (1984). Reciprocity: The supply of public goods through voluntary contributions. *Economic Journal*, 94, 772–787.
Thaler, R. (1980). Towards a positive theory of consumer choice. *Journal of Economic Behavior & Organization*, 1(1), 39–60.
Tversky, A. & Kahneman, D. (1974). Judgment under uncertainty: Heuristics and biases. *Science*, 186, 1124–1131.
van Damme, E., Binmore, K. G., Roth, A. E., Samuelson, L., Winter, E., Bolton, G. E., Ockenfels, A., Dufwenberg, M., Kirchsteiger, G., Gneezy, U., Kocher, M. G., Sutter, M., Sanfey, A. G., Kliemt, H., Selten, R., Nagel, R. & Azar, O. H. (2014). How Warner Guth's ultimatum game shaped our understanding of social behavior. *Journal of Economic Behavior & Organization*, 108, 292–318.

Chapter 6

General equilibrium of an exchange economy

Abstract

General equilibrium theory concerns simultaneous price determination in all markets, which we refer to as the competitive equilibrium of an economy. There are three issues central to competitive equilibrium—its existence, uniqueness and stability. We study these issues assuming a pure endowment–exchange economy, whereby all goods are given as private endowments and no production is undertaken. We then study the welfare properties of general equilibrium. Two welfare theorems are discussed using the notion of Pareto efficiency. An alternative approach of social welfare maximisation is also considered to evaluate competitive equilibrium. Finally, we discuss the concept of core and its relation to competitive equilibrium.

Keywords: Competitive equilibrium, Edgeworth box, Tatonnment, Exchange, Welfare theorem, Pareto efficiency, Core

6.1 Introduction

According to economic historian Eyup Ozveren (2007), the classic *Thousand and One Nights* is not only a folktale of stories told and retold by countless Middle Age travellers and merchants drawn from a vast geography—from China to Morocco—but also a classic story of rivalry between the two major trading cities of the time, Cairo and Baghdad. The fortunes of the cities and even empires rose and fell with trade, as was the case with Cairo, which triumphed over Baghdad in the thirteenth century because of its better access to sea routes. On land, the 6453-km-long ancient Silk Road sustained the global commerce of silk, tea, porcelain, gems and spices from the East and horses, glassware, textiles and manufactured goods from the West for a period of 1500 years until 1435 CE. It is because of global trade that nutmeg from the Banda islands in Indonesia became a sought-after spice in medieval Europe, the potato travelled from South America to Ireland and Indian black pepper became a culinary essential in the rest of the world.

Trade has always been important to mankind—between nations, communities and individuals. The basic principle that in order to buy something one must sell something else has remained unchanged. In modern society, money has liberated us from conducting buying and selling at the same time and at the same place. But participation in multiple markets in opposite roles has remained essential, and therefore, studying multiple markets in tandem is important. This is what the theory of general equilibrium is all about. In this chapter, we discuss a basic version of the general equilibrium theory that saw an explosion of intellectual contributions between 1950 and 1980 led by Kenneth Arrow and Gerard Debreu. The origin of the theory is attributed to late nineteenth-century economists Francis Edgeworth and Leon Walras.

DOI: 10.4324/9781003226994-6

In the previous chapters, prices were assumed to be exogenous. But prices are determined in the marketplace by forces of demand and supply, with the participation of innumerable consumers and suppliers. Consumers pay for one good, by selling another good, for example, labour by a worker or harvest of apples by an apple grower. This conceptualisation of trade forces us to think of an economy as a cluster of interdependent markets, each of which can be described by a pair of demand and supply curves, and by studying their equilibrium in all markets simultaneously, we will be able to understand the functioning of the whole economy.

A crucial assumption in the general equilibrium theory is the **price-taking behaviour** by all participants. This means that all agents must think that they cannot unilaterally influence the price. They will make their decisions as if the prices are exogenous constraints (as assumed in Chapters 3 and 4). Their decisions—supply or demand—will respond to price changes, but their unilateral decisions will not change the price, nor will they engage with fellow consumers to alter the price. This is equivalent to saying that competition is so intense on either side of each and every market that there is no room for bargaining over price. We call such a situation *perfect competition*. The price-taking behaviour on everybody's part is the bedrock of perfect competition.

As the first step to studying general equilibrium, we will assume that agents trade based on an exogenous endowment of goods. There is no production. The issue of trade based on production is briefly taken up in a later chapter after we introduce technology and the theory of the firm.

6.2 Pure exchange and the Edgeworth box economy

Suppose there are two consumers/agents, A and B. Each is born with an endowment of two goods $\omega_i = (\omega_{1i}, \omega_{2i}), i = A, B, \omega_A \neq \omega_B$ and $\omega_i \geq 0$. This means that they have strictly positive endowment of at least one good. They have no cash. In this two-person economy, the total supply of good 1 is $\omega_{1A} + \omega_{1B} = \bar{x}_1$, and the same of good 2 is $\omega_{2A} + \omega_{2B} = \bar{x}_2$. Agent i's budget constraint is

$$p_1 x_{1i} + p_2 x_{2i} = p_1 \omega_{1i} + p_2 \omega_{2i} \left(\equiv M_i\right). \tag{6.1}$$

Their preferences over the two goods are given by a pair of quasi-concave utility functions, $u_i = u(x_1, x_2), i = A, B$. Above all, they are price takers. These three specifications, namely, their endowments, their preferences and their price-taking behaviour, completely describe our economy.

6.2.1 An example with the Cobb–Douglas preference

For the sake of concreteness, assume the preferences are of the Cobb–Douglas variety:

$$u^i = x_{1i}^{\alpha_i} x_{2i}^{(1-\alpha_i)}, \quad i = A, B. \tag{6.2}$$

Agent i maximises (6.2) subject to (6.1). Recall our utility maximisation problem learnt in Chapter 3. Demands for goods 1 and 2 of individual i are as follows:

$$x_{1i}(p_1, p_2) = \alpha_i \frac{p_1 \omega_{1i} + p_2 \omega_{2i}}{p_1}, \qquad x_{2i}(p_1, p_2) = (1 - \alpha_i) \frac{p_1 \omega_{1i} + p_2 \omega_{2i}}{p_2}. \tag{6.3}$$

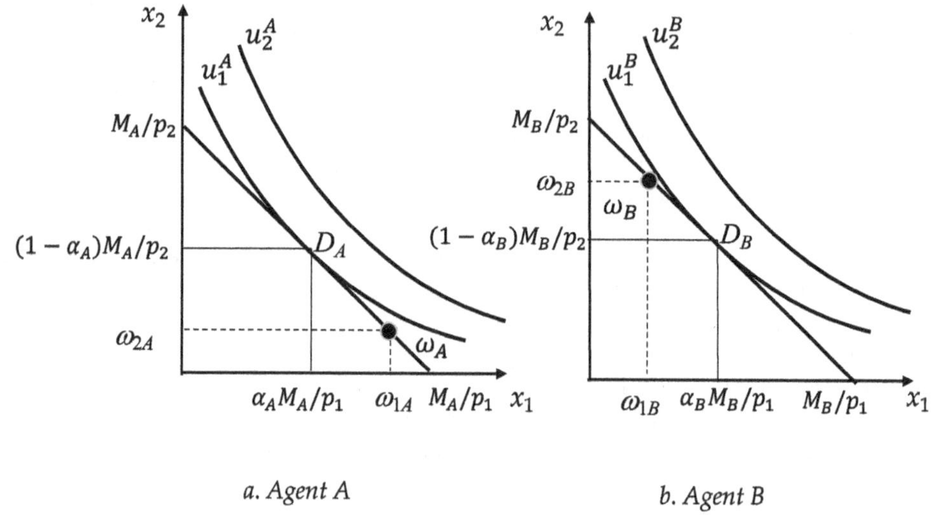

Figure 6.1 Demands and endowments

Straight away we should note that the Marshallian demand functions here are homogeneous of degree zero in prices (and not prices and income). Remember now that we are in a world where income is endogenous via the valuation of the endowment. Therefore, increasing all prices means that income is increased. In this chapter, whenever we refer to homogeneity of demand, we would mean homogeneity of degree zero (only) in prices.

In Figure 6.1, we present the agents' utility maximisation problem and their Marshallian demand curves. The graphs have been drawn in reference to the Cobb–Douglas preference assumed earlier, but that is just illustrative; they apply to general preferences as well. In the left panel, agent A's problem is shown, and in the right panel agent, B's problem is shown. Their respective endowment points are ω_A and ω_B. The sole purpose of trade is to consume at a point different to own endowment point. At an arbitrary price pair (p_1, p_2) (taken by them as given), we draw their budget lines, which must pass through their endowment point because they have the choice of 'buying their own endowment bundle from themselves'. But it is more interesting to consider the case in which they want to consume a different bundle, say, D_A and D_B. It is important not to overlook the simple fact that for D_A and D_B to be different, we need some difference between the two individuals—either in preference or in endowment or both.

To illustrate the scope for trade, without loss of generality, we have placed D_A on the left of ω_A and D_B on the right of ω_B. That is, for agent A, $x_{1A}(p_1, p_2) < \omega_{1A}$; she wishes to consume less of good 1 in reference to what she has. By the implication of her budget constraint, she must have $x_{2A}(p_1, p_2) > \omega_{2A}$. That means, she must consume good 2 in excess of what she has. In other words, if she is a net consumer of good 2, then she must be a net supplier of good 1. But where can she find the extra amount of good 2, and how does she pay for it? The answer lies in the right panel and, to be more precise, in the position of point D_B vis-à-vis ω_B. As shown in the figure, B is a net buyer of good 1 ($x_{1B}(p_1, p_2) > \omega_{1B}$). Then A can approach B to sell the amount of her good 1 endowment that she does not want to consume and, in return, buy some good 2. If these two offers match, then both can shift their consumption points to D_A and D_B from their respective endowment points. If they do, we will say that the economy is in *equilibrium*. As you may expect, equilibrium will depend on what prices they base their demands on.

The fact that the agents experience excess demand for one good and excess supply for the other good makes the two markets mutually interdependent. The two markets can reach equilibrium only in unison. This is a straightforward implication of budget balancing by all individuals, and there are only two goods. In the general n-good case, ensuring $n-1$ markets to be in equilibrium ensures that the remaining nth market must be in equilibrium. This is called Walras law. Focusing, without loss of generality, on the good 1 market, we can write the equilibrium condition as the supply of good 1 by individual A matching the demand for good 1 by individual B:

$$\omega_{1A} - \alpha_A \frac{p_1\omega_{1A} + p_2\omega_{2A}}{p_1} = \alpha_B \frac{p_1\omega_{1B} + p_2\omega_{2B}}{p_1} - \omega_{1B}. \tag{6.4}$$

The next question is, What will be the right price to buy and sell at? We need to solve Eq. (6.4) in terms of p_1 and p_2. But there is only one equation in two unknowns. So we set one price, say, $p_2 = 1$, and solve for p_1 or, equivalently, the relative price of good 1, p_1 / p_2. This also means that we are treating good 2 as a *numeraire* good (or money). Thus, we solve for the competitive equilibrium (relative) price as

$$p_1^* = \frac{\alpha_A\omega_{2A} + \alpha_B\omega_{2B}}{(1-\alpha_A)\omega_{1A} + (1-\alpha_B)\omega_{1B}}.$$

In the next three figures, we illustrate our competitive equilibrium with the help of an Edgeworth box, which is a graphical technique of combining two panels of Figure 6.1 into one (with panel b flipped sideways and upside down). The dimension of the Edgeworth box on each side as shown in Figure 6.2 is given by the total availability of each good, $\bar{x}_1$ and $\bar{x}_2$. We measure agent A's consumption and endowment starting from the bottom-left corner (going north-east), and agent B's consumption and endowment from the top-right corner (by coming down south-west). Then both agents' endowments can be simultaneously shown by a point inside the box, such as $\omega = \{(\omega_{1A}, \omega_{2A}), (\omega_{1B}, \omega_{2B})\}$. A point inside the box corresponds to a

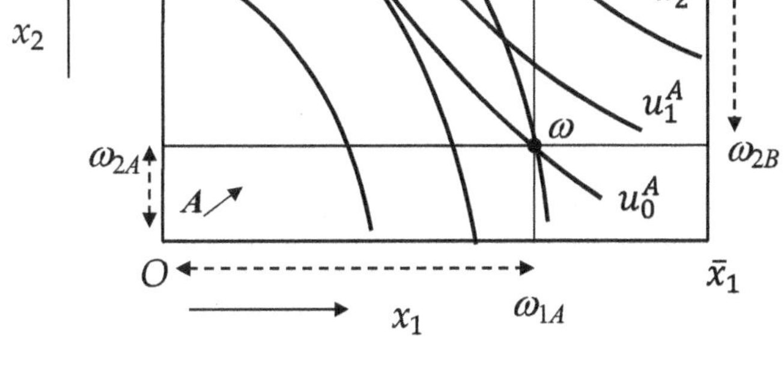

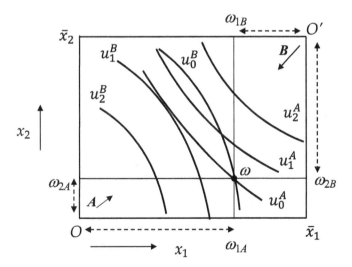

Figure 6.2 Edgeworth box

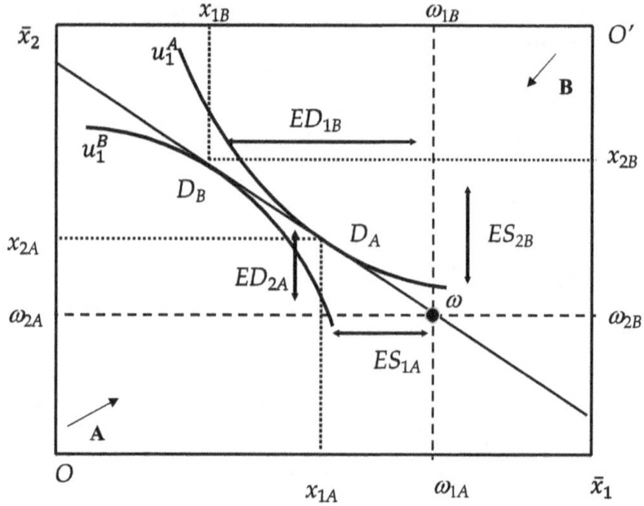

Figure 6.3 State of disequilibrium

particular allocation of the two goods between two agents. We also draw the indifference curves of the two agents, such as u_0^A, u_1^A and u_2^A for A and u_0^B, u_1^B and u_2^B for B. Of these, u_0^A and u_0^B pass through the endowment point implying that the agent A can enjoy at least u_0^A and agent B at least u_0^B without engaging in trade. But, of course, with trade they will be better off, as they move forward from their endowment points.

In Figure 6.3, we show a state of disequilibirum or scope for trade. At a given (arbitrary) price pair, agent A is a net supplier of good 1, and agent B is the net consumer of good 1. But the amount of good 1 agent A wants to supply (at the price assumed), ES_{1A}, is less than the amount of good 1 agent B wants to buy, ED_{1B}. Equivalently, the amount of good 2 agent A wants to buy is too little compared to what agent B wants to sell.

Clearly, the price is not right. In response to the excess demand for good 1 its price should rise, or equivalently the excess supply of good 2 should dampen the price of good 2. In relative terms, the price of good 1 must rise to clear the market. Figure 6.4 shows competitive equilibrium, where the excess demand for good 1 from A exactly matches the excess supply of good 1 from B; a similar match occurs with good 2. The solid budget line that passes through the endowment point has a slope exactly equal to the equilibrium price p_1^* as derived in Eq. (6.5). Agents' consumption bundles D_A and D_B fall on the same budget line and tangent to the respective agent's indifference curve. An alternative graphical way of presenting the competitive equilibrium is to show it as an intersection point of two *offer curves*. An offer curve is the price-consumption path of an agent—the graph of her optimal choices in response to price changes.

6.2.1.1 *Properties*

We can make several observations on the competitive equilibrium price, based on the earlier Cobb–Douglas example, most of which are more general:

1. **Replication neutrality.** If the economy is replicated by multiplying the number of both type A and type B agents k times with the same preference and endowments, the competitive equilibrium price will not change.

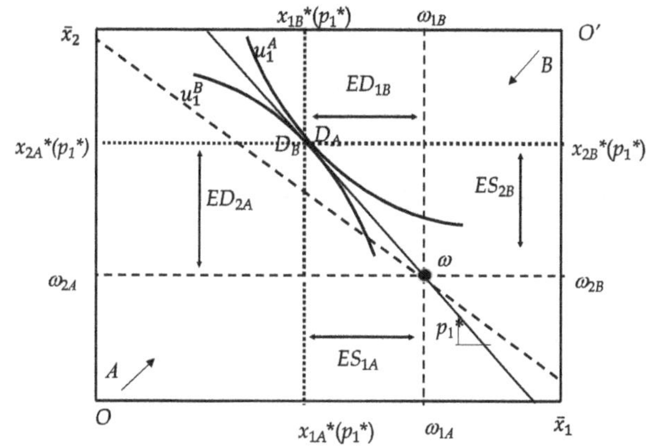

Figure 6.4 Competitive equilibrium

2. **Abundant goods are cheaper.** If ω_{1A} or ω_{1B} increases, the equilibrium price p_1^* will fall; conversely, an increase in ω_{2A} or ω_{2B} will raise p_1^*.
3. **More preferred goods are dearer.** If the consumer's relative preference for x_1 increases, p_1^* will increase.
4. **Homothetic preference.** If consumers' preferences are homothetic, the following would be true:

   a. **Homogeneity in endowments.** The equilibrium price is homogeneous of degree zero in endowments (ω_A, ω_B).
   b. **Independence of distribution of endowments.** If preferences are identical (but endowments differ) and there are only two goods, then the equilibrium price will be an increasing function of the ratio of the two aggregate endowments, $\frac{\bar{x}_2}{\bar{x}_1}$. More precisely, we can write $p_1^* = f\left(\frac{\bar{x}_2}{\bar{x}_1}\right)$, with $f'(.) > 0$.

The first property is very general. If we multiply the number of agents k times both for type A and type B along with their endowments, then in Eq. (6.4), each term is multiplied by n on both sides. Hence, the solution does not change. This will be true regardless of the preferences. The second and third properties are also general. If the total endowment of a good increases, its price should fall. Similarly, if there is a shift of preference in favour of a good, its price should rise.

With homothetic preference, as illustrated by the Cobb–Douglas case, the equilibrium price will remain unchanged if everybody's endowment is doubled, leaving the distribution of endowments unchanged. Furthermore, if individuals have identical preferences, the competitive equilibrium will depend on the ratio of the aggregate endowments of the two goods; the distribution of endowments does not matter.

The preceding claim can be easily proved. Recall from Chapter 3 that homothetic preference means that if bundle x is indifferent to bundle y, then λx is also indifferent to λy, where $\lambda > 0$ is a scalar. Individual demand curves are linear in individual income. For an n-good and I-agent economy, the individual i's demand for good j at a price vector $p = (p_1, p_2, \dots p_n)$ is of the form $x_{ji} = a_{ij}(p) M_i(p)$, where $a_{ij}(p)$ is a function of p involving preference parameters of individual i and $M_i(p) = \sum_j p_j \omega_{ji}$.

The aggregate demand for good *j* is

$$\sum_{i=1}^{I} x_{ij}(p) = \sum_{i=1}^{I} a_{ji}(p) M_i(p) = \sum_{i=1}^{I} a_{ji}(p) \left[\sum_{j=1}^{n} p_j \omega_{ji} \right], \quad j = 1, 2, \ldots, n,$$

and the excess (market) demand for good *j* (summing over *i*) is

$$Z_j = \sum_{i=1}^{I} x_{ij}(p) - \sum_{i=1}^{I} \omega_{ji} = \sum_{i=1}^{I} \left[a_{ji}(p) \left\{ \sum_{j=1}^{n} p_j \omega_{ji} \right\} \right] - \bar{x}_j, \text{for every } j = 1, 2, \ldots, n.$$

At equilibrium, we must have

$$\sum_{i=1}^{I} \left[a_{ji}(p) \left\{ \sum_{j=1}^{n} p_j \omega_{ji} \right\} \right] - \bar{x}_j = 0, \quad \text{for every } j = 1, 2, \ldots, n.$$

Now let us increase endowments of all goods of all individuals by λ times. The above equation then becomes

$$\sum_{i=1}^{I} \left[a_{ji}(p) \left\{ \sum_{j=1}^{n} p_j \lambda \omega_{ji} \right\} \right] - \lambda \bar{x}_j = 0, \quad \text{for every } j = 1, 2, \ldots, n,$$

$$\text{or,} \quad \lambda \left(\sum_{i=1}^{I} \left[a_{ji}(p) \left\{ \sum_{j=1}^{n} p_j \omega_{ji} \right\} \right] - \bar{x}_j \right) = 0, \quad \text{for every } j = 1, 2, \ldots, n.$$

Clearly, the equilibrium price vector does not change. Thus, for homothetic preferences competitive equilibrium is homogeneous of degree zero in endowments.

Next, assume $n = I = 2$ and preferences to be identical, which means $a_{jA} = a_{jB}$. With $p_2 = 1$, we set the excess demand for good 1 to be zero to write

$$a_1(p_1)\bar{x}_2 = (1 - p_1 a_1(p_1))\bar{x}_1, \quad \text{or,} \quad \frac{1 - p_1 a_1(p_1)}{a_1(p_1)} = \frac{\bar{x}_2}{\bar{x}_1}.$$

A solution to this equation is $p_1^* = f(\bar{x}_2 / \bar{x}_1)$, a function of the ratio of total endowments.

6.2.2 *Example: quasi-linear preference*

Now consider a different preference. Suppose two agents are identical in preference but have different endowments. Assume their preferences are quasi-linear (which is not homothetic): $u = x_2 + 2\sqrt{x_1}$. Setting $p_2 = 1$ and maximising u subject to $p_1 x_{1i} + x_{2i} = p_1 \omega_{1i} + \omega_{2i}$, we derive the demand functions of agent *i* as

$$x_{1i} = \begin{cases} 1/p_1^2 & \text{if} \quad p_1 \omega_{1i} + \omega_{2i} \geq \dfrac{1}{p_1} \\ \omega_{1i} + \dfrac{\omega_{2i}}{p_1} & \text{otherwise} \end{cases},$$

and

$$x_{2i} = \begin{cases} \dfrac{p_1^2\omega_{1i} + p_1\omega_{2i} - 1}{p_1} & \text{if} \quad p_1\omega_{1i} + \omega_{2i} > \dfrac{1}{p_1} \\ 0 & \text{otherwise} \end{cases}.$$

The demand functions recognise the fact that the consumption of x_2 is positive only when the consumption of x_1 is met at its optimal level $1/p_1^2$. The competitive equilibrium is simply obtained from $2/p_1^2 = \bar{x}_1$ as $p_1^* = \sqrt{2/\bar{x}_1}$. Both agents consume the same amount of x_1 regardless of their endowment differences (because of their identical preferences). This means that the total endowment of good 1 is just divided equally between the two. Then depending on their individual budgets, they may have a positive consumption of x_2.

In Figure 6.5, we present the equilibrium for quasi-linear preference. In panel *a*, agents consume both goods. Agent *A*'s consumption path is *OCG*, while agent *B*'s consumption path is *O'GC*. Both agents must consume in equilibrium $\bar{x}_1/2$ (due to identical preference). So the competitive equilibrium must lie between *C* and *G* on the line *CG*. If the endowment point ω is to the right of the *CG* line, as shown in panel *a*, then agent *A* must sell $\omega_{1A} - \dfrac{\bar{x}}{2}$ to agent *B* and, in return, buy $x_{2A} - \omega_{2A}$. The equilibrium price p_1^* is the slope of the budget line passing through the endowment point.

In panel *b*, we show two possible corner solutions. In one, equilibrium is at point *C*, when the endowment point is to the left of $\bar{x}_1/2$. Here, agent *A* is not consuming x_2. She sells her entire endowment of x_2 to buy $\bar{x}_1/2 - \omega_{1A}$ of x_1. Agent *B* consumes both goods; in fact, she consumes the entire endowment of x_2. This possibility arises if agent *A*'s budget is balanced with $x_2 = 0$:

$$p_1^*\omega_{1A} + \omega_{2A} = p_1^* x_1^* \rightarrow \frac{\sqrt{2}}{\sqrt{\bar{x}_1}}\omega_{1A} + \omega_{2A} = \frac{\sqrt{\bar{x}_1}}{\sqrt{2}}.$$

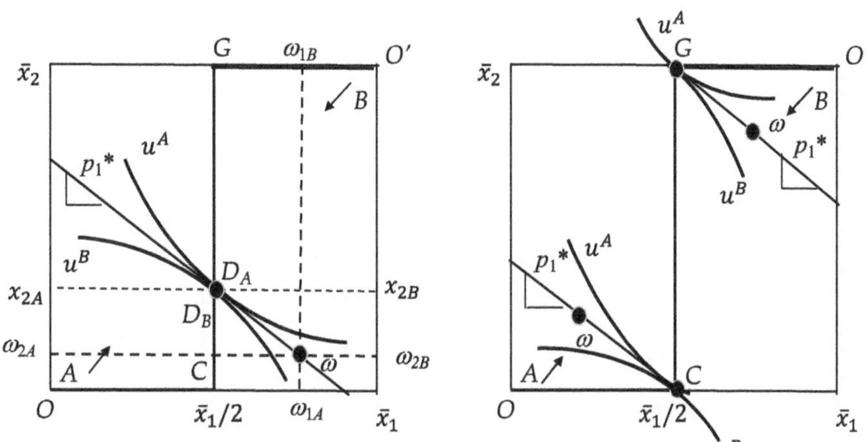

a

a. *Positive consumption of both goods* b. *Zero consumption of* x_2

Figure 6.5 Equilibrium under quasi-linear preference

The other corner equilibrium is point G, when the endowment point is to the right of $\bar{x}_1/2$. Agent B does not consume x_2 now. This possibility arises if

$$p_1^*\omega_{1B} + \omega_{2B} = p_1^* x_1^* \rightarrow \frac{\sqrt{2}}{\sqrt{\bar{x}_1}}\omega_{1B} + \omega_{2B} = \frac{\sqrt{\bar{x}_1}}{\sqrt{2}}.$$

Note that since p_1^* does not depend on the distribution of endowment, the budget lines are always parallel to each other regardless of where ω is.

6.3 Theory: existence, uniqueness and stability of general equilibrium

Now we consider a more general version of the pure exchange–endowment model and examine the predictive power of the general equilibrium theory. Three issues are central: existence, uniqueness and stability of general equilibrium. Before we get to the theory, let us motivate our discussion by considering three graphs in Figure 6.6. We draw three very different types of preferences. The first graph (panel *a*) presents a case in which agent A has a non-convex preference. A non-convex preference implies preferring extremes to their averages; her consumption will register discrete jumps from a small price change. The Edgeworth box diagram shows that this economy does not have a competitive equilibrium. The budget line that passes through the endowment point ω is tangent to the indifference curves of the two agents at different points. While agent A maximises her utility at two points D and E, agent B maximises her utility at point C. But because C is different from D and E, the supply and demand of the two goods do not match. Therefore, there is no equilibrium. Clearly, the consumers cannot trade. They must consume their own endowment.

The second problem we need to be concerned with is the multiplicity of equilibrium. Panel *b* presents a case in which both agents have convex, but not strictly convex, preferences. The budget line that passes through ω is tangent to both agents' indifference curves at infinitely many points between C and D. Here, although the equilibrium price is unique, the vectors of equilibrium allocations (x_1, x_2) are infinitely many. Here, we are unable to predict what consumption the agents should undertake. Thus, we have a multiplicity of allocations. This is due to the perfect substitutability of the two goods in the consumers' preferences. However, we

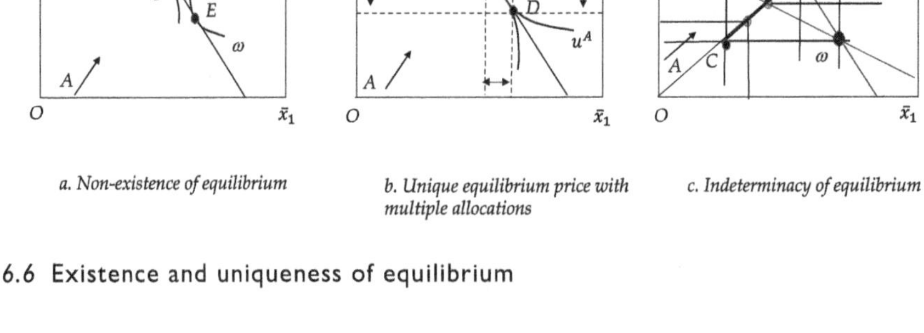

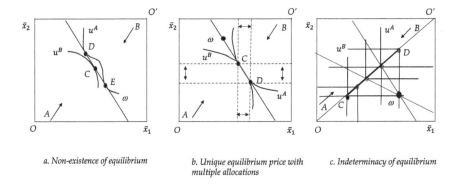

a. Non-existence of equilibrium

b. Unique equilibrium price with multiple allocations

c. Indeterminacy of equilibrium

Figure 6.6 Existence and uniqueness of equilibrium

shall see that the multiplicity of equilibrium prices is a bigger problem than the multiplicity of allocations.

Panel *c* shows an interesting case, in which both agents have identical Leontief preference, which is weakly monotonic and convex but not strictly convex. Their L-shaped indifference curves touch each other at the optimal proportion that the goods should be consumed. Recall that the notion of MRS does not apply here. Consequently, there are many budget lines that can pass through the endowment point and the optimal proportion of the two goods. We have drawn two such budget lines either of which will clear the market. In fact, any budget line (and there are infinitely many) that passes through ω and the line *CD* gives an equilibrium price. Clearly, the equilibrium price is indeterminate and any combination of x_1 and x_2 on the line segment *CD* is market-clearing.

Compare Figure 6.6 with Figure 6.5. The quasi-linear preference on which Figure 6.5 is based is strongly monotonic and strictly convex. This gives us some clues about the existence and uniqueness in the general case. However, we should not conclude from Figure 6.6 that weak monotonicity or weak convexity (or even non-convexity) rules out competitive equilibrium altogether. Some exercises at the end of the chapter will help you understand this point. All we are saying is that in these cases, existence or uniqueness is not guaranteed.

6.3.1 *Existence of equilibrium*

A presentation of the existence theorem requires introducing some further notations and definitions. Suppose there are n goods and I consumers. Every consumer has a positive endowment of at least one good; that is, $\omega_i = (\omega_{1i}, \omega_{2i}, \ldots, \omega_{ni}) \geq 0$. Consequently, the aggregate endowment vector of the economy $\omega = (\overline{x}_1, \overline{x}_2, \ldots, \overline{x}_n)$ is strictly positive, where $\overline{x}_j = \sum_{i=1}^{I} \omega_{ji}$.

First, we define a feasible allocation of goods, which is essentially any bundle that is available to this economy.

Definition 5. *An* ***allocation*** *is a collection of consumption vectors assigned to* I *consumers, which is denoted as* $x = (x_1, x_2, \ldots, x_I) \in X \subset R_+^n$, *where* $x_i = (x_{1i}, x_{2i}, \ldots, x_{ni})$. *An allocation is* ***feasible*** *if for every good* $j = 1, 2, .., n$, $x_{j1} + x_{j2} + \ldots + x_{jI} \leq \overline{x}_j$.

Now consider the consumers' preferences. Assume each consumer's preference to be continuous, strictly convex and locally non-satiated. We should recall from Chapter 2 that preference is locally non-satiated when there is always a sufficiently close bundle that increases the consumer's utility. Preferences that are monotonic (strong or weak) satisfy local non-satiation; in general, non-satiation means the consumer may not increase consumption of some goods because they do not add to their utility.[1] Under this assumption the formal theory of general equilibrium is presented without much complication. We take up the case of strong monotonicity, which is more familiar to us, later.

We first define individual demand functions, from which by aggregation we can derive aggregate demand for any good j and then subtract from it the total endowment of good j to get its excess demand. Note that due to the strong convexity of preferences, we get unique demand at any price vector, and it is also continuous because preferences are continuous. The excess demand functions inherit the homogeneity of degree zero (in prices) property from the demand functions. They also have a negative lower bound, meaning that an excess supply of a good cannot exceed its total endowment. The excess demand functions always satisfy the Walras law at any price, which means the sum of the value of all excess demands must be zero.

Definition 6. *A feasible allocation* $x_i^*(p)$ *is called Marshallian/Walrasian* ***demand*** *vector of consumer* i *at a price vector* $p=(p_1,p_2,\ldots,p_n)$, *if* x_i^* *maximises* $u_i(x_i)$ *subject to the constraint* $\sum_{j=1}^{n} p_j x_{ji} = \sum_{j=1}^{n} p_j \omega_{ji}$. *Note,* $x_{ji}^*(p)$ *must be homogeneous of degree zero in prices for every* j *and* i.

Definition 7. *A vector* $(z_{1i}(p), z_{2i}(p),\ldots,z_{ni}(p))$ *defined over all price vectors* $p \geq 0$ *is called the* ***excess demand*** *vector of consumer* i, *where* $z_{ji}=x_{ji}^*(p)-\omega_{ji}$. *Since every* x_{ji}^* *satisfies the budget constraint of every consumer* i, *the excess demand vector must contain both positive and negative elements. The aggregate excess demand for good* $j, z_j(p_1,p_2,\ldots,p_n)=\sum_{i=1}^{I}\left[x_{ji}(p_1,p_2,\ldots,p_n)-\omega_{ji}\right]$ *is also homogeneous of degree zero in all prices for every good* j *and it has a negative lower bound for every good* j *and all* $p \geq 0$, *which is* $-\bar{x}_j$.

Definition 8. Walras law *The sum of the value of all excess demands must be equal to zero at any price:* $\sum_{j=1}^{n} p_j z_j(p_1,p_2,\ldots,p_n)=0$. *This is implied by consumers' balanced budgets.*

A small but important point to note is that we have defined our excess demand function with respect to non-negative price vectors. That means some prices can be zero. This is a direct implication of the assumption of local non-satiation. If consumers are satiated with respect to some good or if a good is bad, the consumers will not increase their consumption even if its price falls to zero. Therefore, zero price is consistent only with the good not being demanded or desirable, leaving the market of that good in excess supply. We call such goods **free goods**.[2] Competitive equilibrium, as we define next, allows the presence of free goods and thus permits non-clearance of the market of these goods; the market clears only for goods that are desirable, and prices of the desirable goods must be strictly positive.

Definition 9. Competitive equilibrium *Suppose preferences are continuous, strictly convex and locally non-satiated, and all agents' endowments are non-negative. A non-negative price vector* $p^*=(p_1^*,p_2^*,\ldots,p_n^*)$ *and an associated Marshallian/Walrasian demand vector of* I *consumers* $x^*=(x_1(p^*),x_2(p^*),\ldots,x_I(p^*))$ *constitute the* ***competitive (or Walrasian) equilibrium*** *of this* n-*good* I-*agent economy if and only if the excess demand for every good is non-positive, that is,* $z_j(p^*) \leq 0$ *for every* $j=1,2,\ldots,n$.

Definition 10. *Suppose* $p^* \geq 0$ *is a competitive equilibrium and* $z_j(p^*)<0$, *that is, good* j *is in excess supply in equilibrium, then* $p_j^*=0$ *and good* j *must be a* ***free good***.

Now we state our existence theorem. Under non-satiation barring the markets of free goods, all markets clear resulting in strictly positive prices and a positive allocation. It is reassuring that other than very general assumptions on preferences and (private) ownership of endowments, no onerous condition is needed to guarantee that people will be able to voluntarily trade among themselves and be strictly better off than consuming their own endowments.

Theorem 2. *Suppose for every consumer* i, *preference is continuous, strictly convex and locally non-satiated, and their endowments are non-negative. Then there exists a competitive equilibrium* $(p^*, x(p^*))$ *with* $p^* \geq 0$.

The proof of the theorem is straightforward, but for its length, it is placed in Section 6.8. Here, we discuss the proof informally. The key requirement of the proof is to show that a system of n simultaneous equations of market clearing has a solution. The solution gives p^*, which in turn gives the allocation $x(p^*)$. The most common method of showing that a solution exists is to invoke **Brouwer's fixed-point theorem**, which says that if a continuous function (or a vector of functions) $g(p)$ maps a convex, closed and bounded set to itself, then there is a point p such that $g(p)=p$. For a vector of functions, $g_1(p)=p_1, g_2(p)=p_2,\ldots$ and so on. Our excess demand functions and prices do not meet these conditions directly, but with a slight adjustment, they will.[3]

Suppose that, instead of setting a good to be numeraire we write $p_1+p_2\ldots+p_n=1$, a slightly different normalisation. Then our prices are taken from a set, called **unit simplex**, that is convex, closed and bounded. Next, we need to define the fixed-point map as a vector of functions $g(p)=(g_1(p), g_2(p),\ldots,g_n(p))$, which need to be a convenient conversion of the excess demand functions in such a manner that each function $g_j(p)$ will be a non-negative number between 0 and 1. That is, $g(p)$ also belongs to the unit simplex. Then by Brouwer's fixed-point theorem we will get $g(p)=p$, and the construction of $g(p)$ is such that $g(p)=p$ will occur whenever the excess demands for all goods are zero.

As an illustration, for the two-good case the following is an example of $g_1(p)$:

$$g_1(p)=\frac{p_1+\max(0,z_1(p))}{1+\max(0,z_1(p)+\max(0,z_2(p))}$$

where $z_1(.)$ and $z_2(.)$ are the excess demand functions. Similarly, $g_2(p)$ can be defined. Note that although $z_1(.)$ or $z_2(.)$ can be negative, the fixed-point function $g_1(.)$ or $g_2(.)$ will remain non-negative and strictly less than 1. Thus, they become amenable to the fixed-point theorem.

Figure 6.7 illustrates the two-good case. We have a 1 × 1 box. On the horizontal axis, we measure p_1 going from left and p_2 going from right to left. By construction $p_2=1-p_1$. The function $g_1(.)$ is drawn against p_1, holding p_2 fixed at p_2^*, while $g_2(.)$ is drawn against p_2, holding p_1 at p_1^*. By construction, $g_2(.)=1-g_1(.)$. The fixed points are given by E and E', where $g_1(p_1)=p_1$ and $g_2(.)=p_2$ at p_1^* and p_2^*, respectively. Note that the fixed points must be aligned on the same vertical line as shown here; otherwise, they will not be the fixed points. If these two functions are continuous, then you can see that they must cross their respective 45-degree lines. That means, an equilibrium must exist. If $z_1(p_1^*)=0$ and $z_2(p_1^*,p_2^*)=0$, then clearly, we have $g_1(.)=p_1^*$ and $g_2(.)=p_2^*$.

An alternative way to present the graph of the equilibrium is to directly refer to the price and excess demand vectors along with the vector of the fixed-point functions, as shown in Figure 6.8. The first two graphs relate to the two-good case, and the third one to a three-good economy. In the case of two goods, the unit simplex is just the $p_1+p_2=1$ line. When there are three goods, as shown in panel *c*, the unit simplex is the entire triangle formed by points (1,0,0), (0,1,0) and (0,0,1).

Let us consider panel *a* to understand the geometry of the vector of functions $g(p)$. Take an arbitrary price vector $\left(\frac{1}{3},\frac{2}{3}\right)$ from the price simplex. Suppose that at this price, the excess demand vectors are $z(p)=\left(1,-\frac{1}{2}\right)$. Check that $pz(p)=\left(1\times\frac{1}{3}\right)-\left(\frac{1}{2}\times\frac{2}{3}\right)=0$. The excess demand vector is drawn as a perpendicular or orthogonal to the vector p. Then we can calculate $g_1(p)=\frac{p_1+\max(0,z_1(p))}{1+\max(0,z_1(p))+\max(0,z_2(p)}=\frac{\frac{1}{3}+1}{1+1}=\frac{2}{3}$ and $g_2(p)=\frac{\frac{2}{3}}{1+1}=\frac{1}{3}$. The vector

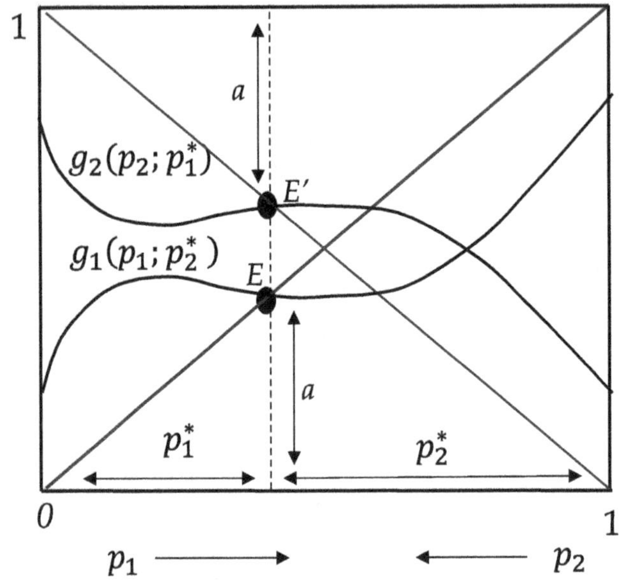

Figure 6.7 Equilibrium in a two-good model

$g(p) = (2/3, 1/3)$ falls on the vector $p + \max(0, z(p))$. As, $g_1(p) > p_1$ and $g_2(p) < p_2$, clearly p is not an equilibrium price. In panel *b*, the equilibrium price is shown, where $z(p^*) = (0,0)$ and $g(p^*) = p^*$.

In the two-good case, all prices must be strictly positive because trade must occur on both goods and no good can be free good. With three goods, the possibility of a free good emerges. In panel *c*, we show this possibility by selecting a point on the line that connects (1,0,0) and (0,1,0) as our equilibrium, so $p_3^* = 0$, which requires the excess demand for good 3 to be negative. The excess demand functions are shown by the orthogonal vector $(0, 0, -z_3(p^*))$.

You should note that several factors played important roles in Theorem 2. Refer to Figure 6.7. The fixed-point maps $g_1(p)$ and $g_2(p)$ are *functions* (and not correspondences) and they are continuous. Continuity is implied by the continuity of excess demand functions, which follow the continuity of preferences. That $g_1(p)$ and $g_2(p)$ are functions is ensured by the uniqueness of demand, which is guaranteed by the strict convexity of preferences. The existence theorem makes these two assumptions explicit. However, when we have more than two goods, the possibility of a free good, although a bit unrealistic, is admitted in equilibrium. This is a direct consequence of the assumption of non-satiated preferences. With non-satiation, the consumer can afford to not consume one good and increase the consumption of other goods to increase her utility. But non-satiation helps us present the proof in a simpler way by making use of the price simplex. Next, we replace the axiom of non-satiation with strong monotonicity and restate the existence theorem.

6.3.1.1 *Strongly monotonic preferences*

When preferences are strongly monotonic, no good will be a free good, so the equilibrium price for every good must be strictly positive. If the price of a good is sufficiently close to zero,

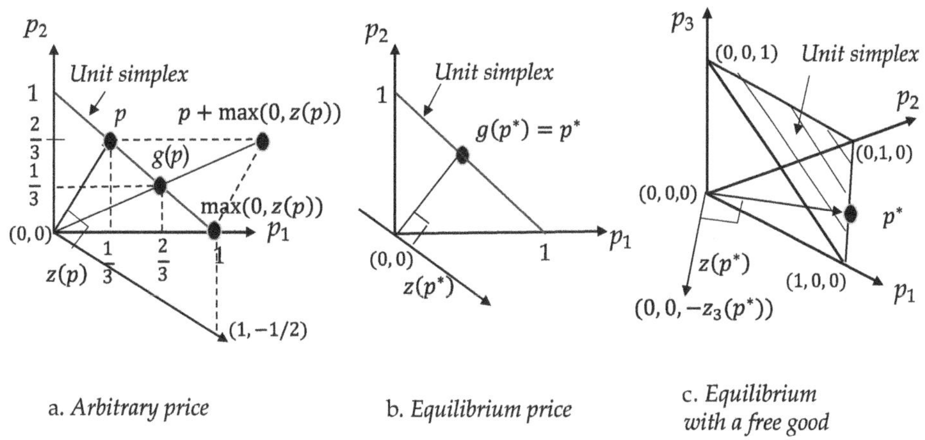

Figure 6.8 Fixed-point graphs

excess demand for that good will be infinitely large. This is stated in the form of Proposition 9 that follows. But proving the existence theorem in this case involves technical complications (for more than two goods). Nevertheless, the existence of a Walrasian equilibrium is guaranteed.

Proposition 9. *Suppose every consumer's preferences are continuous, strictly convex and strongly monotonic. Then the excess demand vector* $(z_{1i}(p), z_{2i}(p), \ldots, z_{ni}(p))$ *defined over all price vectors* $p > 0$ *is homogeneous of degree zero in all prices for every* j *and has a negative lower bound for every good* j *and all* $p > 0$. *Moreover, if a price sequence goes to* p, *which contains* $p_j = 0$ *for some* j, *then the excess demand for good* j *goes to infinity.*

Theorem 3. *Suppose for every consumer* i, *preference is continuous, strictly convex and strongly monotonic. Then there exists a competitive equilibrium* $(p^*, x(p^*))$, *where* $p^* > 0$ *and* $z_j(p^*) = 0$ *for every* $j = 1, 2, \ldots, n$.

The proof of Theorem 3 involves the construction of an upper hemi-continuous fixed-point correspondence and the use of the **Kauktani fixed-point theorem**, which is fit for dealing with correspondences. See Chapter 16 for fixed-point theorems. The issue of a fixed-point correspondence should not be mixed up with excess demand correspondence. The fixed-point correspondence is just a construction to prove the theorem with maximum ease.[4] The fixed-point correspondence needs to be convex-valued and upper hemi-continuous for the application of the Kakutani fixed-point theorem.[5] The formal proof of the theorem is advanced, and we skip it.[6]

Fortunately, the proof for the two-good case is straightforward. We do not need to invoke any fixed-point theorem. Let us revert to the earlier normalisation setting $p_2 = 1$ and restrict our attention to the excess demand for good 1 (because it is sufficient to do so by Walras law). As $p_1 \to 0$, we know that $z_1(p_1) \to \infty$ and that as $p_1 \to \infty$, $z_1(p_1) \to -\omega_1$. Since, $z_1(p_1)$ is continuous, by the intermediate value theorem, there must exist a price, p_1^*, such that $z_1(p_1^*) = 0$. That is precisely our equilibrium.

Next, we present some graphical examples in Figure 6.9 to understand how the existence of equilibrium is affected when we drop the axiom of strict convexity. Panel *a* presents an example where agent *A*'s indifference curves are not convex in the middle region, as a result of which agent *B*'s indifference curves are not tangent to them at the 'right' places. By 'right places', we mean the region through which their respective budget line will pass through.

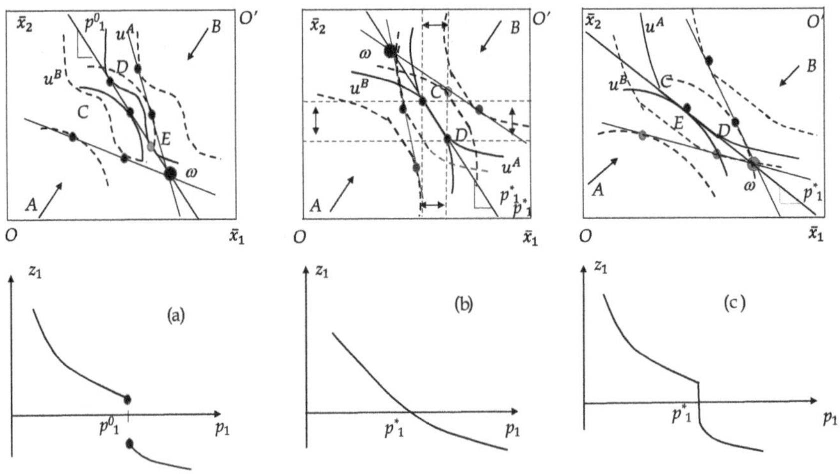

Figure 6.9 Excess demand correspondences and equilibrium

We have assumed $p_2 = 1$ and focus only on p_1. At price p_1^0, agent *B* has a unique optimal bundle *C* (because her preference is convex), while agent *A* has two optimal bundles, *D* and *E*. Compare *B*'s demands with her endowments; she wants to consume more of good 1 and less of good 2 than she has. So her excess demand is positive for good 1, and her excess demand for good 2 is negative. Agent *A* demands less of good 1 and more of good 2 than she has, at both demand points *D* and *E*. But her excess supply of good 1 is greater than *B*'s excess demand for good 1. So the aggregate excess demand for good 1 when bundles *C* and *D* are considered is strictly negative. In contrast, when *C* and *E* are considered *B*'s excess supply of good 1 is smaller than *B*'s excess demand for good 1. So the combined excess demand for good 1 is strictly positive. Thus, at p_1^0, there are two values of excess demand for good 1, z_1, which is shown in the bottom part of panel *a*.

The excess demand map z_1 is a correspondence, because of the two values, it takes at p_1^0. But there is gap between these two values, or put it correctly, the excess demand correspondence is not convex-valued. Therefore, there is no equilibrium. At other prices, $z_1(p)$ is either positive or negative. In the top part of panel *a*, we consider two other prices; the flatter budget line corresponds to a price lower than p_1^0, and the steeper budget line corresponds to a higher price. In both instances, agent *A*'s optimal bundle is unique. But compare them with agent *B*'s optimal bundle, and you can figure out that at $p_1 < p_1^0$, the aggregate excess demand for good 1 is strictly positive and that at $p_1 < p_1^0$, the aggregate excess demand is strictly negative, as shown in the bottom part of panel *a*.

Panel *c* reinstates convexity on agent *A*'s preference but only a weak convexity. As a result, at p_1^*, agent *A*'s demand bundles are infinitely many between points *C* and *D*, of which bundle *E* is common with *B*'s choice. By comparing *A*'s demands with *B*'s, we note that the excess demand for good 1 is now a convex-valued correspondence; note the solid vertical line of $z_1(p)$ at p_1^*. As it meets the conditions of Theorem 2, we have an equilibrium at p_1^*. You can easily check that excess demand for x_1 is strictly positive at $p_1 < p_1^*$ and strictly negative at $p_1 > p_1^*$.

Panel *b* reproduces the case of both agents having identical weakly convex preferences from Figure 6.6. Here, both agents demand infinitely many bundles between *C* and *D*, and their respective excess demand for one good perfectly matches the excess supply of that good. Although this is a perfect example of multiple equilibrium allocations, the equilibrium price is unique. This is shown in the bottom part, where the excess demand function is zero at a unique value of p_1.

You can try to draw the excess demand function of the third figure (panel *c*) of Figure 6.6. Here, $z_1(p_1)$ is a flat line on the horizontal axis, with $z_1(p_1) = 0$ at all prices. This is a case of infinitely many equilibria, a point to which we now turn our attention.

A final word of caution. The conditions specified in Theorems 2 or 3 are *sufficient* conditions but not necessary. This means that it is possible to obtain equilibrium by violating those conditions. For example, in panel *a* of Figure 6.8, we violated convexity in a convenient way to show non-existence. But one can tweak the example to place non-convexity in a region where the indifference curves are unlikely to be tangent to each other and show that an equilibrium exists. A key insight of the preceding discussion is that trade requires diversity, but the diversity has to be of the 'right' kind.

6.3.2 *Local uniqueness of equilibrium*

Uniqueness of equilibrium is a very desirable property, particularly for the purpose of prediction. It turns out that there is no guarantee that we will get a globally unique equilibrium. We have seen from Figure 6.6 panel *c* that equilibrium prices can be too many.

Since, in general, global uniqueness is hard to guarantee, we should look for local uniqueness. What we mean by 'local uniqueness' is that equilibrium points must be isolated when they are many. Each equilibrium must be distinct. In a mathematical sense, the number of equilibrium points must be finite. Consider the two graphs of excess demand function in Figure 6.10. The left one has three equilibria, and the right one has an infinite number. But you can see that if the excess demand function is not flat on the horizontal axis (as is the case with the right figure), we will have local uniqueness, which is ensured if $z'(p) \neq 0$. The following definition takes the first step in this direction when we generalise this idea.

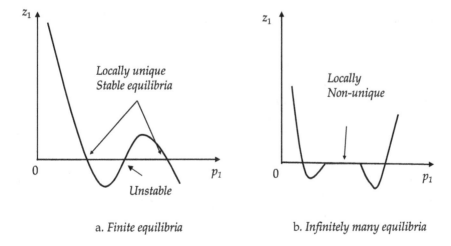

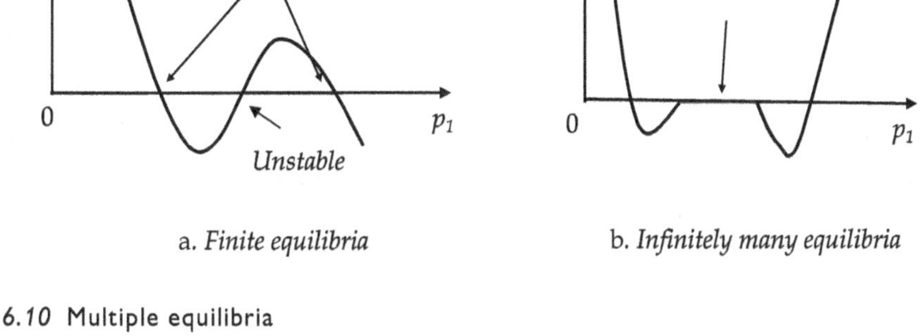

Figure 6.10 Multiple equilibria

Suppose every consumer's preference is continuous, strictly convex and strongly monotonic so that excess demand functions are defined over strictly positive prices. Let $p=(p_1,p_2,\dots,p_{n-1},1)$ be an equilibrium price vector, and let $z(p)=(z_1(p),z_2(p),\dots,z_{n-1}(p))$ be the equilibrium aggregate excess demand vector of $n-1$ goods. By the definition of equilibrium $z_j(p)=0$ for every $j=1,2,\dots,n$.

Now differentiate $n-1$ excess demand equations with respect to $p_1,\dots,p_{n-1}$ and collect the derivatives $z_{jk}=\partial z_j/\partial p_k$ for $j,k=1,2,\dots,n-1$ in an $(n-1)\times(n-1)$ matrix, as shown in the Jacobian matrix of the excess demand system. The generalisation of $z'(p)\neq 0$ is that the matrix $Dz(p)$ should be non-singular (i.e., should have a non-zero determinant).

$$Dz(p)=\begin{bmatrix} z_{11} & z_{12} & \cdots & z_{1(n-1)} \\ z_{21} & z_{22} & \cdots & z_{2(n-1)} \\ \cdots & \cdots & \cdots & \cdots \\ z_{(n-1)1} & z_{(n-1)2} & \cdots & z_{(n-1)(n-1)} \end{bmatrix} \tag{6.6}$$

Definition 11. *An equilibrium price p is* ***regular*** *if the matrix $Dz(p)$ is non-singular. If every equilibrium price vector of an economy is regular, then we say that the economy is* ***regular.***

Theorem 4. *Suppose every consumer's preference is continuous, strictly convex and strongly monotonic. Then any regular equilibrium price vector $p=(p_1,p_2,\dots,p_{n-1},1)$ is* ***locally isolated.*** *That is, there is an ϵ such that if $p'\neq p$ with $p'_n=p_n=1$, and $|p'-p|<\epsilon$, then $z(p')\neq 0$. Moreover, if the economy is regular, then the number of (normalised) equilibrium price vectors are finite.*

Proof of Theorem 4. Suppose p is a regular equilibrium; that is, $Dz(p)$, is non-singular. Then for any tiny changes in p such that $dp\neq 0$, $Dz(p).\,dp\neq 0$. That means we are no longer in equilibrium. This is same as saying that at prices sufficiently close to the proposed equilibrium price p, say p', the excess demand vector $z(p')$ cannot be zero.

The finiteness follows from the fact that due to strong monotonicity of preferences, every price in equilibrium must be strictly positive and finite. If some p_j were arbitrarily close to zero, by Proposition 9, $z_j(p)$ would be strictly positive and large, and that will violate the equilibrium condition. However, if some p_j were arbitrarily large, then $z_j(p)\to -\omega_j$; hence, that cannot be described as equilibrium either. Thus, p will be bounded. Furthermore, since $z(.)$ is a continuous function, the prices at which $z(p)=0$ forms a closed set in R^{n-1}. In other words, as we take arbitrarily close values of $z(p)$ around 0, we will see that the associated prices are also arbitrarily close to the equilibrium price. A set that is closed and bounded in R^{n-1} and discrete (because of local isolation) must be finite.

Now that we know the number of equilibrium will be finite, when $|Dz(p)|\neq 0$, can we say whether there will be an odd or even number of equilibrium points? The answer is yes. As shown in Figure 6.10 for the two-good case (panel *a*), the number of equilibrium points will be odd (e.g., three in this case), and the same holds for the n-good case as well.[7]

One way to describe the finiteness result is to count the equilibria by assigning an index +1, whenever $z(p)$ is negatively sloped (at equilibrium), and assigning an index −1 if it is positively sloped (at equilibrium). The sum of all these indices is exactly +1, no matter how many equilibrium points there are. This is called the **index theorem.** But first formally define an index.

Definition 12. *Suppose that* $p^l = \left(p_1^l, p_2^l, \ldots, p_{n-1}^l, 1\right)$ *is the lth regular equilibrium of the economy,* $l \geq 1$. *Then we denote the*

$$index\ p^l \equiv \rho^l = (-1)^{n-1}\ sign\left|Dz\left(p^l\right)\right|,$$

where $\left|Dz\left(p^l\right)\right|$ is the determinant of the $(n-1)\times(n-1)$ matrix $Dz\left(p^l\right)$.

When there are only two goods (and p_2 is normalised to be 1), the sign of $|Dz(p)|$ is just $z_1'(p_1)$. If $z_1'(p_1) < 0$, then the index of p is $+1$, and if $z_1'(p_1) > 0$, the index of p is -1. Apply the index rule on the left graph of Figure 6.10 and see that the sum of indices comes to $+1$.

In the case of three or more goods, the sign of $|Dz(p)|$ depends on $z_j(p)$ decreases in the direction of an increase in p_j. If $Dz(p)$ is a (locally) negative definite matrix, then its determinant will alternate in sign starting from negative for $n = 2,3,4\ldots$, and when it is multiplied by $(-1)^{n-1}$, our index value of the equilibrium is always $+1$ for every $n \geq 2$.

However, if $z_j(p)$ decreases in the direction of an increase in p_j, the sign of $|Dz(p)|$ will be reversed.[8] Then the index value of the equilibrium will be -1. By adding these index values, we get $+1$ if the number of equilibria is odd and -1 if it is even. The following theorem tells us that in a regular economy, the number of equilibria is always odd.

Theorem 5. *(The Index Theorem) For any regular economy with* $l(\geq 1)$ *equilibria, we have*

$$\sum_l \rho^l = +1.$$

That is, the number of equilibria is odd.

It is noteworthy that the index theorem tells us that there is at least one equilibrium. It also allows global uniqueness. If the $(n-1)\times(n-1)$ matrix $Dz(p)$ has positive determinant at all equilibria, then there is only **one** equilibrium.

When goods are gross substitutes for each other, we are guaranteed of a globally unique equilibrium. Based on what we have learnt in Chapter 3, we say that if $\frac{\partial z_k}{\partial p_j} > 0$ then good k is gross substitute for good j. We now conclude our discussion with a general result.

Proposition 10. *Suppose preferences are continuous, strictly convex and strongly monotonic, and excess demand functions of all goods satisfy the gross substituteness property. Then there is a unique Walrasian equilibrium.*

Proof of Proposition 10. To the contrary of our claim, suppose there are two equilibrium price vectors $p = (p_1, p_2, \ldots, p_n)$ and $p' = (p_1', p_2', \ldots, p_n')$; that is, $z(p) = z(p') = 0$. Now let us define a scalar by taking the largest number of the vector $\left(\frac{p_1'}{p_1}, \frac{p_2'}{p_2}, \ldots, \frac{p_n'}{p_n}\right)$. Without loss of generality, let this be $m \equiv \frac{p_1'}{p_1} > 1$. Note that by the homogeneity property of the excess demand function, $z(mp) = 0$ because $z(p) = 0$

Now consider the vector $mp = (p_1', mp_2, \ldots, mp_n)$. Note that by construction, $mp_2 > p_2', \ldots, mp_n > p_n'$. That is to say, $p' \leq mp$ with $p_1' = mp_1$; then in the price vector mp, the prices of all goods but good 1 have risen in comparison to the vector p'. Therefore, by the gross substituteness property, the excess demand for good 1 must rise at price mp: $z_1(p') < z_1(mp) = 0$. But this is a contradiction to our assumption that p' is an equilibrium price vector. Therefore, both p and p' cannot be equilibrium. We must have a unique equilibrium.

6.3.3 *Stability*

Stability concerns the following question: If an equilibrium of the economy is perturbed due to some underlying factors, then will the equilibrium be restored, or will the economy reach a new equilibrium or simply move around aimlessly? For instance, if the endowment of one good changes, say, due to a bountiful harvest, surely the equilibrium will change, and we expect the economy to travel to a new equilibrium. Generally, we restrict our attention to the two endpoints of this journey, an exercise called **comparative static analysis**, and ignore the question *of how the travel will take place*.

To give a cosmic example of stability, all the planets of our solar system have stable orbits around the Sun, and so do their moons. If a spacecraft is sent to the Moon, it has to be slingshot from the Earth's orbit to the Moon's and then use the Moon's gravity to land there. Our comparative static analysis resembles this journey from one stable equilibrium to another, and we know the journey will be successful (because of the stability of equilibrium). Comparative static analysis is meaningful only when each equilibrium is stable. If an equilibrium is not stable, a slight disturbance of the price around the equilibrium will make the economy move away, and it may never come back to the original equilibrium. Therefore, we need to check the stability of equilibrium.

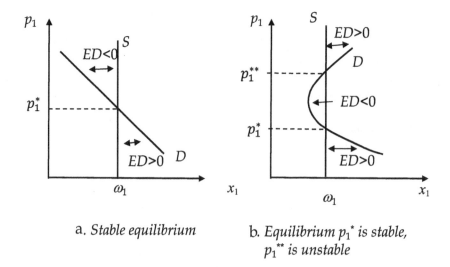

In Figure 6.11, we have drawn two pictures. We claim that the first graph represents a stable equilibrium. The second graph shows two equilibria, of which p_1^* represents a stable equilibrium and p_1^{**} represents an unstable equilibrium. The key difference between the two

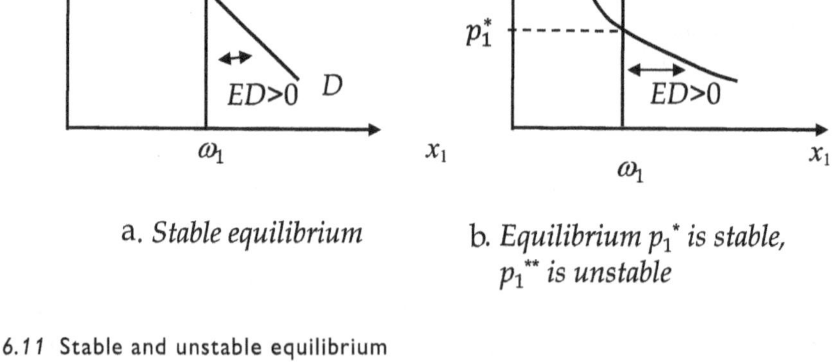

Figure 6.11 Stable and unstable equilibrium

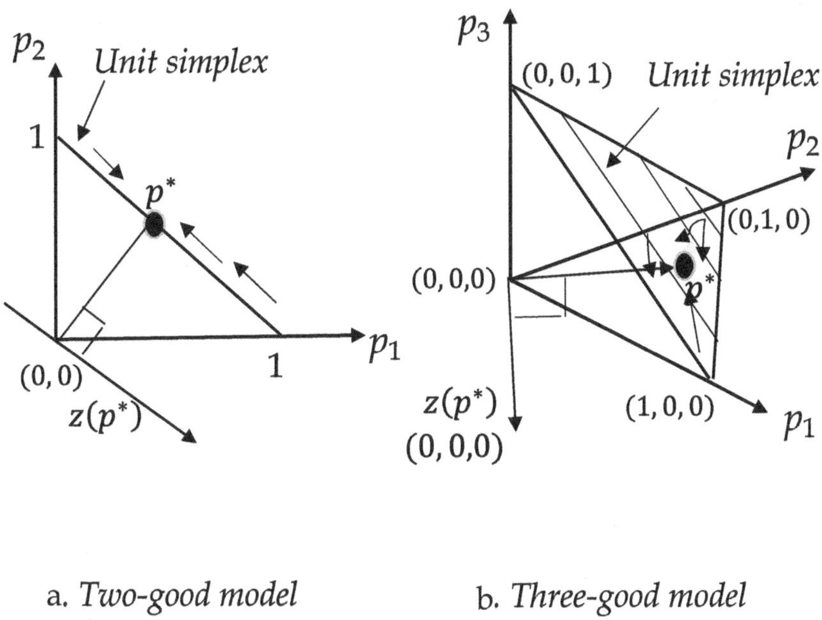

Figure 6.12 Stability of equilibrium

equilibria is the slope of the demand curves, which is a key requirement of stability as we shall shortly see. Figure 6.12 explains how we will test the stability of an equilibrium, say, p^*, in a two-good economy (panel *a*) or in a three-good economy (panel *b*). Checking the stability of an equilibrium in either case comes down to picking an arbitrary point in the neighbourhood of the equilibrium and see if the economy returns to the equilibrium. As a visual analogy, if a ball and a cube are placed on a table, a slight shake of the table will make the ball fall but not the cube.

We need to tell a story of how the economy behaves when it is not in equilibrium. In the context of our exchange economy, we need to specify *how the consumers trade when they are not in equilibrium*. So far, we have said that the consumers are price takers. But if there is a need to change the price to reach equilibrium, who will change the price?

6.3.3.1 *The Tatonnement process*

Walras himself suggested a mechanism of price setting, which is called the **Tatonnement** process. It works as follows. Suppose agents present themselves as buyers and/or sellers in the market. There is an auctioneer, who without any profit motive announces a price vector. All agents register how much they want to buy or sell of each good. The auctioneer then adds up the demands and supplies all goods. For each good, if both sides match, that is just the right price vector; agents carry out the transactions. But if the two sides do not match for any of the goods, the auctioneer will revise the prices. He will raise the prices of those goods which have registered positive excess demand and lower the prices of those goods that have registered negative excess demand. This process will be repeated until demands meet supplies.

Two important points to note here. First, the Tatonnement process prescribes a price adjustment rule that directly follows excess demand, and second, time has quietly crept into our otherwise timeless world. Thus, our price vector becomes a state variable $p(t)$ (in the terminology of dynamical systems). The changes to the state variable are described by a set of differential equations as

$$\begin{aligned}
\frac{dp_1}{dt} &= G_1\left(z_1\left(p_1(t), p_2(t), \dots, p_{n-1}(t)\right)\right) \\
\frac{dp_2}{dt} &= G_2\left(z_2\left(p_1(t), p_2(t), \dots, p_{n-1}(t)\right)\right) \\
\dots\dots & \quad \dots \\
\frac{dp_n}{dt} &= G_n\left(z_n\left(p_1(t), p_2(t), \dots, p_{n-1}(t)\right)\right),
\end{aligned} \tag{6.7}$$

where the function $G_j(.)$ is a smooth sign-preserving function of $z_j(.)$ and the price vector $p(t)$ belong to the unit simplex $\Sigma_j p_j(t) = 1$ at all t.

A solution to the preceding differential equation system is a function $p: R \to S^{n-1}$ such that $\frac{dp}{dt} = G(z(p(t)))$ for all t, which is called a price **trajectory**.[9] The initial price vector is said to be p_0 and is obtained from the trajectory by plugging a t of choice; thus, $p_0 = p(t = 0)$.

The **equilibrium** of the preceding dynamical system is p^* such that $G\left(z\left(p^*(t)\right)\right) = 0$ for all t. Once the economy reaches the state of equilibrium, price will not change any more. The dynamic system is **globally stable** if for any initial price vector p_0, we have $\lim_{t \to \infty} p(t) = p^*$.

We are now going to construct a function that captures the price adjustment process. Suppose

$$V(p(t)) = \sum_{j=1}^{n} \left[\left(p_j - p_j^*\right)^2 \right].$$

The function $V(.)$ adds the square of the distance from any p_j from its equilibrium counterpart p_j^*.

This function has a minimum at $p = p^*$. Now let us check the derivative property of this function:

$$\frac{dV(p(t))}{dt} = \sum_{j=1}^{n} \left[2\left(p_j - p_j^*\right) \frac{dp_j}{dt} \right].$$

Next, consider the following form $G(z(p(t)) = \beta z(p(t))$, where $\beta > 0$ is a scalar. Then we have $\frac{dp_j}{dt} = \beta z_j(p(t))$. Substituting this relation into the derivative of $V(.)$, we write

$$\begin{aligned}
\frac{dV(p(t))}{dt} &= \sum_{j=1}^{n} \left[2\left(p_j - p_j^*\right) \beta z_j(p(t)) \right] = 2\beta \left[\sum_{j=1}^{n} \left(p_j z_j(p(t)) - \sum_{j=1}^{n} p_j^* z_j(p(t)) \right) \right] \\
&= 0 - 2\beta \sum_{j=1}^{n} p_j^* z_j(p(t)).
\end{aligned}$$

What is the sign of $\Sigma_{j=1}^{n} p_j^* z_j\left(p(t)\right)$? As such without further assumption on the demands we cannot ensure its sign. We take recourse to an intuitive restriction with the help of the weak axiom of revealed preference (WARP). Ignore for the time being the time variable and recall that by definition, $x(p)$ is revealed preferred at price vector p and that $x\left(p^*\right)$ is revealed preferred at price vector p^*. If $x(p)$ is directly revealed preferred to $x\left(p^*\right)$, then $px(p) \geq px\left(p^*\right)$, and therefore, when $x\left(p^*\right)$ is chosen, WARP implies that $x(p)$ was not available at p^*, that is, $p^* x(p) \geq p^* x\left(p^*\right)$. In other words, if $px(p) \geq px\left(p^*\right)$, then we must have $p^* x(p) > p^* x\left(p^*\right)$. Subtracting $p\omega$ and $p^*\omega$, respectively, from both sides of the two inequalities we can say that

$$\text{if } px(p) - p\omega \geq px\left(p^*\right) - p\omega, \text{ then } p^* x(p) - p^*\omega > p^* x\left(p^*\right) - p^*\omega,$$

$$\text{or} \quad \text{equivalently, } pz(p) \geq pz\left(p^*\right) \text{ implies } p^* z(p) > p^* z\left(p^*\right).$$

By the definition of equilibrium $z\left(p^*\right) = 0$ for every j, and by Walras law, $pz(p) = 0$ at all p. Therefore, we have $pz(p^*) \leq 0$ and $p^* z(p) > 0$.

Since these relations hold for any arbitrary p (given p^* as an equilibrium) at any time period t, we have

$$\frac{dV(.)}{dt} = -2\beta p^* z\left(p(t)\right) < 0.$$

Thus, our proposed adjustment function $V\left(p(t)\right)$ has a minimum at p^* and $V\left(p(t)\right)$ is strictly downward-sloping at all $p(t) \neq p^*$. Therefore, $V(.)$ is a **Liaponov function** and by the **Liaponov theorem** p^* is unique and a globally stable equilibrium.[10] That means any arbitrary price vector we start from, it will converge to p^*. For more on this read Varian (1992) and Mas-Colell et al. (1995).

To summarise the preceding discussion, we can identify a competitive equilibrium by solving a set of market-clearing conditions, but to determine whether that equilibrium is stable or not, we need to provide a story or a behavioural premise of trade that should clearly specify the process of price adjustments when the economy is not in equilibrium. Walrasian Tatonnement is one such story. For a two-good economy, this suffices to ensure not just local but also global stability. With more than two goods, stability requires a bit more. We have shown that WARP can give us global stability and unique equilibrium. A similar result can be obtained with the assumption of the gross substituteness property for all goods.

In the literature, several non-Tatonnement processes have been introduced to overcome some of the restrictive assumptions of Tatonnement. For instance, Tatonnement permits trade only at the equilibrium price, and goods are assumed perishable. If we allow trades to take place on a trial-and-error basis, leading to the discovery of equilibrium, then if goods are storable, agents' endowments will also change in the process. Furthermore, quantities may be adjusted as well. But in all these stories, with some reasonable assumptions, we can make the competitive equilibrium stable.

6.4 Welfare properties of the Walrasian equilibrium

Competitive equilibrium has several important welfare properties, where welfare is defined in terms of the widely accepted principle of Pareto optimality. If we agree with the Pareto principle, we will have to accept that competitive equilibria are socially desirable. This is essentially a confirmation of Adam Smith's invisible hand argument, which says that if we all pursue our individual private interests, the market will do social good.

Definition 13. *An allocation* x *in an economy with* n *agents is* ***Pareto-efficient or optimal*** *if there is no other allocation* x' *with* $x_i' \succeq_i x_i$ $(or,\ u^i(x') \geq u^i(x))$ *for* $i = 1,2,\ldots,I$ *and* $x_i' \succ_i x_i$ $(i.e.,\ u^i(x') > u^i(x))$ *for some* i.

In other words, with respect to an allocation x, if there is another allocation x', which at least one agent strictly prefers and all others weakly prefer, then x is not Pareto-efficient. Note that Pareto efficiency does not make any reference to endowments.

Once again let us consider our Edgeworth box as drawn in Figure 6.13 for a two-good, two-consumer economy. Consider allocation E through which indifference curves u^A and u^B pass through. Allocation E is not Pareto-efficient, because we see that allocation D makes consumer B strictly better off, while leaving consumer A indifferent. So allocation D **Pareto dominates** allocation E. Therefore, E is not Pareto-efficient.

Is allocation D Pareto-efficient? The answer is yes, because consumer A's indifference curve is tangent to consumer B's indifference curve. Therefore, we will not be able to find any other point in the Edgeworth box that will be preferred by at least one while leaving the other indifferent. The same logic applies to points like F, C and all the points on the solid curve joining points O and O'. All these points are given by tangency between the two consumers' indifference curves. This curve is called the **Pareto efficiency curve or Pareto frontier**.

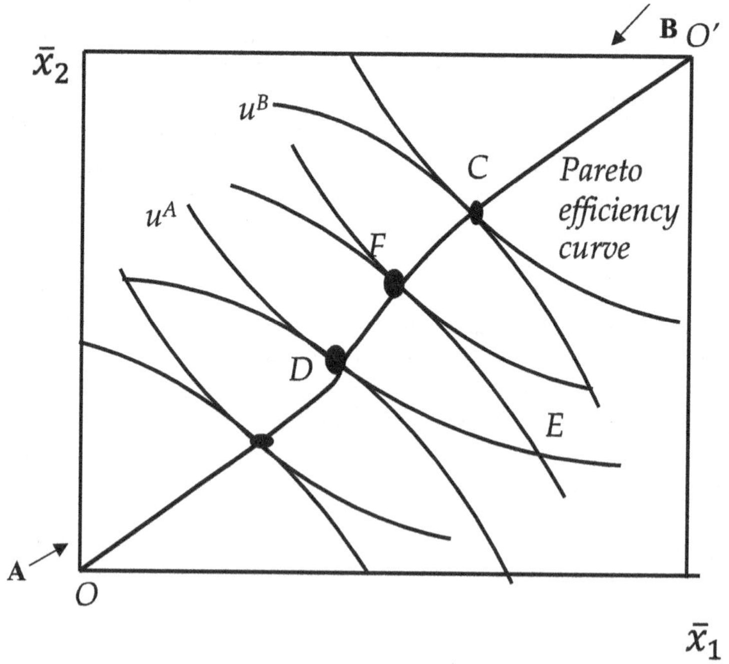

Figure 6.13 Pareto-efficient allocations

Returning to our general model of I individuals and n goods, we derive the Pareto-efficient allocations by solving the following maximisation problem.

$$\begin{aligned}
&\text{Max} && u^1 = u^1(x_{11}, x_{21}, \ldots, x_{n1}) \\
&\text{subject to} && u^2(x_{12}, x_{22}, \ldots, x_{n2}) = \bar{u}^2 \\
& && \ldots \\
&\text{subject to} && u^I(x_{1I}, x_{2I}, \ldots, x_{nI}) = \bar{u}^I \\
&\text{and} && \sum_{i=1}^{I} x_{ji} = \bar{x}_j, \quad j = 1, 2, \ldots, n.
\end{aligned}$$

The Pareto efficiency problem is a maximisation of one consumer's utility subject to holding others' utility constant and the feasibility constraint. The preceding maximisation problem can be written as

$$\text{Max} \quad \mathcal{L} = u^1(x_{11}, x_{21}, \ldots, x_{n1}) + \sum_{i=2}^{I} \lambda_i \left[\bar{u}^i - u^i(x_{1i}, x_{2i}, \ldots, x_{ni})\right] + \sum_{j=1}^{n} \mu_j \left[\bar{x}_j - \sum_{i=1}^{I} x_{ji}\right]$$

Differentiating $\mathcal{L}$ with respect to x_{11} and x_{21} for individual 1 and setting the first-order condition to zero we write the MRS for individual as

$$\frac{\partial u^1(.)}{\partial x_{11}} \bigg/ \frac{\partial u^1(.)}{\partial x_{21}} = \mu_1 / \mu_2,$$

or, in general for consumer i and for any two goods j and k, we obtain

$$MRS^i_{jk} = \mu_j / \mu_k, \quad j \neq k = 1, 2, \ldots, n.$$

Since μ_j / μ_k is independent of i, we can write for any two individuals, say, 1 and 2,

$$MRS^1_{jk} = MRS^2_{jk},$$

and this will be true for all individuals for any pair of goods. Thus, the indifference curves of any two consumers must be tangent to each other.

Example. Let us consider two goods and two consumers with Cobb–Douglas utility functions. Suppose consumer A's utility function is $u^A = x_{1A}^{\alpha} x_{2A}^{1-\alpha}$ and consumer B's utility function is $u^B = x_{1B}^{\beta} x_{2B}^{1-\beta}$. Total availability of goods is $(\bar{x}_1, \bar{x}_2)$. Then the tangency condition becomes

$$\frac{\alpha}{(1-\alpha)} \frac{x_{2A}}{x_{1A}} = \frac{\beta}{(1-\beta)} \frac{x_{2B}}{x_{1B}}.$$

Next, substitute the feasibility constraint as $x_{1B} = \bar{x}_1 - x_{1A}$ and $x_{2B} = \bar{x}_2 - x_{2A}$ to obtain the Pareto efficiency curve as

$$x_{2A} = \left[\frac{\beta(1-\alpha)\bar{x}_2}{\alpha(1-\beta)\bar{x}_1 + (\beta-\alpha)x_{1A}} \right] x_{1A}. \tag{6.8}$$

If preferences were identical, the Pareto efficiency curve would be linear.

A key result in welfare economics is that competitive equilibrium is Pareto-efficient. This means that we cannot find another way of making both consumers better off than they are under a competitive market equilibrium. This result is known as the First Fundamental Theorem of Welfare Economics.

Theorem 6. (First Fundamental Theorem of Welfare Economics) *If preferences are locally non-satiated, and if* (x^*, p^*) *is a Walrasian (competitive) equilibrium, then* x^* *is Pareto-efficient.*

The proof of the theorem is in Section 6.8. But it is straightforward. Note that we do not need strong monotonicity or even convexity of preferences, because we know equilibrium can exist even without them. What this theorem claims is that if there is a competitive equilibrium, the outcome of it will be desirable from a collective point of view, even though resources are privately owned and all individuals act with private motives.

The converse of the first welfare theorem is also true, and it has a stronger implication. We can support every Pareto-efficient allocation by market prices and an appropriate redistribution of endowments or wealth. In other words, to support any Pareto-efficient allocation, we can always find some endowment point such that a budget line can be drawn to run through both the Pareto-efficient allocation and the endowment point. This is called the Second Fundamental Theorem of Welfare Economics.

There are two ways that we can think about the second welfare theorem. If we think about the *redistribution of endowments*, then it suffices to show that if $x^* = (x_A^*, x_B^*)$ (for two agents) is Pareto-efficient, then giving people $x_i^* = \omega_i^*$ is a way to support the Pareto-efficient allocation as a competitive equilibrium. It may sound trivial, because in equilibrium people will not be trading. Therefore, the second welfare theorem requires proving that there exists a positive price vector at $\omega = x^*$. It turns out that this will be true provided preferences satisfy properties more than just local non-satiation, which was enough for the first welfare theorem.

Theorem 7. (Second Fundamental Theorem of Welfare Economics) *Suppose* $x^* = x > 0$ *is a Pareto-efficient allocation in which every agent has a strictly positive allocation of every good. If preferences of every consumer are strictly convex, continuous and strongly monotonic, there exists a price vector* $p > 0$ *such that* (x^*, p) *is a competitive equilibrium if the individual* i*'s endowment is* $\omega_i = x_i^*$.

Proof of the second welfare theorem is a bit more involved (see Section 6.8). Typically, x^* is distributed as an initial endowment, and then by using the convexity of preference assumption a preferred set is defined, which is convex. Given the convex preferred set, one can use the **separating hyperplane theorem** to establish that there exists a set of prices at which any element of the preferred set will lie outside the budget set generated by the initial endowment x^* and the price vector. Then it is shown that such prices must be strictly positive. This is enough to show that the Pareto-efficient allocation x^* is just a competitive equilibrium. The main implication of the second welfare theorem is that we can always redistribute wealth in an economy and achieve any Pareto-efficient allocation we like to arrive at by the decentralised process of competitive equilibrium.

The technical requirement for the second theorem to hold is much greater than the first theorem. In particular, the convexity and continuity of preference are crucial. Furthermore, the preferences are made strongly monotonic so that equilibrium prices must be strictly positive. If this were not the case, redistribution of endowment may not fully work because some goods can be free good, and then the redistribution of it would not have much impact on the demand.

Consider Figure 6.14. In panel *a*, we have an Edgeworth box with standard preferences that give rise to a Pareto efficiency curve with strictly positive allocations. Note that if our endowment point is E, then we can draw a budget line travelling through E and D on the Pareto efficiency curve. Then, clearly, the associated price p^* is a competitive equilibrium; this is our first welfare theorem. But suppose for some reason the social planner wants to implement point C as a competitive equilibrium. Point C is Pareto-efficient. Clearly, from the endowment point E, allocation C cannot be supported as a competitive equilibrium. But the social planner can take away some of the endowments of both goods from agent A and give them to agent B. This exercise takes the economy to endowment point E'. Now you can see that there is a price vector that supports allocation C as a competitive equilibrium. This price is also unique and happens to be same p^*, but that is just by accident.[11] You can also see from the two parallel budget lines that we have reduced the wealth of consume$A$r and increased the same of consumer B. But E' is not the only endowment that supports allocation C as a competitive equilibrium; the endowment point E' or any other points on the same budget line (induced by p^*) including point C will also help us achieve the same goal. The equilibrium price is still the same.

Side by side in panel *b*, we present an example where the Pareto-efficient allocations are not strictly positive. Here, consumer A's preference is strictly increasing in x_1 but independent of x_2; therefore, her preference is weakly convex and weakly monotonic. Her indifference curves are vertical. Consumer B's indifference curves are standard. In this case, the standard tangency

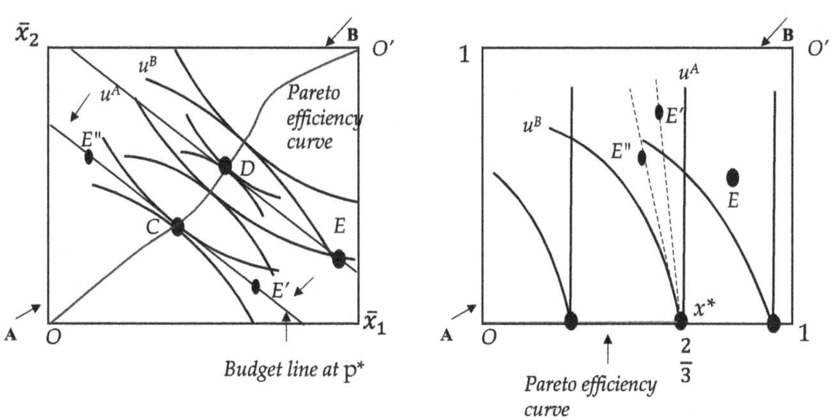

a. *Redistribution of wealth and the second theorem holds*

b. *The second theorem does not hold despite redistribution of wealth*

Figure 6.14 The second welfare theorem

condition for Pareto efficiency does not hold. Yet Pareto-efficient allocations exist, and we can see that the horizontal axis itself constitutes the Pareto efficiency curve. Now can we implement a Pareto-efficient allocation, say, $x^* = ((2/3,0),(1/3,1))$ as a competitive allocation? The answer is 'no'. In order to do that, we have to have $p_1 = 0$ (and by default $p_2 = 1$), which means that no matter what the initial endowment of this economy is, the wealth of consumer A will be reduced to zero. In short, wealth of A is $M_A = 0\times 2/3+1\times 0=0$ and wealth of B will be $M_B = 0\times 1/3+1\times 1=1$. At $p_1 = 0$, consumer A would like to buy $x_1 = 1$ (if not more). This means that x^* is not a competitive equilibrium. In fact, you can recall that in our definition of the competitive equilibrium, if $p_j = 0$, then good j is a free good and it must be in excess supply. That condition is not met here. You can also see that if we select the endowment point E', then there is a budget line with $p_1 > 0$ and $p_2 > 0$ that supports allocation x^*, but then we can draw many such budget lines (such as the one passing through E'') that does the same job. The problem is that there are infinitely many such prices, and therefore, the equilibrium is indeterminate. The point of this graph is that when we violate both convexity and monotonicity the second welfare theorem may not hold.[12]

From a technical point of view, if we want to extend the second welfare theorem to Pareto-efficient allocations that are not strictly positive, then we need to weaken the notion of competitive equilibrium to allow for zero price and non-clearing of market. That means individual budgets may not be satisfied with equality. All we require is that if a consumer prefers an allocation more than the Pareto allocation then the preferred allocation must be outside her budget, and the total demands must match the total supply. This notion of competitive equilibrium is called *quasi-equilibrium*. Usually, any Pareto-efficient allocation is supportable as quasi-equilibrium with wealth redistribution. See Mas-Colell et al. (1995, pp. 522–525 and pp. 551–558) for a comprehensive treatment of the Second Fundamental Theorem of Welfare Economics.

6.5 Welfare maximisation

The Pareto efficiency curve presents infinitely many possible allocations, from which the competitive market picks one (or just a few). But the competitive market is a special mechanism that is not easy to create. The outcome of the competitive market may not necessarily be very popular. A social planner, who is acting on behalf of society, may want to choose a different allocation to the competitive equilibrium. Once that is done, it can be implemented through a competitive market by redistributing endowments.

The simplest way to think about the social planner's choice is to assume that the social planner has a utility function $W = W(u^A, u^B)$, where $W(.)$ is a social welfare function. The case can be easily extended to n consumers. The Pareto efficiency curve can be seen as a frontier of feasible allocations of utility that consumers A and B can obtain from various allocations of (x_1, x_2). Figure 6.15 shows two such utility frontiers. The underlying preferences of the consumers determine the shape of the utility frontier. We show two variations, but there could be many. Panel *a* shows that the feasible utility set is convex, implied by the concave shape of the frontier. Panel *b* shows that the feasible set may not be convex. The highest u^A is $\bar{u}^A$, which corresponds to the allocation that gives the endowment of both goods to consumer A; consumer B's utility is then assumed to be zero. Likewise, consumer B's highest utility $\bar{u}^B$ corresponds to the allocation that gives the whole endowment to consumer B and none to consumer A.

The social welfare function can also be of different forms. We present two of them. Suppose $W = u^{A\alpha} u^{B\beta}$, where $\alpha, \beta > 0$ are weights on the consumers' utilities. If $\alpha = \beta$ then both

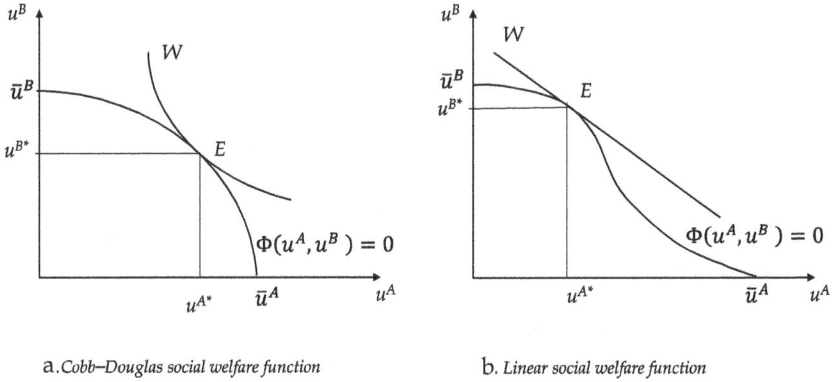

Figure 6.15 Social welfare maximisation

consumers are treated equally. If $\alpha > \beta$ then consumer A is favoured over consumer B. For instance, in the United States, the policy of affirmative action encourages preferential treatment of ethnic minority workers in federal offices. The social welfare function can also be linear as shown in panel $b: W = \alpha u^A + \beta u^B$.

Writing the utility frontier implicitly as $\Phi\left(u^A, u^B\right) = 0$, we can solve the social planner's problem as

$$\text{Max} \quad W = W\left(u^A, u^B\right) \quad \text{sub.to } \Phi\left(u^A, u^B\right) = 0,$$

or, equivalently,

$$\text{Max} \quad \mathcal{L} = W\left(u^A, u^B\right) - \lambda\Phi\left(u^A, u^B\right).$$

The first-order conditions give rise to $\frac{\partial W}{\partial u^A} \Big/ \frac{\partial W}{\partial u^B} = \Phi_1 / \Phi_2$, the slope of the social welfare function equal to the slope of the utility frontier. For panel a, this condition becomes $\frac{\alpha u^B}{\beta u^A} = \frac{\Phi_1}{\Phi_2}$, and for panel b, $\alpha / \beta = \Phi_1 / \Phi_2$. The solutions we have depicted are based on the assumptions that $\alpha > \beta$ for panel a and $\alpha < \beta$ for panel b. In both cases, we have a unique solution $\left(u^{A*}, u^{B*}\right)$, which we can then trace back to the Pareto efficiency curve.

Even if we did not start with Pareto efficiency curve or if we start with utilities of the consumers as the primitive of the model, then one can show that the utility frontier curve is essentially the Pareto efficiency curve on the underlying goods space. If that were not the case, one consumer's utility could be increased without reducing the utility of the other. It can also be shown that the social welfare maximum is supportable as a competitive equilibrium, provided preferences satisfy certain conditions. This is essentially a restatement of the second welfare theorem.[13]

6.6 Core

As we emphasised earlier, a competitive market is one of many mechanisms that a society may create to solve its economic problems. One can think of nonmarket interactions among individuals of a very general nature, and then see if one can arrive at a notion of equilibrium. For instance, instead of going through market and price mechanisms, two neighbours can do some give-and-take of their endowments. It turns out that when there are only two individuals, such give-and-take agreements coincide with the Pareto-efficient allocations, subject to one caveat. The caveat is that consumers will now consider what they can do on their own, and therefore, any give-and-take agreement they arrive at must not leave them worse off than what they can do in isolation. This caveat is imposed by the market mechanism as well (because all exchanges are voluntary), but for Pareto efficiency, this consideration is not taken into account. Recall that Pareto efficiency is defined without considering endowments.

When the option of not accepting any allocation that makes one worse off than being at the original endowment point is taken into account, we arrive at a subset of Pareto-efficient allocations, which is the **contract curve** or **core**, as illustrated in Figure 6.16 panel *a*. The Pareto efficiency curve is the entire curve $ODFCO'$, while the contract curve is only the segment DFC, because anywhere on this segment both consumers are getting a higher utility than at their own endowment points (denoted by ω).

The idea of the contract curve was originally proposed by Edgeworth himself. But you can see that if we have just two consumers, then consuming their own endowment is the only other option they have. But with three or more consumers, various other possibilities open up. Even if a Pareto-efficient allocation is proposed, two out of three consumers or three out of four or any subset of them can form a coalition and see that within the coalition they can make themselves strictly better off by reallocating their endowments. In a multi-agent framework, the idea of core then becomes relevant. In other words, while the contract curve and core are equivalent in a two-agent economy, in multi-agent settings, the core becomes a subset of the contract curve.

Definition 14. *An allocation* $x = (x_1, x_2, \ldots, x_I)$ *is said to* ***improve upon*** *or* ***block*** *another allocation* $x' = (x_1', x_2', \ldots, x_I')$ *if and only if* $x_i \succ_i x_i'$ *for every agent* $i = 1, 2, \ldots, I$ *and* x *is feasible; that is,* $\sum_{i=1}^{I} x_{ji} \le \sum_{i=1}^{I} x_{ji}'$ *for every good* $j = 1, 2, \ldots, n$.

Definition 15. An allocation $x^* = \left(x_1^*, x_2^*, \ldots, x_I^*\right)$ **cannot be improved upon** or is **unblocked** if there is no allocation $x' = (x_1', x_2', \ldots, x_I')$ such that $x_i' \succ_i x_i^*$ for every agent $i = 1, 2, \ldots, I$ and $\sum_{i=1}^{I} x_{ji}' \le \sum_{i=1}^{I} x_{ji}^*$ for every good $j = 1, 2, \ldots, n$.

Definition 16. *The core of an economy is the set of all unblocked allocations.*

Assuming two agents and two goods, we have drawn the contract curve on panel *a* in Figure 6.16. All allocations on the contract curve are unblocked, because they are Pareto superior to the (endowment) allocation ω. So this is also the core of this economy.

6.6.1 *Example 1*

The idea of the core can be fully appreciated if we add more agents to the economy. Suppose there are four agents; two are type A, and two are type B, where the agents' diversity is restricted to only two types (just for simplicity). Let us take an example where type A is described by preference $u^A = x_{1A} x_{2A}$ and endowment (1/2,1), and type B is described by preference $u^B = x_{1B} + x_{2B}$ and endowment $(1,0)$. Thus, the aggregate endowments of this economy are 3 units of x_1 and 2 units of x_2. On panel *b* of Figure 6.16, we depict this case with a standard box of two consumers. The economy in this case is just twice the size of the Edgeworth box drawn,

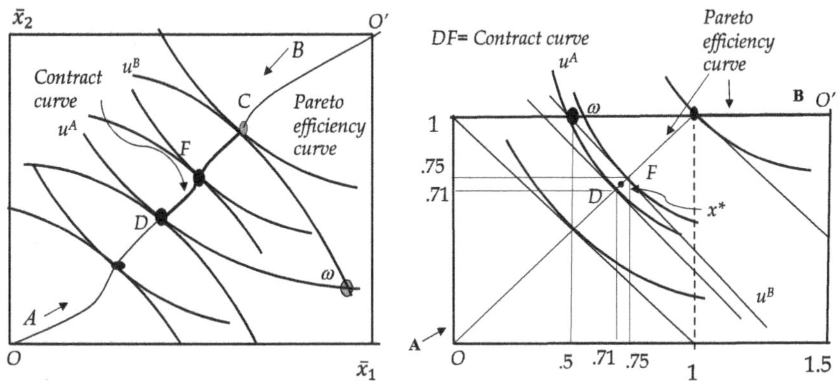

a. Contract curve as core

b. Replication of the economy

Figure 6.16 The core of an economy

which still refers to a single pair of type A and type B agents. The Pareto efficiency frontier is given by the equality of the two indifference curves up to the bundle $(1,1)$ and thereafter by the corner solutions at $x_{2B} = 0$. Thus, the straight line from the origin and the horizontal axis of agent B give the Pareto-efficient allocations, out of which the segment DF is the contract curve. Four agents do not change the contract curve, because of the replication of identical agents. Thus, the contract curve is

$$C = \{(x_{1A}, x_{2A}), (x_{1B}, x_{2B}) \mid 0.71 \le x_{1A} = x_{2A} \le 0.75, 0.75 \le x_{1B} \le 0.79,$$
$$0.25 \le x_{2B} \le 0.29, x_{1A} + x_{1B} = 3/2, x_{2A} + x_{2B} = 1\}.$$

What is the core of this economy? Is it going to be the whole contract curve? Can there be a coalition that can do better than a point on the contract curve? To determine that we need to first consider all possible coalitions. Let $C(k)$ be a coalition of k agents. Then we have the following coalitions:

$$C(1) = \{(A_1), (A_2), (B_1), (B_2)\},$$
$$C(2) = \{(A_1, A_2), (A_1, B_1), (A_2, B_1), (A_1, B_2), (A_2, B_2), (B_1, B_2)\}$$
$$C(3) = \{(A_1, A_2, B_1), (A_1, A_2, B_2), (B_1, B_2, A_1), (B_1, B_2, A_2)\},$$
$$C(4) = \{(A_1, A_2, B_1, B_2)\},$$

where A_i and B_i refer to the ith member of type A and B, respectively, $(i = 1, 2)$. $C(4)$ is called the grand coalition. The unblocked pay-offs of the grand coalition are our core. First, note that the coalitions of one individual are trivial. It only tells us that a type A consumer should not get utility less than $u^A(\omega^A) = 1/2$ and type B should not get utility less than $u^B = 1$. A coalition between two individuals of the same type is meaningless; they cannot make each other better off. Coalitions of two different individuals like (A_i, B_j) cannot improve on any contract curve allocations because they are Pareto-efficient.

So now it remains to be seen if $C(3)$ can block an allocation of the contract curve. Let us denote an allocation x^* on the contract curve as (x_A^*, x_B^*) with $x_A^* = (0.75\lambda, 0.75\lambda)$ and $x_B^* = (3/2 - 0.75\lambda, 1 - 0.75\lambda)$, where $\frac{71}{75} \leq \lambda \leq 1$ for a type A and a type B agent. Their utilities are $u^A = (.75\lambda)^2$ and $u^B = \frac{5-3\lambda}{2}$.

Now consider a coalition of $C(3) = (A_1, A_2, B_1)$; their aggregate endowment is (2,2). Suppose the type B agent is offered $x_B' = (1.5 - 0.75\lambda + \epsilon, 1 - 0.75\lambda)$. Clearly, she will be strictly better off than at allocation x^*. Each of the two type A agents then receive $x_A' = \left(\frac{2 - 1.5 + 0.75\lambda - \epsilon}{2}, \frac{2 - 1 + 0.75\lambda}{2}\right)$, yielding

$$u^A(x_A') = \left(\frac{1}{4} + \frac{0.75}{2}\lambda - \frac{\epsilon}{2}\right) \times \left(\frac{1}{2} + \frac{0.75\lambda}{2}\right).$$

Setting $u^A(x_A') > u^A(x_A^*)$ we arrive at

$$1 + \frac{9}{4}\lambda - (2 + 1.5\lambda)\epsilon - \frac{27}{8}\lambda^2 > 0.$$

Now let $\epsilon \to 0$, then the preceding inequality is valid if $\lambda > \frac{2.914}{3} = \frac{72.85}{75}$.

Next, consider the other possible coalition of three consumers: (B_1, B_2, A_1). Aggregate endowment is now (5/2,1). Consider $x_A' = (0.75\lambda + \epsilon, 0.75\lambda)$, which will give $u^A(x_A') > u^A(x_A^*)$. Each of the type B agents in the coalition gets $x_B' = \left(\frac{2.5 - 0.75\lambda - \epsilon}{2}, \frac{1 - 0.75\lambda}{2}\right)$, and their resultant utility is $u^B(x') = \frac{1}{4}[7 - 3\lambda - 2\epsilon]$. Setting $u^B(x_B') > u^B(x_B^*)$ and letting $\epsilon \to 0$, we get $7 - 3\lambda > 10 - 6\lambda$, which is possible if $\lambda > 1$, a contradiction. $\lambda > 1$ will take us outside the contract curve. Thus, coalitions (B_1, B_2, A_1) or (B_1, B_2, A_2) cannot block any allocations on the contract curve. Therefore, the core of this economy with four consumers is now a reduced set:

$$C^*(4) = \{(x_{1A}, x_{2A}), (x_{1B}, x_{2B}) \mid 0.728 \leq x_{1A} = x_{2A} \leq 0.75, 0.75 \leq x_{1B} \leq 0.772,$$
$$0.25 \leq x_{2B} \leq 0.272, x_{1A} + x_{1B} = 3/2, x_{2A} + x_{2B} = 1\}.$$

In Figure 6.17, we illustrate this on the leftmost figure. To enlarge the area of the core, which we are mainly interested in, the axes have not been drawn to the scale. It is noteworthy that in this example, the competitive equilibrium allocation is (0.75,0.75) for A and (0.75,0.25) for B, which means the type B agent is not better off than being in isolation. This is an artefact of the linear indifference curve, because to render positive consumption of all goods to all individuals in the market equilibrium type B's indifference curve must coincide with the budget line passing through the endowment point.

As we replicate our economy from two agents to four agents some of the Pareto allocations get blocked. In other words, the core shrinks. But note the shrinkage occurs only from the left corner. The competitive equilibrium is preserved in the right corner. Intuitively, the type *B* agents' capacity to bribe a type *A* agent to break away from the grand coalition and form another coalition is very limited, because a type *B* agent does not have good 2. Type *A* agents are clearly in a superior position, and therefore, they can fully eliminate those allocations that give them the lowest or close to the lowest utility from the contract curve.

6.6.2 *Example 2*

In our second example, both types of agents have convex preferences, Cobb–Douglas to be precise. As before there are two type *A* agents and two type *B*. The type *A*'s preference is as before $u^A = x_{1A}x_{2A}$, and the endowment is also unchanged at (1/2,1). Type *B* have the same Cobb–Douglas preference, $u^B = x_{1B}x_{2B}$, but each has an endowment of (1,1/2). Each pair's total endowment is (3/2,3/2). The competitive equilibrium for the economy is $p_1/p_2 = 1$ and (0.75,0.75) for both type *A* and type *B* agents. You can also derive the contract curve to be the set of following allocations: $0.71 \le x_{1A} = x_{2A} \le 0.79$ and $0.71 \le x_{1B} = x_{2B} \le 0.79$, with the feasibility restriction $x_{1A} + x_{1B} = 3/2$ and $x_{2A} + x_{2B} = 3/2$.

Now let us try to find the set of allocations that will remain unblocked. Once again, we need to consider only the coalitions (A_1, A_2, B_1) and (A_1, B_1, B_2) for reasons explained in Example 1. As before, let x^* denote an allocation on the contract curve as $x_A^* = (0.79\lambda, 0.79\lambda)$ and $x_B^* = (3/2 - 0.79\lambda, 3/2 - 0.79\lambda)$, where $\frac{71}{79} \le \lambda \le 1$. Their utilities are $u^A = (.79\lambda)^2$ and $u^B = (3/2 - 0.79\lambda)^2$. Now consider the coalition of (A_1, A_2, B_1) with an aggregate endowment

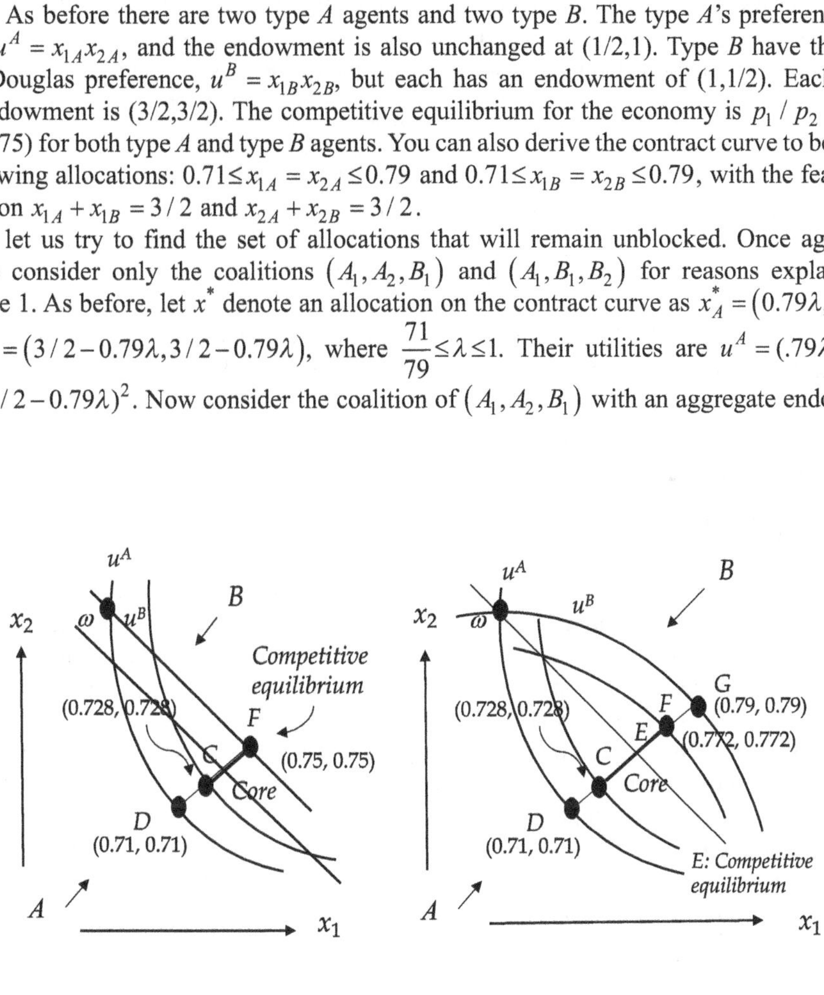

Figure 6.17 Shrinkage of the core with replication

of (2,5/2). Suppose the type B agent is offered $x'_B = (1.5 - 0.79\lambda + \epsilon, 1.5 - 0.79\lambda)$, which makes her strictly better off. Each type A agent gets $x'_A = \left(\frac{2 - 1.5 + 0.79\lambda - \epsilon}{2}, \frac{2.5 - 1.5 + 0.79\lambda}{2}\right)$, and

$$u^A(x'_A) = \frac{1}{4}\left(\frac{1}{2} + 0.79\lambda - \epsilon\right) \times (1 + 0.79\lambda).$$

As before, let $\epsilon \to 0$ and then see that $u^A(x'_A) > u^A(x^*_A)$ if

$$1 + (0.79) \times 3\lambda - (0.79)^2 \times 6\lambda^2 > 0,$$

which gives us a lower bound of 72.83/79 on λ.

Next, consider the coalition (A_1, B_2, B_1), whose endowment is (5/2,2). Consider another bundle on the contract curve $x^{**} = (0.79\mu, 0.79\mu)$ for type B and $(1.5 - 0.79\mu, 1.5 - 0.79\mu)$ for A, where $71/79 \le \mu \le 1$. Note that this is just a swap of the role between A and B. Considering an allocation $x'_A = (1.5 - 0.79\mu + \epsilon, 1.5 - 0.79\lambda)$, and $x'_B = \left(\frac{2.5 - 1.5 + 0.79\mu - \epsilon}{2}, \frac{2 - 1.5 + 0.79\mu}{2}\right)$, we find symmetrically the lower bound on μ as 72.83/79. Combining the two bounds on λ and μ, we get the following bounds on the core allocations:

$$0.728 \le x_{1A} = x_{2A} \le 0.772 \quad \text{and} \quad 0.728 \le x_{1B} = x_{2B} \le 0.772.$$

Panel b of Figure 6.17 illustrates how the core shrinks with the replication of the economy. Note that the shrinkage here is from both ends, and as before, the competitive equilibrium is preserved inside the core.

6.6.3 Properties of the core

It should be clear by now that core allocations are robust to opportunistic behaviours of the agents seeking better deals on the side. Therefore, picking any allocation from the core has the advantage of not being rejected by any subset of agents, and at the same time, the allocation will not be far from the competitive equilibrium, which as such requires well-functioning market mechanisms and price-taking behaviours by all agents. This means that economies, which lack advanced institutions to support competitive trade, can still try to approximate the market equilibrium simply by ensuring what people can get by engaging in various side contracts with fellow participants. Of course, a downside of this exercise is that it may not always be possible to satisfy everybody's alternative opportunities, and indeed there are many occasions where the core of an economy may be empty.

Keeping aside the preceding pessimistic conclusion (i.e., empty core), let us reiterate that core has two attractive properties. The first one is equal treatment within the core, and the second one is the contraction of the core to the competitive equilibrium in a very large economy.

6.6.3.1 Property 1

Suppose preferences are continuous, strongly monotonic and strictly convex. Then in the n-*replication core, any two identical agents must receive identical allocations.*

Proof. Suppose that our economy has $2n$ agents of two types in equal numbers. Two individuals of the same type have the same endowments and same the preferences. Without a loss of generality, assume that only one type A agent receives less of x_1 while all other type A agents are treated identically, and so are all type B agents. Suppose that the agent who has been discriminated against gets $x'_{1A} = \bar{x}_{1A} - \epsilon$, where $\bar{x}_{1A}$ is the average allocation of x_1 amongst the type A agents. By feasibility, $x'_{1A} + (n-1)x_{1A} + nx_{1B} = n\omega_{1A} + n\omega_{1B}$, and if $x_{1A} < \omega_{1A}$, then $x_{1B} > \omega_{1B}$. Then the discriminated type A agent can offer $x_{1B} + \frac{\epsilon}{2}$ to a type B agent and keeps to herself $\omega_{1A} + \omega_{1B} - x_{1B} - \frac{\epsilon}{2}$. This will also improve the discriminated type A agent's pay-off, because $\omega_{1A} + \omega_{1B} - x_{1B} - \frac{\epsilon}{2} > x'_{1A} = \bar{x}_{1A} - \epsilon$, since $\omega_{1A} + \omega_{1B} - x_{1B} - \frac{\epsilon}{2} = \frac{x'_{1A} + (n-1)x_{1A} + nx_{1B}}{n} - x_{1B} - \frac{\epsilon}{2} = \bar{x}_{1A} - \frac{\epsilon}{2}$, which is strictly greater than $\bar{x}_{1A} - \varepsilon$. Therefore, the original allocation x'_{1A} could not be in the core. That is a contradiction.

6.6.3.2 Property 2

Suppose preferences are continuous, strongly monotonic and strictly convex, and there exists a unique competitive equilibrium given the initial endowment of the agents. Then the core of any n*-replication of this economy will contain the competitive equilibrium. Furthermore, as* n *increases, the core shrinks, and in the limit, as* $n \to \infty$*, the core will converge to the competitive equilibrium.*

The proof of Property 2 is straightforward but lengthy, so we have placed it in Section 6.8. Two points we establish in the proof. The competitive equilibrium can never be blocked when it exists. Consider point C in Figure 6.18. By definition, the competitive equilibrium is the common point on any two agents' budget lines, and the equilibrium allocation is their most preferred bundles as well, within the budget set generated by the equilibrium price. Clearly, in any n-replication of the economy, there cannot be any coalition that can make all the coalition members strictly better off, because if it could then the same allocation would have been selected by the competitive equilibrium itself.

The second part of the property is proved by showing that if a core allocation is not a competitive equilibrium, then in some replication of this economy, it will be blocked. As the economy is expanded by replicating the same types of agents, the scope for forming many coalitions is greatly enhanced. In Figure 6.18, consider allocation $\tilde{x}$ on the contract curve DF. Clearly, $\tilde{x}$ is in the core of a two-person economy, but it is not the competitive equilibrium. Now let us join the endowment point ω and $\tilde{x}$ and take an allocation $\beta = (\beta_A, \beta_B)$ on the line joining ω and $\tilde{x}$. It is obvious that β_A will be strictly preferred by all type A agents (and β_B will make type B agents strictly worse off) in comparison to $\tilde{x}$. So, if we give β_A to type A agents and $\tilde{x}_B$ to type B agents, then type A agents would be better off, and the type B agents will remain indifferent.

But we can tweak these two allocations a bit. Let us take ϵ from β_A such that $\beta_A - \epsilon$ is still preferred by a type A agent to $\tilde{x}_A$, and then distribute the total deduction of ϵ equally among the type B agents in addition to giving them $\tilde{x}_B$. With these adjustments, we create β'_A and $\tilde{x}'_B$. Note that now a type B agent would strictly prefer $\tilde{x}'_B$. Thus, allocation $(\beta'_A, \tilde{x}'_B)$ is a strong candidate that can block the allocation $\tilde{x}$.

The question is, Can we find a coalition that can make this allocation feasible? The answer is yes. As is obvious from the figure the proposed allocation is a mix of two different

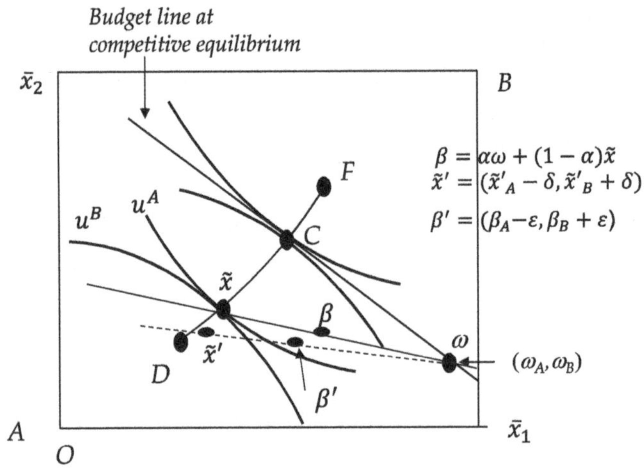

Figure 6.18 Competitive equilibrium and the core

parts of two allocations taken from the Edgeworth box, and therefore, it is not feasible in a two-person economy or in the grand coalition of any n-replication economy. But if we take a subset of the agents, say, n_A and n_B of an n-replication, then it will be feasible in such a coalition.

Extending this logic, we can say that any core allocation of a smaller economy will eventually get eliminated in a larger economy (larger in the sense of replication), except the competitive equilibrium. In the limit then, the core must shrink to a single point, the competitive equilibrium.

An important qualifier to the limiting result is that the competitive equilibrium must exist. If there is no competitive equilibrium (for reasons discussed in Section 6.3.1), then the core will eventually disappear. This is a result of sheer instability unleashed by the opportunistic behaviours of too many agents. In the following section, we demonstrate in two examples that when the incentive to form a grand coalition is stronger, the core will prevail, and when it is otherwise, the core will not be formed.

6.6.4 *Example 3*

Suppose agent A has £50, B has £25 and C also has £25. If at least two of them come together to contribute to a common fund, the government will match their contribution to encourage saving. Thus, if two of them contribute, then the government will contribute either £75 or £50 depending on whether A and B or C contribute or only B and C contribute. Upon cooperation, the total fund available to the coalition is £150 or £100. If all three contribute, the government will contribute £100, and the total fund available to the grand coalition is £200. The Pareto-efficient allocations are any three-way partition of £200, and the contract curve allocations (x_A, x_B, x_C) are $50 \le x_A \le 150, 25 \le x_B \le 125$ and $25 \le x_C \le 125$. The core of this economy is $x_A = 100, x_B = 50$, and $x_C = 50$. This cannot be improved upon by any coalition of A and B or A and C or B and C. Suppose A and B form a coalition; then their total fund will be 150. This is not large enough to make both A and B better off. The same argument applies to the coalition of B and C. You can also check that (102,49,49) cannot be in the core, because B and C can break away and form a coalition to create a fund of 100 and each can get 50.

Now let us make a small change in this example. Suppose the government has fund constraint. It can match the contributions of two persons but gives slightly less than the matching amount if three people contribute. For example, the coalition of A and B gets £75 (and so does the coalition of A and C), and the coalition of B and C gets £50 from the government. However, the grand coalition gets only £80. You can check the core is empty here. The simple test of it is that whatever allocation of the grand coalition we propose, two members can break away and do better. For example, take an allocation of the grand coalition (90,45,45). Clearly, A and B can break away and create a fund of £150 due to the government's contribution rule and both will do better. But this coalition in itself is unstable. The left-out member C, who cannot enjoy more than £25 on his own, can bribe B £60 to form a coalition with him and keep £40 for himself. But then A can break this coalition by offering £45 to C and so on. In effect, there is no core here.

Based on the intuition of this example, you can verify yourself that if the government's contribution rule is modified to give more than proportionately to the grand coalition than to any sub-coalition, then there will be more allocations in the core.

6.7 Conclusion

A major simplification in this chapter is that we have assumed away production. This is because we need to first understand how we can describe production. This will be taken up later. It turns out that the fundamental insights that we have gained from the exchange model will remain largely intact even if we allow production, as long as the production technology remains of a particular variety. As such, the general equilibrium theory is vast. We have presented it with great economy and in its most essential form. For more general versions of the existence theorem and stability, one can look at more advanced books. The notion of the core also has been extended in many dimensions. Again, these topics are beyond the scope of this book.

Summary

1. We graphically and mathematically explained competitive equilibrium using an Edgeworth box.
2. We explained when a competitive equilibrium may not exist.
3. Equilibrium will be unique if all goods are gross substitutes. If not, under some conditions, equilibrium is locally unique.
4. With the Walrasian Tatonnement process, the equilibrium will be stable as well.
5. Competitive equilibrium has desirable welfare properties. It is always Pareto-efficient.
6. The core of an economy always contains competitive equilibrium if the competitive equilibrium exists and is unique.
7. In very large economies, the core will be almost equal to the competitive equilibrium.

6.8 Appendix

6.8.1 *Proof of Theorem 2*

[Adapted from Varian (1992), p. 321] First, note that because of continuous, strictly convex and locally non-satiated preferences, we have a unique and continuous Marshallian demand function $x_{ji}(p)$ for every i and j at any given price vector p. Therefore, the excess demand function for every good $x_{ji}(p)-\omega_{ji}$ is also continuous and unique.

Now we are going to make a different normalisation on prices instead of setting one price equal to 1. Let us set $p_1+p_2+\ldots+p_n=1$, then we define a set $S^{n-1}=\{(p_1,p_2,\ldots,p_n)\mid p_1+p_2+\ldots+p_n=1\}$ as a $n-1$ dimensional unit simplex. By definition, a simplex is a non-empty, compact and convex set, and therefore, the set of our prices S^{n-1} is non-empty, compact and convex.

Our next step is to use the aggregate excess demand function for good i to create a new function g_j as follows. Consider a vector of functions $g(p)=(g_1(p),g_2(p),\ldots,g_n(p))$, where

$$g_1(p)=\frac{p_1+\max(0,z_1(p))}{1+\sum_{j=1}^{n}\max(0,z_j(p))} \tag{6.9}$$

$$g_2(p)=\frac{p_2+\max(0,z_2(p))}{1+\sum_{j=1}^{n}\max(0,z_j(p))} \tag{6.10}$$

$$\ldots \qquad \ldots\ldots$$

$$g_n(p)=\frac{p_n+\max(0,z_n(p))}{1+\sum_{j=1}^{n}\max(0,z_j(p))}. \tag{6.11}$$

Note that by construction g itself belongs to a S^{n-1} simplex, because

$$\sum_j g_j(p)=\frac{\sum_j p_j+\sum_{j=1}^{n}\max(0,z_j(p))}{1+\sum_{j=1}^{n}\max(0,z_j(p))}=1.$$

Therefore, the vector g is a continuous map from S^{n-1} to S^{n-1}. That is, for any p from $\Sigma_j p_j=1$, we will get n values of $g_j(p)$ with $\Sigma_j g_j=1$. Therefore, mathematically, this is a fixed-point problem of finding a solution to the vector of equation $g(p)=p$.

By the **Brouwer's fixed-point theorem**, we know that if $g(p)$ is continuous, then there exists a price vector p^* such that $g(p^*)=p^*$. For our vector of functions, this means

$$g_1(p^*)=p_1^*, g_2(p^*)=p_2^*,\ldots g_n(p^*)=p_n^*.$$

Finally, we need to check if these prices are indeed the Walrasian equilibrium prices. In order to show that, let us write $g_1\left(p^*\right) = p_1^*$ in Eq. (6.9) and write it as

$$p_1^* = \frac{p_1^* + \max\left(0, z_1\left(p^*\right)\right)}{1 + \sum_{j=1}^{n} \max\left(0, z_j\left(p^*\right)\right)}.$$

$$\text{or, } p_1^* \sum_{j=1}^{n} \max\left(0, z_j\left(p\right)\right) = \max\left(0, z_1\left(p\right)\right)$$

Now multiply both sides by $z_1\left(p^*\right)$:

$$z_1\left(p^*\right) p_1^* \left[\sum_{l=1}^{n} \max\left(0, z_n\left(p\right)\right)\right] = z_1\left(p^*\right) \max\left(0, z_1\left(p\right)\right).$$

Repeating the same exercise for every good $j = 1, 2, \ldots, n$, we get

$$z_1\left(p^*\right) p_1^* \left[\sum_{j=1}^{n} \max\left(0, z_n\left(p\right)\right)\right] = z_1\left(p^*\right) \max\left(0, z_1\left(p\right)\right),$$

$$z_2\left(p^*\right) p_2^* \left[\sum_{j=1}^{n} \max\left(0, z_2\left(p\right)\right)\right] = z_2\left(p^*\right) \max\left(0, z_1\left(p\right)\right),$$

.....

$$z_n\left(p^*\right) p_n^* \left[\sum_{j=1}^{n} \max\left(0, z_j\left(p\right)\right)\right] = z_n\left(p^*\right) \max\left(0, z_n\left(p\right)\right).$$

Adding the preceding n equations on both sides, we get

$$\left[\sum_{j}^{n} \max\left(0, z_j\left(p^*\right)\right)\right] \sum_{j}^{n} p_j^* z_j\left(p^*\right) = \sum_{j}^{n} z_j\left(p^*\right) \max\left(0, z_j\left(p^*\right)\right).$$

By Walras law, $\Sigma_j^n p_j^* z_j\left(p^*\right) = 0$ on the left-hand side of this equation. So, from the right-hand side, we should also have

$$\sum_{j}^{n} z_j\left(p^*\right) \max\left(0, z_j\left(p^*\right)\right) = 0.$$

Each term in this expression is either 0 or z_j^2 (which cannot be negative) with $z_j > 0$. But $z_j > 0$ is ruled out for the preceding equality to be valid. That means either $z_j\left(p^*\right) < 0$ or $z_{j'} = 0$. That is precisely our competitive equilibrium.

6.8.2 *Proof of Theorem 6*

Since x^* is Walrasian equilibrium, $\Sigma_j p_j^* x_{ji}^* = \Sigma_j p_j^* \omega_{ji}$ for every $i, i = 1,2,\ldots,I$. That is, each agent's Walrasian allocation satisfies the budget constraint. Furthermore, x_i^* is the most preferred (or utility-maximising) bundle from agent i's budget set. That is to say, if there is any $x_i \succ x_i^*$, then $p^* x_i > p^* x_i^*$.

Now assume that there is an allocation x' that is not competitive equilibrium, but Pareto dominates x^*. That is to say, $x_i' \succeq x_i^*$ for all $i = 1,2,\ldots,I$ and $x_i' \succ x_i^*$ for some i.

But by the definition of the Walrasian equilibrium of $x^*, p^* x_i' \geq p^* x_i^* = p^* \omega_i$ for all i and $p^* x_i' > p^* x_i^* = p^* \omega_i$ for some i. Now summing over i on both sides, we have

$$p_1^* x_1' + p_2^* x_2' + \ldots + p_n^* x_n' > p_1^* \bar{x}_1 + p_2^* \bar{x}_2 + \ldots + p_n \bar{x}_n$$

or

$$p_1^* (x_1' - \bar{x}_1) + p_2^* (x_2' - \bar{x}_2) + \ldots + p_n^* (x_n' - \bar{x}_n) > 0.$$

That means allocation $x' = (x_1', x_2', \ldots, x_I')$ cannot be feasible. Hence, the counter-claim that competitive equilibrium is not Pareto-efficient cannot be true.

6.8.3 *Proof of Theorem 7*

[Adapted from Varian (1992, p. 327)]

Suppose $x^* = (x_1, x_2, \ldots, x_n) > 0$ and Pareto optimal, where $x_{ji} > 0$ for every $j = 1,2,\ldots,n$ and $i = 1,2,\ldots,I$. In reference to x^*, let us define a preference set $V_i = \{x_i \mid x_i \succ x_i^*\}$; due to preferences being continuous, strictly convex and strongly monotonic, the set V_i is convex. Furthermore, we can define $V = \{y : y = \Sigma_{i=1}^{I} x_i, x_i \in V_i\}$. As V is the sum of convex sets V_is, V is a convex set.

Let $\Sigma_{i=1}^{I} \omega_{ji} = \Sigma_{i=1}^{I} x_{ji}$ for every good $j = 1,2,\ldots,n$. Since $\omega = x^*$, we cannot redistribute it and make Pareto improvement. Therefore, $\omega \in V$; that is, ω is outside the set V. Note that ω is also a set with a single point and thus (trivially) convex. The **separating hyperplane theorem** says that when two disjoint sets are convex, there exists a hyperplane that separates the two sets.

In our context, that means there is a price vector $p \neq 0$ such that $py \geq p\Sigma_{i=1}^{I} x_i^*$ for every y in the set V or, equivalently, $p(y - \Sigma_{i=1}^{I} x_i^*) \geq 0$ for every y in V. We need to show that p is strictly positive, and at p consumer i's demand for good j is indeed x_{ji}^*.

To establish that, first rule out that p cannot contain any negative numbers. To see that consider a bundle $y' = (x_1^*, x_2^*, \ldots, x_j^* + \delta, \ldots, x_n^*) > x^*$ for some $\delta > 0$. Then by strong monotonicity of preferences, $y' \succ x^*$ and thereby $y' \in V$. We then see that $py' - px^* = px^* + p_j \delta_j - px^* = p_j \delta \geq 0$. That means $p_j \geq 0$. Since this is true for any arbitrary j, we can ensure that no p_j can be negative.

Next, consider a vector of allocations assigned to I consumers, $y = (y_1, y_2, \ldots, y_I)$ and assume consumer 1 strictly prefers her allocation to x_1^*, while consumer 2 is indifferent between y_2 and x_2^*, consumer 3 is indifferent between y_3 and x_3^* and so on. Then we can construct a bundle $\tilde{y} = (\tilde{y}_1, \tilde{y}_2, \ldots, \tilde{y}_n)$ by reducing y_1 slightly, say, by a factor of δ, and equally distributing them to all other consumers. That is, $\tilde{y} = \left(y_1(1-\delta), y_2 + \frac{\delta y_1}{n-1}, \ldots, y_n + \frac{\delta y_1}{n-1} \right)$. By strong monotonicity of preference, $\tilde{y} \succ x^*$ for every consumer i and $\tilde{y}$ must belong to the set V. Then it must follow that $p\tilde{y}_i \geq px_i^*$ for every consumer i. Since by definition x_i^* is part of a Pareto allocation, any bundle preferred to x_i^* must not cost less than x_i^* at our price vector p, which we have already shown to be non-negative.

Finally, we show that any vector strictly preferred to x_i^* must be costlier than x_i^*. That is if $y_i \succ x_i^*$, then we must have $py_i > px_i^*$. Suppose that is not the case; instead, $py_i = px_i^*$. Then we can create a new allocation θy_i with $0 < \theta < 1$ so that $\theta y_i \succ x_i^*$ (by consumer i). By continuity of preferences such a bundle always exists. Then we will have $\theta py_i < px_i^*$ (because $\theta < 1$). This contradicts the fact that if a bundle is preferred to x_i^*, then it must not cost less than x_i^*; that is, $\theta py_i \geq px_i^*$. That is a contradiction.

Therefore, we must have $py_i = px_i^*$ for every consumer i, which, in combination with the fact $x_i^* > 0$ (for every good j for every consumer i), shows that p must also be strictly positive and x_i^* is the utility maximising bundle at price p and endowment $\omega_i = x_i^*$. Since for every good j, $\sum_{i=1}^{I} x_{ji}^* = \sum_{i=1}^{I} \omega_{ji}$ (by construction), $\left(x^*, p\right)$ is a competitive equilibrium.

6.8.4 Proof of Property 2

Suppose there are two types, A and B, of consumers with strictly convex, continuous and strongly monotonic preferences, and there is a competitive equilibrium p^* and a corresponding allocation x^*; this allocation is unique by strict convexity. See point C in Figure 6.18. By the definition of competitive equilibrium, x_A^* is the most preferred bundle of type A in her budget set at p^* and so is x_B^* for type B. That is, $p^* x_A^* = p^* \omega_A$ and $p^* x_B^* = p^* \omega_B$.

Now, consider any n-replication of this economy. In the competitive equilibrium allocation and the core of the replicated economy, any two identical agents must receive the same allocations (for facing the same prices and by implication of Property 1, respectively).

We can easily show that the competitive allocation will always be in the core. Suppose not. Then there is an allocation x' and a coalition of S of n_A and n_B agents $\left(n_A \leq n, n_B \leq n\right)$, such that $x' \succ_i x^*$ for every $i \in S$. That is, x' is strictly preferred by both type A and type B members of the coalition S. Then it must be the case that $p^* x'_A > p^* x_A^*$ for all $n_A \in S$ and $p^* x'_B > p^* x_B^*$ for all $n_B \in S$, which implies $n_A x'_A + n_B x'_B > n_A \omega + n_B \omega_B$. This means that x' is not feasible for the coalition S. Therefore, the competitive equilibrium cannot be blocked.

Next, we show that any core allocation of a smaller economy that is not a competitive equilibrium can be eventually blocked by some replication. Consider an allocation $\tilde{x}$ (see Figure 6.18) that is in the core of a two-person economy but not a competitive equilibrium. Then we can construct a bundle β that is a convex combination of ω and $\tilde{x}$. Suppose $\beta = \alpha\omega + (1-\alpha)\tilde{x}$. By construction, β is on the line joining ω and $\tilde{x}$, and β_A is strictly preferred by all type A agents. That is,

$$\beta_A = \alpha\omega_A + (1-\alpha)\tilde{x}_A, \beta_B = \alpha\omega_B + (1-\alpha)\tilde{x}_B, 0 < \alpha < 1.$$

Note that β_A is above the indifference curve. We can find two allocations, say, $\left(\beta' = \beta'_A, \beta'_B\right)$ and $\tilde{x}' = \left(\tilde{x}'_A, \tilde{x}'_B\right)$, where $\beta'_A = \beta_A - \epsilon$ and $\tilde{x}' = \tilde{x}_B + \delta$, such that β'_A is strictly preferred by all type A agents and $\tilde{x}'_B$ is strictly preferred by all type B agents, due to strict convexity and strong monotonicity of preference.[14]

Then it can be shown that there is a coalition S in some n-replication of this economy that can support an allocation β'_A to its type A members and $\tilde{x}'_B$ to its type B members. Refer to Figure 6.18. Be aware that these two allocations are not at the same point of the Edgeworth box, because the box is drawn for a pair of agents (or a replication of it). For a coalition of unequal members, the Edgeworth box of that coalition will be different. So we need to check the feasibility mathematically.

Let us suppose this coalition has n_A type A members and n_B type B members, with $n_A > n_B$. Define $\alpha = \frac{n_A - n_B}{n_A}$. Then we can write the elements of β'_A as (for ϵ_1 and ϵ_2 small)

$$\beta'_{1A} = \frac{n_A - n_B}{n_A}\omega_{1A} + \frac{n_B}{n_A}\tilde{x}_{1A} - \epsilon_1$$

$$\beta'_{2A} = \frac{n_A - n_B}{n_A}\omega_{2A} + \frac{n_B}{n_A}\tilde{x}_{2A} - \epsilon_2,$$

and $\tilde{x}'_B$ as

$$\tilde{x}'_{1B} = \tilde{x}'_{1B} + \delta_1 = \tilde{x}'_{1B} + \frac{n_A \epsilon_1}{n_B}$$

$$\tilde{x}'_{2B} = \tilde{x}'_{2B} + \delta_2 = \tilde{x}'_{2B} + \frac{n_A \epsilon_2}{n_B}.$$

As can be seen, from each type A member of the coalition ϵ_1 of good 1 and ϵ_2 of good 2 are taken away and distributed among the type B members. We now check if this allocation is feasible to the coalition S. For good 1,

$$\begin{aligned} n_A \beta'_{1A} + n_B \tilde{x}'_{1B} &= n_A\left[\frac{n_A - n_B}{n_A}\omega_{1A} + \frac{n_B}{n_A}\tilde{x}_{1A} - \epsilon_1\right] + n_B\left[\tilde{x}_{1B} + \frac{n_A \epsilon_1}{n_B}\right] \\ &= (n_A - n_B)\omega_{1A} + n_B \tilde{x}_{1A} - n_A \epsilon_1 + n_B \tilde{x}_{1B} + n_A \epsilon_1 \\ &= (n_A - n_B)\omega_{1A} + n_B(\tilde{x}_{1A}\tilde{x}_{1B}) \\ &= n_A \omega_{1A} - n_B \omega_{1A} + n_B(\omega_{1A} + \omega_{1B}) \\ &= n_A \omega_{1A} + n_B \omega_{1B}. \end{aligned}$$

Similarly, we can show

$$n_A \beta'_{2A} + n_B \tilde{x}'_{2B} = n_A \omega_{2A} + n_B \omega_{2B}.$$

Clearly, the allocation $(\beta'_A, \tilde{x}'_B)$ is feasible for the coalition of S that has (n_A, n_B) members.

6.9 Exercises

1. Consider a two-person two-good economy. The consumers' preferences and endowments are $u^A = u^B = \sqrt{x_1} + \sqrt{x_2}$ and $\omega_A = (a,b), \omega_B = (b,a), a \neq b$.
   a. Derive the competitive equilibrium of this economy. Discuss if the equilibrium is unique what condition of uniqueness has been satisfied.
   b. Graphically illustrate your answer for question 1(a).
   c. Derive the Pareto-efficient allocations.
   d. Show the contract curve on the graph. Explain why every allocation on the contract curve will remain unblocked in this two-person economy but that will not be so if this economy is replicated.

Table 6.1 Excess demand systems

A	*B*	*C*
$x_1 : \frac{p_2}{p_1} + p_3$	$x_1 : \frac{p_3 - p_2}{p_1}$	$x_1 : \frac{p_2^2}{p_1^2} - \frac{p_3}{p_1}$
$x_2 : \frac{p_1 p_3}{p_2}$	$x_2 : \frac{p_1 - p_3}{p_2}$	$x_2 : \frac{-p_2 + p_3}{p_1}$
$x_3 : -\frac{p_2}{p_3}$	$x_3 : \frac{p_2 - p_1}{p_3}$	$x_3 : -\frac{p_2}{p_1}$

2. Suppose $u^A = \alpha\sqrt{x_1} + \beta\sqrt{x_2}$ and $u^B = x_1 x_2$ and $\omega_A = (a,b), \omega_B = (b,a), a \neq b$.
   a. Derive the competitive equilibrium of this economy, and illustrate your answer with an Edgeworth box diagram.
   b. Derive the Pareto-efficient allocations, and identify the contract curve.
3. Suppose consumer A's preference is strictly convex, but consumer B's preference is non-convex. They have positive endowments of two goods. Explain graphically that for this economy there is a core, but a competitive equilibrium may not exist.
4. Consumer A's preference is given by $u^A = x_1^{\alpha} x_2^{1-\alpha}, 0 < \alpha < 1$. Consumer B's preference is given by $u^B = \min[x_1, x_2]$ and $\omega_A = (a,b), \omega_B = (b,a), a \neq b$.
   a. Derive the competitive equilibrium of this economy. Comment on the nature of this equilibrium.
   b. Graphically illustrate the Pareto-efficient allocations.
5. Consumer A's preference is $u^A = \min[ax_1, bx_2]$ and $u^B = \min[bx_1, ax_2]$, and their endowments are $\omega_A = (2,1)$ and $\omega_B = (1,2)$.
   a. What conditions do you need to impose on a and b to ensure that there is a competitive equilibrium?
   b. Derive all Pareto-efficient allocations for this economy. Graphically illustrate them.
   c. Identify the core of this economy.
6. Suppose p_1, p_2 and p_3 are three prices for goods x_1, x_2 and x_3, respectively. Then determine which of the sets of equations (A, B and C) in Table 6.1 could be an excess demand system.
7. In a two-person two-good economy, preferences of A and B are $u^A = -\frac{\left[x_1^{-2} + x_2^{-2}\right]}{2}$ and $u^B = x_1 x_2$, respectively. Their initial endowments are $\omega_A = (a,0)$ and $\omega_B = (0,b)$.
   a. Assuming price-taking behaviour, derive the demand functions.
   b. How many equilibria are there?
   c. Show if $a = b$, then the only equilibrium (relative) price is 1.
8. In a two-good economy, excess demand equation for a good is given by $z = -p^2 + 3.5p - 3.5 + \frac{1}{p}$, where p is the relative price of the two goods. Find the equilibria of this economy. By drawing a graph of z, determine which equilibrium is stable.

9. Consider a two-person two-good economy with endowments $\omega_A = \left(\frac{4}{5}, \frac{1}{5}\right)$ and $\omega_B = \left(\frac{1}{5}, \frac{4}{5}\right)$. Suppose there is an allocation in the core of this economy, which is not a competitive equilibrium. Let this allocation be $x^*A = \left(\frac{2}{5}, \frac{3}{5}\right)$ and $x_B^* = (3/5, 2/5)$ for A and B, respectively. Construct a bundle $y_A = \frac{x_A^*}{2} + \frac{1}{2}\omega_A$ and $y_B = x^*{}_B$. Assume (y_A, y_B) blocks (x_A^*, x_B^*) if (y_A, y_B) becomes feasible. If this economy is replicated there exists a coalition of n_A and n_B agents that can make (y_A, y_B) feasible. Derive n_A and n_B (assume n_A and n_B need not be integers).
10. Suppose A, B and C make accessories for cricket. A specialises in pads, which are interchangeable between left and right legs. B and C make gloves, but B is better in making right-hand gloves, while C is better in left-hand gloves. Suppose A makes 10 pairs of pads. B makes 6 right-hand gloves and 3 left-hand gloves, while C makes 6 left-hand gloves and 3 right-hand gloves. Players are willing to pay more if they buy pads and gloves in pairs. Suppose the price of a pair of gloves or pads is £20, but when sold separately, each item will fetch only £7. Furthermore, if pads and gloves are bought from the same place, then players make a 'thank you' payment of £3. Assume the production cost is fixed. What will be the core of this little economy?

Notes

1 An example of non-satiation is bliss-point utility functions, where, except at the bliss point, everywhere else local non-satiation holds. You can draw circular indifference curves and see that utility can be raised even by reducing the consumption of both goods. When some goods are 'bad' preferences satisfy non-satiation.
2 We should note that if we assume strict monotonicity, then there cannot be any free good in equilibrium. All prices must be positive, and all markets will clear.
3 One can use a direct method of applying the implicit function theorem on the system of excess demand equations. But this would require differentiability of the excess demand functions. The argument is based on the verification of the local conditions of a solution.
4 As preferences are strictly convex, our excess demand $z(p)$ will continue to be single-valued, and therefore, it is a function. But because of strong monotonicity at very small $p_j, z_j(p)$ will be infinitely large. So the search for an equilibrium should look for prices that can reduce the excess demand of j sufficiently. Conceptually, it means at the given p, we need to find a set of prices, say, q, that will maximize the value of $z(p)$; that is, $qz(p) \geq q'z(p)$ for any q, q' from the unit simplex. Clearly, at least one such q_j must be greater than p_j, and there are many such vectors q. This procedure makes $g(p)$ multi-valued, and we need to argue in terms of correspondence.
5 Upper hemi-continuity is the appropriate notion of continuity for correspondence, which is a set in itself. Convexity of this set is important to guarantee existence of a fixed point. Formally, since $p \in S^{n-1}$ and $g(p) \subset S^{n-1}$, with upper hemi-continuity and convexity of $g(p)$, we will have $p^* \in g(p^*)$. In the environment of correspondence, equilibrium means p^* must belong to the set $g(p^*)$.
6 You can read the proof in Mas-Colell et al. (1995, pp. 586–587).
7 When we have n goods, we need to recognise multiple cross-price effects. But generally, the direct effects are stronger.

8 Clearly, then $Dz(p)$ is not (locally) negative definite. As such the opposite direction of $z(p)$ involves changing vector orientation. For example, the determinants of the following two matrices are exactly opposite. $\mathcal{A}$ is negative definite, $\mathcal{B}$ is not.

$$\mathcal{A} = \begin{bmatrix} -1 & 0 & 0 \\ 0 & -1 & 0 \\ 0 & 0 & -1 \end{bmatrix} \quad \text{and} \quad \mathcal{B} = \begin{bmatrix} 0 & 0 & -1 \\ 0 & -1 & 0 \\ -1 & 0 & 0 \end{bmatrix}$$

9 Note that $p(t)$ is a map from the set of real number to the $n-1$ dimensional unit simplex.

10 The Liaponov theorem says that for a dynamical system if a Liaponov function exists, then its equilibrium is globally stable and a globally stable equilibrium must be unique.

11 The same price vector is a result of the way we have aligned the indifference curves. It should not be confused as multiple equilibria problem. We may have the same p^*, but our endowment has changed.

12 One should not mix up zero quantity of a good with zero price of a good, as part of competitive equilibrium. Zero price must be associated with negative excess demand. Zero quantity with positive price can be consistent with competitive equilibrium; the converse, however, can be problematic. Figure 6.14 panel *b* shows a case where the theorem does not work. But if we have *A*'s indifference curve linear (both goods are desirable now), then we can make the second theorem hold even with a corner solution.

13 However, there is a technical point we need to keep in mind. When we start from utilities as a primitive to create a feasible set of utilities, we need to assume that utilities are transferable across consumers. It is a bit of a strong assumption, because utilities are just ordinal assignments to describe preference orderings. But in this case, we need utilities also to be cardinal.

14 It is obvious that $\beta'_B = \beta_B + \epsilon$ and $\tilde{x}'_A = \tilde{x} - \delta$. But we do not need to consider these two allocations.

References and further readings

Debreu, G. & Scarf, H. (1963). A limit theorem on the core of an economy. *International Economic Review*, 4, 235–246.

Edgeworth, F. Y. (1881). *Mathematical Psychics*. London: Kegan Paul.

Hildrenbrand, W. & Sonnenschein, H. (Eds.). (1991). *Handbook of Mathematical Economics*, Vol. IV. Amsterdam: North-Holland.

Mas-Colell, A., Whinston, M. D. & Green, J. R. (1995). *Microeconomic Theory*. New York: Oxford University Press.

Ozveren, E. (2007). Bazaars of the *Thousand and One Nights*. *European Journal of History of the Economic Thought*, 14(4), 629–655.

Varian, H. R. (1992). *Microeconomic Analysis*, 3rd ed. New York: Norton.

Walras, L. (1874). *Elements of Pure Economics* [English translation 1954]. Homewood, IL: Irwin.

Chapter 7

Choice under uncertainty

Abstract

Expected utility theory has remained the most popular theory of decision making under uncertainty. Because of its simplicity, the theory found its way into every area of economics over the last 78 years. But it has never been smooth sailing. Soon after its creation, the theory faced criticism for making unrealistic predictions about certain choices people would make under uncertainty (Allais paradox). The criticisms have only grown since then. In this chapter we present the expected utility theory, its many applications, and its criticisms along with major developments in non-expected utility theories.

Keywords: Certainty equivalent, Risk premium, Insurance premium, Betting, Allais paradox, Prospect theory, Regret theory, Ellsberg paradox

7.1 Introduction

Consider the following three examples:

Example 1: A family wants to celebrate their 5-year-old's birthday at a nearby child-friendly leisure centre. However, the weather forecast suggests a significant chance of rain, which may affect the invited children's preference for dessert—hot pudding or ice cream. The family expects that half of the children may switch from ice cream to hot pudding if it rains. But the caterer points out that without a prior order, they cannot offer hot pudding. They insist that either a precise number of hot puddings be determined 24 hours in advance or an order for *both* pudding and ice cream be placed so that regardless of the weather, all children's choices can be met.

Example 2: You have invested $10,000 in a portfolio of stocks and bonds. This is your hard-earned money; you anxiously check the value of your portfolio every day by logging into your bank's website. Because of the unpredictability of the financial markets, you worry whether your investment will grow steadily or get wiped out in a single day of turbulence. After six months and a modest gain on your investment, you may wonder whether you should sell your portfolio and move the money into gold instead; gold seems to be holding steady.

Example 3: Mr Banerjee detests any form of gambling. But he has been hearing about a weekly postcode lottery that many of his neighbours are into. The lottery company puts all postcodes in England into a large lottery drum and then a random draw determines the winning postcode, which means those who have bought the ticket and live in that postcode will share the

DOI: 10.4324/9781003226994-7

prize money. Mr Banerjee is in a dilemma. On one hand, gambling is not his cup of tea, but on the other hand, if his postcode wins, his ticket-holding neighbours will celebrate non-stop for days, much to his envy and regret. Should he also buy a ticket?

All these examples illustrate many familiar circumstances of uncertainty. Our responses to uncertainty vary depending on our attitude to *risk*, our perception of the likelihood of risky events, and the presence or absence of instruments to deal with the risk. So what sort of theory can help us understand consumers' decision-making in these circumstances?

Fortunately (or unfortunately), there are several theories. The most commonly used theory is the *expected utility theory* according to von Neumann and Morgenstern (1944). The expected utility (EU) theory in some sense extends the standard utility theory by taking into account the alternative levels of utility a consumer will experience depending on what state of nature is realised and then computing expected utility with the help of the probabilities associated with those states of nature.

But this theory has been challenged, and a consensus for developing a decision theory 'not based on expected utility' is building up. Two important developments in this regard are *prospect theory and regret theory*. We postpone a discussion of these theories or the criticisms of the expected utility theory until later. First, we show how the expected utility theory is used to model decision-making under uncertainty.

7.2 Expected utility approach

Suppose there are n states of nature, which lead to n possible outcomes or consequences of an event as $(x_1, x_2, \ldots, x_n)$. x_i can be a monetary return or reward in the context of investment or physical quantity of a crop or simply an occurrence such as rain, snow or sun. The probabilities of each state of nature are known or can be computed accurately.[1] Let these probabilities be $(p_1, p_2, \ldots, p_n)$, $\sum p_i = 1$.

Any uncertain event that affects an agent's income or utility is called a lottery or gamble. We will use both terms interchangeably without implying any value judgement. In many cultures, gambling is considered immoral, and in all societies, caution is strongly advised when a large sum of money is placed at stake. But from a formal point of view, gambling in a casino or buying a lottery ticket at the supermarket is no different from making a career choice or deciding on the best pension plan. All are gambles or lotteries. A lottery with a vector of promised state contingent returns $x = (x_1, x_2, \ldots, x_n)$ and their associated probabilities $p = (p_1, p_2, \ldots, p_n)$, $\Sigma_1^n p_i = 1$ are denoted as $\mathcal{L}(x, p)$. Thus, another lottery that promises a different profile of returns, or the same x with different probabilities is a different lottery. That is, $\mathcal{L}(x, p) \neq \mathcal{L}'(x, p')$ if $p \neq p'$ or $x \neq x'$ or both. A compound lottery of over two or more simple lotteries is also a lottery.

Let us now accept as a premise that our consumer knows what her utility would be (or how she would feel) in each of these states of nature. This is, however, not an easy thing to accept, as we shall see later. But let us assume that the consumer knows all her potential utility levels. Then she can compute her expected utility in a simple way:

$$Eu = p_1 u(x_1) + p_2 u(x_2) + \ldots + p_n u(x_n) = \sum_{i=1}^{n} p_i u(x_i).$$

Like decision-making under certainty, she can decide on the basis of the highest expected utility, a seemingly natural extension of rational choice to uncertainty.

That the consumer should care about state-specific utility than monetary pay-offs when such pay-offs apply is quite important. To understand this, let us consider the following lottery. Suppose a coin is to be flipped 50 times at most. If heads comes up the first time at the nth $(n \leq 50)$ flip, you are given $\$2^n$ and the game ends. If heads does not come up, the coin is flipped again until the 50th round comes. The question is, How much are you willing to pay for this lottery? By simply looking at the money you would receive, in expected terms, is

$$\frac{1}{2}\times 2+\frac{1}{2^2}\times 2^2+\frac{1}{2^3}2^3+\ldots+\frac{1}{2^{50}}\times 2^{50}=\$50.$$

Note that the probability of getting a head at the nth flip is1/2, time$(1/2)^{n-1}$, the probability of getting $n-1$ tails in a row. Thus, at every round, the expected prize is exactly \$1, and for 50 rounds, the expected prize is \$50. Therefore, it is 'fair' to charge \$50. By fair we mean that the expected prize of a lottery is equal to the actual cost of the lottery. Despite being a fair lottery, how many (in reality) would be willing to pay \$50 to play it? Probably not too many. This is known as the *St. Petersburg paradox*.

There are several plausible explanations as to why people would be unwilling to play this fair gamble. One good explanation, which illustrates our case in point, is that people consider utility from the prize rather than the prize itself. If we consider the same problem in an expected utilitarian framework, then paying is worthwhile if

$$\frac{1}{2}\times u(2)+\frac{1}{2^2}\times u\left(2^2\right)+\frac{1}{2^3}u\left(2^3\right)+\ldots+\frac{1}{2^{50}}\times u\left(2^{50}\right)>u(50).$$

Assuming an increasing utility function, we can see that on the left-hand side, the utility in the first five terms is strictly less than $u(50)$ and in the remaining terms by how much the utility exceeds $u(50)$ depends on how concave the utility function is. Therefore, for many individuals, the left-hand side of the preceding inequality may not exceed the right-hand side, while in monetary terms, the gamble is fair for everybody. However, there is another argument. Many would say that to recover \$50 there must be five tails in a row, which demands extraordinary luck. Therefore, it is unwise to bet \$50. Note that in this argument, the emphasis is on the *ex post* gains and losses. But under uncertainty, once a decision is made, *ex post* gains and losses are irrelevant.

7.2.1 Risk aversion

Under the expected utility approach, we are able to incorporate how the attitude to risk can vary from individual to individual. For some individuals losing \$5000 on a risky stock may not be a big deal, but for many, it could be too much; they might just play safe by keeping their money in fixed deposits. Different risk attitudes should be reflected in their utility functions. In terms of attitude to risk, a consumer can be *risk-averse*, a *risk-loving* or *risk-neutral*. She is defined to be *risk-averse* if and only if

$$u(p_1x_1+\ldots+p_nx_n)>\sum_{i=1}^{n}p_iu(x_i)\ \text{or}\ u(Ex)>Eu.$$

Alternatively, the consumer is defined to be a *risk-loving* if and only if

$$u\left(p_1x_1+\ldots+p_nx_n\right)<\sum_{i=1}^{n}p_iu\left(x_i\right) \text{ or } u\left(Ex\right)<Eu,$$

and *risk-neutral* if and only if

$$u\left(p_1x_1+\ldots+p_nx_n\right)=\sum_{i=1}^{n}p_iu\left(x_i\right) \text{ or } u\left(Ex\right)=Eu.$$

It is easy to see that risk aversion implies (and is implied by) strict concavity of the utility function $u(.)$. Similarly, risk loving implies (and is implied by) by a strictly convex $u(.)$ function, and risk neutrality implies linear $u(.)$ function. See Figure 7.1. Suppose a lottery promises £5 with probability 1/2 and £15 with probability 1/2. The expected prize is £10. In panel *a*, the expected utility of the lottery is less than the utility of the expected prize; in panel *b*, it is reversed. The risk neutrality corresponds to linear utility functions.

In general, geometrically, if we have two points, a $a=\left(x_1,u\left(x_1\right)\right)$ and point $b=(x_2,u(x_2))$, then a convex combination of a and b is a point $c=\left(px_1+\left(1-p\right)x_2,pu\left(x_1\right)+\left(1-p\right)u\left(x_2\right)\right)$, which is shown in panel a. Point $x^*=px_1+\left(1-p\right)x_2$ is the expected prize from the lottery that promises x_1 with probability p and x_2 with probability $\left(1-p\right)$. The height c at point x^* represents the expected utility of the lottery.

Most people are believed to be risk-averse, while some people love taking risks, such as high-stakes gamblers, rope walkers, 'free' rock climbers, snake handlers and the like. Frenchman Alain Robert earned the nickname 'Spiderman' for climbing without any safety gears many tall skyscrapers and structures, including Dubai's Burg Khalifa, the tallest building on Earth. Firms and businesses are thought to be risk-neutral.

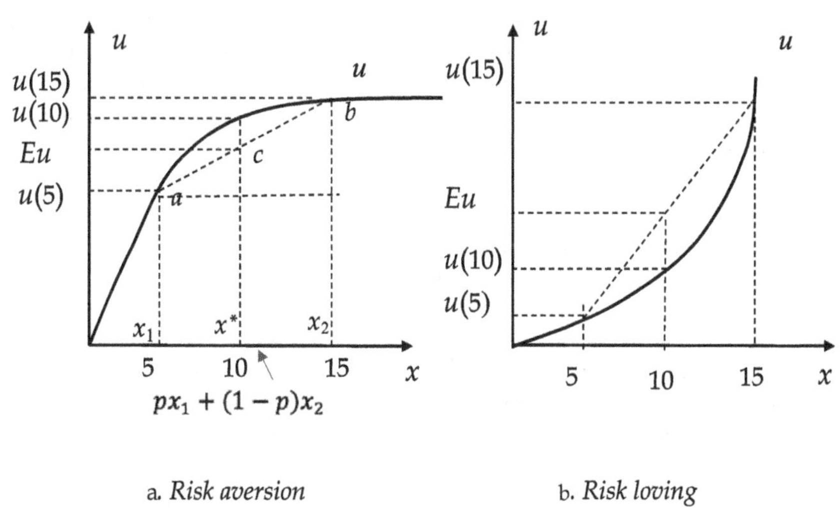

Figure 7.1 Utility functions for risk aversion and risk-loving

It is convenient to have a measure of risk aversion. Intuitively, the more concave the expected utility function, the more risk-averse the consumer. A well-known measure is the *Arrow-Pratt* measure of *risk aversion* (Arrow, 1971; Pratt, 1964):

$$r(x) = -\frac{u''(x)}{u'(x)}.$$

This is also known as the measure of absolute *risk aversion*. There is a related measure called *relative risk aversion*, which is defined to be the degree of absolute risk aversion relative to x:

$$\rho(x) = r(x)x = -\frac{xu''(x)}{u'(x)}.$$

Often, we use utility functions that display constant absolute risk aversion (CARA) or constant relative risk aversion (CRRA). An example of CARA utility functions $u(x) = \frac{1}{r}\left[1 - e^{-rx}\right]$, while $u = \sqrt{x}$ exhibits CRRA.

7.2.2 Risk premium

Risk imposes significant utility costs on risk-averse individuals. Therefore, it is not surprising that most people are willing to pay a premium to avoid risks or protect themselves from potential losses. For example, people pay higher rents to reside in a low-crime area. People with beach-front properties buy extra insurance against storm surge damages. We install an extra lock on our doors if a neighbour's house has been burgled.

Let us first consider the risk-avoidance strategy. Imagine an ardent Leicester City fan has placed a £20 bet on his team's winning the Premier League title (as it did in 2015–16). Should that extremely unlikely event happen, he will win £100,000. But 30 matches later (and only 8 to go), that suddenly becomes a possibility; in fact, the chance is 70 percent, by the estimates of the experts. Fearing potentially large payouts, the betting firm comes up with an offer: Take £50,000 and surrender the bet. What should our fan do—take the cash-out offer or hold on to the bet? The second option has the risk of getting nothing, but it gives an expected prize of £70,000. His choice clearly depends on how risk-averse he is. If his expected utility from the gamble is less than his utility from £50,000, he should trade the bet. Giving up £20,000 from a gamble is worthwhile to get a certainty payment of £50,000. This is the idea of risk premium.

Let us define **certainty equivalent** *(CE)* as the level of 'sure' income that makes a risk-averse individual indifferent between taking a gamble and giving up the gamble by taking the sure income. That is, $u(CE) = Eu(x)$. Then **risk premium** (θ) is defined as $\theta = \bar{x} - CE$, where $\bar{x} = Ex$. In Figure 7.2, we present a scenario in which a lottery has two possible prizes, x_1 and x_2, that give an expected reward of $px_1 + (1-p)x_2$ and an expected utility of $Eu(x) = pu(x_1) + (1-p)u(x_2)$. But the same utility can be obtained at an equivalent sure income of *CE*. That is, if someone offers *CE* to buy the lottery ticket from our consumer, she should sell. Any price bigger than *CE* is great, and any price less than *CE* should be rejected. For a risk-averse individual, *CE* is always strictly less than $\bar{x}$. But how much less will depend on the degree of risk aversion. There is an important relationship between risk premium and the degree of absolute risk aversion.

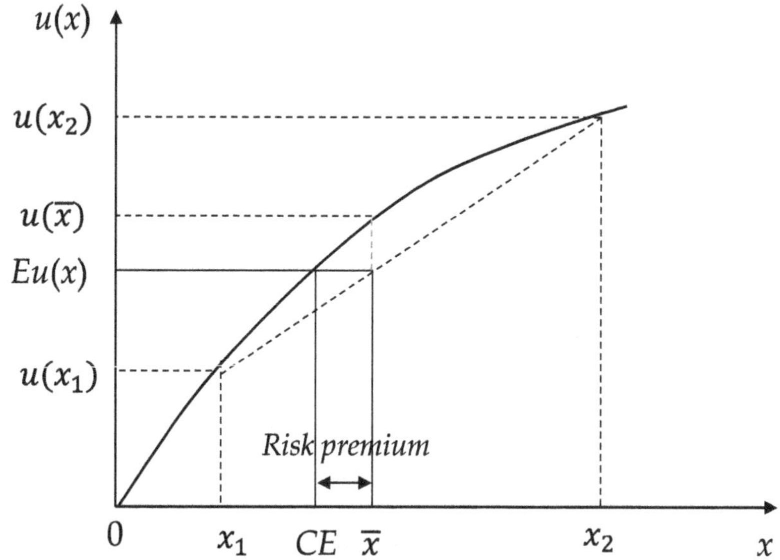

Figure 7.2 Risk premium

Lemma 1. *Suppose the distribution of returns* x *from a lottery is fully characterised by mean* $\overline{x}$ *and variance* σ^2*. Then a risk-averse consumer's risk premium for the lottery,* $\theta(x)$ *is strictly declining in* x *if and only if the degree of absolute risk aversion* $r(x)$ *is declining around the mean return* $\overline{x}$*. Furthermore, the certainty equivalent can be written as*

$$CE = \overline{x} - r(\overline{x})\frac{\sigma^2}{2}.$$

Proof. We first note that by Taylor expansion around $\overline{x}$, we can write

$$u(x) \approx u(\overline{x}) + u'(\overline{x})(x-\overline{x}) + u''(\overline{x})\frac{(x-\overline{x})^2}{2} + \ldots \tag{7.1}$$

Taking the expectation of the preceding (ignoring the terms beyond the second derivative):

$$Eu(x) \approx E\left\{u(\overline{x}) + u'(\overline{x})(x-\overline{x}) + u''(\overline{x})\frac{(x-\overline{x})^2}{2} + \ldots\right\}$$

$$\approx u(\overline{x}) + u''(\overline{x})\frac{\sigma^2}{2} \text{ since } E(x-\overline{x}) = 0.$$

Similarly, expand $u(CE)$ around $\overline{x}$ (now ignoring the terms beyond the first derivative) as

$$u(CE) \approx u(\overline{x}) + u'(\overline{x})(CE-\overline{x}) + \ldots.$$

Since by definition $u(CE) = Eu(x)$, it must be that the right-hand-side expressions of the previous two equations are (approximately) equal:

$$\begin{aligned} u(\bar{x})+u'(\bar{x})(CE-\bar{x}) &\approx u(\bar{x})+u''(\bar{x})\frac{\sigma^2}{2} \\ \bar{x}-CE &\approx \left[-\frac{u''(\bar{x})}{u'(\bar{x})}\right]\frac{\sigma^2}{2}, \\ CE &\approx \bar{x}-\left[-\frac{u''(\bar{x})}{u'(\bar{x})}\right]\frac{\sigma^2}{2} = \bar{x}-r(\bar{x})\frac{\sigma^2}{2}. \\ \theta &\approx r(\bar{x})\frac{\sigma^2}{2}, \text{ (equivalently).} \end{aligned} \quad (7.2)$$

Corollary 2. *Suppose the distribution of the returns* x *of a lottery is normally distributed. Then if the consumer's preference exhibits CARA, her risk premium will be constant. If her preference exhibits CRRA, then her relative risk premium will be constant.*

This corollary is evident from Eq. (7.1). For CARA utility functions, $r(x)$ is constant, say, at r, and for CRRA, $r(x)x$ is constant. Hence, for the former, the risk premium is constant, while for the latter the relative risk premium (i.e., \$θ x\$) is constant.

An important implication of the expected utility theory is that consumers decide on which lottery to buy based on which lottery yields the highest *CE*. Those whose utility functions are of the CARA type will find that their *CE* is constant and entirely determined by the mean return and variance of returns of the lottery. Take a CARA utility function $u(x) = \frac{1}{r}\left[1-e^{-rx}\right]$. The expected utility of this individual is then $Eu(x) = \frac{1}{r}\left[1-e^{-r(CE)}\right]$, because by the definition of *CE*, $u(CE) = Eu(x)$. Now if a lottery gives returns that are normally distributed, then using Eq. (7.1), we can write $Eu(x) = \frac{1}{r}\left[1-e^{-r\left(\bar{x}-\frac{r}{2}\sigma^2\right)}\right]$. The certainty income varies positively with respect to mean and negatively with respect to variance. This is known as the *mean-variance preference*. In portfolio selection, the well-known Sharpe ratio is based on this principle; consumers are advised to select the portfolio that gives the highest Sharpe ratio when comparing two or more portfolios of stocks. The numerator of the Sharpe ratio has the mean return of the stock relative to a risk-free rate, and the denominator has the standard deviation of the returns. Of course, some consumers are more sensitive to big losses than to big gains. The downside risk or 'tail risk' then is more important than just variance, and the Sharpe ratio will not be a very useful guide.

7.2.3 *Insurance premium*

A risk-averse person does not need to avoid risk by trading for a risk-free option. Insurance against risk can be bought, if the risk is insurable. Not all risks are insurable, but many are. We buy medical insurance, travel insurance, insurance against theft and fire and so on. The expected utility theory helps us understand how much insurance a risk-averse individual would demand and what premium she would be willing to pay.

Suppose a risk-averse consumer has wealth W, which may be lost by an amount L with probability p and may remain intact with probability $1-p$. The expected wealth of the consumer is $\bar{x} = p(W-L)+(1-p)W = W - pL$. Examples can be an event of flood that destroys a farmer's rice crops, very high temperature leading to grapes being too sweet and losing their aroma, a house fire and many such unfortunate events. Let us call the loss state a bad state of nature and the no-loss state a good state. We denote the consumer's income in the bad state as x_B and in the good state as x_G.

The consumer can buy insurance with a cover D for which she has to pay premium γD, $0<\gamma<1$. That means, if the bad state strikes, she will receive D from the insurance company. Thus, her wealth would be $x_B = W - L + D - \gamma D$ in the bad state and $x_G = W - \gamma D$ if the good state prevails. Her expected utility from buying insurance is

$$Eu = pu(W-L+D-\gamma D)+(1-p)u(W-\gamma D) = pu(x_B)+(1-p)u(x_G).$$

We ask, How much insurance coverage is optimal for the consumer? The answer is obtained by maximising Eu with respect to D. The first-order condition is

$$\begin{aligned} &pu'(x_B)\frac{\partial x_B}{\partial D}+(1-p)u'(x_G)\frac{\partial x_G}{\partial D}=0,\\ \text{or,}\quad &pu'(x_B)(1-\gamma)-(1-p)u'(x_G)\gamma=0,\\ \text{or,}\quad &p\left[\frac{u'(x_B)}{pu'(x_B)+(1-p)u'(x_G)}\right]=\gamma. \end{aligned} \tag{7.3}$$

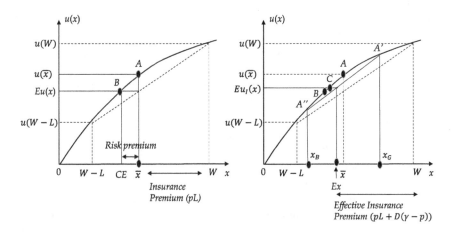

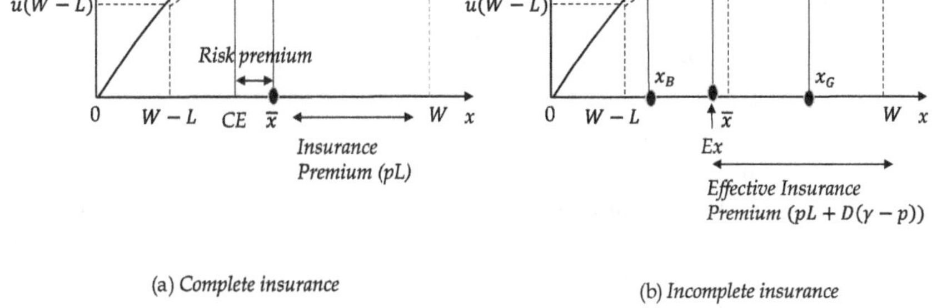

Figure 7.3 Insurance premium

The optimal cover should be such that the ratio of the expected marginal utility in the bad state to the overall expected marginal utility is equal to the rate of premium γ. Clearly, the left-hand side is less than 1 to match the premium rate of the right-hand side.

Now, let us try to determine γ. Suppose the insurance market is competitive and firms can earn only zero expected profit (from every customer). That is,

$$E\pi = -p(1-\gamma)D + (1-p)(\gamma D) = 0, \text{ or } \gamma = p.$$

The insurance premium rate γ when equal to the probability of the bad state p is called the *actuarially fair insurance premium rate.* It is so called because for the insurance firm, the act of selling insurance is also a gamble, and if it earns zero expected profit from it, then it is taking a fair gamble. Substituting $\gamma = p$ into Eq. (7.3), we get

$$u'(x_B) = u'(x_G), \text{ or } x_B = x_G, \text{ or } D = L.$$

The consumer's optimal demand for D is exactly L. That is, she will go for 'full coverage' so that her marginal utilities of wealth/income are equalised across all states of nature, which is called *complete insurance.* In consequence, her net income will be the same regardless of the states; that is, $x_B = x_G = W - pL$. It can also be seen that if $\gamma > p$ (which is likely to be true if the insurance market is not competitive) the consumer's optimal demand D will be strictly less than L. In that case, Eq. (7.3) implies $\dfrac{u'(x_B)}{pu'(x_B)+(1-p)u'(x_G)} > 1$ or $x_B < x_G$ or $D < L$.

Proposition 11. *If the insurance premium rate is equal to the probability of loss, a risk-averse consumer will demand complete insurance and full cover of the loss. If the insurance premium rate is greater than the probability of loss, she will demand incomplete insurance.*

Figure 7.3 demonstrates the difference between risk premiums and insurance premiums. While a 'fair insurance premium' allows the consumer to maintain her income at $\bar{x}$ and thus $u(\bar{x})$ with certainty, a 'risk premium' guarantees a certainty income and utility $Eu(x)$ when avoiding taking the risk. In other words, the risk premium determines the price at which one wants to sell a risky asset, and the insurance premium tells us at what price one can protect a risky asset. Panel *a* demonstrates full protection, while panel *b* demonstrates partial protection ($\gamma > p$). In the latter case, incomplete insurance means the original lottery is being transformed into a new lottery with less variability, given by points A' and A'' (or, in income terms, x_G and x_B), the convex combination of which gives the new expected income Ex and a lower expected utility $Eu_I(x)$ given by point C. Because of incomplete insurance, the expected utility is now lower than the utility under complete insurance, $u(\bar{x})$, but it is still greater than that from 'no insurance' (point B). This shows that the consumer is always better off by buying insurance against risks even when the insurance cover is partial. Of course, if the insurance premium rate becomes so high that her utility falls below point B, then she can sell the risky asset. A related question is, Under incomplete insurance, does the consumer pay a greater or smaller total premium; that is, is $\gamma D > pL$? The answer depends on how risk-averse the consumer is. However, we can calculate an 'effective' insurance premium, which is the difference between W and Ex, $pL + D(\gamma - p)$ or $\gamma D + p(L - D)$. When $\gamma > p$, the effective insurance premium is greater than both the fair premium pL and the actual premium γD. The consumer sacrifices an effectively larger amount of her wealth.

We end the discussion of this section by making two important observations. First, the tendency to seek complete insurance, that is, to equalise marginal utilities of income across all states of nature, is a common feature of any optimisation under uncertainty. In agricultural tenancy models, credit contracts, investment models, labour contracts and similar circumstances, the same phenomenon is observed. Risk-averse agents will try to transfer income across different states so that variability in utility is reduced.

Second, for the idea of insurance to work, we need another agent whose wealth should not be affected in the same way as that of the insured person or who is risk-neutral. The example we considered is the one in which insurance is provided by a risk-neutral insurance firm. However, in many situations, such as in employment contexts an employee cannot buy market-based insurance against her income uncertainty; see our example in the next section. The employer then can provide implicit insurance through a carefully designed wage contract. Two risk-averse agents being at two opposite ends of a transaction also can provide some insurance to each other, although neither of them can absorb the full risk. In other situations, there may not be any scope for risk sharing at all. For instance, small businesses may suffer from international price movements. In such instances, they can bet in favour of adverse price movements in a specialised betting market, which is called *hedging*. If the adverse price movement occurs, they will suffer business losses but will also earn a payment from their bets. In the financial market there are many instruments, broadly classified as *derivatives* that are used to offset risk in one asset (or investment) by investing in another, which are linked by the same uncertainty but give returns in opposite directions. Securities, such as swaps, options, futures and the like, are some of the commonly used derivatives. Farmers are often contracted by traders well before the harvest to sell their crops at a pre-specified price (*future contract*), but the contract may entail an *option* for the trader not to buy the crop if its market price falls below a certain level. Similarly, the farmer may also want to retain an option not to sell at the agreed price if the market price rises above a threshold. Modern financial markets provide a range of ways to reduce risk exposures for individuals and businesses alike.

7.3 Applications

7.3.1 *Share tenancy*

In many developing countries, especially in Asia, landowners are seen to lease out lands in return for a share of the harvest. The tenant bears the production cost himself, although sharing the cost of some non-labour inputs, such as fertilisers is also common. The output sharing rule can be fixed or variable depending on the amount of harvest, which is subject to weather uncertainty. Farmers and landowners agree beforehand by which proportion the output will be shared.

This type of tenancy arrangement involves two issues: (1) efficient input use and (2) efficient risk sharing. The first question concerns if the total surplus is maximised. The second question concerns whether output sharing implies optimal risk sharing.

Suppose a tenant leases a plot of land and employs labour l (assuming away other non-labour inputs) at a cost wl. To allow for cost sharing let μ be the tenant's share of the cost, $0 < \mu \leq 1$. The production function is $Q = \theta_i f(l)$, where θ_i is a harvest-affecting parameter that varies between two states of nature, good and bad, $i = G, B$; $\theta_G > \theta_B$. The bad state is realised with probability p. The price of the crop is fixed at unity. Let α_G and α_B be the state-dependent output shares retained by the tenant; the remaining shares go to the landowner. The function $f(l)$ is monotonic and concave in l. The tenant's utility function is $u_T = u_T(x)$, and the landowner's utility function is $u_L = u_L(y)$, where x and y are their respective state-contingent incomes. We can specify $x_G = \alpha_G \theta_G f(l) - \mu wl$ and $x_B = \alpha_B \theta_B f(l) - \mu wl$, while $y_G = (1-\alpha_G)\theta_G f(l) - (1-\mu)wl$, and $y_B = (1-\alpha_B)\theta_B f(l) - (1-\mu)wl$.

Let us assume that the tenant applies labour after θ is realised.[2] The weather uncertainty here is more like unexpected rain just before the sowing season. Therefore, his optimal labour use is given by maximising his state-dependent utility, $u_T = u_T(x_B)$, with respect to l_B, or $u_T(x_G)$, with respect to l_G. We consider two cases of cost sharing: (1) $\mu_B = \alpha_B$ and $\mu_G = \alpha_G$ and (2) $\mu = 1$. In the first case, costs and outputs are shared by the same proportion. In the second case, the tenant bears all production costs.

7.3.1.1 *First best*

We start with the tenant's optimal labour use after θ is realised and costs that are shared at the rate α_B and α_G. The first-order conditions for labour are

$$\theta_B f'(l_B) = w \text{ and } \theta_G f'(l_G) = w. \tag{7.4}$$

Evidently, labour is optimally used to maximise not just the tenant's income but the joint surplus of the two parties. Thus, *production efficiency* is achieved. Optimal labour l_B^* and l_G^* are independent of the sharing proportions.

Now we turn to the issue of risk sharing. Suppose the landowner determines α_G and α_B (before θ_i-s are realised) by maximising her expected utility subject to the tenant's expected utility held at $\bar{u}$ with perfect anticipation of the future labour use l_B^* and l_G^*.

$$\begin{aligned} &\text{Max} \quad Eu_L = pu_L\left(y_B\left(l_B^*\right)\right) + (1-p)u_L\left(y_G\left(l_G^*\right)\right) \\ &\text{sub. to} \quad Eu_T = pu_T\left(x_B\left(l_B^*\right)\right) + (1-p)u_T\left(x_G\left(l_G^*\right)\right) = \bar{u}. \end{aligned}$$

Forming a Lagrangian, we derive three first-order conditions for α_B, α_G and λ (the Lagrange multiplier) as

$$\begin{aligned} &pu_L'(y_B)\left\{-\theta_B f\left(l_B^*\right)\right\} + \lambda\left[pu_T'(x_B)\left\{\theta_B f\left(l_B^*\right)\right\}\right] = 0, \\ &pu_L'(y_G)\left\{-\theta_G f\left(l_G^*\right)\right\} + \lambda\left[pu_T'(x_G)\left\{\theta_G f\left(l_G^*\right)\right\}\right] = 0, \\ &pu_T\left(x_B\left(l_B^*\right)\right) + (1-p)u_T\left(x_G\left(l_G^*\right)\right) - \bar{u} = 0. \end{aligned}$$

The first two equations can be rearranged to write

$$\frac{u_L'(y_B)}{u_T'(x_B)} = \lambda, \text{ and } \frac{u_L'(y_G)}{u_T'(x_G)} = \lambda \Rightarrow \frac{u_T'(x_B)}{u_T'(x_G)} = \frac{u_L'(y_B)}{u_L'(y_G)}. \tag{7.5}$$

The optimal output (and cost) sharing proportions should be such that the marginal rate of substitution of income between bad and good states must be the same for both agents. Equivalently, the ratio of marginal utilities of the two agents must be the same across the two states. This is known as *efficient risk sharing*. As both agents are risk-averse, total risk is to be shared in this manner.

In the special case of the landowner being risk-neutral (who just cares for profit), we have $u_L'(y_B) = u_L'(y_G) = 1$, which implies that the tenant should have complete insurance in $x_B = x_G$ or $\alpha_B^*\left[\theta_B f\left(l_B^*\right) - w l_B^*\right] = \alpha_G^*\left[\theta_G f\left(l_G^*\right) - w l_G^*\right]$, leading to $u_T'(x_B) = u_T'(x_G)$. Since the bad-state surplus is smaller than the good-state surplus, we should expect $\alpha_B^* > \alpha_G^*$. The tenant should receive a bigger share of the surplus in the bad state. Thus, we show that both production efficiency and risk-sharing efficiency are achieved.

7.3.1.2 Second best

Now we consider the more realistic case of the labour cost being fully borne by the tenant. By setting $\mu_B = \mu_G = 1$, we now solve the problem again.

Let us first derive the optimal labour conditions as

$$u_T'(x_B)\left[\alpha_B\theta_B f'(l_B) - w\right] = 0, \text{ and } u_T'(x_G)\left[\alpha_G\theta_G f'(l_G) - w\right] = 0. \quad (7.6)$$

Let $l_B^* = l(\alpha_B)$ and $l_G^* = l(\alpha_G)$ be the optimal labour amounts used by the tenant. For each labour level, the tenant equalises the wage with his *own marginal returns*, which is just the α proportion of the marginal product of labour. It can be easily checked that $\frac{\partial l_B^*}{\partial \alpha_B} = -\frac{f'\left(l_B^*\right)}{\alpha_B f''\left(l_B^*\right)} > 0$ and $\frac{\partial l_G^*}{\partial \alpha_G} = -\frac{f'\left(l_G^*\right)}{\alpha_G f''\left(l_G^*\right)} > 0$. Since α_B and α_G are fractions, Eq. (7.6) confirms that total (state-dependent) surplus is not maximised under the share tenancy arrangement (without cost sharing); rather, the tenant's state-dependent incomes x_B and x_G are maximised. This under-production result is well known since Alfred Marshall wrote about it in his famous critique of the so-called *Metayage* tenancy, an extensively prevalent system of nineteenth-century France. All share tenancy systems (without cost sharing) chronically under-produce and are therefore *productively inefficient*.

To derive the optimal risk-sharing conditions, we need to recognise that α_B and α_G will have two effects: a direct effect on the income of the two parties via their shares of the output for any given level of labour and an indirect effect that works by changing the optimal use of labour. The landowner will experience both effects, while the tenant will experience only the direct effect, because the indirect effect is washed away through his optimisation.

Therefore, we write the first-order condition with respect to α_B as

$$pu_L'(y_B)\left\{-\theta_B f(l_B^*) + (1-\alpha_B)\theta_B f'(l_B^*)\frac{\partial l_B^*}{\partial \alpha_B}\right\} + \lambda\left[pu_T'(x_B)\theta_B f(l_B^*)\right] = 0.$$

The preceding can be simplified and rewritten as

$$p\theta_B f\left(l_B^*\right)\left[u_L'\left(y_B\right)\left\{-1+\frac{\left(1-\alpha_B\right)}{\alpha_B f\left(l_B^*\right)}\frac{f'\left(l_B^*\right)^2}{\left(-f''\left(l_B^*\right)\right)}\right\}+\lambda u_T'\left(x_B\right)\right]=0,$$

or, $$u_L'\left(y_B\right)\left[-1+\left\{\frac{\left(1-\alpha_B\right)}{\alpha_B}\right\}\times\left\{\frac{f'\left(l_B^*\right)l_B^*}{f\left(l_B^*\right)}\right\}\times\left\{\frac{f'\left(l_B^*\right)}{-f''\left(l_B^*\right)l_B^*}\right\}\right]+\lambda u_T'\left(x_B\right)=0$$

or, $$u_L'\left(y_B\right)\left[-1+\left\{\frac{\left(1-\alpha_B\right)}{\alpha_B}\right\}\times\frac{\epsilon_f}{\left|\epsilon_{f'}\right|}\right]+\lambda u_T'\left(x_B\right)=0$$

or, $$u_L'\left(y_B\right)\left[-1+\kappa_B\right]+\lambda u_T'\left(x_B\right)=0,$$

where

$$\epsilon_f=\frac{f'\left(l_B^*\right)l_B^*}{f\left(l_B^*\right)},\quad \left|\epsilon_{f'}\right|=-\frac{f''\left(l_B^*\right)l_B^*}{f'\left(l_B^*\right)}\quad\text{and}\quad \kappa_B=\left\{\frac{\left(1-\alpha_B\right)}{\alpha_B}\right\}\times\frac{\epsilon_f}{\left|\epsilon_{f'}\right|}>0.$$

The two elasticity terms relate to the total output and the marginal product of labour, respectively. In the same way, we can write the first-order condition with respect to α_G as

$$u_L'\left(y_G\right)\left[-1+\kappa_G\right]+\lambda u_T'\left(x_G\right)=0,$$

where $\kappa_G=\left\{\frac{\left(1-\alpha_G\right)}{\alpha_G}\right\}\times\frac{\epsilon_f}{\left|\epsilon_{f'}\right|}$ relates to the good state elasticities. From the two first-order conditions, we see that $\kappa_B$and κ_G both must be strictly less than 1; otherwise, the optimality conditions will not be satisfied for interior α_B and α_G. Thus, combining the two first-order conditions, we write the optimal risk-sharing condition as

$$\frac{u_L'\left(y_B\right)}{u_T'\left(x_B\right)}=\frac{\lambda}{1-\kappa_B}\text{ and }\frac{u_L'\left(y_G\right)}{u_T'\left(x_G\right)}=\frac{\lambda}{1-\kappa_G}\Rightarrow\frac{u_L'\left(y_B\right)}{u_L'\left(y_G\right)}=\left\{\frac{1-\kappa_G}{1-\kappa_B}\right\}\frac{u_T'\left(x_B\right)}{u_T'\left(x_G\right)}. \tag{7.7}$$

Since $\kappa_B\neq\kappa_G$, the ratio of the marginal utilities of the two agents are not same across the two states. Hence, risk is not efficiently shared. Thus, we see that production inefficiency leads to inefficient risk allocation. Even in the special case of a risk-neutral landowner, we obtain $u_T'\left(x_B\right)\neq u_T'\left(x_G\right)$—incomplete insurance for the tenant.

Since Marshall, economists have examined why people engage in inefficient tenancy when Pareto superior alternatives are available. Among the explanations offered are the difficulty of the landowner to verify the tenant's actual cost and asymmetric information about the state of nature. See Basu (2003) and Ray (1998) for further reading.

7.3.2 Implicit contract

In the labour literature, there is a body of work that examines the twin issues of efficiency and insurance as part of employment contracts. Uncertainty creates common concerns for employers and employees, and both may wish to share the risk by tying wages to labour hours rather than fixing an hourly wage rate. This literature came to be known as the implicit contract literature, not because the contract offered to the workers is implicit or informal but because the contract carries an implicit insurance element.

Let us use the same set-up as in the section of share tenancy except that the landowner is now called the employer and the tenant the employee. Let the output be as before $Q_B = \theta_B f(l)$ and $Q_G = \theta_G f(l)$, which occur with probability p and $1-p$. Suppose the employment contract specifies a state-specific wage bill (i.e., total wage payment) W_B and W_G and employment l_B and l_G.[3] The employment contract, is by construction a Pareto optimal programme. The employer maximises his expected utility subject to the employee's expected utility held at a reservation level $\bar{u}$. The employee's (state-specific) utility is $u = u(W, l)$, with $u_W > 0$, and $u_{WW} < 0$, $u_{ll} > 0$, while the employer's (state-specific) utility is $v = v(\pi)$, where $\pi = \theta f(l) - W$. The implicit contracting problem is

$$\begin{aligned} &\text{Max} \quad Ev = pv\left(\theta_B f(l_B) - W_B\right) + (1-p)v\left(\theta_G f(l_G) - W_G\right) \\ &\text{sub. to} \quad Eu = pu\left(W_B, l_B\right) + (1-p)u\left(W_G, l_G\right) = \bar{u}. \end{aligned}$$

Again, following the standard Lagrangian procedure we derive the first-order conditions with respect to l_B, W_B, l_G and W_G, respectively, as follows:

$$pv'(\pi_B)\{\theta_B f'(l_B)\} + \lambda p \frac{\partial u}{\partial l_B} = 0 \tag{7.8}$$

$$-pv'(\pi_B) + \lambda p \frac{\partial u}{\partial W_B} = 0 \tag{7.9}$$

$$(1-p)v'(\pi_G)\{\theta_G f'(l_G)\} + \lambda(1-p)\frac{\partial u}{\partial l_G} = 0 \tag{7.10}$$

$$-(1-p)v'(\pi_G) + \lambda(1-p)\frac{\partial u}{\partial W_G} = 0 \tag{7.11}$$

Substituting Eq. (7.9) into (7.8) and (7.11) into (7.10), we get the production efficiency conditions

$$\theta_B f'(l_B) = MRS_B \quad \text{and} \quad \theta_G f'(l_G) = MRS_G, \tag{7.12}$$

where MRS_B and MRS_G represent the MRS of the worker between wage and employment in the bad and good states, respectively. Eq. (7.12) says that in each state the marginal (revenue) product of the firm must equate the marginal rate of substitution of the worker. This is production efficiency.

In addition, dividing Eq. (7.9) by Eq. (7.11), we obtain the risk-sharing condition as

$$\frac{\frac{\partial u}{\partial W_B}}{\frac{\partial u}{\partial W_G}} = \frac{v'(\pi_B)}{v'(\pi_G)}. \tag{7.13}$$

The marginal rate of substitution (MRS) of the worker from transferring 1 unit of income (i.e., wage bill) from the bad state to the good state must be the same as that of his employer. Therefore, the employment contract ensures both production efficiency and efficient risk sharing.

In the special case of risk-neutral employer, $v'(.) = 1$ and we get from Eq. (7.13) $\frac{\partial u}{\partial W_B} = \frac{\partial u}{\partial W_G}$. That is, the marginal utility of income of the worker must be invariant across states. Once again, the *complete insurance* condition holds for the employee. However, caution should be taken in suggesting that the employee's income will remain constant. This will be true only if the employee's utility is separable in wage bill and labour, as in $u = h(W) - g(l)$. Here, the employee will enjoy a constant wage bill, but his utility in the good state will be lower than that in the bad state, because he will be asked to work more in the good state.

The basic point of this exercise is that when two agents engage in a mutually beneficial agreement, they would try to share risk optimally as well as maintain productive efficiency if the contracting is organised in an unconstrained way. However, a broader point of the implicit contract literature is that contracting will be constrained either because of informational asymmetry, union agreements or other factors, leading to an inflexible wage and/or unemployment as rational outcomes. See Azariadis (1975), Azariadis and Stiglitz (1983) and Newberry and Stiglitz (1987).

7.3.3 Medical insurance

The insurance problem we discussed earlier applies to those circumstances in which the insurance companies know the probability of the bad state for each and every client. Examples of such circumstances are burglary, fire, flooding and the like. Medical insurance is one case in which this assumption is easily violated. Insurance companies may know the average probability of prostate cancer for all males between 50 and 60 but will not be able to ascertain the true probability of a given individual for that age group. Moreover, the individual males of that age group may have a different belief to the average probability of the group. This difference can have important implications for medical insurance.

Suppose we have a continuum of agents of mass 1, all having wealth W and facing a risk of losing L (e.g., losing income due to illness). But the probability of losing L, denoted by p, varies from person to person. We assume p to be uniformly distributed over [0, 1] with density 1 and probability p. Each individual knows his own probability (or what he believes to be his true likelihood). But the insurance companies know only the average probability, which is 1/2 (due to the uniform distribution assumption).

In order to make their expected profit non-negative, an insurer needs to set the premium rate at least equal to 1/2. Let this premium rate be denoted as γ and the cover be a full cover so that anybody who is buying insurance will enjoy a fixed income $W - \gamma L$. Consider an individual, whose probability of loss is (an arbitrary) p and compare his utility from insurance

$Eu_I = u(W - \gamma L)$ with the same from not buying insurance $Eu_0 = pu(W - L) + (1 - p)u(W)$. Buying insurance is optimal if and only if

$$p \geq \frac{u(W) - u(W - \gamma L)}{u(W) - u(W - L)} \equiv \hat{p}(\gamma).$$

That is, if an individual's own probability exceeds a critical level, which makes their *CE* of not buying the insurance no larger than $W - \gamma L$, then and only then the individual will buy. In fact, all individuals with a probability greater than $\hat{p}$ will buy the insurance, and all other individuals (for whom $p < \hat{p}$) will not buy the insurance. Now note that an individual whose own probability is exactly γ will enjoy $u(W - \gamma L; p = \gamma) > u(CE; p = \gamma) = Eu_0(p = \gamma)$. That is, $W - \gamma L > CE(p = \gamma)$. The indifferent individual for whom $u(W - \gamma L) = Eu_0(\hat{p})$ must have $CE(\hat{p}) = W - \gamma L$. As *CE* increases with a decrease in *p*, we must have $\hat{p} < \gamma$. Also, $\hat{p}$ will be increasing in γ.

Now consider a representative insurer's problem. He knows that only $1 - \hat{p}$ proportion of the people will buy the policy, giving it an expected revenue of $(1 - \hat{p}(\gamma))\gamma L$, while the expected payout is $\int_{\hat{p}(\gamma)}^{1} pLdp = L\left[1 - \hat{p}(\gamma)^2\right]/2$. The expected profit is

$$E\pi = \left[(1 - \hat{p}(\gamma))\gamma - \frac{1 - \hat{p}(\gamma)^2}{2}\right]L = \left[1 - \hat{p}(\gamma)\right]\left[\gamma - \frac{1 + \hat{p}(\gamma)}{2}\right]L.$$

But unless $\gamma > \frac{1 + \hat{p}}{2}$, the insurance company cannot make positive profit. In fact, if γ is set at the average probability 1/2, then it will clearly make losses. Maximising $E\pi$ with respect to γ, we get the optimal γ from the equation:

$$1 - \hat{p} - \hat{p}'(\gamma)\left[\gamma - \hat{p}\right] = 0.$$

If there is an optimal $\gamma \in (1/2, 1)$ satisfying $(1 + \hat{p})/2 < \gamma$, then and only then the insurance option will be available in the market.

The preceding problem is often referred to as the **adverse selection** problem of insurance (commonly associated with health or medical insurance) that leads to market failures. Here, only those people who are at high risk buy the insurance, jeopardising the viability of insurance businesses.[4] One way out is making medical insurance mandatory so that everybody must participate (just as automobile insurance is mandatory). The US Affordable Care Act, 2010, popularly known as Obamacare, makes it mandatory for employers to offer health insurance to their workers, which essentially has strengthened the viability of private health insurance businesses. An alternative solution is to have state-run health care funded through direct taxation, as is the case in Europe. Another option pursued in many countries such as India is to offer income tax incentives for buying medical (or life) insurance. This also enables many low-risk individuals to participate in the insurance market.

7.3.4 *Search*

Expected utility theory can be useful even when risk does not inflict loss in utility. With the assumption of risk neutrality, we study problems like job and price search and betting.

7.3.4.1 *Job search*

We continue to look for better jobs even when we have a good one. Suppose a risk-neutral worker currently earns w^*, but she believes that there are better jobs out there which will give a higher wage up to $\overline{w}$. Finding these jobs is probabilistic. Let $F(w)$ be the probability of finding a job that pays w or less and $f(w)$ be the probability density function of a job that pays exactly w. Job search means sampling from the pool of jobs. If the draw brings up a job that gives a wage higher than w^*, she will take it. Otherwise, she will stay in her current job. There is a search cost of c.

Her expected income from job search is

$$v = -c + w^* \int_0^{w^*} f(w)dw + \int_{w^*}^{\overline{w}} wf(w)dw = -c + F(w^*)w^* + (1 - F(w^*))\omega(w^*),$$

where $\omega(w^*)$ is the conditional expected wage given w^*, where

$$\omega(w^*) = \int_{w^*}^{\overline{w}} w\left\{\frac{f(w)}{1-F(w^*)}\right\}dw, \quad \Rightarrow \quad \int_{w^*}^{\overline{w}} wf(w)dw = (1-F(w^*))\omega(w^*).$$

The second term in the equation for v says that she remains in her current job with probability $F(w^*)$, and the third term says that she gets a higher expected wage $\omega(w^*)$ with probability $1-F(w^*)$.

Our question is, At what w^* will she stop searching? The answer is that if her current wage w^* exceeds v, she will not search. The highest w^* is such that $v(w^*) - w^* = 0$.

$$v - w^* = (1-F(w^*))\left[-\frac{c}{1-F(w^*)} + \omega(w^*) - w^*\right] = 0 \tag{7.14}$$

To solve the problem explicitly, let us assume uniform wage distribution, $f(w) = 1/\overline{w}$ and $F(w) = w/\overline{w}$. This helps us write:

$$\begin{aligned} v - w^* &= -c + \frac{w^{*2}}{\overline{w}} + \left(1 - \frac{w^*}{\overline{w}}\right)\left(\frac{\overline{w} + w^*}{2}\right) - w^* \\ &= \frac{1}{2\overline{w}}\left[w^{*2} - 2\overline{w}w^* + \overline{w}(\overline{w} - 2c)\right]. \end{aligned}$$

$v - w^* \leq 0$ if and only if $w^* \geq \overline{w} - \sqrt{2\overline{w}c} = \overline{w}\left[1 - \sqrt{\frac{2c}{\overline{w}}}\right]$. If the worker is already earning $\overline{w}\left[1 - \sqrt{\frac{2c}{\overline{w}}}\right]$ or more, she will not search for another job. Note that the threshold wage is decreasing in c and less than $\overline{w}$ if $0 < c < \overline{w}/2$.

What if she repeats her search until she finds a better job? Mind that every round of search requires incurring a cost c, and conditional on not getting a wage offer above w^*, the search in any period is same as the search in the previous round. Here, we are assuming that the entire pool of jobs is searched again. There is no reason to assume that a previously found job offering a wage lower than w^* cannot offer a higher wage next time around.[5] The worker's expected income from job search is then modified as

$$\tilde{v} = -c + F(w^*)\tilde{v} + (1 - F(w^*))\omega(w^*).$$

With probability $F\left(w^*\right)$, she will repeat her search, incur cost c every time and should face the same expected income $\tilde{v}$ as in the current round. She searches for $\frac{1}{1 - F\left(w^*\right)}$ (expected) number of times, and her net gains from the search should be zero at the threshold wage:

$$\tilde{v} - w^* = -\frac{c}{1 - F\left(w^*\right)} + \omega\left(w^*\right) - w^* = 0,$$

which gives the identical threshold wage as in Eq. (7.14). Thus, regardless of whether she searches only once or repeatedly, the critical wage is still the same. This is because there is no discounting in the future in our simple setting.

7.3.4.2 *Price search*

Consumers search for the best bargains; prices vary from store to store and from week to week (if not between days). Imagine our consumer is looking for a (good but reasonably priced) kitchen appliance. Although most stores today have an online presence, not all deals are posted online. Visiting the stores is always a good idea. But going to a store has some cost. Let this be c and constant between stores. Since stores often have surprises, let the price of the appliances p be a random variable, where p has a probability density function $f(p)$. The cumulative distribution function $F(x) = \int_0^x f(p)\,dp$ refers to the probability that price will be less than or equal to some level x; $F(\infty) = 1$, $F(0) = 0$.

The consumer's bargain hunting is similar to the job search problem, with one slight modification. The stopping price is to be determined, while in the job search problem, the current wage was given. We present a simple model of price search following McAfee (2006).

Since in the price search problem, the consumer's utility from the appliance is the same, what matters is the total cost of the appliance (including the search cost), and to keep the total cost minimum, she needs to decide on a cut-off price, say, p^*, at which she will look no further. This is also a case of repeated search, and the entire pool of stores is searched every time.

Let us denote the expected total cost of purchase by $G(p^*)$. If her expected cost of purchase is $G(p^*)$, then her future expected cost of purchase conditional on not getting $p < p^*$ is also $G(p^*)$.

Thus, we write

$$G(p^*) = c + \int_0^{p^*} pf(p)dp + G(p^*)\int_{p^*}^{\infty} f(p)dp$$
$$= c + \int_0^{p^*} pf(p)dp + G(p^*)(1 - F(p^*))$$
$$= \frac{c + \int_0^{p^*} pf(p)dp}{F(p^*)}.$$

The consumer's cost consists of the 'expected search cost' and the expected price, both conditional on finding a price lower than p^*. The expected number of searches to find a price less than p^* is $\frac{1}{F(p^*)}$, which gives an expected search cost $\frac{c}{F(p^*)}$ and an expected price $\frac{\int_0^{p^*} pf(p)dp}{F(p^*)}$.

To find out the minimum cost, we need to set $G'(p^*) = 0$ and verify that $G''(p^*) > 0$.

$$G'(p^*) = \frac{1}{F(p^*)^2}\left[F(p^*)\frac{\partial}{\partial p^*}\left\{\int_0^{p^*} pf(p)dp\right\} - \left\{c + \int_0^{p^*} pf(p)dp\right\}f(p^*)\right].$$

The first term on the numerator involves differentiating a term under integration, whose upper limit is itself the differential variable.[6] This turns out to be

$$G'(p^*) = \frac{p^* f(p^*)}{F(p^*)} - \frac{f(p^*)\left[c + \int_0^{p^*} pf(p)dp\right]}{F(p^*)^2} = \frac{f(p^*)}{F(p^*)}\left[p^* - \frac{c + \int_0^{p^*} pf(p)dp}{F(p^*)}\right]$$
$$= \frac{f(p^*)}{F(p^*)}\left[p^* - G(p^*)\right] = 0 \Rightarrow p^* = G(p^*).$$

The first-order condition requires that p^* must be a fixed point, at which it must equal the expected total cost of purchasing the good.[7]

To illustrate the optimal reservation price of the consumer, let us assume that p is uniformly distributed over $[a,b]$. Then we derive the expected total cost as

$$G\left(p^*\right)=\frac{c+\int_0^{p^*} pf(p)dp}{F\left(p^*\right)}=\frac{c+\int_a^{p^*} p\frac{1}{b-a}dp}{\frac{p^*-a}{b-a}}$$

$$=\frac{c(b-a)+\frac{1}{2}\left(p^{*2}-a^2\right)}{p^*-a}=\frac{1}{2}\left(p^*+a\right)+\frac{c(b-a)}{p^*-a}.$$

The cost function $G\left(p^*\right)$ is minimised at

$$G'\left(p^*\right)=\frac{1}{2}-\frac{c(b-a)}{\left(p^*-a\right)^2}=0,\Rightarrow p^*=a+\sqrt{2c(b-a)}.$$

Several observations can be made here. First, as $c\to 0,\ p^*\to a$. If search has no direct cost, people will search forever until they find the lowest possible price a. Second, $p^*<b$ if $2c<(b-a)$. If the maximum gain from price search is less than or equal to twice the search cost, then one should not search (under uniform distribution). Third, there is also a general observation that the optimal expected search cost $G\left(p^*\right)$ is a concave function of c. This follows from the fact that $\frac{\partial G\left(p^*\right)}{\partial c^*}=\frac{1}{F\left(p^*\right)}$ by the envelope theorem (because $G\left(p^*\right)$ is minimised at the optimum p^*), and $\frac{\partial^2 G\left(p^*\right)}{\partial c^2}=-\frac{f\left(p^*\right)}{F\left(p^*\right)^2}\frac{\partial p^*}{\partial c}$. Since $\frac{\partial p^*}{\partial c}>0$ we must have $\frac{\partial^2 G\left(p^*\right)}{\partial c^2}<0$. Total cost rises in the search cost, but it rises at a decreasing rate.

7.3.5 Betting

Bets are state-contingent claims with finite lives that are linked to a specific event. Who will win the soccer World Cup? Who is going to be the new Super Bowl champion? Which film will win the Oscars? These are just a few examples of innumerable opportunities that bookmakers offer for betting enthusiasts. While horse racing is one of the oldest forms of legal betting operations around the world, illegal betting on all sorts of things is also common. Such is the popularity of betting.

There are broadly two types of bookmaking (or betting systems). Under *fixed-odds* betting, the bookmakers set inflexible odds, specifying how much money will be paid per dollar of bet if outcome x occurs. Slot machines and devices that have winning chances mechanically (and secretly) preset are also prime examples of fixed-odds betting. Since betting odds are relative, they also convey some assessment of the bookmaker about which outcome is likely. Bettors play against the bookmaker or betting house (just as in blackjack). Horse racing and high-street betting in the United Kingdom are run on a fixed-odds basis. A slightly different system is *parimutuel betting*, where bettors on two sides are pitted against each other with the winners sharing the losers' collective bet. All jackpot lotteries are organised on a parimutuel basis. Here, betting odds keep changing depending on which side attracts more bets. The bookmaker's role is to organise betting in exchange for a small commission, usually from the winning side. There is also a third system, a recent phenomenon called *betting exchanges* (mostly online), where two bettors from opposite sides are matched and one is pitted against the other. This is individual-to-individual betting.

We now present a simple model of fixed-odds betting for a monopoly betting market. Suppose there is a two-team contest resulting in a win or loss; a draw is not a possibility. A monopolist bookmaker offers betting opportunities on a team's win. He sells two tickets, indexed 1 and 2, at prices π_1 and π_2, $(\pi_1, \pi_2 < 1)$, respectively. The tickets are nothing but a promise that if team 1 wins, ticket 1 holders will get 1 dollar each, and if team 2 wins, ticket 2 holders will get 1 dollar each. The losing team's ticket holders will get nothing. Price π_1 corresponds to betting odds on team i of $\frac{1-\pi_i}{\pi_i}:1$. Conversely, betting odds of $x:y$ for team i corresponds to $\pi_i = \frac{y}{x+y}$.

There is a continuum of bettors or punters, having \$1 each to bet; their collective wealth is also \$1. They are parameterised by individual beliefs, denoted by q, about the probability of team 1's win. Belief q is distributed over [0,1] by a cumulative distribution function $F(q)$ with probability density $f(q) > 0$ for $q \in [0,1]$. A bettor with $q = 0$ believes team 1 can never win, and a bettor with $q = 1$ believes team 1 will surely win. We impose an assumption on the distribution function to ensure some regularity results. The assumption is easily satisfied under uniform distribution.

Assumption 3.

$$\frac{1-F(q)}{f(q)} \text{ and } \frac{F(1-q)}{f(1-q)} \text{ are decreasing in } q.$$

There is an important difference between the bettors' beliefs and the bookmaker's belief. The bookmaker is professional, and he has specialist knowledge to figure out the true probability of team 1's win, which is denoted by p. By comparison, the bettors bet out of loyalty for their favourite team or simply for fun; as a result, their beliefs are uncorrelated with the true probability.

From a modelling point of view, the difference between these two beliefs can be borne out in the following way. Suppose Mother Nature makes a draw to determine team 1's winning chance. The bookmaker observes Nature's draw, and therefore, he correctly learns the probability p, while the bettors do not observe Nature's draw; instead, they draw their own and independent signals about the fate of the contest, which will be completely uncorrelated to the nature's draw. Clearly, these beliefs are non-rational, and this is why in the betting literature, these bettors are often referred to as 'naive' bettors just like the noise traders in the financial markets (see Shin, 1991; and Bag and Saha, 2011).

From every ticket the bookmaker sells, he expects to make $\left(1-\frac{p}{\pi_1}\right)$ profit if it is ticket 1 and $\left(1-\frac{1-p}{\pi_2}\right)$ profit if it is ticket 2. Clearly, these profits are non-negative only if $p \le \pi_1$ and $1-p \le \pi_2$. Since he is a monopolist, we can focus only on positive profit, which implies $\pi_1 + \pi_2 > 1$. The restriction that $\pi_1 + \pi_2$ cannot be strictly less than 1 is also intuitive. If it were so, then a bettor could split his \$1 on two bets and ensure getting either $\$(1/\pi_1)$ or $\$(1/\pi_2)$, both being greater than 1, a clear positive return with certainty. Therefore, $\pi + \pi_2 \geq 1$ is essential. This is called the *Dutchbook or no free money* restriction.

Having seen the prices (π_1, π_2) a bettor figures out that he can spend all his wealth (\$1) by buying $1/\pi_1$ ticket 1 tickets, or $1/\pi_2$ ticket 2 tickets. Based on his belief, his expected receipt from ticket 1 is $\frac{q}{\pi_1} \times 1$ dollars and from ticket 2 is $\frac{1-q}{\pi_2} \times 1$ dollars.

Given our Dutchbook restriction, which also implies $\pi_1 > 1 - \pi_2$, we can have one of the following three configurations for any $q \in [0,1]$:

$$(i)\ \frac{q}{\pi_1} > 1 > \frac{1-q}{\pi_2}, \qquad (ii)\ \frac{1-q}{\pi_2} > 1 > \frac{q}{\pi_1}, \qquad (iii)\ \max\left\{\frac{q}{\pi_1}, \frac{1-q}{\pi_2}\right\} < 1.$$

A bettor of belief q buys ticket 1 instead of ticket 2 if i applies, buys ticket 2 instead of ticket 1 if (ii) applies, and buys neither if (iii) applies.

So, all bettors with $q \geq \pi_1$ will buy ticket 1, and all bettors with $q \leq 1 - \pi_2$ will buy ticket 2, and all bettors with $1 - \pi_2 < q < \pi_1$ will not buy any tickets at all. Thus, the number of ticket 1 tickets sold will be $\int_{\pi_1}^{1} f(q)\,dq$, and the number of ticket 2 tickets sold will be $\int_0^{1-\pi_2} f(q)\,dq$. This leads to the monopolist bookmaker's expected profit as follows:

$$E\Pi = \int_{\pi_1}^{1} \left(1 - \frac{p}{\pi_1}\right) f(q)\,dq + \int_0^{1-\pi_2} \left(1 - \frac{1-p}{\pi_2}\right) f(q)\,dq$$
$$= 1 - F(\pi_1) - \frac{p}{\pi_1} + p\frac{F(\pi_1)}{\pi_1} + F(1-\pi_2) - (1-p)\frac{F(1-\pi_2)}{\pi_2}.$$

Intuitively, the exclusion of bettors whose beliefs are between $1 - \pi_2$ and π_1 is crucial for the bookmaker's profit, because his own belief also lies in this interval. Therefore, he cannot make money from the bettors whose beliefs are close to his (and nature's true draw); he can make money only from those whose beliefs are far from his, either to the right of π_1 or to the left of $1 - \pi_2$. Of course, by reducing the ticket prices, the exclusion zone can be reduced and more revenues can be raised, but it may also imply greater payouts. Optimal prices strike a balance by creating an appropriate gap between π_1 and $1 - \pi_2$.

The first-order conditions for profit maximisation are

$$\frac{\partial E\Pi}{\partial \pi_1} = \frac{pf(\pi_1)}{\pi_1^2}\left[\frac{1-F(\pi_1)}{f(\pi_1)} - \frac{(\pi_1 - p)}{p}\pi_1\right] = 0, \tag{7.15}$$

$$\frac{\partial E\Pi}{\partial \pi_2} = \frac{(1-p)f(1-\pi_2)}{\pi_2^2}\left[\frac{F(1-\pi_2)}{f(1-\pi_2)} - \frac{(\pi_2 - (1-p))}{1-p}\pi_2\right] = 0. \tag{7.16}$$

The following lemma shows that optimal prices $\pi_i\ (i = 1,2)$ are strictly increasing in the bookmaker's beliefs about the team's winning chances.

Lemma 2. (monotonic prices) *Suppose Assumption 3 holds. Then the optimal prices* (π_1, π_2) *that solve Eqs. (7.15) and (7.16) have the following properties:* $\partial \pi_1 / \partial p > 0$, $\partial \pi_2 / \partial p < 0$. *Also,* $\pi_1(0) = 0$ *and* $\pi_1(1) = 1$. *Symmetrically,* $\pi_2(p = 1) = 0$ *and* $\pi_2(p = 0) = 1$.

The resultant expected profit of the bookmaker will be a U-shaped curve with the highest profit being equal to 1 at either end of the probability spectrum.

Proposition 12. (bookmaker's preference for unbalanced contests) *The bookmaker's profit* $E\Pi(p)$ *is U-shaped and has a unique minimum at* p^* *where the following relation holds:*

$$\frac{1-F\left(\pi_1\left(p^*\right)\right)}{\pi_1\left(p^*\right)} = \frac{F\left(1-\pi_2\left(1-p^*\right)\right)}{\pi_2\left(1-p^*\right)}.$$

If $f(.)$ *is symmetric, then* $p^* = 1/2$, *and* $\pi_1(1/2) = \pi_2(1/2)$.

Under uniform distribution, where $f(q) = 1$ and $F(q) = q$, the expected profit is

$$E\Pi = 1 - \pi_1 - \frac{p}{\pi_1} + p + 1 - \pi_2 - (1-p)\frac{1-\pi_2}{\pi_2} = 3 - \pi_1 - \pi_2 - \frac{p}{\pi_1} - \frac{1-p}{\pi_2}.$$

Optimal prices then follow a simple square root rule: $\pi_1 = \sqrt{p}$ and $\pi_2 = \sqrt{1-p}$. The corresponding betting odds are $\frac{1-\sqrt{p}}{\sqrt{p}}:1$ for team 1 and $\frac{1-\sqrt{1-p}}{\sqrt{1-p}}:1$ for team 2. The resultant profit function is then

$$E\Pi(p) = 3 - 2\sqrt{p} - 2\sqrt{1-p}.$$

This highest profit curve is drawn in Figure 7.4. The key point is that the bookmaker makes most money when the contest is truly uneven. Because the bettors bet blindly guided by their stubborn beliefs, the bookmaker can induce most people to bet on team 1 when it is truly an underdog. The inducement is given by reducing the ticket price sufficiently. The opposite can be done when it is truly a favourite. In either case, his profit is maximum. Of course, if the contest is near even, then he does not find it optimal to steer the bettors too much in one way or another. Bettors then bet evenly on either side, and the bookmaker's expected profit becomes low.

Of course, in reality, all bettors are not naive. Many do thorough research on teams before placing a bet. These people may acquire similar information as that of the bookmaker and can win a big sum if the bookmaker is unaware of their presence. Some bettors may go further to acquire even more accurate information about some team's true ability to perform (due to some players' undisclosed injuries). In that case, these bettors will have privileged or superior information than the betting house. Shin (1991, 1992) modelled such cases of insider information. It is also possible that some players are secretly bribed by a corrupt punter to underperform, which then becomes a case of match-fixing. The bookmaker's knowledge of such possibilities can lead to interesting types of equilibria in the betting markets. Bag and Saha (2011, 2017a, 2017b) have studied this problem in several settings. Then there are cases of abusing performance-enhancing drugs (doping) and undermining the opponent's capability to perform (sabotage). Preston and Szymanski (2003) have discussed a range of such problems of cheating in contests.

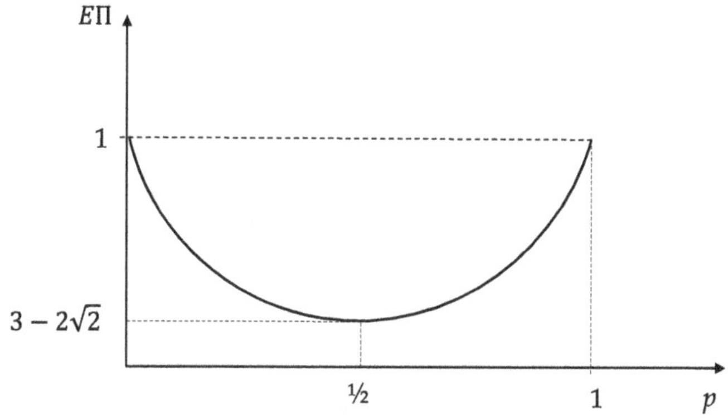

Figure 7.4 Expected highest profit of the bookmaker

7.3.6 *Temptation and self-control preferences*

The North Norfolk coastline is one of the most beautiful places in the east of England because of its lovely cliffs, greenery and pebbled beaches. A day trip to one of the seaside towns is always very enjoyable, but after being there, one finds it hard to resist the temptation of deep-fried fish and chips that are inseparable from these places. Although a cholesterol-conscious middle-aged man may promise himself before the journey to avoid 'unhealthy' food at all costs, the promise may be easily broken once the time comes. Similar dilemmas abound in our everyday lives. We academics promise to spend more time reading and writing research papers and spend less time following politics or watching television, but we fail to do so for lack of self-control. New Year resolutions of doing more exercises are broken within weeks.

Behavioural economists have addressed this problem as one of *dynamic inconsistency*. In such contexts, they invoke hyperbolic discounting of the future, which accommodates the possibility that the consumers may see a given length of delay now, say, between today and tomorrow, differently to the one occurring in future. For example, if one is asked to take $1 today as opposed to $1.50 tomorrow, one may take $1 today, but if the same choice is to be exercised one month from now, the consumer may prefer to wait one extra day to get 50% more. Such preferences are referred to as present-biased preferences, and hyperbolic discounting seems to explain this anomaly. Nobel Prize–winning economist Richard Thaler once famously described how he experimented with his dinner guests by quietly moving a bowl of tasty cashew nuts away from their sight after noticing that the irresistible nuts were disappearing faster than the healthier snacks that he laid out. A little *nudge*, in his words, solved the self-control problem of his guests.

The problem of self-control has always been seen as a counter-example of where the rational choice theory can go wrong. More choices, in classical theory, are always better, but in the presence of temptation, that may not hold. A body of recent works, such as Gul and Pesendorfer (2001) and Chatterjee and Krishna (2009), has tried to provide a theory of self-control preferences by adopting expected utility. The key idea is that the consumer has two different preferences, one is 'long run' (or normal), which makes her better off, and the other is 'short term' or temptation, which gives a spurt only in temporary enjoyment but inflicts disutility over the longer term. Chatterjee and Krishna (2009) call it *alter-ego or dual-self* preference, which may emerge with some probability.

The problem is usually posed as a two-stage decision problem. The first stage concerns the selection of a menu, and the second stage concerns the selection of an item from the chosen menu. As an example, one may first need to decide which restaurant to go to—a fully vegetarian South Indian restaurant or a buffet restaurant that offers all sorts of choices or a sizzler place that offers only meat and chicken. Each restaurant is like a menu. If we denote x as a menu, b as a healthy option in the menu and a as an unhealthy option, then the South Indian restaurant can be seen as a menu $\{b\}$, the buffet restaurant as $\{b,a\}$ and the sizzler restaurant as $\{a\}$. The menu of the restaurants is then $x = \{\{b\},\{b,a\},\{a\}\}$.

If the first or third restaurant is chosen, there is no possibility of experiencing a conflict between two egos. But if the buffet restaurant is chosen, then the consumer is facing a dual-self problem going into the second stage. While her normal ego prefers b to a and this preference is described by a von Neuman–Morgenstern utility function $u(x)$, her alter ego would prefer a to b and the alter ego's preference is described by a function $v(x)$. Thus, $u(b) > u(a)$ and $v(a) > v(b)$. Overall, we can write $\{b\} \succ \{a,b\} \succeq \{a\}$. A person with greater self-control would never go to a sizzler place; that is, for her, $\{b\} \succ \{a,b\} \succ \{a\}$. She strictly prefers to have the healthy option on the menu than a menu of only unhealthy options. But if someone has strong temptation, then she might feel indifferent between the second and the third menus; that is, $\{a,b\} \sim \{a\}$.

The dual-self preference then can be seen as an expected utility problem, in which upon arriving at the buffet restaurant, the dual self decides on the food with probability ρ and the normal self decides with probability $1-\rho$. The dual self or the alter ego will zero in on the unhealthy section of the buffet counter, which is a subset $B_v(x)$ of x that satisfies the alter ego most; the healthier section is irrelevant to this self. The normal self, by comparison, will consider the whole menu x. However, the consequence of the choice made by either self will be borne by the consumer's normal or long-run self. Therefore, by denoting β as a choice variable (to be selected from x), the expected utility can be written as

$$Eu(x) = (1-\rho)\max_{\beta \in x} u(\beta) + \rho \max_{\beta \in B_v(x)} u(\beta).$$

Note the difference in the domains of the choice of the two selves, while the utility functions being $u(.)$ in both parts. Gull and Pesendorfer (2001) posed the problem slightly differently, where the dual self is a non-stochastic decision-maker and temptation directly inflicts a utility cost. The formalisation of the self-control problem in both papers has taken the route of the expected utility approach and suitably modified the axioms of preferences that underpin the expected utility theory, to which we now turn attention.

7.4 Logical premise of the expected utility theory

So far, we have not discussed the theoretical foundation of the expected utility approach. Instead, we learnt about its various useful applications. In most of these cases, we considered lotteries as variations in the monetary prizes, while maintaining the same probability distribution over the states of nature. However, the concept of lottery is more general. If the prizes are the same but their probabilities are different, then the lotteries are also different. Therefore, we can define lotteries entirely on the probability space, and each probability mix represents a different lottery. A lottery with n possible outcomes is simply denoted by a probability vector $(p_1, p_2, \ldots, p_n)$

and another lottery by $(p'_1, p'_2, \dots, p'_n)$. Two boxes containing unequal combinations of different coloured balls represent two different lotteries.

How do we define an indifference curve on the probability space? For the benefit of working with numbers, let us first assume that there are two outcomes: $x_1 = \$100$ and $x_2 = \$400$. The consumer's utility function is $u(x) = \sqrt{x}$. Thus, if state 1 occurs, she gets utility 10, and if state 2 occurs, she gets 20. Let the probability of realising x_i be p_i. Formally, a lottery is $\mathcal{L} = (p; x)$, where $p = (p_1, p_2)$, with $p_1 + p_2 = 1$ and $x = (x_1, x_2)$. Utility from this lottery is $\mathcal{U}(\mathcal{L}) = Eu = p_1 u(x_1) + p_2 u(x_2)$. Clearly, Eu is strictly decreasing in p_1 (because $x_1 < x_2$). In panel *a* of Figure 7.5, we depict this case, where the probability space is just the $p_1 + p_2 = 1$ line, and every point on this line is an indifference curve. As we move from right to left, the expected utility increases.

Let us now move to a more interesting case in which we add a third state of nature with x_3 and let $x_3 = 900$ giving utility 30. Now our probability space is a three-dimensional simplex $p_1 + p_2 + p_3 = 1$, which is often referred to as a **Marschak–Machina triangle** in the uncertainty literature. It is essentially an equilateral triangle as shown in panel *b* of Figure 7.5. A point anywhere inside the triangle is a strictly positive probability triplet (p_1, p_2, p_3), and a point on any of the edges of the triangle has one probability zero. By convention, the left bottom corner corresponds to the certainty case of getting prize x_1 (the lowest pay-off). Clearly, it represents the lottery (1,0,0). The bottom-right corner corresponds to getting the prize x_2 with certainty; it represents the lottery (0,1,0). The top corner represents the lottery (0,0,1) that awards prize x_3 with certainty. The line that connects the left and the top corners has $p_2 = 0$ everywhere and maps a declining p_1 as we move upward and trace $p_3 = 1 - p_1$. The line that connects the two bottom corners maintains $p_3 = 0$ and from left to right p_1 decreases. Likewise, on the line connecting the top and right corners, we have $p_1 = 0$, and an upward movement along the line signifies a decline in p_2. Any line inside the triangle that is parallel to the base maintains the same p_3 everywhere, just as a line parallel to the right side has a fixed p_1 and a line parallel to the left side has a fixed p_2.

Now, consider an expected utility level $Eu = 20$. Then two lotteries that can give $Eu = 20$ are (1/2,0,1/2) and (0,1,0), which are shown by points *A* and *B*, respectively, in Figure 7.5 panel *b*. Then by taking any convex combination of these two lotteries, we can create another lottery that gives exactly $Eu = 20$. Point $\mathcal{L}_2$ is one such lottery. Therefore, the entire straight line connecting points *A* and *B* is the indifference curve that gives $Eu = 20$. Similarly, the line connecting points *C* and *D* gives expected utility $Eu = 25$. At *C*, we have (1/4,0,3/4) and at *D* (0,1/2,1/2).

It should be clear from this example that if we adopt the expected utility approach, then our indifference curves would be linear and downward-sloping as shown in Figure7.5 panel *b*. It will be neither flat nor upward-rising. It will not be flat because on a flat line (in a Marschak–Machina triangle) p_3 is constant, and going from left to right, p_2 increases and p_1 falls, which implies that Eu must rise. Similarly, on an upward-rising line Eu must rise because p_3 keeps rising (going upward). So the only possibility is that the indifference curve must be falling in the direction of the intermediate pay-off.

Essentially, this is the crux of the expected utility theory developed by von Neuman and Morgenstern (1944). If lottery $\mathcal{L}_1$ is preferred (or indifferent) to lottery $\mathcal{L}_2$, then the expected utility of $\mathcal{L}_1$ must be greater than (or equal to) the expected utility of $\mathcal{L}_2$ and vice versa.

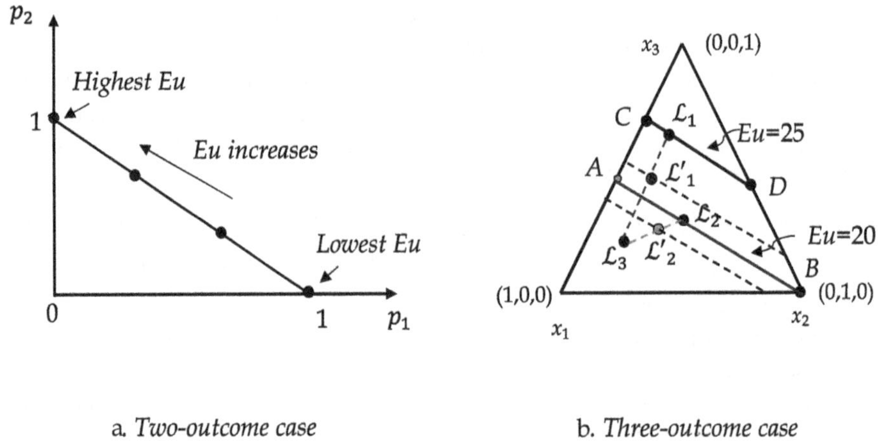

Figure 7.5 Expected utility indifference curves

7.4.1 Axioms of preference over lotteries

Let us now formally state the axioms that underpin the existence of an expected utility function. Let us continue to use the general definition of a lottery $\mathcal{L} = (p;x)$, where $p = (p_1, p_2, \ldots, p_n)$, $\sum_i^n p_i = 1$ and $x = (x_1, x_2, \ldots, x_n)$. Unless stated otherwise, $\mathcal{L}$ is always a simple lottery. A compound lottery over two simple lotteries $\mathcal{L}'$ and $\mathcal{L}''$ is denoted by $\mathcal{L}_c = p' \times \mathcal{L}' + (1-p') \times \mathcal{L}''$.

1. **Completeness:** For any pair of simple lotteries $(\mathcal{L}_1, \mathcal{L}_2)$, either $\mathcal{L}_1 \succeq \mathcal{L}_2$ or $\mathcal{L}_2 \succeq \mathcal{L}_1$ or both. That is, the consumer can rank every possible lottery in her preference ordering.
2. **Transitivity:** If $\mathcal{L}_1 \succeq \mathcal{L}_2$ and $\mathcal{L}_2 \succeq \mathcal{L}_3$, then $\mathcal{L}_1 \succeq \mathcal{L}_3$.
3. **Continuity:** The preference relation $\succeq$ is continuous if for any $\mathcal{L}_1$, $\mathcal{L}_2$ and $\mathcal{L}_3$, the following two sets of compound lotteries are closed:

$$\{\alpha \in [0,1] : \alpha \times \mathcal{L}_1 + (1-\alpha) \times \mathcal{L}_2 \succeq \mathcal{L}_3\}$$

and

$$\{\alpha \in [0,1] : \mathcal{L}_3 \succeq \alpha \times \mathcal{L}_1 + (1-\alpha) \times \mathcal{L}_2\}.$$

That the preceding two sets are closed means that a small change in probabilities should not change the nature of the ordering of two lotteries. If we take a sequence of compound lotteries over $\mathcal{L}_1$ and $\mathcal{L}_2$ and if every element of that sequence is preferred to $\mathcal{L}_3$ then the limit of the sequence is also preferred to $\mathcal{L}_3$. Intuitively, if 'jogging in the park' is preferred to 'walking on a treadmill' only when there is no rain, then walking on a treadmill should continue to be preferred if rain reduces from heavy to light and from light to a mere drizzle.

The preceding three axioms are non-controversial and can be regarded as a natural inheritance from the theory of choice under certainty. The next axiom is, however, special, and it is critical for the expected utility approach.

4. **Independence:** For any trio of lotteries $(\mathcal{L}_1, \mathcal{L}_2, \mathcal{L}_3)$ and $\alpha \in (0,1)$, we say $\mathcal{L}_1 \succeq \mathcal{L}_2$ if and only if $\mathcal{L}_1' \succeq \mathcal{L}_2'$, where

$$\mathcal{L}_1' = \alpha \times \mathcal{L}_1 + (1-\alpha) \times \mathcal{L}_3 \text{ and } \mathcal{L}_2' = \alpha \times \mathcal{L}_2 + (1-\alpha) \times \mathcal{L}_3.$$

In other words, the preference ordering between two lotteries should be judged in reference to a third lottery, an irrelevant alternative. If we create two compound lotteries by combining each of the two and the third lottery, then the preference ordering between the two compound lotteries must be same as that between the two simple lotteries.

In Figure 7.5 panel *b*, we illustrate the independence axiom by taking a lottery $\mathcal{L}_3$ (which gives $Eu < 20$) and compare lotteries $\mathcal{L}_1$ and $\mathcal{L}_2$. As drawn in the figure, $\mathcal{L}_1 \succ \mathcal{L}_2 \succ \mathcal{L}_3$. The compound lotteries with respect to $\mathcal{L}_3$ are denoted by $\mathcal{L}_1'$ and $\mathcal{L}_2'$. Clearly, $\mathcal{L}_1' \succ \mathcal{L}_2'$ for every $\alpha \in (0,1)$. This will always be true if the indifference curves are linear and parallel to each other (as drawn in the graph).

An important implication of the independence axiom is that for any $\alpha \in (0,1)$ and $\mathcal{L}^* = \alpha\mathcal{L} + (1-\alpha)\mathcal{L}'$, if $\mathcal{L} \succeq \mathcal{L}'$, then $\mathcal{L}' \preceq \mathcal{L}^* \preceq \mathcal{L}$. To see this, suppose $\mathcal{L} \succ \mathcal{L}'$, but $\mathcal{L}^* \prec \mathcal{L}' \prec \mathcal{L}$. Then if we take $\mathcal{L}$ as the third lottery, the preference relation $\mathcal{L}^* \prec \mathcal{L}'$ implies by the independence axiom $\beta\mathcal{L} + (1-\beta)\mathcal{L}^* \prec \beta\mathcal{L} + (1-\beta)\mathcal{L}'$. Taking α very close to 1, we get $\mathcal{L}^* \approx \mathcal{L} \prec \beta\mathcal{L} + (1-\beta)\mathcal{L}'$—a contradiction. A similar contradiction can be established for $\mathcal{L}' \prec \mathcal{L} \prec \mathcal{L}^*$ by taking β very close to zero.

With the preceding four axioms, we now can state the expected utility theorem according to von Neuman and Morgenstern (1944), the proof of which is given in Section 7.7.

Expected utility theorem. Suppose the preference relation $\succeq$ satisfies axioms 1–4. Then we can assign a number u_i to each element of the outcome vector $x = (x_1, x_2, \ldots, x_n)$ such that for any two lotteries $\mathcal{L} = (p; x)$ and $\mathcal{L}' = (p'; x)$, $\mathcal{L} \succeq \mathcal{L}'$ if and only if $\sum_{i=1}^n p_i u_i \geq \sum_{i=1}^n p_i' u_i$. In other words, $\mathcal{U}(\mathcal{L}) = \sum_{i=1}^n p_i u_i$ and $\mathcal{U}(\mathcal{L}') = \sum_{i=1}^n p_i' u_i$, and $\mathcal{U}(\mathcal{L}) \geq \mathcal{U}(\mathcal{L}')$ implies $\mathcal{L} \succeq \mathcal{L}'$.

7.4.2 *Criticisms of the expected utility approach*

With completeness, transitivity and continuity, we get the existence of a utility function just like preference under certainty. But the independence axiom tells us that the indifference curves must also be linear and parallel on the probability space. Without them, we cannot express preference ordering in terms of an expected utility comparison. One implies the other. But this point is controversial. Many experimental studies, as well as observed empirical behaviours, are inconsistent with parallel or even linear indifference curves.

Before we investigate this issue more formally, let us first take note of an extreme simplification that the expected utility approach makes. Here, the consumer is asked (or assumed) to care about the utilities she will have *ex post* in the realised state, which as the theory assumes will depend only on the 'prize' of that state. Invoking this specific notion of state-specific utility, she then calculates her expected utility. But in reality, our *ex post* utilities are not devoid of emotions. We feel elated if we made the right call or feel dejected if we made the wrong call or get disappointed if something beyond our control went wrong. And at the time of making a decision, we know that we might feel this way afterwards. This consideration can significantly influence the choices we make.

7.4.2.1 Allais paradox

One criticism that goes back to the early days of the expected utility theory is the *Allais paradox* due to Allais (1953). The paradox demonstrates that the insistence of the expected utility to have a linear and parallel indifference curve can lead to 'unreasonable' predictions that most people will inevitably violate. Let us continue with our example of $x_1 = 100$, $x_2 = 400$ and $x_3 = 900$ along with $u = \sqrt{x}$.

Consider two lotteries $\mathcal{L}_1 = (0,1,0)$ and $\mathcal{L}_1' = (0.08, 0.85, 0.07)$. By computing expected utility we can see

$$\mathcal{U}(\mathcal{L}_1) = 20 > \mathcal{U}(\mathcal{L}_1') = 0.08 \times 10 + 0.85 \times 20 + 0.07 \times 30 = 0.8 + 17 + 2.1 = 19.9.$$

The consumer prefers lottery $\mathcal{L}_1$ over $\mathcal{L}_1'$. This preference necessarily implies that the consumer must prefer lottery $\mathcal{L}_2$ over lottery $\mathcal{L}_2'$, where

$$\mathcal{L}_2 = (0.85, 0.15, 0) \text{ and } \mathcal{L}_2' = (0.93, 0, 0.07).$$

To see this, let us start with the inequality $(\mathcal{U}(\mathcal{L}_1) > \mathcal{U}(\mathcal{L}_1'))$

$$u(x_2) > 0.08u(x_1) + 0.85u(x_2) + 0.07u(x_3).$$

Now adding $0.85 \times u(x_1)$ to both sides of this inequality and rearranging terms, we get

$$\begin{aligned}
&0.85u(x_1) + u(x_2) > 0.93u(x_1) + 0.85u(x_2) + 0.07u(x_3) \\
&0.85u(x_1) + 0.15u(x_2) > 0.93u(x_1) + 0.07u(x_3) \\
&8.5 + 3 = 11.5 > 9.3 + 2.1 = 11.4 \\
&\mathcal{U}(\mathcal{L}_2) > \mathcal{U}(\mathcal{L}_2').
\end{aligned}$$

In Figure 7.6 panel *a*, we illustrate the implication of $\mathcal{L}_1 \succ \mathcal{L}_1'$. In the Marschak–Machina triangle, the right corner represents lottery $\mathcal{L}_1$ where the consumer gets \$400 with certainty. Then we draw a small equilateral triangle that has three corners (0.15, 0.85, 0), (0, 1, 0) and (0, 0.85, 0.15). Lottery $\mathcal{L}_1'$ lies on the left edge of this triangle where all along we maintain $p_2 = 0.85$ and p_3 gradually rises from 0 to 0.15 at the expense of p_1, as we move from bottom left to top right. We should note that lottery $\mathcal{L}_3 = (0, 0.85, 015)$ must have the same height as lottery (0, 85, 0, 0.15) because these two lotteries should have same p_3. Likewise, lotteries $\mathcal{L}_1'$ and $\mathcal{L}_2'$ should also be on the same height because both maintain $p_3 = 0.07$.

Similarly, we can construct another (equilateral) little triangle combining the lotteries (1,0,0), (0.85,0.15,0) and (0.85,0,0.15). Lottery $\mathcal{L}_2$ corresponds to the bottom-right corner of this little triangle. As we have shown mathematically, the consumer must prefer $\mathcal{L}_2$ to $\mathcal{L}_2'$ if she prefers $\mathcal{L}_1$ to $\mathcal{L}_1'$. Although we demonstrated this implication with our example $u(x) = \sqrt{x}$, the point is more general, and it holds for any specification of $u(x)$. We must have $\mathcal{L}_2 \succeq \mathcal{L}_2'$ if and only if $\mathcal{L}_1 \succeq \mathcal{L}_1'$, as long as we adhere to the notion of utility from a lottery as $\mathcal{U}(\mathcal{L}) = \Sigma_i \, p_i u(x_i)$.

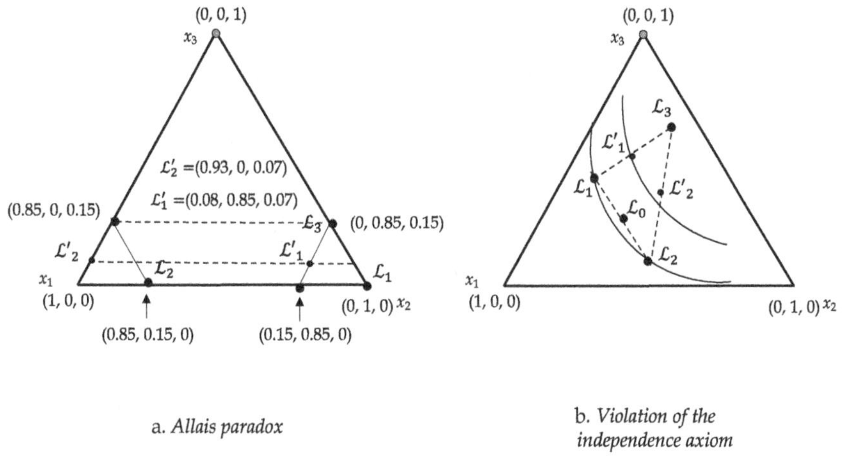

Figure 7.6 Allais paradox and violation of the independence axiom

But one may ask, How reasonable is the preference of $\mathcal{L}_2$ over $\mathcal{L}_2'$? Under $\mathcal{L}_2'$, one gets \$900, with a probability 0.07 and \$400 with a zero probability, while under $\mathcal{L}_2$, the probability of getting \$900 is zero but the probability of getting \$400 is 0.15. In both cases, the chance of getting \$100 is very high. Then it is quite reasonable for one to prefer $\mathcal{L}_2'$ over $\mathcal{L}_2$; after all the chance of getting the biggest prize is significant (though less than 0.15). Given a choice like this, most people may go for $\mathcal{L}_2'$, disobeying the *instruction* of the expected utility theory. We can imagine that such flipping of preference (in the sense of expected utility) would be almost universal if the gap between the highest prize and the second-highest prize gets sufficiently big. Imagine what would be your temptation to pick $\mathcal{L}_2'$ if $x_3 = \$10,000$!

The expected utility theory is attractive for its elegant simplicity. The indifference curves are linear and parallel, which are extremely helpful in so many applications as we have seen in the last section. But the theory should also be seen as a normative theory, because it is instructing consumers *how they should rank* different lotteries, but their actual preference may be quite different. Allais paradox and many such examples do demonstrate that people's preference in reality can indeed violate the expected utility theory. Of the four axioms, the most vulnerable one is the independence axiom.

There are at least two ways we can modify the expected utility approach. One is to drop linearity. That is, allow $Eu = \sum_i \phi(p_i)u(x_i)$ with $\sum_i \phi(p_i) = 1$. For instance, in our three-outcome case, we could have $\phi(p_1) = \sqrt{p_1}$, $\phi(p_2) = \sqrt{p_2}$ and $\phi(p_3) = 1 - \sqrt{p_1} - \sqrt{p_2}$. An immediate implication of this approach is that the indifference curves will no longer be linear. Figure 7.6-*b* represents one such case where the indifference curves become the more familiar convex-shape. Here, straight away we see that a compound lottery (such as $\mathcal{L}_0$) is strictly preferred to two indifferent simple lotteries (such as $\mathcal{L}_1$ and $\mathcal{L}_2$), a big departure from the expected utility theory. Furthermore, such indifference curves may also violate the independence axiom. Take lottery $\mathcal{L}_3$ and construct two compound lotteries $\mathcal{L}_1'$ and $\mathcal{L}_2'$ using same randomisation. There is no guarantee that $\mathcal{L}_1'$ and $\mathcal{L}_2'$ will be on the same indifference curves. We can also show that once we give up the independence axiom, neither the linearity of the indifference curve nor their being parallel to each other is guaranteed.

The other possibility is that we abandon the state-specific utility being solely dependent on the prize but retain the linearity in the probabilities. As discussed several times, after the realisation of an outcome, the decision-maker may have certain emotions, such as rejoice if the call was right and regret if the call is wrong. Such emotions may be inseparable from the utility derived from the monetary prize. In the context of our example (and Allais paradox), when facing the dilemma of choosing between $\mathcal{L}_2$ and $\mathcal{L}_2'$, the consumer may foresee how she would regret if x_3 realises and she has picked $\mathcal{L}_2$. If the regret is overbearing, she would pick $\mathcal{L}_2'$ and escape the Allais paradox.

7.5 Non-expected utility theories

7.5.1 *Prospect theory*

The Israeli Nobel Prize-winning psychologist and economist Daniel Kahneman and his long-time co-author and fellow psychologist Amos Tversky wrote an article in 1979 that became one of the most influential papers in the last 40 years.[8] Kahneman and Tversky (1979) produced a volume of results from many experiments they conducted in three countries—Israel, Sweden and the United States—all showing that people systematically violate the normative prescriptions of the expected utility theory. They then proposed an alternative theory called the prospect theory that would explain the 'anomalies' in people's choices under uncertainty.

We begin by recalling some of their experiments in which the subjects were asked to make a choice between two alternative lotteries or prospects, as Kahneman and Tversky called them. Table 7.1 reports these experiments and outcomes. The figures in brackets represent the percentage of subjects who chose that prospect. A single superscript asterisk represents the usual 10% statistical significance level. The prizes are in a monetary unit.

Experiment 1 offers a choice between 2400 with certainty (prospect B) and 2500 with a probability of 0.33 and 2400 with a probability of 0.66, probabilities almost equal, leaving a tiny probability of nothing (prospect A). If we are ready to disregard the extremely low probability event of getting nothing (under prospect A), prospect A should dominate prospect B. Under A then, people are almost guaranteed to get 2400 and possibly more. And yet 82% of the subjects

Table 7.1 Kahneman–Tversky experiments (1979, pp. 267–268)

Experiment	*Prospect*	*Prospect*
1	A: 2500 with prob. 0.33; 2400 with prob. 0.66; 0 with prob. 0.01	B: 2400 with certainty
Outcome	[18%]	[82%]*
2	C: 2500 with prob. 0.33; 0 with prob. 0.67	D: 2400 with prob. 0.34; 0 with prob.0.66
Outcome	[83%]*	[17%]
3	A: 4000 with prob. 0.80; 0 with prob. 0.20	B: 3000 with certainty
Outcome	[20%]	[80%]*
4	C: −4000 with prob. 0.80; 0 with prob. 0.20	D: −3000 with certainty
Outcome	[92%]*	[8%]

chose prospect B. It seems that the presence of a certainty option makes people behave in a risk-averse manner. The fear of losing 2400 (even with a tiny chance) forces people to select B. Kahneman and Tversky called it the *certainty effect*.

The same subjects were then offered experiment 2, in which there is no certainty of payment and both prospects offer almost the same probability to get a sizeable sum. In fact, prospect C offers a bigger amount with almost the same probability as prospect D. The outcome shows a complete swing from the first experiment; 83% of the subjects now prefer prospect C, which is almost the same as prospect A of experiment 1. Now that the certainty option has been removed, the subjects focus on the bigger prize while treating the two probabilities as almost equal.

Are these two behaviours consistent with the expected utility theory? The answer is no. Assuming $u(0) = 0$ from the choice of experiment 2, we see that

$$0.33u(2500) > 0.34u(2400), \text{ or } \frac{u(2500)}{u(2400)} > \frac{34}{33}.$$

But the same subjects then chose prospect B in experiment 1. That means

$$u(2400) > 0.33u(2500) + 0.66u(2400) \text{ or } \frac{u(2500)}{u(2400)} < \frac{34}{33}.$$

Clearly, between the two experiments the subjects' preference over the outcome pay-offs has flipped, and that is inconsistent with the expected utility theory.

Experiment 3 produces another certainty effect. In this case, a higher expected value of the prize (3200) from prospect A does not sway the subjects. They still behave like risk-averse agents. But experiment 4 reveals something very interesting. It is simply experiment 3 with the pay-offs changed to negative. But the subjects do not choose the certainty prospect. Instead, almost everybody (92%) goes for C, which is much riskier than D. So in this case, we see that they are behaving like 'risk-takers'.

Experiments 3 and 4 together show that when outcome pay-offs are positive, people tend to show an aversion to risk, but when pay-offs are negative, they become risk lovers. This will be again inconsistent with the expected utility theory. The authors argue that both phenomena are reflections of *loss aversion*. Consumers hate to lose their wealth or income. When pay-offs are positive loss aversion forces them to protect their certainty income. When pay-offs are negative, loss aversion encourages them to take a risky gamble because that allows the possibility of losing nothing (albeit with a probability of 0.20). This is called the *reflection effect*.

Now we move on to a formal presentation of the prospect theory. We assume that consumers try to simplify their understanding of the prospects in terms of relative gains and losses by cancelling out the common elements.[9] A prospect is written in the form $(x, p; y, q)$. This means that x occurs with probability p and y occurs with probability q and nothing with probability $1 - p - q$. Often two prospects (500, 0.25; 200, 0.40; −20, 0.35) and (500, 0.25; 250, 0.45; −50; 0.30) are written as (200, 0.40; −20, 0.35) and (250, 0.45; −50; 0.30) after removing the common prize of 500.

For assessment of the outcomes, two elements are important: value functions, namely, $v(x)$ and $v(y)$, and 'decision weighting' of probability p, which reflects the impact of p on the overall value of the prospect. The weighting functions are $\pi(p)$ and $\pi(q)$, but they are not probabilities, and hence, generally $\pi(p) + \pi(q) \leq 1$.

A prospect is called a strictly positive prospect if $x > y > 0$ and a strictly negative prospect if $x < y < 0$, where in both cases, $p+q=1$. A consumer's valuation of a strictly positive or strictly negative prospect is

$$\mathcal{V}(x,p;y,q) = v(y) + \pi(p)\left[v(x) - v(y)\right].$$

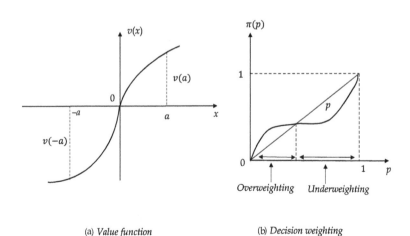

The value function is written in the form of gain/loss. The first term refers to assured utility (gain or loss). The second term refers to an additional utility gain or loss. Note that the decision weight is applied to the additional loss or gain term only.

A prospect is a *regular* prospect if either $p+q<1$ (in which case there is residual probability of getting nothing) or $p+q=1$ with $x \geq 0 \geq y$ or $x \leq 0 \leq y$. The prospect value function in this case is

$$\mathcal{V}(x,p;y,q) = \pi(p)v(x) + \pi(q)v(y).$$

The consumer selects the prospect that gives her the highest $\mathcal{V}(.)$. We should conclude this section by noting that both $v(.)$ and probability weighting functions take particular shapes which is shown in Figure 7.7. Panel *a* of Figure 7.7 shows that $v(x)$ will be concave when $x>0$ and convex when $x<0$. This is implied by loss aversion. One additional implication is that $v(x) < -v(-x)$. Consumers value losses much more than they value gains. Secondly, the probability weighting function tends to fall below high probability and rise above low probability. Very unlikely outcomes get over-weighted, and very likely outcomes get under-weighted. See panel *b* of Figure 7.7. The weights conform to an empirical regularity borne out by experimental studies. In general, $\pi(0) \neq 0$ and $\pi(1) \neq 1$ are permitted.

In the betting market, punters often are believed to apply the following weighting rule:

$$\pi(p_i)\begin{cases} \geq p_i & \text{if} \quad p_i < 1/2 \\ = p_i & \text{if} \quad p_i = 1/2 \\ \leq p_i & \text{if} \quad p_i > 1/2. \end{cases}$$

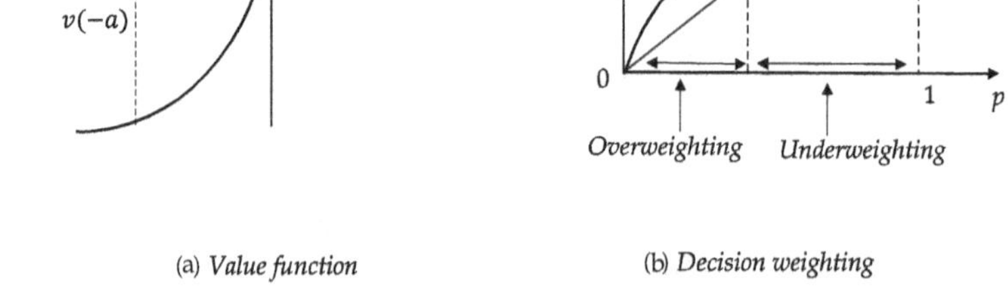

Figure 7.7 Value function and probability weight function

This is justified by saying that agents are less used to evaluating very low or very high probability events for which they might feel anxious. Bettors over-weight the chance of winning by long shots and under-weight the chance of winning by favourites, a phenomenon referred to as the 'favourite long-shot bias' in the betting literature.

7.5.1.1 *Rank-dependent expected utility theory (RDEU)*

One of the unsatisfactory features of the original prospect theory was that the decision weights do not necessarily add up to 1. For this reason, lotteries are not always comparable in terms of stochastic dominance.[10] Quiggin (1982) proposed to assign decision weights based on a non-linear transformation of cumulative probabilities of the outcomes so that they will be dominance comparable.

Consider a lottery with monetary outcomes: $\mathcal{L}=(x_1,p_1;x_2,p_2;\ldots,x_n,p_n)$, where $x_1 \le x_2 \le x_3 \ldots \le x_n$. The rank of x_j is given by its cumulative probability $\Sigma_{i=1}^{j} p_i$. Clearlyx_n is top-ranked.

A consumer while considering which outcomes to concentrate on may pay much greater attention to the worst outcome (if she is a pessimist), the best outcome (if she is an optimist), more to the intermediate outcomes (if she is neither very pessimist nor very optimist) or more to both extreme outcomes than to the intermediate ones (if the extremes are salient). This is the rationale behind considering the rank of an outcome in determining the decision weights. The following assumption is important.

Assumption 4. *The decision weight π_j associated with the* j*th outcome solely depends on its probability p_j and its rank (which is given by its cumulative probability).*

An implication of this assumption is that if two lotteries present two different outcomes with equal rank and equal probability, then those two outcomes should receive the same decision weight. For instance, in $\mathcal{L}_1=\left(5,\frac{1}{4};10,\frac{1}{2};15,\frac{1}{4}\right)$ and $\mathcal{L}_2=\left(9,\frac{1}{4};10,\frac{1}{2};15,\frac{1}{4}\right)$, outcome 9 of $\mathcal{L}_2$ should receive the same decision weight π_1 as outcome 5 of $\mathcal{L}_1$ because their ranks and probabilities are identical. However, between $\mathcal{L}_3=\left(10,\frac{1}{2};12,\frac{1}{4};15,\frac{1}{4}\right)$ and $\mathcal{L}_1$ we cannot assign the same decision weight to 10 for their differential ranks.

Assumption 4 also implies that the decision weights should also follow certain consistency (Diecidue and Wakker, 2001). Consider the following two lotteries and assume that their preference relations are as follows:

$$(10,p_1;2,p_2;1,p_3) \sim (12,q_1;2,q_2;0,q_3)$$

and

$$(10,p_1;3,p_2;1,p_3) \succeq (12,q_1;3,q_2;0,q_3).$$

Then by Assumption 4, the decision weight π_2 applied to the second outcome of the left two lotteries must be identical, and the decision weight π_2' applied to the second outcome of the two right lotteries must also be identical. Furthermore, if the preference relations are valid, then it must follow that $\pi_2 \ge \pi_2'$. Note that no assumption has been made about p_2 and q_2.

For the best outcome of any lottery, the rank does not matter, and therefore, the decision weight should be entirely dependent on its probability. As x_n is specified to be the best outcome, let $\pi_n = w(p_n)$ *be the best outcome decision weight*, where $w(.)$ is an increasing function of p with restrictions $w(0)=0$ and $w(1)=1$.

In general, for a lottery $(x_1, p_1; x_2, p_2; \ldots; x_n, p_n)$ with $x_1 < x_2 < \ldots < x_j < x_{j+1} < \ldots < x_n$, one can derive the following weights:

$$\pi_n = w(p_n)$$

$$\pi_{n-1} = w(p_{n-1} + p_n) - w(p_n)$$

$$\pi_{n-2} = w(p_{n-2} + p_{n-1} + p_n) - w(p_{n-1} + p_n)$$

$$\ldots$$

$$\ldots$$

$$\pi_2 = w\left(\sum_{i=2}^{n} p_i\right) - w\left(\sum_{i=3}^{n} p_i\right)$$

$$\pi_1 = 1 - w\left(\sum_{i=2}^{n} p_i\right).$$

Finally, the consumer's rank-dependent expected utility (RDEU) function over the lottery $\mathcal{L} = (x_1, p_1; x_2, p_2, \ldots, x_n, p_n)$, where $x_1 < x_2 < \ldots < x_j < x_{j+1} < \ldots < x_n$, is

$$\mathcal{U}(\mathcal{L}) = \pi_1 u(x_1) + \pi_2 u(x_2) + \ldots + \pi_n u(x_n).$$

She selects the lottery that gives the highest $\mathcal{U}(\mathcal{L})$.

7.5.1.3 *Cumulative prospect theory*

Quiggin's contribution led to a refinement of the prospect theory by Kahneman and Tversky themselves. Tversky and Kahneman (1992) modified their original version of the prospect theory by adopting the cumulative probability ranks while still retaining the useful binary classifications of gains and losses. Suppose that a lottery $\mathcal{L} = (x_1, p_1; x_2, p_2; \ldots; x_n, p_n)$ is a regular prospect with $x_1 < x_2 < \ldots < x_j < 0 < x_{j+1} < \ldots < x_n$.

Then the gains and losses outcomes can be segregated and two mini lotteries—$\mathcal{L}_G$ for gains and $\mathcal{L}_L$ for losses—can be created by introducing a no-loss–no-gain outcome, say, $x_0 = 0$ as follows,

$$\mathcal{L}_G = \left(x_0, p_0^G; x_{j+1}, p_{j+1}; \ldots; x_n, p_n\right) \text{ and } \mathcal{L}_L = \left(x_1, p_1; x_2, p_2; \ldots; x_j, p_j; x_0, p_0^L\right),$$

where

$$p_0^G = \sum_{i=1}^{j} p_i \text{ and } p_0^L = \sum_{i=j+1}^{n} p_i.$$

On $\mathcal{L}_G$, we can derive the ranks of x_0, and $x_{j+1} - x_n$ by their cumulative probabilities and then set $\pi_n^G = w_G(p_n)$ and, working backward, derive $\left(\pi_{n-1}^G, \ldots, \pi_{j+1}^G\right)$. Similarly, on $\mathcal{L}_L$, we treat x_0 as the best outcome and set $\pi_0^L = w_L\left(p_0^L\right) = w_L\left(p_{j+1} + \ldots + p_n\right)$. However, at $p_0^L = p_{j+1} + \ldots + p_n$, the two weighting functions $w_L(.)$ and $w_G(.)$ should be equal. This means that by setting $\pi_0^L = w_G\left(p_{j+1} + \ldots + p_n\right)$, we work backward to derive $\left(\pi_j^L, \ldots, \pi_1^L\right)$. Of course, $w_G(0) = 0$, $w_G(1) = 1$, $w_L(0) = 0$ and $w_L(1) = 1$.[11]

Combining the preceding decision weights on the outcomes of the two mini lotteries and dropping π_0^G and π_0^L from them, we get the decision weights for the whole lottery as

$$\pi_n^G = w_G(p_n)$$

$$\pi_{n-1}^G = w_G(p_{n-1} + p_n) - w_G(p_n)$$

$$\ldots\ldots \quad \ldots\ldots$$

$$\pi_{j+1}^G = w_G\left(p_{j+1} + \ldots + p_n\right) - w_G\left(p_{j+2} + \ldots + p_n\right)$$

$$\pi_j^L = w_L\left(p_j + p_{j+1} + \ldots + p_n\right) - w_G\left(p_{j+1} + \ldots + p_n\right)$$

$$\pi_{j-1}^L = w_L\left(p_{j-1} + p_j + \ldots + p_n\right) - w_L\left(p_j + \ldots + p_n\right)$$

$$\ldots \quad \ldots$$

$$\pi_1 = w_L(p_1 + p_2 + \ldots + p_n) - w_L(p_2 + \ldots + p_n) = 1 - w_L(p_2 + \ldots + p_n).$$

We can see that the weights are non-negative and do add up to 1. The consumer's assessment of a prospect is

$$\mathcal{U}(\mathcal{L}) = \sum_{i=1}^{j} \pi_i^L v_L(x_i) + \sum_{i=j+1}^{n} \pi_i^G v_G(x_i).$$

Let us conclude the discussion of this section by noting some key differences between EU, RDEU and cumulative prospect theory (CPT). First, all three theories prescribe a preference function (over the lottery space) that is linear in decision weights, but the way the weights relate to the probability of an outcome crucially differs between EU and the other two theories. In EU, the weights are just given by the probabilities, whereas in CPT and RDEU, they are non-linear functions of the probabilities. Second, both EU and RDEU work with outcome-based utility $u(x)$ which is entirely determined by the pay-off under that outcome. But in CPT (and, of course, prospect theory [PT]) assessment or value function of an outcome $v(x)$ can be defined in many ways, such as by considering gains and losses relative to a reference point. Next, we will see that another way of departing from EU is by changing the notion of outcome-based utility altogether while retaining the basic role of the probabilities as decision weights.

7.5.2 Regret theory

We have already mentioned that the possibility of regret and rejoice influences our preferences in lotteries. *Regret theory* formalises the idea (Bell, 1982; Loomes and Sugden, 1982). At the heart of this theory lies a clever construction of the concept of regret and rejoice based on the

Table 7.2 Pay-offs from two lotteries

Roll of a die	1	2	3	4	5	6
$\mathcal{L}_1 : x(\$)$	9	9	9	64	64	64
$u(x)$	3	3	3	8	8	8
$\mathcal{L}_2 : x(\$)$	0	9	9	9	0	484
$u(x)$	0	3	3	3	0	22
If $\mathcal{L}_1$ is chosen	rejoice	neither	neither	rejoice	strong rejoice	strong regret

differential between two lottery-dependent utilities for every given state. The probabilities are 'objective' probabilities as in the expected utility theory. Regret theory does not rely on decision weights, and it works mainly through a modified notion of utility.

Here we present a simple example, following the classic paper by Loomes and Sugden (1982). Consider a game of dice that offers two different sets of prizes giving rise to two different lotteries, which are shown in Table 7.2. The first lottery gives \$9 if the die throws up 1, 2 or 3 and \$64 if any other number comes up. The second lottery gives \$0 if 1 or 5 comes up; \$9 if 2, 3 or 4 comes up; and finally gives \$484 if 6 comes up. Assume $u = \sqrt{x}$. Clearly, lottery $\mathcal{L}_2$ is a bit riskier. Since a die gives equal probability to all six numbers, going by expected utility, we can say that our consumer should prefer $\mathcal{L}_1$ over $\mathcal{L}_2$, because

$$\mathcal{V}(\mathcal{L}_1) = 3 \times \frac{1}{6} \times 11 = 5.5 > \mathcal{V}(\mathcal{L}_2) = \left(3 \times \frac{1}{6} \times 3\right) + \left(\frac{1}{6} \times 22\right) = 5.16.$$

But she is aware of the possibility of rejoice and regret about any choice she makes. If $\mathcal{L}_1$ is chosen and 6 comes up, she would strongly regret for not choosing $\mathcal{L}_2$, which would have given \$484. Likewise, there will be strong rejoice if 5 was the realisation. In this instance, not only has she avoided getting nothing, but she has also ensured a sizeable pay-off. The consumer's choice between these two lotteries will then depend on how she psychologically evaluates these potential utility losses and gains. This is where we need to define a state-specific rejoice function as

$$R_i = R\left(u(x_i \mid \mathcal{L}_1) - u(x_i \mid \mathcal{L}_2)\right).$$

Regret can be defined as the *negative of rejoice* $(= -R_i)$. Then we can compute the expected rejoice (or expected utility where utility is redefined as rejoice) of choosing lottery $\mathcal{L}_1$ as (using $R_2 = R_3$)

$$\mathcal{R}(\mathcal{L}_1) = \frac{R_1 + R_4 + R_5 + R_6}{6} + \frac{R_2}{3}.$$

Since by definition $R_i(\mathcal{L}_1) = -R_i(\mathcal{L}_2)$, we must have $\mathcal{R}(\mathcal{L}_1) = -\mathcal{R}(\mathcal{L}_2)$. If $\mathcal{R}(\mathcal{L}_1) > 0$ then the consumer will choose lottery $\mathcal{L}_1$. Clearly, the consumer's choice depends on the shape of the rejoice function (or the strength of rejoice). If R_i is linear, such as $R_i = a\left[u(x_i \mid \mathcal{L}_1) - u(x_i \mid \mathcal{L}_2)\right]$, the regret theory collapses to the expected utility theory. So the rejoice function must be non-linear. Suppose $R_i = y_i^3$, where $y_i = u(x_i \mid \mathcal{L}_1) - u(x_i \mid \mathcal{L}_2)$. Then we can calculate

$$\mathcal{R}(\mathcal{L}_1) = \frac{R(0)}{3} + \frac{1}{6}\left[R(3) + R(5) + R(8) - R(14)\right] = \frac{27 + 125 + 512 - 2744}{6} = -346.67.$$

So the consumer should choose lottery $\mathcal{L}_2$ instead of $\mathcal{L}_1$. The possibility of experiencing strong regret associated with the realisation of 6 discourages her to select $\mathcal{L}_1$.

Regret theory supports many experimental observations in which the transitivity of preferences does not hold. The rejoice function can also accommodate an intercept term other than $R(.)$. For more see, Loomes and Sugden (1982). However, regret theory appeals strongly when the choice is restricted to two lotteries. For a more general set of choices, there are some additional requirements on the properties of the rejoice function. This problem has been addressed by Loomes and Sugden (1987), Sugden (1993) and Quiggin (1994). Nevertheless, two criticisms have remained with regret theory. First is that the theory does not permit the consumer to think of other realisations of the same lottery. For instance, upon choosing lottery $\mathcal{L}_1$ and seeing the realisation of 1, why would not one wish that the realisation was between 4 to 6? Clearly, this thought is not *regret* but one of *disappointment*. Gul (1991) has incorporated this idea to build a model of disappointment aversion. The second criticism raised by Bikhchandani and Segal (2011) is that when more than two lotteries are considered, any regret-based preference fails to be transitive, and if such preferences are made transitive, they collapse to expected utility preferences.

7.5.3 Ellsberg paradox

In 1961, humanist and former US military analyst Daniel Ellsberg wrote a paper presenting a number of lotteries whose predictions seemed to defy conventional wisdom in decision theory. As subsequent studies did produce evidence and experimental results to confirm Ellsberg's predictions, these problems came to be known as the Ellsberg paradox, which we illustrate with the following two examples.

7.5.4 Problem 1

Suppose there are two urns, both containing 100 balls, red (r) or blue (b). In urn I, the mix of r and b is unknown, while in urn II, the mix is 50 : 50, and it is commonly known. A random ball is drawn from either urn I or urn II. Based on the colour of the ball drawn and the urn from which it is drawn, one receives \$100 or nothing. This gives rise to the following four lotteries:

R_I: Receive \$100 if a red ball is drawn from urn I and nothing otherwise.
R_{II}: Receive \$100 if a red ball is drawn from urn II and nothing otherwise.
B_I: Receive \$100 if a blue ball is drawn from urn I and nothing otherwise.
B_{II}: Receive \$100 if a blue ball is drawn from urn II and nothing otherwise

Ellsberg's prediction was that most people would be indifferent between R_I and B_I and between R_{II} and B_{II}, but they would prefer R_{II} to R_I and B_{II} to B_I. Since the probability of winning \$100 is 1/2 in both R_{II} and B_{II}, preference of R_{II} over R_I implies that the probability of drawing a red ball from urn I is strictly less than 1/2, and similarly preference of B_{II} over B_I implies the probability of drawing a blue ball from urn I is also strictly less than 1/2. But both cannot be true at the same time. That is a paradox.

7.5.5 *Problem 2*

This time there is only one urn, and it contains 90 balls, of which 30 are red (r), the remaining balls are blue (b) or yellow (y) in an unknown mix. Four lotteries are suggested.

R: Receive \$100 if a red ball is drawn; otherwise, nothing.
B: Receive \$100 if a blue ball is drawn; otherwise, nothing.
RY: Receive \$100 if a red or yellow ball is drawn; otherwise, nothing.
BY: Receive \$100 if a blue or yellow ball is drawn; otherwise, nothing.

Ellsberg's prediction for problem 2 was that most people would prefer lottery R to B and prefer BY to RY. We see that $\text{prob}(r)+\text{prob}(b\cup y)=1$ with $\text{prob}(r)$ being 1/3 and prob $(b\cup y)$ being 2/3. Likewise, $\text{prob}(b)+\text{prob}(r\cup y)=1$. But we do not know $\text{prob}(b)$ or $\text{prob}(r\cup y)$. If R is preferred to B, then it should be the case that $\text{prob}(b)<1/3$, which implies $\text{prob}(r\cup y)>2/3$. So if BY is preferred to RY, then a lottery with greater chance of winning the same prize is rejected. That is also a paradox.

Ellsberg paradox raises a fundamental question about how people make decisions when probabilities are unknown. In problem 1, their behaviour (or choice) seems to suggest that they are computing/estimating unknown probabilities incorrectly. In problem 2, they are violating the principle of first-order stochastic dominance, which says that one should not reject a lottery that has a higher probability of giving the same prize.

A large body of empirical studies has supported Ellsberg's prediction, and new literature has emerged to explain why this anomaly happens. The anomaly is a paradox if we assume that people are making decisions using first-order stochastic dominance or computing probabilities in the way mathematicians do. Instead, we should consider the possibility that the fact of *ambiguity* in probability affects the way we make a choice. When probabilities are unknown, one needs to make assumptions to arrive at some estimates. It is not surprising that many people would be averse to such ambiguities. This concern has given rise to the ambiguity aversion literature. While early work in this literature adopted a rank-dependent preference approach (see for instance Segal (1987)) a more common approach is to assume that the consumer considers a distribution over distribution functions from which the unknown probabilities are drawn. For more, see Klibanoff et al. (2005, 2022) and Cerreia-Vioglio (2022).

7.6 Conclusion

The expected utility theory has made a long journey. Nearly 80 years on, the theory still remains very popular for its simplicity and wider applicability, as we have seen with problems of contracting, insurance, search, and betting, despite its continued criticisms and proven behavioural anomalies that dogged the expected utility theory almost from its inception. While the non-expected utility theories are very good for incorporating some fundamental facts of how people behave under uncertainty, their proponents have failed to present a unified theory of decision-making under uncertainty. But make no mistake, going by the recent explosion of interest in *reference-dependent preferences* we can only say that the hunt for a common and unified non-expected utility theory is very much on.

Summary

In this chapter, we learnt the following.

1. The expected utility theory provides a simple way to model decision-making under uncertainty.
2. A risk-averse individual wishes to surrender a risk premium in order to avoid risk. The minimum price to sell a risky asset is the certainty equivalent.
3. An actuarially fair insurance premium ensures that the consumer gets a fixed income across all states of nature.
4. When two risk-averse individuals engage in a gainful contract, such as employment or share tenancy, they would try to share the risk in an efficient manner while also ensuring production efficiency. If there are constraints on contracting, there will be a trade-off between efficiency and insurance.
5. Even when risk sharing is not an issue, expected utility theory can be very useful in determining optimal job/price search and for profit-maximising betting odds.
6. The logical premise of the expected utility theory has been challenged time and again by demonstrating that the prediction of the expected utility theory does not often match with actual choices people make. The Allais paradox is one of many examples.
7. Prospect theory provides an alternative theory, which draws on empirical evidence of how people make choices when facing uncertainty.
8. In prospect theory, there is an asymmetry between the valuation of losses and gains. Loss aversion is a key feature of prospect theory.
9. We also learnt about rank-dependent expected utility theory and cumulative prospect theory; both are further developments of the prospect theory.
10. Regret theory argues that often our choices are based on regret aversion.

7.7 Appendix

1. **Proof of Lemma 2.** First, we show that the second-order conditions (S.O.C.) are satisfied by Assumption 3 and the fact of $\pi_1 > p$ and $\pi_2 > 1-p$:

$$\frac{\partial^2 E\Pi}{\partial \pi_1^2} = -\frac{\left[f(\pi_1)\right]^2 + \left(1-F(\pi_1)\right)f'(\pi_1)}{\left[f(\pi_1)\right]^2} - \frac{2\pi_1 - p}{p} < 0,$$

$$\frac{\partial^2 E\Pi}{\partial \pi_2^2} = -\frac{\left[f(1-\pi_2)\right]^2 - F(1-\pi_2)f'(1-\pi_2)}{\left[f(1-\pi_2)\right]^2} - \frac{2\pi_2 - (1-p)}{1-p} < 0.$$

Next, we show the existence of a unique interior solution. Consider Eq. (7.15). For any given $p \in (0,1)$, neither $\pi_1 = 0$ nor $\pi_1 = 1$ can be a solution. At $\pi_1 = 0$ the bracketed expression is $\left[\frac{1}{f(0)} - 0\right] > 0$, and at $\pi_1 = 1$, it is $\left[0 - \frac{1-p}{p}\right] < 0$. Furthermore, $\frac{\partial E\Pi}{\partial \pi_1}$ is continuous and strictly decreasing in π_1 by the S.O.C. Hence, by the intermediate value theorem, there must be a unique $\pi_1 \in (0,1)$ such that $\frac{\partial E\Pi}{\partial \pi_1} = 0$. A similar reasoning applies Eq. (7.16) for π_2 (but going from $p=1$ to $p=0$).

To establish monotonicity of $\pi_1(p)$, we derive from Eq. (7.15)

$$\frac{\partial^2 E\Pi}{\partial \pi_1^2}\frac{\partial \pi_1}{\partial p} + \frac{\partial^2 E\Pi}{\partial \pi_1 \partial p} = 0, \quad \text{or} \quad \frac{\partial^2 E\Pi}{\partial \pi_1^2}\frac{\partial \pi_1}{\partial p} + \frac{\pi_1^2}{p^2} = 0.$$

Since $\frac{\partial^2 E\Pi}{\partial \pi_1^2} < 0$ we must have $\frac{\partial \pi_1}{\partial p} > 0$.

To see $\pi_1(0) = 0$ and $\pi_1(1) = 1$, rewrite Eq. (7.15) as $\left[p(1-F(\pi_1)) - (\pi_1 - p)\pi_1 f(\pi_1)\right] = 0$. Let $p \to 0$; then we must have $\pi_1 \to 0$ since $f(.) > 0$. Similarly, let $p = 1$, and from the preceding, we get $\left[1 - F(\pi_1) - (\pi_1 - 1)\pi_1 f(\pi_1)\right] = 0$. Now if $\pi_1 \neq 1$, then $\pi_1 < 1$ (since π_i cannot exceed 1), in which case $\left[1 - F(\pi_1) - (\pi_1 - 1)\pi_1 f(\pi_1)\right] > 0$. Hence, π_1 must be raised until $\pi_1 = 1$.

A symmetric argument establishes $\frac{\partial \pi_2}{\partial (1-p)} > 0$ from Eq. (7.16), and in turn $\frac{\partial \pi_2}{\partial p} < 0$.

2. **Proof of Proposition 12.** Substituting $\pi_1(p)$ and $\pi_2(1-p)$ in $E\Pi(.)$ we write $E\Pi(p) \equiv E\Pi(\pi_1(p), \pi_2(1-p))$ and apply the envelope theorem to derive:

$$\frac{\partial E\Pi(p)}{\partial p} = -\frac{1 - F(\pi_1(p))}{\pi_1(p)} + \frac{F(1 - \pi_2(1-p))}{\pi_2(1-p)}. \tag{7.17}$$

From Eq. (7.17), we further derive

$$\frac{\partial}{\partial p}\frac{1 - F(\pi_1)}{\pi_1} = -\frac{\pi_1 f(\pi_1) + (1 - F(\pi_1))}{(\pi_1)^2}\pi_1'(p) < 0,$$

$$\frac{\partial}{\partial p}\frac{F(1 - \pi_2)}{\pi_2} = -\frac{\pi_2 f(1 - \pi_2) + (F(1 - \pi_2))}{(\pi_2)^2}\pi_2'(p) > 0.$$

This implies that the $E\Pi_h(p)$ curve is convex:

$$\frac{\partial^2 E\Pi(\pi_1, \pi_2)}{\partial p^2} = -\frac{\partial}{\partial p}\frac{1 - F(\pi_1)}{\pi_1} + \frac{\partial}{\partial p}\frac{F(1 - \pi_2)}{\pi_2} > 0.$$

Furthermore, since $\pi_2(p=1) = \pi_1(p=0) = 0$ and $\pi_1(p=1) = \pi_2(p=0) = 1$, we get

as $p \to 0$ $\quad \frac{1 - F(\pi_1)}{\pi_1} \to \infty$ and $\frac{F(1 - \pi_2)}{\pi_2} \to 0$

as $p \to 1$ $\quad \frac{1 - F(\pi_1)}{\pi_1} \to 0$ and $\frac{F(1 - \pi_2)}{\pi_2} \to \infty.$

So the $E\Pi(p)$ curve must be U-shaped. At its minimum, $\frac{1-F(\pi_1)}{\pi_1}=\frac{F(1-\pi_2)}{\pi_2}$, and they are equal only at a unique value of p, say, p^*. If $f(q)$ is symmetric, then we must have $p^*=1/2$, implying $f(1-\pi_2)=f(\pi_1)$ and $F(1-\pi_2)=1-F(\pi_1)$. Therefore, $\pi_1=\pi_2$ at $p=1/2$.

3. **Proof of the expected utility theorem.** The following proof is adapted from Mas-Colell et al. (1995, pp. 176–178). There are several steps to follow.
Step 1: Our feasible set of lotteries with outcomes $(x_1,x_2,\ldots,x_n)$, $x_1<x_2<\ldots<x_n$, contains n certainty outcomes:

$$\underline{\mathcal{L}}=(1,0,..,0),\mathcal{L}_2^0=(0,1,..,0),\ldots,\mathcal{L}_{n-1}^0=(0,0,..,1,0),\bar{\mathcal{L}}=(0,0,..,1).$$

By the order of the outcomes x_i, $\bar{\mathcal{L}}$ is our best lottery and $\underline{\mathcal{L}}$ is our worst lottery, and

$$\mathcal{U}(\underline{\mathcal{L}})<\mathcal{U}(\mathcal{L}_2^0)<\ldots<\mathcal{U}(\mathcal{L}_{n-1}^0)<\mathcal{U}(\bar{\mathcal{L}}).$$

This follows from the fact that $x_1\prec x_2\prec\ldots\prec x_n$.
Since $\bar{\mathcal{L}}\succ\underline{\mathcal{L}}$, then by completeness axiom for any other lottery, say, $\mathcal{L}$, in our feasible set, we must have $\bar{\mathcal{L}}\succeq\mathcal{L}\succeq\underline{\mathcal{L}}$. Then we show that for any $\alpha\in(0,1)$ and any two lotteries $\mathcal{L}$ and $\mathcal{L}'$ if $\mathcal{L}\succ\mathcal{L}'$ then $\alpha\mathcal{L}+(1-\alpha)\mathcal{L}'\succ\mathcal{L}'$. This can be seen as follows:

$$\mathcal{L}=\alpha\mathcal{L}+(1-\alpha)\mathcal{L}\succ\alpha\mathcal{L}+(1-\alpha)\mathcal{L}'\succ\alpha\mathcal{L}'+(1-\alpha)\mathcal{L}'=\mathcal{L}'.$$

Step 2: For two compound lotteries of $\bar{\mathcal{L}}$ and $\underline{\mathcal{L}}$, $\beta\bar{\mathcal{L}}+(1-\beta)\underline{\mathcal{L}}\succ\alpha\bar{\mathcal{L}}+(1-\alpha)\underline{\mathcal{L}}$ if and only if $\beta>\alpha$. To see this let us write

$$\begin{aligned}\beta\bar{\mathcal{L}}+(1-\beta)\underline{\mathcal{L}}&=\frac{\beta}{1-\alpha}(1-\alpha)\bar{\mathcal{L}}+(1-\beta)\underline{\mathcal{L}}\\&=\frac{\beta-\alpha\beta-\alpha+\alpha}{1-\alpha}\bar{\mathcal{L}}+\frac{(1-\beta)}{1-\alpha}(1-\alpha)\underline{\mathcal{L}}\\&=\frac{\beta-\alpha}{1-\alpha}\bar{\mathcal{L}}+\left(1-\frac{\beta-\alpha}{1-\alpha}\right)\left[\alpha\bar{\mathcal{L}}+(1-\alpha)\underline{\mathcal{L}}\right]\\&\succ\alpha\bar{\mathcal{L}}+(1-\alpha)\underline{\mathcal{L}}.\end{aligned}$$

The last step follows from Step 1, if $\beta>\alpha$. The first lottery (i.e., the β-lottery) is simply a compound lottery of $\bar{\mathcal{L}}$ and the second lottery (i.e., α-lottery). Then the β-lottery must be preferred to the α-lottery.
Step 3: For any two lotteries $\mathcal{L}^*$ and $\mathcal{L}$, there exist α^* and α, respectively, such that $\alpha^*\bar{\mathcal{L}}+(1-\alpha^*)\underline{\mathcal{L}}\sim\mathcal{L}^*$ and $\alpha\bar{\mathcal{L}}+(1-\alpha)\underline{\mathcal{L}}\sim\mathcal{L}$. This is ensured by the axiom of continuity of preferences.

Step 4: Step 3 implies that there always exists a unique α_i such that $\mathcal{L}_i^0 \sim \alpha_i \overline{\mathcal{L}} + (1-\alpha_i)\underline{\mathcal{L}}$. That is, each certainty lottery, except the best and the worst, is indifferent to a unique compound lottery of the best and the worst lotteries.
Step 5: Let us write $\mathcal{U}(\mathcal{L}) = \alpha$, where $\mathcal{L} = \alpha\overline{\mathcal{L}} + (1-\alpha)\underline{\mathcal{L}}$. Then from Step 4,

$$\mathcal{U}(\underline{\mathcal{L}}) = u(x_1) = 0 \text{ since } \underline{\mathcal{L}} \sim 0 \times \overline{\mathcal{L}} + 1 \times \underline{\mathcal{L}}$$

$$\mathcal{U}(\mathcal{L}_2^0) = u(x_2) = \alpha_2 \text{ since } \mathcal{L}_2^0 \sim \alpha_2 \times \overline{\mathcal{L}} + (1-\alpha_2) \times \underline{\mathcal{L}}$$

$$\ldots \qquad \ldots\ldots$$

$$\mathcal{U}(\mathcal{L}_{n-1}^0) = u(x_{n-1}) = \alpha_{n-1} \text{ since } \mathcal{L}_{n-1}^0 \sim \alpha_{n-1} \times \overline{\mathcal{L}} + (1-\alpha_{n-1}) \times \underline{\mathcal{L}}$$

$$\mathcal{U}(\overline{\mathcal{L}}) = u(x_n) = 1 \text{ since } \overline{\mathcal{L}} \sim 1 \times \overline{\mathcal{L}} + 0 \times \underline{\mathcal{L}}.$$

Note that $u(x_1) = 0$ and $u(x_n) = 1$ can be regarded as an implied normalisation that follows from the construction of the utility function as a weight on the best lottery. $\mathcal{U}(\mathcal{L}) = \alpha$ is clearly an increasing function.
Let us now consider the previously mentioned compound lotteries that are indifferent to certainty lotteries, and randomise over them with probability weights $p_1, p_2, \ldots, p_n$.

$$\begin{aligned}
p_1 \times \underline{\mathcal{L}} &\sim p_1 \times \left[0 \times \overline{\mathcal{L}} + 1 \times \underline{\mathcal{L}}\right] \\
p_2 \times \mathcal{L}_2^0 &\sim p_2 \times \left[\alpha_2 \times \overline{\mathcal{L}} + (1-\alpha_2) \times \underline{\mathcal{L}}\right] \\
\ldots & \qquad \ldots\ldots \\
p_{n-1} \times \mathcal{L}_{n-1}^0 &\sim p_{n-1} \times \left[\alpha_{n-1} \times \overline{\mathcal{L}} + (1-\alpha_{n-1}) \times \underline{\mathcal{L}}\right] \\
p_n \times \overline{\mathcal{L}} &\sim p_n \times \left[1 \times \overline{\mathcal{L}} + 0 \times \underline{\mathcal{L}}\right].
\end{aligned}$$

We denote the preceding compound lottery (on the left-hand side) as $\mathcal{L} = p_1 \times \underline{\mathcal{L}} + p_2 \times \mathcal{L}_2^0 + \ldots + p_{n-1} \times \mathcal{L}_{n-1}^0 + p_n \times \overline{\mathcal{L}}$. Note that by construction, $\mathcal{L}$ is a compound lottery that assigns strictly positive probability over all certainty lotteries. Equivalently, we can write $\mathcal{L} = (x_1, p_1; x_2, p_2; \ldots; x_{n-1}, p_{n-1}; x_n, p_n)$.
Next, by adding the right-hand-side expressions, we write the following indifference relation.

$$\begin{aligned}
\mathcal{L} &\sim [p_1 \times 0 + p_2\alpha_2 + \ldots + p_{n-1}\alpha_{n-1} + p_n \times 1]\overline{\mathcal{L}} \\
&\qquad + \left[p_1 + p_2(1-\alpha_2) + \ldots + p_{n_1}(1-\alpha_{n-1}) + p_n \times 0\right]\underline{\mathcal{L}} \\
&\sim \left[\underbrace{p_1 \times u(x_1) + p_2 u(x_2) + \ldots + p_{n-1} u(x_n) + p_n u(x_n)}_{\gamma}\right]\overline{\mathcal{L}} \\
&\qquad + \left[\underbrace{1 - \{p_2 u(x_2) + \ldots + p_{n_1} u(x_{n-1}) + p_n u(x_n)\}}_{1-\gamma}\right]\underline{\mathcal{L}} \\
&\sim \gamma\overline{\mathcal{L}} + (1-\gamma)\underline{\mathcal{L}}.
\end{aligned}$$

Our compound lottery $\mathcal{L}$ is indifferent to a lottery that assigns a weight γ on the best lottery and $1-\gamma$ on the worst lottery. Then by the construction of our utility function $\mathcal{U}(\mathcal{L})$, we arrived at

$$\mathcal{U}(\mathcal{L}) = \gamma = p_1 \times u(x_1) + p_2 u(x_2) + \ldots + p_{n-1} u(x_{n-1}) + p_n u(x_n).$$

This is just our expected utility function which we wanted to prove. For any other lottery $\mathcal{L}' = (x_1', p_1'; x_2', p_2'; \ldots; x_n', p_n')$, we can derive γ in the same way such that

$$\mathcal{L}' \sim \gamma' \overline{\mathcal{L}} + (1-\gamma)\underline{\mathcal{L}} \Rightarrow \mathcal{U}(\mathcal{L}') = \gamma'.$$

Then by Step 2, $\mathcal{L} \succ \mathcal{L}'$ if and only if $\gamma > \gamma'$. This completes the proof.

7.8 Exercises

1. A consumer's utility function is $u = \sqrt{y}$, where y refers to wealth. He has an asset W, which may lose 50% of its value with a probability of 25% or may remain intact with a 75% probability. Of the following three options, which one should the consumer take?

    a. Buy insurance against loss from a perfectly competitive market.
    b. Sell the asset to an investor.
    c. Do nothing and live with the risk.

2. Peter is contemplating selling a risky asset that gives £625 with a probability of 0.60 and £100 with a probability of 0.40. Peter's utility from income/wealth is given by $u = \sqrt{y}$.

    a. If Peter currently does not have insurance for the risky asset, how much will he be willing to accept for this asset?
    b. If Peter currently has insurance with full cover from a perfectly competitive insurance market, how much will he be willing to accept to sell the asset? Explain your answer.

3. a. An individual's wealth W includes, among other things, a house valued V and a painting valued Z (kept in the house); $W \geq V + Z$. The painting may get stolen with a probability of 0.10. There is also a chance that the house may catch fire with a probability of 0.05, in which case the painting will also get destroyed. His utility function is $u = \sqrt{y}$, where y refers to his net income/wealth. Assuming a perfectly competitive market for insurance, calculate his optimal insurance covers against burglary and fire.
    b. If instead of buying insurance against burglary if a burglar alarm were to be installed, how much would he be willing to spend on it? Also, comment if the insurance market was not competitive how his demands for insurance may change.
4. Suppose a car valued at £10,000, has the risk of being stolen with probability 0.05. The owner of the car has a utility function $u = 10\sqrt{y}$, where y denotes the value of the car. If there is a competitive market for insurance, what would be the premium rate, and how much cover would he like to buy? Is he better off with insurance than without it?
5. a. Mr Jones's home is worth \$200,000, which can lose its value by \$100,000 if there is a subsidence, which can occur with a probability of 10%. Mr Jones's utility function is $u = \sqrt{y}$. Assuming that the insurance market is competitive, how much insurance Mr Jones would like to buy?

b. Suppose Mr Jones runs another risk following the subsidence—the risk of losing £36,000 from his business that he runs from his home. The probability of losing his business following a subsidence is 50%. How would Mr Jones's insurance demand change? (For this question, assume y is wealth plus income.)

6. Mr Marshall has invested \$5000 in a portfolio of stocks that can be worthless (i.e., lose 100%) with a probability of 0.30 and with the remaining probability it can give 100% return. Marshall's utility function is $u = \sqrt{y}$.

   a. Calculate Marshall's expected utility of holding the portfolio, and then compute the minimum price he is willing to accept to sell his portfolio to another investor.
   b. Consider another option. While holding on to the stock, Marshall can buy an insurance contract (a type of derivative) that will give him x in the event his stock portfolio becomes worthless and nothing otherwise, provided he pays an insurance premium of $0.3x$. The amount x is Marshall's choice. What is the optimal value of x?
   c. Now, a financial expert points out that Marshall's risk of losing everything is 0.10 only under normal circumstances, but if the economy is hit with a recession, which has a 50% chance, then his stocks will be worthless with a 60% probability. In the event his stock survives the adverse shock, it will gain 100% in value as before. Should Marshall try to sell his portfolio, and if so at what price? Alternatively, if he goes for insurance, how will the insurance company revise their policy?

7. Pablo's gross wealth is W, which includes a house valued V and a painting gifted by his friend Henri, valued Z. The artwork may get stolen by burglars with a probability of 0.10 on a normal night. But if Pablo's area gets flooded, which can happen with a 0.30 probability, the chance of burglary jumps to 1. Flooding reduces the value of the house by 25%. Pablo's utility function is $u = \sqrt{y}$.

   a. Calculate Pablo's optimal insurance covers against possible losses and the amounts of insurance premia he will be paying.
   b. Assuming Pablo buys insurance (from a competitive market) what is the minimum price of the painting he will be willing to accept to sell it?
   c. Now suppose the local government builds a good flood barrier and the risk of flood is fully eliminated. But due to lack of policing resources, the burglary rate remains constant at 0.30 throughout the year. The insurance industry is still perfectly competitive, but all insurance firms pay back only 90% of the cover as 10% of the cover now goes to cover the administration charges of the claim (which was previously absent). How would Pablo's insurance demand be affected by this change to the insurance rule?

8. Mrs Hawthorne owns a John Constable that is valued \$100,000. But she lives in an area that is prone to burglary. The probability of burglary on any given night is 0.20. But if she forgets to close her living room window, which can happen with a probability of 0.10, the probability of burglary increases to 0.40. In addition to the painting, she has wealth valued at \$10,000. But it is the painting that is what the burglars are interested in. Mrs Hawthorne's utility function is $u = \sqrt{y}$, where y refers to her aggregate wealth.

   a. In the absence of any insurance option for the painting, what is the minimum price she will be willing to accept to sell the painting?
   b. Now suppose there is a competitive insurance market. The insurance companies know her habit of forgetting to close the window, as well as the probability of burglary in the area. If she wishes to insure the painting, how much cover will she buy, and what premium will she pay?

c. In the presence of the option to buy insurance, how does her reservation price for selling the painting change?
d. Let us now introduce yet another option for Mrs Hawthorne—contributing \$7000 to a neighbourhood watch fund, which helps reduce the burglary probability to 0.10 when her window is closed and to 0.30 when her window is open. Do you think she should contribute and still buy insurance or not buy insurance and just contribute?

9. Suppose the probability of a serious illness is uniformly distributed over a population of size N, where each has income m. If the illness strikes, one loses m entirely; otherwise, m remains intact. Each individual knows their own probability of illness p, but the insurance companies don't. They only know the group average. Everybody has the same utility function $u = \sqrt{y}$.

   a. Assuming full cover is offered along with a premium rate γ, determine the critical value of p at which an individual will be indifferent to buying insurance and not buying insurance.
   b. If the government offers a subsidy s on the insurance premium rate, how does your answer to question 9(a) change? If the subsidy is a fixed amount of the total premium, will your answer remain the same?
   c. Now in the same set-up, relax the assumption of full cover. Let D be the cover, $D \leq m$, and consumers are asked to choose their optimal cover against the premium rate γ. Derive the individual demands for cover. Will the indifferent consumer demand full cover? Write the indifference condition for not buying the insurance.

10. Consider the tenancy problem of Section 7.3.1. Assume that labour is applied *before* the uncertainty is resolved. Then derive the tenant's optimal choice of labour for the case where he will fully bear the labour cost himself.
11. Consider the same set-up as in Section 7.3.5. Assume uniform distribution for the naive bettors' beliefs and suppose the collective wealth is y. If there is a bettor with wealth z who knows exactly which team will win and the bookmaker knows the existence of this (privately informed) bettor, then what prices will he set for the two tickets?
12. Consider a betting problem for a two-team contest, which ends with one team's win. Suppose there are 100 naive bettors. Sixty of them believe that team 1 will win with a probability of 3/4, and 40 of them believe that team 2 will win with a probability of 3/4. Each of them has £10 to bet. A monopolist knows that the true probability of win by team 1 is 1/2. Derive the monopolist bookmaker's optimal ticket prices (or betting odds). Does your answer change if there is a bettor whose belief is exactly same as the bookmaker?
13. Consider the roll of a die and two lotteries that assign different utilities to different outcomes as shown in Table 7.3. Assume $u_1 < u_2 < \ldots < u_6$ and a rejoice function is given by $R_i(\mathcal{L}_2) = \left[u_j(\mathcal{L}_2) - u_j(\mathcal{L}_1)\right]^3$. Applying regret theory, determine which lottery is preferable and how the conclusion differs from the expected utility theory.

Table 7.3 Pay-offs from two lotteries

Roll of a die	*1*	*2*	*3*	*4*	*5*	*6*
$\mathcal{L}_1 : u(x)$	u_1	u_2	u_3	u_4	u_5	u_6
$\mathcal{L}_2 : u(x)$	u_6	u_4	u_4	u_3	u_5	u_1

Notes

1 Frank Knight in his 1921 book *Risk, Uncertainty, and Profit* proposed to distinguish between risk and uncertainty on the ground that for risk probabilities are known and for uncertainty the probabilities are not known. We will not make this distinction. Where probabilities are not known, we will assume that the agents have beliefs or subjective probabilities. However, how the beliefs are formed or where the subjective probabilities come from is not a trivial question. Recent research explores such issues.

2 One can easily extend the analysis to the case in which θ is realised after labour is applied, like rain just before harvesting. The analysis will be similar except that the production efficiency will have to be stated in terms of expected output.

3 One can use an alternative formulation of two wage rates w_B and w_G. The result should be same.

4 A similar problem is the 'lemon' problem, where second-hand bad cars/appliances are referred to as lemons. In the markets for used cars, the quality of a car is not known to the potential buyers, and hence, the buyers are not willing to give a good price. Knowing that the sellers of bad cars only participate in the market. A successful trade is very likely to be a 'sour' deal for the buyer, hence the term *lemon*.

5 Essentially sampling from the pool of jobs follows the 'replacement' protocol. If we discard the previously found low-paying jobs, the problem will not be a stationary one, and the analysis will be more complex.

6 Here we need to apply the **Leibniz integral rule**, which gives a formula for the differentiation of a definite integral whose limits are functions of the differential variable. This rule is as follows:

$$\frac{\partial}{\partial z}\int_{a(z)}^{b(z)} g(x,z)dx = \int_{a(z)}^{b(z)}\frac{\partial g}{\partial z}dx + g(b(z),z)\frac{\partial b}{\partial z} - g(a(z),z)\frac{\partial a}{\partial z}.$$

For our problem, $z = p^*$, $a(z) = 0$, $b(z) = p^*$; $g(x,z) = pf(p)$ independent of p^*. This gives

$$\frac{\partial}{\partial p^*}\left[\int_0^{p^*} pf(p)dp\right] = p^* f(p^*).$$

7 We verify the second-order condition as follows.

$$G''(p^*) = \frac{d}{dp}G'(p^*) = \frac{d}{dp}\left[\frac{f(p^*)}{F(p^*)}(p^* - G(p^*))\right]$$

$$= \left[\frac{d}{dp}\frac{f(p^*)}{F(p^*)}\right]\left(p^* - G(p^*) + \frac{f(p^*)}{F(p^*)}\left[1 - G'(p^*)\right]\right.$$

$$= \frac{f(p^*)}{F(p^*)} > 0 \text{ since } G'(p^*) = p^* - G(p^*) = 0.$$

8 Unfortunately, Tversky passed away in 1996, six years before Kahneman was awarded the Nobel Prize. It is widely believed if Tversky was alive, he would have been a co-recipient. The Swedish Academy acknowledged his contribution in their citation.

9 According to Kahneman and Tversky (1979), consumers break down the complex process of decision-making into two phases, editing and assessment or evaluation. In the editing phase, the consumer is trying to digest all the information regarding the prospects, the structure of uncertainties and so on. Her tendency would be to simplify and, in particular, define pay-offs as gains and losses with respect to a reference point.

10 A cumulative distribution function $G(x)$ *first-order stochastically dominates* another cumulative distribution function $F(x)$ if $G(x) \leq F(x)$ at every x. That means under the distribution function $G(x)$ the chance of getting more than x is always higher.

11 Wakker (2010) showed that outcomes can be ranked by redefining them as 'getting more than x_n' as least likely and 'getting more than as x_1' as most likely. Then starting with $w_L(0) = 0$ on the least likely event, one can derive the remaining weights in a bottom-up manner.

References and further readings

Allais, M. (1953). Le comportement de l'homme rationel devant le risque: critique des axioms et postulates de l'école americaine. *Econometrica*, 21, 503–546.

Arrow, K. J. (1971). *Essays in the Theory of Risk-Bearing*. Chicago, IL: Markham.

Azariadis, C. (1975). Implicit contracts and under-employment equilibria. *Journal of Political Economy*, 83, 1183–202.

Azariadis, C. & Stiglitz, J. E. (1983). Implicit contract and fixed price equilibria. *Quarterly Journal of Economics*, 98, 1183–202.

Bag, P. K. & Saha, B. (2011). Match-fixing under competitive odds. *Games and Economic Behavior*, 73, 318–344.

Bag, P. K. & Saha, B. (2017a). Match-fixing in a monopoly betting market. *Journal of Economics Management Strategy*, 26(1), 257–289.

Bag, P. K. & Saha, B. (2017b). Corrupt bookmaking in a fixed odds illegal betting market. *Economic Journal*, 127, 624–652.

Basu, K. (2003). *Analytical Development Economics, the Less Developed Economy Revisited.* Cambridge, MA: MIT Press.

Bell, D. E. (1982). Regret in decision making under uncertainty. *Operations Research*, 30, 961–981.

Bikhchandani, S. & Segal, U. (2011). Transitive regret. *Theoretical Economics*, 6, 95–108.

Cerreia-Vioglio, S., Maccheroni, F. & Massimo M. M. (2022). Ambiguity aversion and wealth effects. *Journal of Economic Theory*, 199, 104898.

Chatterjee, K. & Krishna, V. (2009). A "dual self" representation of stochastic temptation. *American Economic Journal: Microeconomics*, 1(2), 148–167.

Diecidue, E. & Wakker, P. (2001). On the intuition of rank-dependent utility. *Journal of Risk and Uncertainty*, 23(3), 281–298.

Ellsberg, D. (1961). Risk, ambiguity and the Savage axioms. *Quarterly Journal of Economics*, 75, 643–669.

Gul, F. (1991). A theory of disappointment aversion. *Econometrica*, 59(3), 667–686.

Gull, F. & Pesendorfer, W. (2001). Temptation and self-control. *Econometrica*, 69(6), 1403–1435.

Kahneman, D. & Tversky, A. (1979). Prospect theory: An analysis of risk under uncertainty. *Econometrica*, 47(2), 263–291.

Klibanoff, P., Marinacci, M. & Mukerji, S. (2005). A smooth model of decision making under ambiguity. *Econometrica*, 73, 1849–1892.

Klibanoff, P., Mukerji, S., Kyoungwon, S. & Stanca, L. (2022). Foundations of ambiguity models under symmetry: α-MEU and smooth ambiguity. *Journal of Economic Theory*, 199, 105202.

Loomes, G. & Sugden, R. (1982). Regret theory: An alternative theory of rational choice under uncertainty. *The Economic Journal*, 98(368), 805–824.

Loomes, G. & Sugden, R. (1987). Some implications of a more general form of regret theory. *Journal of Economic Theory*, 41, 270–287.

Machina, M. J. (1982). "Expected utility" analysis without the independence axiom. *Econometrica*, 50, 277–323.

Mas-Colell, A., Whinston, M. D. & Green, J. R. (1995). *Microeconomi Theory*. New York: Oxford University Press.

McAfee, R. P. (2006). *Introduction to Economic Analysis*. www.introecon.com [available under the terms of the *Creative Commons Attribution License (CC BY)* https://creativecommons.org/licenses/by/4.0/].

Newberry, D. M. & Stiglitz, J. E. (1987). Wage rigidity, implicit contracts and unemployment and economic efficiency. *The Economic Journal*, 97, 416–430.
Pratt, J. W. (1964). Risk aversion in the small and in the large. *Econometrica*, 32, 122–136.
Preston, I. & Szymanski, S. (2003). Cheating in contest. *Oxford Review of Economic Policy*, 19, 612–624.
Quiggin, J. (1982). A theory of anticipated utility. *Journal of Economic Behavior and Organization*, 3(4), 332–382.
Quiggin, J. (1994). Regret theory with general choice sets. *Journal of Risk and Uncertainty*, 8, 153–165.
Ray, D. (1998). *Development Economics*. Princeton, NJ: Princeton University Press.
Segal, U. (1987). The Ellsberg paradox and risk aversion: An anticipated utility approach. *International Economic Review*, 28(1), 175–202.
Shin, H. (1991). Optimal betting odds against insider traders. *Economic Journal*, 101, 1179–1185.
Shin, H. (1992). Prices of state contingent claims with insider traders, and the favourite-longshot bias. *Economic Journal*, 102, 426–435.
Sugden, R. (1993). An axiomatic foundation for regret theory. *Journal of Economic Theory*, 60, 159–180.
Tversky, A. & Kahneman, D. (1992). Advances in prospect theory: Cumulative representation of uncertainty. *Journal of Risk and Uncertainty*, 5(4), 297–323.
von Neumann, J. & Morgenstern, O. (1944). *Theory of Games and Economic Behavior*. Princeton, NJ: Princeton University Press.
Wakker, P. P. (2010). *Prospect Theory: For Risk and Ambiguity*. Cambridge: Cambridge University Press.

Chapter 8

Firm theory

Abstract

In this chapter, we take up the case of production. Our first task is to describe and characterise technology. Then we discuss a competitive firm's profit maximisation problem, in which the firm directly decides on the optimal input levels. After characterising the profit function and input demand functions, we consider the problem of cost minimisation, whereby the firm is trying to decide on the least cost input bundle to produce a given level of output. After explaining both short- and long-run cost functions and their properties we study duality relations between production and cost.

Keywords: Returns to scale, Returns to factor, Hotelling's lemma, LeChatelier principle, Shephard's lemma, Short-run and long-run costs, Elasticity of cost

8.1 Introduction

The human endeavour to make something new out of a few natural materials has come a long way since the discovery of agriculture 10,000 years ago in the Fertile Crescent. For thousands of years, technological progress had been slow, but it did not take long to move from the eighteenth-century Industrial Revolution to arrive at the modern age of computers and robots. Our capacity to learn, adapt and invent has given us a limitless possibility of consumption and production. And yet the notion of technology, regardless of whether it is as simple as planting strawberries or as complex as building the James Webb Space Telescope, can be summarised in a very simple and abstract way. It is a transformational relationship between *inputs* and *outputs*. Treating this relationship very generally and therefore viewing it as a black box, we restrict our attention to things that go in into a production process, (inputs or factors of production) and things that come out of it (outputs).

Almost everywhere you need human labour. Even in highly automated industries, human intervention is needed (as of now) to fix any malfunctioning of robots. Other inputs can be natural materials like seeds, coal, steel and so on. We denote the list of all possible inputs as $x = (x_1, x_2, \ldots, x_n)$ and the output y. Sometimes, the output also appears on the input side. You need potatoes to grow potatoes, steel to make steel and electricity to make electricity. Our x vector then includes y but calls it some x_i. Although we focus exclusively on the case of a single output, there is no denying that production sometimes leads to joint outputs. A peach grower sells honey as well, because peaches attract honeybees. A slaughterhouse sells both meat and hides. A wheat farmer sells both wheat and hay bales. A poultry farmer sells eggs and chickens. And so on and so forth. The theory that we consider next can be extended to multi-product firms with some modifications. But we will not pursue that.

DOI: 10.4324/9781003226994-8

A firm in our theory is characterised by two things: a technology that it uses and an objective, such as profit maximisation. Non-profit objectives, such as social welfare maximisation or sales maximisation, can also be accommodated. Our first job is to formalise the idea of technology and then analyse the firm's input demands and output supply.

8.2 Technology

We begin by defining a production function:

$$y = f(x_1, x_2, \ldots, x_n),$$

where y is the highest (technically efficient) possible output obtained by employing a bundle of n inputs. A natural property any production function should have is $\frac{\partial f(\cdot)}{\partial x_i} \equiv f_i \geq 0$. That is, the marginal product of an input (MP_i) cannot be negative. Furthermore, for $y > 0$, the input vector must contain at least one element strictly positive. That is, one cannot produce something out of nothing. We will also assume that production functions are continuous.

There are two related notions of technology that are very useful—*production set* and *input requirement set*. A production set is the set of all input bundles and their corresponding feasible output levels. That is,

$$Y = \{(x_1, x_2, \ldots, x_n, y) \mid y \leq f(x_1, x_2, \ldots, x_n)\} \subset R_+^{n+1}.$$

An implicit assumption in the notion of a production set is that we can always throw away some outputs that an input bundle can efficiently produce. For instance, if $y_0 = f(x_0)$ is the highest output, the input bundle x_0 can produce, then by throwing away half of y_0 at no cost, we make $y_0 / 2$ always feasible for the input bundle x^0. This assumption is called the **free disposal** assumption. Figure 8.1 shows a production set when only one input is used. The entire area under the production function $y = f(x)$ is the production set. At input level x_0, the highest possible output

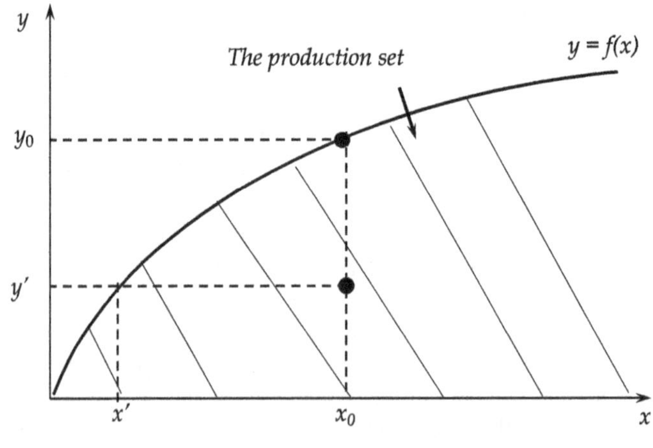

Figure 8.1 Production set of the one input case

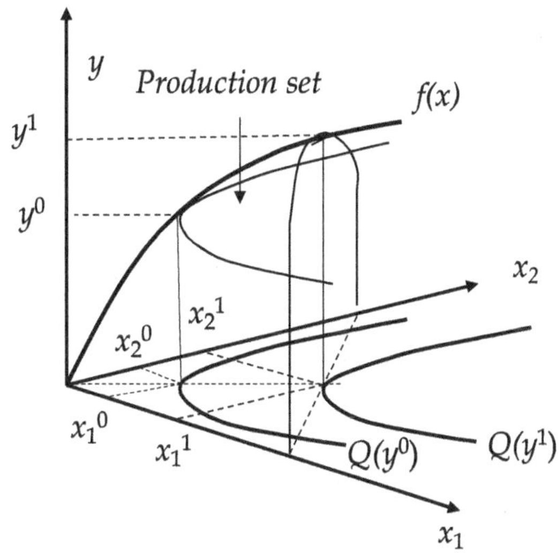

Figure 8.2 Production function of two inputs and its associated production set

is y_0, but any $y < y_0$ is also feasible. The rest can be thrown away. We have depicted a case in which our production function $y = f(x)$ is a strictly concave function, which makes the production set convex. It should be clear that if the production function is not convex, our production set will not be convex. The convexity of the production set is important, as we shall shortly see. Figure 8.2 shows the production set generated by a two-input production function.

An *input requirement set* is a set of input bundles that can produce at least y. Formally, for any given output level y the input requirement set is

$$V(y) = \{(x_1, x_2, \ldots, x_n) \mid f(x_1, x_2, \ldots, x_n) \geq y\} \subset R_+^n.$$

Once again, you can see that our free disposal assumption is at work.

From the production function, we can also derive *isoquants*. An isoquant is a set of input bundles that give exactly the output level y. Formally, for any output level y, an isoquant is

$$Q(y) = \{(x, x_2, \ldots, x_n) \mid f(x_1, x_2, \ldots, x_n) = y\}.$$

Two graphs of isoquants are shown in Figure 8.2, namely, $Q(y^0)$ and $Q(y^1)$, which include input bundles (x_1^0, x_2^0) and (x_1^1, x_2^1), respectively, as shown in the graph. The isoquants are mapped by tracking the same heights, y^0 or y^1, from the floor formed by two axes x_1 and x_2.

Isoquants should not be upward-sloping. If they did, then our assumption $\partial f(.)/\partial x_i \geq 0$ will be violated. Isoquants should be continuous, and they should not cross one another. The continuity of isoquants is guaranteed by the continuity of the production function. Crossing isoquants contradicts the premise that MP_i – s cannot be negative.

We may further define the *marginal rate of technical substitution* (MRTS) between any two inputs as the ratio of their marginal products. That is, $MRTS_{ij} = f_i / f_j$. This is a production analogue to our previously learnt marginal rate of substitution (MRS) in Chapter 2.[1] For two-input production functions, the slope of an isoquant is given by the negative value of MRTS; that is, $\frac{dx_2}{dx_1} = -\frac{f_1}{f_2}$. Like MRS, MRTS is decreasing if the production function $f(x)$ is quasi-concave (see Chapter 2). That is,

$$\frac{dM\,RTS}{dx_1} = \left[\frac{f_2^2 f_{11} - 2f_{12}f_1f_2 + f_{22}f_1^2}{f_2^3(.)}\right] = -\frac{\Delta f}{f_2^3} < 0$$

if and only if

$$\Delta f = \left[-f_2^2 f_{11} + 2f_{12}f_1f_2 - f_{22}f_1^2\right] > 0.$$

A function $f(x)$ is (strictly) quasi-concave if $\Delta f > 0$. We may assume $f_{ii} \leq 0$ while leaving f_{ij} unsigned. If $f_{12} > 0$ two inputs will be called *net complements* and if $f_{12} < 0$, they are *net substitutes*.

Now we specify a few assumptions to ensure that the production set and the input requirement set have some desirable properties:

1. *Axiom of monotonicity*. If $x \in V(y)$ and $x' \geq x$ then $x' \in V(y)$. That is, the input requirement set $v(y)$ include x' when no element of x' is smaller than x, which is capable of producing y. Similarly, if $(y,x) \in Y$ and $y' \leq y$, then $(y',x) \in Y$. If the production set includes y for a given input vector x, then it must also include a lower level of output for the same input vector. You can see that this is the assumption of free disposal at work.
2. *Axiom of closedness*. Both $V(y)$ and Y are closed sets. If $x \in V(y)$ and if we take a sequence $\{x_n\} \in V(y)$, then the limit of the sequence x^0 must also be in $V(y)$. Similarly, if $(x,y) \in Y$ and if we take a sequence $\{(x_n, y_n)\} \in Y$, then the limit of the sequence (x^0, y^0) must also be in Y.
3. *Axiom of convexity*. (a) If $x, x' \in V(y)$, then for every $\lambda \in [0,1], x^* = \lambda x + (1-\lambda)x' \in V(y)$. (b) Similarly, if $(x,y),(x',y') \in Y$, then for every $\lambda \in [0,1], (x^*, y^*) = (\lambda x + (1-\lambda)x', \lambda y + (1-\lambda)y') \in Y$. Convexity of production set is not always needed.

The property of closedness is a technical one. Here, the idea is that if x can produce y (or more than y), then we can always find an arbitrarily close input bundle x' that can also produce y. Along with free disposal, continuity of the production function also helps us understand why the limit of the sequence will remain in the set. Convexity of the input requirement set asserts that if there are two ways we can produce y, then by taking a convex combination of the two ways we can produce y. For instance, two firms can produce 50 units of output by using two different input bundles, say (10,20), and (20,10). Then we can think of a combined technology that uses (15,15), to make the same 50 units. This is an abstract way of generalising substitution possibilities between the above two technologies. Convexity of the input requirement set is supported under a wider set of production functions, and it is to be taken as a general requirement.

But the convexity of a production set is neither always necessary nor easily implied. Taking the previous example forward, here we ask the following: Is it possible to ask one firm to use (5,10), to produce 25 units of the output and another firm (10,5) to produce another 25 units so that we can get 50 units of output from (15,15)? We are not sure if proportionate scaling back is always possible. But if it is, then we can say that our production set is convex. If not, in particular if scaling up is possible but not scaling down, then the production set will not be convex. In that case, an average of two processes may not be able to produce the average of the two outputs they individually can produce. The idea of scaling production up or down is formalised shortly.

Fact 1

1. *If $V(y)$ is convex, then $f(x)$ is quasi-concave.*
2. *If Y is convex, then $V(y)$ is also convex, but a convex $V(y)$ does not imply a convex Y.*

Proof.

1. Suppose $x, x' \in V(y)$ and $x^* \in V(y)$, where $x^* = \lambda x + (1-\lambda)x'$. Then by definition, $\min\{f(x), f(x')\} \geq y$. If $x^* = \lambda x + (1-\lambda)x'$ is also in $V(y)$, then $f(x^*) \geq y$ by the monotonicity of $V(y)$. This means that $f(x^*) \geq \min\{f(x), f(x^*)\}$, which is just the definition of a quasi-concave function.
2. If $(x,y),(x',y') \in Y$, then a convex Y implies $(\lambda x + (1-\lambda)x', \lambda y + (1-\lambda)y') \in Y$, meaning $f(\lambda x + (1-\lambda)x') \geq \lambda y + (1-\lambda)y'$. Suppose without loss of generality, $y' > y = f(x)$ and $x' > x$, then by monotonicity $x' \in V(y)$ and $f(\lambda x + (1-\lambda)x') > y$. Then clearly, $x^* \in V(y)$. This means that $V(y)$ is convex.
   Now consider the converse. Suppose $V(y)$ is convex and take $x' > x$ such that $f(x) = y$ and $f(x') = y' > y$. Then clearly both $x, x' \in V(y)$. Correspondingly, $(x,y),(x',y') \in Y$. Now define $x < x^* = \lambda x + (1-\lambda)x' < x'$, so that $f(x) < f(x^*) < f(x')$. Assume $f(x) < f(x^*) < \lambda f(x) + (1-\lambda)f(x') < f(x')$. Then, because $f(x^*) > f(x), x^* \in V(y)$, implying that $V(y)$ is convex, but $(x^*, \lambda f(x) + (1-\lambda)f(x')) \notin Y$, which means Y is not convex.

8.2.1 *Examples of production function*

We now take note of the most commonly used production functions, assuming there are only two inputs:

1. **Cobb–Douglas production function:**

   $y = Ax_1^{\alpha} x_2^{\beta}$, $A, \alpha, \beta > 0$.

   If $\alpha + \beta < 1$, the production function will be strictly concave.

2. **Quasi-linear production function:**

   $y = ax_2 + z(x_1)$,

   where $z'(.) > 0, z''(.) < 0$.

3. **Linear production function:**

   $y = ax_1 + bx_2$.

   Here, the marginal product of each input is constant.

4. **Leontief production function:**

   $$y = \min\{ax_1, bx_2\}.$$

   This is our familiar case of inputs being perfect complements. Production increases only if all the inputs are increased in a given proportion.

5. **Constant elasticity of substitution (CES) production function:** Similar to the CES utility function, our production function is now

   $$y = \left[ax_1^{\rho} + bx_2^{\rho}\right]^{\frac{1}{\rho}}.$$

   The elasticity of substitution is defined analogously as $\sigma = \frac{d(x_2/x_1)}{dMRTS}\frac{MRTS}{(x_2/x_1)} = \frac{1}{1-\rho}$. See the appendix of Chapter 2 (Section 2.5).

All the properties of these functions discussed in Chapter 2 apply here as well. The isoquants will be exactly of the same shape as the indifference curves for the corresponding utility functions. Therefore, we skip repeating them.

8.2.2 Productivity

We want to define productivity in a clear way so that we can compare two technologies, or predict profitability of expanding a firm's production operation. Productivity can be understood on three dimensions: (1) How does the total output change if only one input is changed, holding all other inputs unchanged? This is *returns to factor*. (2) How does the output change if all inputs are simultaneously changed by the same proportion? This is called *returns to scale*. (3) How does the output change if the function $f(.)$ itself changes? This is called *technical progress*. When referring to productivity, empirical economists and growth theorists refer to technical progress. Microeconomists, by comparison, refer to returns to factor and returns to scale.[2]

8.2.2.1 Returns to factor

Assuming all $n-1$ inputs being held fixed, if input i is increased its marginal contribution to output is its MP_i (or f_i). *Returns to factor i* is said to be increasing, decreasing or constant if and only if $f_{ii} > 0, < 0$, or $= 0$. A closely related notion of productivity is the change in the *average product of input* i (AP_i), or $f(.)/x_i$. You can easily check that AP_i increases when $MP_i < AP_i$, remains constant when $MP_i = AP_i$ and decreases when $MP_i < AP_i$.[3] Therefore, we can define $\epsilon = \frac{f_i(.)x_i}{f(x)}$ as a measure of productivity, and checking $\epsilon > 1$ or $\epsilon < 1$ is equivalent to checking whether the average productivity of input i is rising or falling. While both measures (change in MP_i and AP_i) are useful, in empirical work the second measure is more commonly used. The main reason for it is that in reality, firms cannot change all inputs at will within a short time.

8.2.2.2 Returns to scale

In this case, we change all inputs together by a common proportion. From a temporal point of view, returns to scale is a long-run concept, and it tells us about the potential, rather than actual,

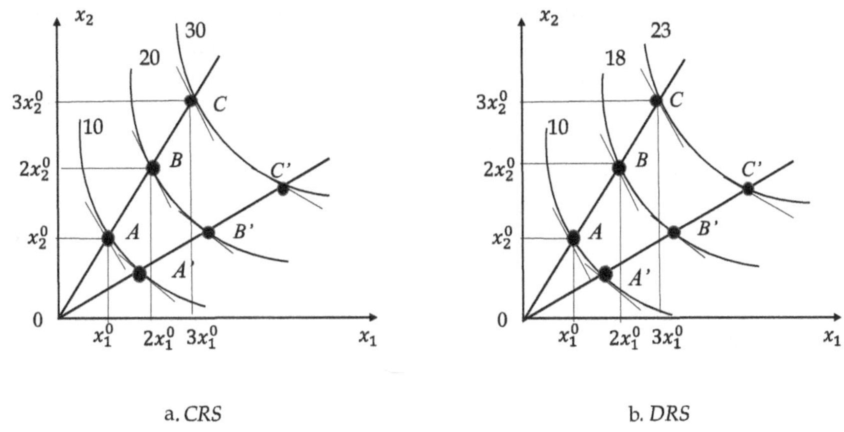

Figure 8.3 Returns to scale

productivity of technology. If we double or treble all our inputs, how does our output change?[4] The following definitions give three classifications:

1. *Increasing returns to scale (IRS):* $f(x)$ exhibits IRS, if $f(\lambda x) > \lambda f(x)$ for $\lambda > 1$, where $x = (x_1, x_2, \ldots, x_n)$. That is, if inputs are doubled (say, $\lambda = 2$), output must be *more* than doubled. Equivalently, for $\lambda < 1, f(\lambda x) < \lambda f(x)$.
2. *Decreasing returns to scale (DRS):* $f(x)$ exhibits DRS, if $f(\lambda x) < \lambda f(x)$ for $\lambda > 1$. That is, if inputs are doubled (say, $\lambda = 2$), output must be *less* than doubled. Equivalently, for $\lambda < 1, f(\lambda x) > \lambda f(x)$.
3. *Constant returns to scale (CRS)*: $f(x)$ exhibits CRS, if $f(\lambda x) = \lambda f(x)$ for $\lambda > 0$. That is, output must rise with the inputs in the same proportion.

In Figure 8.3 we illustrate two types of returns to scale with the help of three isoquants. In panel *a*, we show that as inputs are doubled from (x_1^0, x_2^0) to $(2x_1^0, 2x_2^0)$, output is doubled from 10 to 20. Furthermore, when inputs are increased 1.5 times from $(2x_1^0, 2x_2^0)$ to $(3x_1^0, 3x_2^0)$, output increases 1.5 times (from 20 to 30). This is CRS. A given ray passing through the origin along which we are scaling production up or down by holding the input proportion unchanged is often referred to as a *production process*. Along a given *production process*, output is scaled up by the same rate as the inputs are scaled up.

In panel *b* we illustrate DRS. First, we see that doubling of inputs leads to less than doubling of output, and then as inputs are raised 1.5 times output rises only 1.27 (= 23/18) times. Note that graphically, the difference between the two returns to scale is summarised only at the output label of the isoquants.

Conceptually, returns to scale refer to scaling up or scaling down production, which is also the same as replicating upward or downward. Under DRS, downward replication is feasible, and therefore the production set will be convex. Conversely, under IRS, replicating upward is always feasible, but not replicating downward. Hence, the production set will not be convex under IRS.

We illustrate this difference with two technologies, A and $B : y_A = (x_1 x_2)^{1/3}$ and $y_B = x_1 x_2$. Technology A demonstrates DRS while technology B demonstrates IRS. If we want to produce

3 units of output under technology A, we can use either $(3,9)$, or $(9,3)$, or a convex combination of the two $(6,6)$. All can produce 3 units of output; in fact, $f(6,6)>3$. Therefore, $(6,6)\in V(3)$ just as $(3,9),(9,3)\in V(3)$. We can take any convex combination of $(3,9)$ and $(9,3)$ and make a similar conclusion. Thus, $V(3)$ is convex. Similarly, under technology B, we can use any of the three input bundles and any of their convex combination to produce at least 27 units of output. Thus, the input requirement set $V(y)$ is convex in both cases. But the production set under technology B is not convex. $f_B(3,3)=9<f_B(6,6)/2=18$, whereas $f_A(3,3)=9^{1/3}>f_A(6,6)/2=36^{1/3}/2=(4^{1/3}/2)9^{1/3}$. This is equivalent to saying that the convex combinations of $(f(0,0),0,0)$ and $(f(6,6),6,6)$ (with equal weight) are in Y under technology A but not under technology B. For this reason, increasing returns are often referred to as nonconvex technology.[5]

Fact 2

If $f(x)$ is a strictly convex function, then the production set $Y=\{(x,y)\,|\,y\le f(x)\}$ is nonconvex. Conversely, if $f(x)$ is a concave function then the production set Y *is convex.*

Proof. Let $f(x)$ be a convex function. That is, for any $\lambda\in(0,1)\,f(\lambda x+(1-\lambda x')<\lambda f(x)+(1-\lambda)f(x')$. Without loss of generality, set $x'=0$, and we have $f(\lambda x)<\lambda f(x)$, which implies IRS. But as $f(\lambda x)=f((\lambda x+(1-\lambda)0)<\lambda f(x)+(1-\lambda)f(0)$, clearly $(\lambda x,\lambda f(x))$ does not belong to the set Y, while $(0,0)$ and $(x,f(x))$ do. The converse can be analogously proved by setting $f(x)$ (weakly) concave.

We should also note that the above definitions of returns to scale apply to any input vector x and scalar $\lambda>0$. Therefore, they refer to *global* returns to scale. But if a function does not satisfy any of the three global returns conditions, then we need to examine what *local returns to scale* it exhibits. A function can pass through different phases of all three returns to scale. To study such varying returns to scale, we should use a local measure called *elasticity of output with respect to scale* or simply **elasticity of scale.** This is,

$$E_{y,\lambda}=\frac{\partial f(\lambda x_1,\lambda x_2,\ldots,\lambda x_n)}{\partial\lambda}\frac{\lambda}{f(\lambda x)}.$$

After expanding the right-hand side, we get

$$E_{y,\lambda}=\left[\frac{\partial f(.)}{\partial\lambda x_1}\frac{\partial\lambda x_1}{\partial\lambda}+\ldots+\frac{\partial f(.)}{\partial\lambda x_n}\frac{\partial\lambda x_n}{\partial\lambda}\right]\frac{\lambda}{f(\lambda x)}.$$

Next evaluate this expression at $\lambda=1$:

$$E_{y,\lambda}\,|_{\lambda=1}=[f_1(.)x_1+f_2(.)x_2+\ldots+f_n(.)x_n]\frac{1}{f(x)}.$$

In other words,

$$E_{y,\lambda}=\sum_i^n\epsilon_i\quad\text{where}\quad\epsilon_i=\frac{f_i(.)x_i}{f(x)}.$$

The elasticity of scale is the sum of all individual factor elasticity terms. A production function $f(x)$ exhibits at a given x IRS, if $E_{y,\lambda} > 1$, DRS if $E_{y,\lambda} < 1$ and CRS if $E_{y,\lambda} = 1$. Furthermore, it follows that $f(x)$ exhibits global IRS (or DRS or CRS) if it exhibits local IRS (or DRS or CRS) at *every* input bundle x. Thus, the two measures are equivalent (only) when the returns to scale are global. In particular, if $f(x)$ is *homogeneous* of degree r, then $E_{y,\lambda} = r$. If $r > 1$, we have global IRS; if $r < 1$, we have global DRS; and if $r = 1$, it is CRS.

If a production function $g(x)$ is a positive monotonic transformation of a CRS production function $f(x)$, then $g(x)$ is a **homothetic production function**. Our previous definition of homothetic functions introduced in Chapter 2 holds here as well. That is for a homothetic production function $g(x)$ the $MRTS_{ij}$ is a function of x_i / x_j alone.[6]

In the case of production, however, there is a difference in economic interpretation. While utility can be relabelled preserving the ordering of preference over bundles (this is what positive monotonic transformation does) with no consequence for choice, such relabelling for production would mean a fundamental change in productivity, which can change a firm's choice of inputs. Therefore, in the context of production, we need to take note of the following.

Fact 3

1. *If the production function* $g(x)$ *is homothetic and a positive monotonic transformation of* $f(x)$ *then* $g(x)$ *may or may not share the same returns to scale as* $f(x)$.
2. *If* $g(x)$ *is both homothetic and homogeneous, then* $g(x)$ *exhibits global returns to scale.*

To illustrate this fact, assume $f(x) = \sqrt{x_1 x_2}$ and $g(x) = A + x_1 x_2$ with $g(0) = 0$. Note that $f_1 / f_2 = g_1 / g_2 = MRTS$. But in contrast to $f(2x) = 2f(x)$ (CRS), we have $g(2x) = A + 4x_1x_2 = 2A + 2x_1x_2 - A + 2x_1x_2 = 2g(x) - (A - 2x_1x_2)$. This means that for $g(x)$, doubling of all inputs may not double the output; it depends on the input bundle.

8.3 Profit maximisation

Firms, unlike consumers, do not have *intrinsic preference* over input bundles. They select those bundles that give maximum profit:

$$\tilde{\pi}(x) = pf(x_1, x_2) - w_1x_1 - w_2x_2.$$

In order to understand how the firms make their choice over input bundles, we will assume that they are *price takers* in both the output market and input markets. That is to say, they are perfectly competitive firms, or equivalently they do not have *market powers* in any markets they participate in. They are free to buy any input bundle they wish, but they cannot change the prices of those inputs and that of the resultant output. Here, we should point out that zero profit means 'normal' profit, where every input, including the entrepreneur's skill, is rewarded based on its opportunity cost. Positive profit means super-normal profit, which goes to the entrepreneur or the shareholders of the firm.

Mathematically, profit is maximised by solving the following two first-order conditions:

$$(\partial\tilde{\pi} / \partial x_1) \equiv \tilde{\pi}_1(x) = pf_1(x_1, x_2) - w_1 = 0 \tag{8.1}$$

$$(\partial\tilde{\pi} / \partial x_2) \equiv \tilde{\pi}_2(x) = pf_2(x_1, x_2) - w_2 = 0. \tag{8.2}$$

Assuming that the second-order condition holds, the optimal inputs are $x_i = x_i(p, w_1, w_2)$ for $i = 1, 2$. Let us now quickly examine what the second-order condition is. Note that the profit maximisation problem is an unconstrained problem, and the second-order condition is that the following Hessian matrix of the objective function must be **negative definite**:

$$\begin{bmatrix} \tilde{\pi}_{11} & \tilde{\pi}_{12} \\ \tilde{\pi}_{21} & \tilde{\pi}_{22} \end{bmatrix} = \begin{bmatrix} pf_{11} & pf_{12} \\ pf_{21} & pf_{22} \end{bmatrix}.$$

The principal minors (or the determinants of the principal minors) of the preceding matrix must alternate in sign **starting from negative**:

$$\tilde{\pi}_{11} = pf_{11} < 0, \qquad \text{and} \qquad \tilde{\pi}_{11}\tilde{\pi}_{22} - \tilde{\pi}_{12}\tilde{\pi}_{21} = p^2[f_{11}f_{22} - (f_{12})^2] > 0. \tag{8.3}$$

This means that $f(x_1, x_2)$ must be a strictly concave function. As a concave production function exhibits DRS, profit maximisation is consistent only with DRS technology.

In Figure 8.4, we show the graph of profit maximisation for both one-input (panel *a*) and two-input cases (panel *b*). The two panels not only correspond to two different input cases but also show alternative presentations of the graph. the profit maximisation problem can be seen as finding the iso-profit curve from the production set. Panel *a* shows that iso-profit curve is a line $y = (\tilde{\pi} + wx)/p$, where profit is fixed at a level $\bar{\pi}$. There is a family of iso-profit curves drawn as parallel lines, of which $\bar{\pi}$ represents the highest profit, which is obtained if the point (x^*, y^*) is selected from the production set. Since at (x^*, y^*) the iso-profit line is tangent to the production function, we must have $pf'(x^*) = w$. In panel *b*, we show profit as difference between revenue $pf(x_1, x_2)$ and total cost $C = w_1x_1 + w_2x_2$. The vertical distance between the planes is profit. The input bundle that gives the highest profit is then mapped on the (x_1, x_2) plane. The edge of the cost curve is drawn as an iso-cost line $wx_1 + w_2x_2 = \bar{C}$, and from the height of the revenue function, we derive the iso-revenue curve on the (x_1, x_2) plane. Two curves are tangent to each other at (x_1^*, x_2^*), where we must have $\frac{w_1}{w_2} = \frac{f_1}{f_2} (\equiv MRTS)$.

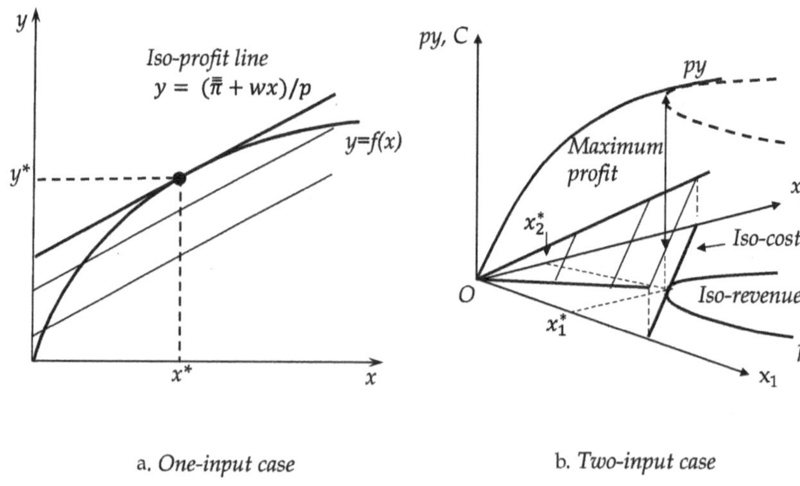

Figure 8.4 Graph of profit maximisation

8.3.1 Examples

1. Let us take the Cobb–Douglas production function $y = Ax_1^{\alpha} x_2^{\beta}$ with the restriction $\alpha + \beta < 1$. We want to maximise $\tilde{\pi} = py - w_1x_1 - w_2x_2$. If we substitute the production function into the profit expression, our problem becomes an unconstrained maximisation problem. From the two first-order conditions of maximisation, we get $x_2 = \dfrac{\beta w_1}{\alpha w_2} x_1$, and substituting that into one of the two equations, the input demand functions can be derived as follows:

$$x_1 = \left[A\alpha^{(1-\beta)}\beta^{\beta}\right]^{\frac{1}{1-r}} \left[\frac{p}{w_1^{(1-\beta)} w_2^{\beta}}\right]^{\frac{1}{1-r}} \quad \text{and} \quad x_2 = \left[A\alpha^{\alpha}\beta^{(1-\alpha)}\right]^{\frac{1}{1-r}} \left[\frac{p}{w_1^{\alpha} w_2^{(1-\alpha)}}\right]^{\frac{1}{1-r}} \tag{8.4}$$

where $r = \alpha + \beta < 1$. Substituting the preceding into the production function, we can obtain the output supply function as

$$y = p^{\frac{r}{1-r}} \left[\frac{A\alpha^{\alpha}\beta^{\beta}}{w_1^{\alpha} w_2^{\beta}}\right]^{\frac{1}{1-r}}. \tag{8.5}$$

Next, by substituting the optimal values of x_1, x_2 and y into the expression of $\tilde{\pi}$, we derive maximum profit called *profit function*:

$$\begin{aligned}
\pi &= \left[\frac{pA\alpha^{\alpha}\beta^{\beta}}{w_1^{\alpha} w_2^{\beta}}\right]^{\frac{1}{1-r}} - w_1\left[\frac{pA\alpha^{(1-\beta)}\beta^{\beta}}{w_1^{(1-\beta)} w_2^{\beta}}\right]^{\frac{1}{1-r}} - w_2\left[\frac{pA\alpha^{\alpha}\beta^{(1-\alpha)}}{w_1^{\alpha} w_2^{(1-\alpha)}}\right]^{\frac{1}{1-r}} \\
&= \left[\frac{pA\alpha^{\alpha}\beta^{\beta}}{w_1^{\alpha} w_2^{\beta}}\right]^{\frac{1}{1-r}} - \left[\frac{pA\alpha^{(1-\beta)}\beta^{\beta}}{w_1^{\alpha} w_2^{\beta}}\right]^{\frac{1}{1-r}} - \left[\frac{pA\alpha^{\alpha}\beta^{(1-\alpha)}}{w_1^{\alpha} w_2^{\beta}}\right]^{\frac{1}{1-r}} \\
&= (1-r)\left[\frac{p}{w_1^{\alpha} w_2^{\beta}}\right]^{\frac{1}{1-r}} \left(A\alpha^{\alpha}\beta^{\beta}\right)^{\frac{1}{1-r}}.
\end{aligned} \tag{8.6}$$

Note the importance of $r = \alpha + \beta < 1$. Without this restriction profit will not be positive.

2. Now consider $y = 2[\sqrt{x_1} + \sqrt{x_2}]$. Profit maximisation leads to the following input demand, output supply and profit functions:

$$x_1 = \frac{p^2}{w_1^2},\ x_2 = \frac{p^2}{w_2^2}, \qquad y = \frac{2p(w_1 + w_2)}{w_1 w_2}, \text{ and} \qquad \pi = \frac{p^2(w_1 + w_2)}{w_1 w_2}. \tag{8.7}$$

Several points from the preceding two examples are noteworthy. By examining Eqs. (8.1)–(8.7), we note the following:

1. Input demand functions are decreasing in their own prices and increasing in the output price. The output supply function is increasing in the output price.
2. The input demand functions do not change if all prices, namely, (p, w_1, w_2), change by the same proportion. And that is true also for the output supply function.
3. In contrast, profit will change by the proportion in which all prices (p, w_1, w_2) are changed. For example, if all prices are doubled, profit will be doubled too.

We will shortly see that all these properties are very general. They will hold for any production function that exhibits local decreasing returns to scale. Before taking up the general case, let us take note of a constrained version of profit maximisation with the help of the earlier Cobb–Douglas production function.

8.3.2 *Constrained profit maximisation*

It is plausible to argue that firms, in reality, are not able to promptly adjust all of their inputs in response to any price change. An apple grower cannot quickly acquire an additional plot of land to increase his export when the international price of apples goes up. A tool-making factory may not be able to buy a new lathe machine within a short period. A corner store cannot expand its business until it is able to rent a bigger premise. This sort of inflexibility arises from input supply constraints. But contractual agreements can also be a factor. For instance, a firm might have an agreement with its workers' union not to cut employment at will if the price of the output falls. In general, there are three possibilities: (1) an input's level is fixed—it can be neither increased nor decreased, (2) an input can be adjusted only downwardly, and (3) an input can be adjusted only upwardly. All these cases can be thought of as *short-run* problems when the constraint in some way bites. If we allow a sufficiently long time, any constraint can be overcome. In conceptual terms, long run is the regime of unconstrained optimisation.

So, how do constrained profit curves compare to the unconstrained profit curve? Let us take the Cobb–Douglas case and assume x_2 is fixed at $\overline{x}_2$. The firm's problem is then to maximise $\tilde{\pi} = pAx_1^{\alpha}\overline{x}_2^{\beta} - w_1x_1 - w_2\overline{x}_2$. Optimal x_1 is $x_1^c = \left(\frac{pA\alpha}{w_1}\right)^{\frac{1}{1-\alpha}} \overline{x}_2^{\frac{\beta}{1-\alpha}}$, which yields the constrained or short-run profit as

$$\pi^c = (1-\alpha)\left(\frac{pA\alpha^{\alpha}}{w_1^{\alpha}}\right)^{\frac{1}{1-\alpha}} \overline{x}_2^{\frac{\beta}{1-\alpha}} - w_2\overline{x}_2.$$

It should be intuitively clear that the short-run profit cannot exceed the long-run profit, because all inputs are not optimally adjusted in the short run. Two profits will be equal only at price $\overline{p}$ at which optimal $x_2 = \overline{x}_2$. We can determine $\overline{p}$ as

$$\overline{x}_2 = \overline{p}^{\frac{1}{1-r}}\left[\frac{A\alpha^{\alpha}\beta^{(1-\alpha)}}{w_1^{\alpha}w_2^{(1-\alpha)}}\right]^{\frac{1}{1-r}} \quad \Rightarrow \quad \overline{p} = \overline{x}_2^{1-r}\frac{w_1^{\alpha}w_2^{(1-\alpha)}}{A\alpha^{\alpha}\beta^{(1-\alpha)}}.$$

In panel *a* of Figure 8.5, we show that at $p \neq \overline{p}$, the long-run or unconstrained profit is strictly greater than the short-run or constrained profit. At $\overline{p}$, two curves are tangent to each other. Furthermore, $w_2\overline{x}_2$ is a fixed cost, which can be covered only if $p \geq \underline{p}$, where $\underline{p}$ sets $\pi^c = 0$. Thus, if price falls to a very low level, the firm will incur a loss. In panels *b* and *c*, we show two other cases, $x_2 \leq \overline{x}_2$ and $x_2 \geq \overline{x}_2$. When x_2 can be reduced below $\overline{x}_2$ but cannot be increased, the short-run profit will be same as the long-run profit at $p \leq \overline{p}$ because with a fall in p, input x_2 can be adjusted downward. This is shown on panel *b*. The case of an upward adjustment of x_2 is shown on panel *c*. Similar graphs can be drawn against w_1 and w_2.

The short-run profit curve shifts to the right if we fix x_2 at a higher value. The tangency of the two profit curves will then occur at a higher profit level. Then it should be apparent that we can

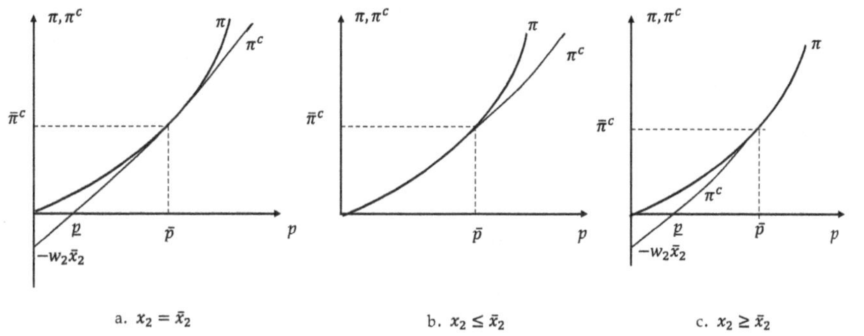

Figure 8.5 Short- and long-run profit curves

maximise the short-run profit with respect to $\bar{x}_2$, and by plugging the optimal value of $\bar{x}_2$, we should get back the long-run profit. Indeed,

$$\frac{\partial \pi^c}{\partial \bar{x}_2} = (1-\alpha)\left(\frac{pA\alpha^\alpha}{w_1^\alpha}\right)^{\frac{1}{1-\alpha}} \frac{\beta}{1-\alpha}\bar{x}_2^{-\frac{1-r}{1-\alpha}} - w_2 = 0 \Rightarrow \bar{x}_2^* = \left(\frac{pA\alpha^\alpha \beta^{1-\alpha}}{w_1^\alpha w_2^{1-\alpha}}\right)^{\frac{1}{1-r}},$$

which is the same as in Eq. (8.4).

8.3.3 *Properties of the profit and input demand functions*

We first take note of three important properties of the (unconstrained) profit function for a general production function that is consistent with profit maximisation. For any given (p, w_1, w_2), we can derive the firm's maximum profit from the profit function, which is

$$\pi(p, w_1, w_2) = pf(x_1(p, w_1, w_2), x_2(p, w_1, w_2)) - \sum_i w_i x_i(p, w_1, w_2).$$

1. **Hotelling's lemma.** $\pi(p, w_1, w_2)$ has the following derivatives:

$$\frac{\partial \pi(.)}{\partial p} = f(x_1(.), x_2(.)), \qquad \frac{\partial \pi(.)}{\partial w_1} = -x_1(.), \qquad \frac{\partial \pi(.)}{\partial w_2} = -x_2(.).$$

This means that $\pi(p, w_1, w_2)$ is increasing in p and decreasing in w_1 and w_2.
Proof. This follows from the envelope theorem. Let us differentiate $\pi(p, w_1, w_2)$ with respect to p.

$$\begin{aligned}\frac{\partial \pi(.)}{\partial p} &= f(x_1(.), x_2(.)) + \left\{\underbrace{pf_1(.) - w_1}_{=0 \text{ by FOC}}\right\}\frac{\partial x_1(.)}{\partial p} + \left\{\underbrace{pf_2(.) - w_2}_{=0 \text{ by FOC}}\right\}\frac{\partial x_2(.)}{\partial p} \\ &= f(x_1(.), x_2(.))\end{aligned}$$

The derivatives $\frac{\partial \pi(.)}{\partial w_1}$ and $\frac{\partial \pi(.)}{\partial w_2}$ can be derived in the same way.

2. **Convexity.** $\pi(p, w_1, w_2)$ is a convex function of (p, w_1, w_2).
   Proof. Take two price vectors (p, w_1, w_2) and (p', w_1', w_2'), and define (p'', w_1'', w_2'') as $p'' = \alpha p + (1-\alpha)p'$, $w_1'' = \alpha w_1 + (1-\alpha)w_1'$ and $w_2'' = \alpha w_2 + (1-\alpha)w_2'$ for any $0 \le \alpha \le 1$. We have to show that $\pi(p'', w_1'', w_2'') \le \alpha\pi(p, w_1, w_2) + (1-\alpha)\pi(p', w_1', w_2')$, by the definition of a convex function.
   By profit maximisation, $\pi(p'', w_1'', w_{2''}) = \text{Max}\,[p''f(x_1, w_2) - w_1''x_1 - w_2x_2''] = \text{Max}\,[\{\alpha p + (1-\alpha)p'\}f(x_1, x_2) - \sum_i \{\alpha w_i + (1-\alpha)w_i'\}x_i = [\alpha\{pf(x) - \sum_i w_ix_i\} + (1-\alpha)\{p'f(x_1, x_2) - \sum_i w_i'x_i\}]$. This expression is the maximum of a weighted sum of two terms. It must be less than the weighted sum of two maximised terms, which is $\alpha[\text{Max}(pf(x_1, x_2) - \sum_i w_ix_i)] + (1-\alpha)[\text{Max}(p'f(x_1, x_2) - \sum_i w_i'x_i)] = \alpha\pi(p, w_1, w_2) + (1-\alpha)\pi(p', w_1', w_2')$. Therefore, $\pi(p'', w_1'', w_2'') \le \alpha\pi(p, w_1, w_2) + (1-\alpha)\pi(p', w_1', w_2')$.
3. **Homogeneity** $\pi(p, w_1, w_2)$ is homogeneous of degree 1: $\pi(\lambda p, \lambda w_1, \lambda w_2) = \lambda\pi(p, w_1, w_2)$.
   Proof By definition $\pi(p, w_1, w_2)$ is the maximum value of $\pi = pf(x_1, x_2) - \sum_i w_ix_i$, and $\pi(\lambda p, \lambda w_1, \lambda w_2)$ is the maximum value of $\pi = (\lambda p)f(x_1, x_2) - \sum_i (\lambda w_i)x_i$, which is same as $\lambda \times \text{Max}[pf(x_1, x_2) - \sum_i w_ix_i] = \lambda\pi(p, w_1, w_2)$.

Hotelling's lemma applies not only to the long-run profit function but to the short-run as well. We then get in the short-run case

$$\frac{\partial \pi^s(.)}{\partial p} = f(x_1^s(.), \bar{x}_2), \qquad \frac{\partial \pi^s(.)}{\partial w_1} = -x_1^s(.).$$

From the previously mentioned three properties of the profit function, several properties of the output supply function and the input demand functions follow.

Corollary 3.

1. *The output supply function* $f(x_1(p, w_1, w_2), x_2(p, w_1, w_2))$ *is always increasing in* p.
2. *The input demand function* $x_i(p, w_1, w_2)$ *is decreasing in* w_i.
3. *Cross-price effects of the input demand functions and the output supply functions are symmetric:* $\frac{\partial x_1(.)}{\partial w_2} = \frac{\partial x_2(.)}{\partial w_1}$, $\frac{\partial y(.)}{\partial w_1} = \frac{\partial x_1(.)}{\partial p}$ *and* $\frac{\partial y(.)}{\partial w_2} = \frac{\partial x_2(.)}{\partial p}$.
4. *The input demand functions as well as the output supply function are homogeneous of degree zero in* (p, w_1, w_2).

Proof.

1. The profit function is a convex function of (p, w_1, w_2). This means

$$\pi_{11} > 0, \qquad \begin{vmatrix} \pi_{11} & \pi_{12} \\ \pi_{21} & \pi_{22} \end{vmatrix} > 0, \qquad \begin{vmatrix} \pi_{11} & \pi_{12} & \pi_{13} \\ \pi_{21} & \pi_{22} & \pi_{23} \\ \pi_{31} & \pi_{32} & \pi_{33} \end{vmatrix} > 0.$$

By the Hotelling's lemma,

$$\frac{\partial \pi}{\partial p} = y(p, w_1, w_2), \qquad \frac{\partial \pi}{\partial w_1} = -x_1(p, w_1, w_2), \qquad \text{and} \qquad \frac{\partial \pi}{\partial w_2} = -x_2(p, w_1, w_2).$$

Therefore,

$$\frac{\partial^2 \pi}{\partial p^2} = \frac{\partial y(.)}{\partial p}, \qquad \frac{\partial^2 \pi}{\partial w_i^2} = -\frac{\partial x_i(.)}{\partial w_i}.$$

As cross partial derivatives are always symmetric, we must have for $i \neq j$ $\frac{\partial^2 \pi}{\partial p \partial w_i} = \frac{\partial y(.)}{\partial w_i} = -\frac{\partial x_i(.)}{\partial p}$, and $\frac{\partial^2 \pi}{\partial w_i w_j} = -\frac{\partial x_i(.)}{\partial w_j} = -\frac{\partial x_j(.)}{\partial w_i}$.

Convexity of $\pi(.)$ implies

$$\frac{\partial y(.)}{\partial p} > 0, \qquad p^2\left[-\frac{\partial y(.)}{\partial p}\frac{\partial x_1(.)}{\partial w_1} - \left(\frac{\partial x_1(.)}{\partial w_2}\frac{\partial x_2(.)}{\partial w_1}\right)\right] > 0.$$

For the second inequality to hold, we must have $\frac{\partial x_1(.)}{\partial w_1} < 0$.

Since convexity of $\pi(.)$ in (p, w_1, w_2) holds regardless of the ordering of the variables, by swapping the place of x_1 for x_2 and consequently swapping the place of w_1 for w_2, we can conclude (following the earlier procedure) that $\frac{\partial x_2(.)}{\partial w_2} < 0$.

Finally, if a function is homogeneous of degree r, its first derivatives are homogeneous of degree $r-1$. The first derivatives of $\pi(.)$ are by Hotelling's lemma are $y(.)$, $x_1(.)$ and $x_2(.)$, which must be homogeneous of degree zero.

8.3.3.1 The LeChatelier principle

One important observation can be made from Figure 8.5. The slope of the short-run profit function cannot exceed the slope of the long-run profit function at any given p, and furthermore, the output supply response will be stronger in the long run. Intuitively, the firm can always adjust all inputs in the long run to its best interest and therefore, its profit should rise or fall at a greater rate.

This can be formally established by combining Hotelling's lemma and the fact that both curves are positively sloped and the long-run profit cannot be smaller than the short-run profit. Suppressing the input prices, we write $\pi(x_1(p), x_2(p)) \geq \pi^s(x_1(p), \bar{x}_2)$. Then it follows that $\frac{\partial \pi}{\partial p} \geq \frac{\partial \pi^s}{\partial p}$ at all p, and at $\bar{p}$, the two slopes are equal, because $\bar{x}_2$ is optimal at $\bar{p}$. That means if we define $g(p) \equiv \pi(p) - \pi^s(p)$, then $g(p)$ is U-shaped with a minimum at $\bar{p}$. The convexity of $g(p)$ implies $g''(p) > 0$ or, equivalently, $\frac{\partial^2 \pi(p)}{\partial p^2} > \frac{\partial^2 \pi^s(p)}{\partial p^2}$. Since by Hotelling's lemma $\frac{\partial \pi}{\partial p} = y(p)$ and $\frac{\partial \pi^s}{\partial p} = y^s(p; \bar{x}_2)$, what we have proved is that $\frac{\partial y(p)}{\partial p} > \frac{\partial y^s(p)}{\partial p}$.

You should also note that we have not said much about the cross-price effects and the effects of the output price on individual input demands. The reason is that these effects are ambiguous in general. A direct algebraic method will be helpful for deriving the conditions needed to ascertain their signs, which we show next.

8.3.3.2 *Comparative statics*

The derivative properties of the input demand functions can be algebraically derived by using the comparative statics method. Suppose we wish to know the effects of an increase in w_1 on $x_1(.)$ and $x_2(.)$. Essentially, we need to derive $\frac{\partial x_1}{\partial w_1}$ and $\frac{\partial x_2}{\partial w_1}$ from the two first-order conditions (8.1) and (8.2). Carrying out differentiation with respect to w_1, we write

$$pf_{11}(.)\frac{\partial x_1}{\partial w_1}+pf_{12}(.)\frac{\partial x_2}{\partial w_1}=1$$

$$pf_{21}(.)\frac{\partial x_1}{\partial w_1}+pf_{22}(.)\frac{\partial x_2}{\partial w_1}=0$$

or, equivalently,

$$\begin{bmatrix} pf_{11} & pf_{12} \\ pf_{21} & pf_{22} \end{bmatrix}\begin{bmatrix} \frac{\partial x_1}{\partial w_1} \\ \frac{\partial x_2}{\partial w_1} \end{bmatrix}=\begin{bmatrix} 1 \\ 0 \end{bmatrix}.$$

This is a system of two linear equations in two unknowns: $\frac{\partial x_1}{\partial w_1}$ and $\frac{\partial x_2}{\partial w_1}$, which we will try to solve using the *Cramer's rule* or *matrix inversion method*. By using the Cramer's rule, we write

$$\frac{\partial x_1}{\partial w_1}=\frac{\begin{vmatrix} 1 & pf_{12} \\ 0 & pf_{22} \end{vmatrix}}{\begin{vmatrix} pf_{11} & pf_{12} \\ pf_{21} & pf_{22} \end{vmatrix}}=\frac{f_{22}}{p\left[f_{11}f_{22}-f_{12}^2\right]}<0. \tag{8.8}$$

The preceding sign is ascertained by the fact that the numerator is strictly negative and the denominator is strictly positive, both implied by the strict concavity of $f(x_1,x_2)$. Following the same procedure, we can derive

$$\frac{\partial x_2}{\partial w_1}=\frac{\begin{vmatrix} pf_{11} & 1 \\ pf_{21} & 0 \end{vmatrix}}{\begin{vmatrix} pf_{11} & pf_{12} \\ pf_{21} & pf_{22} \end{vmatrix}}=-\frac{f_{21}}{p\left[f_{11}f_{22}-f_{12}^2\right]}<0 \text{ if } f_{21}>0. \tag{8.9}$$

Similarly, by differentiating the first-order conditions with respect to w_2, we derive the comparative static properties of $x_2(.)$ as

$$\frac{\partial x_1}{\partial w_2} = -\frac{f_{12}}{p[f_{11}f_{22} - f_{12}^2]} = \frac{\partial x_2}{\partial w_1}, \tag{8.10}$$

and

$$\frac{\partial x_2}{\partial w_2} = \frac{\begin{vmatrix} pf_{11} & 0 \\ pf_{21} & 1 \end{vmatrix}}{\begin{vmatrix} pf_{11} & pf_{12} \\ pf_{21} & pf_{22} \end{vmatrix}} = \frac{f_{11}}{p\left[f_{11}f_{22} - f_{12}^2\right]} < 0. \tag{8.11}$$

Note that the signs of $\partial x_i / \partial w_j$ depend crucially on the sign of f_{12}, which can be positive or negative. That is whether they are *net* complements or substitutes.

Now let us examine the effects of an increase in p.

$$pf_{11}(.)\frac{\partial x_1}{\partial p} + pf_{12}(.)\frac{\partial x_2}{\partial p} = -f_1$$

$$pf_{21}(.)\frac{\partial x_1}{\partial p} + pf_{22}(.)\frac{\partial x_2}{\partial p} = -f_2$$

From the preceding then, we derive

$$\frac{\partial x_1}{\partial p} = \frac{\begin{vmatrix} -f_1 & pf_{12} \\ -f_2 & pf_{22} \end{vmatrix}}{\begin{vmatrix} pf_{11} & pf_{12} \\ pf_{21} & pf_{22} \end{vmatrix}} = \frac{-f_1 f_{22} + f_2 f_{12}}{p\left[f_{11}f_{22} - f_{12}^2\right]}, \tag{8.12}$$

and

$$\frac{\partial x_2}{\partial p} = \frac{-f_2 f_{11} + f_1 f_{21}}{p[f_{11}f_{22} - f_{12}^2]}. \tag{8.13}$$

Note that the two signs are both ambiguous. In particular, if $f_{12} > 0$, that is, the inputs are net complements, both signs will be positive, and the inputs will be called *normal* inputs. But if $f_{12} < 0$, that is, the two inputs are net substitutes, and if $|f_2 f_{12}| > |f_1 f_{22}|$, then we have $\frac{\partial x_1}{\partial p} < 0$. The input x_1 is then called an *inferior input*.

But we can easily verify that both inputs cannot be inferior at the same time. To see this, suppose both inputs are inferior. Then we must have $|f_2 f_{12}| > |f_1 f_{22}|$ and $|f_1 f_{21}| > |f_2 f_{11}|$. Then we must have $f_1 f_2 f_{12}^2 > f_1 f_{22} \times f_2 f_{11}$, or $f_{12}^2 > f_{11} f_{22}$, which violates the assumption that $f(x_1, x_2)$ is strictly concave in (x_1, x_2). Alternatively, we can see that $\frac{\partial y}{\partial p} = f_1 \frac{\partial x_1}{\partial p} + f_2 f_1 \frac{\partial x_2}{\partial p} > 0$ implies that both inputs cannot be inferior at the same time.

If the production technology is homothetic then no input can be inferior. Whatever be the technology, the optimal input combinations must satisfy $w_1 / w_2 = MRTS$. For a homothetic production function *MRTS* does not change unless x_2 / x_1 changes. Therefore, if x_1 rises in response to an increase in *p*, x_2 must rise by the same proportion. Therefore, both inputs must be normal at all times.

We summarise the preceding discussion in the following fact.

FACT 4

1. *Input* x_i *is a gross complement to (or substitute for) input* x_j *if they are net complements (or substitutes). That is,* $\partial x_i / \partial w_j < (>) 0$ *if and only* $f_{12} > (<) 0$.
2. *Both inputs cannot be inferior at the same time.*
3. *For homothetic technology, all inputs are normal.*

8.4 Cost minimisation

Firms often break their profit maximisation problem into two steps: they first minimise cost subject to a given output level and then use the cost function to choose the output level freely to maximise profit. This is also due to the fact that in modern firms, input and output decisions are compartmentalised. Also, from a theoretical point of view, cost functions are very useful for analysing a firm's behaviours in imperfectly competitive markets.

The firm's problem is to minimise $\tilde{c} = w_1 x_1 + w_2 x_2$ subject to $f(x_1, x_2) = y$. Formally, the problem is identical to the consumer's expenditure minimisation problem learnt in Chapter 4, and therefore, we avoid repetition of many details. As before, we set the Lagrangian as to minimise $\mathcal{L} = w_1 x_1 + w_2 x_2 + \mu[y - f(x_1, x_2)]$ with respect to (x_1, x_2, μ). The three first-order conditions are

$$w_1 - \mu f_1(.) = 0 \tag{8.14}$$

$$w_2 - \mu f_2(.) = 0 \tag{8.15}$$

$$y - f(x_1, x_2) = 0. \tag{8.16}$$

These three equations are solved for x_1, x_2 and μ. Combining the first two equations, we get $\frac{f_1}{f_2} = \frac{w_1}{w_2}$, or $MRTS = w_1 / w_2$. Panel *a* in Figure 8.6 shows that taking an isoquant given at output *y*, the firm is searching for the lowest iso-cost line, which must be tangent to the given isoquant, as shown by point *A*.

The second-order condition for cost minimisation is that *MRTS* must decrease with an increase in x_1, which will be true if the following bordered Hessian matrix is positive definite, or equivalently, its border-preserving principal minors are all negative.[7]

$$\begin{bmatrix} -\mu f_{11} & -\mu f_{12} & -f_1 \\ -\mu f_{21} & -\mu f_{22} & -f_2 \\ -f_1 & -f_2 & 0 \end{bmatrix}$$

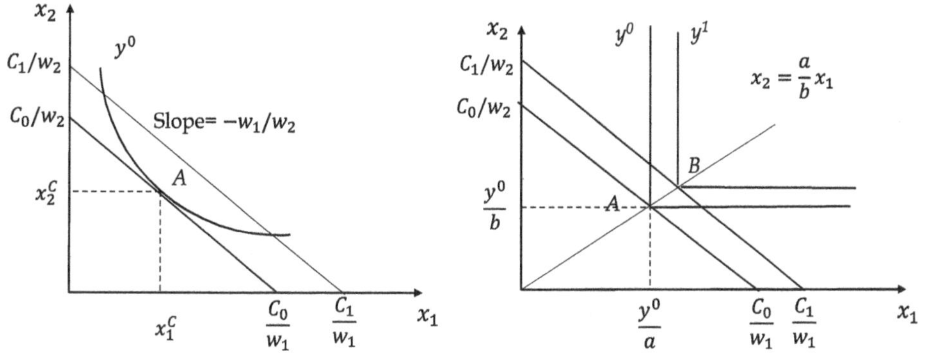

a. Cost minimisation for imperfect substitute inputs

b. Cost minimisation for Leontief technology

Figure 8.6 Optimal input choice for cost minimisation

After expanding the determinant and setting it to be negative, we get

$$-\mu\Delta f \equiv -\mu[-f_{11}f_2^2 + 2f_{12}f_1f_2 - f_{22}f_1^2] < 0 \quad \Rightarrow \quad \Delta f > 0.$$

This means that the production function must be (strictly) quasi-concave. Note that this is a weaker requirement than profit maximisation. A solution to our cost minimisation problem gives two **conditional input demand** functions:

$$x_1 = x_1(w_1, w_2, y) \text{ and } \quad x_2 = x_2(w_1, w_2, y).$$

Once we substitute the conditional input demand functions into the cost equation, we get our *cost function*, which gives us the lowest cost of producing a given y, $c(w_1, w_2, y) = w_1x_1(w_1, w_2, y) + w_2x_2(w_1, w_2, y)$.

8.4.1 Examples

1. Consider the CES production function. The firm wishes to minimise $\tilde{c} = w_1x_1 + w_2x_2$ subject to $y = [ax_1^\rho + bx_2^\rho]^{\frac{1}{\rho}}$. Taking μ as the Lagrange multiplier, we write the three first-order conditions as

$$w_1 - \mu\left[ax_1^\rho + bx_2^\rho\right]^{\frac{1-\rho}{\rho}} ax_1^{\rho-1} = 0$$

$$w_2 - \mu\left[ax_1^\rho + bx_2^\rho\right]^{\frac{1-\rho}{\rho}} bx_2^{\rho-1} = 0$$

$$y - \left[ax_1^\rho + bx_2^\rho\right]^{\frac{1}{\rho}} = 0.$$

Dividing the first equation by the second one, we get $x_2 = x_1\left[\frac{bw_1}{aw_2}\right]^{\frac{1}{1-\rho}}$, a linear relationship between the optimal x_2 and optimal x_1 as expected from a homothetic production function. Substituting this into the technology constraint we write

$$y = \left[ax_1^{\rho} + bx_1^{\rho}\left(\frac{bw_1}{aw_2}\right)^{\frac{\rho}{1-\rho}}\right]^{\frac{1}{\rho}}$$

$$= \frac{x_1}{(aw_2)^{\frac{1}{1-\rho}}}\left[a^{\frac{1}{1-\rho}}w_2^{\frac{\rho}{1-\rho}} + b^{\frac{1}{1-\rho}}w_1^{\frac{\rho}{1-\rho}}\right]^{\frac{1}{\rho}}.$$

From the preceding, we derive the conditional input demand for x_1 as

$$x_1 = \frac{y(aw_2)^{\frac{1}{1-\rho}}}{\left[a^{\frac{1}{1-\rho}}w_2^{\frac{\rho}{1-\rho}} + b^{\frac{1}{1-\rho}}w_1^{\frac{\rho}{1-\rho}}\right]^{\frac{1}{\rho}}},$$

and symmetrically

$$x_2 = \frac{y(bw_1)^{\frac{1}{1-\rho}}}{\left[a^{\frac{1}{1-\rho}}w_2^{\frac{\rho}{1-\rho}} + b^{\frac{1}{1-\rho}}w_1^{\frac{\rho}{1-\rho}}\right]^{\frac{1}{\rho}}}.$$

The firm's cost function is

$$c(w_1, w_2, y) = y\frac{[(aw_2)^{\frac{1}{1-\rho}}w_1 + (bw_1)^{\frac{1}{1-\rho}}w_2]}{\left[a^{\frac{1}{1-\rho}}w_2^{\frac{\rho}{1-\rho}} + b^{\frac{1}{1-\rho}}w_1^{\frac{\rho}{1-\rho}}\right]^{\frac{1}{\rho}}} = y\frac{w_1w_2\left[a^{\frac{1}{1-\rho}}w_2^{\frac{\rho}{1-\rho}} + b^{\frac{1}{1-\rho}}w_1^{\frac{\rho}{1-\rho}}\right]}{\left[a^{\frac{1}{1-\rho}}w_2^{\frac{\rho}{1-\rho}} + b^{\frac{1}{1-\rho}}w_1^{\frac{\rho}{1-\rho}}\right]^{\frac{1}{\rho}}}$$

$$= y\frac{w_1w_2}{\left(a^{\frac{1}{1-\rho}}w_2^{\frac{\rho}{1-\rho}} + b^{\frac{1}{1-\rho}}w_1^{\frac{\rho}{1-\rho}}\right)^{\frac{1-\rho}{\rho}}}.$$

Note that the cost function is linear in y, a direct implication of the production function being homogeneous of degree one (CRS). Equally, the conditional input demands are also linear in y. Thus, for any CRS technology, the average cost c/y and the marginal cost $\partial c/\partial y$ are both constant. Also, note that the conditional input demand functions are homogeneous of degree zero in (w_1, w_2) while the cost function is homogeneous of degree one in (w_1, w_2).

2. The CES example demonstrates the algebra of cost minimisation when the technology can be described by a differentiable production function. But cost minimisation applies to non-differentiable technologies as well. Take the Leontief technology for instance. The firm's cost minimisation problem is to minimise $\tilde{C} = w_1x_1 + w_2x_2$ subject to the constraint $y = \min\{ax_1, bx_2\}$. Panel *b* of Figure 8.6 shows that in this case, there is only one combination of (x_1, x_2) that is optimal regardless of w_1 and w_2. If the output is given at y^0, the firm should choose $(y^0/a, y^0/b)$ at point *A*. If output is given at a higher level, such as y^1, the optimal input mix would move to point *B*. Thus, the conditional input demands and cost are

$$x_1 = y/a, \qquad x_2 = y/b, \qquad \text{and} \qquad c = y\frac{bw_1 + aw_2}{ab}.$$

3. Finally, consider the Cobb–Douglas technology $y = Ax_1^\alpha x_2^\beta$. From the first-order conditions, we will get $x_2 = \left(\frac{\beta w_1}{\alpha w_2}\right)x_1$. Substituting this relation for x_2 into the production function, we derive

$$x_1 = \left(\frac{y}{A}\right)^{\frac{1}{\alpha+\beta}}\left[\frac{\alpha w_2}{\beta w_1}\right]^{\frac{\beta}{\alpha+\beta}} \qquad \text{and} \qquad x_2 = \left(\frac{y}{A}\right)^{\frac{1}{\alpha+\beta}}\left[\frac{\beta w_1}{\alpha w_2}\right]^{\frac{\alpha}{\alpha+\beta}}.$$

The resultant cost function is

$$c(w_1, w_2, y) = (\alpha+\beta)y^{\frac{1}{\alpha+\beta}}\left(\frac{w_1^\alpha w_2^\beta}{A\alpha^\alpha\beta^\beta}\right)^{\frac{1}{\alpha+\beta}}.$$

The average (AC) and marginal cost (MC) functions are

$$\frac{c}{y} = (\alpha+\beta)y^{\frac{1-\alpha-\beta}{\alpha+\beta}}\left(\frac{w_1^\alpha w_2^\beta}{A\alpha^\alpha\beta^\beta}\right)^{\frac{1}{\alpha+\beta}}, \qquad \text{and} \qquad \frac{\partial c}{\partial y} = y^{\frac{1-\alpha-\beta}{\alpha+\beta}}\left(\frac{w_1^\alpha w_2^\beta}{A\alpha^\alpha\beta^\beta}\right)^{\frac{1}{\alpha+\beta}}.$$

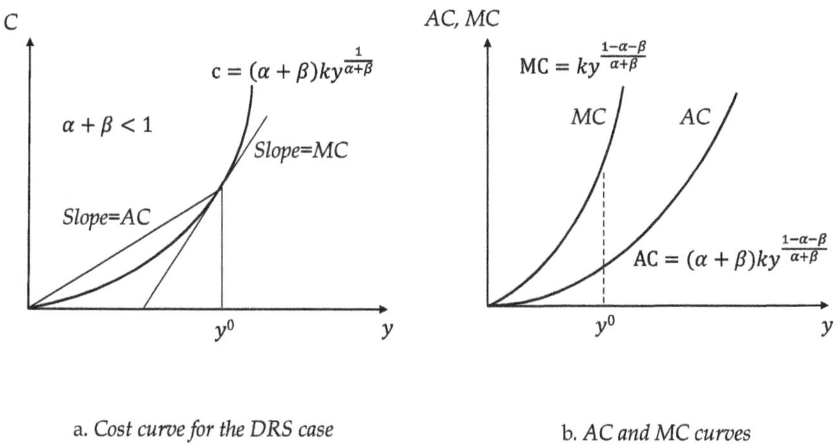

Figure 8.7 Total cost, average cost and marginal cost curves for Cobb–Douglas technology

The average cost is increasing if and only if $\alpha + \beta < 1$, that is, when the technology is exhibiting DRS. Alternatively, the average cost will be constant or decreasing if there are CRS (i.e., $\alpha + \beta = 1$) or IRS ($\alpha + \beta > 1$).

Figure 8.7 depicts for the Cobb–Douglas technology the total cost curve in the left panel and AC and MC curves in the right panel, assuming there is DRS. The total cost then increases at an increasing rate, which means that the MC curve must be rising as well. At output y^0, we take note of MC by the slope of the tangent line. The average cost at y^0 is given by the slope of the line passing through the origin. Clearly, the tangent line is steeper, and this is true at every y on the total cost curve. Therefore, MC must be above the AC curve as shown on the right panel.

8.4.1.1 *Constrained or short-run cost function*

As in the case of profit maximisation, here, too, we look at the implications of inflexibility in the adjustment of certain inputs. Once again, we demonstrate this case with the Cobb–Douglas technology by holding our input x_2 fixed at $\bar{x}_2$. If output is held given at y and x_2 at $\bar{x}_2$, the optimal input x_1 is just given by the production function as $x_1 = \left(\frac{y}{A\bar{x}_2^{\beta}}\right)^{\frac{1}{\alpha}}$. The short-run cost function is then $C^S(w_1, w_2, y; \bar{x}_2) = w_1\left(\frac{y}{A\bar{x}_2^{\beta}}\right)^{\frac{1}{\alpha}} + w_2\bar{x}_2$. The second term is the fixed cost. Let us also note that the short-run average cost (SAC) function, as

$$(SAC \equiv)\frac{c^S(y;\bar{x}_2)}{y} = w_1 y^{\frac{1-\alpha}{\alpha}}\left(\frac{1}{A\bar{x}_2^{\beta}}\right)^{\frac{1}{\alpha}} + \frac{w_2\bar{x}_2}{y}.$$

If $\alpha \geq 1$, SAC will be a decreasing function of y. But if $\alpha < 1$, then SAC may rise or fall depending on y. More precisely, when $\alpha < 1$,

$$\frac{\partial SAC}{\partial y} = \frac{(1-\alpha)}{\alpha}\left(\frac{w_1}{(A\bar{x}_2^{\beta})^{\frac{1}{\alpha}}}\right) y^{\frac{1-2\alpha}{\alpha}} - \frac{w_2\bar{x}_2}{y^2} < (\geq) 0$$

$$\text{if and only if} \qquad y < (\geq) A\bar{x}_2^{\alpha+\beta}\left[\frac{\alpha w_2}{(1-\alpha)w_1}\right]^{\alpha} \equiv \bar{y}.$$

In Figure 8.8, we first show the long-run AC (LAC) curves on the left panel for the Cobb–Douglas production function. Under CRS ($\alpha + \beta = 1$), the average cost will be a flat line and equal to MC. Under IRS, AC will be downward-sloping and under DRS upward-sloping.

The right panel of Figure 8.8 shows that if we fix an input the average cost (SAC) will look like a U-shaped curve when there are diminishing returns to the variable factor (x_1 in this case). If there are increasing or constant returns to the variable factor, the total cost is either rising linearly or rising at a decreasing rate. Therefore, the SAC must decrease. But when there are diminishing returns, the average variable cost is increasing, and average fixed cost is decreasing, leaving the direction of change in their sum ambiguous.

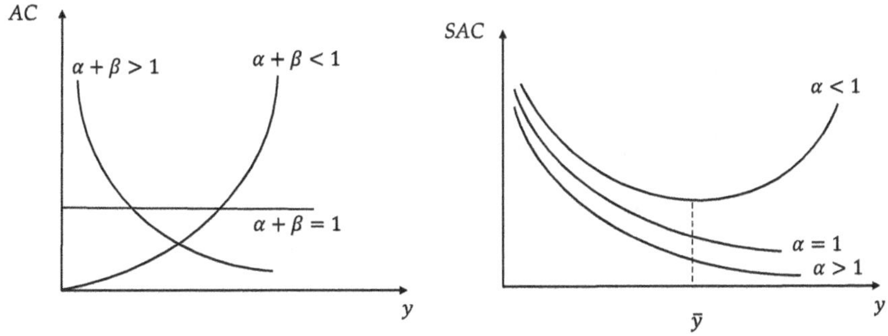

a. *Long-run average cost*

b. *Short-run average cost*

Figure 8.8 Long- and short-run average cost curves for Cobb–Douglas technology

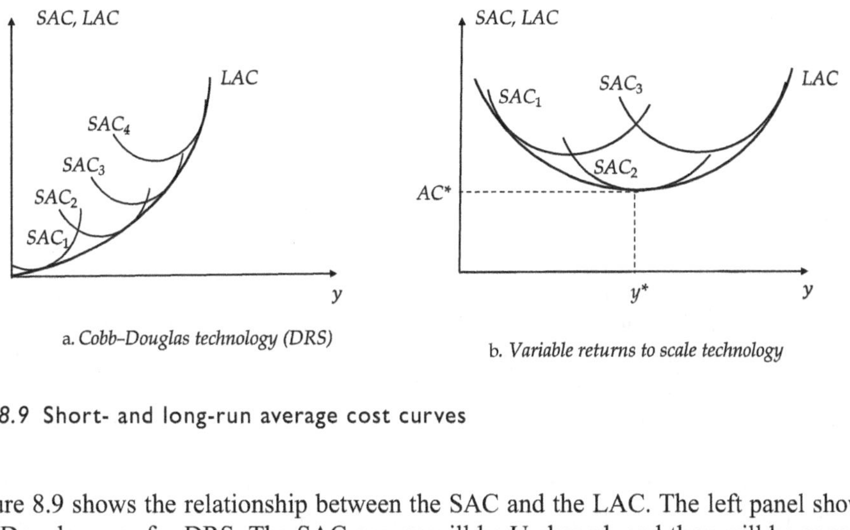

a. *Cobb-Douglas technology (DRS)*

b. *Variable returns to scale technology*

Figure 8.9 Short- and long-run average cost curves

Figure 8.9 shows the relationship between the SAC and the LAC. The left panel shows the Cobb–Douglas case for DRS. The SAC curves will be U-shaped, and they will be encased by the LAC curve, which is rising. The picture will be the same for any production function that exhibits DRS at any output level. But if the technology is such that the returns to scale are variable, then the LAC will be U-shaped showing IRS at low levels of output and DRS at higher levels of output. At y^*, the average cost is minimum. y^* is often referred to as the *minimum efficient scale*.[8] In the short run, the firm may be at SAC_1, SAC_2 or any other possible SAC curves. Whatever the SAC curve is, it must be above the LAC curve everywhere except at a point of tangency, which must be the output level, where the fixed-input level $\bar{x}_2$ turns out to be optimal. Therefore, LAC is always an envelope of all SAC curves.

Mathematically, it should be clear that (for any production function) when the AC is falling, the MC must remain below the AC, and when the AC is rising, the MC must remain above the AC. You can verify this from the fact that $\frac{\partial(c/y)}{\partial y} = \frac{(\partial c/\partial y)-(c/y)}{y} > (\leq) 0$ if and only

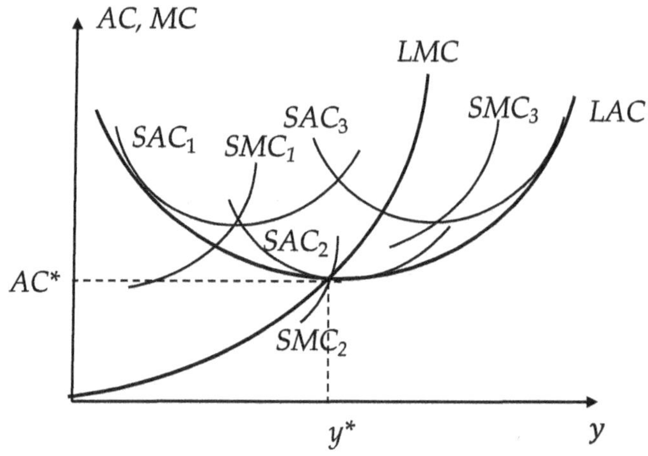

Figure 8.10 Average and marginal cost curves for variable returns to scale technology

if $\partial c / \partial y > (\leq) c / y$. This general property can be stated in terms of *the elasticity of cost with respect to output*, $E_{c,y} = \dfrac{\partial c}{\partial y}\dfrac{y}{c}$.

FACT 5

If $E_{c,y} > 1$, *the AC must be rising, and if* $E_{c,y} < 1$, *the AC must be falling.*

Figure 8.10 shows the relationship between MC and AC clearly for both the short- and long-run cases. For each of the short-run cases, MC cuts the AC curve from below at AC's minimum point. For SAC_2, the short-run MC (SMC) coincides with the long-run MC (LMC) at y^0, where both SAC_2 and LAC have the same minimum. But at all other output levels, SMC_2 will be different from *LMC*. That is because SMC_2 corresponds to a fixed x_2, while *LMC* allows x_2 to be optimised along with x_1.

We should also be mindful of the difference between *economies of scale* and *IRS*. Both refer to the declining phase of the average cost curves, but the first one applies to the SAC curve, while returns to scale, as explained before, apply to the long run only. The presence of any fixed input creates economies of scale even if the variable inputs have strong diminishing returns to factor.

8.4.2 Properties of the cost function and the conditional input demand functions

Mathematically, the firm's cost function is identical to the consumer's expenditure function. Both functions have the same properties that we have discussed and proved in Chapter 4. Therefore, we do not repeat their proofs.

1. The cost function $c(w_1, w_2, y)$ is homogeneous of degree 1 in input prices(w_1, w_2).
2. $c(w_1, w_2, y)$ is a concave function of (w_1, w_2).

3. **Shephard's lemma:** The first derivatives of the cost function are

$$\frac{\partial c(.)}{\partial w_1} = x_1(w_1, w_2, y), \qquad \frac{\partial c(.)}{\partial w_2} = x_1(w_1, w_2, y), \qquad \frac{\partial c(.)}{\partial y} = \mu(w_1, w_2, y).$$

Therefore, $c(w_1, w_2, y)$ is increasing in (w_1, w_2, y).

From the properties of the cost function, we derive the following properties of the conditional input demand functions.

1. Conditional input demand functions are homogeneous of degree zero in (w_1, w_2).
2. The conditional input demand function $x_i(w_1, w_2, y)$ is strictly decreasing in w_i and increasing in w_j. Moreover, $\frac{\partial x_i(.)}{\partial w_j} = \frac{\partial x_j(.)}{\partial w_i}$.

That conditional input demand functions are homogeneous of degree zero in (w_1, w_2) follows from the fact that the cost function is homogeneous of degree 1 and the conditional input demand functions are the first derivatives of the cost function. The concavity of the cost function means

$$c_{11} < 0, \quad \begin{vmatrix} c_{11} & c_{12} \\ c_{21} & c_{22} \end{vmatrix} = \quad c_{11}c_{22} - c_{21}^2 > 0 \quad \Rightarrow \quad c_{22} < 0.$$

$c_{ii} < 0$ implies x_i is strictly decreasing in w_i. Furthermore, homogeneity of $x_1(w_1, w_2, y)$ means $w_1 \frac{\partial x_1}{\partial w_1} + w_2 \frac{\partial x_1}{\partial w_2} = 0$. Since $\frac{\partial x_1}{\partial w_1} < 0$, we must have $\frac{\partial x_1}{\partial w_2} > 0$. Also, $c_{ij} = c_{ji}$ since they are cross partial derivatives, and therefore, $\frac{\partial x_i(.)}{\partial w_j} = \frac{\partial x_j(.)}{\partial w_i}$.

We should also note that from the properties of the cost function, nothing could be said about the relationship between the conditional input demands and y. Conceptually, if the isoquant shifts out reflecting an increase in y, the new tangency point (between the new isoquant curve and a new iso-cost line) may not necessarily lie north-east of the old tangency point. It necessarily will if the two inputs are *net complements*. For homotheteic technology, not only are two inputs net complements, but they are also used in an unchanged proportion when output is increased or decreased (holding the input prices unchanged) regardless of the returns to scale. In this case and all other cases of net complements, all conditional inputs are *normal* inputs meaning they will rise with output. But if the two inputs are net substitutes, the new tangency point can involve lesser demand for one of the inputs. If it does then the input, which is demanded less, is called *inferior conditional input*.

We illustrate this possibility by directly examining the comparative statics of the conditional input demand functions given by Eqs. (8.14)–(8.16) with respect to y:

$$\begin{bmatrix} \mu f_{11} & \mu f_{12} & f_1 \\ \mu f_{21} & \mu f_{22} & f_2 \\ f_1 & f_2 & 0 \end{bmatrix} \begin{bmatrix} \partial x_1^C / \partial y \\ \partial x_2^C / \partial y \\ \partial \mu / \partial y \end{bmatrix} = \begin{bmatrix} 0 \\ 0 \\ 1 \end{bmatrix}.$$

Then by applying Cramer's rule, we derive (as we have done for profit maximisation)

$$\frac{\partial x_1^C}{\partial y} = \begin{vmatrix} 0 & \mu f_{12} & f_1 \\ 0 & \mu f_{22} & f_2 \\ 1 & f_2 & 0 \end{vmatrix} \times \begin{vmatrix} \mu f_{11} & \mu f_{12} & f_1 \\ \mu f_{21} & \mu f_{22} & f_2 \\ f_1 & f_2 & 0 \end{vmatrix}^{-1} = \frac{f_2 f_{12} - f_1 f_{22}}{\Delta f > 0}$$

and

$$\frac{\partial x_2^C}{\partial y} = \begin{vmatrix} \mu f_{11} & 0 & f_1 \\ \mu f_{21} & 0 & f_2 \\ f_2 & 1 & 0 \end{vmatrix} \times \begin{vmatrix} \mu f_{11} & \mu f_{12} & f_1 \\ \mu f_{21} & \mu f_{22} & f_2 \\ f_1 & f_2 & 0 \end{vmatrix}^{-1} = \frac{f_1 f_{21} - f_2 f_{11}}{\Delta f},$$

where (let us recall) $\Delta f = -f_{11} f_2^2 + 2 f_{12} f_1 f_2 - f_{11} f_2^2 > 0$ by quasi-concavity of $f(.)$. If $f_{12} = f_{21} > 0$, then both signs are positive. Otherwise, the signs are ambiguous, and one of the inputs can become inferior. With $f_{12} < 0$, if $| f_2 f_{12} | > | f_1 f_{22} |$, then x_1^C becomes an inferior input. However, both inputs can never be inferior at the same time. If they were, then quasi-concavity of $f(x_1, x_2)$ would be violated.[9]

Similar comparative statics, such as $\partial x_i(.) / \partial w_j$, $i, j = 1,2$ can be derived in the same way. You may also look at the appendix of Chapter 4 (Section 4.7), where the same method has been applied to consumers' expenditure minimisation.

8.4.3 Production–cost duality

Unlike the utility theory, the firm theory does not yield a rich set of duality results. This is because profit maximisation and cost minimisation are not equivalent. Nevertheless, there is a close relation between technology and cost. Iso-cost curves and isoquant curves bear close connections through their slopes and curvatures. Furthermore, while technology is described by pure productivity conditions, such as returns to scale or returns to factors without any reference to output or input prices, cost data invariably involve input prices. So in firm theory, duality analysis centres on two issues: (1) How does one read technology from cost information, and how does one infer cost curves from technology? and (2) Can we recover technology (i.e., the input requirement set) from conditional input demand curves?

Both questions are important from an empirical point of view, because technology may not be observable to independent researchers, but cost functions can be estimated by using published data, and they use duality relations that one can decipher the type of technology being used. However, answering the second question in the general case is a bit more advanced. It may suffice to know that the conditional input demand functions generate a larger set that will include the input requirement set $V(y)$ and possibly much more, unless $V(y)$ is closed, non-empty, convex and monotonic. In other words, the type of production functions we commonly use will give us $V(y)$ exactly. That is, we can reconstruct the technology exactly starting from the conditional input demand function. We demonstrate this with the Cobb–Douglas or CES technology.

1. Let us first turn our attention to the first question. There is an important relation between the summary technological information *elasticity of output with respect to scale* and the summary cost information *elasticity of cost with respect to output.*

Lemma 3. *a. The elasticity of output with respect to scale is equal to the inverse of the of cost with respect to output. That is,* $E_{y,\lambda}|_{\lambda=1}=\frac{1}{E_{c,y}}$.

b. If $f(x_1,x_2)$ *is homogeneous of degree 1, then the cost function must be of the form* $c(w_1,w_2,y)=yc(w_1,w_2,1)$.

c. If $f(x_1,x_2)$ *is homogeneous of degree r, then the cost function must be of the formc*$(w_1,w_2,y)=y^{\frac{1}{r}}c(w_1,w_2,1)$.

Proof:

a. Let us recall that $E_{y,\lambda}|_{\lambda=1}=\frac{\partial f(x_1,\lambda x_2)}{\partial\lambda}\frac{\lambda}{f(\lambda x_1,\lambda x_2)}|_{\lambda=1}$, which becomes

$$E_{y,\lambda}|_{\lambda=1}=[f_1(.)x_1+f_2(.)x_2]\frac{1}{f(x)}.$$

We wish to evaluate this elasticity at some x which minimises cost given some arbitrary (w_1,w_2,y). From the first-order conditions for cost minimisation, we get $f_i=\frac{w_i}{\mu}$, where μ is the Lagrange multiplier for cost minimisation. Next, replace x_i with the compensated input demand functions $x_i(w,y)$. So we can write

$$E_{y,\lambda}|_{\lambda=1}=\left[\frac{w_1}{\mu(w_1,w_2,y)}x_1(w_1,w_2,y)+\frac{w_2}{\mu(w_1,w_2,y)}x_2(w_1,w_2,y)\right]\frac{1}{f(x_1(.),x_2(.))}.$$

Since $\sum_i w_ix_i(.)=c(w_1,w_2,y)$ and $f(x_1(w_1,w_2,y)),x_2(w_1,w_2,y))=y$, we have

$$E_{y,\lambda}|_{\lambda=1}=\frac{c(w_1,w_2,y)}{\mu(w_1,w_2,y)y}.$$

By Shephard's lemma, $\frac{\partial c(w_1,w_2,y)}{\partial y}=\mu$. Therefore,

$$E_{y,\lambda}|_{\lambda=1}=\frac{\frac{c(w_1,w_2,y)}{y}}{\frac{\partial c(w_1,w_2,y)}{\partial y}}=\frac{AC}{MC}\equiv\frac{1}{E_{c,y}}.$$

This is what we wanted to prove.

b. Suppose (x_1^0,x_2^0) is the least cost input bundle for producing 1 unit of y. That is, $c(w_1,w_2,1)=\min\{\sum w_ix_i^0\}$ subject to $f(x)=1$. If $f(.)$ is homogeneous of degree 1, then (yx_1^0,yx_2^0) must produce exactly y. That is, we can always scale up or scale down production to y units. Then $c(w_1,w_2,y)=\min\{\sum w_iyx_i\}$ sub. to $f(x)=y$ must be given by $yc(w_1,w_2,1)$.

c. If $f(x_1,x_2)$ is homogeneous of degree r, then $E_{y,\lambda}|_{\lambda=1}=r$. Then $E_{c,y}=1/r$, which means the cost function must be of the form $c=y^{\frac{1}{r}}k$, where $k>0$ involves (w_1,w_2) but not $y(\neq 1)$.

Since $c(.)$ must be homogeneous of degree 1 in (w_1, w_2) at all y, including $y = 1$, k must be $c(w_1, w_2, 1)$.

2. Now we show that if the production technology is Cobb–Douglas or CES, we can exactly recover the isoquant from the conditional input demand functions. Let us recall that the conditional input demand functions for the Cobb–Douglas case are

$$x_1 = \left(\frac{y}{A}\right)^{\frac{1}{\alpha+\beta}} \left[\frac{\alpha w_2}{\beta w_1}\right]^{\frac{\beta}{\alpha+\beta}} \quad \text{and} \quad x_2 = \left(\frac{y}{A}\right)^{\frac{1}{\alpha+\beta}} \left[\frac{\beta w_1}{\alpha w_2}\right]^{\frac{\alpha}{\alpha+\beta}}.$$

From this, we can write

$$x_1^{\alpha} = \left(\frac{y}{A}\right)^{\frac{\alpha}{\alpha+\beta}} \left[\frac{\alpha w_2}{\beta w_1}\right]^{\frac{\alpha\beta}{\alpha+\beta}} \quad \text{and} \quad x_2^{\beta} = \left(\frac{y}{A}\right)^{\frac{\beta}{\alpha+\beta}} \left[\frac{\beta w_1}{\alpha w_2}\right]^{\frac{\alpha\beta}{\alpha+\beta}}.$$

Then multiplication of the two expressions give

$$x_1^{\alpha} x_2^{\beta} = \left(\frac{y}{A}\right)^{\frac{\alpha+\beta}{\alpha+\beta}} \left[\frac{\alpha w_2}{\beta w_1}\right]^{\frac{\alpha\beta}{\alpha+\beta}} \left[\frac{\beta w_1}{\alpha w_2}\right]^{\frac{\alpha\beta}{\alpha+\beta}} \quad \Rightarrow \quad y = A x_1^{\alpha} x_2^{\beta}.$$

Similarly, from the conditional input demand functions for the CES technology as derived in Section 8.4.1, you can write

$$a x_1^{\rho} = \frac{y^{\rho} w_2^{\frac{\rho}{1-\rho}} a^{\frac{1}{1-\rho}}}{\left[a^{\frac{1}{1-\rho}} w_2^{\frac{\rho}{1-\rho}} + b^{\frac{1}{1-\rho}} w_1^{\frac{\rho}{1-\rho}}\right]},$$

and

$$b x_2^{\rho} = \frac{y^{\rho} w_1^{\frac{\rho}{1-\rho}} b^{\frac{1}{1-\rho}}}{\left[a^{\frac{1}{1-\rho}} w_2^{\frac{\rho}{1-\rho}} + b^{\frac{1}{1-\rho}} w_1^{\frac{\rho}{1-\rho}}\right]}.$$

Adding the two terms we get

$$a x_1^{\rho} + b x_2^{\rho} = y^{\rho} \quad \Rightarrow \quad y = \left[a x_1^{\rho} + b x_2^{\rho}\right]^{\frac{1}{\rho}}$$

In both cases, we are able to retrieve the production function exactly.

8.5 Conclusion

Cost functions are much more useful than profit functions, because cost functions can be applied to a wider set of the market and types of firms, while the profit function is consistent only with diminishing returns (scale or factors) and price-taking behaviours of firms. Even for diminishing returns, technology and price-taking firms the cost functions and the two-step procedure of profit maximisation are far more instructive to uncover many nuances of the short-run and long-run output decision. We explore these issues in the next chapter.

Summary

In this chapter, we have studied the following:

1. How to describe technology and characterise the notion of productivity has been discussed.
2. The effect of a single input on the total output is described by *returns to factor*, while the effect of all inputs (changed by the same proportion) on the output is described by *returns to scale*. The former is a short-run concept while the latter relates to the long run.
3. The profit function states the maximum profit for any given set of input and output prices in both the short run and the long run.
4. Hotelling's lemma and the LeChatelier principle describe many nice properties of the profit function.
5. Cost function states the minimum cost of producing a given y for given input prices. Note that the output price p does not enter the cost function.
6. Shephard's lemma describes some nice properties of the cost function.
7. Long-run average cost curve is an envelope of all short-run average cost curves.
8. Economies of scale arise from fixed cost, and thus, it relates to short runs only. It makes the average cost fall.
9. When the AC is falling, the MC must be below the AC, and when the AC is rising, the MC must be above the AC.
10. There are production–cost duality relations. Returns to scale can be read from the cost function and vice versa.

8.6 Exercises

1. True or false?

   a. The input requirement set to $y = \max\{x_1, x_2\}$ is convex.
   b. From a long-run cost function, it follows that $rMC = AC$, where the underlying production function is homogeneous of degree r.
   c. $\dfrac{\partial MC}{\partial w_1} = \dfrac{\partial x_1(w_1, w_2, y)}{\partial y}$.
   d. The following pair of functions are legitimate conditional input demand functions:
   $$x_1 = \frac{A^{\frac{1}{2}} y w_2}{w_1} \text{ and } x_2 = \frac{A^2 y w_1}{w_2}.$$
   e. $E_{C,w_1} + E_{C,w_2} + E_{C,y} = 1$.

2. Show the following:

   a. For a production function homogeneous of degree r, $(r < 1)$, $\dfrac{E_{\pi,p}}{E_{\pi,p} - 1} = \dfrac{1}{r}$.
   b. For $f(x_1, x_2) = a x_1^{1/2} + x_1^{1/3} x_2^{1/6} + b x_2^{1/2}, a, b > 0$ always $MC > AC$.
   c. If the production function is homogeneous of degree r, then $E_{MC,y} = (1 - r)/r$.
   d. If the MC is decreasing in some input price, then that input must be an inferior input.

3. Derive the elasticity of substitution and the conditional input demand functions from the following production function:

$$y = \left[ax_1^{-\rho} + (1-a)x_2^{-\rho}\right]^{-\frac{h}{\rho}}, \; 0 < a < 1, \; h > 0, \; \rho > -1.$$

4. Identify the intervals of x for which the production function, $y = ax + bx^2 - cx^3$, $a, b, c > 0$, exhibits increasing, constant and decreasing returns (to factor).
5. Suppose $f(x) = a \ln x_1 + (1-a)\ln x_2$, $a > 0, x_1, x_2 > 1$. Find the values of x_1 and x_2 for which the production function locally exhibits constant returns to scale.
6. Consider a price-taker firm with technology $y = 6x_1^{1/2}x_2^{1/4}$, where x_2 cannot exceed an availability constraint $\bar{x}_2$. Prices of y, x_1 and x_2 are p, 3 and 1. respectively.

   a. Derive the profit-maximising levels of x_1 and x_2. Are they gross substitutes or complements?
   b. Write the profit function. What restriction on $\bar{x}_2$ is necessary to ensure that production is worthwhile?
   c. Draw the profit curve against p and compare it with the case in which there is no constraint on x_2.

7. A farmer has a fixed plot of land L which can be used to produce two crops, food y_1 and fodder y_2, both saleable in the market at fixed prices p_1 and p_2. The production technologies of the two crops are $y_1 = F(L_1)$ and $y_2 = G(L_2)$, where $F(.)$ and $G(.)$ are both increasing and strictly concave. L_i is the plot of land devoted to the production of the ith crop; $L_1 + L_2 = L$.

   a. Derive the production possibility curve, that is, the most efficient combinations of y_1 and y_2 that can be produced using the entire plot of land L.
   b. Assume zero production cost. Determine his optimal allocation of land between the two crops. Show it on a graph.
   c. If the farmer gets additional land through land reform, how will his choice of L_1 and L_2 be affected?

8. For $y = a \ln x_1 + b \ln x_2$, $a, b > 0$ find the optimal profit-maximising inputs and check the second-order condition. In order to ensure $y > 0$, what restrictions should you impose on p?
9. Consider a firm that sells a product y at a fixed price p^0 using technology $y = \sqrt{l} + \sqrt{k}$, where l and k stand for labour and capital. The wage rate is fixed at w^0, and the price of capital is fixed at r.

   a. Derive the optimal input demands and the profit function.
   b. Now suppose the product price falls from p^0 to $\frac{1}{2}p^0$. In response, the firm finds it optimal to fire some workers and reduce the use of capital. Can you tell us how many workers are to be fired, and what would be the firm's profit?
   c. Imagine that the workers' union opposes any firing, and if their demand is met, how would the firm's profit be affected?
   d. What if the union concedes to take a wage cut, but still insists on no firing. It is agreed between the firm and the union that the wage cut will leave the firm's profit exactly halfway between the two alternative options of no firing and firing all redundant workers. What would be the reduced wage rate?

10. Consider a price taker firm that has two plants in two regions—1 and 2. In region 1, labour is cheaper and in region 2 raw materials are cheaper; that is, $w_1 < w_2$, and $r_1 > r_2$. Technology for each region is $y_i = l_i^{1/2} + k_i^{1/2}$.

a. Derive the input demand functions for the two regions, and write the regional profit functions.
b. If for some reason the wage rate is equalised between the regions at $\hat{w} = (w_1 + w_2)/2$, how would the total as well as regional employment of this firm be affected?

11. Draw an isoquant and derive the cost function for each of the following two technologies: $y = \min\{ax_1, x_1 + bx_2\}$, $b > 0, a > 1$ and $y = \min\{ax_1, bx_2\} + x_2$, $a, b > 0$.
12. A farmer rents in a fixed plot of land $\hat{L}$ that can be used to produce two crops, food y_1 and fodder y_2. The production technologies of the two crop are as follow:

$$y_1 = AL_1^{\alpha} K_1^{\beta}, \qquad 0 < \alpha + \beta < 1, \qquad \text{and} \qquad y_2 = \min\{aL_2, bK_2\}; \qquad L_1 + L_2 = \hat{L}.$$

Rent per unit of land is t and the price of capital is r.

a. Derive the cost function for food and fodder.
b. Also, derive their marginal costs.
c. If the assumption of land constraint is slightly modified as $L_1 + L_2 \le \hat{L}$, how does your answer to the questions 12(a) and 12(b) change?

13. Consider the following technology of a firm: $y = el^{1/2}$. Let $e = f(k), f'(k) > 0, f''(k) < 0$. The prices of k and l are fixed at r and w, respectively.
Short Run: Suppose k, which is rationed by the government, and it is fixed at k^0.

a. Derive the short-run cost function of this firm. Distinguish between the variable and the fixed cost.
b. Derive the AC and the MC curves and present them graphically. Show the usual relation between the AC and the MC. Calculate the critical value of y at which the MC crosses the AC.

Long Run: Next consider the case where k is freely available in the market.

a. Derive the long-run cost function.
b. If the firm has to pay a tax at the rate of t on the value of capital used, then what would be its $\frac{\partial c}{\partial t}$, where c is the total cost.

14. Derive the cost function for the technology $y = \min\left\{\frac{x_1}{a}, \frac{x_2}{b}\right\}$, where the price of x_1 is w_1 and the price of x_2 is $w_2 = w_2^0 + x_2$. Write the AC and the MC.
15. Consider the case of linear technology: $y = l + k$. The wage rate per worker is an increasing function of l. That is, $w = w(l), w'(.) > 0, w''(.) > 0$. The price of capital is, however, fixed (r).

a. Write the cost minimisation problem.
b. Discuss various possible solutions and present them graphically using iso-cost and iso-quant curves.
c. Consider a solution where both $l, k > 0$ and write the conditional input demand functions.
d. Write the cost function when l and k are both positive. Verify the Shephard's lemma.

Notes

1 Do not be confused if you come across $MRTS_{ij} = -f_i / f_j$ in some textbooks. Many authors include a negative sign to directly interpret the slope of an isoquant as *MRTS*. Both are correct. As long as the negative sign is consistently carried through, both will lead to the same results.

2 Of course, for technical progress, one may ask, Where does technology come from? Is there a production function for technology? Research and development are one way to create technology, but dissemination of knowledge and social learning also help.

3 Differentiate $f(.)/x_i$ with respect to x_i, which gives $\partial(f/x_i)/\partial x_i = \frac{f_i - (f/x_i)}{x_i} \geq 0$ if and only if $f_i \geq f/x_i$.

4 When we are changing all inputs, we need to change them in the same proportion; otherwise, it will be difficult to compare the outputs before and after the change of input mix.

5 Be mindful of the difference between '*nonconvex technology*' and *convex production function*. The latter implies the former, which relates to the production set.

6 Mathematically, a homothetic function is a positive monotonic transformation of a homogeneous function. But then any homogeneous function of degree r can be expressed as a positive monotonic transformation of another homogeneous function of degree 1. Hence, it is useful to say that a homothetic production function is a positive monotonic transformation of a CRS production function.

7 We need only positive semi-definiteness of the bordered Hessian matrix or non-increasing *MRTS*.

8 The term *minimum* is used to allow for a flat bottom part of the LAC curve.

9 Suppose both inputs are inferior: $f_2 f_{12} - f_1 f_{22} < 0$ and $f_1 f_{21} - f_2 f_{11} < 0$. Multiplying the first inequality with f_1 and the second with f_2, we get $f_2 f_1 f_{12} - f_1^2 f_{22} < 0$ and $f_1 f_2 f_{21} - f_2^2 f_{11} < 0$. Adding the two inequalities, we get $-f_2^2 f_{11} + 2 f_1 f_2 f_{12} - f_1^2 f_{22} = \Delta f < 0$, which means that $f(x_1, x_2)$ is *quasi-convex*.

Further readings

Henderson, J. H. & Quandt, R. E. (1980). *Microeconomic Theory: A Mathematical Approach*, 3rd ed. Singapore: McGraw-Hill.

Hotelling, H. (1932). Edgeworth's taxation paradox and the nature of demand and supply function. *Journal of Political Economy*, 40, 577–616.

Mas-Colell, A., Whinston, M. D. & Green, J. R. (1995). *Microeconomic Theory*. New York: Oxford University Press.

Samuelson, P. A. (1983). *Foundations of Economic Analysis*. Cambridge, MA: Harvard University Press.

Shephard, R. (1953). *Cost and Production Functions*. Princeton, NJ: Princeton University Press.

Varian, H. R. (1992). *Microeconomic Analysis*, 3rd ed. New York: Norton.

Chapter 9

Perfect competition

Abstract

When markets are perfectly competitive, a firm's output decision depends on two things—the presence of any sunk or unavoidable cost and the price level it takes as given. If some costs are unavoidable even when the production plants are shut down, the firm will be willing to stay in operation as long as it is able to minimise loss. This is a consequence of facing a shorter time frame that does not allow optimal adjustments of certain inputs. In the long run, firms can exit freely and avoid any loss, but any profit opportunities will also disappear quickly. After studying the output choice of a firm, we analyse the welfare implication of a perfectly competitive market. Any tax or subsidy creates a welfare loss. We then return to the theme of general equilibrium studied earlier and examine, under some special assumptions, how exchange and trade can be incorporated into a framework of production.

Keywords: Sunk cost, Shut-down price, Tax incidence, Walrasian and Marshallian stability, Dead-weight loss, Production possibility frontier, Pareto-efficient input allocations, Stolper-Samuelson theorem, Rybcszynski theorem

9.1 Introduction

In developing countries, much of their stark poverty is found in the rural areas where farmers struggle to make ends meet despite spending long hours in the field. If their technology is not modern by global standard, think of the perils of the highly mechanised American farms. They have been disappearing. The number of family farms in the United States, according to the US Census of Agriculture, has steadily declined from its peak, 6.8 million, in 1935 to a mere 2.1 million in 2002. Rapid urbanisation may be an important factor behind the struggles of agriculture everywhere. But intense competition among farmers and their universal inability to set prices also have contributed to their declining incomes. The history of the spice trade gives many accounts of monopolies giving way to competition. Vanilla, once grown only in Mexico and an exclusive monopoly of Spain in the sixteenth century, is now sourced from many tropical countries, with Indonesia and Madagascar topping the list. Saffron is another example. Still the most expensive spice in the world (1 kilogram costs around £2000), saffron was introduced to the world by Spain, but Iran now holds the near-monopoly position with almost 90% of the global export coming from there. Similar are the stories of nutmeg, peppercorn, cinnamon, clove and other spices. With colonial conquests and the diffusion of plantation techniques, the production of these spices spread across continents. In just 300 years, what were once the exclusive consumables of the royalties have become culinary essentials of the whole world.

DOI: 10.4324/9781003226994-9

Economists for long conceptualised an ideal system of trade, perhaps as a legacy of the unprecedented rise in commerce and maritime trade from the sixteenth century onward, in which neither any buyer nor any seller would have power to influence the price. The goods they will be buying and selling should be largely homogeneous, as agricultural goods tend to be, and the industrial goods were at the early stage of the Industrial Revolution. Henry Ford, the famous automobile entrepreneur, once said, "Any customer can have a car painted any color that he wants so long as it is black". Furthermore, trade-related information should be widely spread to disallow one to exercise undue advantage. This is the notion of perfect competition. Although in reality no market perfectly fits the bill of perfect competition, it has remained an ideal benchmark against which all systems of trade can be evaluated.

We have already introduced the price-taking behaviours in Chapter 6 while studying the theory of exchange in a multi-market framework. In this chapter, we focus on the functioning of a single market, but we now allow production. You have already dealt with technology and production in Chapter 8 and input choice. Here, we take a different perspective by focusing on the output choice and the aggregate impact of competition.

9.2 Distinction between short run and long run

Before we proceed to determine output supply, we need to make a clear distinction between short and long runs for firms and industry. While studying cost function, we discussed how in the short run, a firm is constrained in its ability to adjust some of the inputs. As a result, some input costs become fixed, that is, invariant to output. We call this *fixed-input cost* (*FIC*). Now we introduce another type of fixed cost, usually associated with an early stage of the firm. This is called set-up cost. Examples include creating infrastructural facilities in and around a production plant, warehousing, workers' rest facilities, car parks and so on. We denote the set-up cost as I. Although both FIC and I are grouped under fixed cost FC, we should be mindful about their differences.[1]

An obvious difference between short and long runs (for firms) is that in the long run, FIC is transformed into variable costs, because all inputs can be optimally adjusted. But set-up costs may remain. If it is inherently a business start-up cost, it will have to be incurred regardless of the time frame we are looking at. However, for small firms, set-up costs can be insignificant. But then the scale of the firm—small or large—should also be a result of competition in the marketplace.

The short run also refers to a situation in which the total fixed cost ($FC = FIC + I$) may not be recoverable (by reselling the idle equipment, land or other assets) or avoidable (by reneging on contractual obligations) in part or entirety, if the firm shuts down or exits (exit and shut down are synonymous).[2] The unavoidable part of the fixed cost is called **sunk cost**. This applies to both FIC and set-up costs. To elaborate further, 'sunk' fixed costs largely come from machines and immovable assets. However, contractual agreements with landlords, long-term suppliers of inputs and even with a section of the workers who are on permanent contract can also give rise to sunk costs. But in all contracts, exit clauses are included to reduce the financial burden of the firm in the event of adverse business conditions.[3] Therefore, the entire fixed cost may not necessarily be sunk.

In the long run, however, there is no sunk cost. The firm can recover the set-up cost, if any, along with the cost of any capital goods. The basic idea is that any physical asset that has not been fully depreciated can be resold at its 'book value'. The long run permits the search for a buyer for these assets. Alternatively, if the sunk cost arises due to contractual obligations, with the expiry of the term of the contract, the 'sunk' nature of the cost disappears. To summarise, in

Table 9.1 Short and long run

	Short run	*Long run*
Firm	Fixed-input cost, set-up cost, sunk cost	All inputs are adjusted, set-up cost, no sunk cost
Industry	Restricted entry, costly exit	Free entry, free exit

the short run (1) there may be both FICs and set-up costs, and (2) some of these costs are sunk in part or full. In the long run, there are no sunk costs, but non-sunk set-up costs may remain.

For industry, the short run means no new entry, and the maximum number of firms that can remain in operation is fixed, which implies that some firms may choose to leave or shut down. As a result, the existing firms will earn super-normal profits from high prices and suffer losses from low prices due to unavoidable fixed costs. In the long run, entry and exit are seamless as super-normal profits attract new entries and losses induce exit, because all costs are avoidable upon exit. Table 9.1 summarises these distinctions.

The notion of the sunk cost can be formally borne out by the following specification:

$$\begin{aligned} c(y) &= F + c_v(y) \qquad \text{if} \quad y > 0 \\ &= \gamma F \qquad \text{if} \quad y = 0. \end{aligned}$$

Here, $0 < \gamma < 1$ proportion of the fixed cost F is sunk. If $\gamma = 0$, no cost is sunk.

9.3 Output supply in the short run

Two decisions confront any firm: (1) Whether to stay in business or shut down, and (2) if business is to continue, then how much output to produce?

Let us start with the output decision. The firm maximises $\pi = py - c(y)$ with respect to y.[4] The optimal output is determined by the equation

$$\pi'(y) \equiv p - c'(y) = 0, \qquad \text{or,} \quad p = MC(y).$$

The second-order condition is $\pi''(y) < 0$, or $c''(y) > 0$. That is, the marginal cost (MC) curve must be increasing at the optimal output. It should be obvious that $c'(y) = c_v'(y)$. Here, we can straight away rule out increasing returns to scale or factor (or economies of scale) as well as constant returns to scale or factor. In those cases, the MC is not increasing, and therefore, the profit will not be maximum, or the output will be indeterminate. This means that we must have decreasing returns to scale (in the long run) or decreasing returns to factor (in the short run) for profit maximisation to be consistent with price taking behaviour.

Now let us turn our attention to the first question—the one of staying in business. In light of the distinction between sunk and fixed costs, let us write the following:

$$\begin{aligned} FC &= \text{Sunk fixed cost}(FC_S) + \text{non-sunk fixed cost}(FC_{NS}) \\ VDC &= FC_{NS} + VC \quad \text{(Total avoidable cost)} \\ TC &= FC_S + VDC = FC_S + FC_{NS} + VC = FC + VC. \end{aligned}$$

In the preceding, it is noteworthy that FC_{NS} is a common term for FC and VDC. This is because it is fixed with respect to output but not with respect to time. That costs vary on two dimensions—time and output—is an important fact to bear in mind. It is crucial to understand the short-run behaviours of the firm.

If the price of the output is such that the firm is not able to earn a positive profit, it will compare losses from two alternative options: close down or continue. By closing down, it will suffer a loss equal to the sunk cost. By continuing to produce (by the $p = MC$ rule), it will earn a revenue that may or may not cover the total avoidable costs (variable costs and avoidable fixed costs). If it covers the entire avoidable costs and little more, then its loss will be lower than the sunk cost. It should stay in business. Alternatively, if the revenue is not large enough to cover even the (total) avoidable cost, clearly shutting down is the best option. Thus, the firm should shut down if

$$p < \text{average avoidable cost}\,(AAC = VDC / y).$$

Therefore, the shut-down price is the minimum value of average avoidable cost (AAC). When the fixed cost is entirely sunk ($AAC = AVC$, or average variable cost), the shut-down price is the minimum value of AVC.

Figure 9.1 depicts the short-run MC, average cost (AC) and AVC curves, assuming that the entire fixed cost is sunk. So the firm will supply a positive output if $p > AVC_m$. If the price is p_1, as shown in panel *a*, the firm chooses output y_1 by setting $p = MC$ at point A. Since $p_1 >$ SAC (short-run average cost) at y_1, the firm earns strictly positive profit, which is marked by the rectangular area. The vertical difference between SAC and the AVC gives AFC (average fixed cost). On panel *b*, we show the firm's supply response to a much lower price, p_0, which is strictly less than SAC but above AVC. The firm cannot break even, but by closing down, it will lose FC, the sunk cost, while by producing y_0 at point B (where $p_0 = MC$), it will earn a surplus over and above the variable cost. The surplus goes to cover part of the fixed/sunk cost.

The supply curve of the firm is then given by the SMC curve above the minimum point of the AVC curve. If the price falls below p_1, the minimum value of AVC, the firm will supply zero output, or exit so to speak. This is shown on panel *a* of Figure 9.2.

We can also present a case, where $FC > FC_S$. Suppose γFC is the sunk cost, $\gamma < 1$. Panel *b* of Figure 9.2 shows this possibility. Here, $AAC = AVC + (1-\gamma)AFC > AVC$. As a result, the shut-down price $\bar{p}_2$, the minimum value of AAC, is higher than the case in which the whole

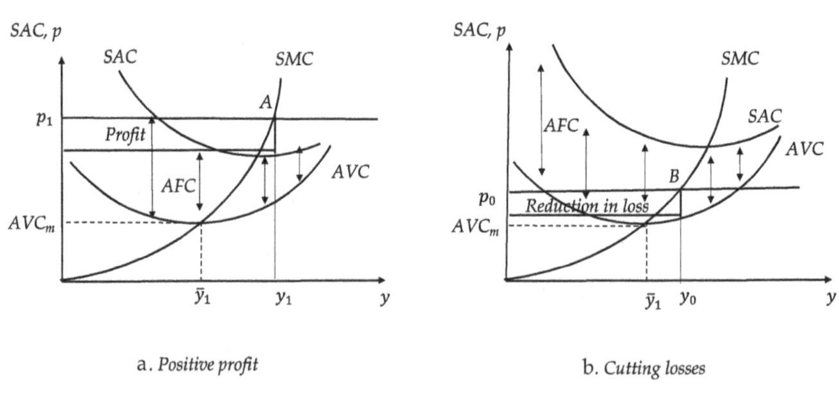

Figure 9.1 Firm's short-run optimal outputs ($FC = FC_S$)

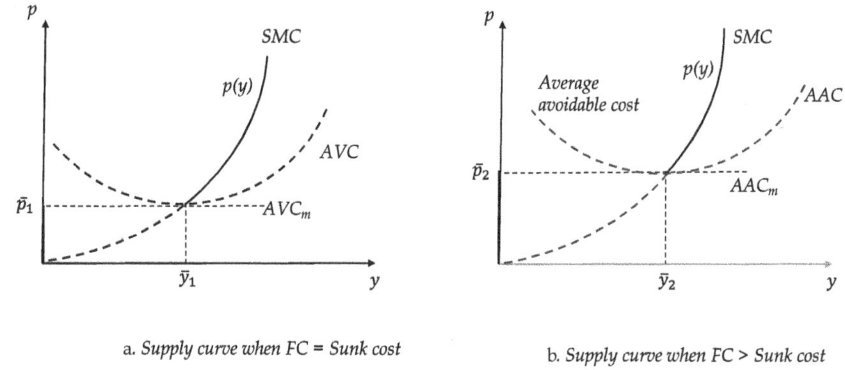

Figure 9.2 Firm's short-run supply curves

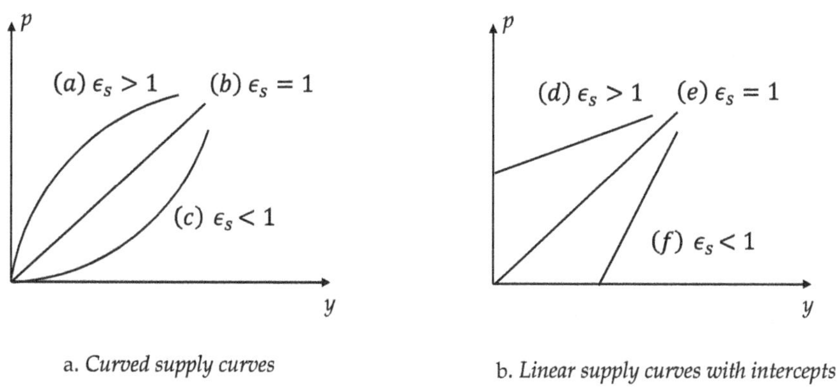

Figure 9.3 Price elasticity of supply

fixed cost is sunk (panel *a*). The supply curve is given by the SMC curve above the minimum point of AAC. We write the firm supply curve as $y(p)$ and its inverse function as $p(y)$ as shown in Figure 9.2.

9.3.1 Price elasticity of supply

We can also study the price elasticity of a firm's supply, just like we did for consumers. Let us assume that a firm's supply function is given by $y = kp^\theta$, with $k, \theta > 0$. The price elasticity of supply is $\epsilon_s \equiv \frac{\partial y}{\partial p}\frac{p}{y} = \theta$. The supply curve is elastic (inelastic) if $\theta >$ (<)1. When $\theta > 1$ the supply curve is a convex function of p, and the inverse supply curve is concave (while passing through the origin). Such a supply curve will be price elastic. The firms will respond more than proportionately to price rises. Conversely, if the inverse supply curve is convex, it is price inelastic, and if linear, it is unitary elastic. Figure 9.3 panel *a* shows the inverse supply curves for the function $y = kp^\theta$ for different values of θ.

It turns out that in the linear case, a positive or negative intercept makes a difference to the supply elasticity. Take $p = d + cy$ and verify that $\epsilon_s > 1$ if $d > 0$, $\epsilon_s < 1$ if $d < 0$ and $\epsilon_s = 1$ if $d = 0$, as shown in panel *b* of Figure 9.3. Why is the supply curve (*d*) of the right panel similar to the supply curve (*a*) of the left panel and curve (*f*) to curve (*c*)? The answer is that the presence of a positive intercept makes the linear (inverse) supply curve of panel *b* (weakly) concave. Similarly, the negative intercept of curve (*f*) turns it into a convex curve. Hence, they share the same elasticity property. However, unlike the price elasticity of demand, the supply elasticity does not reveal any interesting insight into the firm's revenue.

9.3.2 Market supply curve

In the short run, the number of firms is fixed, of which all or some may be operative depending on the price relative to their AACs. Thus, a horizontal summation of individual supply curves across the operative firms gives the market supply curve.[5] To illustrate this clearly, let us retrieve the Cobb–Douglas example from the last chapter. The short-run cost curve (holding x_2 fixed) is

$$c^S(w_1, w_2, y; \bar{x}_2) = ky^{\frac{1}{\alpha}} + w_2\bar{x}_2, \quad \text{where } k = w_1\left(\frac{1}{A\bar{x}_2{}^{\beta}}\right)^{\frac{1}{\alpha}}.$$

From this, we obtain

$$SAC = ky^{\frac{1-\alpha}{\alpha}} + \frac{w_2\bar{x}_2}{y} \qquad \text{and} \qquad SMC = \frac{k}{\alpha}y^{\frac{1-\alpha}{\alpha}}.$$

Assume $\alpha < 1$ and note that SAC is minimum at

$$\bar{y} = A\bar{x}_2^{\alpha+\beta}\left[\frac{\alpha w_2}{(1-\alpha)w_1}\right]^{\alpha}.$$

Setting $p = SMC$, we get the output response of a firm as

$$\phi(p) = p^{\frac{\alpha}{1-\alpha}}\left[\frac{A\alpha^{\alpha}\bar{x}_2^{\beta}}{w_1^{\alpha}}\right]^{\frac{1}{1-\alpha}}.$$

Suppose there are n_1 identical firms that differ from another set of n_2 identical firms in terms of the extent of the sunk cost; $n_1 + n_2 = n$. For type 1 firms (first group), the entire $w_2\bar{x}_2$ is sunk, while for type 2, only $\gamma w_2\bar{x}_2$ ($\gamma < 1$) is sunk.

For type 1 firms, the AAC is the same as AVC. The minimum point of AVC is zero, while for type 2 firms, their minimum point of $AAC = ky^{\frac{1-\alpha}{\alpha}} + (1-\gamma)\frac{w_2\bar{x}_2}{y}$ occurs at

$$\bar{y}_2 = A\bar{x}_2^{\alpha+\beta}\left[\frac{\alpha(1-\gamma)w_2}{(1-\alpha)w_1}\right]^{\alpha},$$

giving rise to the minimum of AAC as

$$\bar{p} \equiv AAC_m = (1-\gamma)^{1-\alpha}\left[\frac{w_1^{\alpha} w_2^{1-\alpha} \bar{x}_2^{1-\alpha-\beta}}{A\alpha^{\alpha}(1-\alpha)^{1-\alpha}}\right].$$

Note that if $\gamma = 1$, $\bar{p} = 0$. Likewise, if $\gamma = 0$, $\bar{p} = AC_m$ (the minimum point of AC). The resultant supply curves of a type 1 firm and a type 2 firm are

$$y_1^S = \phi(p) \quad \text{for} \quad p \geq 0 \qquad \text{and} \qquad y_2^S = \begin{cases} \phi(p) & \text{for} \quad p \geq \bar{p}, \\ 0 & \text{for} \quad p < \bar{p}. \end{cases}$$

The market supply is the sum of the two supply curves with the appropriate number of operative firms accounted for. The supply curve is thus given by the following equation:

$$Y_S = \begin{cases} n\phi(p) & \text{for} \quad p \geq \bar{p}, \\ n_1\phi(p) & \text{for} \quad p < \bar{p}. \end{cases}$$

Let the market demand be given by a linear function $p = a - bY$. Setting demand equal to supply, we get the market equilibrium. For illustrative purposes, assume $\alpha = 1/2$, so that our supply curve is also linear as

$$Y_S = \begin{cases} \dfrac{n}{2k} p & \text{for} \quad p \geq \bar{p}, \\ \dfrac{n_1}{2k} p & \text{for} \quad p < \bar{p}, \end{cases} \tag{9.1}$$

where let us recall $k = w_1\left(\dfrac{1}{A\bar{x}_2{}^{\beta}}\right)^{\frac{1}{\alpha}}$. Equating demand and supply (of n firms), we get

$$Y^* = \frac{na}{2k+nb}, \qquad p^* = \frac{2ka}{2k+nb}. \tag{9.2}$$

In Figure 9.4 on panel a, we have drawn the supply curve as given by Eq. (9.1). $p(y)$ is a firm's supply curve with the shut-down price being zero for type 1 firms and $\bar{p}$ for type 2 firms. n_1 type 1 firms supply up to $n_1\bar{y}_2$ at price $\bar{p}$, when n_2 type 2 firms also join and the total supply increases up to $n\bar{y}_2$. At $p > \bar{p}$, all n firms are operative. In panel b, we have drawn three demand curves and have shown three possible equilibria. At point E_2, the price is high enough to allow all n firms to operate. In contrast, the demand curve Y_D'' is so low that only n_1 firms can operate. With intermediate demand Y_D', the equilibrium price is $\bar{p}$, and some of the type 2 firms may shut down because of a lack of demand. We can verify that

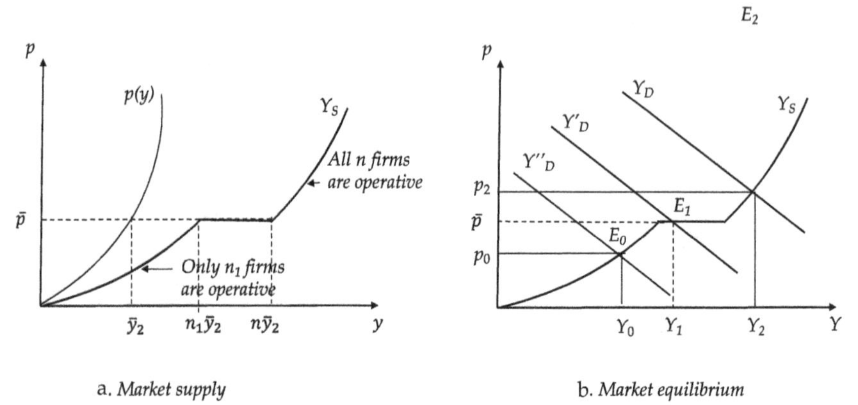

Figure 9.4 Market equilibrium with two types of firms

$$p^* > \bar{p} \quad \text{if} \quad a > \bar{p}\left(1+\frac{nb}{2k}\right)$$

$$p^* = \bar{p} \quad \text{if} \quad \bar{p}\left(1+\frac{n_1 b}{2k}\right) \le a \le \bar{p}\left(1+\frac{nb}{2k}\right)$$

$$p^* < \bar{p} \quad \text{if} \quad a < \bar{p}\left(1+\frac{n_1 b}{2k}\right).$$

9.4 The long-run case

In the long run, firms can adjust all inputs. So there cannot be FICs. But the set-up cost may remain. This means that the shut-down price is the minimum value of the long-run average cost (LAC). But the output supply decision is still taken by the $p = LMC$ rule. Thus, all decisions are based on the long-run MCs and ACs.

But remember the number of firms is not fixed. Free entry and exit imply that any super-normal profit will disappear promptly, and so will any losses. As firms will be able to fully optimise on all inputs and find the best available technology, all firms that are able to operate must have the same AC and the same minimum efficient scale (MES).

Take, for example, a long-run cost function

$$c^L = \begin{cases} F + \frac{c}{2}y^2, & \text{for} \quad y > 0 \\ 0 & \text{for} \quad y = 0. \end{cases}$$

Here, the firm can avoid the set-up cost F simply by exiting. The LAC curve ($LAC = F / y + cy / 2$) gives rise to a unique efficient scale $y^* = \sqrt{\frac{2F}{c}}$ (where $LMC = LAC$).

The industry supply curve is then a flat line at price $p(y^*)$, the total supply will be given $Y_D(p(y^*))$ and the number of firms will be $n^* = Y_D(p(y^*)) / y^*$. This leads to two dramatic

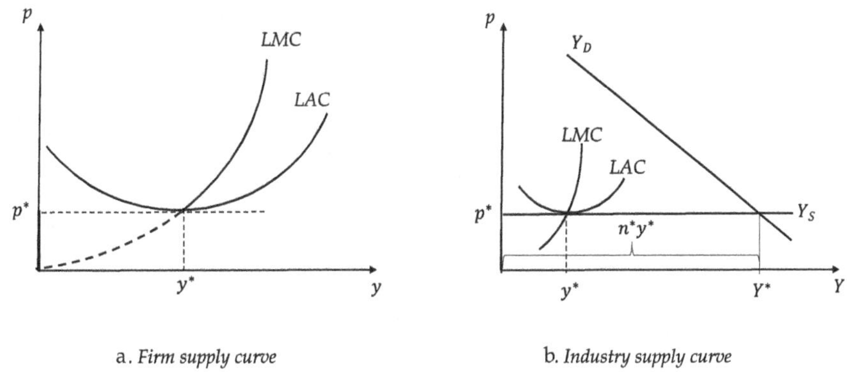

Figure 9.5 Long-run supply curve and market equilibrium

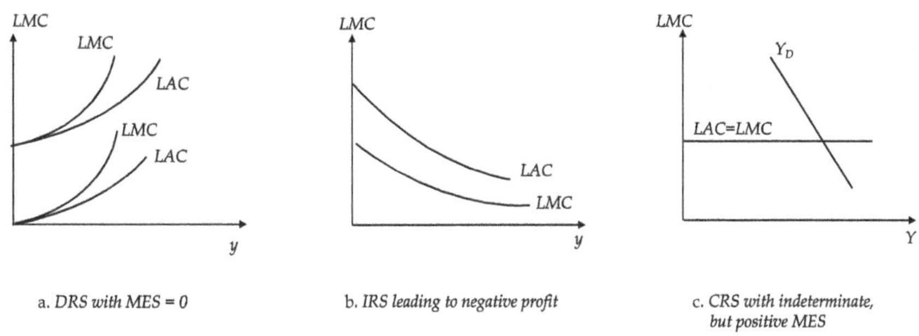

Figure 9.6 Incompatibility of long-run equilibrium

conclusions: (1) MES (y^*) must be strictly positive, and (2) there is no 'long-run supply curve for the industry', while the long-run supply curve of the firm is still given by its *LMC* above *LAC*.

See Figure 9.5. The long-run supply curve for a firm is shown on panel *a*. The firm will supply y^* units if price is p^*, zero if $p < p^*$ and, according to $p = LMC$, if $p < p^*$. On the right, panel *b* shows industry supply. Under free entry, the equilibrium price cannot exceed p^* because new firms will enter and drive profits to zero. The price cannot fall below p^* either. Then n^* firms will enter, each producing y^* so that the total demand y^* is met.

For consistency of long-run equilibrium we need MES to be strictly positive. That means either the technology exhibits all three returns to scale or there is a set-up cost. Figure 9.6 shows some scenarios that are incompatible with the notion of a long-run competitive equilibrium. Panel *a* shows two pairs of *LAC* and *LMC* that exhibit a decreasing returns to scale but both showing $MES = 0$. So if any positive output is supplied, it will earn zero profit. Panel *b* shows the case of increasing returns to scale (IRS), where price-taking behaviour rules out positive profit altogether, because $LMC < LAC$. The third figure is a tricky one. Here, any positive output can be supplied by a firm and zero profit can be sustained. So total demand can be met at zero profit. But the number of firms as well as an individual supply of each firm will both be indeterminate. This case is not fully incompatible, but any number of firms and any MES can be supported in equilibrium.

9.5 Stability: price and quantity adjustment models

Our static representation of equilibrium in a perfectly competitive market can be seen as a limiting version of dynamic trading processes seen in the real world. Prices go through ups and downs to finally reach the market-clearing level. But how do we know that we will arrive at our (usually) unique equilibrium if we start from an arbitrary point away from it? As you would recall from the discussion of general equilibrium in Chapter 6, this is a question of stability of equilibrium. Just to remind ourselves, stability relates to the issue of preserving a stationary state. Think about an object placed on a table. Will the object fall onto the ground if we shake the table gently? The answer is no if the object is a cube, but it will if it is a ball. The ball is an unstable object, while the cube is not. In the context of market equilibrium, we want to know if the equilibrium survives any perturbation. Generally, the story of stability is kept hidden from the static presentation of equilibrium. It needs to be separately told. Here, we briefly discuss three models of price and/or quantity adjustment that will provide stability to our equilibrium. This means that once away from equilibrium, if price/quantity is adjusted by the rules specified, we should be able to return to our equilibrium.

9.5.1 *Walrasian price adjustment*

Let us recall the Walrasian *Tatonnement* process from Chapter 6. Suppose there is an auctioneer who announces an arbitrary price and producers and consumers have to declare how much they would like to sell and buy at that price. If the consumers' declaration (quantity demanded) exceeds the firms' declaration (quantity supplied), then the auctioneer will increase the price and repeat the process until the two declarations match. The goods change hands at that point. He will do the reverse if the firms' declaration exceeds the consumers' declaration.

If we describe the auctioneer's announcement as $p(t)$, then the previously discussed process is essentially a description of how $p(t)$ converges to the equilibrium price p^*. The price adjustment process can be described by postulating the following function:

$$\frac{dp}{dt} = H(Y_D(p(t)) - Y_S(p(t)), \qquad \text{with} \quad H(0) = 0, H'(.) > 0.$$

The right-hand-side expression, $H(p(t))$, can be written using Taylor expansion in the neighbourhood of the equilibrium price, p^*, as

$$H(p(t)) = H(Y_D(p^*) - Y_S(p^*)) + \underbrace{H'(p^*)\left(\frac{\partial Y_D(p^*)}{\partial p} - \frac{\partial Y_S(p^*)}{\partial p}\right)}_{\equiv h(p^*)}(p(t) - p^*) + \ldots$$

$$= 0 + h(p^*)(p(t) - p^*) + \ldots$$

Note $h(p^*)$ is constant with respect to $p(t)$. Our price adjustment equation is then

$$\frac{dp}{dt} = h(p^*)(p(t) - p^*), \qquad \Rightarrow \qquad \frac{dp}{dt} - h(p^*)p(t) = -p^* h(p^*).$$

This is a differential equation is of the form

$$\frac{dz}{dt} + \alpha z(t) = \beta, \qquad \alpha, \beta > 0.$$

A typical solution *z*(*t*) is a sum of a complementary function z_c and a particular integral z_p. Let $z_c = Be^{-\alpha t}$, where *B* is an arbitrary constant that can be specified in a number of ways. z_p takes the value of *z* when *z* is constant; hence, $z_p = \beta / \alpha, \alpha \neq 0$. Thus $z(t) = Be^{-\alpha t} + \beta / \alpha$. Now we can specify *B* by setting $t = 0$, $z(0) = B + \beta / \alpha$ or $B = z(0) - \beta / \alpha$. Since *z*(0) is known, *B* is specified.

Following the preceding rule, the solution to our differential equation is

$$p(t) = p^* + (p^0 - p^*)e^{h(p^*)t}, \tag{9.3}$$

where p^0 refers to the initial price. The stability of equilibrium requires that

$$\lim_{t \to \infty} p(t) = p^*,$$

which, in turn, implies that $h(p^*) < 0$ or, equivalently, $\left(\frac{\partial Y_D(p^*)}{\partial p} - \frac{\partial Y_S(p^*)}{\partial p} \right) < 0$ (since $H'(p^*) > 0$). There are three possibilities:

1. The demand curve is negatively sloped, and the supply curve is positively sloped. In this case, the stability condition is easily met.
2. (Giffen good) Both curves are positively sloped around the equilibrium. The stability condition then requires $\frac{\partial Y_D(p^*)}{\partial p} < \frac{\partial Y_S(p^*)}{\partial p}$.
3. (Backward-bending supply curve) Both curves are negatively sloped. The stability condition holds

   if $\left| \frac{\partial Y_D(p^*)}{\partial p} \right| > \left| \frac{\partial Y_S(p^*)}{\partial p} \right|$.

Graphically, since we draw inverse demand and supply curves, the slope conditions are to be taken in their inverse form.

9.5.2 Marshallian quantity adjustment

Marshall suggested a similar mechanism that uses quantity as the adjustment variable. Our imaginary auctioneer now announces an arbitrary quantity for sale and asks the consumers and firms how much they are 'willing to pay' and 'willing to accept', respectively. If the willingness to pay or the so-called demand price exceeds, the willingness to accept the auctioneer revises his quantity on sale by increasing it. He decreases the output when the demand price falls short of the supply price and leaves the output unchanged when the two prices match. Trade takes place thereafter. Because quantity is the adjustment variable here, let us write the quantity adjustment equation in terms of the inverse demand function *p*(*Y*).

We postulate the quantity adjustment process as

$$\frac{dY}{dt} = G(p_D(Y(t)) - p_S(Y(t))) \qquad \text{with} \quad G(0) = 0, G'(.) > 0.$$

Like before, $Y(t)$ is the auctioneer's placement of Y at time and Y^* is the equilibrium output. By Taylor, expansion around Y^*

$$G(Y(t)) = G(p_D(Y^*) - p_S(Y^*)) + \underbrace{G'(Y^*)\left(\frac{\partial p_D(Y^*)}{\partial Y} - \frac{\partial p_S(Y^*)}{\partial Y}\right)}_{\equiv g(Y^*)}(Y(t) - Y^*) + \ldots$$

$$= 0 + g(Y^*)(Y(t) - Y^*).$$

Note $g(Y^*)$ does not involve t. The adjustment equation is a first-order differential equation:

$$\frac{dY}{dt} - g(Y^*)Y(t) = -g(Y^*)Y^*,$$

which is solved as

$$Y(t) = Y^* + (Y^0 - Y^*)e^{g(Y^*)t}. \tag{9.4}$$

The stability requirement is $g(Y^*) < 0$, and since $G'(.) > 0$, we must have

$$\frac{\partial p_D(Y^*)}{\partial Y} - \frac{\partial p_S(Y^*)}{\partial Y} < 0.$$

Once again, there are three possibilities:

1. In the regular case of downward-sloping demand and upward-sloping supply curves, the stability condition is automatically satisfied.
2. (Giffen good) Both curves are positively sloped around the equilibrium. The stability condition now requires $\frac{\partial p_D(Y^*)}{\partial Y} < \frac{\partial p_S(Y^*)}{\partial Y}$.
3. (Backward-bending supply curve) Both curves are negatively sloped. The stability condition requires $\left|\frac{\partial p_D(Y^*)}{\partial Y}\right| > \left|\frac{\partial p_S(Y^*)}{\partial Y}\right|$.

9.5.2.1 Comparison

It would be instructive to compare the price adjustment versus quantity adjustment mechanisms as suggested by Eqs. (9.3) and (9.4), respectively. When the demand and supply curves are of

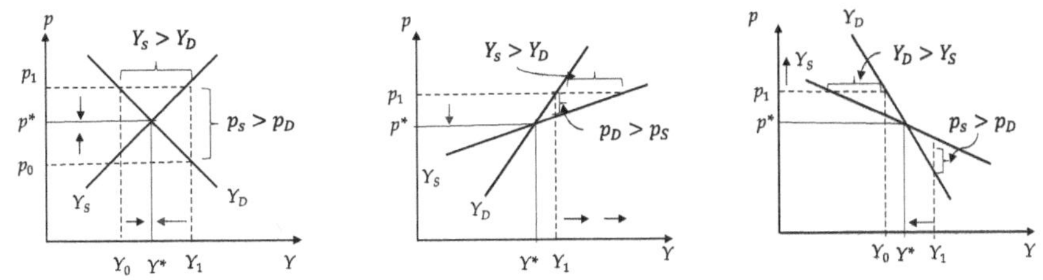

a. *Both W-stable and M-stable* b. *W-stable, but M-unstable* c. *W-unstable, but M-stable*

Figure 9.7 Stability of equilibrium

regular shape, both stability conditions are met. That is, the equilibrium of the regular demand and supply curves are both *W-stable* (stable by the Walrasian mechanism) and *M-stable* (stable by the Marshallian mechanism). Panel *a* of Figure 9.7 shows this case. Fix price at p_1 and see that the sellers want to sell more than the buyers want to buy, so by the Walrasian mechanism, the price needs to be reduced toward p^*. Alternatively, fix Y at Y_1 and see that the sellers want a higher supply price than what the consumers are willing to pay. Hence, the output is reduced toward Y^*. Thus, this case is stable by both mechanisms.

The preceding equivalence between the two mechanisms breaks down if one of the two curves has an irregular slope, at least around equilibrium if not everywhere. Panel *b* shows the case in which the demand curve is upward-sloping. At $p_1 > p^*$, we still have excess supply, and the Walrasian stability condition requires the auctioneer to reduce the price. So the equilibrium is W-stable, but note that at $Y_1 > Y^*$, consumers post a higher willingness to pay than the sellers' willingness to accept, so the auctioneer needs to increase the output by the Marshallian mechanism. That means the adjustment process will move away from equilibrium. Hence, the equilibrium here is M-unstable. Panel *c* shows the case of equilibrium being M-stable but W-unstable.

If you wonder why the supply curve would be backward-bending, recall from Chapter 3 that the labour supply curve can be backward-bending. Similarly, a backward-bending supply curve can also emerge from endowment incomes. You may also ask which stability model should be used when one of the two curves becomes non-regular. It usually depends on the researcher's preference and the research problem. Generally, the Walrasian mechanism is more commonly used because price adjusts more quickly than quantity.

9.5.3 *A discrete-time model of price and quantity adjustments*

One can argue that neither price nor quantity can be adjusted instantaneously, and certainly, quantity adjustments are seen to be more time-consuming than price adjustments. Firms often base their expectation about future prices on current prices (an act of adaptive expectation). When such realism is incorporated, we have a discrete-time model of supply and demand. A popular version of this model is the *cobweb model*, which specifies a pair of demand and supply equations as

$$Y_D(t) = a - bp_t \qquad \text{and} \qquad Y_s(t) = \delta + \sigma p_{t-1}.$$

We assume $a > \delta$ to allow for positive gains of trade. The condition $Y_D(t) = Y_S(t)$ generates a first-order linear difference equation:

$$p_t + \frac{\sigma}{b} p_{t-1} = \frac{a-\delta}{b}.$$

Note that by setting $Y_D(t) = Y_S(t)$ at every time period t, we do not get equilibrium. Because of the asymmetry in time, sensitivities of demand and supply prices will not match despite the quantities being matched. In equilibrium, both quantity and price should be stationary.[6] By setting $p_t = p_{t-1}$ for every t, we get the stationary or equilibrium price as $p^* = \frac{a-\delta}{b+\sigma}$.

Let us briefly digress to difference equations. For a first-order linear difference equation of the form $x_t + \alpha x_{t-1} = k$, the solution is sum of a particular solution x_p, and a complementary solution x_c. That is $x_t = x_p + x_c$. A standard practice is to try a complementary solution of the form, $x_t = B\beta^t$, for which we must solve for both B and β by trying out the homogeneous part of the equation $x_t + \alpha x_{t-1} = 0$ (i.e., ignore k). This gives us $B\beta^t + \alpha B\beta^{t-1} = 0$ or $\beta = -\alpha$. The particular solution can be obtained by considering the full equation $x_t + \alpha x_{t-1} = k$. We can take the stationary value of x and write $\bar{x} + \alpha\bar{x} = k$ or $\bar{x} = k/(1+\alpha)$. Now combining the complementary and the particular solution, we write $x_t = B\beta^t + \frac{k}{1+\alpha} = B(-\alpha)^t + \bar{x}$. Finally, setting $t = 0$, we derive the initial value $x_0 = B + \bar{x}$, from which we solve for $B = x_0 - \bar{x}$. This gives us the full solution as $x_t = [x_0 - \bar{x}](-\alpha)^t + \bar{x}$.

Our price adjustment equation has the same form, and we write its solution as

$$p_t = \left[p_0 - \frac{a-\delta}{b+\sigma}\right]\left(-\frac{\sigma}{b}\right)^t + \frac{a-\delta}{b+\sigma} = (p_0 - p^*)\left(-\frac{\sigma}{b}\right)^t + p^*. \tag{9.5}$$

For the equilibrium to be stable, starting from any p_0, the price adjustment path must converge to p^* as time goes to infinity. This will happen only if $\sigma < b$; that is, $\partial Y_S / \partial p < |\partial Y_D / \partial p|$. Thus, along a convergent price path, the market price (as given by Eq. (9.5)) assumes the following values:

$$p_t = \begin{cases} p_0 & \text{at } t = 0 \\ -\frac{(p_0 - p^*)\sigma}{b} + p^* & \text{at } t = 1 \\ \frac{(p_0 - p^*)\sigma^2}{b^2} + p^* & \text{at } t = 2 \\ -\frac{(p_0 - p^*)\sigma^3}{b^3} + p^* & \text{at } t = 3 \\ \cdots & \cdots\cdots \\ p^* & \text{as } t \to \infty. \end{cases}$$

This path looks like a cobweb. Starting from a price below p^*, it jumps the next period to a price greater than p^* (at $t = 1$), then falls back below p^* at time period 2, jumps back above p^*

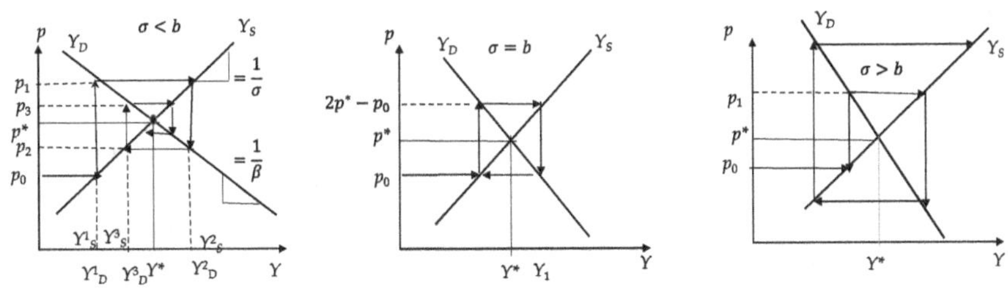

a. *Stable* b. *Unstable: Uniform cycle* c. *Unstable: Explosive cycle*

Figure 9.8 The cobweb model

the period after and so on. But each time it jumps up or down, the magnitude of rise or fall gets smaller, thus converging to p^* eventually. Figure 9.8 shows this in panel *a*. We start from p_0. In period 0, there is no supply response yet. But it gives rise to p_1 by the equilibrium price rule. At p_1, we get Y_D^1, which responds to p_1 while we get Y_S^1 responding to p_0. Both quantities are equal, although their underlying prices are not. Given p_1, the supply response of period 2 will be Y_S^2, which will be equal to Y_D^2, but Y_D^2 will correspond to p_2 and p_2 will be less than p^*. But note that p_2 is closer to p^* than p_0 was, and p^3 will be closer to p^* than p_1 was. Thus, the cycles are dampening, and the price adjustment path will take us to p^*. The equilibrium is stable, and the stability condition is $\sigma < b$.

But if $\sigma = b$ the adjustment path will endlessly travel around p^* with uniform jumps from excess demand to excess supply. The cycles will be uniform between p_0 and $-p_0 + 2p^*$, as shown (see panel *b* of Figure 9.8):

$$p_t = \begin{cases} p_0 & \text{at} \quad t = 0 \\ -p_0 + 2p^* & \text{at} \quad t = 1 \\ p_0 & \text{at} \quad t = 2 \\ -p_0 + 2p^* & \text{at} \quad t = 3 \\ \cdots & \ldots.. \end{cases}$$

Finally, if $\sigma > b$, the adjustment path will never converge, and with ever-amplifying cycles, it will move far and far away from the equilibrium as shown in panel *c* of Figure 9.8.

The stability condition of the cobweb model may seem odd at first glance, considering that in the other two models of stability, we did not encounter this condition. In fact, both the Walrasian and Marshallian mechanisms guarantee stability if the demand and supply curves are regularly sloped. The cobweb model says that in addition to the two curves being regular, the supply curve must be less steep than the demand curve.[7] Why is it so? Note that the other two mechanisms only recommend a particular rule of price or quantity adjustments without saying what microstructure of the market would make those adjustments possible. The cobweb model, by comparison, takes a conscious step in this direction by introducing minimal friction on the supply side via sellers' adaptive expectations. The friction is just enough to generate price cycles, some of which can be very destabilising.

9.6 Welfare

We learnt in Chapter 6 that when all markets are competitive and are in a state of general equilibrium, there is no scope for Pareto improvement. That means no individual can be made better off without making someone else worse off. The framework we adopted there did not allow production. Here, within the framework of a single market, we establish that the Pareto optimality result holds with production as well. The single-market framework is also very useful in studying the welfare or efficiency aspects of various market-specific policies like tax, subsidy or price controls.

The idea that no buyer or seller can be made better off without making another seller or buyer worse off is demonstrated by showing that the gains of two sides—buyers and sellers—are maximum in an 'un-interfered' market equilibrium. The collective gains of the buyers are given by consumer surplus (CS), that is, the area under the market demand curve minus their total spending, and the collective gains of the sellers are given by producer surplus (PS), that is, total revenue minus the area under the market supply curve. Since the area under the supply curve captures the total variable cost, producer surplus is profit plus fixed cost if any.[8] The sum of consumer surplus and producer surplus is called social welfare. The competitive equilibrium realises the maximum social welfare possible, leaving no dead-weight loss (DWL).

Socially optimal output is obtained by maximising

$$SW(Y) = CS + PS = \int_0^Y p_D(x)dx - c_v(Y), \tag{9.6}$$

and the following first-order condition implicitly gives Y^*:

$$SW'(Y) = 0 \qquad \Rightarrow \qquad p_D(Y^*) = \frac{\partial c_v(Y^*)}{\partial Y}.$$

The socially optimal output equates price with the social marginal cost of production. Note that the fixed cost or set-up cost, and equally, a lump-sum tax/subsidy does not affect the welfare-maximising output or social welfare. A competitive market selects equilibrium $Y^c = Y^*$ because every firm follows the $p = MC$ rule. Maximum social welfare is achieved through the market. But that will change if a per unit tax/subsidy is applied.

9.6.1 *Welfare loss due to distortionary taxes and subsidies*

Let us take the case of a proportional tax imposed on the suppliers. Suppose, for simplicity, the variable cost of producing any output level, say, Y^0, is affected in the following way. $c_v(Y^0;t) = \left(\int_0^{Y^0} \frac{\partial c_v(Y)}{\partial Y} dY\right)(1+t)$. Competitive equilibrium in the presence of tax, $Y^c(t)$, is given by

$$p_D(Y^c) = \frac{\partial c_v(Y^c)}{\partial Y}(1+t) \qquad \Rightarrow \quad Y^c(t) < Y^*.$$

Similarly, for subsidy s the output $Y^c(s)$ is given by

$$p_D(Y^c) = \frac{\partial c_v(Y^c)}{\partial Y}(1-s) \qquad \Rightarrow \quad Y^c(s) > Y^*.$$

It can be easily verified that $SW(y^c) < SW(Y^*)$ for both t and s. First, consider

$$SW(Y^c(t)) = \int_0^{Y^c} p_D(Y)dY - c_v(Y^c(t)) = \int_0^{Y^c}\left[p_D(Y) - \frac{\partial c_v(Y)}{\partial Y}\right]dY.$$

Note that to calculate SW we have subtracted only the production cost of Y^c but not the tax part, because tax is not part of the true social cost of production. For social welfare, what matters is the utility consumers get and what truly costs to provide it. In the previous equation, by subtracting and adding $SW(Y^*)$, we rewrite $SW(Y^c)$ as

$$SW(Y^c(t)) = \int_0^{Y^*}\left[p_D(Y) - \frac{\partial c_v(Y)}{\partial Y}\right]dY + \int_0^{Y^c}\left[p_D(Y) - \frac{\partial c_v(Y)}{\partial Y}\right]dY - \int_0^{Y^*}\left[p_D(Y) - \frac{\partial c_v(Y)}{\partial Y}\right]dY$$

$$= SW(Y^*) - \int_{Y^c}^{Y^*}\left[\underbrace{p_D(Y) - \frac{\partial c_v(Y)}{\partial Y}}_{>0 \text{ for } Y^c(t)<Y^*}\right]dY. \tag{9.7}$$

Thus, $SW(Y^c(t)) < SW(Y^*)$. Similarly, when there is subsidy, we can write

$$SW(Y^c(s)) = SW(Y^*) + \int_{Y^*}^{Y^c}\left[\underbrace{p_D(Y) - \frac{\partial c_v(Y)}{\partial Y}}_{<0 \text{ for } Y^c(s)>Y^*}\right]dY. \tag{9.8}$$

In either case, the DWL is given by

$$SW(Y^*) - SW(Y^c(t)) = \int_{Y^c}^{Y^*}\left[p_D(Y) - \frac{\partial c_v(Y)}{\partial Y}\right]dY \qquad (DWL \text{ due to tax}),$$

$$SW(Y^*) - SW(Y^c(s)) = \int_{Y^*}^{Y^c}\left[\frac{\partial c_v(Y)}{\partial Y} - p_D(Y)\right]dY \qquad (DWL \text{ due to subsidy}).$$

The social welfare loss due to taxation or subsidy is given by the area between the MC curve (or the supply curve) and the demand curve between Y^c and Y^*.

9.6.1.1 *Example*

An example may be useful. Take a linear (inverse) demand curve $p = a - bY_D$ and a linear (inverse) supply curve $p = d + cY_S$. The equilibrium is $Y^* = \frac{a-d}{b+c}, p^* = \frac{ac+bd}{b+c}; a > d$. We calculate CS and PS as

$$CS = \int_0^{Y^*} (a - bY)dY - p^*Y^* = \frac{b(a-d)^2}{2(b+c)^2}$$

$$PS = p^*Y^* - \int_0^{Y^*} (d + cY)dY = \frac{c(a-d)^2}{2(b+c)^2}.$$

The gains from trade or maximum social welfare is

$$SW = \frac{(c+b)(a-d)^2}{2(b+c)^2} = \frac{(a-d)^2}{2(b+c)}.$$

9.6.1.1.1 SALES TAX

Let us now consider a sales tax, also called goods and services tax or value-added tax, that is applied to the value of the good (*ad valorem tax*). Suppose the price received by the producers is r (producer price) and the price paid by the consumers is p (market price), while $p = r(1+t)$. The tax t is imposed on the producer price as a fixed percentage. Thus, our market is described by the following three equations:

$$p = a - bY_D, \qquad r = d + cY_S, \qquad \text{and} \qquad p = r(1+t).$$

The equilibrium output, producer price and market price are

$$Y^c = \frac{a - d(1+t)}{b + c(1+t)}, \qquad r^c = \frac{ac+bd}{b+c(1+t)}, \qquad p^c = \frac{ac+bd}{b+c(1+t)}(1+t).$$

9.6.1.1.1.1 Tax incidence A frequently asked question is, To what extent will the final price increase after the tax? An increase in market price reflects the consumer's burden of the tax. In general, consumers do not bear the full burden of the tax increase; it is allocated between the consumers and producers, and the allocation depends on the price elasticity of demand. Only in some special cases will consumers fully bear the tax burden.

Here, we should be careful in calculating how much of the tax is applied per unit of the output. If the sales tax is 20% of the price of the good, which is say \$5 (received by the producers), then the *tax burden per unit of output* is \$1. This is because the sales tax is a proportional tax. By comparison, if the tax is an excise tax, which is applied directly to per unit of output, then a tax of \$1 is also the tax burden per unit of output regardless of what price is charged. An excise tax is also called a unit tax or a fixed-per-unit tax. But in the proportional case, like the example shown here, the tax burden (per unit of Y) is rt, a proportion of the producer price. In our example, from an increase in the tax rate of t, the tax burden (per unit of output) increases to

$$\frac{\partial(tr^c)}{\partial t} = r^c + t\frac{\partial r^c}{\partial t} = r^c - \frac{ctr^c}{b+c(1+t)} = \frac{(b+c)}{b+c(1+t)}r^c. \tag{9.9}$$

This is the effect of the tax rate on the tax burden per unit of output, and the consumers' share in it is reflected in the *increase* in the market price, while the producers' share is reflected in the *decrease* in the producer price. That is,

$$\text{Increase in tax burden:} \quad \left|\frac{\partial r^c}{\partial t}\right| + \frac{\partial p^c}{\partial t} = \frac{\partial(tr^c)}{\partial t},$$

which can be verified by the following derivatives:

$$\frac{\partial r^c}{\partial t} = -\frac{c(ac+bd)}{(b+c(1+t))^2} = -\frac{cr^c}{b+c(1+t)}, \qquad \frac{\partial p^c}{\partial t} = \frac{b(ac+bd)}{(b+c(1+t))^2} = \frac{br^c}{b+c(1+t)}.$$

The consumers' share of the tax burden will get larger if b increases, that is, if the demand curve gets steeper. In particular, starting from a situation of $t = 0$ (where $r^* = p^*$), if a tax is introduced consumers' tax burden will be (as a ratio of the initial price):

$$\left.\frac{\partial p^c}{\partial t}\right|_{t=0} = \frac{b}{(b+c)}\frac{(ac+bd)}{(b+c)} = \frac{b}{b+c}p^c \qquad \text{or,} \quad \left.\frac{\partial p^c/\partial t}{p^c}\right|_{t=0} = \frac{b}{b+c} < 1.$$

In the extreme case of a fully inelastic demand curve where $b \to \infty$, the entire tax burden will be borne by the consumers. This applies to goods like medicine, food grains and extremely necessary goods. The other extreme case is $c \to \infty$, where the supply curve is vertical. In that case, the producers cannot cut back production and have to fully absorb the tax burden. The market price obviously will not change.

9.6.1.1.2 CONSUMER SUBSIDY

During the COVID-19 pandemic, the UK government ran a temporary restaurant support scheme in England called 'Eat out to Help out' in which the restaurants were to receive per diner a subsidy of 50% of the bill with a subsidy cap of £10.[9] The Indian government runs a cooking gas subsidy programme in which consumers pay the market price and the subsidy arrives in their bank accounts. These subsidy stories can be modelled in the same way as the tax case by writing $t = -s$. It does not matter whether we incorporate tax/subsidy on the demand side or supply side, the formal analysis is equivalent to each other. Here we will show how the subsidy can be introduced on the demand side.

The demand and the supply curves are as before, but we modify the producer price as $r = p(1+s)$. That is, the producers collect the subsidy as a percentage of the market price, which is paid by the consumers.[10] Here, the relation between the producer price and the market price is $r = p(1+s)$. The equilibrium quantity and prices are

$$Y^c = \frac{a(1+s)-d}{c+b(1+s)}, \qquad p^c = \frac{ac+bd}{c+b(1+s)}, \qquad r^c = \frac{ac+bd}{c+b(1+s)}(1+s).$$

The subsidy per unit of output is sp^c, which changes from an increase in s as follows:

$$\frac{\partial(sp^c)}{\partial s} = p^c - \frac{bsp^c}{c+b(1+s)} = \frac{b+c}{c+b(1+s)} p^c. \tag{9.10}$$

An increase in the subsidy rate increases the subsidy benefit per unit of output, and it will be distributed between the producers and the consumers. The producer's share of the marginal subsidy benefit is given by the increase in r^c and the consumers' share of the marginal subsidy benefit is given by the fall in the market price p^c. Therefore,

$$\frac{\partial r^c}{\partial s} + \left|\frac{\partial p^c}{\partial s}\right| = \frac{cp^c}{c+b(1+s)} + \frac{bp^c}{c+b(1+s)} = \frac{b+c}{c+b(1+s)} p^c = \frac{\partial(sp^c)}{\partial s}.$$

Figure 9.9 illustrates the previously discussed tax and subsidy stories. In panel a, we show how the tax case can be illustrated by shifting the supply curve. Before tax, we have the usual efficient equilibrium (Y^*, p^*). After tax, the equilibrium moves to (Y^c, p^c). The tax component creates a wedge between what the producers receive (r^c) and what the consumers pay (p^c). The social welfare after the tax can be decomposed into CS, PS and tax revenue. Mind that tax revenue is a fund vested with the government that can be used for some social purposes. Therefore, it should be counted as part of social welfare. However, as the equilibrium output Y^c is strictly less than the efficient output Y^*, some gains from trade go unexploited. This is our DWL marked by the triangle. We can calculate it as

$$DWL(t) = (Y^* - Y^c)\frac{tr^c}{2} = \frac{(ac+bd)^2}{2(b+c)[b+c(1+t)]^2} t^2.$$

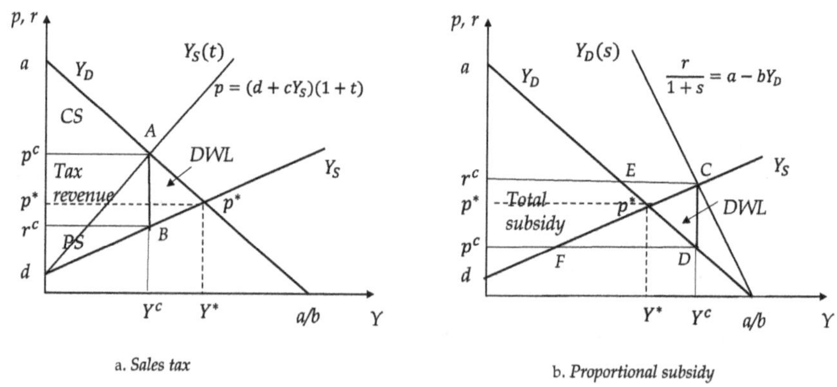

Figure 9.9 Tax, subsidy and welfare loss

In panel *b*, we show the subsidy case, but we work through the demand curve to demonstrate that you can shift either curve for graphical illustration, as well as how to define what consumers pay and what producers receive. Subsidy here is sent to the producers, so it is shown to be applied on the market price p, which the consumers actually pay. If the market price is p^c, then the consumers' demand matches with the supply, because based on p^c, the producers receive $r^c = p^c(1+s)$, exactly what is needed to supply Y^c. To determine the output, we therefore equate the actual supply curve with the 'effective demand curve' $Y_D(s)$ (expressed as a function of r) given by the equation $\frac{r}{1+s} = a - bY_D$, and once we derive Y^c, we read the market price from the actual demand curve. Note here that the market price p^c is strictly less than p^* and the output Y^c exceeds the efficient output Y^*.

Social welfare in the subsidy case should be read as [*CS* + *PS* – Total subsidy], because to provide the subsidy, the government may have to borrow and a debt obligation will be inflicted on the society. However, there are compensating gains as well but only up to a point. Total subsidy is given by the area $p^c r^c CD$, which can be decomposed into three parts: (1) area $p^c FCr^c$, which goes to the producers as part of their producer surplus; (2) area FDp^*, which goes to the consumer as part of their consumer surplus; and (3) area $p^* DC$, which covers the production cost of additional output $(Y^c - Y^*)$. But the additional production uses up too many resources that cost more relative to their social benefits (at the margin). So this part is our DWL, which is exactly

$$DWL(s) = (Y^c - Y^*)\frac{sp^c}{2} = \frac{(ac+bd)^2}{2(b+c)[c+b(1+s)]^2}s^2.$$

We should be mindful that in the tax case, the DWL is due to *underproduction* and consequent non-realisation of full potential, while in the subsidy case, it is due to *overproduction* and wastage of resources.

9.7 Contestable market

A closely related idea of the long-run equilibrium of perfect competition is contestability. Baumol et al. (1982) proposed a new theory of competition called the theory of contestable markets, in which firms can have market powers (in the sense that they can set any price they want) but they face a constant threat of entry. The constant threat of entry is underpinned by the assumption that there is no sunk cost. Because of this threat, existing firms' profits will always be zero and so will any entrant's. But since they are not necessarily price takers, in equilibrium, price can deviate from MC, yet $p = AC$ equality will be maintained. In contrast, under perfect competition, we must always have $p = MC = AC$ in the long run.

An important implication of $p = AC \neq MC$ is that IRS technology can be accommodated into this framework. In other words, contestable markets do not impose any restriction on production technology, except that there is no sunk cost. But a sunk cost (as explained earlier) does not always have to be technological; economic factors (such as a rental clause) also determine sunk cost. Once we remove sunk costs, the fear of *hit-and-run* entry will keep the existing firms at bay so that they will charge a price just large enough to cover their costs and yet collectively serve the whole market. With this notion of competition, a contestable market can have a single firm, yet it will fail to earn any super-normal profit.

Some interesting examples of contestable markets are trucking, telecommunications, airlines, railways etc. Roads are publicly owned. So if there is an active rental market for trucks (in general there is), entry and exit into and from the trucking industry would be easy. The same argument applies to airlines, because of the aircraft lease markets and because ownership of an airport is usually vested with a different entity than airlines. Previously (up to the early 1980s), ownership of telephone cable network permitted a monopoly in the downstream telephone services. However, with the famous break-up of AT&T (in the United States) and subsequent decoupling of the call provision from cable usage for carrying calls the telecommunication market became contestable. The American experience was emulated in many countries. Later, with the advent of mobile communication technology, that monopoly completely disappeared. However, railways are a much trickier case, because the rail lines and their associated infrastructure require high and recurrent costs for maintenance and upgrades. A similar argument applies to the electricity industry as well. Sunk costs in these industries are so large that they can be removed from the firms by deregulation, but they cannot be made to disappear from the industry. So for these markets, achieving contestability through privatisation and deregulation has remained a big challenge. Here, contestability is likely to be restricted only at end uses, such as passenger ferrying, goods freight and electricity retailing.

Some economists, such as Schwartz and Reynolds (1983) and Weitzman (1983), questioned to what extent hit-and-run entry is possible to make contestability work where perfect competition does not. After all, the time to enter a market (or entry cost in general) is rarely insignificant. Even for an airline until a plane is filled to capacity, cost can hardly be reduced to minimum on an average basis. Baumol et al. (1983) argued that it is not the length of time to enter a market that is crucial. A potential entrant (as in the case of airlines) can sell tickets in advance *conditional* on entry (or subject to filling the plane, in the airline example). That is enough to force the incumbent firms to lower their price and surrender the profit to the consumers.

The idea of contestability has been well received in modern industrial economics. The theory of contestable markets can be seen as a generalisation of the notion of competition. All perfectly competitive markets are contestable markets, but all contestable markets are not perfectly competitive. The parable of perfect competition relies on *actual* competition, but that of contestable markets directs our attention to *potential* competition.

9.8 General equilibrium with production

9.8.1 *The Crusoe economy*

We now briefly return to the theme of general equilibrium but this time by allowing production *albeit* in a rudimentary way. Our goal is to demonstrate that production can be integrated with exchange in the equilibrium framework and the simplest way to do that is to consider a one-producer–one-consumer economy, commonly called the Crusoe economy in reference to the fictional shipwrecked sailor Robinson Crusoe who was marooned in an uninhabited island. His survival can be seen as running a one-person economy, where he had to act like a producer employing himself as a worker in the morning and then turns into a consumer in the afternoon. Essentially, his three selves—a producer, a worker and a consumer—are engaged in trade.

Crusoe as producer has a (strictly concave) technology to produce $y = f(L)$ from labour input L supplied by himself as a worker. In return, he receives wL as wages and then later, as a producer, profit from production. All profit and wages are combined into the income of Crusoe the consumer. All actors are price takers.

As producer, he maximises profit $\pi = pf(L) - wL$. From the first-order condition, $pf'(L) - w = 0$, we derive his labour demand function $L_d(p,w)$. We also have a supply function as $y = f(L(p,w))$, or simply $y_s(p,w)$, and, in turn, his profit $\pi(p,w)$.

Crusoe the consumer maximises utility $u(y,l)$ subject to his total budget constraint $py \le w(T-l) + \pi(p,w)$, where l is his leisure consumed out of his total available time T; the rest of the time is his labour. His demand for the good as $y_d(p,w)$ and the supply of labour as $L_s(p,w) = T - l(p,w)$.

A Walrasian equilibrium in this economy is a price pair (p^*, w^*) such that

$$y_d(p^*,w^*) = y_s(p^*,w^*) \qquad \text{and} \qquad L_d(p^*,w^*) = L_s(p^*,w^*).$$

In Figure 9.10, we draw Crusoe's twin problem of production and consumption. In the left panel, we have drawn his production function by going leftward from point T to read his labour supply on the horizontal axis. Going rightward from the origin, we read leisure. His preference for the final good y and leisure l is shown by the indifference curve u. As a producer, he is searching for the highest iso-profit line, $\pi = py - wL$, which is tangent to the production function at point D_F. This means that his profit is maximum at labour demand L_F, which produces y_F. The profit generated by (L_F, y_F) constitutes the budget $B(p,w)$ for Crusoe the consumer. The budget line is given by the same iso-profit line. The budget line is tangent to his indifference curve at D_C, which means as a consumer, Crusoe wants to have l_C hours of leisure and consume y_C amount of the good. Since his labour supply falls short of his labour demand, and correspondingly his output supply is greater than his output demand, we have to conclude that the prices are not right at point D_F. For both labour and output markets, to clear his indifference curve must be tangent to the production function, in which case the budget line or the iso-profit line should pass through

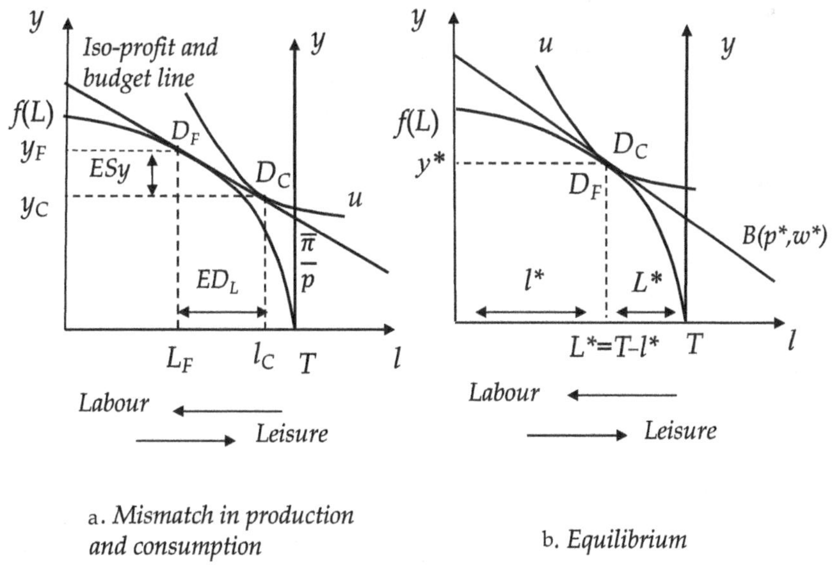

Figure 9.10 Equilibrium in a Crusoe economy

between them, as shown on the right panel. Points D_F and D_C coincide here, and therefore, the supply and demand in both markets perfectly match. The budget line now has a different slope given by the price ratio w^* / p^*, which is precisely our general equilibrium price in this one-consumer–one-producer economy. This equilibrium is also Pareto optimal, because anywhere else, Crusoe the producer cannot do better without making Crusoe the consumer worse off.

9.8.2 *A two-factor two-good model*

A general equilibrium model of multiple factors and goods can be constructed by extending our exchange model of Chapter 6 by incorporating production. Two important issues should be paid attention to. First, production technologies should be convex; that is, they should exhibit non-increasing returns to scale. Second, all income from profit and factor ownership should be distributed among consumers, because all factors and firms are privately owned. With these modifications, all the insights and results of the endowment exchange model will hold. So we will not pursue that here.[11]

Instead, we will take up a simple two-by-two model with some special assumptions, which we have adapted from Mas-Colell et al. (1995, pp. 535–537). Let us think of an extension of our Crusoe economy. Imagine Crusoe shares the island with his brother. Together, they own all the physical resources of this economy, which we denote by x_2, and their labour input is denoted by x_1. Each input has a total availability constraint: $x_1 \leq \bar{x}_1$ and $x_2 \leq \bar{x}_2$. More importantly, we assume that neither the resources, including their leisure time, nor the goods they produce have any direct utility to them. They sell their goods overseas and import foreign goods to consume. Thus, our problem reduces to analysing the problem of two firms, that must optimally allocate two resources to maximise their profits. Let us call them firm A and B. Since each firm produces one good, their identity is synonymous with the identity of the good. In the spirit of perfect competition, both firms are assumed to be price takers for all goods and resources.

Our special set-up rules out solving for the goods' prices, which are determined in the international market. So our sole objective is to determine the equilibrium factor prices and factor allocations between the two firms. For a formal presentation of the model, let us denote x_{ij} as the allocation of input j in firm i. Thus, x_{1B} is the labour (input 1) used in firm B. Let us now specify our key assumptions.

Assumption 5.

1. *The input availability constraints are* $x_{1A} + x_{1B} \leq \bar{x}_1$ and $x_{2A} + x_{2B} \leq \bar{x}_2$.
2. *Production technologies are:* $y_A = F(x_{1A}, x_{2A})$ and $y_B = G(x_{1B}, x_{2B})$, $F(.) \neq G(.)$.
3. *Both* F(.) *and* G(.) *exhibit constant returns to scale.*
4. *Firms are price takers, and they maximise profits.*
5. *Prices of the goods are fixed at* p_A *and* p_B, *respectively.*

There are several points to note:

1. The input availability constraints give rise to an Edgeworth box for resources, in a very similar way to the endowment exchange model. The size of the box is given by $(\bar{x}_1, \bar{x}_2)$ and we can map each factor allocation vector onto the output space (y_A, y_B) via firms' isoquants. However, there is a difference. There is no endowment point for the firms. That is because the resources have no direct consumption value to the firms (or our Crusoe brothers). It is irrelevant which firm owns how much of each of the resources. The resources are valued at

the market price and bought and sold as desired. This is why we did not specify any market features of the inputs.

Having said that, we should recognise that in reality, things can be different due to market imperfections. For instance, in developing countries, when leasing out his land, a landowner may face a lower income prospect than if he organises production himself. Factor endowment creates a self-employment option, which may affect an individual's income. But in our set-up, it will not.

2. Technological asymmetry is important. If firms use identical technology, then the only source of their choice difference would be the difference in the product prices. But we are interested in their differences of factor intensity. We would like to see that in equilibrium, one firm is intensive in factor 1 and the other firm in factor 2.
3. We have specified CRS for production technologies and profit maximisation as a firm objective. How can these two be compatible? Earlier we said that profit maximisation is compatible only with diminishing returns technology. That argument is correct when firms do not face any input supply constraint. But in the special set-up of the two-factor two-good model, input supply constraints and technological asymmetry work together to bring in diminishing returns.

To elaborate the preceding points further, we first show that the following two problems are identical.

Market problem:

$$\text{Max} \quad \pi_A = p_A F(.,.) - \sum_{j=1}^{2} w_j x_{jA} \qquad \text{Max} \quad \pi_B = p_B G(.,.) - \sum_{j=1}^{2} w_j x_{jB}$$

$$\text{sub. to} \quad x_{1A} + x_{1B} = \bar{x}_1 \qquad \text{sub. to} \quad x_{1A} + x_{1B} = \bar{x}_1$$

$$x_{2A} + x_{2B} = \bar{x}_2 \qquad x_{2A} + x_{2B} = \bar{x}_2$$

and the *social planner's problem*:

$$\text{Max} \quad R_A + R_B = p_A F(x_{1A}, x_{2A}) + p_B G(x_{1B}, x_{2B})$$

$$\text{sub. to} \quad x_{1A} + x_{1B} = \bar{x}_1$$

$$x_{2A} + x_{2B} = \bar{x}_2$$

The first problem is a decentralised decision-making problem in which two firms individually try to maximise their profits within the framework of a market where input prices guide them to make the correct decisions. The second problem is a *centralised* decision-making problem in which the social planner, who looks after only the collective interests, tries to decide how many units of each input should go to each firm. Here market prices of the inputs are absent. This problem resembles that of a cartel formed by the two brothers, except that the cartel has no price-setting power.

The solution to the market problem is $\{(x_{1A}^*, x_{2A}^*), (x_{1B}^*, x_{2B}^*), (w_1^*, w_2^*)\}$, which is given by the following set of equations:

$$p_A F_1(x_{1A}^*, x_{2A}^*) = w_1^* \qquad p_A F_2(x_{1A}^*, x_{2A}^*) = w_2^*,$$

$$p_B G_1(x_{1B}^*, x_{2B}^*) = w_1^* \qquad p_B G_2(x_{1B}^*, x_{2B}^*) = w_2^*,$$

$$x_{1A}^* + x_{1B}^* = \bar{x}_1, \qquad \text{and} \qquad x_{2A}^* + x_{2B}^* = \bar{x}_2.$$

The solution to the social planner's problem is $\{(x_{1A}^*, x_{2A}^*), (x_{1B}^*, x_{2B}^*)\}$ given by

$$p_A F_1(x_{1A}^*, x_{2A}^*) = p_B G_1(x_{1B}^*, x_{2B}^*), \qquad p_A F_2(x_{1A}^*, x_{2A}^*) = p_B G_2(x_{1B}^*, x_{2B}^*),$$
$$x_{1A}^* + x_{1B}^* = \bar{x}_1, \qquad \text{and} \qquad x_{2A}^* + x_{2B}^* = \bar{x}_2.$$

Two sets of equations give exactly the same allocations of inputs. Therefore, the two problems are equivalent. In the left panel of Figure 9.11, we have drawn the production possibility frontier (PPF) that describes how much y_B can be efficiently produced for any given amount of y_A. The PPF reflects both the availability constraints $\bar{x}_1$ and $\bar{x}_2$ and the production technologies $F(.)$ and $G(.)$. The frontier itself maps the Pareto- (or technically) efficient allocations of inputs (PEIAs) that are shown on the right panel inside the Edgeworth box. From the left origin O, we draw firm A's isoquants; three such isoquants are marked by y_A^0, y_A^* and y_A'. The bottom horizontal axis reads firm A's use of input x_1 while the left vertical axis reads firm A's use of input x_2. The top horizontal axis and the right vertical axis read firm B's use of inputs x_1 and x_2, respectively. Origin O' is the starting point of B. Two isoquants of B are y_B^* and y_B'. The PEIAs are given by the tangency points of the two firms' isoquants. The dashed curve OO' is the set of Pareto-efficient allocations consisting of the points like A, B and C. Pareto-efficient allocations (x_1, x_2) correspond to (y_A, y_B) on the PPF. The shape of the PPF is given by the PEIA curve OO'. For CRS technology, if the PEIA curve deviates from the diagonal line, the corresponding PPF will be as shown in Figure 9.11.

Given the goods prices (p_A, p_B), the social planner would pick point E, where the joint revenues are maximised by producing (y_A^*, y_B^*). Then moving on to panel b, he selects point B, which gives the optimal allocation of inputs to produce y_A^* and y_B^*. The same solution is also the decentralised choice of firms that are individually made through market. The iso-cost line with slope w_1 / w_2 is tangent to both firms' optimal isoquants. Thereby, the equilibrium input price ratio is also determined.

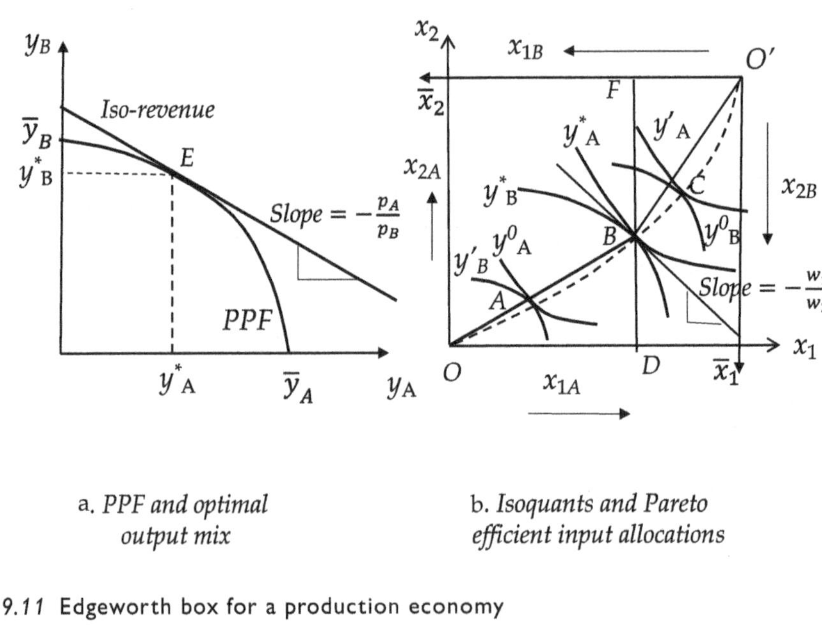

Figure 9.11 Edgeworth box for a production economy

Here, we take note of an important feature of the PEIAs. From panel *b* we see that in equilibrium, firm *A*'s factor intensity x_{2A} / x_{1A} is given by the slope of the line *OB*, while firm *B*'s factor intensity is given by the slope of the line *O′B* (which is equal to $BF / O'F$). Clearly, as we have drawn, the factor intensity of firm *B* is greater, which means that firm *B*'s production is intensive in input x_2 and that firm *A*'s production is intensive in input x_1. You can see that firm *A*'s greater factor intensity in input x_1 holds true not just at equilibrium point *D* but at all points on the PEIA curve *OO′*.

9.8.2.1 *Example*

Let us learn a bit more about Pareto allocations with an example. Suppose $F(x_{1A}, x_{2A}) = x_{1A}^{\frac{2}{3}} x_{2A}^{\frac{1}{3}}$ and $G(x_{1B}, x_{2B}) = x_{1B}^{\frac{1}{3}} x_{2B}^{\frac{2}{3}}$. Substituting the availability constraints we can write $G(.,.) = (\bar{x}_1 - x_{1A})^{\frac{1}{3}} (\bar{x}_2 - x_{2A})^{\frac{2}{3}}$. From this, we derive

$$MRTS_A = 2\frac{x_{2A}}{x_{1A}}, \qquad MRTS_B = \frac{1}{2}\frac{(\bar{x}_2 - x_{2A})}{(\bar{x}_1 - x_{1A})}.$$

Setting $MRTS_A = MRTS_B$ we get the equation for PEIA:

$$x_{2A} = \frac{x_{1A}\bar{x}_2}{4\bar{x}_1 - 3x_{1A}} \qquad \text{with} \qquad \frac{\partial x_{2A}}{\partial x_{1A}} = \frac{4\bar{x}_1\bar{x}_2}{(4\bar{x}_1 - 3x_{1A})^2} > 0 \quad \text{and} \quad \frac{\partial^2 x_{2A}}{\partial x_{1A}^2} > 0.$$

The relation between the PEIA and the PPF is shown in Figure 9.12. A diagonal PEIA curve (line *B*) has equal factor intensity for the two goods, and it will correspond to a linear PPF as shown by line *B* on panel *a*. If the PEIA curve is below the diagonal line, output y_A is intensive in input x_1 (relative to the equal factor intensity line), and output y_B is intensive in input x_2. That is,

$$\frac{x_{1A}(w_1^*, w_2^*)}{x_{2A}(w_1^*, w_2^*)} > \frac{x_{1B}(w_1^*, w_2^*)}{x_{2B}(w_1^*, w_2^*)},$$

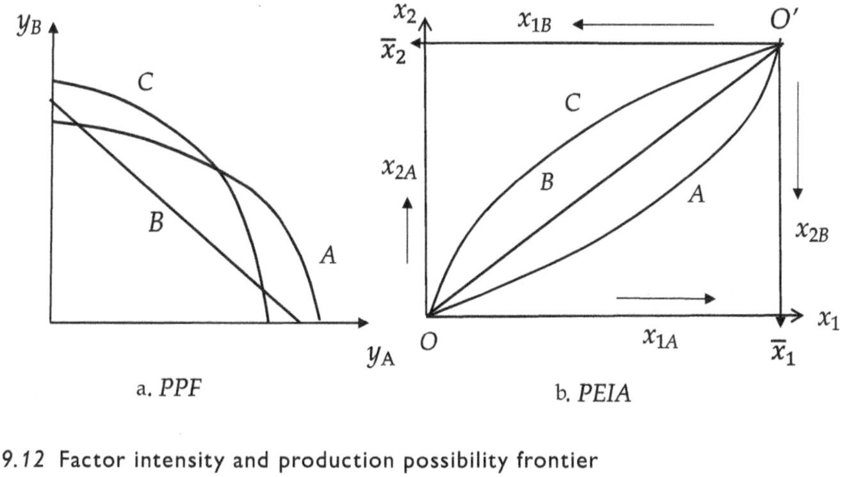

Figure 9.12 Factor intensity and production possibility frontier

which is evident from the lower ratio x_{2A}/x_{1A} than x_{2B}/x_{1B} along the PEIA curve A. Its associated PPF is as shown by curve A on the left panel. A PEIA curve above the diagonal line, like C, shows output y_B being intensive in input x_1. Its PPF will also be concave-shaped but with a greater y_B (curve C). Three PPFs are drawn based on the assumption that $\bar{x}_1 > \bar{x}_2$ as we have depicted on panel b. The PPF intercepts vary depending on which factor is in relative abundance and which good is intensive in the abundant input. The y_A intercept of PPF marked A is largest because here, y_A is intensive in the abundant input x_1.

9.8.2.2 *Comparative statics*

Now we turn our attention to two important comparative static results. The first result concerns the effect of an increase in the (relative) product price. How does an increase in p_A impact the equilibrium input prices? To answer this question, let us start with a key implication of the assumption of CRS: firms must make zero profit. In addition, the cost function of both firms must be of the form $c_i(w_1, w_2, y_i) = y_i c(w_1, w_2, 1)$ for $i = A, B$. Remember that under CRS, cost simply scales up or down proportionately with the output being scaled up or down. Therefore, zero profit means in equilibrium:

$$c_A(w_1^*, w_2^*, 1) = p_A \qquad \text{and} \qquad c_B(w_1^*, w_2^*, 1) = p_B. \tag{9.11}$$

For an increase in p_A, we can derive the comparative static effects (using Shephard's lemma and Cramer's rule) as

$$\frac{\partial w_1^*}{\partial p_A} = \frac{\begin{vmatrix} 1 & \dfrac{\partial c_A(.)}{\partial w_2} \\ 0 & \dfrac{\partial c_B(.)}{\partial w_2} \end{vmatrix}}{\begin{vmatrix} \dfrac{\partial c_A(.)}{\partial w_1} & \dfrac{\partial c_A(.)}{\partial w_2} \\ \dfrac{\partial c_B(.)}{\partial w_1} & \dfrac{\partial c_B(.)}{\partial w_2} \end{vmatrix}} = \frac{\begin{vmatrix} 1 & x_{2A}^* \\ 0 & x_{2B}^* \end{vmatrix}}{\begin{vmatrix} x_{1A}^* & x_{2A}^* \\ x_{1B}^* & x_{2B}^* \end{vmatrix}} = \frac{x_{2B}^*}{x_{1A}^* x_{2B}^* - x_{1B}^* x_{2A}^*}. \tag{9.12}$$

Similarly,

$$\frac{\partial w_2^*}{\partial p_A} = \frac{\begin{vmatrix} x_{1A}^* & 1 \\ x_{1B}^* & 0 \end{vmatrix}}{\begin{vmatrix} x_{1A}^* & x_{2A}^* \\ x_{1B}^* & x_{2B}^* \end{vmatrix}} = -\frac{x_{1B}^*}{x_{1A}^* x_{2B}^* - x_{1B}^* x_{2A}^*}. \tag{9.13}$$

The denominator is positive if y_A is intensive in x_1. From this analysis, an important theorem follows.

Theorem 8. (Stolper–Samuelson theorem) *Suppose that in a two-factor two-good economy, technologies are CRS, inputs are non-reproducible and non-traded (externally), firms are price takers and goods prices are exogenously given. Then an increase in* p_A *will lead to an increase in* w_1 *and a decrease in* w_2 *if and only if* y_A *is intensive in input* x_1*. The converse is true if and only if* y_B *is intensive in* x_1*. Formally,*

$$\frac{\partial w_1^*}{\partial p_A} > 0 \quad \text{and} \quad \frac{\partial w_2^*}{\partial p_A} < 0, \quad \text{if and only if} \quad \frac{x_{1A}^*}{x_{2A}^*} > \frac{x_{1B}^*}{x_{2B}^*}. \tag{9.14}$$

Consequently, the factor intensity x_{1A} / x_{2A} *will fall while* x_{1B} / x_{2B} *will rise while still good* A *remains intensive in input 1.*

The key result of the Stolper–Samuelson theorem as given by Eq. (9.14) is a direct implication of Eqs. (9.12) and (9.13). The key message of the theorem is that gains from export will be passed on to the workers if the exported good is labour-intensive. Alternatively, if, in the international market, capital-intensive goods become dearer, then workers will lose. An additional point of the theorem is that despite wage gains and reduced employment output *A* will be supplied in greater volume, and it will remain labour-intensive if its production technology has a bias toward labour (as reflected in the PEIA curve). The theorem appeared in a 1939 classic paper by Wolfgang Stolper and Paul Samuelson and has remained a fundamental building block of neoclassical trade theory.[12]

Figure 9.13 illustrates how the Stolper–Samuelson theorem works. In panel *a*, we register the increase in p_A by a right and downward shift of the iso-revenue curve. The new tangency point moves to E' showing that the output of y_A must increase and that of y_B must decrease. In panel *b*, we show the firms' zero-profit condition on the (w_1, w_2) plane by drawing an iso-cost curve for each firm for one unit of output. This cost must be equal to the price of the good to ensure zero profit. Thus, at the initial price vector (p_A, p_B), we have $c_A(w_1, w_2, 1) = p_A$ and $c_B(w_1, w_2, 1) = p_B$. Their intersection at point *D* gives the initial equilibrium input prices (w_1^*, w_2^*).

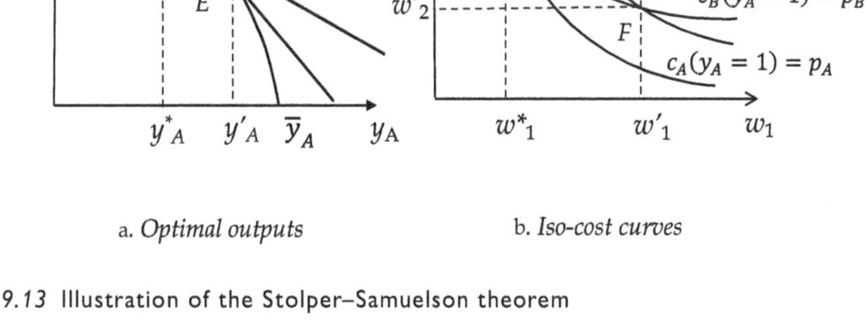

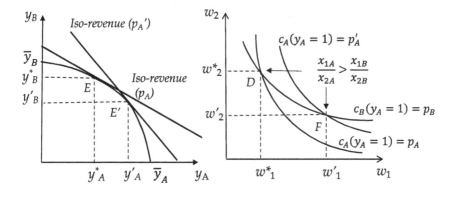

a. *Optimal outputs* b. *Iso-cost curves*

Figure 9.13 Illustration of the Stolper–Samuelson theorem

The assumption that good A is intensive in input x_1 is reflected in the fact that $c_A(.)$ is steeper than $c_B(.)$ at their intersection point. Recall that by Shephard's lemma, the slope of the cost function gives the ratio of input demand functions. That is,

$$\frac{\partial c_A(.)}{\partial w_1} / \frac{\partial c_A(.)}{\partial w_2} = \frac{x_{1A}(w_1, w_2)}{x_{2A}(w_1, w_2)} \quad \text{and} \quad \frac{\partial c_B(.)}{\partial w_1} / \frac{\partial c_B(.)}{\partial w_2} = \frac{x_{1B}(w_1, w_2)}{x_{2B}(w_1, w_2)}.$$

So the steeper $c_A(.)$ curve confirms that $x_{1A} / x_{2A} > x_{1B} / x_{2B}$.

Now with an increase in p_A, the cost curve $c_A(.)$ shifts upward to match the higher price at P_A'. But $c_B(.)$ does not move. Consequently, a new intersection occurs at point F, registering a rise in w_1 and a fall in w_2. This means the ratio of the inputs x_1 / x_2 must fall for output A and must rise for output B. Despite this fall in the input mix in firm A, the factor intensity, however, will not be reversed.

In the second question, we ask if one of the two inputs is available in a greater quantity how our equilibrium prices and factor allocation will change. This question was answered by Tadeusz Rybcszynski in a 1955 paper that also went on to become a fundamental result in trade theory. The result, known as the Rybcszynski theorem, states that if an input's availability increases in our special model, the relative input prices will not change, but the production of the good in which the 'more available' input is intensively used in equilibrium will expand and the production of the other good will contract. To state it formally, let us assume without loss of generality that $\bar{x}_1$ increases.

Theorem 9. (Rybcszynski theorem) *In a two-factor two-good economy of the kind described earlier, an increase in $\bar{x}_1$ (the total availability of x_1) will leave the price ratio of inputs unchanged and lead to an increase in the production of y_A and a decrease in the production of y_B, if and only if y_A is intensive in input x_1. Similarly, an increase in $\bar{x}_2$ will lead to a contraction of y_A and an increase in y_B if y_B is intensive in x_2.*

The Rybcszynski result is striking, and the claims are remarkably strong. There are two parts which may appear puzzling. First, one may jump to conclude that if more labour is available then the wage rate relative to the price of capital should fall (a natural effect of competition in the labour market), and second, the PPF of this economy will shift out unambiguously, making an increase in the production of both goods a possibility. But that does not happen. Why? In other words, what is stopping both industries from hiring more workers and increasing production?

The answer lies in the assumption of CRS. Because of CRS, our Eq. (9.11) must hold for every unit of y_A and y_B. From panel b of Figure 9.13, we see that $c_A(.)$ and $c_B(.)$ will not move. That neither curve moves despite an increase in the equilibrium output of y_A is an artefact of the assumption of scale neutrality. Therefore, the factor intensity of neither industry will change. This means that firm A will expand the application of the two inputs proportionately and expand its output, which will then require firm B to proportionately reduce its use of both inputs. This is shown in Figure 9.14. Line A represents factor intensity for firm A, and line B represents the same for firm B. In panel a, we show an increase in $\bar{x}_1$. The initial equilibrium is at point C. Since the factor intensities of neither industry will change after an increase in $\bar{x}_1$, two (factor intensity) lines can cross each other only at point D. Therefore, the equilibrium output of y_A must rise and that of y_B must fall. The case of an increase in $\bar{x}_2$ is shown on panel b of Figure 9.14.

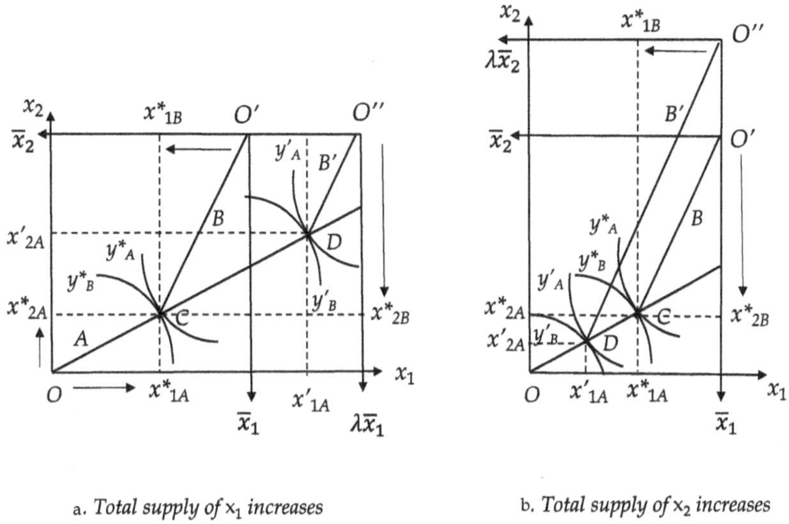

Figure 9.14 Illustration of the Rybcszynski theorem

You should convince yourself why the opposite does not happen. Why doesn't firm B expand and firm A contract when $\bar{x}_1$ increases? With a few steps, you can prove this. Suppose $\bar{x}_1$ increases to $\lambda\bar{x}_1$ where $\lambda > 1$, and the associated equilibrium input allocations change from $\{(x_{1A}^*, x_{2A}^*), (x_{1B}^*, x_{2B}^*)\}$ to $\{(x_{1A}', x_{2A}'), (x_{1B}', x_{2B}')\}$. The factor market equilibrium and factor intensities must satisfy the following:

$$x_{1A}^* + x_{1B}^* = \bar{x}_1, \qquad x_{2A}^* + x_{2B}^* = \bar{x}_2,$$

$$x_{1A}' + x_{1B}' = \lambda\bar{x}_1, \qquad x_{2A}' + x_{2B}' = \bar{x}_2,$$

$$x_{1A}^* / x_{2A}^* = \theta_1 = x_{1A}' / x_{2A}', \qquad x_{1B}^* / x_{2B}^* = \theta_2 = x_{1B}' / x_{2B}'.$$

Let us assume $\theta_1 > \theta_2$; that is, y_A is intensive in x_1. Then we can write $\theta_1 = \theta_2 + \delta$, where $\delta > 0$. From the two equilibrium conditions of the factor market for x_1, before and after the increase in $\bar{x}_1$, we can write

$$\begin{aligned}(\lambda - 1)\bar{x}_1 &= (x_{1A}' - x_{1A}^*) + (x_{1B}' - x_{1B}^*)\\ &= \theta_1(x_{2A}' - x_{2A}^*) + \theta_2(x_{2B}' - x_{2B}^*)\\ &= (\theta_2 + \delta)(x_{2A}' - x_{2A}^*) + \theta_2(x_{2B}' - x_{2B}^*)\\ &= \theta_2(x_{2A}' + x_{2B}') - \theta_2(x_{2A}^* + x_{2B}^*) + \delta(x_{2A}' - x_{2A}^*)\\ &= \delta(x_{2A}' - x_{2A}^*).\end{aligned}$$

Since the left-hand side is positive, we must have $x_{2A}' > x_{2A}^*$, which then implies $x_{2B}' < x_{2B}^*$ because $\bar{x}_2$ is unchanged. Clearly, we must also have $x_{1A}' > x_{1A}^*$ and $x_{1B}' > x_{1B}^*$ to maintain the constant factor intensities θ_1 and θ_2, respectively. This implies that y_B must contract and y_A must expand. Under the alternative factor intensity assumption of $\theta_1 < \theta_2$, we have $\delta < 0$, and then it must follow that$x'_{2A} < x^*_{2A}$.

The Stolper–Samuelson theorem and the Rybcszynski theorem both show how the many insights of the general equilibrium theory can be understood by studying the factor intensity of the traded goods. Ronald Jones (1965) later showed that the two theorems bear a duality relation. It should be clear to you that trade models are a special case of general equilibrium in which production and consumption may be separated by geographical boundaries and different sets of rules, laws and restrictions. Only in a completely globalised world with complete integration of factor and product markets will we have the full general equilibrium model. Until then, the international economy will look like our special two-factor two-good model.

It also turns out that none of the features of this special model is too special. In the trade literature, all the special assumptions of this model have been relaxed. The qualitative results remain largely valid. Even the assumption we made about having just two firms is not special. But what remains crucial is the price-taking behaviour of the firms. In the next few chapters, we will study how economic outcomes change if firms have market power.

9.9 Conclusion

Perfect competition is a hallmark of the economic paradigm. Adam Smith's vision of the invisible hand is intricately linked to markets being perfectly competitive. In this chapter, we looked at a single market and studied in detail the behaviour of firms. A key insight is when technology exhibits diminishing returns, firms' profit-maximising objectives are consistent with their price-taking behaviour, and in consequence, markets will allocate goods efficiently. Perfect competition can be easily extended to multiple markets by incorporating production into the framework of general equilibrium. We did this in a simplistic and special way and showed that the outcome of this model confirms the first fundamental theorem of welfare economics. Welfare in a competitive equilibrium cannot be improved on in the sense of Pareto.

Summary

We learnt the following:

1. The fixed cost of a firm consists of the FIC and the set-up cost, of which the FIC can remain fixed and unavoidable (or sunk) only in the short run. No cost is unavoidable in the long run. Long run differs from short run only in terms of the presence of a sunk cost in the short run.
2. For industry, *short run* means there is a fixed number of firms. In the long run, firms can freely enter or exit.
3. Profit maximisation is consistent with price-taking beahviour only with diminishing returns to factor/scale depending on short/long run.
4. There is no long-run supply curve for industry. Zero profit and identical technology dictate the long-run equilibrium price to be the minimum point of the LAC curve, at which the market demand determines how many firms can operate.
5. The market equilibrium creates maximum social welfare in the absence of any tax or subsidy. Tax creates DWL via underproduction and subsidy creates DWL via overproduction.

6. A two-good two-factor model with exogenous product prices is a useful framework for studying the implications of perfect competition in a multi-market framework.
7. The Stolper–Samuelson theorem and the Rybcszynski theorem show that interesting insights can be gained from this framework about the role of factor intensity in determining the distribution of gains from trade.

9.10 Exercises

1. Suppose n identical firms operate in a market characterised by the demand curve $p = a - Q$. firm's cost function is $c = hq^2 + H$, where γH is a sunk cost, and assume $H > \dfrac{a^2 h}{(2h+n)^2}$.

   a. Derive a firm's and the industry's short-run supply curve. Calculate the equilibrium price and output.
   b. How does your answer change if H is not a sunk cost?
   c. Derive the long-run equilibrium price, output and the equilibrium number of firms.

2. There are n_1 identical firms with cost function $C_1 = aq - bq^2 + c_1q^3 + F$, where γF is a sunk cost ($\gamma < 1$). Another n_2 identical firms have the cost function $C_2 = aq - bq^2 + c_2q^3$. Assume $c_2 > c_1$. The market demand curve is $p = A - Q$.

   a. Derive the typical short-run supply curve of a representative firm from each group. Write the aggregate supply equation and draw its graph.
   b. Discuss and distinguish between two market equilibria (in terms of output and prices), one of which corresponds to the case where only n_1 firms operate, and the other where all firms operate.
   c. Finally, consider the following long-run scenario, where $F = 0$ and $c_1 = c_2$. What would be the long-run price and market output, and equilibrium number of firms? Calculate social welfare.

3. Consider a perfectly competitive market with N identical firms each with the following cost function:

$$C = y^2 + 4 \quad \textit{for } y > 0$$
$$= 0 \quad \textit{for } y = 0.$$

   The market demand curve is given as $p = 100 - 2Y$. Assume $N < 24$.

   a. Derive the firm and industry supply curves. Obtain the equilibrium price and output. Draw a demand–supply diagram to illustrate the equilibrium.
   b. Calculate consumer surplus, individual firm profit and social welfare in the given equilibrium. Check if social welfare increases in N.

4. In a perfectly competitive market served by N identical firms each having the cost function, $C = ay^2$. The market demand curve is linear: $p = A - Y$, where Y refers to the aggregate output.

   a. Derive the equilibrium price and the market output.
   b. Now interpret the cost and demand parameters in the following way. The cost parameter a is a function of excise tax t, $a'(t) > 0$, and the demand parameter A is a function of income

tax rate τ, $A'(\tau) < 0$. Show that the equilibrium output (for the market) decreases in both t and τ, when t and τ are separately changed. Calculate DWL.

c. Next, consider a scenario where the government wants to reduce the excise tax rate t and raises τ while maintaining $d\tau / \tau = -dt / t$. Further, assume that $A(\tau) = B / \tau$ and$a(t) = \alpha t$. What will be the effect on the equilibrium output in this market when t is reduced and simultaneously τ is increased? Illustrate your answer graphically.

5. A competitive market is served by 6 identical firms each with a cost function $C = 10 + q^3 - q^2 + (5/4)q$. The market demand is given by $p = \frac{51}{12} - \frac{Q_D}{3}$.
   a. Derive the short-run equilibrium price, firm supply and social welfare.
   b. Suppose in the long run, the cost function changes to $C = q^3 - q^2 + (5/4)q$. Derive the long-run price, market output and social welfare. How many firms will operate in the long run?

6. In developing countries, many industries are characterised by technological dualism. Consider such an industry in which two groups of firms N_1 and N_2 use two different technologies so that their cost functions are $C_1 = F_1 + aq^2$ and $C_2 = F_2 + q^2$, with the restrictions $F_1 < F_2$ and $a > 1$. The market demand curve is $p = A - Q$.
   a. Derive the individual firm supply curves in the short run (assume F_1 and F_2 are sunk).
   b. Calculate the short-run equilibrium price, output and social welfare.
   c. Assume new entry into the industry is not permitted, but switching from one technology to another is. Now suppose type 2 firms are making less profit than type 1 firms, and many type 2 firms want to switch to type 1 technology. A switch will simply mean a decline in N_2 exactly matched by an increase in N_1. Can you show that industry output will decline but that an individual firm's output will increase regardless of the technologies they are using?
   d. If there is a fixed switching cost E, and if n firms (from an initial group of N_2 firms) switch from type 2 technology to type 1, then which *condition* do you need to consider to solve for n?

7. Consider an industry with n identical firms. A representative firm's total costs are given as, $C(q) = F + kq^2$, where F is sunk in the short run. The market demand curve is $p = a - bQ$, $k < a$.
   a. Calculate the short-run equilibrium price and market output.
   b. Suppose firms are making losses. To help them, the government announces a policy of giving a subsidy, but the total amount of subsidy is fixed at F for the entire industry. How does the firm's supply curve change?
   c. Is it possible that firms may stop producing because of the subsidy policy?

8. Consider a two-sector open economy with two inputs and two price-taking firms producing good A and good B, respectively. Prices of the two goods are determined internationally. Input prices are determined domestically. The supplies of two inputs are exogenously given at 1 each. Firm A's production technology is $y_A = \min\{x_{1A}, bx_{2A}\}$, $b > 1$, and firm B's production technology is $y_B = \sqrt{x_{1B}x_{2B}}$.
   a. Derive the PEIAs of the two firms and show them on an Edgeworth box diagram. Identify the factor intensity of each firm.
   b. Derive and draw the PPF of this economy.

c. Write the condition for deriving the optimal outputs (denote p_A and p_B as prices of the two goods).
d. What would be the equilibrium input price ratio? Can you comment on the effect of an increase in p_A?

Notes

1 Of course, many small businesses or modern-day digital product/service firms can run on very few fixed costs. Some of these can operate from home using the existing utilities meant for consumption like an internet connection.
2 Despite referring to different time frames, basic firm theory does not distinguish between temporary shut-down and permanent closure. The distinction is important in reality. To formally address this issue, one needs to incorporate the firm's expectations of future. Such issues are addressed in the industrial organisation literature.
3 A relevant point is that a sunk cost is not always technological; it can be economic too.
4 Note that the cost function $c(y)$ is nothing, but $c(w_1, w_2, y)$, which we derived in Chapter 8. Since the input prices are not particularly important here, we have suppressed them.
5 *Horizontal summation* refers to the convention of representing y on the horizontal axis of a supply graph.
6 Trade does not take place until the stationary equilibrium is reached.
7 You can check that the Giffen good case is captured by $b < 0$ and the backward-bending supply curve case by $\sigma < 0$. In both cases, the cobweb model generates explosive cycles (because $-\sigma / b > 0$). The only remaining case is $\sigma < 0$ and $b < 0$. But that is an absurd case.
8 Assume for this part that the entire fixed cost is sunk in the short run.
9 The subsidy here is applied to the price posted by the producers.
10 If the subsidy is directly paid to the consumers, then the market price and the producer price should be the same. But then we should define a consumer price as $\rho = p(1-s)$, where p refers to the market price. The demand curve should be written as $\rho = a - bY_D$ and the supply curve as $p = d + cY_S$. Also note that when we write $r = p(1+s)$, the basis of subsidy is the price paid by the consumers, which is slightly different to the 'Eat out to Help out' programme. Therefore, caution should be taken in defining the basis of the tax as well as the consumer and producer prices. We call the consumer price as the market price.
11 For more advanced treatment of the problem, see Mas-Colell et al. (1995).
12 In modern trade theory, it is acknowledged that factor intensity can get reversed under certain conditions. See Feenstra (2015) for theoretical arguments and Kiyota and Kurokawa (2022) for empirical evidence.

References and further readings

Baumol, W. J. (1982). Contestable markets: An uprising in the theory of industry structure. *American Economic Review*, 72, 1–15.

Baumol, W. J., Panzar, J. C. & Willig, R. D. (1982). *Contestable Markets and the Theory of Industry Structure*. San Diego: Harcourt Brace Jovanovich.

Baumol, W. J., Panzar, J. C. & Willig, R. D. (1983). Contestable markets: An uprising in the theory of industry structure: Reply. *The American Economic Review*, 73(3), 491–496.

Chiang, A. C. (1984). *Fundamental Methods of Mathematical Economics*, 3rd ed. Singapore: McGraw-Hill.

Feenstra, R. C. (2015). *Advanced International Trade: Theory and Evidence*, 2nd ed. Princeton, NJ: Princeton University Press.

Henderson, J. H. & Quandt, R. E. (1980). *Microeconomic Theory: A Mathematical Approach*, 3rd ed. Singapore: McGraw-Hill.

Johnson, H. G. (1971). *The Two-Sector Model of General Equilibrium*. Chicago, IL: Aldine-Atherton.

Jones, R. W. (1965). The structure of simple general equilibrium models. *Journal of Political Economy*, 73(6), 557–572.

Kiyota, K. & Kurokawa, Y. (2022). Factor intensity reversals redux: Feenstra is right! *Review of International Economics*, 30, 885–914.

Mas-Colell, A., Whinston, M. D. & Green, J. R. (1995). *Microeconomic Theory*. New York: Oxford University Press.

Rybcszynski, T. M. (1955). Factor endowments and relative commodity prices. *Economica*, 88, 336–341.

Schwartz, M. & Reynolds, R. J. (1983). Contestable markets: An uprising in the theory of industry structure: Comment. *American Economic Review*, 73(3), 488–900.

Stolper, W. F. & Samuelson, P. A. (1941). Protection and real wages. *Review of Economic Studies*, 9, 58–73.

Weitzman, M. L. (1983). Contestable markets: An uprising in the theory of industry structure: Comment. *American Economic Review*, 73(3), 486–487.

Chapter 10

Monopoly

Abstract

Monopoly is the least preferred market from society's point of view, except when there are economies of scale or increasing returns, or there is need for encouraging innovations. We study monopolist's pricing behaviours and their implications for social welfare. Charging a non-discriminatory single price is generally not the most profitable strategy for the monopolist. He does better by engaging in price discrimination. We discuss three types of price discrimination. Furthermore, for durable goods the monopolist experiences a significant loss in his monopoly power due to opportunities of recycling, renting and consumers' rational expectation of the monopolist's future behaviours, about which he is unable to commit in the present.

Keywords: Price-cost mark up, Natural monopoly, Regulation, Price discrimination, Two-part tariff, Durable goods monopoly, Coase conjecture

10.1 Introduction

> In 1865, when Mr. John D. Rockefeller began in a small way to refine petroleum at Cleveland, Ohio, the oil industry was in a singularly inchoate state. . . . By 1863 boats had begun transporting petroleum down Oil Creek, and small pipe-lines and branch railway lines had been built. In 1866 a more efficient cylinder refining-still was invented, casing and torpedoes were coming to be used in drilling, the tank-car began to replace the clumsy flat-car with its wooden tubs, and pipe-lines regularly transported petroleum from the wells to the railroad. . . . To secure these economies in refining, small concerns must either increase their capital to about $500,000 or else combine into this larger and more efficient unit of production. Mr. Rockefeller was among the first to see the exigency; . . .
>
> (Montague, 1902)

The preceding excerpt is a 'sympathetic' account of the meteoric rise of the Standard Oil Company from its inception in 1865 to a giant monopoly in 1878 controlling 95 per cent of the oil market in America. Mr Rockefeller's business instinct and ability to mobilise capital gave him (and his company) extraordinary success that soon proved to be ignominious. In 1879, the state of New York launched an investigation into the company's extremely favourable contracts with railroad companies that were allegedly killing competition. But the company's fortune continued to grow, and so did allegations of unfair practices. In 1890, the US Congress passed the Sherman Antitrust Act, the centre piece of monopoly prevention regulation. Two decades, later in 1911, the US Justice Department broke Standard Oil up into 43 pieces. However, this

DOI: 10.4324/9781003226994-10

was by no means a permanent end to monopoly. Out of those scattered pieces, some new giants emerged—ExxonMobil and Chevron being two of them.

In major democracies, there is a general distaste for monopolies so much so that cartels are banned and monopolies are permitted only on limited grounds, such as public interest and technological innovations. In this chapter, we study why monopoly is problematic for market economies and where the limits of monopoly lie.

10.2 Optimal price

The polar opposite market of perfect competition is monopoly, the case of a single seller. The producer can charge any price without being undercut. The only constraint he faces is consumers' response; if he charges a high price, he will sell less and vice versa. His problem is to maximise $\pi = p(y)y - c(y)$, where $p(y)$ is the inverse market demand function with $p'(y) < 0$ and $c(y)$ is the cost function, $c'(y) \geq 0$. The first order condition for maximisation gives rise to the familiar marginal revenue (MR) equal to marginal cost (MC) condition:

$$p(y) + yp'(y) - c'(y) = 0 \quad \Rightarrow \quad p(y)\left[1 - \frac{1}{|\epsilon|}\right] = c'(y), \tag{10.1}$$

where $\epsilon = \frac{\partial y(p)}{\partial p}\frac{p}{y} < 0$ is the price elasticity of direct demand. Note that when differentiable $p(y)$ is singled-valued, and so we write $p'(y) = 1/y'(p)$. MR is increasing in the absolute value of the elasticity. Clearly, $MR \geq 0$ if $|\epsilon| \geq 1$ and $MR < 0$ if $|\epsilon| < 1$. Eq. (10.1) defines the price-cost mark-up or degree of monopoly by $[p(y) - c'(y)]/p(y) = 1/|\epsilon|$.

If the demand curve is linear and of the form $p = \bar{p} - by$, then $MR = \bar{p} - 2by$ as shown in Figure 10.1. The highest output the monopolist can sell is $\bar{y} = \bar{p}/b$. But his $MR = 0$ at $\bar{y}/2$ and $MR = MC$ can hold only at $y < \bar{y}/2$. In general, Eq. (10.1) implies that when marginal cost is positive monopolist's output must lie in the elastic part of the demand curve.

The required second-order condition for maximisation is $2p'(y) + yp''(y) - c''(y) < 0$, which is easily met if $p''(y) \leq 0$ and $c''(y) \geq 0$. That is to say, we do not want the (inverse) demand curve to be extremely convex. In Figure 10.1, the $MR = MC$ condition is met at point A, yielding output y_m and price p_m. Since $p_m > AC_m = AC(y_m)$ profit is strictly positive, which is shown by the rectangular area AC_mBCp_m. The triangular area $\bar{p}p_mC$ gives the consumer surplus (CS), and the area below AC_m and above MC up to y_m gives the fixed cost (FC). Thus, the social welfare is $CS +$ Profit $+ FC$, and it is strictly less than the welfare achievable under perfect competition, which is given by point E where $MC = p(y)$. The shaded area AEC gives the dead-weight loss (DWL) due to monopoly.

Proposition 13. *The degree of monopoly or price-cost mark-up is inversely related to the absolute value of the price elasticity of demand. Thus, the lower the elasticity, the greater the mark-up and consequently greater the DWL due to monopoly.*

10.2.1 Source of monopoly

An obvious question is why monopoly is allowed to exist in the real world if it inflicts harm on society. The answer is that legislation in most countries forbids monopoly practices, such as predatory pricing and creating barriers to entry. Such legal oversight makes monopolies short-lived. However, there are three situations that deserve some discussion. First, having one firm in the market in itself

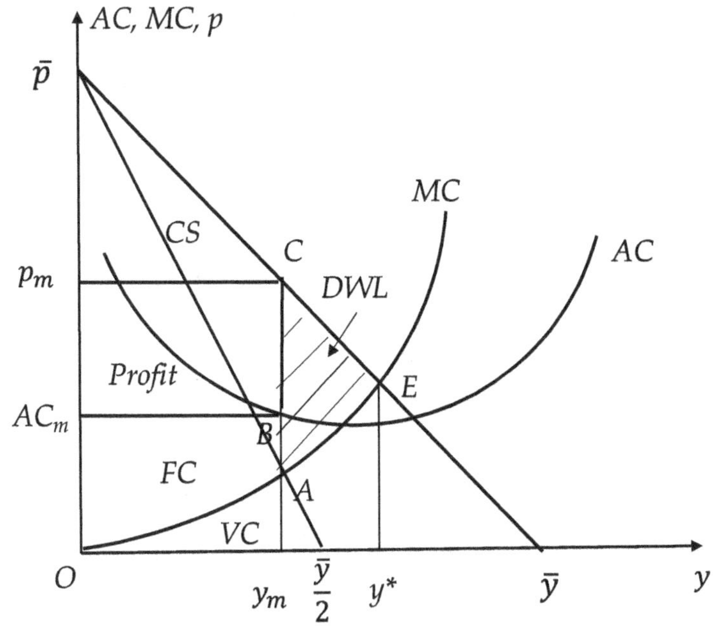

Figure 10.1 Monopolist's output choice

does not guarantee that it will earn a high profit and cause DWL. Remember the contestable markets from the last chapter. If there is no sunk cost, even a single firm cannot exploit its market power. Its profit will be zero, and the social welfare will be maximum or close to maximum.

Second, government itself often grants monopoly or exclusive business rights to some firm, usually on a time-bound basis. Most common example is pharmaceutical and industrial patents. Pharmaceutical companies are granted monopoly rights over drugs they develop for a period of 20 years. Granting a monopoly right via patents is a way to incentivise firms to undertake research and development that has obvious social benefits.

Third, there are industries in which production involves large set-up costs and very little operational costs. A water supply company needs to invest in water storage, purification facilities and crucially an extensive pipe network. Once these are done, the subsequent cost of supplying water is very little. Similar points can be made about electricity supplies and railways. These types of industries are called natural monopolies (also referred to as utilities), because of their natural preclusion of any additional provider. There is just no room for two.

Before we study natural monopolies in detail, it is worth pointing out that except protection from competition, there is nothing intrinsic about monopoly that guarantees a high profit. In Figure 10.1, that $AC_m < p_m$ guarantees positive profit. But if we had $AC_m > p_m$, the monopolist could do nothing but shut down.

10.2.2 Natural monopoly

Historically, the term *natural monopoly* meant owning a natural resource that bestows a monopoly right over the sale or use of it in downstream production. Owning a mountain means exclusive control over water springs (if any) and thereby monopoly rights over selling mineral water. Ownership of a coal mine can allow local monopoly over electricity generation. But profits earned in this way are actually rent that comes from ownership rather than any productive activity. In modern economies, natural monopolies refer to those industries in which average costs (ACs) are falling over a long interval of output so that MES or the minimum point of the AC curve is too large relative to the market demand.

Consider a firm with the cost function $C = F + cy$ and the market demand curve $p = \overline{p} - by$. The MES of this firm is infinitely large, so it is a natural monopoly. Two diagrams of this firm are drawn in Figure 10.2. In the left panel, the size of the fixed cost is moderate so that the monopolist makes a positive profit, while in the right panel, the fixed cost is so large that the monopolist barely breaks even.

In either case, there is no room for a second firm. Just to convince yourself, do the following thought experiment. Suppose the incumbent is producing profitably at some output say y_1 and selling at a price p_0. A second firm tries to enter, for which it must incur the fixed cost F and produce y_2. For this entry to be profitable and for the market to have two firms, it is necessary to have $p(y_1 + y_2)(y_1 + y_2) \geq 2F$ (even if we ignore the variable costs). Clearly, that may not be possible because with entry price will fall while individual average cost will rise (due to economies of scale). However, firms can do better by merging and avoiding duplication of the fixed cost. Consumers also benefit from such a merger. Because of the falling AC curve, a monopoly is socially desirable.

But the social desirability of monopoly does not guarantee that the consumers will benefit from having only one firm. Left alone, the monopolist will maximise its profit by charging p_m, much too higher than the marginal cost c. By setting $MC = MR$, we get

$$y_m = \frac{\overline{p} - c}{2b}, \qquad p_m = \frac{\overline{p} + c}{2}, \quad \pi_m = \frac{(\overline{p} - c)^2}{4b} - F,$$

$$PS_m = \frac{(\overline{p} - c)^2}{4b}, \quad CS_m = \frac{(\overline{p} - c)^2}{8b}, \quad SW_m = \frac{3(\overline{p} - c)^2}{8b}.$$

The monopolist makes a positive profit only if $F < (\overline{p} - c)^2 / 4b$. But does this lead to a DWL of social welfare? Let us derive the socially optimum output and social welfare by setting $p = MC$, which gives us

$$y^* = \frac{\overline{p} - c}{b}, \quad p^* = c, \quad PS^* = 0, \quad CS^* = \frac{(\overline{p} - c)^2}{2b}, \quad SW^* = \frac{(\overline{p} - c)^2}{2b}.$$

Therefore, $DWL = SW^* - SW_m = \frac{(\overline{p} - c)^2}{8b}$. One caution here: the equality of CS_m and DWL is just an artefact of linearity of the demand curve and constant marginal cost.

10.2.2.1 Elimination of DWL

What policy can eliminate the DWL? The conventional solution of breaking up a monopoly does not work here, because we have already seen that having multiple firms to induce competition is just wasteful. So we need to think about other types of intervention aiming to directly affect the firm's output choice. There are two ways to do it: public ownership and regulation.

10.2.2.1.1 PUBLIC OWNERSHIP

Suppose that the natural monopoly is nationalised. Public ownership means that the firm's objective changes from profit maximisation to social welfare maximisation. Here we can have two versions: full nationalisation and partial nationalisation. Let us propose the objective function of a public-sector firm as

$$V = \theta\pi(y) + (1-\theta)SW(y),$$

where θ represents the degree of private ownership in the publicly owned firm. Contrary to popular beliefs, public firms are not always 100 per cent owned by the government, nor are private firms always entirely devoid of the stakes held by government entities (such as banks and financial institutions). In reality, control is more important than ownership, and majority shareholding gives control.[1] But we abstract from the control issue and allow θ to vary continuously between 0 and 1. $\theta = 0$ represents full nationalisation, $\theta = 1$ represents full private ownership and $0 < \theta < 1$ represent partial nationalisation.

Let us now write social welfare as

$$SW(y) = \int_0^y p(x)dx - cy = \int_0^y (\bar{p} - bx)dx - cy$$
$$= (\bar{p} - c)y - b\frac{y^2}{2},$$

substituting $\pi = (\bar{p} - by)y - cy - F$ and the above expression of SW into the objective function of the partially nationalised firm, we write

$$V = (\bar{p} - c)y - (1+\theta)b\frac{y^2}{2} - \theta F. \tag{10.2}$$

The partially nationalised firm achieves its highest pay-off by setting

$$\tilde{y}(\theta) = \frac{\bar{p} - c}{(1+\theta)b}. \tag{10.3}$$

Note if the firm is fully nationalised ($\theta = 0$), the output will be $\tilde{y}(0) = y^* = (\bar{p} - c)/b$, and if the firm is fully privately owned, $\tilde{y}(1) = (\bar{p} - c)/2b$ is the monopoly output. The partially nationalised firm's profit is

$$\tilde{\pi}(\theta) = \frac{\theta(\bar{p} - c)^2}{b(1+\theta)^2} - F = \frac{(\bar{p} - c)^2}{b}\Big[\frac{\theta}{(1+\theta)^2} - \underbrace{\frac{bF}{(\bar{p} - c)^2}}_{\equiv k}\Big].$$

The degree of nationalisation should not be such that the firm runs into losses. So we require $\tilde{\pi}(\theta) \geq 0$, which boils down to

$$\theta^2 k - \theta(1-2k) + k \leq 0, \quad \Rightarrow \quad \theta \geq \frac{1}{2k}[1 - \sqrt{1-4k}] - 1 \equiv \underline{\theta}.$$

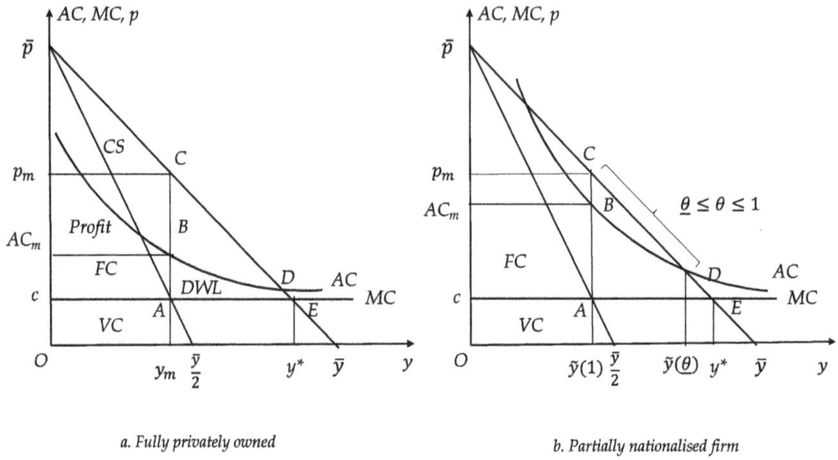

Figure 10.2 Natural monopoly

The lowest θ to ensure non-negative profit should be $\underline{\theta}$. You can check that $\underline{\theta} > 0$ because $(1-2k)^2 > 1-4k$, and at $\theta = \underline{\theta}$, the output of the public firm will be $\tilde{y}(\underline{\theta})$ at which $\pi(\tilde{y}(\underline{\theta})) = 0$. Solving the zero-profit equation $(\bar{p}-c)y - by^2 - F = 0$, we obtain $y^+ = \frac{(\bar{p}-c)}{2b}[1+\sqrt{1-4k}]$. Now set $y^+ = \tilde{y}(\theta)$,

or

$$\frac{(\bar{p}-c)}{2b}[1+\sqrt{1-4k}] = \frac{\bar{p}-c}{b(1+\theta)} \Rightarrow \quad 1-4k = \frac{(1-\theta)^2}{(1+\theta)^2}.$$

The preceding equation reduces to $k + k\theta^2 - (1-2k)\theta = 0$, which has a unique solution $\theta = \underline{\theta}$.

We present the partially nationalised firm's case on panel *b* of Figure 10.2. Any point between *C* and *E* on the demand curve can be mapped by varying θ between 0 and 1. Point *D* corresponds to $\underline{\theta}$, the zero-profit point, and point *C* to a fully private firm.

10.2.2.1.2 REGULATION

But public ownership is not universal. While in Asia and Africa it is more common, in North America, natural monopolies are large private corporations. Europe historically had many public-sector utilities, but over the last 30 years, the public ownership has been diluted. When a natural monopoly is privately held, it can be regulated through a government agency, whereby the firm is asked to produce a certain level of *y* or charge a certain price per unit. See Spulber (1989) for a comprehensive efficiency and welfare analysis of regulation covering both single- and multi-product firms.

A general principle of regulating a natural monopoly is that the regulator should try to pursue the second-best Pareto optimal pricing, which is called in the literature the Ramsay–Boiteux rule, following Ramsay (1927) and Boiteux (1956). The second-best Pareto optimal pricing is solved in terms of prices rather than quantities, subject to a non-negative profit constraint.

In the context of our example, suppose that there are n identical consumers with utility function $u = \bar{p}y - \frac{b}{2}y^2 + x$ and income m, where x is a second good, the price of which is fixed at 1. Each consumer's demand is then given by $p = \bar{p} - by$, and the market demand is simply $p = \bar{p} - b(Y/n)$, where Y is the market demand. Substituting demand $y = (\bar{p} - p)/b$ into the utility function we derive the indirect utility function as $v = \bar{p}\frac{(\bar{p}-p)}{b} - \frac{(\bar{p}-p)^2}{2b} = \frac{(\bar{p}-p)}{b}\left[\bar{p} - \frac{\bar{p}-p}{2}\right] = \frac{\bar{p}^2 - p^2}{2b}$. The regulator's optimal price, that is, the second-best Pareto optimal price, is p^* that maximises aggregate indirect utility or $nv = n\frac{\bar{p}^2 - p^2}{2b}$ subject to the zero-profit constraint $p = c + \frac{F}{yb}$. The indirect utility strictly increases if price is steadily reduced. The stopping point is where $p = AC$. This is precisely our point D in Figure 10.2. The solution reduces the DWL to a minimum (subject to the no-subsidy constraint).

The moot point is that natural monopolies pose a dilemma to society. We need them, but left to themselves, they will abuse the monopoly power to the detriment of society. Through regulation or nationalisation, the DWL can be reduced but not fully eliminated without giving a subsidy to the firm. With subsidy, the monopolist can be asked to produce y^* (at point E of Figure 10.2). Without subsidy, it can be asked to produce at point D, where output will not be fully efficient.

Proposition 14. *Nationalisation and regulation are two alternative ways to improve social welfare in a natural monopoly. However, neither can fully eliminate the DWL without giving a subsidy to the monopolist.*

One may ask, If public ownership and regulation are equivalent, why there is so much objection to nationalisation? The answer is that the choice is partly political and party history-dependent. Keeping the political issues aside, one can still find some economic differences between these two alternatives. Generally, public-sector enterprises are seen to be 'inefficient' both technologically and input cost–wise. Private firms are better on these counts. But regulating a private firm has its own challenges too. The biggest obstacle is information about the true cost of the firm. A regulator, despite her best effort, may not be able to learn all the relevant costs and thus will have to concede some profits by setting a price slightly higher than she would have liked. Besides the cost, there are other complexities. For example, in the electricity market, production and distribution must do a complex balancing act of meeting the demand 'on demand'. Because consumers' peak demand times vary geographically, a smooth supply requires being part of a large electricity grid. Regulating an industry of this kind involves coordination across multiple jurisdictions. Over the last few decades, production has been left to large corporate firms, while the distribution of electricity has been subjected to a mixture of private competition and regulation. In the United Kingdom, many energy retailers compete for end users, who benefit from low prices. But the regulator keeps a watch on the wholesale price. If, for some reason, the wholesale price goes up significantly, the retail price may be capped, as was done in 2022–23.

10.3 Price discrimination

Our claim that the monopolist earns maximum profit by setting $MR = MC$ needs to be qualified by saying that it is true only if we restrict to a non-discriminatory or uniform price. The monopolist can increase his profit further by resorting to price discrimination. He can charge different prices from different buyers based on their individual or group attributes (such as student discount) and the quantities they buy.[2] When prices are made conditional on both the quantity bought and the identity or attribute of the consumer, it is called *first-degree* price discrimination. If the discrimination is only based on the quantity bought, it is called *second-degree* price discrimination (such as a buy-one-get-one-free offer). Finally, if the discrimination is only based on the consumer's identity (such as student discounts), it is called *third-degree* price discrimination.

We explain the three discrimination cases with a simple example. Suppose our monopolist has CRS technology with no fixed cost so that his cost function is simply $C = cy$. There are two consumers, with demand curves $p_1 = a_1 - b_1 y_1$ and $p_2 = a_2 - b_2 y_2$. They are called type 1 and type 2 consumers, respectively, with the latter being regarded as high type for her willingness to pay a higher price. Also note that our assumption of one consumer of each type is a mere simplification. It means that the two types of consumers are in equal proportion in the market. One can easily relax this assumption.[3]

From the individual demand curves, we derive the market demand (denoted as $y = y_1 + y_2$) and its inverse function as

$$y = \begin{cases} \dfrac{a_2}{b_2} - \dfrac{p}{b_2} & \text{for } p > a_1 \\[2ex] \dfrac{A}{\beta} - \dfrac{p}{\beta} & \text{for } p \le a_1 \end{cases} \quad \text{and} \quad p = \begin{cases} a_2 - b_2 y & \text{for } y < \dfrac{a_2 - a_1}{b_2} \\[2ex] A - \beta y & \text{for } y \ge \dfrac{a_2 - a_1}{b_2} \end{cases}, \tag{10.4}$$

where

$$A \equiv \frac{a_2 b_1 + a_1 b_2}{b_1 + b_2} \text{ and } \beta \equiv \frac{b_1 b_2}{b_1 + b_2}.$$

It can be easily verified that $a_1 < A < a_2$ given our assumption $a_1 < a_2$.

10.3.1 *No price discrimination*

Let us first consider the case where only a single price is charged. The monopolist will have two options: set a high price and sell only to the high-type consumer or set a low price and sell to both types of consumers. Which one is profitable remains to be determined.

Taking the market demand curve as given in Eq. (10.4), the monopolist maximises his profit and sets $MR = MC$ with respect to the market segment he wishes to operate in. If he aims at the type 2 market, p must exceed (or be equal to) a_1. For this market,

$$y_2 = \frac{a_2 - c}{2b_2} \quad p_2 = \frac{a_2 + c}{2} \quad \text{and} \quad \pi_2 = \frac{(a_2 - c)^2}{4b_2}.$$

For this price to be out of reach for the type 1 consumer, we should have $p_2 \ge a_1$ or, equivalently, $c \ge 2a_1 - a_2$. Otherwise, the high-type segment alone cannot be targeted. So let us assume

$c > 2a_1 - a_2$. The alternative option of selling to both types of consumers gives rise to the following output, price and profit:

$$y_m = \frac{A-c}{2\beta} \quad p_m = \frac{A+c}{2} \quad \text{and} \quad \pi_m = \frac{(A-c)^2}{4\beta}.$$

The combined market profit is greater than selling only to the high-type consumer if $\frac{(A-c)^2}{4\beta} > \frac{(a_2-c)^2}{4b_2}$. This inequality boils down to

$$\underbrace{\frac{\sqrt{b_1}}{b_2}\left(\sqrt{b_1+b_2}-\sqrt{b_1}\right)}_{\equiv k \text{ (say)}} < \frac{a_1-c}{a_2-c} \quad (\leq 1).$$

Note that we have not made any assumption on the relative magnitudes of b_1 and b_2. Therefore, it is not guaranteed that $k < 1$. If the preceding condition is satisfied, the monopolist will prefer to sell to both customers; otherwise, he will sell only to the high type. This condition also says that the low type's willingness to pay should not be too low relative to the high type's willingness to pay.

Let us assume that indeed the previous condition holds and that both consumers are served at a common price $p = (A+c)/2$. Panel *a* of Figure 10.3 shows the monopolist's preferred option of selling to both consumers. Because of the kink in the (Average revenue) AR curve (given by Eq. (10.4)), the MR curve is discontinuous at $y = (a_2 - a_1)/b_2$ and non-monotonic. The first segment of the MR curve is given by the equation $MR = a_2 - 2b_2 y$ and the second segment by $MR = A - 2\beta y$. The equilibrium is given by the intersection of the second segment of the MR curve and the MC curve, which gives $p_m < a_1$. Since $p_m > c$, clearly there is a DWL, marked by a triangle. The magnitude of the loss is $\text{DWL} = (A-c)^2/8\beta$. We would like to see if price discrimination helps reduce the DWL.

10.3.2 First-degree price discrimination

Imagine a village doctor somewhere in India who charges his patients based on how much one is able to pay, which is common knowledge in a rural community. You would probably guess

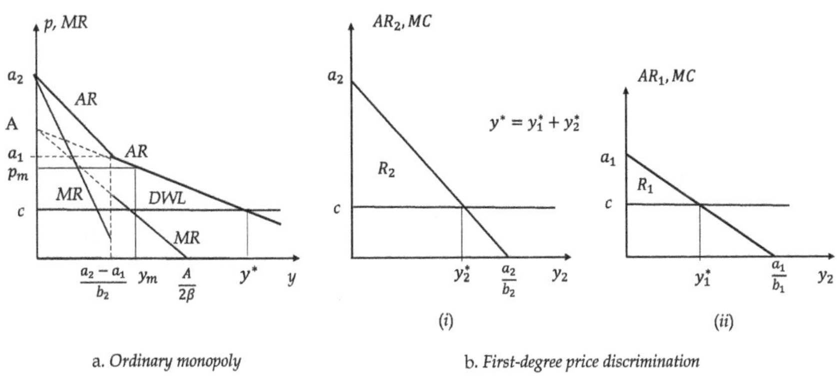

Figure 10.3 First-degree price discrimination

that the well-off in the village see him as a greedy and exploitative character, while the poor see him as kind and generous. It is not hard to see that if he charged everybody the same fee fair and square, he would have treated fewer patients and made less money. This is first-degree price discrimination. But this is possible, because he holds a local monopoly in that village. In a city where lives are anonymous, such discrimination would be nearly impossible. The closest thing we come across is personalised Uber Eats offers or supermarket deals delivered to our smartphones. Nevertheless, the special example of the 'greedy' village doctor gives us a benchmark of what a monopolist can do.

Let us return to the two-consumer example laid out earlier. The monopolist knows both consumers, and he can insist on the following individualised quantity and payment offers/schedules (which are also called *two-part tariffs* or *non-linear prices*), which the consumers will not reject.

$$\text{For type 2 consumer: pay } T_2^* = \frac{(a_2 - c)^2}{2b_2} + cy_2^* \quad \text{and buy } y_2^* = \frac{a_2 - c}{b_2} \tag{10.5}$$

$$\text{For type 1 consumer: pay } T_1^* = \frac{(a_1 - c)^2}{2b_1} + cy_1^* \quad \text{and buy } y_1^* = \frac{a_1 - c}{b_1}. \tag{10.6}$$

If the type 2 consumer buys y_2^* at the unit price c, her consumer surplus will be $(a_2 - c)^2 / 2b_2$; see the marked triangle R_2 of Figure10.3 panel $b(i)$. The fixed payment part of T_2^* is precisely R_2. Of course, by agreeing to buy at the specified payment schedule the consumer's utility (or the final consumer surplus) will be zero, which is no less than what she can get by not buying. In fact, to make her strictly better off the monopolist can return her just a penny. Exactly the same argument applies to the type 1 consumer for the payment schedule (y_1^*, T_1^*).

But note that not only has the monopolist made more money but he has eliminated the DWL completely. The combined output $y_1^* + y_2^*$ equals the social optimum $y^* = (A - c) / \beta$. Therefore, we can say that a monopoly yields the maximum social welfare if the monopolist is *able to price discriminate by first degree*. But there is a crucial condition to be met. He needs to have full information about the consumers.

Proposition 15. *A first-degree price-discriminating monopoly produces the highest social welfare just like a competitive market, but the monopolist also earns the highest profit.*

10.3.3 Second-degree price discrimination

The informational requirement for first-degree price discrimination is extreme. The monopolist may not be able to identify who is type 1 and who is type 2. When his knowledge is restricted in this way, he still can use price discrimination but not to the fullest extent. He can make the price contingent on the quantity bought on the premise that the quantities bought will correlate with the consumers' types. The discriminating payment schedules will incentivise the buyers to self-select. To proceed further, let us make some assumptions about the differences in the two demand curves.

Assumption 6.

$$a_2 \geq a_1, a_1 - c > a_2 - a_1 \textit{ and } b_2 \leq \left(\frac{a_2 - c}{a_1 - c} \right) b_1.$$

The second part of our assumption ensures that the low type is adequately profitable so that serving two types of consumers is worthwhile. The third part of our assumption ensures that $y_1^* = (a_1 - c)/b_1 < y_2^* = (a_2 - c)/b_2$.

Let us first see the problems the monopolist might face if he wanted to pursue first-degree price discrimination, when he is not able to identify the consumers. Suppose the buyers are presented with offers $\mathcal{B}^* = \{(y_1^*, T_1^*), (y_2^*, T_2^*)\}$ as given in Eqs. (10.5) and (10.6). Let us define the consumer surplus of type i when she selects a generic offer (y_j, T_j) as

$$u(j \mid i) = \int_0^{y_j} [a_i - b_i x] dx - T_j = a_i y_j - b_i \frac{y_j^2}{2} - T_j, \quad \text{for} \quad i, j = 1, 2.$$

Thus, $u(j \mid i)$ is the consumer surplus when the type i consumer selects the offer intended for j. We can check that type 1 consumer will select the offer (y_1^*, T_1^*) because by selecting (y_2^*, T_2^*), her consumer surplus becomes negative. But the type 2 consumer will also select (y_1^*, T_1^*), because (y_2^*, T_2^*) leaves her with zero consumer surplus, while (y_1^*, T_1^*) leaves her with a positive surplus. See panel a of Figure 10.4. A type 2 consumer has to be content with buying less, but because she pays also less, she will have a positive consumer surplus marked by the area $a_1 a_2 D E_1$. Therefore, the offer (y_2^*, T_2^*) will not be selected at all, and first-degree price discrimination is not optimal in the absence of perfect information.

So what offer can the monopolist come up with that type 2 will take up? As a start, let us note that if T_2 is tweaked a bit, say by offering a discount by the magnitude of $a_1 a_2 D E_1$ to buy y_2^*, then type 2 should select y_2^*, because it leaves her with the same consumer surplus as the offer (y_1^*, T_1^*) would.

However, in panel b, we demonstrate that the discount $a_1 a_2 D E_1$ is too generous. The monopolist can increase her profit by tweaking the bundle intended for type 1 as well. If y_1 is reduced below y_1^* and T_1 from R_1, profit from type 1 will fall, but the discount to be offered to type 2 will also fall, which means profit from type 2 rises, and this rise is greater than the fall in profit from type 1. The optimal point to stop is where the marginal consumer surplus of type 1 is exactly equal to the marginal consumer surplus of type 2, because these are exactly the marginal loss and gain from type 1 and 2, respectively, from a reduction of y_1. In panel b, we show that at $\tilde{y}_1$,

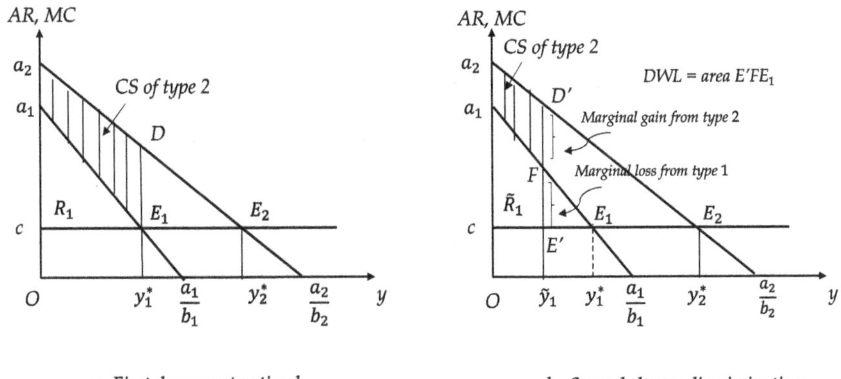

Figure 10.4 Second-degree price discrimination

the marginal loss and gain are equal. So the second-degree price discrimination modifies the first-degree offer as

$$\left(y_2^*,\tilde{T}_2\right):\quad \text{pay } \tilde{T}_2=\frac{\left(a_2-c\right)^2}{2b_2}+cy_2^*-\left[\left(a_2-a_1\right)-\left(b_2-b_1\right)\frac{\tilde{y}_1}{2}\right]\tilde{y}_1 \quad \text{and buy } y_2^*$$

$$\left(\tilde{y}_1,\tilde{T}_1\right):\quad \text{pay } \tilde{T}_1=\tilde{R}_1+c\tilde{y}_1 \quad \text{and buy } \tilde{y}_1.$$

As can be seen, the monopolist's second-degree price discrimination scheme, $\mathcal{B}$, boils down to finding $\tilde{y}_1$ that maximises profit $\pi\left(y_1,T_1\right)+\pi\left(y_2,T_2\right)$ subject to a constraint

$$u(2\,|\,2)\geq u(1\,|\,2)\Rightarrow\int_0^{y_2}\left(a_2-b_2x\right)dx-T_2\geq\int_0^{y_1}\left(a_2-b_2x\right)dx-T_1.$$

The constraint is called the **incentive compatibility** or **self-selection constraint** of the type 2 consumer, because she is made to feel better off (or indifferent) by selecting $\left(y_2,T_2\right)$ instead of $\left(y_1,T_1\right)$. Substituting the expressions for profit and consumer surplus into the incentive compatibility constraint and making it bind, we write the monopolist's problem as

$$\begin{aligned}
\max\quad & \pi_1+\pi_2=T_1-cy_1+T_2-cy_2\\
\text{sub. to}\quad & T_1=a_1y_1-b_1\frac{y_1^2}{2},\\
\text{and}\quad & T_2=\left[a_2y_2-b_2\frac{y_2^2}{2}\right]-\left[a_2y_1-b_2\frac{y_1^2}{2}\right]+T_1\\
& \quad=\left[a_2y_2-b_2\frac{y_2^2}{2}\right]-\left[(a_2-a_1)y_1-(b_2-b_1)\frac{y_1^2}{2}\right].
\end{aligned}$$

Substituting T_1 and T_2 into the expression of profit, we write

$$\pi_1+\pi_2=\left[\left(2a_1-a_2\right)y_1-\left(2b_1-b_2\right)\frac{y_1^2}{2}-cy_1\right]+\left[a_2y_2-b_2\frac{y_2^2}{2}-cy_2\right]. \tag{10.7}$$

The monopolist maximises (10.7) w.r.t. y_1 and y_2. The first-order conditions yield

$$\tilde{y}_1=\frac{2a_1-a_2-c}{2b_1-b_2}\quad\text{and}\quad\tilde{y}_2=\frac{a_2-c}{b_2}\left(\equiv y_2^*\right). \tag{10.8}$$

For $\tilde{y}_1>0$, it is necessary that $2a_1>a_2+c$ (or $a_1-c>a_2-a_1$) and $2b_1>b_2$, both satisfied by Assumption 6. Let us also note that under second-degree price discrimination, the DWL does not get eliminated, because $\tilde{y}_1<y_1^*$. The DWL given by the triangle $E'FE_1$ in panel b of Figure 10.4 and denoted by ω is

$$
\begin{aligned}
\omega &= \left(a_1 - b_1\tilde{y}_1 - c\right)\frac{\left(y_1^* - \tilde{y}_1\right)}{2} \\
&= \frac{1}{2}\left[\left(a_1 - c\right)\frac{b_1 - b_2}{2b_1 - b_2} + \left(a_2 - a_1\right)\frac{b_1}{2b_1 - b_2}\right] \times \left[\left(a_1 - c\right)\frac{b_1 - b_2}{b_1\left(2b_1 - b_2\right)} + \frac{(a_2 - a_1)b_1}{b_1(2b_1 - b_2)}\right] \qquad (10.9) \\
&= \frac{1}{2b_1}\left[\left(a_1 - c\right)\lambda + \left(a_2 - a_1\right)(1 - \lambda)\right]^2, \quad \left(\text{where} \quad \lambda = \frac{b_1 - b_2}{2b_1 - b_2}\right).
\end{aligned}
$$

The magnitude of the DWL depends on three factors $a_1 - c, a_2 - a_1$ and $b_1 - b_2$. While $a_2 - a_1$ and $b_1 - b_2$ directly reduces $\tilde{y}_1, a - c$ increases the difference $y_1^* - \tilde{y}_1$ as well. Thus, each of these factors increases DWL.

Now we write the optimal payments:

$$
\tilde{T}_1 = T_1^* - \omega - c\left(y_1^* - \tilde{y}_1\right) \quad \text{and} \quad \tilde{T}_2 = T_2^* - \frac{\tilde{y}_1}{2}\left[\left(a_1 - c\right)\lambda + \left(a_2 - a_1\right)(2 - \lambda)\right].
$$

Clearly, the payments under second-degree price discrimination are strictly less than that under first-degree price discrimination$\left(T_1^*, T_2^*\right)$, leading to

$$
\text{Loss of profit } = \omega + \frac{\tilde{y}_1}{2}\left[\left(a_1 - c\right)\lambda + \left(a_2 - a_1\right)(2 - \lambda)\right].
$$

A decrease in the quantity sold to the type 1 consumer (from y_1^*) has two opposite effects. On one hand, it decreases profit from the low-type consumer and thus increases the DWL, but on the other hand, it reduces the required discount to be conceded to the high type (to maintain her incentive compatibility constraint) and thus increases profit. Profit is maximum where the marginal loss from the low type is just equal to the marginal gain from the high type, as shown in Figure 10.4.

Proposition 16. *Suppose Assumption 6 holds. Under second-degree price discrimination, the high-type consumer is conceded a consumer surplus, but there is no social welfare loss vis-à-vis her, while the low-type consumer is sold below the first-degree price discrimination output level, giving rise to a DWL. The low type is left with no consumer surplus.*

10.3.4 Role of demand elasticity

So far, we have assumed that the high-type consumers' demand is fairly elastic, so offering bigger discount to them is profitable. But if their demand is very inelastic, then the previous conclusion can change. Let us now modify our Assumption 6 so that the high type's demand curve becomes so steep that y_2^* falls below y_1^*. Will the monopolist's pricing strategy change? To study this problem let us assume the following.

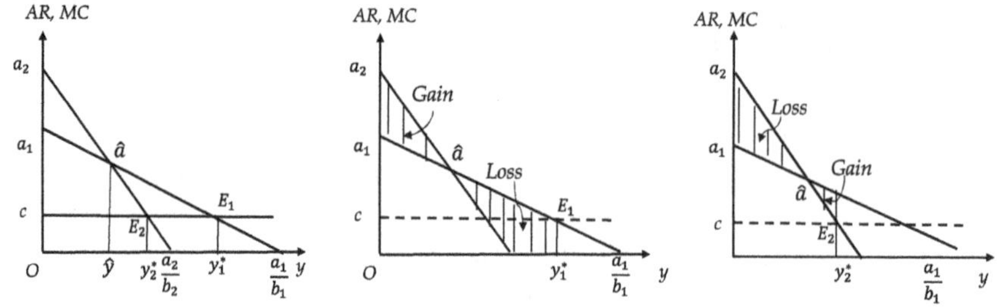

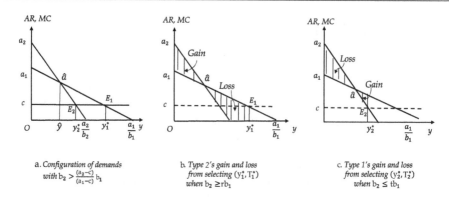

a. *Configuration of demands with* $b_2 > \frac{(a_2-c)}{(a_1-c)} b_1$

b. *Type 2's gain and loss from selecting* (y_1^*, T_1^*) *when* $b_2 \geq rb_1$

c. *Type 1's gain and loss from selecting* (y_2^*, T_2^*) *when* $b_2 \leq tb_1$

Figure 10.5 Feasibility of the first-degree offers when $b_2 > b_1$

Assumption 7. *Suppose* $a_2 > a_1, a_1 - c > a_2 - a_1, b_2 > b_1$ and $b_2 > \left(\frac{a_2 - c}{a_1 - c}\right) b_1$.

Figure 10.5 represents this case. In panel *a*, we see that the two demand curves cross each other at $\hat{y} = \frac{a_2 - a_1}{b_2 - b_1}$; as a result, $y_1^* > y_2^*$, and we cannot (unconditionally) call type 2 as a high type. Here, some interesting possibilities emerge. In the other two panels, we show that if the first-degree price discrimination offers $\mathcal{B}^*$ are on display, the type 2 consumer will not select (y_1^*, T_1^*) (panel *b*) and the type 1 consumer will not select (y_2^*, T_2^*) (panel *c*). In panel *c*, we see that type 1's gain is strictly less than the loss from selecting (y_2^*, T_2^*). Thus, first-degree price discrimination is very likely. To examine this possibility, we check the incentive compatibility condition for type 1. That is, the type 1's consumer surplus from selecting (y_2^*, T_2^*) must be non-positive:

$$CS(2^* \mid 1) = u(y_2^*; 1) - T_2^* = \int_0^{y_2^*} (a_1 - b_1 x) dx - \int_0^{y_2^*} (a_2 - b_2 x) dx \leq 0$$

$$= y_2^* \left[\left\{ a_1 - b_1 \frac{y_2^*}{2} \right\} - \left\{ a_2 - b_2 \frac{y_2^*}{2} \right\} \right] \leq 0$$

$$= y_2^* \left[\left\{ \frac{2a_1 b_2 - b_1(a_2 - c)}{2b_2} \right\} - \frac{a_2 + c}{2} \right] \leq 0 \left(\text{since } y_2^* = \frac{a_2 - c}{b_2} \right).$$

Simplifying this expression, we get the condition

$$b_2 \leq \left(\frac{a_2 - c}{2a_1 - a_2 - c} \right) b_1 \quad (\equiv tb_1). \tag{10.10}$$

Similarly, in panel *b*, we note the gain and loss of type 2 from selecting (y_1^*, T_1^*). Note that when the type 2 consumer selects y_1^*, she gets utility only up to $y = a_2 / b_2$, and beyond that, her utility is zero. But she has to pay T_1^*. By imposing incentive compatibility, we require

$$CS(1^* \mid 2) = u(y_1^*;2) - T_1^* = \int_0^{\frac{a_2}{b_2}} (a_2 - b_2 x)dx - \int_0^{y_1^*} (a_1 - b_1 x)dx \leq 0$$

$$= \frac{a_2^2}{2b_2} - \left(a_1 - b_1 \frac{y_1^*}{2}\right) y_1^* \leq 0$$

$$= \frac{a_2^2}{2b_2} - \frac{a_1^2 - c^2}{2b_1} \leq 0.$$

The required inequality reduces to

$$b_2 \geq \left(\frac{a_2^2}{a_1^2 - c^2}\right) b_1 \quad (\equiv rb_1). \tag{10.11}$$

To compare between r and t, we write $u(1^* \mid 2)$ in terms of $u(2^* \mid 1)$ as follows:

$$CS(1^* \mid 2) = \int_0^{y_2^*} [(a_2 - a_1) - (b_2 - b_1)x]dx - \left[\int_{y_2^*}^{y_1^*} (a_1 - b_1 x)dx - \frac{c^2}{2b_2}\right]$$

$$= -CS(2^* \mid 1) - \left[\underbrace{\int_{y_2^*}^{y_1^*} (a_1 - b_1 x)dx - \frac{c^2}{2b_2}}_{\kappa > 0}\right].$$

When $b_2 > tb_1$, $CS(2^* \mid 1)$ is necessarily positive, which implies that we must have $CS(1^* \mid 2) < 0$, or $b_2 > rb_1$. Alternatively, if $CS(1^* \mid 2) > 0$, it must be that $b_2 < rb_1$, which, in turn, requires that $CS(2^* \mid 1) < 0$. Together, these two facts imply $r < t$.

If conditions (10.11) and (10.10) are both satisfied, that is, if $rb_1 \leq b_2 \leq tb_1$, the first-degree price discrimination offers $\{(y_1^*, T_1^*), (y_2^*, T_2^*)\}$ satisfy the incentive compatibility conditions for both type 1 and type 2, and he will simply put these offers before the consumers, who will then self-select. Thus, even when the monopolist lacks the necessary information to carry out first-degree discrimination, the low-demand elasticity of the high type allows him to still implement the first-degree offers.

In panel *a* of Figure 10.6, we depict the configurations of demand slopes b_1 and b_2 (assuming $a_2 > a_1$). When $b_2 > b_1$ in the region falling between $b_2 = tb_1$ and $b_2 = rb_1$, the first-degree price discrimination offers are perfectly implementable via the self-selection method, and thereby, the DWL is eliminated.[4] In the region to the right of $b_2 = rb_1$ we have the second-degree price discrimination offers with $\tilde{y}_1 < y_1^*$ as already discussed.

What remains to be seen is the optimal prices for the region of $b_2 > tb_1$, where y_1^* continues to be greater than y_2^*. Here, if the first-degree offers are presented type 1 will select (y_2^*, T_2^*), while type 2 will stick to her (y_2^*, T_2^*). This is the reverse problem seen in the region of $b_2 < rb_1$. The monopolist will then reduce y_2 below y_2^* to extract more surplus from type 1, but this exercise is not a mirror image of the case seen earlier. We show a graphical solution to this problem in panel *b* of Figure 10.6, without taking recourse to algebra.

Consider panel *b* of Figure 10.6, where $b_2 > tb_1$. If $\mathcal{B}^*$ is offered, type 1 will select (y_2^*, T_2^*) despite the fact that she will suffer a disutility (negative CS) from y up to $\hat{y}$ (or to the left of point $\hat{a}$), as she is paying more than her total benefit up to $\hat{y}$. But after $\hat{y}$, her consumption

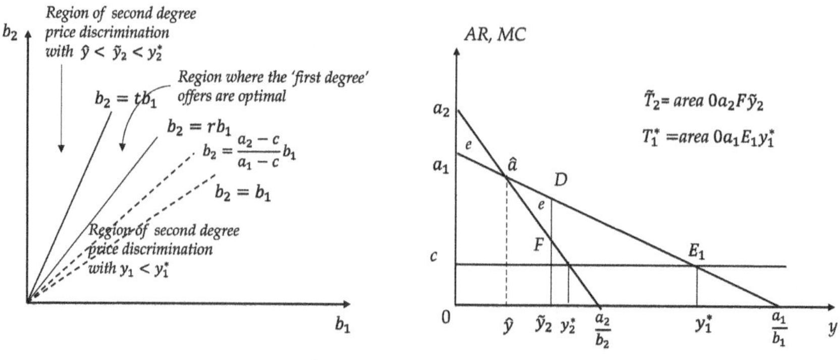

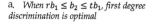

a. *When $rb_1 \leq b_2 \leq tb_1$, first degree discrimination is optimal*

b. *When $b_2 > tb_1$ second degree discrimination with $\hat{y} < \tilde{y}_2 < y_2^*$ is optimal*

Figure 10.6 Parametric space of (b_1, b_2)

begins to yield a positive consumer surplus. Overall gain will exceed the loss if $y_2 = y_2^*$. The monopolist's optimal strategy is then to reduce y_2 until type 1's gains and losses become equal. $\tilde{y}_2$ is precisely such an optimal output level. Therefore, she will be left with no surplus regardless of whether she selects $\tilde{y}_2$ or y_1^*. The type 2 consumer will buy $\tilde{y}_2$ and pay $\tilde{T}_2$, because her selecting (y_1^*, T_1^*) is ruled out. Thus, the most interesting observation here is that neither type of consumer is left with any surplus. But the DWL is not fully eliminated, because of inefficiency in y_2.

Proposition 17. *Suppose Assumption 7 holds.*

1. *Further assume $rb_1 \leq b_2 \leq tb_1$. Then despite not being able to identify the consumers' types, the monopolist secures highest profit and thereby completely eliminates DWL by offering the first-degree price discrimination offers, which the consumers self-select.*
2. *If $b_2 < rb_1$ the monopolist sets $\{(\tilde{y}_1, \tilde{T}_1), (y_2^*, \tilde{T}_2)\}$, where $\tilde{y}_1 < y_1^*$ and there is DWL vis-à-vis type 1.*
3. *If $b_2 > tb_1$, the schedule $\{(y_1^*, T_1^*), (\tilde{y}, \tilde{T}_2)\}$ is optimal for the monopolist, where $\hat{y} < \tilde{y}_2 < y_2^*$ and $\tilde{T}_2 = \int_0^{\tilde{y}_2} (a_2 - b_2 x) dx$ so that $u((\tilde{y}_2, \tilde{T}_2) \mid 1) = 0$. Both consumers have zero consumer surplus, and there is DWL vis-à-vis type 2.*

We conclude this section by noting that second-degree price discrimination is one specific response to the general problem of the monopolist lacking sufficient information that is necessary to exercise his full monopoly power. In a later chapter, we will revisit this issue while addressing the question of asymmetric information in a more general context.

10.3.5 Third-degree price discrimination

The most common form of price discrimination practised in reality is third-degree discrimination, whereby everybody pays a per unit fixed price but some pay less depending on a qualifying criterion, such as being a student. Bus and train tickets are the most common example of this. Many restaurants advertise that "Kids eat free".

In a model of general demand curves, the output choice rules are

$$p_2\left[1-\frac{1}{|\epsilon_2|}\right]=c \text{ and } p_1\left[1-\frac{1}{|\epsilon_1|}\right]=c.$$

The monopolist will set a higher price and sell a lower quantity in that market where the demand is relatively less elastic. In the context of our linear demand example, optimal prices are $p_2=(a_2+c)/2$ and $p_1=(a_1+c)/2$. The corresponding quantities sold are $y_2=(a_2-c)/2b_2$ and $y_1=(a_1-c)/2b_1$. Let us now see if the DWL decreases with price discrimination. Assuming that the monopolist was previously serving both types of consumers, recall from Section 10.3.1 that the monopolist was selling $y_m=(A-c)/2\beta$. After the price discrimination, the combined output of the two markets is

$$y_1+y_2=\frac{a_2-c}{2b_2}+\frac{a_1-c}{2b_1}=\frac{a_2b_1+a_1b_2-c(b_1+b_2)}{2b_1b_2}=\frac{\frac{a_2b_1+a_1b_2}{b_1+b_2}-c}{\frac{2b_1b_2}{b_1+b_2}}=\frac{A-c}{2\beta}.$$

So, in the linear demand case, there is no difference in terms of output or welfare. The DWL remains unchanged.

However, in general, the effect of third-degree price discrimination on social welfare is ambiguous. It depends on the shape of the demand functions and the type of utility functions assumed. See Varian (1985, 1989, 1992) for a detailed welfare analysis.

The most positive impact of third-degree price discrimination is felt when previously some market was not served, possibly because of the consumers' lower willingness to pay. From Section 10.3.1, assume that previously the monopolist was selling only to the high-value consumers and the low-value consumers were not served. Previously, he was selling $y_2=(a_2-c)/2b_2$ at a price $p_2=(a_2+c)/2>a_1$, which implies $a_2-2a_1-c>0$.[5] Now if the monopolist sells $y_2=(a_2-c)/2b$ in the high-value market and $y_1=(a_1-c)/2b_1$ in the low-value market, social welfare inevitably improves.

10.4 Durable goods monopoly

So far, what we discussed applies to goods that do not have recurrent utility to the consumers. All non-durable goods are clearly of this nature. Some durable goods also effectively become non-durable due to their restricted use—a child's buggy, for example, or toys. Despite being perfectly fit for recycling rarely are they reused. But for a refurbished iPhone or a college textbook, the story is different. Recycling is good for the environment but certainly creates a problem for their monopolist sellers. Textbooks are not updated every year, and a good number of the current-year books are likely to be recycled, causing a dent to the publisher's future sales. A more acute problem is faced when the recycled good is an intermediate good, like aluminium or steel. Recycled aluminium can be perfectly substituted for newly made aluminium in many production processes.

Durability creates another problem that is not present in the textbook market. Take the case of hard-cover books for fiction. You want to read Salman Rushdie's new novel *Victory City*, but it is available only in hardcover at £22.00. You may wonder whether it is worth waiting six months in the hope of seeing the price come down or a paperback version hitting the bookstores. That you and many others may wait influences what price the publisher should set today. Thus, in a durable good monopoly, the monopolist's power is curbed by two indispensable factors: (1) recycling scope and (2) consumer's expectation about future price. In the first case, the future demand is reduced by the current supply and to what extent this reduction will take place depends on the feasibility of recycling. In the second case, the two selves of the monopolist—the present one and the future one—compete with each other. You may read Bulow (1982, 1986) and Tirole (1989, Chapter 1.5) for a deeper understanding.

We first present a brief formal analysis of both recycling and renting.[6] Suppose our good lasts for two periods and it can be produced in either period at a constant marginal cost c. The units bought in period 1 can serve their owner over two periods if recycled or retained. The units bought in period 2 are useful only for one period (by definition). Let $p = a - by$ by be the per period demand for the services provided by the durable good.

10.4.1 Recycling

Let us assume that y is a metal (like aluminium) used in production for other goods. If in period 1 y_1 amount of metal is sold and used, then in period 2, we assume ρy_1 is recycled, $0 \le \rho \le 1$. To the downstream producers, the new and recycled metals are perfect substitutes. After having sold y_1 in the first period the monopolist will sell y_2 to maximise $\pi_2 = [a - b(\rho y_1 + y_2) - c]y_2$. The solution to his problem is $y_2^*(y_1) = \dfrac{a - b\rho y_1 - c}{2b}$, resulting in the second-period profit $\pi_2^*(y_1) = \dfrac{(a - b\rho y_1 - c)^2}{4b}$. The second-period solution recognises the fact that $\rho y_1 / 2$ fewer units will be sold than the standard monopoly output.

In the first period, the monopolist then maximises $\Pi = \pi_1 + \delta\pi_2^*(y_1) = (a - by_1 - c)$ $y_1 + \delta \dfrac{(a - b\rho y_1 - c)^2}{4b}$ with respect to y_1, where δ represents the discount factor for future ($\delta \le 1$). The solution is as follows:

$$\frac{\partial \Pi}{\partial y_1} = (a - c - 2by_1) - \delta\rho \frac{(a - c - b\rho y_1)}{2} = 0$$

$$= (a - c)\frac{(2 - \delta\rho)}{2} - by_1 \frac{(4 - \delta\rho^2)}{2} = 0$$

$$\Rightarrow y_1^* = \frac{(a - c)}{b}\left[\underbrace{\frac{2 - \delta\rho}{4 - \delta\rho^2}}_{= \gamma \text{ (say)}}\right].$$

You can check $\gamma < 1/2$ because of $\delta\rho < 1$. The profit profile due to recycling is, therefore,

$$\pi_1^* = \frac{(a - c)^2}{b}(1 - \gamma)\gamma, \qquad \pi_2^* = \frac{(a - c)^2}{4b}(1 - \rho\gamma)^2,$$

and $$\Pi^* = \frac{(a - c)^2}{b}\left[(1 - \gamma)\gamma + \delta\frac{(1 - \rho\gamma)^2}{4}\right].$$

Note that $\Pi^* < \Pi^*(\rho = 0) = \frac{(a-c)^2(1+\delta)}{4b}$. Total profit under recycling is strictly less than the total profit of the non-recycling case.

10.4.2 Renting

For many durable goods, like small planes, limousine services, farm equipment like tractors in developing countries and, of course, cars have strong rental markets. Libraries are also an example of (book) renting. Just two decades ago, video rental stores dotted street corners of every major city in the United States. Imagine that our monopolist rents and does not sell. Let the demand for rental services be $r = a - by$. If production does not involve any variable cost, the monopolist should produce $y = a/2b$ in the first period and rent these units out in both periods. However, given $MC = c$, producing somewhere between $a/2b$ and $(a-c)/2b$ units will be optimal.

Let y_1 be his first-period production, which is then rented out in both periods; no production is needed in the second period. $\pi_2 = (a - by_1)y_1$ is the second-period rental income. In the first period, then the monopolist should maximise $\Pi = (a - by_1 - c)y_1 + \delta(a - by_1)y_1$. The optimal output and profits are

$$y_1^* = \frac{a(1+\delta)-c}{2b(1+\delta)}, \quad y_2^* = 0, \quad \text{and} \quad \Pi^* = \frac{(a(1+\delta)-c)^2}{4b(1+\delta)}. \tag{10.12}$$

We can verify that $(a-c)/2b < y_1^* < a/2b$. The durable good monopolist produces a bit more than the static monopoly level but less than the pure renter's optimal level (because production is costly). This is the highest profit the monopolist can get.

10.4.3 Selling

Now consider the case of selling. Here, there are two cases to consider: without commitment and with commitment. For the sake of concreteness, assume that the buyers are not the final consumers, but they are renters who operate in a competitive market, and they can ensure that the first-period buyers cannot rent out the good in the next period.[7]

1. **Selling without commitment** Suppose the monopolist cannot commit to a profile of $\{y_1, y_2\}$. Instead, he chooses them in sequence. The monopolist can sell in both periods if he so wishes. Let us begin with the last period when there is no difference between renting and selling. Already y_1 has been sold and rented out in period 1, and these units are being rented out again in period 2. The seller sells y_2 units to maximise $\pi_2(y_1) = (a - by_1 - by_2 - c)y_2$. Optimal y_2 is $y_2^*(y_1) = (a - by_1 - c)/2b$ and $p_2 = r_2 = (a - by_1 + c)/2$, which yield $\pi_2(y_1) = (a - by_1 - c)^2/4b$.

   In period 1, the monopolist maximises $\Pi = (p_1 - c)y_1 + \delta\pi_2$ with respect to y_1. The buyers hold rational expectations about the future prices when they calculate the present value of the durable good generating $r_1 = (a - by_1)$ and $r_2 = (a - by_1 + c)/2$ as the streams of rental income per unit of y_1. We impose the rational expectation condition as

$$p_1 = r_1 + \delta r_2 = (a - by_1) + \delta\frac{(a - by_1 + c)}{2} = \frac{(a - by_1)(2+\delta) + c\delta}{2}. \tag{10.13}$$

Substituting Eq. (10.13) into Π, we write

$$\Pi = \left[\frac{(a-by_1)(2+\delta)+c\delta}{2} - c\right]y_1 + \delta\frac{(a-by_1-c)^2}{4b}.$$

The solution to this profit maximisation is

$$y_1^s = \frac{2[a-c(1-\delta)]}{b(4+\delta)} \quad \text{and} \quad y_2^s = \begin{cases} \dfrac{a(2+\delta)-c(2+3\delta)}{2b(4+\delta)} & \text{if } c < a\left(\dfrac{2+\delta}{2+3\delta}\right) \\ 0 & \text{if } a\left(\dfrac{2+\delta}{2+3\delta}\right) \le c < a \end{cases}. \tag{10.14}$$

We can check that $y_1^s < y_1^*$, where y_1^* is given in Eq. (10.12). The monopolist recognises that his first-period production will find their way back into the market in the second period through the competitive renters, and the residual demand for his second-period sale will be significantly smaller. So he tries to reduce the loss of the second-period demand by cutting back production in the first period (from y_1^*). Note that if c is sufficiently close to a (i.e., $a(2+\delta)/(2+3\delta) \le c < a$), the monopolist does not produce at all in the second period. His behaviour becomes identical to that of a renter. His profit will also be the same as that of a renter. Although the resulting profit of selling $\{y_1, y_2\}$ as opposed to renting is difficult to compare, intuitively renting gives the highest profit.

2. **Selling with commitment** Now consider the case where the monopolist can commit to a profile $\{y_1, y_2\}$ at the beginning of the two periods. Then he would maximise the following with respect to (y_1, y_2) and announce both outputs at the beginning:

$$\max \Pi = [(a-by_1-c)+\delta(a-by_1-by_2)]y_1 + \delta(a-by_1-by_2-c)y_2.$$

The solution is obtained from two first-order conditions:

$$\frac{\partial \Pi}{\partial y_1} = [(a(1+\delta)-c)-2b(1+\delta)y_1] - 2\delta b y_2 = 0 \tag{10.15}$$

$$\frac{\partial \Pi}{\partial y_2} = -\delta b y_1 + \delta[(a-c-by_1)-2by_2] = 0. \tag{10.16}$$

It can be verified that the solution to y_2 is negative, which means that y_2 must be set zero. Then the optimal period 1 output is $y_1 = \dfrac{a(1+\delta)-c}{2b(1+\delta)}$, exactly what a renter would produce as derived in Eq. (10.12).

If profit from 'selling without commitment' was higher than 'selling with commitment', then the monopolist could easily commit to the same output profile. But that is not the case. Thus, we have proved that selling with commitment, which is equivalent to renting, always gives higher profit.

Proposition 18. *Suppose the durable good monopolist has two alternative options: either (1) sell to competitive renters (without commitment) or (2) directly rent to the final consumers (but do not sell). Under the selling option, if he could commit to outputs in advance, he would sell only in period 1, and then the sell option becomes equivalent to the rent option. This gives him the highest profit. But if he cannot commit, then he ends up selling in both periods and charges a lower price in the second period. The 'no commitment' profit is lower than the renting profit.*

An obvious question is, Why doesn't the monopolist restrict his selling only to one period? The problem lies in the fact that the buyers have rational expectations and that the monopolist often lacks the necessary means to make the commitment. His decisions are inherently sequential. No matter what he says at the outset, he will not be able to resist the temptation of selling a bit in the second period and will make more money *ex post*. This inevitably means that he will compete with the commercial renters in the second period. However, the renters perfectly anticipate this likely behaviour, and therefore, they will be willing to pay a lower price in the first period. The monopolist is then forced to cut his sales in the first period and will lose much more overall. His inability to commit and the buyers' rational expectations both play crucial roles in eroding his monopoly power.

In practice, the durable goods producers take a number of actions to mitigate their predicament. (1) Periodically, they introduce variations in the features of the product and sometimes discontinue the older models. This is equivalent to killing the good prematurely (Bulow, 1986). In the markets for mobile phones, cars, computers and cameras, this is a routine practice. (2) Another strategy can be to alter the production technology such that the marginal cost of production *increases* with time. Bulow (1982) has discussed this possibility. Recall that in our model if $c > a(2+\delta)/(2+3\delta)$, the monopolist would find the second-period production costly, and thereby, he avoids the 'commitment' problem. (3) The seller can offer a price-match guarantee over an extended time. If he sells in the second period, he will have to partially refund the first-period sales. Such a promise would credibly deter him from selling in the next period. (4) Finally, renting, although more profitable under ideal conditions, is not without certain problems. Taking due care of the good is an obvious one. Most durable goods, from cars to machines, are subject to moral hazard (sloppy users causing some damage). Where such problems are significant renting may not be a practical option.

10.4.4 The Coase conjecture

The durable goods monopolist faces yet another problem that we only hinted about. That is the buyers' willingness to wait when they anticipate a price fall in future. As we said earlier, even an avid Rushdie fan may want to wait a few more months for the price of the new novel to come down. The buyers form this anticipation because the seller cannot make a credible commitment to hold the price unchanged in future. The seller will indeed lower his price in response to make buyers' expectations self-fulfilling. If the price adjustments become rapid, most buyers will find waiting even more rewarding, forcing the monopolist to settle for a very low price much more quickly. In the extreme case of rapid price falls, as Ronald Coase (1972) conjectured, all buyers will wait until the price drops to the marginal cost wiping out profit completely.

The Coase conjecture highlights the disadvantage of future flexibility of price manoeuvering, which applies to many set-ups including monopoly. The formal proof of the Coase conjecture is more complex, as one needs to consider an infinite time horizon and model both the behaviours of the individual buyers, especially their waiting strategy, and the seller's sequential decisions about price reductions. In equilibrium, both sides should have rational expectations about each other's strategy. With a model of this kind and a continuum of buyers Gul et al. (1986) proved that the Coase conjecture indeed holds where all trade collapses to one period and price to the marginal cost. However, their finding is not robust. Bagnoli et al. (1989) showed that in a model of discrete demand, there are multiple equilibria and that in one equilibrium, the monopolist is able to perfectly price discriminate, contrary to the Coase conjecture. Cason and Sharma (2001) extended this literature to two types of consumers with private information (about their types). They showed that in a limiting form of their game equilibrium is unique and trade takes place over at most two periods (displaying the so-called Coasian dynamics or inter-temporal price discrimination). Cason and Sharma (2001) notably provided the first empirical evidence of the Coase conjecture using laboratory experiment.

The general point of the durable goods monopoly is that if commitment is possible a seller should commit to future prices, because by not doing so he triggers anticipation of future price reductions amongst his buyers and his profits will be in peril. By committing today and thereby sacrificing future freedom, he can earn at least what he could earn without commitment. But commitment is not easy to make. The moral of the story is that a durable good monopolist does not really have that much monopoly power.

10.5 Conclusion

In this chapter, we studied many facets of monopoly, much of it based on the assumption that the good is a non-durable good. While monopolies are condemned for making super-normal profits and causing maximum loss of social welfare, in reality, monopolies are relatively short-lived. That is because technological advantage disappears over time or patent protection has its predetermined shelf life. Natural monopolies have special concerns that should be addressed through regulation. For long-lasting goods, the monopolist faces competition from his own future self because of the rationality of consumers. There is another type of monopoly we did not discuss here, that is, cartels formed by a group of producers. Cartels have a special problem of being internally unstable, and this instability is best understood only with the help of game theory, which we plan to study next. We conclude this section with a brief discussion of auctions in Section 10.6.

Summary

1. The degree of monopoly power is inversely related to the price elasticity of demand.
2. When a firm is a natural monopoly, that is, when its average cost is declining, monopoly is the only desirable form of market. But it needs to be regulated or nationalised.
3. Price discrimination increases monopoly profit and reduces DWL. In particular, under first-degree price discrimination, the monopolist earns the highest possible profit and completely eliminates DWL.
4. The second-degree price discrimination, which involves charging different prices for different quantities bought, reduces DWL but does not fully eliminate it.
5. In some special cases, when the high-value consumers' demand is very inelastic, the second-degree price discrimination can coincide with the first-degree price discrimination.
6. When a good is durable, its monopolist producer faces a loss in demand due to recycling or renting.
7. The durable good monopolist experiences a loss in profit when he is unable to commit to future prices. His best option is to rent out every period instead of selling.

10.6 Appendix: auctions

When a single seller confronts many potential buyers as in monopoly or a single buyer confronts many potential sellers as in monopsony and if the good to be bought and sold is an indivisible unit, then the analyses we have conducted earlier regarding optimal price and quantity do not perfectly apply. Auctions are the most common form of market for such situations. The single seller can trigger a bidding competition among the potential buyers and award the good to the winner in exchange for a payment specified in the auction rule. This is the common method by which art objects, houses, antiques and the like are sold. Likewise, a single buyer can organise a bidding contest among sellers, as governments do for building roads, buying arms and ammunition, among other things. Auctions for variable quantities are also common, as seen in the wholesale fish trade, the Amsterdam Flower Market and the way supermarkets buy their produce. But variable quantity auctions are complicated to model. Hence, we restrict our attention to the buying and selling of 1 unit of good.

Auctions vary in terms of the rules and formats, open bidding or secret bidding and so on. But they can be seen as some variant of one of the following four auctions:

1. Ascending-bids open auction (also known as the English auction)
2. Second-price sealed-bid auction (also known as the Vickrey auction)
3. First-price sealed-bid auction
4. Descending-bids open auction (also known as the Dutch auction)

As for the bidders' valuations of the object to be auctioned, there are two main classes: private value and common value. In the private-value case, each bidder values the object independently of others' valuations. Someone who appreciates art and collects it for private enjoyment would be one such example. The common-value case refers mainly to commercial bidders who are buying the good with the sole purpose of reselling in future. Their bids are likely to be correlated with the estimate of the future commercial value. Even though they estimate the future value privately, their estimates are likely to have a large common component. We first discuss auctions in a private-value setting.

10.6.1 English auction

Here the auctioneer starts from a low bid. The bidders openly bid and gradually drop out until the last bid stands. The last bidder is declared the winner, and he pays the price equal to the bid he has made. Here the bidder's strategy is simple—bid slightly higher than the last bid, provided his valuation is strictly greater than the last bid. The end result is that all bidders except the highest valuation bidder drop out. Bidders have a dominant strategy to bid all the way up to their individual valuation. The highest-valuation bidder bids the second-highest valuation and wins. Thus, the outcome of an English auction is efficient, meaning that the good goes to the bidder who values it most.

10.6.2 Vickrey auction

All bidders submit their bids in sealed envelopes. The auctioneer declares the highest bidder as the winner and asks him to pay the second-highest bid as the price. This auction was proposed by Canadian American economist William Vickrey.[8] This auction rule mimics the English auction, and every bidder has a dominant strategy to bid equal to his valuation. The outcome is also the same with the highest-valuation bidder becoming the winner. The English auction and the Vickery auction are equivalent in terms of the player strategies and the game outcome. Both auctions are information-revealing.

10.6.3 First-price sealed bid

This auction sounds similar to the Vickrey auction but is strategically very different. Here, all bidders submit their bids in sealed envelopes. The highest bidder wins, and he pays the bid he was written. Here, the bidders have an incentive to bid a lower value from their own valuation. But how much lower is not obvious. Clearly, it depends on the distribution of the valuation of the other bidders and beliefs about others' bidding strategies.

Suppose there are m risk-neutral bidders and all bidders' valuation v is distributed in the interval [0, 1] following the uniform distribution. Let $\tilde{v}$ be the valuation of a bidder, and he bids b; assume $\tilde{v} > 0$. Then his expected pay-off is $Eu = [\{\tilde{v} - b\}$. Prob. of wins]. Now consider the possibility that all bidders follow a symmetric bidding strategy that is linear in their valuation. Then the uniform distribution of valuations will also translate into a uniform distribution of bids. Suppose the resulting bids will be uniformly distributed over the support $[\underline{b}, \bar{b}]$, where $0 \le \underline{b} < 1$ and $0 < \bar{b} \le 1$.

Using this rule, one can calculate the Prob. of win $= \dfrac{mb^{m-1}}{[\bar{b} - \underline{b}]^{m-1}}$. The probability that an individual bidder's bid will not exceed b is $\dfrac{b}{\bar{b} - \underline{b}}$, and for $m-1$, bidders to have bids less b together is $\dfrac{b^{m-1}}{[\bar{b} - \underline{b}]^{m-1}}$. There are m such possible scenarios. So the expected utility from bidding b is

$$Eu(\tilde{v}) = [\tilde{v} - b]m\frac{b^{m-1}}{[\bar{b} - \underline{b}]^{m-1}}.$$

Maximising $Eu(\tilde{v})$ with respect to b, we get

$$b^*(\tilde{v}) = \frac{m-1}{m}\tilde{v} \qquad \text{for all} \quad \tilde{v} > 0.$$

The lowest-valuation bidder bids $b = 0$. Under this special and simple strategy of bidding, each bidder bids a fraction of his valuation, where the fraction depends on the number of bidders. But in general, the first-price sealed-bid auction strategies can be complex. Although *ex ante* the object is expected to go to the highest-valuation bidder, *ex post* that is not guaranteed because of the nature of the auction.

10.6.4 Dutch auction

The famous Aalsmeer Flower Market of Amsterdam is home to selling flowers following a descending-bid auction method. A clock (taking the role of an auctioneer) starts with an opening price and then at a predetermined interval keeps reducing it. Bidders are equipped with a device to stop the clock whenever they wish, and the first bidder to stop the clock wins and pays the price at which he has stopped the clock. Here, the bidders face a dilemma between waiting too long (and risk missing the chance to buy) and stopping the clock too early to secure a buy. It turns out that this auction is identical to the first-price sealed-bid auction in terms of the strategy and outcome.

10.6.5 Revenue equivalence

There is a well-known result that all four auctions are revenue equivalent. Therefore, a seller should be indifferent between all of them. This can be seen as follows: in the English auction, the bidding strategy is $b^*(v) = v$, and in the Dutch auction, $b^*(v) = \frac{m-1}{m}v$. Under the English auction, the seller receives

$$ER = \int_0^1 [v \cdot \text{Prob. of second-highest bid}]dv.$$

The probability of v being the second-highest bid is $m(m-1)v^{m-2}(1-v)$. Thus,

$$ER = \int_0^1 \left[vm(m-1)v^{m-2}(1-v)\right]dv = m(m-1)\int_0^1 \left[v^{m-1} - v^m\right]dv = \frac{m-1}{m+1}.$$

Under the Dutch auction (or the first-price auction), the probability of v being the highest-valuation bidder is mv^{m-1}, which gives

$$ER = \int_0^1 \left[\frac{m-1}{m}v\right]mv^{m-1}dv = \int_0^1 (m-1)v^m dv = \frac{m-1}{m+1}.$$

Thus, from the seller's perspective, all four auctions are equivalent. For more on auctions and revenue equivalence in particular and empirical evidence, see Phlips (1988, Chapter 4).

10.6.6 Common-value auction

The bidding strategy for common-value auctions is complicated. Here, there is a special problem of winner's curse. Every bidder has an estimate of the true value of the object, but he does not know whether other bidders' estimates are above or below his estimate. If he wins, then his valuation must be on the higher side than others'; he might then regret overestimating the value of the object.

10.7 Exercises

1. Consider a monopolist with a cost function $c = y^2/2$ facing market demand $p = 2 - y$.
    a. Derive the firm's output, price and profit.
    b. Calculate the DWL.
    c. Suppose the firm has two plants. Plant i (i=1, 2) gives rise to the cost function $C_i = c_i y^2$, with the restriction that $c_1 < 1 < c_2$. Derive the firm's optimal output and profit.

2. Suppose a market with demand $p = a - Q$ is served by a single producer whose cost function is $C = \frac{cQ^2}{2} + F$, where F observes the following restriction:

$$\frac{ca^2}{2(1+c)^2} < F < \frac{a^2}{2(2+c)}.$$

   a. Derive the monopolist's output, price and profit. Verify if profit is positive.
   b. Now consider a government intervention, in which the firm is asked to produce at the *competitive* level. What will be the firm's profit at this prescribed output?
   c. If the government offers a subsidy on the fixed cost, how much subsidy should it offer to make the monopolist indifferent between intervention and no intervention?

3. A public-sector monopoly has a cost function $C = cq$, and q depends solely on labour by the production function $q = al$. The market demand curve is $p = A - q$.

   a. First derive the public sector's optimal employment and the economy's social welfare. What is the wage rate of this firm?
   b. Now consider a scenario where wages have gone up and the marginal cost increases to $\tilde{c}$. Calculate the redundancy of this firm and the impact on social welfare.
   c. Now suppose the management finds it hard to lay off workers and all workers are retained. Calculate the effect on social welfare.
   d. An economist advises the government to privatise the public-sector firm to a single buyer and, from the proceeds of privatisation, pay severance pay to the redundant workers. What is the maximum value a private buyer will be willing to pay to buy the firm, and how much severance pay per redundant worker can be offered?

4. For a market with demand function $p = A - y$ and a monopolist producer with cost function $C = y^2 + F$, where $F = A^2/16$ is an advertising expenditure dependent on the size of the market, derive the profit-maximising price, output and social welfare. Show that the DWL of this market increases with A.

5. A monopolist has only two periods to do business, and the good is not a durable good. His cost conditions in two periods are given as

$$C_1 = kq_1 + F_1, \quad \text{and } C_2 = c_2 q_2 + F_2, \quad \text{where} \quad c_2 = k - \alpha q_1.$$

   The parameter α $(\alpha < 1)$ represents the degree of learning by doing. Let δ be the discount factor. The market demand curve $p = a - q$ is stable over time.

   a. Derive the optimal period-wise outputs and prices. Verify if $q_2 \geq q_1$.
   b. Consider an alternative case in which the learning effect accrues to fixed cost. Set $\alpha = 0$ and write $F_2 = F_1 - \beta q_1$. Derive the optimal outputs and prices.
   c. How do the period-wise outputs and prices compare now? Can you comment on which type of learning is more profit-enhancing?

6. Consider a monopolist with marginal cost c, $0 < c < 1$, and two buyers whose demand curves are $p = 1 - y$ and $p = 2 - y$. The buyers know their type, but the monopolist does not.

   a. First consider the benchmark case of no price discrimination assuming that the monopolist can identify the buyers. Derive the optimal output and profit. Continuing with the assumption of full information derive the first-degree discrimination prices and profit.

b. Assuming imperfect information derive the second-degree discrimination prices and the DWL.
c. How does your answer to part (b) change if the number of buyers is 5 and two of them are type 2 and three of them are type 1?

7. Suppose a fragrance market is monopolised. On the demand side, it is populated by two types of consumers: θ_L and θ_H, $\theta_L < \theta_H$. The mix of the consumers is 50:50. The marginal cost of fragrance production is 2. Two types of consumers' demand functions are $p_H = 10\theta_H - q$ and $p_L = 10\theta_L - q$. The monopolist wishes to discriminate price between the consumers to the extent optimal for him.

   a. Derive the menu of price-quantity pairs that the monopolist would charge under full information.
   b. Derive the second-best price-quantity pairs and compare them with the first-best case.
   c. Produce a graph of the optimal price discrimination.

8. Consider a durable goods monopoly with a rental demand curve of $r = 1 - y$. The market lasts for two periods. Production involves only a fixed cost F, but renting involves a marginal cost c. The monopolist's discount factor is δ. Assume there is no scope for accumulating inventory, and every time production is carried out F must be incurred.

   a. Derive the output and profits separately for renting and selling.
   b. Determine under what conditions renting is preferred to selling.
   c. Next, assume that γ fraction of the output sold in the first period is recycled back in the second period. How attractive is the selling option now?

Notes

1 Although in theory 51% of shareholding gives outright control of the firm, in reality, holding a much smaller proportion of shares gives control if all other investors' shares are small.
2 This should not be confused with discriminatory practices forbidden under anti-discrimination laws. Discrimination on the basis of gender, age, religion, or colour of skin, among other aspects, is illegal because they are exclusionary. Price discrimination, even when based on age, is inclusive.
3 Another way to think is that the type 1 demand curve is the aggregate demand curve of group 1 and that type 2 demand curve is the aggregate demand curve of group 2, where each group consists of certain number of identical consumers. Two groups do not have to be identical.
4 By the second-degree method we mean that the monopolist cannot ask the consumers to 'buy this and pay that' as he would under first degree, but he would lay out all possible offers, and the consumers will self-select.
5 Note this condition is just the exclusion condition for type 1. The optimality of serving both markets or just the high-demand market requires specifying a much stronger condition, which we have done in Section 10.3.1.
6 The model presented here is a simplified version of the problem based on the analysis of Bulow (1982, 1986) and Tirole (1989, Chapter 1.5).
7 The assumption of selling to commercial renters is just a modelling trick. Competition rules out any further mark-up. The key aim is to prevent renting out by consumers.
8 Sadly, Vickery died in a road accident in 1996 just three days after receiving the news that he was selected for that year's Nobel Prize.

References and further readings

Bagnoli, M., Salant, S. W. & Swierzbinski, J. E. (1989). Durable-goods monopoly with discrete demand. *Journal of Political Economy*, 97, 1459–1478.

Boiteux, M. (1956). Sur la gestion des Monopoles Publices astreints a l'Equilibre Budgetaire. *Econometrica*, 24, 22–40 [Translated as "On the management of public monopolies subject to budget constraints." *Journal of Economic Theory*, 1971, 3, 219–240].
Bulow, J. I. (1982). Durable goods monopolists. *Journal of Political Economy*, 15, 314–332.
Bulow, J. I. (1986). An economic theory of planned obsolescence. *Quarterly Journal of Economics*, 51, 729–750.
Cason, T. N. & Sharma, T. (2001). Durable goods, Coasian dynamics, and uncertainty: Theory and experiments. *Journal of Political Economy*, 109(6), 1311–1354.
Coase, R. H. (1972). Durability and monopoly. *Journal of Law and Economics*, 15, 143–149.
Gul, F., Sonnenschein, H. & Wilson, R. B. (1986). Foundations of dynamic monopoly and the Coase conjecture. *Journal of Economic Theory*, 39, 155–190.
Montague, G. H. (1902). The rise and supremacy of the Standard Oil company. *The Quarterly Journal of Economics*, 16(2), 265–292.
Phlips, L. (1988). *The Economics of Imperfect Information*. Cambridge: Cambridge University Press.
Ramsay, F. P. (1927). A contribution to the theory of taxation. *Economic Journal*, 37, 47–61.
Spulber, D. F. (1989). *Regulation and Markets*. Cambridge, MA: The MIT Press.
Tirole, J. (1989). *The Theory of Industrial Organization*. Cambridge, MA: The MIT Press.
Varian, H. R. (1985). Price discrimination and welfare. *American Economic Review*, 75(4), 870–875.
Varian, H. R. (1989). Price discrimination. In R. Schmalensee & R. Willig (Eds.), *Handbook of Industrial Organization*. Amsterdam: North-Holland.
Varian, H. R. (1992). *Microeconomic Analysis*, 3rd ed. New York: Norton.

Chapter 11

Game theory

Abstract

Game theory is essential for understanding the strategic interactions between firms and individuals or any economic actors. In this chapter we go through the dominance criterion and Nash equilibrium, two main ways to solve static games. We then study subgame perfect equilibrium for sequential games. Next, we analyse both static and sequential games with asymmetric information, where beliefs become an essential part of equilibrium. Finally, a class of games called cheap-talk games is discussed in detail.

Keywords: Dominant strategy, Nash equilibrium, Subgame-perfect equilibrium, Bayesian–Nash equilibrium Signalling, Cheap-talk games

11.1 Introduction

Game theory is now so central to microeconomics that it hardly requires justification to study it independently. Because of game theory, we are now able to model many situations of conflict, such as haggling over a price, location strategies of supermarkets, research and development competition and so on. It is the insight of game theory that informs us how precariously balanced our urge to compete and desire to cooperate are, how important it is to coordinate our actions in social situations and how to sustain peace between two warring parties paradoxically by threatening to destroy each other. Then there are compelling circumstances in which we have to act primarily based on our beliefs and guess about others and the environment around us. Modelling beliefs is complicated. Philosopher Ludwig Wittgenstein wrote in his famous book *On Certainty*, "At the core of all well-founded belief lies belief that is unfounded." The breadth and scope of game theory have expanded so rapidly over the last four decades that you are well advised to study game theory as an independent module/course alongside microeconomics.

In this chapter, we are parsimonious in covering a selection of concepts that will help us study the topics of the next few chapters. By no means do we claim to be comprehensive, nor do we pretend to offer an easier version of the technically demanding variant of game theory that it has become. Yet you will see that good understanding of a handful of key game-theoretic tools and concepts will go a long way to improve your understanding of microeconomics.

11.2 Static games

Games that are played only once and games where all players take their actions simultaneously are commonly called static games, indicating no time lapse between the players' actions. It is also conceivable that a static game might consist of only one player. For instance, the dictator

DOI: 10.4324/9781003226994-11

game in which a single player is to decide how much money she would take for herself from an exogenously given fund is a game of one player. The game is of great interest to experimental economists who study people's social preferences, such as altruism and fairness (as discussed in Chapter 5). But this is less common; most games involve at least two players. We first take up static games with full or symmetric information and later move on to dynamic games with or without symmetric information. With the help of static games, let us first try to understand three methods of solving a game—dominance solvability, Nash equilibrium and rationalisability.

11.2.1 Logic of dominance

Let us start with the most famous of all games, the *prisoner's dilemma*, in which two individuals have been arrested on suspicion of committing a crime together, but the authority lacks incriminating evidence; confession from at least one of them is needed to convict them. In order to extract confession, the authority holds them in two separate prison cells and gives each of them a chance to confess their crime. However, the reward for confessing depends on what the other prisoner does. If one confesses while the other does not, the confessing prisoner is let go and the other prisoner is severely punished with a jail term of 7 years. But if both confess, none gets any special reward or harsher punishment—criminality is proven, and both sent to jail for 4 years. However, if neither opens their mouth, the authority fails to prove the fullest extent of their crime, and the prisoners serve just 1 year for minor offences.

In the language of game theory, the prisoner's dilemma game is a one-shot or **static** game, with two prisoners playing against each other by simultaneously choosing an **action** or **strategy**—confess or not confess. Actions and strategies are not synonymous, but in static games they are. Table 11.1 panel *a* fully describes the game by specifying their strategies and consequent pay-offs in every possible **outcome** of the game. This pay-off matrix representation of the game is called a **normal form** representation. By convention, the first entry of each pay-off vector corresponds to the row player (or player 1) and the second entry to the column player (player 2). In the prisoner's dilemma game, players are identical, evident from the symmetry of their pay-offs. Since the prisoners face jail terms, their pay-offs are negative.

Now let us think how the prisoners will play this game. Prisoner 1 sitting in his cell would wonder what if prisoner 2 confesses; he would then end up for 7 years if he does not confess and 4 years if he confesses. Alternatively, if the other prisoner does not confess, he will get away with a light sentence by not confessing, but he can do better by confessing and picking up the 'go free' reward. Either way, confession is the most attractive option. Since both prisoners think in the same way, both will end up confessing.

Between the strategies of confession and no confession, the former **strictly dominates** the latter. It is natural to expect that any **rational** (i.e., being self-interested) player will never play a strictly dominated strategy. This simple logic of dominance guides the prisoners to confess. The end result of their joint confession is not something they would relish but it is nevertheless inevitable because of their 'rationality'.

Table 11.1 Dominance solvable games

(a) Prisoner's dilemma

	Confess	*Not confess*
Confess	−4, −4	0, −7
Not confess	−7, 0	−1, −1

(b) Cops and robbers

	Escape south	*Escape north*
Chase south	50, −100	0, 100
Chase north	25, −50	25, −50

Notations

Let us now introduce some notations to formally state the logic of dominance. Without loss of generality, assume there are two players, 1 and 2, and each player has n strategies in their disposal, namely, $\{s_{1i}, s_{2i}, ..., s_{ni}\}$, $i = 1, 2$. Let S_i be the **strategy set** of player i. A **strategy profile** is $\sigma = (s_{j1}, s_{k2}), j, k = 1, 2, \ldots, n$, that consists of one strategy of each player. Let $S = S_1 \times S_2$ be the Cartesian product of the players' strategy sets. A typical element of S is σ, and there are n^2 elements or strategy profiles/combinations in S.

Each player has a **pay-off** function, $U_i : S \rightarrow R$, where R is the set of real numbers. U_i specifies the pay-off of player i for each and every possible strategy profile σ. U_i can be monetary or utility and is realised after the game has been played out.

For player 1 strategy, s_{j1} is said to be **strictly dominated** if there exists a strategy $s_{j'1}$ such that for every given strategy of player 2,

$$U_1(s_{j'1};\ s_{k2}) > U_1(s_{j1};\ s_{k2}), \qquad \text{for} \quad k = 1, 2, ..., n.$$

In other words, $U_1(\sigma_j) < U_1(\sigma_{j'})$ for all σ_j and$\sigma_{j'}$, where σ_j and $\sigma_{j'}$ contain the same strategy of player 2, but for player 1, strategy j and j' respectively. An analogous definition applies to strictly dominated strategies of player 2. For player 1 strategy s_j is said to be **weakly dominated** if $U_1(\sigma_j) \leq U_1(\sigma_{j'})$.

For player i, if a strategy is strictly undominated by any other strategy, that strategy is called a **dominant** strategy. In the prisoner's dilemma game, confession is the dominant strategy for each player. Formally, for player 1, $s_{j'1}$ is a dominant strategy if and only if $U_1(s_{j'1}; s_{k2}) > U_1(s_{j1}; s_{k2})$, for all $j \neq j', j = 1, 2, ..., n$, and $k = 1, 2, \ldots, n$.

But what if a game does not have a dominant strategy profile? How to play that game? Consider the pay-off matrix of panel b in Table 11.1. In the underlying story, two robbers are trying to get away in two cars by taking one of the two alternative routes, south and north. In the car boots, they have stashed their even shares of the stolen £100,000. The cops do not know which route they have taken. The southern route is long and traffic-free. So if the robbers flee south and the cops also chase south, robbers get caught and money is retrieved in full. But if the cops mistakenly chase north, the robbers get away. Fleeing by the northern route has a different story; the route is short but congested. Chasing and fleeing both meet with partial success. Because the route is short, the cops can correct their mistake of chasing south midway by turning back and still catch one of the two robbers. Because the route is also congested, even if the cops are on the robbers' toes right from the beginning, they succeed in nabbing only one of them. In all cases, the reward for the cops is 50% of the recovered cash.

We can see that neither of the two sides has a strictly undominated strategy. The cops prefer to chase south if the robbers flee south and to chase north if the robbers have fled north. Clearly, they are in a bind. Fortunately, the robbers have a *weakly* undominated strategy in 'Escape north'. If the cops *reason* that the robbers being rational should never play a weakly dominated strategy, they can rule out the possibility of escaping south, and crucially if the robbers know that the cops would reason this way, and importantly if the cops know that the robbers know that the cops would reason this way, then both sides can look at a truncated version of the game by eliminating 'Escape south' from the strategy set. In the truncated game, cops will have a strictly undominated strategy in 'Chase north'. The game then ends with one robber getting caught on the northern route.

Note that we have now added a *common knowledge* assumption. Each player being rational is not enough to figure out how this game will be played. Each player must assume that a (weakly) dominated strategy will not be played at any stage of the game by any side and that each side must know that the other side knows it at any layer of reasoning. This common knowledge allows each player to step in the other player's shoes and figure out how her opponent decides on the optimal strategy. The force of the common knowledge assumption should be appreciated in light of the fact that the players are able to rule out in no uncertain terms the dominated strategy of 'Escape south'. If some doubt is allowed to creep into the cops' mind about the robbers' thought process, it will be hard to predict the outcome of the game.

The preceding method of eliminating a dominated strategy can be applied successively through iteration. Consider the game presented in Table 11.2 panel *a*. Here, player 2 (column) has a dominated strategy, Left. By playing centre, he is weakly better off. Player 1 then can disregard 2's play of left. Deleting his strategy left, we can write the game as in Table 11.2 panel *b*.

Next, we see that in the reduced game in Table 11.2 panel *b*, player 1 has a dominated strategy Left. Eliminating 1's strategy Left, the game is further reduced to only right and centre for each player as shown in Table 11.2 panel *c*. In that game, player 2's strategy Right is strictly dominated by Centre. So, we eliminate Right from 2's strategy set to arrive at game in Table 11.2 panel *d*, where player 1 strictly prefers to play Centre. Thus, the outcome of the game is that both players play Centre and get 2 each. This method of solving a game is called **iterated elimination of dominated strategies.**

It is noteworthy that in the original game player 1 also has a dominated strategy in Left. Eliminating Left from player 1's strategy set, we can eliminate Left from 2's strategy set and eventually arrive at the same outcome of both playing Centre. However, when we successively eliminate *weakly* dominated strategies, the final outcome can depend on the order of the elimination (which, however, does not happen in our example), but when eliminating *strictly* dominated strategies, the order of elimination does not affect the outcome.

Further experimentation with eliminating dominated strategies should reveal that the logic of dominance solvability has its limitations. The most obvious one is that we may not arrive at a unique strategy combination. How do we predict the outcome of such games? Or should we say, how will the players play such games? This question takes us to an alternative approach, called the equilibrium approach and more specifically to Nash equilibrium.

Table 11.2 Iterated elimination of weakly dominated strategies

(a) Round 1

	Right	Left	Centre
Right	5, 5	2, 4	1/2, 6
Left	4, 5	3, 4	1, 4
Centre	4, 1	4, 3/2	2, 2

(b) Round 2

	Right	Centre
Right	5, 5	1/2, 6
Left	4, 5	1, 4
Centre	4, 1	2, 2

(c) Round 3

	Right	Centre
Right	5, 5	1/2, 6
Centre	4, 1	2, 2

(d) Round 4

	Centre
Right	1/2, 6
Centre	2, 2

11.2.2 Nash equilibrium

Consider another game, called the battle of the sexes game (Table 11.3 panel *a*). The story of the game goes like this. A couple wants to spend an evening together after work. There are two choices, movie or theatre. Absent any mobile communication device, the couple need to guess where their other half will be heading to. The husband has a strict preference for theatre while the wife's preference is for the movies, and they enjoy them most when they are in each other's company. The possibility of being alone in their less preferred destination is the worst outcome that each wants to avoid.

In this game, there is no dominant strategy for any player. It is, therefore, a good idea to think in terms of interlocked strategy pairs. The husband prefers to go to the movies, if he expects his wife to go to the movies as well (and thus get utility 3 instead of 2). Likewise, the wife prefers to go to a movie (than being at the theatre alone) if she expects her husband to do the same. Thus, both opting for the movies is an interlocked pair of strategies from which neither would want to *deviate unilaterally*. Similarly, both going to theatre is another interlocked pair of strategies. Such interlocked strategies are called **Nash equilibrium.**

Definitions: (1) Strategy s^*_{j1} of player 1 is a ***best response*** to strategy s_{k2} of player 2, if and only if
$U(s^*_{j1};s_{k2})) \geq U(s_{j'1};s_{k2})$ for all $j' \neq j$, and $j' = 1,2,...,n$.

(2) The strategy profile $\sigma^* = (s^*_{j1}, s^*_{k2})$ is a **Nash equilibrium** if s^*_{j1} and s^*_{k2} are the mutual best responses to each other.

It is recommended that in games like the battle of the sexes, players should think in terms of a Nash equilibrium while selecting their strategy. The husband's selection of a movie must be justified by his expectation of the wife's selection of a movie. Likewise, the wife's selection of the theatre is justified by an expectation of her husband's selection of the theatre. But expectations can go wrong, especially when there are multiple equilibria as in this game. Therefore, it is impossible to predict a unique outcome. There is no obvious way to determine how the couple would *coordinate* on a specific equilibrium.

In situations like the one portrayed in the chicken game in Table 11.3 panel *b*, failure of coordination has disastrous consequences. In the background story, two motorists are approaching each other on a narrow mountain road. Each takes pride in not swerving and sticking to the middle of the road. Swerving gives them a sense of 'being chicken'. But if neither swerves, they collide and may experience serious harm. There are two equilibria here: (Swerve, Do not swerve) and (Do not swerve, Swerve). The quesiton is, How do they coordinate?

Table 11.3 Coordination games

(a) Battle of the sexes

	Movie	*Theatre*
Movie	5,3	2,2
Theatre	0,0	3,5

(b) Chicken game

	Swerve	*Do not swerve*
Swerve	5, 5	0, 10
Do not swerve	10, 0	−10, −10

In reality, we find many ways to coordinate. Here are some of them:

1. Pareto superiority. If one equilibrium is Pareto superior to the others, then it will have a higher chance of being selected. In our battle of the sexes game, neither equilibria is Pareto-dominated (assuming equal weight to the utility of the husband and the utility of the wife). Hence, the Pareto criterion fails.
2. Pre-play communication. Pre-play communication between the husband and wife would save them from the disaster of going to different places. However, if such communications are merely talks without any backup of commitment, one may see that such communication is not very helpful. But recent advances in the cheap-talk literature shows that such communications are indeed helpful.
3. Sequential move. If the wife is allowed to decide first, she would buy two movie tickets. That would indicate commitment on her behalf and the husband will join her.
4. Focal points are another way to facilitate coordination. Consider the following game: Two brothers are given 100 rupees to split in any way they want. Most people would agree that the brothers would split it in half and half. (The rupee-split game has infinitely many Nash equilibria.) Economist Thomas Schelling found that if people are asked to choose a number from the set of 7, 100, 13, 261 and 99, most people would choose 7. How such focal points are formed is a complex matter.
5. Norms can evolve through repeated plays. In mountainous areas, there may be well established practices of giving right of way to motorists who are driving uphill. The utility from honouring a norm offsets the pride from not swerving.
6. When players need to coordinate on symmetric strategies, as in the battle of the sexes game, the chance of coordination is much greater than that in games where the required coordination should occur on asymmetric strategies (as in the chicken game).

Nash equilibrium and iterated elimination of dominated strategies are just two alternative approaches to solving a game. If there is a unique Nash equilibrium the iterated elimination method also leads to the Nash equilibrium. For instance, the game of Table 11.2 panel *a* has a unique Nash equilibrium (Centre, Centre), which is also obtained by the iterated elimination method. If there are two Nash equilibria, the iterated method will preserve the two equilibria in its maximally reduced form.

11.2.2.1 Non-existence of Nash equilibrium

There are games that have no Nash equilibrium. In the matching penny game (Table 11.4 panel *a*), two brothers play a game of hiding a penny in their hands, holding heads or tails up and then (simultaneously) revealing to see if they match or do not match. If the pennies match, the big brother (row player) gets the little brother's penny, and if they do not match the little brother gets the big brother's penny. In this game, there is no congruence of interest and no Nash equilibrium. The pay-offs presented in the game are in terms of gain and loss.

In the right panel of Table 11.4, we have a more generalised version of the matching penny game, in which the pay-offs do not add up to zero. Imagine two sisters playing hide and seek. The little sister hides in one of the two rooms, and the big sister has to find her. Again, two sisters' interests are not congruent. We also let the pay-offs to vary depending on the room where the hider is found. Similar match–mismatch types of games are penalty shoot-out (in football). These games do not have a Nash equilibrium.

Table 11.4 Matching pennies and hide and seek

(a) Matching pennies

	Head	*Tail*
Head	1, −1	−1,1
Tail	−1,1	1, −1

(b) Hide and seek (a, b > c)

	Hide in 1	*Hide in 2*
Seek in 1	*a*, 1 − *a*	*c*, 1 − *c*
Seek in 2	*c*, 1 − *c*	*b*, 1 − *b*

11.2.2.2 *Mixed strategy*

In the previous discussion, when we said that games like matching pennies do not have equilibrium, we meant equilibrium in pure strategies. *Pure strategy* refers to the deterministic play of a given strategy—either play it or don't play it. *Mixed strategy* refers to playing a strategy with probability, which is a randomisation over pure strategies. Such randomisation occurs when a player is indifferent between some (if not all) pure strategies. Generally, one is indifferent between pure strategies when the other player is randomising over her strategies as well. Real-world examples of mixed strategies include the following: (1) Individuals to be audited for income tax are randomly selected. (2) In the game of cricket, a pace bowler may randomly swing the ball inward or outward to deceive the batter. (3) In penalty shootouts, a footballer's shot at goal should appear random to keep the goalkeeper guessing.

Definition: (1) The mixed strategy of player 1 is a probability distribution $m_1(S_1)$ over her strategy set, such that $m_{j1}(s_{j1})$ is the probability of playing strategy s_{j1} and $m_{11}+m_{21}+\ldots+m_{n1}=1$. The mixed strategy of player 2 is analogously defined as $m_2(S_2)$.

(2) Player 1's mixed strategy $m_1^*(S_1)=(m_{11}^*,m_{21}^*,\ldots,m_{n1}^*)$ is best response to player 2's strategy $m_2(S_2)$ if and only if $EU_1(m_1^*;m_2)\geq EU_1(m_1;m_2)$ for all $m_1\neq m_1^*$, where

$$EU_1(m_1^*,m_2)=\sum_{i=1}^{n} m_{i1}^*\left(\sum_{j=1}^{n} m_{j2}U_1(s_{i1};s_{j2})\right).$$

(3) A mixed strategy profile $\mu^*=(m_1^*;m_2^*)$ is a **Nash equilibrium** if m_1^* and m_2^* are best responses to each other.

Now let us try to derive the equilibrium mixed strategies for the game of matching pennies. Let p (and $(1-p)$) be the probability of selecting head (tail) for the big brother (the row player) and q (and $(1-q)$) be the same for the little brother; $0<p,\ q<1$. The expected pay-off of the big brother from playing head (H) is $Eu_b(H)=[q-1+q]=2q-1$, and the same from playing tail is $Eu_b(T)=1-2q$. Playing H with certainty (which is a pure strategy play, $p=1$) is optimal if $2q-1>1-2q$; that is, $q>1/2$. Playing T with certainty is optimal if $q<1/2$ (i.e., optimal $p=0$). But if $q=1/2$, the big brother is indifferent between playing H or T; any $p\in[0,1]$ is optimal here. Thus, we can write the two brothers' maximum pay-offs (resulting from optimal p against q) as

$$Eu_b=\begin{cases}1-2q & \text{for } q<1/2\\ 0 & \text{for } q=1/2\\ 2q-1 & \text{for } q>1/2\end{cases} \quad\text{and}\quad Eu_l=\begin{cases}1-2p & \text{for } p<1/2\\ 0 & \text{for } p=1/2.\\ 2p-1 & \text{for } p>1/2\end{cases}$$

Note that for both players, there is a range of probabilities which give the same pay-off. If $q = 1/2$, the optimal value of p is any number between 0 and 1. This makes the best response or reaction a correspondence rather than a function. Similarly, if $p = 1/2$ optimal $q \in [0,1]$. Thus, we write the player's reaction correspondences as

$$p^* = \begin{cases} 0 & \text{if } q < 1/2 \\ p_0^1 & \text{if } q = 1/2 \\ 1 & \text{if } q > 1/2 \end{cases} \quad \text{and} \quad q^* = \begin{cases} 1 & \text{if } p < 1/2 \\ q_0^1 & \text{if } p = 1/2, \\ 0 & \text{if } p > 1/2 \end{cases}$$

where $p_0^1 = [0,1]$ and $q_0^1 = [0,1]$ represent the entire interval. Both correspondences have an intersection set containing $p^* = q^* = 1/2$. That is precisely our Nash equilibrium. Panel a of Figure 11.1 shows the two reaction correspondences. If the little brother plays H with probability q > 1/2, the big brother will play H with certainty. Alternatively, if the little brother plays H with probability q < 1/2 the big brother will play T with certainty, and at q = 1/2 he is completely indifferent. From the little brother's perspective being matched is a disaster. That is why when the big brother plays H with probability p > 1/2 the little brother will play T with certainty. The rest of the graph is self-explanatory. The unique mixed strategy equilibrium is $(1/2, 1/2)$.

Although mixed strategies often appear difficult to interpret, in certain contexts, they are quite helpful. For instance, in some games, a mixed strategy may dominate a pure strategy, even if no pure strategy is dominated by another pure strategy. Suppose there are three strategies, *A*, *B* and *C* and none is dominated. But a randomisation over *A* and *C* may dominate the pure strategy *B*. It is also possible that a pure strategy can be the best response to a mixed strategy, while it is not the best response to any pure strategy. Furthermore, when there are multiple Nash equilibria, as in the battle of the sexes game, a mixed-strategy equilibrium can be unique and overcome the problem of coordination.

On panel *b* of Figure 11.1, we draw the reaction correspondences of a wife and husband for the battle of the sexes game. Suppose, p and $1 - p$ are the probabilities of wife going to a movie (*M*) or the theatre (*T*). Likewise, the husband's mixed strategies are q and $1 - q$ for *M* and *T*,

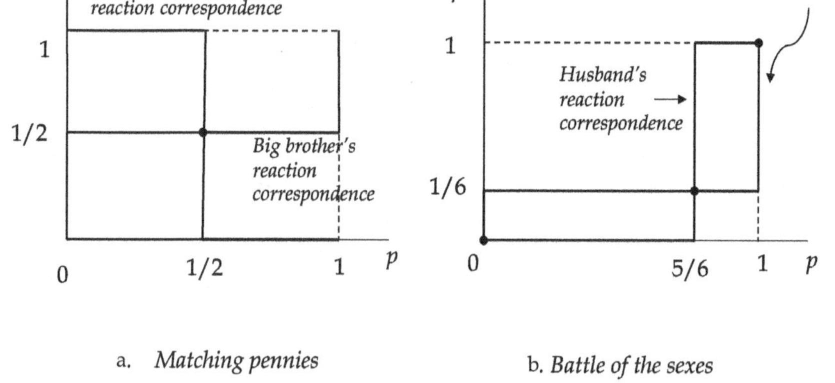

Figure 11.1 Nash equilibrium in mixed strategies

respectively. Let us first calculate the wife's pure strategy response to any mixed strategy of the husband. For a given q, the wife prefers to play M if and only if $5q+2(1-q)>(1-q)3$, which requires $q>1/6$. By comparison, for $q<1/6$, she would surely play T. And for $q=1/6$, she is indifferent, and her response would be the entire $[0,1]$ interval of p. For the husband, the pure-strategy response of playing M is optimal if $3p>2p+5(1-p)$, which requires $p>5/6$. For $p<5/6$, he would surely play T. But at $p=5/6$, he is indifferent, and any value of $q\in[0,1]$ would be his best response. The two best response correspondences of the players contain $p=5/6$ and $q=1/6$ as their common point, and therefore, we have a mixed-strategy Nash equilibrium$(p^*=5/6, q^*=1/6)$. The reaction correspondences meet at two other points, namely, $(p=q=0)$ and $(p=q=1)$. These are two pure-strategy equilibria. However, note that both players make an expected pay-off of $5/2$ under the mixed-strategy equilibrium, which is dominated by either of the pure-strategy equilibrium, where each is assured of at least 3.

At this point, it should be clear that a Nash equilibrium is an intersection point/set of the best response functions/correspondences of all players. Since best responses are mapping from the strategy set to itself, Nash equilibrium is essentially a fixed point. For the existence of a fixed point, we need to satisfy the conditions laid out in Brouwer's and the Kakutani fixed-point theorems. Two key conditions are that the strategy set should be convex and compact, and the best response mapping should be continuous if it is a function and upper hemi-continuous if it is a correspondence. The first condition is ensured by randomisation over discrete strategies, and the second condition is met by the fact that the best responses are maximisers.

11.2.3 Rationalisable strategies

A third approach to solving games, according to Pearce (1984) and Bernheim (1984), is to identify strategies that can never be rationalised as being ever played. Following the British spelling convention, I would call them rationalisable. A strategy is not rationalisable if (1) it is strictly dominated by another pure strategy, (2) it is strictly dominated by a mixed strategy (involving other pure strategies) or (3) it is never the best response strategy to any strategy.

Thus, rationalisable strategies are the strategies that are left after the iterative removal of strategies that are never the best responses. These strategies include Nash equilibrium strategies.

Here, we look for strategies that are not **rationalisable**, or that cannot be justified as a rational response invoking a player's conjectures or beliefs about his opponents' possible choice of strategy. This argument essentially redefines the best response strategies. So far, when we said that strategy s_1 of player 1 is the best response to s_2 of player 2, we almost implied that player 1 will play s_1 if player 2 plays s_2 as if s_1 is optimal against the *actual choice* of s_2. But, in the simultaneous move games, the actual choice of one player is not observable to the other player prior to his own choice.

Therefore, the best response function can be given an alternative interpretation. Player 1's strategy s_1 is the best response when she **conjectures** or **believes** that player 2 will play s_2. This interpretation is equally applicable to both pure and mixed strategies. However, an important requirement of this argument is that players must use their common knowledge to form a conjecture.

While making a conjecture about player 2's strategy s_2, player 1 must put herself in player 2's shoes and imagine what player 2 might believe about player 1's strategies to justify her choice of s_2, and then player 1 has to get back to herself and think about how she would justify her choice of the strategy that player 2 would believe her to play, and so on. As is obvious, this is an infinite chain of reasoning or thinking entirely based on the players' common knowledge and rationality.

Table 11.5 Rationalisable strategies

(a) Game 1

	t_1	t_2
τ_1	2, 1	1, 2
τ_2	1, 2	2, 1

(b) Game-2

	t_1	t_2	t_3	t_4
τ_1	4, 0	1, 1	2, 0	1, −1/2
τ_2	0, 1	2, 4	3, −1	3/2, 2
τ_3	2, −1	1, 3	2, 4	3, 2
τ_4	3, 2	3/2, 1	4, 2	2, 4

When this chain of reasoning goes through a set of strategies, without bumping into irrationality, we can say that these strategies are rationalisable.

Consider the game shown in Table 11.5 panel *a*. First note that this game does not have any Nash equilibrium. Nor does it have any dominated strategy. But are all strategies rationalisable? Start with τ_1. The row player will play τ_1 if she believes that the column player will play t_1. But then she must think that the column player will play t_1 if the column player believes that the row player will play τ_2. Why would the column player believe so? The column player will believe so, because it is rational for the row player to play τ_2 if the row player believes that the column player will play t_2, because it is rational for the column player to play t_2 when she believes that the row player will play τ_1. The row player's choice of τ_1 is rational if she believes that the column player will play t_1. Thus, we are back to the starting point of a loop, where the rationality argument runs through all four strategies for infinite rounds without a halt, $\tau_1 \to t_1 \to \tau_2 \to t_2 \to \tau_1 \to t_1$, and the loop goes on. Hence, all the strategies are rationalisable.

Next, consider the game shown in Table 11.5 panel *b*. What are the rationalisable pure strategies in this game? For either player, no strategy is strictly dominated by another (pure) strategy. However, strategy t_1 is dominated by a mixed strategy $(0,1/2,0,1/2)$, that is, playing t_2 and t_4 with probabilities 1/2 and 1/2. Then the row player cannot rationalise the column player's play of t_1. Once we delete t_1, then the row player cannot ever play τ_1, because τ_1 was best response to t_1. So τ_1 needs to be deleted.

Next, with (τ_1, t_1) out of the picture we can see that (τ_2, t_2) are mutual best responses. Thus, (τ_1, t_2) are a Nash equilibrium and rationalisable as well. Furthermore, τ_3 is best response to t_4, and t_4 is best response to τ_4, while τ_4 is best response to t_3, which the column player would play if she expects the row player to play τ_3. Thus, we have an endless loop $\tau_3 \to t_4 \to \tau_4 \to t_3 \to \tau_3 \to t_4 \ldots$. Combining these with the Nash equilibrium strategies we conclude that (τ_2, τ_3, τ_4) and (t_2, t_3, t_4) are rationalisable.

Note that here we do not necessarily end up with a strategy pair like in Nash equilibrium. But we identify all strategies whose play can be justified by invoking the rationality logic.

11.3 Dynamic games

Games in which players make decisions over time, allowing later movers to have more information than early movers, require us to think of strategies and Nash equilibrium in a slightly different way.[1]

First of all, the sequential nature of decision-making can be brought out by presenting the game through a game tree, which is called an *extensive form* representation. Take the prisoner's dilemma game but assume that prisoner 1 is first given the opportunity to confess (or not confess); after prisoner 1 makes his decision, prisoner 2 learns about it and decides whether to confess or not confess. Panel *a* of Figure 11.2 shows this game. The game tree begins with the decision node of prisoner 1. Following the two alternative decisions of prisoner 1, prisoner 2 has two decision modes, and at each node, he has the same action sets. According to the four paths of play four pay-off vectors are noted.

Here, it is important to make a distinction between actions and strategies. Prisoner 1 has two *actions*, which are also his two strategies. But prisoner 2 has two actions, namely, confess (*C*) and not confess (*NC*), and four strategies. Each strategy for prisoner 2 must spell out what action he would take following every history of the game. His strategies are

1. *CC:* If prisoner 1 has played *C*, play *C*; if prisoner 1 has played *NC*, play *C*.
2. *CNC:* If prisoner 1 has played *C*, play *C*, if prisoner 1 has played *NC* play *NC*.
3. *NCC:* If prisoner 1 has played *C*, play *NC*; if prisoner 1 has played *NC*, play *C*.
4. *NCNC:* If prisoner 1 has played *C*, play *NC*; if prisoner 1 has played *NC*, play *NC*.

After defining strategies this way we can present a dynamic game in normal form (Table 11.6). The pay-offs for the second prisoner have been determined by considering the strategy of the first prisoner. We can easily check that the unique Nash equilibrium of this game is (*C*, *CC*). This means that both prisoners will confess, rendering the same outcome as in the simultaneous game.[2]

Second, in a sequential game context, an early mover must take into account how the late mover will react to her moves. If she fears a threat of retaliation from her rival to her choice of strategy *x*, then she should examine if her rival would indeed carry out the threat should she

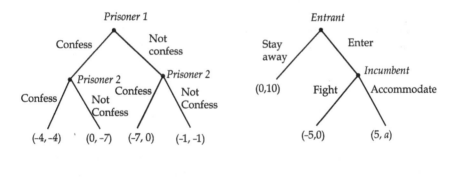

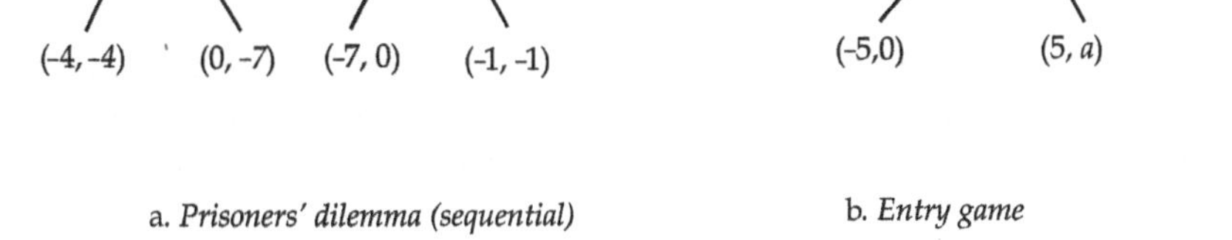

Figure 11.2 Extensive form game

Table 11.6 Sequential prisoner's dilemma

	C	CNC	NCC	NCNC
C	−4, −4	−4, −4	0, −7	0, −7
NC	−7, 0	−1, −1	−7, 0	−1, −1

choose x. Equally, if she anticipates cooperation to her decision y, then her anticipation should be really met *ex post*. Thus, any threat of retaliation or promise of cooperation *must be credible* in the subgame regardless of the history of the game.

Consider the game depicted in panel *b* of Figure 11.2. It is a game of entry. An entrant is contemplating whether to enter or stay out of a market served by a single incumbent. If he stays out, the game ends and the incumbent retains a monopoly pay-off of 10. But if he enters, the incumbent can fight or accommodate entry. The incumbent will fight if $a < 0$ and accommodate if $a > 0$. If $a > 0$, the threat of fighting is not credible and the entrant should enter. Although entry, if met with 'Fight', is costly, the entrant should conclude that the incumbent will never carry out the threat of fighting and instead accommodate entry.

This notion of credibility of threats (or promises) must be an integral feature of the Nash equilibrium. This idea was put forward by Selten (1975). Therefore, in dynamic games, we should talk about **subgame perfect Nash equilibrium** (SPNE), formally which is a profile of mutually best responses at each and every subgame of the game along the equilibrium path. The method of ensuring subgame perfection (or verifying credible threats) is **backward induction**, that is, solving the game by starting from the last stage and going backwards.

In panel *a*, we can see that in either subgame, prisoner 2's optimal action is confess. Travelling upwards along the confess branch (and ignoring prisoner 2's not-confess action), we see that prisoner 1 should choose confess too, because that brings only 4 years of jail term instead of 7-year jail term from not confessing.

To see the importance of credible threat, we can reconsider the entry game in its normal form. The entrant firm has the following strategies: (1) *FF:* If 1 has stayed away, fight; if 1 has entered, fight. (2) *FA:* If 1 has stayed away, fight; if 1 has entered, accommodate. (3) *AF:* If 1 has stayed away, accommodate; if 1 has entered, fight. (4) *AA:* If 1 has stayed away, accommodate; if 1 has entered, accommodate.

The Nash equilibria of the normal-form game are as follows:

1. If $a < 0$ there are two equilibria: (Stay away, *FF*) and (Stay away, *AF*).
2. If $a > 0$ there are four equilibria: (Stay away, *FF*), (Stay away, *AF*), (Enter, *FA*) and (Enter, *AA*).

Consider the case of $a < 0$. These two equilibria imply a unique equilibrium path of play in the extensive form game, in which the entrant stays away and the incumbent plays a dummy strategy, either fight or accommodate. Note that the incumbent does not get a chance to play in equilibrium; however, what he would do in the unreached node, if the entrant (unexpectedly) played 'Enter', works as a credible threat. The second part of the strategies *FF* and *AF* both specify 'Fight' in the event of entry and since $a < 0$ fighting is optimal in the subgame. For the first part of these two strategies, which specifies a dummy action, playing 'accommodate' against staying away while playing 'Fight' against entry is nonsensical. Therefore, we can eliminate the equilibrium (Stay away, *AF*).

Table 11.7 Normal form of the entry game

	FF	*FA*	*AF*	*AA*
Stay away	0, 10	0, 10	0, 10	0, 10
Enter	−5, 0	5, *a*	−5, 0	5, *a*

For the case of $a > 0$, we see two equilibrium paths of play: (1) The entrant stays away, and the incumbent plays a dummy action. (2) The entrant enters, and the incumbent accommodates. Note that the first path of play is based on the presumption that the incumbent will play 'Fight'. But this is not credible, because if entry occurs, the incumbent would prefer to accommodate, get $a > 0$ than to fight and get nothing. Therefore, equilibria (Stay away, *FF*) and (Stay away, *AF*) are to be discarded. From the remaining two, we can further eliminate (Enter, *FA*), because the first part of the strategy of the incumbent is not credible. Thus, (Enter, *AA*) is the unique SPNE as we have derived from the extensive form game.

Definition of SPNE: Suppose players 1 and 2 have finite action sets A_1 and A_2. Their strategy sets S_1 and S_2 are defined on the action sets and the order of play. Let s_{j1} be a typical element of S_1 and s_{k2} of S_2.

(1) Strategy s^*_{j1} of player 1 is a **best response** to strategy s_{k2} of player 2, if and only if

$$U(s^*_{j1}; s_{k2})) \geq U(s_{j'1}; s_{k2}) \text{ for all } j' \neq j.$$

(2) The strategy profile $\sigma^* = (s^*_{j1}, s^*_{k2})$ is an SPNE if s^*_{j1} and s^*_{k2} are the mutual best responses to each other, not only along the equilibrium path of play but also off the equilibrium paths, including the unreached nodes.

The definition of the SPNE differs from the standard Nash equilibrium in two respects. It makes a distinction between actions and strategies, and it enforces credible threats to be an integral feature so that at no point of the play deviation by any party will ever be optimal.

In order to ensure the credibility of threats, we have used backward induction, which is the standard method applied in all dynamic full information games that have a finite length. However, there are some conceptual issues with backward induction, despite its power of forcing a unique equilibrium (in most cases). Backward induction can be a straitjacket leading to a unique, but non-intuitive, equilibrium. Consider the following few examples.

11.3.1 *Finitely repeated prisoner's dilemma*

Consider the story of the two prisoners again. Suppose the prisoners are serial offenders and they play the same game for n periods, every time the game is just a repetition of the same game. The (finitely) repeated prisoners' dilemma game is of great interest for the fact that in the static game, the players end up with 4 years of jail term, while there is a Pareto optimal outcome of both spending just 1 year each. Perhaps, only one time period is an artificial restriction that prevents people from seeing any future reward to present cooperation.

Now let us try to solve this dynamic game by backward induction. Start from the nth period. Whatever the history of the game, the prisoners are in a one-period static game (as it is the last period), and we know that they will play their dominant strategy 'confess'. That is, there is no cooperation in the last period. Moving to the last but one period, each player would consider 'What is the reward for cooperation, because next period we all will confess?' Therefore, in the penultimate period, both will confess. In the $n - 2$ period, the prisoners face the same conundrum, as they perfectly anticipate the inevitability of playing 'Confess' in the next two periods. So, they confess again. Thus, regardless of the number of times the game is repeated, as long as the repetition is finite the prisoners always confess.

However, the failure of the prisoners to cooperate (even after many repetitions) is neither intuitive nor very realistic. But it is the unique outcome of the backward induction reasoning that game theory has come to rely on for solving sequential games. In a sense, backward induction in a finitely repeated prisoner's dilemma creates a paradox by enforcing the static game outcome as the only sustainable solution.

Similar paradoxes have been noted by Selten (1978) in the chain store game and Rosenthal (1981) in the centipede game. In the chain store game, a monopolist has 20 chain stores in 20 different locations and is facing threats of entry one by one (sequentially) into all 20 markets. As such, in a given market, the monopolist is better off accommodating entry than fighting it. But if he fights entry at least in the first few rounds, the entrant firms would stay away, and the monopolist would enjoy a much higher overall pay-off. But backward induction forces us to see that no matter what happens in 19 markets, in the 20th market, the monopolist would always accommodate, and anticipating that the 19th market entrant will definitely enter and force accommodation, and by the similar logic in each and every market entry will be accommodated. Rationality based on backward induction forces entry accommodation in every market, while other types of rationality that do not rely on backward induction can generate deterrence and higher pay-offs for the monopolist. This is the paradox.

The centipede game is shown in Figure 11.3. Two players, A and B, have the option of taking a given allocation of a pot or passing the pot to the other. In passing, the pot gets bigger every round. The taking rule is that player A splits the pot evenly, while player B takes a larger share with exactly £3 more than what his rival gets. The game lasts for nine rounds in this example, with A moving in odd rounds and B in even rounds. In the last round, taking is the only option, and in any round, the choice of the Take the option terminates the game.

Intuitively, it seems rational for players to pass the pot for few rounds before exercising the selfish Take option. In our example, the pot begins with a size of £2, and if the pot is passed eight rounds, the pot will grow to £10. Surely, it is in the players' interest to let the pot grow. Yet, the backward induction reasoning forces us to conclude that the pot will be taken in the very first round. Starting from the eighth round, B sees that getting £6 is better than getting £5 in the next round. So he will play Take. Knowing this A will play Take in the seventh round (because £4 is better than £3) and so on. Once again, we see that backward induction–based rationality does not always produce outcomes that are intuitively 'rational'. Under backward induction, even if a player finds himself in an off-the-equilibrium node (following a mistake of his rival or signalling the intent of cooperation), he will make the most 'selfish' choice. This strong notion of credible threat forces all players (with perfect foresight) to make the safest and most selfish decisions all the way.

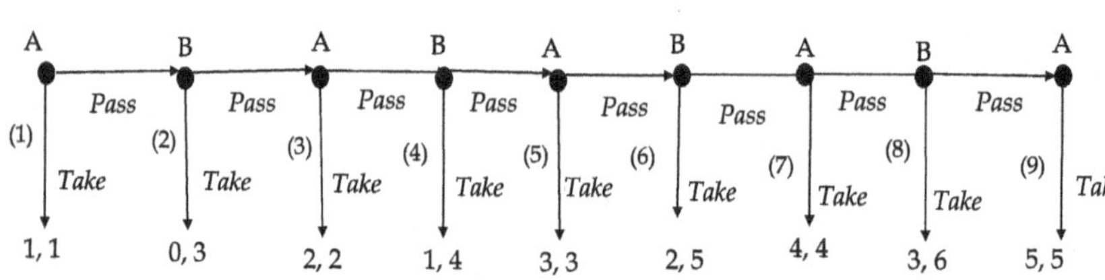

Figure 11.3 Centipede game

11.3.2 *Traveller's dilemma*

The previously mentioned inconsistency is not exclusive to sequential games. It can arise even in single-shot games. Basu's (1994) traveller's dilemma game, in which backward induction works only at the introspective level, demonstrates this problem.

The story goes like this: Two travellers bought identical antiques on a remote island but found their suitcases carrying the antiques damaged by the airline. The airline manager, knowing that the travellers had identical antiques but not knowing their true price, asks them to separately write the price of the antique. Their stated price should be between \$2 and \$100 (as the airline's maximum compensation is \$100). If they quote an identical price $x_i = x_j$, the airline will pay x_i to both of them. If their quotes are different, say, $x_i > x_j$, the lower quote will be taken as the true price, and for traveller *j*'s honesty, he will be given $x_j + 2$ while traveller *i* will be given $x_j - 2$.

What price should the travellers write? At first thought, Traveller 1 would be tempted to write \$100 expecting his counterpart to do the same, but then he tells himself, "Hold on! I can quote \$99 and pick up \$101." The other traveller is also on a similar thought trail, and soon they will revise their quotes to 99, 98, . . . and eventually settle at \$2. Thus, (2, 2) is the unique Nash equilibrium of this game. Note that the players are applying backward induction–based rationality as if they were in a sequential game, but the game is one-shot, yet the force of backward induction reasoning pushes them all the way down to the minimum compensation. One would expect that each player would be able to quote a much higher figure than the minimum with the expectation of the other doing the same. But that is not admitted in the known solution concepts of the game theory.

Empirical evidence on the traveller's dilemma shows that the size of the penalty (reward) of quoting a higher (lower) price matters for the quoted price. Capra et al. (1999) found from laboratory experiments that higher reward/punishment induces the average price quoted by the players to be close to the minimum price, while smaller reward/punishment pushes the average price near the permissible maximum.

At one level, there are philosophical issues of rationality and common knowledge of rationality, and some of these issues are unresolved. In fact, backward induction has come to be accepted as the bedrock of finite-horizon dynamic games.

11.3.3 *Infinitely repeated games*

Infinite repetitions of one-shot games are of particular interest, because it has no end period and thus backward induction becomes inapplicable. Some of the paradoxes mentioned earlier may be avoided in such open-ended dynamic games.

Let us consider the infinite repetition of prisoner's dilemma. In the infinitely repeated game, the one-shot game is called the stage game. Each prisoner/player has a common discount factor $0 < \delta < 1$. We are particularly interested to find if cooperation can be achieved and sustained as an SPNE. Since backward induction cannot be applied here, the *notion* of subgame perfection needs to be enforced in a different way. Here, to support a particular sequence of play as equilibrium, we need to specify another strategy profile as a **punishment path** that must be taken if one of the players deviates from the equilibrium at any point of the play. The subgame perfection is then checked by comparing each player's pay-off from the equilibrium path with that from the punishment path. Let us now demonstrate this notion of equilibrium by two well-known strategies, grim and tit-for-tat.

11.3.3.1 Grim strategy

Under this strategy, both players will begin (*NC*, *NC*; i.e., not confessing which is our desired strategy of cooperation) and will continue to play so until one deviates. If one deviates, both players will have to resort to playing (*C*, *C*) forever. The punishment strategy here is to play the stage-game Nash equilibrium forever. Let us now examine a given player's incentive to play *NC* or deviate to *C* at any given period.

Without loss of generality, consider prisoner 1. When prisoner 2 plays *NC*, by playing *NC* prisoner 1 will suffer a lifetime loss (or a negative pay-off) of

$$\Delta_1^* = -1(1+\delta+\delta^2+\delta^3......) = -\frac{1}{1-\delta}.$$

By unilaterally deviating to *C*, he gets 0 for one period and thereafter −4 forever. His loss will be

$$\Delta^D = 0 - 4\delta[1+\delta+\delta^2+\delta^3+.....] = -\delta\frac{4}{1-\delta}.$$

Deviation to *C* is not optimal if $\delta\frac{4}{1-\delta} > \frac{1}{1-\delta}$, which requires $\delta > 1/4$. The same can be checked for prisoner 2. Thus, if the prisoners' discount factor exceeds 1/4 cooperation will be sustained as an SPNE.

11.3.3.2 Tit-for-tat strategy

When the players are asked to play tit-for-tat, they must start with (*NC*, *NC*) until one deviates to *C*. Following the deviation, the players must play the rival's previous period action. For example, if player 1 deviates to *C* at time *t*, while player 2 still plays *NC*, then at time *t* + 1, player 1 must play *NC* (which was player 2's action at time *t*) and player 2 will play *C* (which was player 1's action in period *t*). Then in period *t* + 2, player 1 must play *C* and player 2 must play *NC*. Thus, we have a sequence of switching back and forth between *C* and *NC* by each player in alternative periods, forming an endless sequence of mutual retaliation.

Again, without loss of generality, consider player 1's incentive to deviate. By deviating to *C*, he will get 0 for one period and thereafter −7 and 0 in alternative periods forever. His pay-off will be

$$\begin{aligned}\pi_1^D &= 0+-7\delta+\delta^2\times 0+\delta^3\times(-7)+\delta^4\times 0+\delta^5\times(-7)+....\\ &= -7\delta[1+\delta^2+\delta^4+....] = -\frac{7\delta}{1-\delta^2}.\end{aligned}$$

Deviation is not optimal if $\frac{7\delta}{1-\delta^2} > \frac{1}{1-\delta}$, which requires

$$\frac{7\delta}{(1-\delta)(1+\delta)} > \frac{1}{1-\delta} \Rightarrow 7\delta > 1(1+\delta), \Rightarrow \delta > 1/6.$$

Here, the minimum value of δ is smaller than that under the grim strategy. That is because under tit-for-tat the punishment is not as severe and return to cooperation is encouraged. Therefore, cooperation is sustained under a slightly weaker condition. The literature on infinitely repeated games is very rich and should be studied separately.

11.4 Games of incomplete information

There are games in which players may have less information about their opponent or pay-offs. For example, a buyer may be less informed than the seller about the quality of the good she wants to buy. Nash equilibrium in such games should be modified to incorporate the uninformed player's beliefs into the calculus of optimal strategy. This notion of Nash equilibrium that incorporates players' beliefs, both prior and updated (where applicable), is called **Bayesian Nash equilibrium.** We first consider a one-shot game of asymmetric information.

11.4.1 Simultaneous games with asymmetric information

Consider the game presented in Table 11.8. Player 2 (the column player) is one of the two types, *a* and *b*, which he knows but player 1 (the row player) does not. Player 2's type determines the pay-off of both players. Player 1, however, believes that nature has assigned to player 2 type *a* with probability μ and *b* with probability $1-\mu$.[3] The belief is common knowledge. The type-dependent pay-offs of the players are shown in matrices *a* and *b*.

In this game, player 1 has just two strategies: τ_1 and τ_2. But player 2 has four strategies: (1) t_1t_1: If type *a*, play t_1; if type *b*, play t_1. (2) t_1t_2: If type *a*, play t_1; if type *b*, play t_2. (3) t_2t_1: If type *a*, play t_2; if type *b*, play t_1. (4) t_2t_2: If type *a*, play t_2; if type *b*, play t_2.

Of these four strategies, the second strategy is the dominant strategy. So the question is, What strategy is optimal for player 1? His expected pay-off from τ_1 is $Eu_1(\tau_1)=3\mu+2(1-\mu)$, and the expected pay-off from τ_2 is $Eu_1(\tau_2)=2\mu+3(1-\mu)$. He will play τ_1 if $\mu>1/2$; otherwise, he will play τ_2. Thus, $(\tau_1,t_1t_2;\mu>1/2)$ is a Bayes–Nash equilibrium, and so is $(\tau_2,t_1t_2;\mu<1/2)$. If $\mu=1/2$, player 1 is indifferent between τ_1 and τ_2.

Definition. To state the definition of Bayesian Nash equilibrium, let us assume that player 2 is of *k*-possible types represented by $\theta=(\theta_1,\theta_2,...,\theta_k)$ which is drawn by nature with probability $\mu=(\mu_1,\mu_2,...,\mu_k)$. Player 1 is the uninformed player. Let $s_2(\theta)$ be the strategy of player 2. A strategy profile $\sigma^*=(s_{i1}^*,s_{j2}^*(\theta))$ is a **Bayesian Nash equilibrium** if (1) $s_{j2}^*(\theta)$ is the best response of player 2 to player 1's strategy s_{i1}^* and (2) $Eu_1(s_{i1}^*,s_{j2}^*(\theta))\geq Eu_1(s_{i1},s_{j2}^*(\theta))$ for $s_{i1}\neq s_{i1}^*$, where the expected utility is computed using μ and player 2's equilibrium strategy.

The Bayesian Nash solution to the preceding game is, in some sense, simple because player 2 has a dominant strategy for each type. Therefore, player 1's strategy is determined by a

Table 11.8 Asymmetric information game 1

(a) Probability μ

	t_1	t_2
τ_1	3, 3	0, 1
τ_2	2, 2	1, 0

(b) Probability $1-\mu$

	t_1	t_2
τ_1	0, 1	2, 3
τ_2	1, 0	3, 2

Table 11.9 Asymmetric information game 2 (modified battle of the sexes)

(a) Probability μ			(b) Probability $1-\mu$		
	M	T		M	T
M	5, 3	2, 2	M	5, 5	2, 0
T	0, 0	3, 5	T	0, 4	3, 3

cutoff value of μ. But the Bayesian Nash equilibrium can be a little bit complicated if the informed player does not always have a dominant strategy. Consider a modified version of the battle of the sexes game presented in Table 11.9. Suppose the husband's preference for movies depends on some random event in his office. The husband's preference swings in favour of theatre with probability μ and in favour of movies with probability $1-\mu$. If it swings in favour of theatre, the resulting pay-off matrix is one of the standard battle of the sexes game, but if it is for the movies, his dominant strategy is go to the movies, and the pay-offs will be as given in panel *b*.

As is obvious, for the wife there are two pure strategies, going to movies (*M*), going to theatre (*T*). For the husband, there are four pure strategies. But for both players, there are mixed strategies as well. First, consider pure strategy plays. Let us examine if both the wife and husband playing *M* can be a Bayesian Nash equilibrium. (*M*, *M*) is a Nash equilibrium regardless of the husband's type. Therefore, the wife's sure pay-off from playing *M* is 5. Against the wife's play of *T*, the husband plays *T* if his type is *a* and *M* if his type is *b*. The wife's expected pay-off is then $Eu_1(T) = 3\mu$. Clearly, she will always play *M*. Thus, both going to movies is a Bayes–Nash equilibrium.

What about a Bayesian Nash equilibrium in mixed strategies? Suppose in this equilibrium, the husband randomises between *M* and *T* if his type is *a*, and plays *M* for sure if his type is *b*. The wife randomises between *M* and *T*. We already know that if the wife plays *M* with probability 5/6 and plays *T* with probability 1/6, the husband will be indifferent between *M* and *T*, and thus his randomisation is optimal when his type is *a*. But we need to derive the probability of husband playing *M* so that the wife remains indifferent between playing *M* and *T*. Let this probability be *q*.

By playing *M* the wife gets $Eu_1(M) = \mu[5q + 2(1-q)] + (1-\mu)5$. By playing *T*, she gets $Eu_1(T) = \mu[3(1-q)]$. If the wife is indifferent between *M* and *T*, then it must be $Eu_1(M) = Eu_1(T)$, which gives $q = 1 - \frac{5}{6\mu}$. For $q \in (0,1)$, it is required that $\frac{5}{6} < \mu$.

Thus, if $\mu > \frac{5}{6}$, the husband will play *M* with probability $q = 1 - \frac{5}{6\mu}$ and *T* with probability $\frac{5}{6\mu}$. Note that if $\mu \to 1$, we return to the standard battle of the sexes game and the husband plays *M* with probability 1/6 (as expected). Alternatively, if $\mu < \frac{5}{6}$, the husband plays *T* with certainty if his type is *a*. Of course, if his type is *b*, he always plays *M*.

To summarise, at any μ both playing *M* is a Bayes–Nash equilibrium. In addition, if $\mu > \frac{5}{6}$, there is a mixed-strategy Bayesian Nash equilibrium involving the wife randomising over *M* and *T*, while the husband randomises if his type is *a* and plays *M* if his type is *b*.

11.4.2 Sequential games with asymmetric information

In many games asymmetrically informed players move sequentially. A better informed seller may quote a price to which the less informed buyer responds by saying yes or no. Similarly, the less informed buyer can also quote a price to which the seller responds. A key feature of such dynamic games is that the less informed player may get a chance to update his belief using Bayes' rule about the better informed player's type after observing his move. Therefore, the equilibrium of such games follows the notion of Bayesian Nash equilibrium along with sub-game perfection.

Suppose player 1 is one of three types $\{\theta_1,\theta_2,\theta_3\}$ and he knows it, while player 2 does not know it. But he knows that player 1 can be of θ_i type with probability $\mu_i > 0, i = 1,2,3, \sum_i \mu_i = 1$. These probabilities are prior beliefs of player 2 about player 1's type. Player 1 has two actions $\{\tau_1,\tau_2\}$, while player 2 has $\{t_1,t_2\}$. Player 1 selects τ_1 or τ_2 (after learning his own type). Player 2 observes τ_1 or τ_2 as the choice of player 1 but can't tell what type of player 1 has made this choice. He then makes a choice from his action sets $\{t_1,t_2\}$. All pay-offs then materialise. The game is shown in Figure 11.4.

Let us first consider the full information version of this game. If player 1 was of θ_1 type, the SPNE would have been player 1 playing τ_1 and player 2 t_1. Similarly, for θ_2 type player 1, the SPNE would be player 1 playing τ_2 and player 2 t_2, while for θ_3 type, the SPNE would call for playing τ_2 and t_1 in sequence.

With asymmetric information, suppose player 2 observes player 1 to play τ_1. He then tries to calculate Prob. $(\theta_1 \mid \tau_1)$, Prob. $(\theta_2 \mid \tau_1)$ and Prob. $(\theta_3 \mid \tau_1)$, that is, the probability that nature has chosen θ_1, θ_2 or θ_3, given that τ_1 has been observed. The probability of observing τ_1 is

$$\text{Prob.}(\tau_1) = \text{Prob.}(\tau_1 \mid \theta_1)\text{Prob.}(\theta_1) + \text{Prob.}(\tau_1 \mid \theta_2)\text{Prob.}(\theta_2) + \text{Prob.}(\tau_1 \mid \theta_3)\text{Prob.}(\theta_3),$$

and the joint probability of (τ_1,θ_1), that is, that of seeing τ_1 after θ_1 being chosen by nature, is

$$\text{Prob.}(\theta_1,\tau_1) = \text{Prob.}(\theta_1 \mid \tau_1)\text{Prob.}(\tau_1) = \text{Prob.}(\tau_1 \mid \theta_1)\text{Prob.}(\theta_1).$$

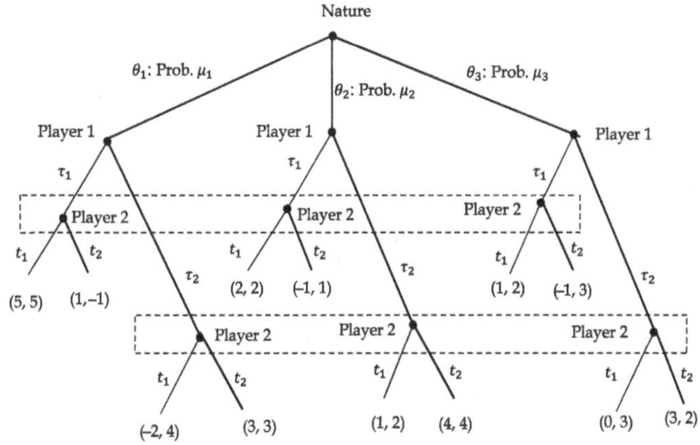

Figure 11.4 Sequential game with asymmetric information

From the above two relations we derive the player 2's belief updating rule as,

$$\text{Prob.}(\theta_1 \mid \tau_1) = \frac{\text{Prob.}(\tau_1 \mid \theta_1)\text{Prob.}(\theta_1)}{\text{Prob.}(\tau_1)}$$

$$= \frac{\text{Prob.}(\tau_1 \mid \theta_1)\text{Prob.}(\theta_1)}{\text{Prob.}(\tau_1 \mid \theta_1)\text{Prob.}(\theta_1) + \text{Prob.}(\tau_1 \mid \theta_2)\text{Prob.}(\theta_2) + \text{Prob.}(\tau_1 \mid \theta_3)\text{Prob.}(\theta_3)}.$$

In a similar way $\text{Prob.}(\theta_2 \mid \tau_1)$ and $\text{Prob.}(\theta_3 \mid \tau_1)$ and the remaining conditional probabilities can be derived.

In the preceding belief-updating rule, $\text{Prob.}(\tau_1 \mid \theta_1)$, $\text{Prob.}(\tau_1 \mid \theta_2)$ and $\text{Prob.}(\tau_1 \mid \theta_3)$ should be derived from the optimal strategy of player 1, as suggested by a proposed equilibrium. This principle reinforces the belief-dependency of Bayesian Nash equilibrium.

11.4.2.1 Equilibrium

Let us now examine how a Bayesian Nash equilibrium can be computed. Intuitively, player 1 should play τ_1 only if he observes θ_1, and his choice of τ_1 should be matched by player 2's choice of t_1. But if player 1 observes θ_2 or θ_3, he would be very tempted to play τ_2 and player 1 would then respond with t_2 if he believes player 2 to be of θ_2 and t_1 otherwise. Let us examine this possibility as a Bayesian Nash equilibrium. Here,

$$\text{Prob.}(\theta_1 \mid \tau_1) = \frac{1 \cdot \text{Prob.}(\theta_1)}{1 \cdot \text{Prob.}(\theta_1) + 0 \cdot \text{Prob.}(\theta_2) + 0 \cdot \text{Prob.}(\theta_1)} = \frac{\mu_1}{\mu_1} = 1.$$

Therefore, player 2 will always play t_1 if he observes τ_1 chosen by player 1. Now suppose player 1 has played τ_2 after observing either θ_2 or θ_3. Then player 2 updates his beliefs as

$$\text{Prob.}(\theta_2 \mid \tau_2) = \frac{1 \cdot \text{Prob.}(\theta_2)}{0 \cdot \text{Prob.}(\theta_1) + 1 \cdot \text{Prob.}(\theta_2) + 1 \cdot \text{Prob.}(\theta_1)} = \frac{\mu_2}{\mu_2 + \mu_3}$$

$$\text{Prob.}(\theta_3 \mid \tau_2) = \frac{1 \cdot \text{Prob.}(\theta_3)}{0 \cdot \text{Prob.}(\theta_1) + 1 \cdot \text{Prob.}(\theta_2) + 1 \cdot \text{Prob.}(\theta_1)} = \frac{\mu_3}{\mu_2 + \mu_3}.$$

The expected pay-off of player 2 from playing t_1 is $Eu_2(t_1) = \frac{\mu_2}{\mu_2 + \mu_3}2 + \frac{\mu_3}{\mu_2 + \mu_3}3$, and the expected pay-off from playing t_2 is $Eu_2(t_2) = \frac{\mu_2}{\mu_2 + \mu_3}4 + \frac{\mu_3}{\mu_2 + \mu_3}2$. Playing t_2 is preferred if $4\mu_2 + 2\mu_3 > 2\mu_2 + 3\mu_3$ or if $\mu_2 > \mu_3 / 2$; otherwise, play t_1.

11.4.2.2 Equilibrium 2

Can there be a Bayesian Nash equilibrium in which player 1 plays τ_1 regardless of his types? Let us examine this possibility. If player 1 always plays τ_1, then player 2 cannot update his beliefs. By playing t_1, his utility is $Eu_2(t_1) = 5\mu_1 + 2(\mu_2 + \mu_3)$, and by playing t_2, his utility is $Eu_2(t_2) = -\mu_1 + \mu_2 + 3\mu_3$. He will play t_1 if $\mu_1 > \frac{\mu_3 - \mu_2}{6}$. Otherwise, he will play t_2.

An important point here is that playing τ_2 by player 1 is not prescribed in the equilibrium. So if player 1 plays τ_2, that will be out-of-equilibrium play, and how will player 2 then update his beliefs, because in the Bayesian updating rule the denominator will have zero, that is, Prob.$(\tau_2 \mid \theta_1) =$ Prob.$(\tau_2 \mid \theta_2) =$ Prob.$(\tau_2 \mid \theta_3) = 0$ by the prescription of the equilibrium? Bayesian Nash equilibrium requires here specifying an out-of-equilibrium belief of player 2. One common practice is to choose any belief that would force player 1 not to deviate from τ_1. We can specify that whenever player 1 plays τ_2, player 2 will assume/believe that player 1's type is θ_1. Such a belief will make him play t_1, which will earn player 1 a pay-off of −2 if his type is θ_1, 1 if his type is θ_2 and 0 if his type is θ_3. In all cases, player 2's pay-off will be lower than that from playing τ_1. So, player 1 will not deviate. When a Bayesian Nash equilibrium is supplemented by out-of-equilibrium beliefs, it is called a **perfect Bayesian Nash equilibrium** or **simply perfect Bayesian equilibrium** (PBE).

Thus, a perfect Bayesian equilibrium of this game is that (1) player 1 will play τ_1 regardless of his type, (2) player 2 will play t_1 if $\mu_1 > (\mu_3 - \mu_2)/6$ and play t_2 otherwise and (3) if player 1 plays τ_2, player 2 will believe that player 1's type is θ_1.

11.4.2.3 Equilibrium 3

Now let us further explore this example to see if we can find a randomised Bayesian Nash equilibrium. Suppose player 1 plays τ_1 if his type is θ_1 , plays τ_2 if his type is θ_2 and randomises between τ_1 and τ_2 if his type is θ_3.[4] When randomising let α be the probability of playing τ_1 and $1-\alpha$ be the same for τ_2. Of course, by observing τ_1, player 1 cannot tell whether player 2 has randomised in state θ_3 or played deterministically in state θ_1. He needs to apply the Bayes' rule.

Player 2 will then update his beliefs as follows:

$$\text{Prob.}(\theta_1 \mid \tau_1) = \frac{\mu_1}{\mu_1 + \alpha\mu_3}, \qquad \text{Prob.}(\theta_2 \mid \tau_1) = 0$$

$$\text{Prob.}(\theta_3 \mid \tau_1) = \frac{\alpha\mu_3}{\mu_1 + \alpha\mu_3}, \quad \text{and}$$

$$\text{Prob.}(\theta_1 \mid \tau_2) = 0, \qquad \text{Prob.}(\theta_2 \mid \tau_2) = \frac{\mu_2}{\mu_2 + (1-\alpha)\mu_3}$$

$$\text{Prob.}(\theta_3 \mid \tau_2) = \frac{(1-\alpha)\mu_3}{\mu_2 + (1-\alpha)\mu_3}$$

After observing player 1 play τ_1, player 2 plays t_1 if

$$Eu_2(t_1 \mid \tau_1) = \frac{5\mu_1 + 2\alpha\mu_3}{\mu_1 + \alpha\mu_3} > Eu_2(t_2 \mid \tau_1) = \frac{3\alpha\mu_3 - \mu_1}{\mu_1 + \alpha\mu_3}$$

or if $\alpha < \dfrac{6\mu_1}{\mu_3}$. Similarly, after observing player 1 play τ_2, player 2 plays t_2 if

$$Eu_2(t_1 \mid \tau_2) = \frac{2\mu_2 + 3(1-\alpha)\mu_3}{\mu_2 + (1-\alpha)\mu_3} > Eu_2(t_2 \mid \tau_2) = \frac{4\mu_2 + 2(1-\alpha)\mu_3}{\mu_2 + (1-\alpha)\mu_3}$$

or if $\alpha < 1 - \frac{2\mu_2}{\mu_3}$. Thus, depending on the magnitude of α player 2 will play t_1 or t_2 following player 1's play of τ_1 orτ_2.

11.5 Signalling

In the sequential game presented in Figure 11.4, we considered three possible equilibria, in which the first and third ones involve player 1 playing τ_1 if his type or state of the world is θ_1. In this state, he is able to perfectly inform player 2 of his true type. In state 2, he is not able to do so; nevertheless, he helps player 2 to update his belief about state 2, and thus, player 2's knowledge about the true state of the world improves. In both instances, player 1 is able to communicate his private information, fully or partially, through his own action, τ_1 or τ_2. This is commonly called *signalling*, that is, an informed player revealing some information. For information revelation, it is critical that the action taken by the informed player must not be optimal for any other type than the one trying to reveal information. The labour market is a prime example of a signalling problem in which workers try to communicate their productivity or innate talents through various costly actions.

Let us consider a variant of Spence's (1973) classic job market signalling model. There are two players: player 1 is a job candidate whose innate ability (a) is known only to her. Player 2 is an employer whose pay-off depends on the worker's (innate) ability.[5] As done before, the informational asymmetry is modelled by assuming that nature selects a, which player 1 observes but player 2 does not. He knows that a can be high or low, $a \in \{a_l, a_h\}$, $a_h > a_l$, and the probability of $a = a_l$ is p, $0 < p < 1$. The candidate's innate ability affects the employer's pay-off. Having learnt her own ability, the candidate acquires education, $e \in [0,1]$, which will be observable to the employer. Note that player 2's action/strategy is now a continuous variable. We will assume that education does not affect her ability but works as a signalling device.[6] To keep the matter simple, assume there is no direct cost of education (as if all paid for by the government), but there is disutility from giving effort for education, and crucially, for the same level of education, a high-ability individual suffers less disutility than a low-ability individual. Let the disutility, or psychological cost of education, be $c(a) = e / a$, where $a = a_h$, a_l.

A high-ability worker produces a revenue R_h, while a low-ability worker produces $R_l (< R_h)$. The employer pays w_h to a high-ability worker and w_l to a low-ability worker when he is sure about their ability. Assume $\pi_h = R_h - w_H > R_l - w_l$ so that he always prefers a high-ability worker to a low-ability worker. Furthermore, let us set $w_h = \theta a_h$ and $w_l = \theta a_l$.

The candidate's utility function is $u = w - \frac{e}{a}$. Here, we need to assume that a high-ability candidate gets higher utility even after suffering the maximum disutility of education.

Assumption 8.

$$w_h - \frac{1}{a_h} > w_l \Rightarrow a_h(w_h - w_l) \equiv a_h \Delta w > 1, where \ \Delta w \equiv w_h - w_l = \theta(a_h - a_l) > 0.$$

The wage differential should be large enough relative to the productivity so that even if the high-ability candidate acquires the highest level of education (1) and the low-ability candidate acquires no education, still the high-ability candidate would still prefer to acquire education and signal her ability. A natural implication of our setting is that the worker, regardless of her type, is guaranteed to receive w_l without incurring any education cost and thus, her reservation utility is $\underline{u}_h = \underline{u}_l = w_l = \theta a_l$.

Our key question is, How much education a candidate will acquire to signal her high ability? A crucial condition is that the high-ability candidate must choose an education level that a low-ability candidate cannot find optimal to choose. A similar condition is also imposed on the low-type candidate to prevent her from pretending to be the high type. These conditions are called *incentive compatibility* conditions, which we specify as

$$\mathrm{IC}_h : u_h(w_h, e_h \mid a_h) \geq u_h(w_l, e_l \mid a_h) \Rightarrow w_h - \frac{e_h}{a_h} \geq w_l - \frac{e_l}{a_h}$$

$$\mathrm{IC}_l : u_l(w_l, e_l \mid a_l) \geq u_l(w_h, e_h \mid a_l) \Rightarrow w_l - \frac{e_l}{a_l} \geq w_h - \frac{e_h}{a_l}.$$

The preceding two incentive compatibility constraints are rewritten as

$$e_l + a_h \Delta w \geq e_h \qquad \text{and} \qquad e_h \geq e_l + a_l \Delta w \qquad \Rightarrow \qquad e_l + a_l \Delta w \leq e_h \leq e_l + a_h \Delta w. \tag{11.1}$$

Figure 11.5 explains the incentive conditions with two alternative graphs. In the left panel, we present the indifference curves of type h and l. Note that we can write the indifference curve/line of type i as $w = \bar{u}_i + \frac{e}{a_i}, i = h, l$. When the utility level $\bar{u}_i$ is held at the minimum level w_l, the indifference curve represents reservation utility. Note that the indifference curve of the low type is steeper, and they can cross each other only once. This is called a *single-crossing* property, crucial for this type of problem. Notably, at their crossing point, the high type's indifference curve will indicate a higher level of utility than the low type's indifference curve (because $a_h > a_l$).

Both types would prefer to be on or above their reservation indifference curves. Thus, the area between the two reservation indifference curves is our main interest, because in this region, the low type does not want to be in and the high type strictly does. Since the high wage is fixed at w_h, we can restrict our attention to this line between points E and F. At point E, the low type is indifferent between pretending to be a high type (by choosing e_h) and revealing her low type (by choosing no education). The same holds for type h at point F. Any point to the right of E violates the low type's *individual rationality* or *participation* constraint, and any point to the right of F

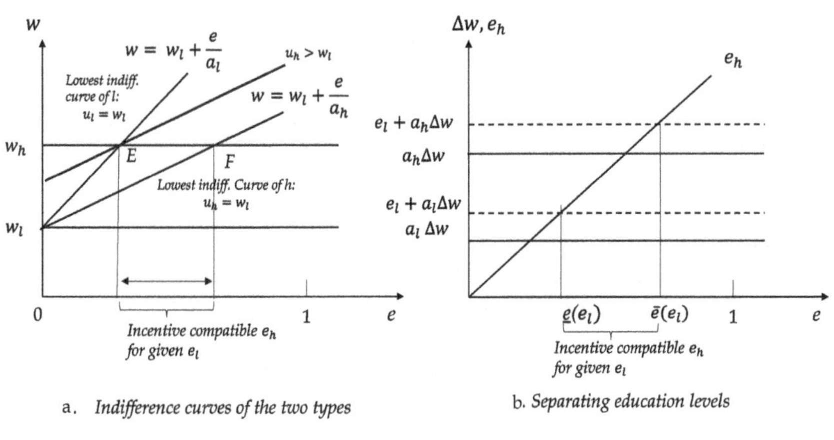

Figure 11.5 Incentive-compatible education levels

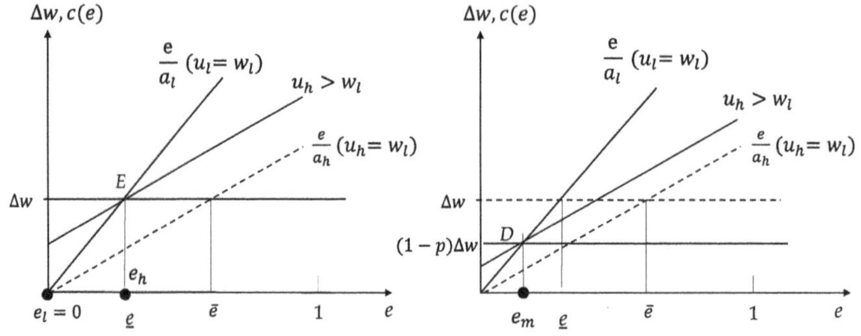

a. *Separating equilibrium* b. *Pooling equilibrium*

Figure 11.6 Separating and pooling equilibrium

violates the high type's individual rationality constraint. Thus, all points between E and F satisfy the incentive constraints of both types.

In the right panel, we present the implication of the incentive constraints in terms of the wage differential. Inequality (Eq. (11.1)) is shown for a given level of e_l. Thus, the interval $[\underline{e}(e_l), \overline{e}]$ represents the equilibrium education levels that reveal the high type's ability. The greater the magnitude of e_l, the greater the minimum level of e_h. However, we can argue that if the high-type candidate acquires a high level of education and credibly signals her ability, then the low type has no incentive to acquire any education; she will set $e_l = 0$.

In Figure 11.6 panel *a*, we show the equilibrium education levels. Once, e_l is set zero, the range of e_h that can credibly signal a high type falls to $[\underline{e}, \overline{e}]$. That means, any education level between $\underline{e}$ and $\overline{e}$ is a separating equilibrium. Each education level induces the correct belief of the employer about the candidate's type, and given this belief, the candidate does not deviate. However, Cho and Kreps (1987) have proposed intuitive criteria to select the Pareto-dominant equilibrium from this interval. Since any education level in this interval gives the same information, the candidate will choose the least cost education, which makes $e_h = \underline{e} = a_l \Delta w$. This education-level Pareto dominates any other separating equilibrium.

Proposition 19. (separating equilibrium) *The perfect Bayesian equilibrium of this game is* $(e_h = \underline{e}, e_l = 0)$, *where* $\underline{e} = a_l \Delta w$ *induces a posterior belief of the employer that* $Prob.(a_h \mid \underline{e}) = 1$. *Furthermore, the employer should also believe that* $Prob.(a_h \mid \underline{e} < e \leq \overline{e}) = 1$. *In addition, he must entertain* $Prob.(a_h \mid e < \underline{e}) = 0$ *and* $Prob.(a_h \mid e > \overline{e}) = 0$ *as out-of-equilibrium beliefs.*

Pooling equilibrium There is also an equilibrium where both types choose the same education level and leave the employer unsure about the candidate's type, in which case the employer will fall back on his priors and offer the candidate an average wage, $w_m = (1-p)w_h + pw_l$. Such an equilibrium is called pooling equilibrium. What will this common education level be?

Intuitively, this education level must be one that violates the incentive compatibility conditions of both types as given by Eq. (11.1). In other words, the pooling equilibrium education must satisfy the following incentive constraints:

$$u_h(w_m, e_m \mid e_h) \geq u_h(w_l, 0 \mid e_h) \Rightarrow w_m - \frac{e_m}{a_h} \geq w_l$$

$$u_l(w_m, e_m \mid e_l) \geq u_l(w_l, 0 \mid e_l) \Rightarrow w_m - \frac{e_m}{a_l} \geq w_l,$$

from which we can obtain

$$(1-p)a_h \Delta w \geq e_m \text{ and } (1-p)a_l \Delta w \geq e_m. \quad (11.2)$$

The new incentive conditions state that both types of candidate should acquire education e_m and hide their identity to get w_m rather than choosing no education and getting w_l. Note the direction of inequality now. Since e_m must be below both thresholds, we must set $e_m \leq (1-p)a_l\Delta w$. This gives us a continuum of education levels between 0 (but not including 0) and e_m that satisfies the pooling equilibrium conditions. See panel *b* of Figure 11.6 and point *D* in particular. e_m corresponds to point *D*, and all points to the left of *D*, excluding 0, can be a pooling equilibrium. At $e = 0$, the employer believes—at least that is how the incentive conditions have been set—that the candidate is low type and offers only w_l. Therefore, the employer's beliefs are crucial for selecting a unique pooling equilibrium.

Proposition 20. (pooling equilibrium) *Education level* $e_m = (1-p)a_l\Delta w$ *is a perfect Bayesian pooling equilibrium, provided the employer believes that* prob.$(a_l \mid e_m) = p$ *and* prob.$(a_l \mid e \neq e_m) = 1$.

Note the crucial importance of the out-of-equilibrium belief condition here. Given that belief, both types are forced to choose e_m and receive w_m, else they will get w_l. Under the rules of PBE any restriction can be imposed on out-of-equilibrium beliefs and hence, the preceding equilibrium is admissible. But clearly at very high education levels, believing a worker to be low ability is neither justifiable nor intuitive.

Furthermore, this pooling equilibrium (and any pooling equilibrium, for that matter) is, welfare-wise, an inferior. Intuitively, why should a player be required to incur a cost to transmit 'no information'? In the absence of any education, the employer will go by their priors and should just offer w_m, and the candidate's utility will be much higher. Therefore, as Cho and Kreps (1987) would argue, in the job market signalling model of Spence, the only sensible equilibrium is the separating equilibrium. To summarise, in equilibrium either a high type will choose education $\underline{e}$ to signal her high ability, or there will be no signalling at all (by any type). The employer will then have to offer w_h (observing $\underline{e}$) or simply w_m (observing no education).

11.6 Cheap talks

When one player is privately informed about the state of the world and that information cannot be communicated through costly actions such as education in a job market signalling model, what can the informed player do? Well, sending messages like texts, reports and deliberations is one option. Experts come on TV to provide investment tips, advisors recommend policies to the government, employers relay their business outlook to their employees and so on. In many instances, such messages are free to send or receive, not verifiable and certainly non-binding. In other words, these messages are cheap talks. But the very fact that the sender of these messages has superior information makes the *cheap talks* (endogenously) costly if they are utterly untrue. A general point is that the cheap talk messages are neither fully truth-revealing nor complete falsehoods; they contain sufficient information to allow the players to improve their welfare relative to the 'no communication' case.

In many economic contexts, such as employer–employee relations or bargaining over an object, both sides have a common interest in sharing some information to make a successful trade, but they also do not want to reveal all in order to drive a hard bargain on the distribution of the surplus arising from the trade. Cheap-talk games show that noisy messages are a compromise on the agents' intrinsic conflicts between sharing and hiding information. We now present a simplified version of the classic model of Crawford and Sobel (1982).[7]

11.6.1 The Crawford–Sobel (1982) model

Suppose there are two players. One of them, whom we call sender (*S*), privately observes the nature's draw of the state the world θ and sends a message to the other player (call him receiver *R*), who then updates his belief (if possible) about the realisation of the state and takes an action, a. Both θ and a affect the pay-offs of both players.

The utility functions of the players are $u^S = -(a-\theta-b)^2$, with $b \geq 0$, and $u^R = -(a-\theta)^2$. Maximising u^S and u^R is equivalent to minimising $v^s = (a-\theta-b)^2$ and $v^R = (a-\theta)^2$. We may use them interchangeably and especially for graphical illustrations work with v^i $(i = S, R)$. As shown in Figure 11.7 panel *a*, the receiver's optimal action is $a^* = \theta$ while the sender prefers the receiver to take action $a^* = \theta + b$. The receiver's optimal action falls short of the sender's most preferred action, by a difference of *b*, which measures the conflict of interest between them, and it is called sender's *bias*. In the figure (panel *a*), we have drawn the $v(.)$ functions against the receiver's actions.

Let us assume $\theta \in [0,1]$. It is common knowledge that θ is uniformly distributed. The sender's messaging strategy is a function $\mu : [0,1] \to M$, where M is the set of messages and m is its typical element. Messages are not backed by evidence and the receiver can believe, disregard or take it with a pinch of salt. A crucial point to note is that messages do not directly enter the utility functions of the players (hence, the term *cheap talk*), unlike in the education signalling model. Messages can be a number, a real line segment or a sentence or texts. There are three types of messages:

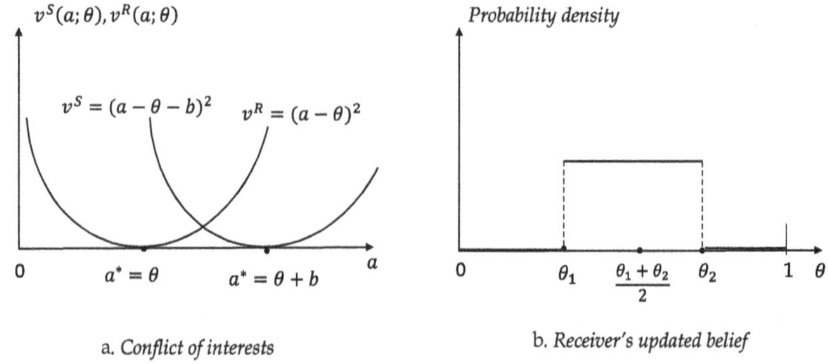

Figure 11.7 Preferences and beliefs

1. If $\mu(\theta) = \theta$, then it is called 'truth-revealing'.
2. If the message says that θ is between 1/4 and 1/3 ($\mu(\theta) = m \in [1/4, 1/3]$), the message is 'noisy' but informative nonetheless as the range of θ is narrowed down.
3. If the message is unclear or incoherent, then it is called 'babbling'; the receiver interprets it as $\theta \in [0,1]$ conveying no information.

After receiving the message, player R processes it and computes the conditional probability of the true state being θ, $G(\theta \mid m)$. In so doing, he needs to use the equilibrium strategy of the sender and the distribution function of θ. If the message is truth-revealing, $G(\theta \mid m) = 1$ is a trivial conclusion. If the message is babbling, the receiver's belief is given by the prior uniform distribution. If the message is noisy, then he needs to update his belief. After processing the message he takes action a, using strategy $\alpha : M \to A$, where A is the set of actions with a as its typical element.

We first note that in the special case of $b = 0$, where the players have no conflict of interests, there are two possible equilibria. In one, $\mu(\theta) = \theta$; that is, the sender always tells the truth, and the receiver believes it and takes action $a^*(\theta) = \theta$. In the other equilibrium, the sender babbles, and the receiver goes by his prior belief to set $a^* = E\theta = 1/2$.

But with $b > 0$, the truth-revealing equilibrium cannot occur, because if the sender chooses $\mu(\theta) = \theta$ and the receiver believes it and sets $a^* = \theta$, then the sender would deviate to an 'untruthful' signal $\theta + b$ to trick the receiver into setting $a^* = \theta + b$ (which is the most preferred action from the sender's perspective). Therefore, truth revelation is ruled out in equilibrium. The babbling equilibrium, however, always remains. Crawford and Sobel (1982) have proved that a PBE of any cheap-talk game will have the following additional properties:

1. The real line continuum $\theta \in [0,1]$ will be finitely partitioned, say, in N intervals, such as $0 = \theta_0(N) < \theta_1(N) < \ldots < \theta_N(N) = 1$, where N depends on the bias b and the distribution function of θ.
2. Within each partition, say, $[\theta_{i-1}, \theta_i]$, the message is the same. That is, $\mu(\theta) = m_i$ for any realisation of $\theta \in [\theta_{i-1}, \theta_i]$. The sender's types are *pooled* within an interval/partition but separated across partitions. In short, in order to reconcile his conflicting incentives, the sender does not reveal the true θ but points to the right partition where θ belongs.

To construct the PBE partitions of the state space, we proceed through the following steps, starting from the last stage.

11.6.1.1 Receiver's optimal action

Suppose the receiver has received a message that true θ lies in the interval $[\theta_1, \theta_2]$. In equilibrium, believing this message he updates his belief about the probability density function $g(\theta)$ as (see Figure 11.7 panel *b*),

$$g(\theta \mid m) = \begin{cases} 0 & \text{for } \theta < \theta_1 \\ \dfrac{1}{\theta_2 - \theta_1} & \text{for } \theta_1 \le \theta \le \theta_2 \\ 0 & \text{for } \theta > \theta_2 \end{cases}.$$

The receiver maximises his expected utility using the preceding beliefs with respect to a:

$$\text{Max}_a\ Eu^R(m) = \int_{\theta_1}^{\theta^2} \left\{ -\frac{(a-\theta)^2}{\theta_2 - \theta_1} \right\} d\theta.$$

His objective function simplifies to

$$Eu^R(m) = \left. \frac{(a-\theta)^3}{3(\theta_2-\theta_1)} \right|_{\theta_1}^{\theta_2} = \frac{(a-\theta_2)^3-(a-\theta_1)^3}{3(\theta_2-\theta_1)}. \tag{11.3}$$

Differentiating Eq. (11.3) with respect to a and setting it equal to zero we, get

$$3[(a-\theta_2)^2-(a-\theta_1)^2]=0 \ \Rightarrow \ a^* = \frac{\theta_2+\theta_1}{2}. \tag{11.4}$$

The receiver's optimal action is equal to the average (mean) value of θ over the interval $[\theta_1, \theta_2]$, which is the midpoint due to uniform distribution (see panel b of Figure 11.7).[8]

11.6.1.2 Sender's messages

To see how the state space is partitioned, consider first only two partitions: $[0, \theta_1]$ and $[\theta_1, 1]$. In Figure 11.8 panel a, we draw the function $v^S(.)$ against θ for two given actions of the receiver, a_1 and a_2, $a_1 < a_2$. It is clear that if $\theta < \theta_1$, the sender would prefer a_1 over a_2 (remember he prefers minimum $v(.)$), and if $\theta > \theta_1$, he prefers a_2 over a_1. And if $\theta = \theta_1$, then he is indifferent between a_1 and a_2. We can also see that for action a_1, the sender's utility is highest in state $\tilde{\theta}_1 = a_1 - b$, and the same is true for action a_2 in state $\tilde{\theta}_2 = a_2 - b$.

From two partitions, there are two messages: $m_1 = [0, \theta_1]$ and $m_2 = (\theta_1, 1]$, which generate optimal actions $a_1^*(m_1) = \theta_1 / 2$ and $a_2^*(m_2) = (1+\theta_1)/2$. The sender's maximum utility is

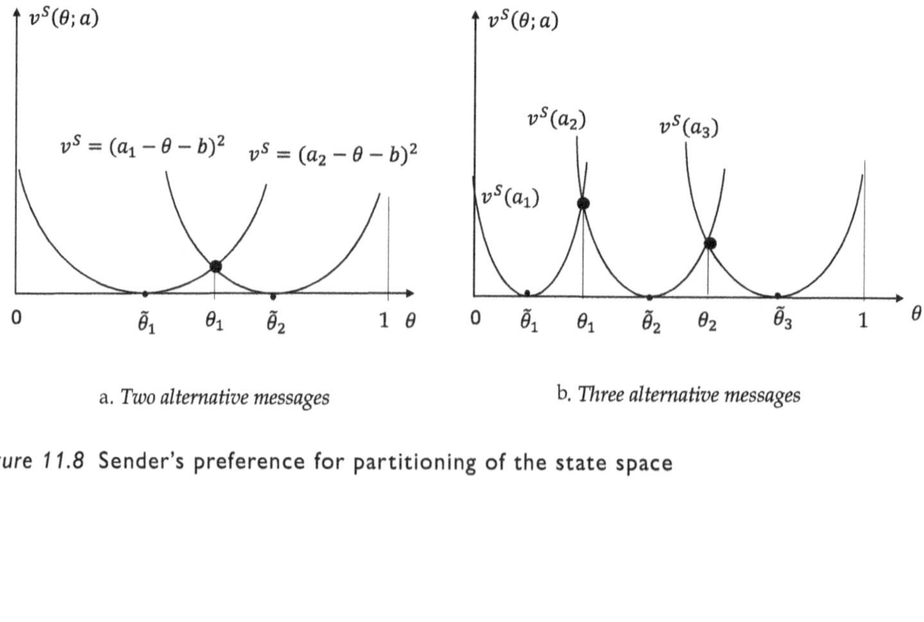

Figure 11.8 Sender's preference for partitioning of the state space

$$u^S(a_1^*(m_1);\theta) = -\left(\frac{\theta_1}{2} - \theta - b\right)^2 \qquad \text{for } \theta \le \theta_1,$$

$$\text{and } u^S(a_2^*(m_2);\theta) = -\left(\frac{\theta_1 + 1}{2} - \theta - b\right)^2 \qquad \text{for } \theta > \theta_1.$$

As we know at θ_1 the sender is indifferent, we must have

$$\left(\frac{\theta_1}{2} - \theta_1 - b\right)^2 = \left(\frac{\theta_1 + 1}{2} - \theta_1 - b\right)^2,$$

which is true only if $\frac{\theta_1 + 1}{2} - \theta_1 - b = \theta_1 + b - \frac{\theta_1}{2}$. This yields

$$\text{(for 2 intervals)}: \qquad \theta_1 = \frac{1}{2} - 2b. \tag{11.5}$$

Note that for $\theta_1 > 0$, we must have $b < 1/4$.

Next, consider a three-interval partition: $[0,\theta_1], (\theta_1,\theta_2]$ and $(\theta_2,1)$. See Figure 11.8 panel *b*. Setting the indifference conditions for θ_1 and θ_2 as

$$\left(\frac{\theta_1}{2} - \theta_1 - b\right)^2 = \left(\frac{\theta_1 + \theta_2}{2} - \theta_1 - b\right)^2$$

$$\left(\frac{\theta_1 + \theta_2}{2} - \theta_2 - b\right)^2 = \left(\frac{1 + \theta_2}{2} - \theta_2 - b\right)^2,$$

we obtain

$$\theta_2 = 2\theta_1 + 4b, \qquad \text{and} \qquad \theta_2 = \frac{1 + \theta_1}{2} - 2b.$$

From this, we solve

$$\text{(for 3 intervals)}: \qquad \theta_1 = \frac{1}{3} - 4b \qquad \text{and} \qquad \theta_2 = \frac{2}{3} - 4b, \tag{11.6}$$

where $\theta_1 > 0$ requires $b < 1/12$.

In the *N*-partition case, from the two adjacent partitions, $[\theta_{i_1}, \theta_i]$, and $[\theta_i, \theta_{i+1}]$, we write the two indifference conditions for θ_i and θ_{i+1} as

$$\frac{\theta_{i+1} + \theta_i}{2} - b - \theta_i = b + \theta_i - \frac{\theta_{i-1} + \theta_i}{2},$$

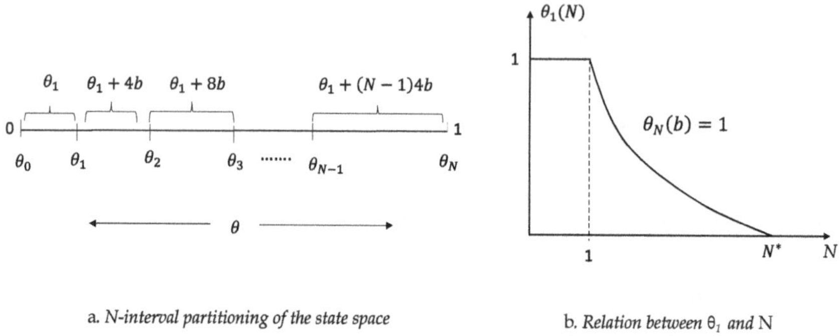

Figure 11.9 N-interval partitioning of the state space

which yields

$$\theta_{i+1} - \theta_i = [\theta_i - \theta_{i-1}] + 4b \Rightarrow \theta_{i+1} = 2\theta_i - \theta_{i-1} + 4b. \tag{11.7}$$

The preceding equation says that the length of the $i + 1$ interval must be bigger than the length of the ith interval by exactly $4b$. See panel a of Figure 11.9, where we have shown N intervals. The length of the successive partitions gets bigger and the difference between any two successive intervals is constant at $4b$.

Now let us note that Eq. (11.7) is a second-order difference equation. We now try to solve this equation. The solution to any difference equation consists of two parts: $\theta_i = \Theta_P + \Theta_C$, namely, the particular and complementary solutions.

Let us rewrite the difference equation as $\theta_{i+2} - 2\theta_{i+1} + \theta_i = 4b$. To derive the particular solution, we can try $\theta_i = ki^2$.[9] Then writing $k(i+2)^2 - 2k(i+1)^2 + ki^2 = 4b$ and simplifying it, we get $k = 2b$. Hence, our particular solution is $\Theta_P = 2bi^2$. Now for the complementary solution Θ_C, let us try $\theta_i = Ac^i i$ and write $Ac^{i+2}(i+2) - 2Ac^{i+1}(i+1) + Ac^i i = 0$. This equation yields $(c-1)^2 + 2c\dfrac{(c-1)}{i} = 0$, which holds for every i if and only if $c = 1$. Thus, $\Theta_C = Ai$. Combining the two solutions, we write $\theta_i = Ai + 2bi^2$. We still need to solve for A. Since setting $\theta_0 = 0$ does not help (as $i = 0$ reduces both sides to zero), by setting $i = 1$, we write $\theta_1 = A + 2b$ or $A = \theta_1 - 2b$. Thus, substituting the value of A into the solution we write the final expression of our solution as

$$\theta_i = \theta_1 i + 2bi(i-1), \qquad i = 1, 2, \ldots, N. \tag{11.8}$$

This is the well-known Crawford–Sobel equation for equilibrium partitions, where N is the number of intervals. Crawford and Sobel (1982) have also shown that if N intervals are feasible in equilibrium, then there are also equilibria involving $N - 1$ intervals, $N - 2$ intervals, $N - 3$ intervals and so on.

It is noteworthy that in the previous equation, θ_1 is unknown; however, as we know that in any N-interval equilibrium $\theta_N = 1$ in Eq. (11.8) by setting $i = N$, we solve for

$$\theta_1 = \frac{1}{N} - 2b(N-1). \tag{11.9}$$

Clearly, when $N = 2$, we have $\theta_1 = \frac{1}{2} - 2b$; when $N = 3$, we have $\theta_1 = \frac{1}{3} - 4b$; and so on, which we have already seen in Eqs. (11.5) and (11.6). Eq. (11.9) can also be used to derive what the upper limit on N is. This can be derived by setting $\theta_1 = 0$ in Eq. (11.9) as

$$N^* = \frac{1}{2} + \frac{1}{2}\left\{\sqrt{1 + \frac{2}{b}}\right\}. \tag{11.10}$$

Since the value obtained in Eq. (11.10) is not necessarily an integer N^*, we should write

$$-\frac{1}{2} + \frac{1}{2}\left\{\sqrt{1 + \frac{2}{b}}\right\} < \text{Largest integer } N \leq \frac{1}{2} + \frac{1}{2}\left\{\sqrt{1 + \frac{2}{b}}\right\} \equiv N^*.$$

The upper limit N^* is inversely related to bias b. When $b \to 0$, $N^* \to \infty$ implies the finest possible partitioning of the state space, leading to the most informative equilibrium. Indeed, at $b = 0$, we have noted that truth-telling is an equilibrium. In Figure (11.9) panel b, we have shown the relationship between N and θ_1; any value of N strictly less than N^* is admissible as an equilibrium partition of the state space.

We summarise the preceding discussion in the following statement of the equilibrium.

Theorem 10. *For every* N, $1 \leq N \leq N^*$ *where* N^* *is given in Eq. (11.10), there exists a PBE of the cheap-talk game described earlier in which the sender partitions the state space in* N *intervals,* $0 = \theta_0(N) < \theta_1(N) < \theta_2(N) < ... < \theta_N(N) = 1$, *and sends signal* $\mu(\theta) = m_i$ *for every* $\theta \in (\theta_{i-1}, \theta_i]$, *which induces the receiver's action* $a^*(m_i) = \frac{\theta_{i-1} + \theta_i}{2}$ *while the following equality holds for the sender's utility at every edge of the state space interval:* $u^S(a^*(m_{i-1}), \theta_i) = u^S(a^*(m_i), \theta_i)$, *or equivalently*

$$-\left(\frac{a_{i-1} + a_i}{2} - \theta_i - b\right)^2 = -\left(\frac{a_i + a_{i+1}}{2} - \theta_i - b\right)^2, \text{ for } i = 1, 2, ..., N - 1.$$

11.6.1.3 Welfare analysis

Now we examine the players' welfare under informative equilibrium. Are they better off than in the completely uninformative (or babbling) equilibrium? To begin with, let us note that in the perfect world, where the true state is observed by both players, the sender's utility would be $u^S = -b^2$ and the receiver's utility would be $u^R = 0$, because the receiver would always set $a = \theta$. But that possibility is ruled out due to asymmetric information. So our benchmark case is the babbling equilibrium, where the state space is not partitioned and the receiver cannot update his belief. The receiver's *ex ante* utility is then $u^R = \int_0^1 -(\frac{1}{2} - \theta)^2 d\theta$. By the uniform distribution assumption, the probability density is 1 and the mean is 1/2, which is also his optimal action. By virtue of the quadratic utility function his utility is equal to $-\sigma^2$, the variance of θ. That is,

$Eu^R = \int_0^1 -(\frac{1}{2} - \theta)^2 d\theta = -\sigma^2$. You can compute σ^2 to be 1/12.[10] For the sender, *ex ante* utility is

$Eu^S = \int_0^1 -(\frac{1}{2} - \theta - b)^2 d\theta = -\sigma^2 - b$.[11]

Now let us consider an *N*-interval equilibrium. The receiver's *ex ante* (before receiving any message) expected utility is

$$Eu^R(N) = \sum_{i=1}^{N} \text{Porb.}(m_i) \int_{\theta_{i-1}}^{\theta_i} -\left(\frac{\theta_{i-1} + \theta_i}{2} - \theta\right)^2 \cdot \frac{1}{\theta_i - \theta_{i-1}} \cdot d\theta. \tag{11.11}$$

Note that since $\frac{\theta_{i-1} + \theta_i}{2} = E(\theta \mid m_i)$, the utility of the receiver in the interval m_i directly gives the (negative of) the conditional variance of θ in m_i, that is,

$$\int_{\theta_{i-1}}^{\theta_i} \{E(\theta \mid m_i) - \theta\}^2 \cdot \frac{1}{\theta_i - \theta_{i-1}} \cdot d\theta = \sigma^2(m_i),$$

and consequently, the receiver's utility is a convex combination of the conditional variances of θ in each of the N intervals:

$$Eu^R(N) = -\sum_{i=1}^{N} \text{Porb.}(m_i) \cdot \sigma^2(m_i) = -\sigma^2(N)$$

Similarly, the *ex ante* expected utility (before observing θ) of the sender is

$$\begin{aligned} Eu^S(N) &= \sum_{i=1}^{N} \text{Porb.}(m_i) \int_{\theta_{i-1}}^{\theta_i} -\left(\frac{\theta_{i-1} + \theta_i}{2} - \theta - b\right)^2 \cdot \frac{1}{\theta_i - \theta_{i-1}} \cdot d\theta \\ &= -\sum_{i=1}^{N} \text{Porb.}(m_i) \int_{\theta_{i-1}}^{\theta_i} (E(\theta \mid m_i) - \theta - b)^2 \cdot \frac{1}{\theta_i - \theta_{i-1}} \cdot d\theta \end{aligned}$$

In this equation, expanding the term inside the integral

$$\int_{\theta_{i-1}}^{\theta_i} \{[E(\theta \mid m_i) - \theta]^2 + b^2 - 2b[E(\theta \mid m_i) - \theta]\} \cdot \frac{1}{\theta_i - \theta_{i-1}} \cdot d\theta,$$

and using the fact that $2b\int_{\theta_{i-1}}^{\theta_i} \{E(\theta \mid m_i) - \theta\} \frac{d\theta}{\theta_i - \theta_{i-1}} = 0$, we can write

$$\begin{aligned} Eu^S(N) &= -\sum_{i=1}^{N} \text{Porb.}(m_i) \int_{\theta_{i-1}}^{\theta_i} \{[E(\theta \mid m_i) - \theta]^2 + b^2\} \cdot \frac{1}{\theta_i - \theta_{i-1}} \cdot d\theta \\ &= -\sigma^2(N) - b^2, \end{aligned} \tag{11.12}$$

The *ex ante* expected utilities of both players are almost entirely accounted for by the variance of θ, reflecting how costly the intrinsic uncertainty is. The sender suffers an unavoidable additional disutility due to his bias. The variance $\sigma^2(N)$ is a common utility loss as the information cannot be transmitted without cost. However, the cost of information transmission depends on how the state space is partitioned. Intuitively, the greater the number of partitions lower the cost of transmission.

11.6.1.3.1 *Derivation of variance*

We now show how the variance of θ endogenously depends on the partitioning of the state space. Consider

$$\sigma^2(N) = \sum_{i=1}^{N} \text{Porb.}(m_i) \int_{\theta_{i-1}}^{\theta_i} \left(\frac{\theta_{i-1} + \theta_i}{2} - \theta \right)^2 \cdot \frac{1}{\theta_i - \theta_{i-1}} \cdot d\theta.$$

Since Porb.$(m_i) = m_i = \theta_i - \theta_{i-1}$, the preceding equation simply can be written as

$$\sigma^2(N) = \sum_{i=1}^{N} \int_{\theta_{i-1}}^{\theta_i} \left(\frac{\theta_{i-1} + \theta_i}{2} - \theta \right)^2 \cdot d\theta.$$

Carrying out integration,

$$\begin{aligned}
\sigma^2(N) &= \sum_{i=1}^{N} -\frac{1}{3} \left(\frac{\theta_{i-1} + \theta_i}{2} - \theta \right)^3 \Bigg|_{\theta i-1}^{\theta_i} \\
&= \sum_{i=1}^{N} -\frac{1}{3} \left[\left(\frac{\theta_{i-1} + \theta_i}{2} - \theta_i \right)^3 - \left(\frac{\theta_{i-1} + \theta_i}{2} - \theta_{i-1} \right)^3 \right] \\
&= \sum_{i=1}^{N} -\frac{1}{24} \left[(\theta_{i-1} - \theta_i)^3 - (\theta_i - \theta_{i-1})^3 \right] \\
&= \sum_{i=1}^{N} -\frac{1}{24} \left[-2(\theta_i - \theta_{i-1})^3 \right] = \frac{1}{12} \sum_{i=1}^{N} (\theta_i - \theta_{i-1})^3.
\end{aligned}$$

Let us now substitute the value of θ_1 as given in Eq. (11.9) into the equation for θ_i as given in Eq. (11.8) to obtain $\theta_i = \frac{i}{N} - 2bi(N-i)$, and similarly, we write $\theta_{i-1} = \frac{i-1}{N} - 2b(i-1)(N-i+1)$. From these two equations, we get

$$\theta_i - \theta_{i-1} = \frac{1}{N} + 2b(2i - N - 1) \qquad \text{for} \qquad i = 1, 2, \ldots, N. \tag{11.13}$$

Thus,

$$\sigma^2(N) = \frac{1}{12} \sum_{i=1}^{N} \left(\frac{1}{N} + 2b(2i - N - 1) \right)^3.$$

Let us write $D \equiv \frac{1}{N} - 2b(N+1)$ and expand the sum of the cubic terms in the previous equation as

$$\sum_{i=1}^{N}(D+4bi)^3 = \sum_{i=1}^{N}\left[D^3 + 12biD^2 + 48b^2i^2D + 64b^3i^3\right]$$

$$= \underbrace{ND^3 + 12bD^2\sum_{i=1}^{N} i}_{\equiv A} + \underbrace{48b^2D\sum_{i=1}^{N} i^2}_{\equiv B} + \underbrace{64b^3\sum_{i=1}^{N} i^3}_{\equiv C}.$$

We now take note of the following rules of summation for series (arithmetic progression, squares and cubes):

$$\sum_{i=1}^{N} i = \frac{N(N+1)}{2}, \qquad \sum_{i=1}^{N} i^2 = \frac{N(N+1)(2N+1)}{6}, \qquad \sum_{i=1}^{N} i^3 = \frac{N^2(N+1)^2}{4},$$

which we will substitute as and when needed in the algebra.[12] First, we can simplify $A = D^2\left[1 + 4bN(N+1)\right]$ and write

$$\begin{aligned}
A + B &= D\left[D\{1 + 4bN(N+1)\} + 8b^2N(N+1)(2N+1)\right] \\
&= D\left[\frac{1}{N} + 2b(N+1) + 8b^2N^2(N+1)\right] \\
&= \left[\frac{1}{N} - 2b(N+1)\right] \times \left[\frac{1}{N} + 2b(N+1)\right] + \left[\frac{1}{N} - 2b(N+1)\right] \times 8b^2N^2(N+1) \\
&= \frac{1}{N^2} - 4b^2(N+1)^2 + 8b^2N(N+1) - C \\
&= \frac{1}{N^2} + 4b^2(N+1)(N-1) - C.
\end{aligned}$$

Therefore, $A + B + C = \frac{1}{N^2} + 4b^2(N^2 - 1)$, and we finally arrive at

$$\sigma^2(N) = \frac{1}{12}\left[\frac{1}{N^2} + 4b^2(N^2 - 1)\right]. \tag{11.14}$$

We can promptly note that when $N = 1$ we return to $\sigma^2 = 1/12$. Furthermore,

$$\frac{\partial \sigma^2(N)}{\partial N} = \frac{1}{12}\left[-\frac{2}{N^3} + 8b^2N\right] < 0 \quad \text{if} \qquad b \le \frac{1}{2N^2}.$$

From our equation of θ_1, Eq. (11.9), we verify that for $\theta_1 \ge 0$, we must have $b \le \frac{1}{2N^2(N-1)}$. So we need to impose a stricter condition on b to ensure the variance to be decreasing in N. Let us recall from Eq. (11.10) that for a given b, we get an upper limit on N as $N^*(b)$. Therefore, by setting $b - \frac{1}{2[N^*(b)]^2} = 0$, we solve for b, say, $\bar{b}$, which will be the upper limit on b, to allow for the lowest N^*. Then for any $b < \bar{b}$, the variance $\sigma^2(N)$ will be decreasing in N. See Figure 11.10 panel *a* for an illustration of the players' *ex ante* disutility (v^S and v^R) changes with N when $b < \bar{b}$. The following proposition summarises the welfare result.

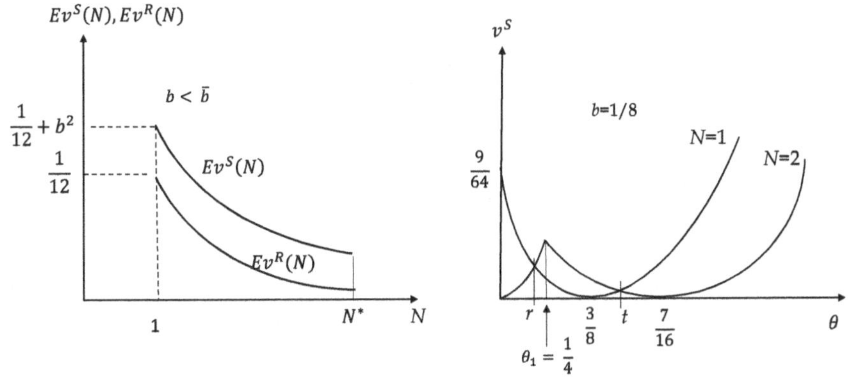

a. Ex ante *disutility of the players*

b. Ex post *disutility of the sender*

Figure 11.10 Ex *ante and* ex *post* disutility

Proposition 21. *Suppose* $b < \bar{b}$ where $\bar{b} - \frac{1}{2[N^*(\bar{b})]^2} = 0$. *Then the players' utilities increase in* N, *that is, with greater partitioning of the state space.*

11.6.1.4 Ex post *utility*

Here, we make another observation. *Ex ante* welfare improvement does not guarantee that the players' *ex post* welfare will always rise with *N*. It may not. For the receiver, *ex post* utility means utility after receiving the message, which is we know $u^R(m_i) = -\sigma^2(m_i)$. For the sender, *ex post* utility refers to his utility after observing θ. His utility will depend on both the actual realisation of θ and the equilibrium strategy he adopts, that is, the number of intervals he chooses. Here, the *ex post* utility may not increase with more partitions of the state space. The reason is that at every interval there is an ideal θ who gets highest utility and how far the true θ is from that ideal point determines the sender's utility. This distance changes with a change in the number of equilibria.

To illustrate this point, let us assume $b = 1/8$. Using Eq. (11.10), we determine that in, at most two intervals, the line $\theta = [0,1]$ can be partitioned. In the no-partition case, where no information is transmitted, $u^S(\theta) = -(\frac{3}{8} - \theta)^2$, which has a maximum at $\theta = 3/8$, as shown in panel *b* of Figure 11.10 in terms of his disutility v^S. Next, consider two partitions. From Eq. (11.9) with $N = 2$, we see that $\theta_1 = 1/4$. Therefore, the sender's (*ex post*) utility is $u^S(\theta) = -(-\theta)^2$ if $\theta \in [0, 1/8]$, and $u^S = -(\frac{7}{16} - \theta)^2$ if $\theta \in (1/4, 1]$. Now note in Figure 11.10 panel *b* that his disutility v^S in the two-interval case first steadily goes up at $\theta \le 1/4$, but thereafter, it falls, reaches zero at 7/16 and rises back again. Therefore, in the interval $\theta \in (r, t)$, the uninformative equilibrium gives lower disutility. Outside this interval, everywhere else his *ex post* disutility is less under the informative equilibrium.

11.6.2 Equilibrium selection

One major issue with the cheap-talk equilibrium is that there are too many equilibria. For any given b, while there is the most informative equilibrium with $N^*(b)$ intervals, there is also the most uninformative equilibrium with no partitioning whatsoever, and then there are all other equilibria with less than $N^*(b)$ partitions. How does the receiver know which equilibrium is played by the sender? We assume that in equilibrium, somehow their beliefs are coordinated. For instance, if the sender follows a two-interval equilibrium and sends his message accordingly, the receiver will 'correctly' believe that (instead of seeing it as a deviation to a three-interval equilibrium). Messages as such do not convey 'deviation' from the equilibrium. Then how does the sender detect deviation? Farell (1993) addressed this issue partially by introducing messages in the form of 'neologism'. That is to say, if the sender deviates from a proposed equilibrium he would send a message that is legible/audible but must contain completely new words with no clear meaning.[13] This refinement is in the spirit of traditional belief-based refinement, as we have seen in Spence's signalling model; however, neologism does not always work well.

Chen et al. (2008) proposed a new type of refinement by imposing a restriction on the lowest type of the sender's pay-off (i.e., $\theta = 0$) called 'no incentive to separate' (NITS). The requirement of NITS is that *type 0 should not get a lower pay-off by sending an equilibrium message that he belongs to the equilibrium interval* $[0,\theta_1]$ *than somehow communicating (for instance, by deviating and sending a message of 'neologism') that he is type* 0. That is to say, he should not have an incentive to separate from any other θ belonging to interval $[0,\theta_1]$. Formally, the NITS condition is

$$u^S(m_1 \mid 0) = -(\frac{\theta_1}{2} - 0 - b)^2 \geq u^S(0 \mid 0) = -(-b)^2 \Rightarrow b \geq \frac{\theta_1}{4}. \tag{11.15}$$

Note that in the equation, revealing his type and making the receiver correctly believe it would result in action $a = 0$.

Chen et al. (2008) have shown that of all the equilibria in the Crawford–Sobel game, only the most informative equilibrium survives the NITS test. This is a very powerful result. It means that once we know the value of b, we can compute the largest integer (from Eq. (11.10)) that gives the maximum number of partitions of the state space and take that as the most important equilibrium; all other equilibria, including the babbling one, can be ignored.

Proposition 22. *Given any* b > 0*, the only equilibrium that survives the NITS test is the most informative equilibrium with* N^* *intervals, where* N^* *is the largest number of intervals of the state space satisfying*

$$-\frac{1}{2} + \frac{1}{2}\sqrt{1+\frac{2}{b}} < N^* \leq \frac{1}{2} + \frac{1}{2}\sqrt{1+\frac{2}{b}}.$$

Proof. Consider the equilibrium with N^*-interval partitioning of the state space. From Eq. (11.9), we write

$$\theta_1(N^*) = \frac{1}{N^*} - (N^* - 1)2b, \qquad \Rightarrow \qquad b < \frac{1}{2N^*(N^* - 1)} \qquad \text{for } \theta_1(N^*) > 0.$$

To satisfy the NITS condition as given in Eq. (11.15), we write $b \geq \frac{1}{4}\left[\frac{1}{N^*} - (N^* - 1)2b\right]$. This yields $b \geq \frac{1}{2N^*(N^* - 1)}$. Thus, both $\theta_1(N^*) > 0$ and NITS are satisfied if and only if

$$\frac{1}{2N^*(N^* + 1)} \leq b < \frac{1}{2N^*(N^* - 1)}. \tag{11.16}$$

Now we need to show that in the preceding interval of b, the equilibrium with $N^* - 1$ intervals of the state space cannot satisfy NITS. To see that, in these two conditions on b, replace N^* by $N^* - 1$. Thus, $\theta_1(N^* - 1) > 0$ requires $b < \frac{1}{2(N^* - 1)(N^* - 2)}$, and for NITS to hold, we must have $b \geq \frac{1}{2N^*(N^* + 1)}$. Together they imply

$$\frac{1}{2N^*(N^* - 1)} \leq b < \frac{1}{2(N^* - 1)(N^* - 2)}. \tag{11.17}$$

Inequalities (11.16) and (11.17) show that the two critical intervals of b do not overlap. It is easy to check that for $N^* - 2$, interval partition as well, the NITS will fail, and so will for any $N < N^* - 2$. Therefore, if NITS holds for N^*, then NITS will fail for every partition that gives strictly less than N^* intervals.

11.6.2.1 *Advanced issues*

In Crawford and Sobel (1982), communication is one-shot and one-sided. In reality, often communications are two-way, even if the receiver has no information to add, and/or messages are sent multiple times, in various forms, such as starting with preliminary chats and culminating in a well-structured written report. Not to mention that the state space is one-dimensional. Many authors have extended the communication stage of the cheap-talk game in several directions, including multiple experts/senders (differing in their biases). A general finding of this line of work is that the informational content of equilibrium can be improved. Even with a fixed bias, one can design the communication game in such a manner that the equilibrium partition of the state space can increase from two to three (or more). See Krishna and Morgan (2001, 2004) for more on this. Also see Bag and Sharma (2019) and Chakraborty et al. (2020) for two interesting applications.

We have assumed that cheap talks are unverifiable and can be utter lies. This unrestricted nature of messages forces the sender to encapsulate the truth with a bit of haziness (i.e., pooling), and the question then surrounds how big or how small the hazy bit is. Typically, with higher types, the interval of pooling gets larger. In reality, of course, messages are often not allowed to be entirely cheap talks. In courts, a prosecutor is required to reveal and share all the evidence he gathers to prove the accused guilty. An economic advisor to the government has to back up his recommendations with data, case studies and models. In such contexts, incentive compatibility constraints of the Crawford–Sobel kind are not important. The sender is committed to telling the truth, but he can control the informational environment pertaining to the truth.

In the context of prosecution, he selectively gathers and presents the evidence that portrays the accused in a bad light in order to 'persuade' the jury or judge to believe that the accused is guilty. The design of information and interpretative manipulation of evidence are subject matters of the Bayesian persuasion literature (Kamenica and Gentzkow, 2011).

A final observation is that the receiver can delegate the choice of action to the sender. This will solve the information problem, but it will involve distortion in the sender's choice of action from the receiver's point of view. However, in some instances, that may still be better than relying on a cheap-talk equilibrium. Another option is that the receiver can write an incentive contract by which the sender will take an action in exchange for an 'incentive payment'. We explore in a later chapter how the incentive contracts work.

11.7 Conclusion

Game theory is vast. We had to leave out many important topics, such as evolutionary games, sequential equilibrium and trembling-hand perfection, the stability of equilibrium and the existence theorems of the Nash equilibrium. For common knowledge and repeated games, we have also been very parsimonious. To learn more about game theory, you are advised to take a dedicated course/module in game theory or read some of the readings listed at the end of the chapter. In the next few chapters, we will come across a wide variety of applications, which will help you understand the importance of nuanced arguments that game theory so delicately depends on.

Summary

In this chapter, we learnt the following:

1. Some games can be solved by using the notions of dominant strategies, iterated elimination of dominated strategies and rationalisable strategies.
2. When a Nash equilibrium in pure and mixed strategies exists.
3. Subgame perfect equilibrium is the appropriate solution concept for full information dynamic games.
4. Bayesian Nash equilibrium is the appropriate solution concept for simultaneous-move incomplete information games.
5. Some sequential games with incomplete information are signalling games. Perfect Bayesian equilibrium for job market signalling was studied.
6. A cheap-talk game of signalling was studied in detail.

11.8 Exercises

1. Consider the game presented in Table 11.10.

    a. Find all the pure strategy Nash equilibria of this game.
    b. Can you try mixed-strategy equilibrium or equilibria?
    c. Consider a sequential version of the game in which the row player moves first and the column player moves next. Find the subgame perfect equilibrium of this game.

Table 11.10 Game 1

	Left	*Centre*	*Right*
Left	(1, 3)	(0, 4)	(2, 5)
Centre	(4, 5)	(2, 2)	(0, 1)
Right	(3, 4)	(3, 5)	(1, 3)

2. Derive the pure and mixed-strategy equilibria of the game shown in Table 11.11.

Table 11.11 Game 2

	Left	*Centre*	*Right*
Left	(1, 3)	(0, 4)	(2, 5)
Centre	(4, 5)	(2, 2)	(3, 1)
Right	(5, 6)	(1, 5)	(1, 3)

3. Derive the Bayesian Nash equilibrium of the game shown in Table 11.12, where the row player can be type 1 with probability α and type 2 with probability $1-\alpha$. Both players move simultaneously.

Table 11.12 Game 3

Probability α			*Probability* $1-\alpha$		
	H	*T*		*H*	*T*
H	3, 5	4, 2	*H*	2, 3	5, 1
T	1, 1	5, 3	*T*	0, 2	4, 3

4. Consider the pay-off matrices presented in Table 11.12 and suppose the row player (who privately knows her type) moves first. Column moves next. Derive the Bayesian Nash equilibrium of this sequential game.
5. Let us revisit the job market signalling model. Suppose education is not free. In addition to the effort cost of education, there is a fixed fee F for acquiring education. Thus, a worker's utility is $u_i = w - \frac{e}{a_i} - F$, where $a_i \in \{a_l, a_h\}$ is the worker's ability. Each worker produces ka_i unit of output, and they are paid λka_i, $0 < \lambda < 1$. The employers know that α proportion of the workers have high ability. They also know that β proportion of the population is poor, and they cannot afford education. But who is poor and who is not is not known to the employers. Total mass of workers is 1. Find the PBE of this game.

Notes

1 It is a trivial point that if the later mover does not get to observe the history of the game, then it is a simultaneous-move or static game.
2 Note in this case, prisoner 1 (row player) has no dominated strategy, but prisoner 2 has a weakly undominated strategy in *CC*.
3 The idea of introducing nature as a neutral player to convert a game of incomplete information into a complete but imperfect game is according to Harsany (1967, 1968a, 1968b). Nature's draw is observable to only one player, while the other player knows only the probability of the draw but not the draw itself. This is just a way of modelling informational uncertainty.
4 In many books, this is referred to as mixed-strategy equilibrium, but that can be misleading, because players randomise between actions, not between strategies.
5 The problem can be posed as a game between a continuum of workers and a set of firms as well.
6 One can make education as contributing to skills or enhancing innate ability. But the basic problem of signalling does not change. However, education may have some other implications, which are worthy of investigation.
7 I gratefully acknowledge discussions with Jaideep Roy on this model.
8 The second-order condition for maximisation is satisfied as $\partial^2 Eu^R(m) / \partial a^2 = -2$.
9 Note that since the coefficients of the left-hand-side terms add up to zero, neither $\theta_i = k$ nor $\theta_i = ki$ would work.

10 Write $\int_0^1 -(\frac{1}{2}-\theta)^2 d\theta = -(\frac{1}{2}-\theta)^3/3\Big|_0^1 = -[\frac{1}{2}-1]^3/3+1/24 = 1/24+1/24 = 1/12$.

11 You can write $Eu^S = -\left[\int_0^1 (\frac{1}{2}-\theta)^2 d\theta + b^2 - 2b\int_0^1 (1/2-\theta)d\theta\right] = \sigma^2 - b^2$, since $\int_0^1 (1/2-\theta)d\theta = 0$.

12 Caution: The following algebra will test your patience.

13 Recall that 'babbling', a message that is not legible/audible, is reserved for communicating no information. A 'neologism' communicates information of deviation.

References and further readings

Bag, P. & Sharma, T. (2019). Sequential expert advice: Superiority of closed-door meetings. *International Economic Review*, 60, 1877–1910.

Basu, K. (1994). The traveler's dilemma: Paradoxes of rationality in game theory. *The American Economic Review, Papers and Proceedings*, 84(2), 391–395.

Bernheim, D. (1984). Rationalizable strategic behavior. *Econometrica*, 52, 1007–1028.

Capra, M. C., Goeree, J. K., Gomez, R. & Holt, C. A. (1999). Anomalous behavior in a traveler's dilemma? *The American Economic Review*, 89(3), 678–690.

Chakraborty, A., Ghosh, P. & Roy, J. (2020). Expert captured democracies. *American Economic Review*, 110(6), 1713–1751.

Chen, Y., Kartik, N. & Sobel, J. (2008). Selecting cheap-talk equilibria. *Econometrica*, 76(1), 117–136.

Cho, I. & Crep, D. M. (1987). Signaling games and stable equilibria. *Quarterly Journal of Economics*, 102(2), 179-222.

Crawford, V. & Sobel, J. (1982). Strategic information transmission. *Econometrica*, 50(6), 1431–1451.

Farell, J. (1993). Meaning and credibility in cheap-talk games. *Games and Economic Behavior*, 5, 514–531.

Harsany, J. (1967). Games with incomplete information played by 'Bayesian' players. Part I. The basic model. *Management Science*, 14(3), 159–182, 32–34, 486–502.

Harsany, J. (1968a). Games with incomplete information played by 'Bayesian' players. Part II. Bayesian equilibrium points. *Management Science*, 14(5), 320–334, 486–502.

Harsany, J. (1968b). Games with incomplete information played by 'Bayesian' players. Part III. The basic probability distribution of the game. *Management Science*, 14(7), 486–502.

Kamenica, E. & Gentzkow, M. (2011). Bayesian persuasion. *The American Economic Review*, 101(6), 2590–2615.

Kartik, N. (2009). Strategic communication with lying costs. *The Review of Economic Studies*, 76, 1359–1395.

Kono, H. & Kandori, M. (2021). Corrigendum to Crawford and Sobel (1982) strategic information *transmission. Econometrica Online Article Corrigendum*, 1–10.

Kreps, D. M. (1990). *Game Theory and Economic Modelling*. Oxford: Clarendon Press.

Krishna, V. & Morgan, J. (2001). A model of expertise. *Quarterly Journal of Economics*, 116, 747–775.

Krishna, V. & Morgan, J. (2004). The art of conversation: Eliciting information from experts through multi-stage communication. *Journal of Economic Theory*, 117, 147–179.

Mas-Colell, A., Whinston, M. D. & Green, J. R. (1995). *Microeconomic Theory*. New York: Oxford University Press.

Nash, J. (1951). Non-cooperative games. *Annals of Mathematics*, 54, 289–295.

Pearce, D. G. (1984). Rationalizable strategic behavior and the problem of perfection. *Econometrica*, 52, 1029–1050.

Rasmusen, E. (1989). *Games and Information: An Introduction to Game Theory*. Oxford: Basil Blackwell.

Rosenthal, R. (1981). Games of perfect information, predatory pricing and the chain store paradox. *Journal of Economic Theory*, 25(1), 92–100.

Selten, R. (1975). Re-examination of the perfectness concept for equilibrium points in extensive games. *International Journal of Game Theory*, 4, 25–55.

Selten, R. (1978). The chain store paradox. *Theory and Decision*, 9(2), 127–159.

Spence, M. A. (1973). Job market signaling. *Quarterly Journal of Economics*, 87(3), 355–374.

Chapter 12

Bargaining

Abstract

Bargaining is a special type of trading situation in which neither side is a price taker. The most common approach to bargaining is the generalised Nash bargaining, which we study in detail. As an application, we analyse different types of bargaining between workers/unions and employers in different settings. Efficiency and distributional implications of such bargaining are discussed. Some additional topics of interest are bargaining in a public-sector enterprise and bargaining through delegates. We also study bargaining under incomplete information. Two models, namely, sealed-offer bargaining and sequential one-sided-offer bargaining, are discussed in detail.

Keywords: Bilateral monopoly, Nash bargaining, Efficient bargaining, Right-to-manage bargaining, Kalai-Smorodinsky solution, Sealed offer bargaining, Bilateral delegation

12.1 Introduction

Markets are meant to tell us at what price a good should be traded and in how much quantity. We have seen how perfect competition and monopoly do this job, and in the next chapter, we will see how imperfectly competitive markets do it. In all these markets, there is competition on at least one side, if not both. In particular, buyers or consumers in all these markets have no power to alter price through their individual purchase decisions. But when competition is absent on both sides of a market, we cannot easily say at what price the good will be traded. Think about someone on your street selling her car and you are interested; surely you would be haggling over the price. In tourist places, buying souvenirs from a roaming vendor involves bargaining. Even when the vendors are located in a fixed place, such as in the Fashion Street market of Mumbai (funnily, Fashion Street is not the street's name), negotiating over the price can be a norm. Among large things, Twitter was bought by Elon Musk in 2022 after six months of negotiations (at US$44 billion).

In all cases of bargaining, the agreed price ultimately depends on the negotiation skill or the bargaining power of the two opposing parties. At the same time, there are risks of delay and disagreement. The theory of bargaining helps us understand these problems.

Two questions will receive most of our attention: whether a bargaining outcome is Pareto-efficient (meaning no wastage, no delay) and whether the outcome is 'fair'. There are two main approaches to studying bargaining: the cooperative or axiomatic approach developed before the game theory era and the non-cooperative approach based on modern game theory. The cooperative bargaining theory requires Pareto efficiency to be a key property of any bargaining solution,

DOI: 10.4324/9781003226994-12

and the focus is then directed to fairness alone. Non-cooperative bargaining theory, by comparison, presents bargaining as a game (static or dynamic); the bargaining solution may or may not be Pareto-efficient. We discuss both types of models but in a selective way.

12.2 Monopsony and bilateral monopoly

Before we get into the models of pure bargaining, let us learn about a specific market called bilateral *monopoly* that consists of one buyer and one seller. A stepping stone toward bilateral monopoly is monopsony, whereby the buyer has monopoly power but the sellers don't. Markets with a buyer's monopoly power work differently than the markets of a seller's monopoly.

Consider a large fruit farmer, who is the sole employer of fruit pickers in his local area. The market where he sells his fruits is competitive, as it is served by sellers from far and away. In the local agricultural labour market, the farmer is a monopsonist. Suppose he wants to maximise $\pi = pf(l) - w(l)l$, where $f(l)$ is the quantity of fruits produced by l units of labour. The labour supply curve is given by the function $w(l)$, which states the minimum wage at which the workers are willing to supply l units of labour. Assume $w'(l) > 0$. Our fruit farmer chooses l by the following first-order condition for profit maximisation:

$$pf'(l) = w(l) + lw'(l). \tag{12.1}$$

The left-hand side of Eq. (12.1) is the familiar value of the marginal product of labour (recall from Chapter 8), VMP. The right-hand side is the marginal expenditure of hiring labour (ME).[1] The average expenditure of hiring labour is just $w(l)$. If the fruit farmer had no market power in the labour market, he would have taken the wage rate $w(l)$ as given, and like a competitive firm, he would set $pf'(l) = w(l)$, as shown by point C in Figure 12.1 panel a. The VMP curve is the standard labour demand curve of a competitive firm. However, being a monopsonist, he would try to increase his profit further by reducing the wage rate. But trying to reduce the wage necessitates hiring fewer workers. So, he would move to the point BM_C where the ME curve intersects the VMP curve. He hires l_{MS} workers and gives a wage rate of $\underline{w}$. Note the fall in wage from the competitive level w_C.

Now consider its polar opposite scenario, where the farmer does not have any market power, that is, he is not a monopsonist, but the workers are united (via a trade union for instance) and able to set the wage as they wish. What level of hiring would they dictate, and what wage should they pay to themselves? The answer can be figured out by letting them step in the farmer's shoes and imagining that they own the fruit farm. Thus, they would employ the same quantity of labour as given by the monopsonist's choice equation (12.1) and give themselves the highest possible wage, which is the VMP at that employment, $\overline{w}$, as shown in Figure 12.1 panel a.

These two extreme cases suggest that if we have a bilateral monopoly the choice of labour will continue to be the same, but the wage will fall in between $\underline{w}$ and $\overline{w}$. Exactly where? Unfortunately, the market does not tell us; it leaves the wage indeterminate. To get an answer, we must turn to bargaining.

Before we move on to bargaining, let us take note of a variant of the bilateral monopoly, in which our fruit farmer is also a monopolist in the fruit market. In that case, he will account for the effect of using an extra unit of labour on the market price of fruit as well. His choice will then be given by

$$f'(l)[p + p'(f(l))f(l)] = w(l) + lw'(l), \tag{12.2}$$

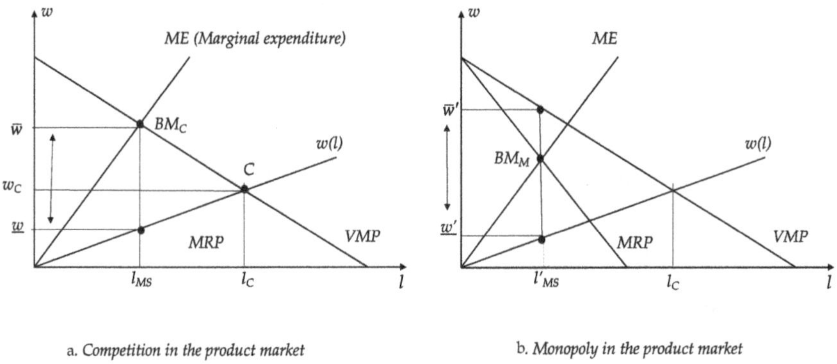

Figure 12.1 Bilateral monopoly

where $f'(l)[p+p'(f(l))f(l)]$ is the marginal revenue product (MRP) of labour. Panel b of Figure 12.1 describes this scenario. As the monopolist in the product market is also a monopsonist in the input market, he equates MRP with ME. Point BM_M shows the optimal hiring of labour, and as before, the wage remains indeterminate with the whole range of possibilities between $\underline{w}'$ and $\overline{w}'$.

12.3 Nash bargaining

Suppose two players have to decide on how to split a pie of size 1. If they are able to agree on an allocation, player 1 gets s and player 2 gets $(1-s)$. If they fail to agree, the pie is lost forever and they get nothing. We first note that any $s \in [0,1]$ is a feasible allocation and that the bargaining possibilities are wide open. This is the simplest bargaining problem we can think of.

A solution to the above problem as proposed by John Nash (1950, 1953) requires maximising a function $B = s(1-s)$ with respect to s, which then yields $s = 1/2$. The suggested solution is not only efficient (not a fraction of the pie has been wasted) but also fair.

The preceding problem, however, can be misleading, because it gives an impression that a 50:50 split is the fairest allocation. In fact, we have not explained at all what fairness means. At the heart of the Nash bargaining theory are two key elements: bargaining powers of the players and disagreement pay-offs, also known as threat points or status quo. Nash, in his original formulation, assumed equal bargaining powers of the players. His solution was generalised by Kalai by allowing asymmetric bargaining powers. The solution obtained by this latter formulation is called a generalised or an asymmetric Nash bargaining solution.

To make the problem a bit more general, let us assume that players care about their utility from the share of the pie, rather than the share itself. That is, player 1 wishes to maximise $u_1 = u_1(s)$ and player 2 $u_2 = u_2(1-s)$; both functions are assumed to be monotonic and concave. Their disagreement pay-offs are $d = (\underline{u}_1, \underline{u}_2)$. Even though in the event of disagreement, they do not get any share of the pie, they might be able to enjoy an alternative pay-off. For example, if a disagreement between employees and employer leads to the closure of the firm, the workers might get redundancy pay and the firm might relocate somewhere else. Disagreement pay-offs give reservation utilities. Let us also introduce a parameter $\alpha \in [0,1]$ which represents the (relative) bargaining power of player 1; $(1-\alpha)$ represents the bargaining power of player 2. Intuitively, if $\alpha = 1/2$, then players have equal bargaining power, and $\alpha < 1/2$ means that player

1 is weaker relative to player 2. Finally, assume that the players' utility functions observe the following restriction:

$$u_1(0) \le \underline{u}_1 < u_1(1) \equiv \bar{u}_1, u_2(0) \le \underline{u}_2 < u_2(1) \equiv \bar{u}_2.$$

The Nash bargaining solution suggests that we solve the following problem:[2]

$$\text{Max } B = \left[u_1(s) - \underline{u}_1\right]^{\alpha} \left[u_2(1-s) - \underline{u}_2\right]^{1-\alpha}.$$

The first-order condition for maximisation is

$$\frac{dB}{ds} = \alpha \left(u_1 - \underline{u}_1\right)^{\alpha-1} \left(u_2 - \underline{u}_2\right)^{1-\alpha} u_1'(.) - (1-\alpha)\left(u_1 - \underline{u}_1\right)^{\alpha} \left(u_2 - \underline{u}_2\right)^{-\alpha} u_2'(.) = 0$$

$$\text{or,} \quad (u_1 - \underline{u}_1)^{\alpha-1}(u_2 - \underline{u}_2)^{-\alpha}\left[\alpha(u_2 - \underline{u}_2)u_1'(.) - (1-\alpha)(u_1 - \underline{u}_1)u_2'(.)\right] = 0.$$

That is,

$$\frac{u_2(1-s) - \underline{u}_2}{u_1(s) - \underline{u}_1} = \frac{(1-\alpha)}{\alpha} \frac{u_2'(.)}{u_1'(.)}. \tag{12.3}$$

Equation (12.3) says that the pie should be split in such a way that the ratio of the players' net utilities $(u_i - \underline{u}_i)$ is equal to the ratio of their respective bargaining powers multiplied by the ratio of the marginal utilities. In the symmetric case of $\alpha = 1/2$ and $\underline{u}_1 = \underline{u}_2$, we have $u_1(s) = u_2(1-s)$ and $u_1'(s) = u_2'(1-s)$, and therefore, $s = 1/2$.

We can also ascertain that if $\alpha > 1/2$, then $s > 1/2$ (assuming $\underline{u}_1 = \underline{u}_2$). To see this, let us differentiate the first derivative of the Nash maximand $B'(s)$ with respect to α at the optimal solution:

$$B''(s)\frac{\partial s}{\partial \alpha} + \frac{\partial B'(s)}{\partial \alpha} = 0$$

$$\text{or,} \quad \frac{\partial s}{\partial \alpha} = -\frac{\partial B'(s)/\partial \alpha}{B''(s)} = -\left[\frac{(u_2 - \underline{u}_2)u_1'(.) + (u_1 - \underline{u}_1)u_2'(.)}{B''(s)}\right] > 0.$$

This relation is strictly positive because $B''(s) < 0$ by the second-order condition of maximisation. Thus, moving from the symmetric solution of $s = 1/2$ at $\alpha = 1/2$, if α increases, s must rise too.

It is worth noting that fairness of an allocation is defined as something relative to the players' bargaining powers as well as their disagreement pay-offs. If one has superior skills in bargaining and/or has a higher disagreement pay-off, it is reasonable to expect that one should be awarded a greater share. Therefore, a player's share as given by the Nash bargaining solution is increasing in his own bargaining power and disagreement pay-off while it is decreasing in the other player's bargaining power and disagreement pay-off.

12.3.1 A general statement of the Nash bargaining solution

The Nash bargaining solution is applicable not just to sharing a fixed pie, but also to situations where the size of the pie itself might be an outcome of bargaining. For example, bargaining over wage and employment is a case where the outcome of bargaining determines the size of the economic surplus. Therefore, we can present the problem of bargaining directly in terms of utilities (instead of share of the pie s). Let $\Omega = \{(u_1,u_2): F(u_1,u_2) \le 0\}$ be the set of utilities that player 1 and player 2 can get from an agreement (over whatever might be the underlying object of bargaining). $F(u_1,u_2)=0$ is the Pareto-efficiency frontier; $\frac{\partial F}{\partial u_1} > 0, \frac{\partial F}{\partial u_2} > 0$. Let $(\bar{u}_1,\bar{u}_2)$ be such that $F(\bar{u}_1,0)=0$ and $F(0,\bar{u}_2)=0$, where the lowest utility of a player is denoted by 0; $\bar{u}_1$ and $\bar{u}_2$ are the highest pay-offs of player 1 and player 2, respectively. As before, denote the disagreement pay-offs as $(\underline{u}_1,\underline{u}_2)$, $\underline{u}_1 < \bar{u}_1$ and $\underline{u}_2 < \bar{u}_2$.

The Nash bargaining solution is obtained by maximising $B = (u_1 - \underline{u}_1)^{\alpha} (u_2 - \underline{u}_2)^{1-\alpha}$ subject to the constraint that $F(u_1,u_2)=0$. Write the Lagrangian as

$$L = (u_1 - \underline{u}_1)^{\alpha} (u_2 - \underline{u}_2)^{1-\alpha} - \lambda F(u_1,u_2).$$

The first-order conditions are

$$\begin{aligned} \frac{\partial L}{\partial u_1} &\equiv \alpha (u_1 - \underline{u}_1)^{\alpha-1} (u_2 - \underline{u}_2)^{1-\alpha} - \lambda F_1 = 0 \\ &(u_1 - \underline{u}_1)^{\alpha-1}(u_2 - \underline{u}_2)^{-\alpha}\left[\alpha(u_2 - \underline{u}_2)\right] = \lambda F_1 \end{aligned} \tag{12.4}$$

$$\begin{aligned} \frac{\partial L}{\partial u_2} &\equiv (1-\alpha)(u_1 - \underline{u}_1)^{\alpha} (u_2 - \underline{u}_2)^{-\alpha} - \lambda F_2 = 0 \\ &(u_1 - \underline{u}_1)^{\alpha-1}(u_2 - \underline{u}_2)^{-\alpha}\left[(1-\alpha)(u_1 - \underline{u}_1)\right] = \lambda F_2, \end{aligned} \tag{12.5}$$

$$\frac{\partial L}{\partial \lambda} \equiv -F(u_1,u_2) = 0.$$

Dividing Eq. (12.4) by Eq. (12.5), we get

$$\frac{u_2 - \underline{u}_2}{u_1 - \underline{u}_1} \frac{\alpha}{(1-\alpha)} = \frac{F_1}{F_2}. \tag{12.6}$$

The right-hand-side expression is clearly the slope of the Pareto frontier. The left-hand side is the slope of the Nash maximand B (it can be easily checked). Thus, the Nash equilibrium occurs where the Nash maximand is tangent to the Pareto frontier. Alternatively stated, Eq. (12.6) becomes

$$\frac{u_2 - \underline{u}_2}{u_1 - \underline{u}_1} = \frac{(1-\alpha)}{\alpha} \frac{F_1}{F_2}. \tag{12.7}$$

Eq. (12.7) is equivalent to Eq. (12.3). To see this, note that from $F(u_1,u_2)=0$ we can write $dF = F_1 du_1 + F_2 du_2 = 0$, from which we get $\frac{F_1}{F_2} = -\frac{du_2}{du_1}$. Next, see that $du_2 = u_2'(1-s)(-1)ds$ and $du_1 = u_1'(s)ds$. Thus, $\frac{F_1}{F_2} = \frac{u_2'(.)}{u_1'(.)}$.

In Figure 12.2, we portray the solution on panel α. The feasible set of utilities over which bargaining takes place is denoted by Ω, and the disagreement point is denoted by d. The Nash maximand is the function B. It is evident that the disagreement pay-offs indirectly reduce the feasible

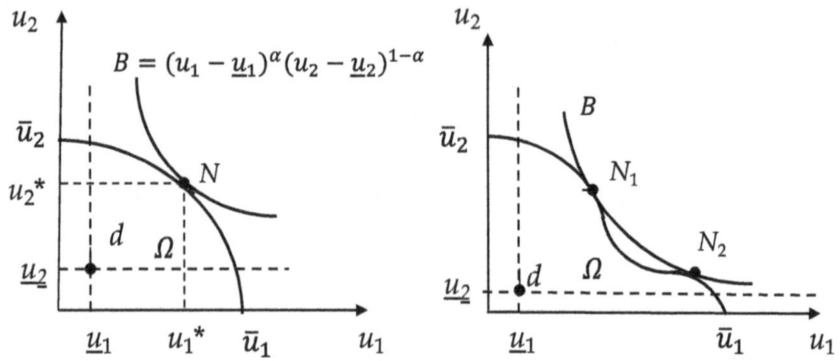

a. *Convex feasible set* b. *Non-convex feasible set*

Figure 12.2 Nash bargaining solution

set of agreements by entering the objective function B. Therefore, for the net utility set to be non-empty, we must have $\underline{u}_i < \bar{u}_i$ (for $i = 1, 2$). The (generalised) Nash solution is given by point N.

One point is worth emphasising here. The solution given by Eq. (12.3) or (12.6) assumes that the bargaining frontier $F(u_1, u_2)$ is differentiable. This need not be the case. Even if $F(.)$ is not differentiable, the Nash solution still can be obtained by identifying the highest curve B from the set Ω. For instance, if $F(.)$ is a rectangular box, the solution will be at the kink, the farthest north-eastern point of the set.

However, one thing is important—the convexity of the set Ω. The feasible set of the utilities must be convex (as in panel *a* of Figure 12.2). If it is not convex, we may have multiple solutions, such as points N_1 and N_2 as shown in panel *b* of Figure 12.2. The bargaining solution in this case, is discontinuous in α, which we want to avoid. Therefore, we generally insist on the convexity of the feasible set of pay-offs.

12.3.2 *Axioms underlying the Nash bargaining solution*

In more general terms, we define a bargaining problem as a pair (Ω, d), $\Omega \subseteq R^2, d \in R^2$, where $\Omega = \{(u_1, u_2) : F(u_1, u_2) \le 0\}$ and $d = (\underline{u}_1, \underline{u}_2)$.[3] The Pareto-efficiency frontier is defined by $\Omega^e = \{(u_1, u_2) \mid F(u_1, u_2) = 0\}$. Let the class of all bargaining games be denoted as $\mathcal{G}$. A bargaining solution is $\phi : \mathcal{G} \to R^2$. That is, for every possible bargaining problem the solution rule assigns a pair of (u_1, u_2).

We now argue that a bargaining solution (i.e., ϕ) should have some desirable (normative) properties stated as axioms and then show that the Nash bargaining solution indeed satisfies these properties.

1. **Independent of utility representations (IUR):** For any bargaining problem (Ω, d) in $\mathcal{G}$ and its bargaining solution ϕ, consider another bargaining game $(\Omega', d') \in \mathcal{G}$ such that

$$d' = (a_1 \underline{u}_1 + b_1, a_2 \underline{u}_2 + b_2)$$
$$\Omega' = \{(a_1 u_1 + b_1, a_2 u_2 + b_2) : (u_1, u_2) \in \Omega\}.$$

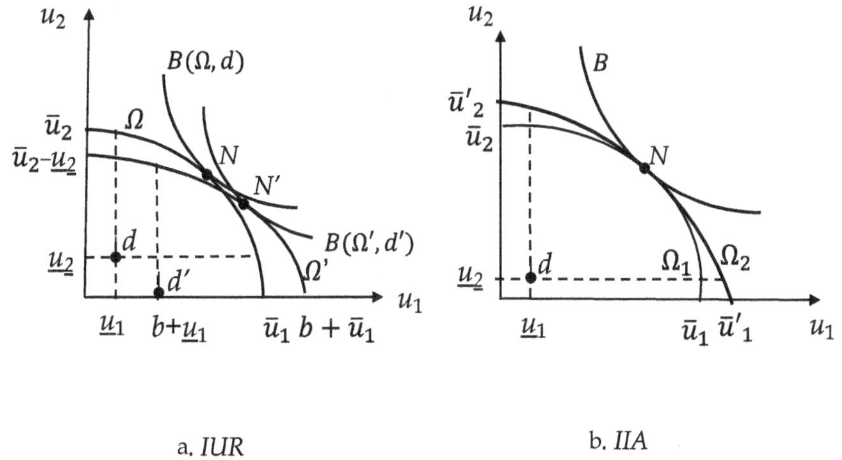

Figure 12.3 Axioms of independent of utility representations and independence of irrelevant alternatives

Then, for $i = 1,2$, $\phi_i(\Omega', d') = a_i\phi_i(\Omega, d) + b_i$.

How we measure utility does not matter. When a game's utilities are linearly (and monotonically) transformed and a new bargaining game is created, the bargaining solution of the transformed game will also be a linear monotonic transformation of the solution of the old game. Panel *a* of Figure 12.3 illustrates the axiom of IUR. The bargaining set Ω' is a monotonic linear transformation of Ω as every element of Ω' has b added to u_1 and $\underline{u}_2$ subtracted from u_2, including the disagreement pay-off d'. The Nash bargaining solution N' of the set Ω' must be a linear transformation of the solution N to the game Ω. That is, $N' = (u_1^* + b, u_2^* - \underline{u}_2)$.

2. **Pareto efficiency:** Fix (Ω, d) and a solution $\phi = (\phi_1, \phi_2)$. It must be that $\phi(.) \in \Omega^e$. There does not exist a utility pair $(u_1, u_2) \in \Omega \cup \{d\}$ such that $u_1 \geq \phi_1(\Omega, d), u_2 \geq \phi_2(\Omega, d)$ and for some i $u_i > \phi_i(\Omega, d)$. That is, there cannot be any Pareto improvement.
3. **Symmetry:** Suppose (Ω, d) is symmetric, meaning that $\underline{u}_1 = \underline{u}_2$ and if $(u_1, u_2) \in \Omega$, then also $(u_2, u_1) \in \Omega$. Then, $\phi_1(\Omega, d) = \phi_2(\Omega, d)$.
The symmetry axiom applies only to the pure Nash bargaining solution, which requires the bargaining powers to be equal. However, in the literature, often the Nash bargaining solution with symmetric bargaining power is loosely referred to as the symmetric solution, even though Ω is not symmetric. The generalised Nash bargaining solution does not satisfy this axiom, because asymmetric bargaining powers are allowed there.
4. **Independence of irrelevant alternatives (IIA):** Fix a bargaining solution $\phi : \mathcal{G} \rightarrow R^2$ and choose two bargaining games: (Ω_1, d_1) and (Ω_2, d_2) such that $d_1 = d_2$, $\Omega_1 \subset \Omega_2$ and $\phi(\Omega_2, d_2) \in \Omega_1$. Then for $i = 1,2, \phi_i(\Omega_2, d_2) = \phi_i(\Omega_1, d_1)$.
That is, if there are two games, one having a larger utility set than the other but sharing a common disagreement pay-off, and if the solution to the larger game belongs to the smaller game's feasible set, then the solutions of the two games are the same. That is to say, the larger game includes many irrelevant alternatives. As shown in panel *b* of Figure 12.3 the set Ω_2 is larger than Ω_1, but the solution to Ω_2, namely, point N, is included in Ω_1. Then N must be a solution for Ω_1; otherwise, N would not have belonged to Ω_1. This seems to suggest that if a choice is optimal against a larger constraint set and remains feasible to a smaller constraint set, then it should continue to be optimal against the smaller constraint set as well.

Proposition 23. (symmetric Nash bargaining solution) *A bargaining solution* $\phi : \mathcal{G} \to R^2$ *satisfies Axioms 1–4 if and only if* ϕ *is given by the unique solution to the following problem:*

$$Max \qquad B = (u_1 - \underline{u}_1)(u_2 - \underline{u}_2),$$

where (u_1, u_2) *belongs to the set* Ω^e *and* $u_1 \geq \underline{u}_1, u_2 \geq \underline{u}_2$. *In other words, the symmetric Nash bargaining solution satisfies Axioms 1–4.*

Proposition 24. (asymmetric or generalised Nash bargaining solution) *For each* $\alpha \in (0,1)$, *a bargaining solution* $\phi_\alpha : \mathcal{G} \to R^2$ *satisfies Axioms 1, 2 and 4 if and only if* ϕ_α *is given by the unique solution to the following problem:*

$$Max \qquad B(\alpha) = (u_1 - \underline{u}_1)^\alpha (u_2 - \underline{u}_2)^{1-\alpha},$$

where (u_1, u_2) *belongs to the set* Ω^e *and* $u_1 \geq \underline{u}_1, u_2 \geq \underline{u}_2$. *The asymmetric Nash bargaining solution satisfies all the previously mentioned axioms except 3 (unless* $\alpha = 1/2$*).*

12.3.3 The Kalai–Smorodinsky solution

Among the previously discussed axioms, the IIA is a subject of criticism, because it makes the Nash bargaining solution completely unaffected by changes in the maximal pay-offs $\overline{u}_1$ and $\overline{u}_2$. If Ω represents the set of all potential gains from engaging in bargaining, then the extreme points measure how the players individually value the 'entire pie'. If one player values it more than the other, the higher valuing player should get a bigger slice of the pie (*ceteris paribus*) to be consistent with the spirit of cooperation. In the Nash bargaining solution, the maximal pay-off is ignored, and the disagreement pay-offs play the most critical role.

Kalai and Smorodinsky (1975) offered a new solution that violates IIA and explicitly incorporates the maximal points of Ω, namely, $(\overline{u}_1, 0)$ and $(0, \overline{u}_2)$. Their proposed solution mimics a randomisation between two alternative 'take-it-or-leave-it' offers of the two parties. In principle, the bargaining solution should be in between the disagreement pay-off and the maximal pay-offs. The players should try to go north-east toward the maximal point $(\overline{u}_1, \overline{u}_2)$ and stop at the Pareto frontier. Note that this solution does not rely on the concept of bargaining power.

Figure 12.4 shows the Kalai–Smordonisky (KS) solution on panel *a* at point K, as compared to the simple Nash solution N (which assumes equal bargaining power). The Nash bargaining solution N is to the right of the KS solution because $\overline{u}_2 > \overline{u}_1$. Of course, under generalised Nash bargaining, we can map every point of the Pareto frontier by varying α, and therefore, there exists some $\alpha < 1/2$ such that point N corresponds to point K. That the KS solution violates IIA is shown on panel b. Here, by construction $K = N$ for the bargaining set Ω_1. The set Ω_2 is larger than Ω_1 with its u_2 intercept increased significantly more than its u_1 intercept. Hence, the new KS solution as given by N' is to the left of the earlier solution K, but the Nash bargaining solution remains unchanged at N. Note that the bargaining set here does not have a smooth frontier. This is deliberately done to demonstrate that both the Nash and KS solutions are applicable even if the Pareto frontier is not differentiable.

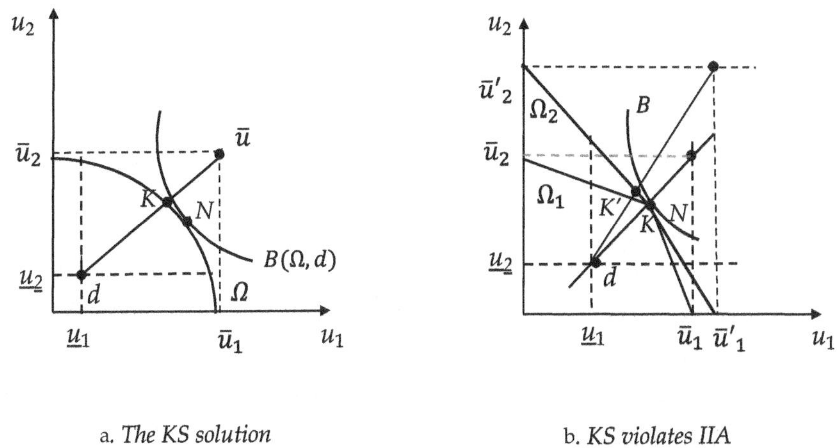

Figure 12.4 The Kalai–Smorodinsky solution

Proposition 25. (Kalai–Smordonisky solution) *For every bargaining game* (Ω, d) *in* $\mathcal{G}$, *there exists a unique bargaining solution* $\phi_K : \mathcal{G} \to R^2$ *that satisfies Axioms 1, 2 and 3 but not Axiom 4 (i.e., IIA), such that* $\phi_1^k \le \bar{u}_1$ *and* $\phi_2^k \le \bar{u}_2$ *along with*

$$\phi_1^k = \lambda \underline{u}_1 + (1-\lambda)\bar{u}_1, \qquad \phi_2^k = \lambda \underline{u}_2 + (1-\lambda)\bar{u}_2$$
$$\text{and} \quad F(\phi_1^k, \phi_2^k) = 0 \qquad \text{for} \quad \lambda \in (0,1].$$

12.4 Non-cooperative bargaining: the alternating-offer game of Rubinstein

Nash bargaining solution is best seen as merely a *proposal* that neither party should refuse. However, in reality, unless there is an arbitrator bargaining may take time to settle and players have to agree to a particular game form, which is often referred to as *bargaining protocol*, before they begin bargaining. Since delay is costly (because players are likely to discount the future) and a game might favour the players asymmetrically, real-world bargaining is likely to be fraught with inefficiencies. Thus, while elegant for axiomatic characterisation, the Nash bargaining solution focuses entirely on the solution of bargaining rather than the *process* of bargaining.

Nash himself in his 1953 paper proposed a simple bargaining game, which has come to be known as the *Nash demand game*. The game is as follows: Suppose two players are trying to bargain over the partition of a pie of size 1. Players simultaneously propose s_1 and s_2. If $s_1 + s_2 \le 1$, the players are awarded s_1 and s_2, but if $s_1 + s_2 > 1$, then players receive zero. It can be shown that for any s_1 the best response of player 2 is to propose $1 - s_1$ and for any s_2 player 1's best response is to propose $1 - s_2$. This leads to any proposal $s_1, s_2 \in [0,1]$ such that $s_1 + s_2 = 1$ being an equilibrium. While the game is non-cooperative, its infinitely many solutions are seen as a major problem.[4]

The first major non-cooperative bargaining game is due to Rubinstein (1982). In this game, as before a pie of size 1 is to be divided between two players. They have infinitely many periods to agree on an allocation of the pie. Player 1 opens the offer with an allocation proposal $(1-s_2, s_2)$. He offers s_2 to player 2 and retains $(1-s_2)$ for himself. Player 2 has the option of accepting it, in which case the game ends. Player 2 can refuse it and make a counter-offer in period 2 $(s_1, 1-s_1)$. That is, he offers s_1 to player 1 and $(1-s_2)$ to himself. Player 1 can accept it, and the game will end; alternatively, he can reject the offer, take the game to period 3 and make a counteroffer. The game will carry on until an offer is accepted. Note that player 1's turn comes in every odd period and player 2's turn in every even period. Both players are impatient. Let δ_1 be the discount factor of player 1 and δ_2 of player 2; $0 < \delta_1, \delta_2 < 1$. Due to discounting, the size of the cake shrinks (but only in valuation).

This is a complete information infinite horizon game. Since there is no terminal period, we cannot apply backward induction straight away to derive the subgame perfect equilibrium. Nevertheless, the stationarity property of the game (i.e., the game looks the same every period regardless of the history of rejection) helps one to restrict attention to only three periods. Using this stationarity argument originally proposed by Shaked and Sutton (1984) we can quickly establish the equilibrium partition.

Suppose in period 3 player 1 is to make an offer, and he anticipates that from the remaining subgame (or continuation game) the best pay-off player 2 can get is x. Then if he offers $\delta_2 x = v_2$ player 2 should not refuse. Player 1 then offers $(1-v_2, v_2)$. In period 2, when player 2 is to make his offer, he can offer $\delta_1(1-v_2)$, the present value of what player 1 can expect to get in period 3. The remaining pie, $1-\delta_1(1-v_2)$, stays with player 2. Now, moving on to period 1, player 1 then can offer $\delta_2[1-\delta_1(1-v_2)]$, which player 2 should not refuse. But note the game in period 1 is no different from the game in period 3, as the pie is stationary. Therefore, his offer in period 1 must be the same as v_2 that player 2 expects to get from the continuation game starting from period 3. That is to say, we must have

$$v_2 = \delta_2\left[1-\delta_1(1-v_2)\right].$$

We then can solve for v_2 as

$$v_2 = \frac{\delta_2(1-\delta_1)}{1-\delta_1\delta_2} = s_2^* \quad \Rightarrow \quad v_1 = 1-v_2 = \frac{1-\delta_2}{1-\delta_1\delta_2} = s_1^*. \tag{12.8}$$

Equation (12.8) is the well-known Rubinstein offer and counter-offer bargaining solution. In the special case of $\delta_1 = \delta_2 = \delta$,

$$s_2^* = \frac{\delta}{1+\delta} \text{ and } s_1^* = \frac{1}{1+\delta}\left(> s_2^*\right).$$

When two players are equally impatient, the first mover—player 1 as assumed—gets a larger share of the pie.

12.4.1 An alternative proof

There is another way of deriving the equilibrium, which is less elegant, but more instructive, provided we accept a modification of the game. Suppose the game lasts only for T periods, T being finite. If the game ever continues up to the last period through rejections of offers and counter-offers, a last period rule is invoked in which the proposer can keep the whole pie. In other words, the last period proposer is a 'dictator' as in a dictator game.[5]

One advantage of this formulation is that backward induction can be applied in a straightforward way. Let us start from $T = 2$; the game lasts only for two periods. If there is a disagreement in the first period, the game goes on to the second and last period. Since this is last period, player 2 gets $s_2 = 1$, $s_1 = 0$. Then moving to period 1, player 1 should offer $s_2^* = \delta_2$, the present value of player 2's future pay-off. Player 2 should agree, and player 1 should get $s_1^* = 1 - \delta_2$.

Now, consider $T = 3$. Here, in the last period, player 1 moves, and he will propose $s_2 = 0$ and $s_1 = 1$. Therefore, in the second period, player 2 should offer $s_1 = \delta_1$, which player 1 should not reject, and thus, player 2 will get $s_2 = (1 - \delta_1)$. In period 1, therefore, player 1 can offer $s_2^* = \delta_2 (1 - \delta_1)$ to player 2, leading to an agreement. In the three-period game, player 1's pay-off is $s_1^* = 1 - \delta_2 (1 - \delta_1)$. You can check that player 2's pay-off falls in this case (for extending the terminal period) and player 1's pay-off improves. So, it seems that whoever is able to make the last move will have some advantage.

Yet again, extend the game by one more period. In period $T = 4$, player 2 will surely get the full pie. So in period 3, player 1 is going to offer δ_2 to player 2 and then retain $(1 - \delta_2)$ for himself. Proceeding in this manner, we arrive at the first-period offer $s_2^* = \delta_2 \left[1 - \delta_1 (1 - \delta_2)\right]$, and he retains for himself $s_1^* = 1 - \left[\delta_2 \{1 - \delta_1 (1 - \delta_2)\}\right]$.

By arranging the previously discussed pay-offs and extending the same calculation for $T = 5, 6$ we see a pattern:

For $T = 1$, $s_1^* = 1$

For $T = 2$, $s_1^* = 1 - \delta_2$

For $T = 3$, $s_1^* = (1 - \delta_2) + \delta_1 \delta_2$

For $T = 4$, $s_1^* = 1 + \delta_1 \delta_2 - \delta_2 - \delta_2^2 \delta_1 = (1 - \delta_2)(1 + \delta_1 \delta_2)$

For $T = 5$, $s_1^* = (1 - \delta_2)[1 + \delta_1 \delta_2] + (\delta_1 \delta_2)^2$

For $T = 6$, $s_1^* = (1 - \delta_2)\left[1 + \delta_1 \delta_2 + (\delta_1 \delta_2)^2\right]$

...

For $T = n$(even), $s_1^* = (1 - \delta_2)\left[1 + \delta_1 \delta_2 + (\delta_1 \delta_2)^2 + \ldots + (\delta_1 \delta_2)^{\frac{n}{2} - 1}\right]$

For $T = n + 1$, $s_1^* = (1 - \delta_2)\left[1 + \delta_1 \delta_2 + (\delta_1 \delta_2)^2 + \ldots + (\delta_1 \delta_2)^{\frac{n}{2} - 1}\right] + (\delta_1 \delta_2)^{\frac{n}{2}}$.

Thus, if the terminal period is an even number, the first player's pay-off forms a GP series, while if the terminal period is an odd number, then it contains an additional term $(\delta_1\delta_2)^{\frac{n}{2}}$. Therefore, we can write the finite GP sum as (for n being even and $n \geqslant 4$)

$$s_1^* = \begin{cases} (1-\delta_2)\dfrac{1-(\delta_1\delta_2)^{\frac{n}{2}}}{1-\delta_1\delta_2} & \text{if } T = n \\ (1-\delta_2)\dfrac{1-(\delta_1\delta_2)^{\frac{n}{2}}}{1-\delta_1\delta_2} + (\delta_1\delta_2)^{\frac{n}{2}} & \text{if } T = n+1. \end{cases}$$

Now by letting $T \to \infty$, as $(\delta_1\delta_2)^{n/2} \to 0$, we arrive at

$$s_1^* = \frac{1-\delta_2}{1-\delta_1\delta_2}, \qquad s_2^* = 1 - s_1^* = \frac{\delta_2(1-\delta_1)}{1-\delta_1\delta_2},$$

which are the same as the ones given by Eq. (12.8).

Two important points to note here. The first point is that the symmetric Rubinstein solution (i.e., $\delta_1 = \delta_2 = \delta$) does not coincide with the symmetric Nash bargaining solution 1/2:1/2. This is of great interest in bargaining theory. It turns out that the length of time lapses between an offer and a counter-offer matters. If this time lapse becomes arbitrarily small (instead of one full unit of time) so that the future becomes almost the same as the present, the Rubinstein pay-offs will converge to 1/2.[6] The second point is that agreement is reached in the very first period. Hence, the outcome is efficient, as no *delay* occurs. Delay in agreement is a measure of inefficiency, as much as physically losing a part of the bargaining pie. However, we should also note that efficiency here is guaranteed by the complete information nature of the game. Later we will see that incomplete information causes inefficiency.

12.5 Bargaining over wage and employment

Now we return to the case of bilateral monopoly in which a single firm (or a confederate of firms) negotiates with a group of employees and apply the Nash bargaining approach. Although in reality, employees are represented by their union and since the union's objective function can significantly differ from an individual worker's utility function, we first restrict our attention to a single employee. Typically, in firm workers' bargaining, the pie is not a fixed one; rather, it is also subject to bargaining via employment.

Here, we take note of certain terminologies relating to bargaining protocols. If wage and employment are both bargained over simultaneously, it is called *efficient bargaining*, a term coined by McDonald and Solow (1981).[7] In some countries, such as the United Kingdom and the United States, employers have right to unilaterally decide on employment without consulting the employees or their union, as encoded in the employers' hiring and firing rights. Wage in this case may be the only thing to negotiate, and once the wage is negotiated, the employer decides on employment. This is called *right-to-manage* bargaining. A special variety of this bargaining is called the *monopoly union* protocol, whereby the workers or their union can unilaterally set the wage.

12.5.1 *Efficient bargaining*

Suppose an employee and an employer bargain over wage and employment. The employee's preference is given by $v = u(wl) - z(l)$ where l is the hours of work and $z(l)$ is disutility from work; $u'(.) > 0, u''(.) < 0, z'(.) > 0, z''(.) > 0$. The employer's profit is given by $\pi = R(l) - wl$, where $R(l)$ is revenue, $R''(.) < 0$. Let the bargaining powers of the employee and the employer be α and $1-\alpha$, respectively. Their disagreement pay-offs are $\bar{v}$ and $\bar{\pi}$.

Let us write the Nash bargaining problem as

$$\text{Max}_{w,l}\ B = \left[u(wl) - z(l) - \bar{v}\right]^{\alpha} \left[R(l) - wl - \bar{\pi}\right]^{1-\alpha}.$$

The first-order conditions are

$$\frac{\partial B}{\partial w} \equiv \left\{[v-\bar{v}]^{\alpha-1}[\pi-\bar{\pi}]^{-\alpha}\, l\right\}\left[\alpha(\pi-\bar{\pi})u'(.) - (1-\alpha)(v-\bar{v})\right] = 0$$

$$\frac{\partial B}{\partial l} \equiv \left\{[v-\bar{v}]^{\alpha-1}[\pi-\bar{\pi}]^{-\alpha}\right\}\left[\alpha(\pi-\bar{\pi})\left[u'(.)w - z'\right] + (1-\alpha)(v-\bar{v})(R'-w)\right] = 0.$$

In these two equations, under any solution, since $v > \bar{v}$ and $\pi > \bar{\pi}$, we must have

$$\alpha(\pi-\bar{\pi})u'(.) = (1-\alpha)(v-\bar{v}) \tag{12.9}$$

$$\alpha(\pi-\bar{\pi})\left[u'(.)w - z'(l)\right] = -(1-\alpha)(v-\bar{v})\left[R'(l) - w\right]. \tag{12.10}$$

Divide Eq. (12.9) by Eq. (12.10) and rearrange terms to get

$$R'(l) = \frac{z'(l)}{u'(wl)}. \tag{12.11}$$

Eq. (12.11) is the *contract curve* between the employer and the employee. On every point of this curve, the marginal rate of substitution (MRS) of the employee between w and l is equal to the slope of an iso-profit curve of the employer. The slope of the employee's indifference curve is $\frac{dw}{dl} = \frac{z'(.) - u'(.)w}{u'(.)l}$, and the slope of an iso-profit curve is $\frac{dw}{dl} = \frac{R'(l) - w}{l}$.

Note that both slopes can be positive or negative depending on the values of w and l. If $z'(l) > u'(wl)w$, the indifference curve is upward-sloping, and if $z'(l) < u'(wl)w$, then it is downward-sloping. When l is extremely small, $z'(l)$ is close to zero (by the convexity of $z(.)$ function), but $u'(wl)$ is infinitely large (by the concavity of $u(.)$ function), so the indifference curve must be downward-sloping. The opposite is true when l is large. There is a critical value of l for every given w at which the slope is zero. Similarly, the iso-profit curve is upward-sloping if $w < R'(l)$ and downward-sloping if $w > R'(l)$. The curve has a flat top at $R'(l) = w$.

Equating the two slopes, we get Eq. (12.11). What will be the slope of the contract curve? Writing Eq. (12.11) as $R'(l)u'(w(l)l) - z'(l) \equiv 0$ and differentiating it with respect to l, we derive

$$\frac{dw}{dl} = -\frac{\left[R''(l)u'(wl) + R'(l)u''(wl)w - z''(l)\right]}{R'(l)u''(wl)l} < 0. \tag{12.12}$$

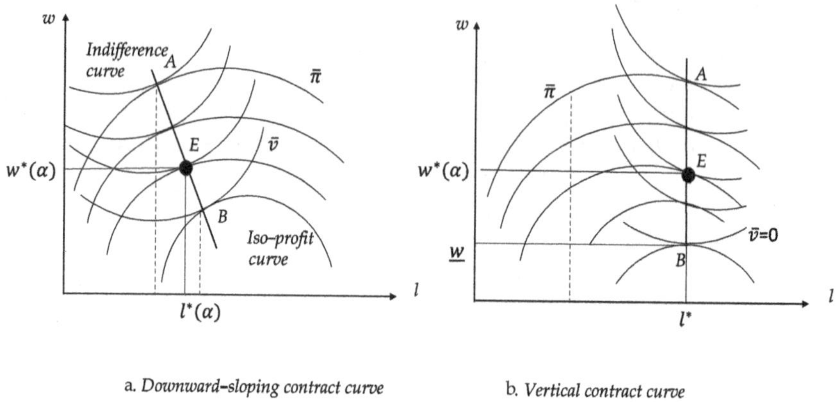

Figure 12.5 Wage–employment contract curves

The numerator and the denominator are both negative, and with the additional negative sign, the whole expression becomes negative. In particular, note that $v''(.) < 0$ is crucial to get the negative slope of the contract curve.

Figure 12.5 panel *a* shows the contract curve. Point *A* corresponds to the lowest iso-profit curve while point *B* to the lowest indifference curve. The bargaining solution occurs at a point like E, the exact location of which depends on α. The solution is clearly Pareto-efficient. Eq. (12.9) (in conjunction with Eq. (12.11)) gives us the bargaining solution, where the ratio of the net pay-offs of the two parties must be proportional to their bargaining powers:

$$\frac{(v-\bar{v})}{(\pi-\bar{\pi})}=\frac{\alpha}{1-\alpha}u'(.).$$

12.5.1.1 *Bargaining with a trade union*

We can easily extend the previous story from one to many identical employees simply by multiplying *v*(.) by the number of employees. But that would be a very simplistic representation of unions. Generally, their objective functions are more focused on two key things, wage and employment, rather than disutility from work, which an individual worker may value. In addition, unions are concerned about wage income rather than utility from wage income.

Suppose there are N workers who form a union. The union's objective is to maximise the aggregate income of its members. If employed a worker receives w and works for a fixed number of hours, say, 1 unit of time (as in one man-day, in the industrial relations parlay). If l number of workers are hired, total income is wl. However, if $l < N$, then the remaining workers receive the minimum wage denoted by $\underline{w}$ from working somewhere. In the case of selecting who will be employed and who will not, we will assume that it is decided randomly; thus, everybody has a l/N probability of being employed.[8]

With these specifications, the union's objective function changes to $\tilde{v}=wl+(N-l)\underline{w}=N\underline{w}+(w-\underline{w})l$. Since $N\underline{w}$ is a fixed term, we can redefine the union's objective function as

$v = \tilde{v} - N\underline{w}$. If there is a disagreement, no worker is employed, and all workers receive $\underline{w}$. Thus, $\overline{v} = 0$. The Nash bargaining problem is then written as

$$\text{Max}_{w,l}\ B = \left[(w - \underline{w})l\right]^{\alpha}\left[R(l) - wl - \overline{\pi}\right]^{1-\alpha}.$$

Proceeding in the same way as earlier, you should get the equation of the contract curve as

$$R'(l) = \underline{w}. \tag{12.13}$$

Now note an important difference. The employment depends on the minimum wage and not on the agreed wage, which means that employment is independent of the bargaining powers. The contract curve is vertical here, as shown by the line AB in panel b of Figure 12.5. Bargaining solely centers on wage. The wage will be chosen at an intermediate point like E.

Proposition 26. *Efficient bargaining with a trade union separates negotiation over wage and employment in two domains. Employment is chosen in reference to the opportunity cost of labour, while wage is chosen to allocate the resulting surplus in accordance with the bargaining powers of the parties.*

12.5.2 Right-to-manage bargaining

Take the same set-up as the above and consider a sequential game whereby the firm and its employees or their union bargain over wage, following which the firm chooses employment. This is right-to-manage bargaining, also often referred to as sequential bargaining.[9]

We consider the case of a single employee and the union separately. In either case, to apply backward induction, we need to start from the last stage. For any wage decided in the first stage, the firm chooses l such that

$$R'(l) = w. \tag{12.14}$$

This is the standard labour demand curve $l(w)$, which is downward-sloping and corresponds to the peak of the iso-profit curves as shown in Figure 12.6 panels a and b. Panel a corresponds to the case of a single employee, while panel b gives the case of a union. The lowest point on the labour demand curve must be given by the point where the employee or the union's utility is lowest at $\overline{v}$. In the case of union, as shown in panel b, this point corresponds to the minimum wage $\underline{w}$. Similarly, the highest point on the labour demand curve is given by the point where the firm's profit is the lowest $\overline{\pi}$ (i.e., its disagreement pay-off).

12.5.2.1 Bargaining with an employee

We take the same utility function of the employee and rewrite the Nash bargaining problem as

$$\text{Max}_{w}\quad B = \left[u(wl(w)) - z(l(w)) - \overline{v}\right]^{\alpha}\left[R(l(w)) - wl(w) - \overline{\pi}\right]^{1-\alpha}.$$

The first-order condition yields

$$(1-\alpha)\left[R'(.)l'(w)) - l(w) - wl'(w)\right](v - \overline{v}) + \alpha(\pi - \overline{\pi})\left[u'(.)\{wl'(w) + l(w)\} - z'(.)l'(w)\right] = 0$$

Making use of the labour demand equation $R'(.) - w = 0$, we write

$$-(1-\alpha)\left[v-\bar{v}\right]l(w)+\alpha\left[\pi-\bar{\pi}\right]\left(u'(.)l(w)\left\{\epsilon+1-\frac{z'(.)}{w}\epsilon\right\}\right)=0.$$

$$\frac{v-\bar{v}}{\pi-\bar{\pi}}=\frac{\alpha}{1-\alpha}\left\{\epsilon+1-\frac{z'(.)}{w}\epsilon\right\}u'(.). \tag{12.15}$$

where $\epsilon = wl'(w)/l(w) < 0$ is the wage elasticity of labour demand.

The ratio of the employee's utility and the firm's profit is proportional to their bargaining powers, adjusted for the wage elasticity of labour demand and the marginal utility of the worker.

12.5.2.2 Bargaining with a trade union

We solve the first-stage problem by applying Nash bargaining. We assume $\bar{\pi} = 0$ and write:

$$\text{Max}_w \quad B=\left[(w-\underline{w})l(w)\right]^{\alpha}\left[R(l(w))-wl(w)\right]^{1-\alpha}.$$

The first-order condition yields

$$(1-\alpha)v\left[l-l'(w)\{R'(l)-w\}\right]=\alpha\pi\left[(w-\underline{w})l'(w)+l\right].$$

Now substitute the firm's labour demand into the preceding equation and rewrite it as

$$\frac{v}{\pi}=\frac{\alpha}{1-\alpha}\left[\frac{(w-\underline{w})l'(w)+l}{l}\right],$$

$$\text{or} \quad \frac{v}{\pi}=\frac{\alpha}{1-\alpha}\left[\bar{\epsilon}+1\right] \tag{12.16}$$

where $\bar{\epsilon} = \dfrac{(w-\underline{w})l'(w)}{l} < 0$ is the (wage) elasticity of labour demand and $|\bar{\epsilon} < 1|$. Figure 12.6 panel b shows the bargaining solution at a point like E. We can rewrite Eq. (12.16) as

$$\frac{(w-\underline{w})}{\frac{R(l)}{l}-w}=\frac{\alpha}{1-\alpha}\left[\bar{\epsilon}+1\right]$$

$$\text{or} \quad w\left(1+\frac{\alpha}{1-\alpha}(1+\bar{\epsilon})\right)=\underline{w}+\frac{R(l)}{l}\frac{\alpha}{1-\alpha}(1+\bar{\epsilon}) \tag{12.17}$$

$$\text{or} \quad w=\underline{w}\left(\frac{1-\alpha}{1+\alpha\bar{\epsilon}}\right)+\frac{R(l)}{l}\left(\frac{\alpha(1+\bar{\epsilon})}{1+\alpha\bar{\epsilon}}\right)=\lambda\underline{w}+(1-\lambda)\left[R(l)/l\right],$$

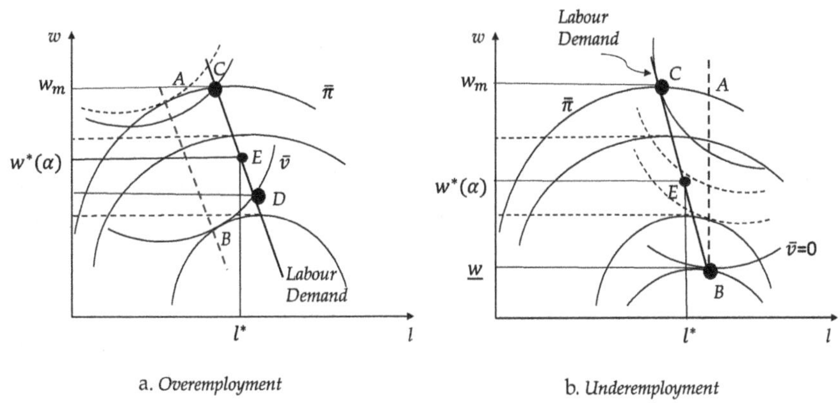

Figure 12.6 Inefficiency of employment choice

where $1-\lambda = \frac{\alpha(1+\bar{\epsilon})}{1+\alpha\bar{\epsilon}} < 1$. Thus, Eq. (12.17) says that the agreed wage is a weighted average of the minimum wage and the average revenue productivity $(R(l)/l)$ of the worker. When $\alpha \to 0, w \to \underline{w}$ and when $\alpha \to 1, w \to \frac{R(l)}{l}$. If the firm has all the bargaining power, it would get away by giving only $\underline{w}$, and alternatively, if the worker had all the bargaining power, it will appropriate the entire surplus and leave the firm only with zero profit.

An important point shared by both the above cases is while wage is negotiated and balances the parties' pay-offs in accordance with their bargaining powers, employment is off the contract curve.

See Figure 12.6. The labour demand curve is off the contract curve—to its right in the left panel and to its left on the right panel. Because the firm will choose its optimal labour from the peak of its iso-profit curve, workers are over-employed when negotiation takes place with a single worker. In contrast, when a union is involved, underemployment occurs.

Proposition 27. *Right-to-manage bargaining is inefficient. Players' bargaining powers matter for both wage and employment.*

12.5.3 Delegation in wage bargaining

Bargaining in modern firms is often conducted via professional negotiators, whom we can call delegates. As such firms are run by managers, appointed by the shareholders, while the unions are run by union leaders appointed by the union members. We can think of the manager and union leader as the delegates of the shareholders and the union members. If the delegates share the same objectives as their employer, then delegation is trivial. But if they are asked to pursue a different objective, which is generally referred to as an incentive scheme, then delegation can alter the outcome of negotiation. Obviously, the most interesting question to ask then is, How does one optimally design incentives to gain advantage against one's opponent? Here, we should note that incentive schemes can be of various types, but usually the literature restricts attention to linear schemes. Here is a delegation model adapted from Chatterjee and Saha (2013).

Suppose, as before, our union of N identical members wants to maximise $v = (w - \underline{w})l$. It appoints a union leader who is asked to maximise the following:

$$y = \rho v(.) + (1-\rho)wl = wl - \rho \underline{w}l. \tag{12.18}$$

Here, the key variable is ρ. If $\rho \neq 1$, then clearly the union leader's objective deviates from the union's own objective. As ρ is not dependent on w or l, it is a case of linear delegation—linear in the principal's objective. If $\rho > 1$, we can say the union leader is oriented to net wage bill
maximisation; alternatively, if $\rho < 1$, he is said to maximise the gross wage bill of the workers.

The firm's profit is as before $\pi = R(l) - wl, R''(l) < 0$. The shareholders appoint a manager, who is asked to maximise

$$z = \mu\pi + (1-\mu)R(l) = R(l) - \mu wl. \tag{12.19}$$

Here, too, $\mu \neq 1$ captures the case of delegation. If $\mu < 1$ we call it a case of sales orientation and if $\mu > 1$ it is a case of profit orientation (or penalising sales).[10]

We will study efficient bargaining between the two delegates. But the game is, by definition, a sequential (two-stage) game, whereby in the first stage, the firm and the union choose their optimal incentives, namely, μ and ρ, and then in the second stage, negotiation takes place between the two delegates. We assume that the union's bargaining power α is transferred to the union leader, just as the firm's bargaining power is transferred to the manager. All parties have disagreement pay-offs of zero.

The second second-stage bargaining is solved by maximising $B = \left[y^{\alpha} z^{1-\alpha}\right]$ with respect to (w, l). Two first-order conditions are

$$\frac{\partial B}{\partial l} = 0 \;\Rightarrow\; y^{\alpha-1}z^{-\alpha}\left[\alpha z(w - \rho\underline{w}) + (1-\alpha)y\{R'(l) - \mu w\}\right] = 0$$

$$\frac{\partial B}{\partial w} = 0 \;\Rightarrow\; y^{\alpha-1}z^{-\alpha}\left[\alpha z - (1-\alpha)y\mu\right]l = 0.$$

The second equation gives $\alpha z = (1-\alpha)y\mu$, which we substitute in the first equation. Then we arrive at the agreed employment and wage as implicitly given by the following two equations:

$$R'(l) = \mu\rho\underline{w}, \tag{12.20}$$

$$wl = (1-\alpha)\rho\underline{w}l + \alpha\frac{R(l)}{\mu}. \tag{12.21}$$

As noted earlier, the employment choice is not directly affected by the bargaining powers; rather, it depends on the minimum wage. However, now there is presence of μ and ρ, and if they depend on α, then the bargaining powers will affect l. Let us denote $w(.) = w(\mu, \rho)$ and $l(.) = l(\mu, \rho)$ as the solution to the above two equations. Also, crucially, $\partial l / \partial\rho < 0$ and $\partial l / \partial\mu < 0$ (because $R''(l) < 0$).

Moving onto the first stage, with the perfect anticipation of future l and w, the shareholders of the firm and the union members calculate their profit and utility as

$$\pi(\rho;\mu) = R(l(.)) - w(.)l(.) = R(l) - \alpha\frac{R(l(.))}{\mu} - (1-\alpha)\rho\underline{w}l(.)$$

$$v(\mu;\rho) = \alpha\frac{R(l(.))}{\mu} + (1-\alpha)\rho\underline{w}l(.) - \underline{w}l(.).$$

Both sides, respectively, maximise the preceding with respect to ρ and μ, and substituting $R'(l) = \rho\mu\underline{w}$ in the first-order conditions, we arrive at

$$\pi'(\mu) = \frac{1}{\mu^2}\left[\mu^2(\mu-1)\rho\underline{w}\frac{\partial l}{\partial\mu} + \alpha R(.)\right] = 0, \tag{12.22}$$

$$v'(\rho) = \underline{w}\left[(\rho-1)\frac{\partial l}{\partial\rho} + (1-\alpha)l\right] = 0. \tag{12.23}$$

These two equations, which are the best response functions of the two parties, are very illuminating. For the firm, for any $\alpha > 0$, regardless of what the union does, choosing $\mu > 1$ improves profit. This is evident from the strictly positive value of $\pi'(\mu)\big|_{\mu=1} = \alpha R(.) > 0$. Its profit will rise until μ exceeds a critical value that sets $\pi'(\mu) = 0$. In the same way, the union's utility always increases, except when $\alpha = 1$ by setting $\rho > 1$ (check $v'(\rho)\big|_{\rho=1} > 0$). This means offering incentives is a dominant strategy for both sides.

We now summarise our findings from the preceding analysis:

1. Since $\partial l/\partial\mu < 0$, Eq. (12.22) would hold with equality if and only if $\mu^* > 1$ when $\alpha > 0$ and $\mu^* = 1$ when $\alpha = 0$.
2. Since $\partial l/\partial\rho < 0$, Eq. (12.23) would hold with equality if and only if $\rho^* > 1$ when $\alpha < 1$ and $\rho^* = 1$ if $\alpha = 1$.
3. Since both $\rho > 1$ and $\mu > 1$, Eq. (12.20) confirms that there will be underemployment relative to the no delegation case.
4. Both sides try to inflate the effective minimum wage or the opportunity cost of labour through incentive delegation.
5. The incentive of each side gets weaker if its bargaining power increases.

12.5.3.1 *Effect of bargaining power*

We now want to see how bargaining power affects the delegation incentives.

Let (μ^*, ρ^*) be the Nash equilibrium incentives satisfying Eqs. (12.22) and (12.23) and assume that the equilibrium is unique and stable. The stability of Nash equilibrium is met by the condition

$$\Delta = \pi''(\mu)v''(\rho) - \frac{\partial\pi'(.)}{\partial\rho}\frac{\partial v'(.)}{\partial\mu} > 0.$$

Differentiating Eqs. (12.22) and (12.23), and using the facts that $\frac{\partial \pi'(\mu)}{\partial \alpha} = \frac{R(l)}{\mu^2} > 0$, $\frac{\partial v'(\rho)}{\partial \alpha} = -\underline{w}l < 0$ and the stability of equilibrium, we derive the comparative static results as

$$\frac{\partial \mu^*}{\partial \alpha} = \frac{1}{\Delta}\left[-\frac{\partial \pi'(\mu)}{\partial \alpha}u''(\rho) + \frac{\partial \pi'(\mu)}{\partial \rho}\frac{\partial u'(\rho)}{\partial \alpha}\right] = -\frac{1}{\Delta}\left[\frac{R(l)}{\mu^2}u''(\rho) + \underline{w}l\frac{\partial \pi'(\mu)}{\partial \rho}\right] > 0$$

$$\frac{\partial \rho^*}{\partial \alpha} = \frac{1}{\Delta}\left[-\frac{\partial u'(\rho)}{\partial \alpha}\pi''(\mu) + \frac{\partial \pi'(\mu)}{\partial \alpha}\frac{\partial u'(\rho)}{\partial \mu}\right] = \frac{1}{\Delta}\left[\underline{w}l\pi''(\mu) + \frac{R(l)}{\mu^2}\frac{\partial u'(\rho)}{\partial \mu}\right] < 0.$$

Lemma 4. *An increase in α reduces ρ^* and increases μ^*.*

A key aspect of delegation in bargaining is that it is a device to overcome the lack of bargaining power. Therefore, with an increase in the exogenous bargaining power, there are two effects on the players' pay-offs. There is a familiar direct and positive effect on the player's pay-off whose bargaining power has gone up (relative to his rival's). This just leads to a bigger slice of the bargaining pie. But then his increased bargaining power will also make his rival hike his incentive to overcome his loss of bargaining power. This will have an indirect negative effect on his pay-off.

Thus, the standard bargaining effect and the induced incentive response from the rival counteract each other.

To see this, we apply the envelope theorem to $\pi(.)$ and $v(.)$ and obtain

$$\pi'(\alpha) = -\left[\underbrace{\frac{R(l^*)}{l^*} - \mu^*\rho^*\underline{w}}_{>0}\right]\frac{l^*}{\mu^*} - \underline{w}\left[\underbrace{(1-\alpha)l^* - \rho^*(\mu^*-1)\frac{\partial l^*}{\partial \rho}}_{>0}\right]\frac{\partial \rho^*}{\partial \alpha}, \tag{12.24}$$

$$v'(\alpha) = \left[\underbrace{\frac{R(l^*)}{l^*} - \mu^*\rho^*\underline{w}}_{>0}\right]\frac{l^*}{\mu^*} - \left[\underbrace{\frac{\alpha s(l^*)}{\mu^{*2}} - (\rho^*-1)\underline{w}\frac{\partial l^*}{\partial \mu}}_{>0}\right]\frac{\partial \mu^*}{\partial \alpha}. \tag{12.25}$$

In these equations, the first terms are the standard bargaining power effect, and the second terms are their rival's incentive effect. You can verify that if $\rho = \mu = 1$ (as in the no-delegation case), the second term will be absent in each of the these two equations, and we will get the standard effects: $v'(\alpha) > 0$ and $\pi'(\alpha) < 0$. Also note that from an increase in α the rival's incentive effect faced by the union is negative while that faced by the firm is positive. This is because an increase in α means a decrease in the firm's bargaining power. Hence, the asymmetry in the incentive effect.

TWO CRITICAL ISSUES

1. Could it be possible that the incentive effect α ever dominates the direct effect? If the answer is yes, then we have a curious case where a player's pay-off falls in his bargaining power. To explore this possibility further, we need to make additional assumptions on the revenue

function of the firm and may also need to carry out a numerical example. Indeed, Chatterjee and Saha (2013) confirmed this possibility. Also see Mukherjee and Saha (2024) for a similar result for the right-to-manage bargaining case.[11]

2. If delegation is going to reduce one's pay-off, why does one delegate? The answer is that delegation is a dominant strategy, like confession in the prisoner's dilemma game. And like prisoner's dilemma, if the rival player does not delegate, then delegation is enormously rewarding. Hence, both end up delegating and thereby reducing the bargaining pie considerably. Still, in comparison to the no-delegation scenario, bilateral delegation makes the union strictly better off in a lower range of α and the firm in a higher range of α. There is a middle range, where both are worse off. In this critical range, both sides have incentives to avoid delegation, but that is not possible unless their option to delegate is taken away. You may see Chatterjee and Saha (2013) for more on this and a full welfare analysis.

Proposition 28. *Delegation in bargaining causes inefficiency, and yet delegation is a dominant strategy of the players. It is more rewarding if the other party does not delegate. But bilateral delegation reduces the bargaining pie severely, so much so that at an intermediate range of* α *both players will be individually better off if they are forbidden to delegate.*

12.5.4 Bargaining with a public-sector firm

There is a widely held view that public sector firms are very 'inefficient'. By inefficiency, commentators often refer to the firm's inability to maintain low cost and this has something to do with its public ownership. Certain input suppliers—labour unions more than anybody else—are blamed for taking advantage of the firm's public ownership. The argument, although very popular, is not easy to establish in a formal model without invoking special settings of firm–union interactions. Nevertheless, the issue of bargaining with a public-sector firm holds an independent interest. Here, we apply efficient bargaining to a partially public firm.

A firm that has θ proportion of its ownership in private hands and $1-\theta$ proportion with the government aims to maximise an objective function, which is a convex combination of profit and social welfare. Let this function be written as $G = \theta\pi + (1-\theta)SW$. If we maintain the same set-up as before (assuming labour is the only input) so that $\pi = R(l) - wl$, and if we assume that the market demand is a standard downward-sloping function $p = p(q(l))$, then $SW \equiv \pi + CS = \int_0^l p(x)dx - wl$. This allows us to derive

$$G = \theta[R(l) - wl)] + (1-\theta)\left[\int_0^l p(x)dx - wl\right] = \theta R(l) + (1-\theta)\int_0^l p(x)dx - wl.$$

The trade union's objective function is $v = (w - \underline{w})l$ as before. Set disagreement pay-offs to zero. Now let us employ efficient bargaining, which calls for maximising $B = v^{\alpha}G^{1-\alpha}$ with respect to w and l. Two first-order conditions are

$$\frac{\partial B}{\partial w} = \left(v^{\alpha-1}G^{-\alpha}\right) \times \left[\alpha lG - (1-\alpha)vl\right] = 0$$

$$\frac{\partial B}{\partial l} = \left(v^{\alpha-1}G^{-\alpha}\right) \times \left[\alpha(w-\underline{w})G + (1-\alpha)v\{\theta R'(l) + (1-\theta)p(l) - w\}\right] = 0$$

The first equation tells us that $\alpha G = (1-\alpha)v$. Substituting this into the second equation and writing out both equations, we get two important conditions for wage and employment, respectively, as

$$w = (1-\alpha)\underline{w} + \alpha\left[\theta\frac{R(l)}{l} + (1-\theta)\frac{\int_0^l p(x)\,dx}{l}\right] \tag{12.26}$$

$$\underline{w} = \theta R'(l) + (1-\theta)p(l). \tag{12.27}$$

Eq. (12.26) shows that the wage rate is a convex combination of the minimum wage and the average 'productivity' of the public-sector firm, which itself is a convex combination of the average revenue and utility of the consumers per worker. The public firm's ownership enters the wage equation via the average productivity term. Eq. (12.27) says that the marginal return from employing an additional worker, which is a convex combination of the marginal revenue productivity of labour and average revenue, must be equal to the minimum wage. If the public firm is fully public, then the price is equal to the minimum wage.

Also as expected, neither the workers' wage nor their bargaining power affects the public firm's employment choice (because of the efficient bargaining protocol). But public ownership does enter the employment equation. The greater the extent of public ownership, the greater the employment, because $p(l) > R'(l)$ for any l (recall the relation between AR and MR).

Proposition 29. *For a partially or fully public firm that engages with workers in efficient bargaining, the following results hold:*

1. *A (partially or fully) public-sector firm always hires more workers than a private firm.*
2. *Workers receive a higher wage bill because of public ownership, but their wage rate may or may not be higher than that in a privately owned firm, nor does it affect the price consumers pay.*

We conclude this section by noting that if the demand curve is linear and production technology is *CRS*, namely, $q = l$, then the wage rate will be completely neutral to the ownership of the firm.

Suppose $p = 1 - l$. Then $R(l)/l = 1 - l$ and $\frac{\int_0^l p(x)\,dx}{l} = 1 - l/2$. Therefore, $\theta\frac{R(l)}{l} + (1-\theta)\frac{\int_0^l p(x)dx}{l} = 1 - l\frac{1+\theta}{2}$. Next, see from the employment equation that $\theta R'(l) + (1-\theta)p(l) = 1 - l(1+\theta)$. Then, we conclude $l^* = \frac{1-\underline{w}}{1+\theta}$ and $w^* = (1-\alpha)\underline{w} + \alpha\frac{1+\underline{w}}{2}$.

Remark 1

If the production technology is constant returns to scale (CRS) and the market demand curve is linear, efficient bargaining will make the wage rate completely neutral to the ownership of the firm, although public ownership will keep the price lower and generate greater consumer welfare.

This remark highlights the fact that when we move to non-CRS technology or non-linear demand, they interact with the firm ownership in a non-trivial way, and these interactions vary across bargaining protocols. Any effect on the wage should be attributed to these interactions, rather than public ownership *per se*.

12.6 Bargaining with incomplete information

So far, we have assumed that the contracting parties know everything about each other. Now we consider a more realistic scenario in which both sides may lack some critical information about each other. Taking the context of selling and buying an indivisible good, assume that the seller may not know what the maximum price the buyer is willing to pay is. Likewise, the buyer may not know the minimum price the seller is willing to accept. In reality, people learn about each other's willingness to pay/accept through a process of negotiation that is inherently time-consuming. There are also bargaining protocols where the players get only one chance to strike a deal. How do the players design their bids and offers, and what are the odds of disagreement? These are the issues we will now look into.

12.6.1 Sealed-offer bargaining

Chatterjee and Samuelson (1983) analysed a simple one-shot bargaining model of incomplete information in which a seller and a buyer simultaneously make offers. They formally established some of the key themes of this literature, such as inefficiency of trade and overstating/understating of offers, that helped subsequent developments in this literature. Saha (1995) later extended this model to markets where an agent can choose to be a seller or a buyer. The following exposition is largely based on Saha (1995).

Consider bargaining over the sale of an indivisible good, a car or a painting, for example. The seller's valuation of the good is v_S, and the buyer's valuation is v_B. But neither side knows the other's valuation. Had they known, they could simply strike a deal at some price between v_s and v_B if $v_S < v_B$; else, they just walk away.

Without knowledge of each other's valuations, they could do many things to arrive at an agreement. Let us take the simplest one. Both sides simultaneously announce an offer they are willing to pay/accept. The buyer announces b, and the seller announces s. If $b > s$, a price-setting rule $p = \alpha b + (1-\alpha)s$ will kick in to complete the trade. α is exogenously fixed. If $b < s$, no trade takes place. They have just one chance to strike a deal.

Player i believes that player j's valuation v_j $(i, j = B, S)$ is uniformly distributed over a common support [0,1]. These beliefs are common knowledge.[12]

Strategies Let the buyer's strategy be $b = \beta(v_B)$ and the seller's strategy be $s = \sigma(v_S)$. The players choose their offers by following these two functions and their choices generate a *distribution of buyers and sellers who can successfully trade*. While quoting b, the buyer knows that the proportion of sellers with *valuations* at mostb is exactly b (because of the uniform distribution of v_S), and out of them, those sellers whose *optimal offers* do not exceed b will constitute a smaller set of sellers. Who are those sellers?

We get an answer from Figure 12.7, where we have drawn two possible offer functions, $\beta(v_B)$ and $\sigma(v_S)$. The linearity of the two functions is just assumed at this stage, and later, we will try to establish their validity as perfect equilibrium offers. What is important at this stage is not the linearity but monotonicty. These offer functions must be strictly increasing; otherwise, they will not be incentive compatible, which can be shown formally (for the proof, see Section 12.8).

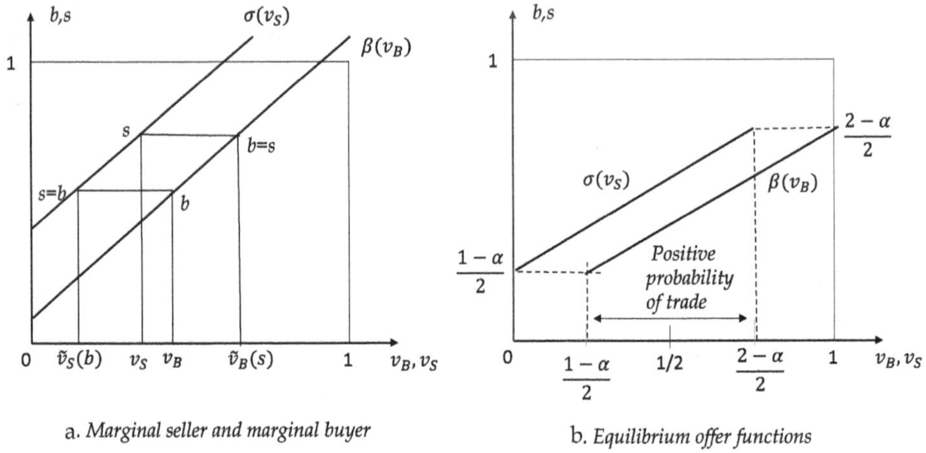

Figure 12.7 Offer functions

Property 3

The incentive-compatible strategy functions are strictly increasing: $\beta'(v_B) > 0$ *and* $\sigma'(v_S) > 0$.

Intuitively, we expect that the buyer would be announcing an offer below v_B and the seller above v_S. Therefore, a seller who is able to strike a deal with a buyer who has announced b must have a valuation strictly less than b. We see from panel *a* of Figure 12.7 that all those sellers whose valuations are less than $\tilde{v}_S(b)$ can trade with the buyer who has quoted b because $\sigma(\tilde{v}_S(b)) = s = b$. We call $\tilde{v}_S(b)$ *marginal seller* for offer b (the last seller to accept the offer b). The mass of these sellers is exactly $\tilde{v}_S(b)$ (by the uniform distribution of valuations).

Therefore, (noting that the density function of v_S is 1 and assuming $\tilde{v}_S \geq 0$) we can write the buyer's expected pay-off as

$$\pi_B = \int_0^{\tilde{v}_S(b)} \left[v_B - \alpha b - (1-\alpha)\sigma(v_S)\right] dv_S. \tag{12.28}$$

Note that when $b < s, \tilde{v}_S < 0$, trade does not occur. The buyer maximises π_B with respect to b.[13] The first-order condition is

$$[v_B - \alpha b - (1-\alpha)b]\frac{\partial \tilde{v}_s(b)}{\partial b} - \alpha \tilde{v}_s(b) = [v_B - b]\frac{\partial \tilde{v}_s(b)}{\partial b} - \alpha \tilde{v}_s = 0. \tag{12.29}$$

Let us note that since $\sigma(\tilde{v}_S) = b$, we can write $\tilde{v}_S = \sigma^{-1}(b)$. Thus, $\dfrac{\partial \tilde{v}_S(b)}{\partial b} = \dfrac{\partial \sigma^{-1}(b)}{\partial b}$ $= \dfrac{1}{\sigma'(\tilde{v}_S)}$ because $\sigma(v_S)$ is monotonic and continuous.[14] Furthermore, $b = s = \sigma(\tilde{v}_S)$ and $v_B = \beta^{-1}(\sigma(\tilde{v}_S))$. Using these facts and rearranging terms, we rewrite Eq. (12.29) as

$$\left[\beta^{-1}\left(\sigma\left(\tilde{v}_S\right)\right)-\sigma\left(\tilde{v}_S\right)\right]-\alpha\tilde{v}_S\left(b\right)\sigma'\left(\tilde{v}_S\left(b\right)\right)=0. \tag{12.30}$$

Now consider the expected profit of a seller. From Figure 12.7 panel *a*, we see that from the seller's offer *s*, there is a *marginal buyer* $\tilde{v}_B\left(s\right)$ such that $\beta\left(\tilde{v}_B\left(s\right)\right)=b=s$. The marginal buyer is the first buyer to accept the offer s, and all buyers above $\tilde{\beta}\left(s\right)$ will also accept s. Thus, we write the seller's expected profit as

$$\pi_S=\int_{\tilde{v}_B(s)}^{1}\left[\alpha\beta\left(v_B\right)+\left(1-\alpha\right)s-v_S\right]dv_B. \tag{12.31}$$

Maximising π_S with respect to s, write the first-order condition as

$$-\left[s-v_S\right]\frac{\partial\tilde{v}_B\left(s\right)}{\partial s}+\left(1-\alpha\right)\left[1-\tilde{v}_B\left(s\right)\right]=0. \tag{12.32}$$

As before, we note that since $\tilde{v}_B=\beta^{-1}\left(s\right)$, $\frac{\partial\tilde{v}_B\left(s\right)}{\partial s}=\frac{\partial\beta^{-1}\left(s\right)}{\partial s}=\frac{1}{\beta'\left(\tilde{v}_B\right)}$. In addition, $s=\beta\left(\tilde{v}_B\left(s\right)\right)$ and $v_S=\sigma^{-1}\left(\beta\left(\tilde{v}_B\left(s\right)\right)\right)$. Therefore, Eq. (12.32) can be written as

$$-\left[\beta\left(\tilde{v}_B\left(s\right)\right)-\sigma^{-1}\left(\beta\left(\tilde{v}_B\left(s\right)\right)\right)\right]+\left(1-\alpha\right)\left(1-\tilde{v}_B\left(s\right)\right)\beta'\left(\tilde{v}_B\left(s\right)\right)=0. \tag{12.33}$$

As Eqs. (12.30) and (12.33) hold for any $\tilde{v}_S$ and $\tilde{v}_B$, $\beta^{-1}\left(\sigma\left(v_S\right)=\tilde{v}_B\left(v_S\right)\right.$ and $\sigma^{-1}\left(\beta\left(v_B\right)\right)=\tilde{v}_S\left(v_B\right)$, we can rewrite the two equations as

$$-\sigma'\left(v_s\right)-\frac{\sigma\left(v_S\right)}{\alpha v_S}+\frac{\tilde{v}_B\left(v_S\right)}{\alpha v_S}=0, \tag{12.34}$$

$$\beta'\left(v_B\right)-\frac{\beta\left(v_B\right)}{\left(1-\alpha\right)\left(1-v_B\right)}+\frac{\tilde{v}_S\left(v_B\right)}{\left(1-\alpha\right)\left(1-v_B\right)}=0. \tag{12.35}$$

These two best response functions constitute a pair of linked first-order differential equations. We now try to solve them to derive the Bayesian Nash equilibrium offer functions.

We attempt a linear solution. Suppose $\sigma\left(v_S\right)$ and $\beta\left(v_B\right)$ are linear so that $\tilde{v}_S$ also becomes a linear function of v_B. Let us write $\tilde{v}_S=m+nv_B$; then by implication, $\tilde{v}_B=\left(v_S-m\right)/n$, where the constant terms m and n are to be determined from the solution of $\sigma\left(v_S\right)$ and $\beta\left(v_B\right)$.[15] Eqs. (12.34) and (12.35) then can be conveniently written as

$$\sigma'\left(v_s\right)+\frac{\sigma\left(v_S\right)}{\alpha v_S}=\frac{v_S-m}{n\alpha v_S}, \tag{12.36}$$

$$-\beta'\left(v_B\right)+\frac{\beta\left(v_B\right)}{\left(1-\alpha\right)\left(1-v_B\right)}=\frac{m+nv_B}{\left(1-\alpha\right)\left(1-v_B\right)}. \tag{12.37}$$

These two equations are no longer linked as we could exploit the linear relation between $\tilde{v}_S$ and v_B, (and between $\tilde{v}_B$and v_S) to express them only in terms of the agent's own valuation.[16] In order to derive the optimal offers within the class of linear functions, let us propose $\sigma(v_S) = c_0 + c_1 v_S$ and $\beta(v_B) = a_0 + a_1 v_B$.

Then by substituting $\sigma(v_S) = c_0 + c_1 v_S$ into Eq. (12.36), we write

$$c_1 \alpha v_S + c_0 + c_1 v_S = \frac{v_S - m}{n}.$$

Let us plug $v_S = 0$ and obtain $c_0 = -m/n$ and substituting it back into the equation we derive $c_1 = \frac{1}{n(1+\alpha)}$.

Similarly, by substituting $\beta(v_B) = a_0 + a_1 v_B$, we write Eq. (12.37) as

$$-a_1(1-\alpha)(1-v_B) + (a_0 + a_1 v_B) = (m + n v_B).$$

Setting $v_B = 1$, we get $a_0 + a_1 = m + n$ and then substituting back $a_0 = m + n - a_1$ into the equation, we derive $a_1 = \frac{n}{2-\alpha}$ and, in turn, $a_0 = m + n\frac{1-\alpha}{2-\alpha}$. Using the values of a_0, a_1, c_0 and c_1, we can now express the equilibrium strategies as functions of m and n:

$$\beta(v_B) = m + n\frac{1-\alpha}{2-\alpha} v_B \tag{12.38}$$

$$\sigma(v_S) = \frac{v_S}{n(1+\alpha)} - \frac{m}{n}. \tag{12.39}$$

Now we impose two boundary conditions on the preceding offer functions:

$$\beta\left(-\frac{m}{n}\right) = -\frac{m}{n} \quad \text{and} \quad \sigma(m+n) = m+n.$$

Setting these two restrictions on $\beta(.)$ and $\sigma(.)$, we derive from Eqs. (12.38) and (12.39)

$$n = \frac{2-\alpha}{1+\alpha} \quad \text{and} \quad m = -\frac{(2-\alpha)(1-\alpha)}{2(1+\alpha)}.$$

Also, the marginal seller and the marginal buyer are

$$\tilde{v}_S(v_B) = \frac{2-\alpha}{1+\alpha} v_B - \frac{(2-\alpha)(1-\alpha)}{2(1+\alpha)} \quad \text{and} \quad \tilde{v}_B(v_S) = \frac{1+\alpha}{2-\alpha} v_S + \frac{1-\alpha}{2}.$$

In addition, by setting $\tilde{v}_S(v_B) = 0$, we can derive the lowest value of $v_B, \hat{v}_B = (1-\alpha)/2$, which expects a positive probability of trade. Similarly, by setting $\tilde{v}_B(v_S) = 1$, we derive $\hat{v}_s = (2-\alpha)/2$, the highest value of v_S that expects a positive probability of trade. These two critical values define the support of the equilibrium offer functions, which we report in the following proposition.

Proposition 30. *In the one-shot sealed offer bargaining game described earlier, the following linear strategies form a Bayesian Nash (or perfect) equilibrium.*

$$\beta(v_B)=\begin{cases}\dfrac{v_B}{1+\alpha}+\dfrac{(1-\alpha)\alpha}{2(1+\alpha)} & \text{for } v_B \geq \dfrac{1-\alpha}{2}\\[2ex] \dfrac{1-\alpha}{2} & \text{for } v_B < \dfrac{1-\alpha}{2}\end{cases} \tag{12.40}$$

$$\text{and } \sigma(v_S)=\begin{cases}\dfrac{v_S}{2-\alpha}+\dfrac{1-\alpha}{2} & \text{for } v_S \leq \dfrac{2-\alpha}{2}\\[2ex] \dfrac{2-\alpha}{2} & \text{for } v_S > \dfrac{2-\alpha}{2}.\end{cases} \tag{12.41}$$

12.6.1.2 *Probability of trade*

Panel *b* of Figure 12.7 shows the equilibrium offer functions as given in Eqs. (12.40) and (12.41). Between 0 and $(1-\alpha)/2$ the buyer's offer falls short of the seller's; hence, there is no trade. On the other extreme, between $(2-\alpha)/2$ and 1, the seller's offer exceeds the buyer's offer, and again, there is no trade. At $v_B=1$ the buyer's offer is exactly $(2-\alpha)/2$.[17] In the intermediate zone where $\beta(v_B)\geq\sigma(v_S)$, the probability of trade is positive.

$$\text{Ex ante prob. of trade } = \text{Prob.}\left(v_B \geq \hat{v}_B\right)\times \text{Prob.}\left(v_S \leq \hat{v}_S\right)=\frac{1+\alpha}{2}\times\frac{2-\alpha}{2}.$$

Contrast this with the complete information case, where $\hat{v}_B=0, \hat{v}_S=1$ and the *ex ante* probability of trade is 1. If a seller of valuation v_S meets a buyer of valuation $v_B \geq v_S$, the trade takes place with certainty, and every seller type has a positive probability of meeting a buyer with whom he can trade. Therefore, for a seller of valuations v_S, the *conditional probability of trade* is $1-v_S$. Under incomplete information, the *conditional probability* of trade is the probability of $v_B \geq \tilde{v}_B(\sigma(v_S)) = 1-\tilde{v}_B < 1-v_S$. The smaller probability of trade under incomplete information, either *ex ante* or conditional, reflects inefficiency.

Saha (1995) has shown that an agent is more likely to choose to be a seller when his own valuation is very low. He does so in order to avoid a low probability of trade. Likewise, if an agent's valuation is very high, he is more likely to choose to be a buyer. However, while, by choosing a particular side, they can improve their expected probability of successful trade, they also face a new uncertainty—matching uncertainty. The combined effect of the two uncertainties can reduce the chance of trade significantly.

12.6.1.3 *Overstating and understating*

Note that all buyers except the first buyer, $\hat{v}_B$ (or $(1-\alpha)/2$), always quote *below* their valuation. The extent of their understatement increases as α, the bias in the pricing rule that favours the seller, increases. Check that $\beta(v_B)$ shifts downward as α increases. By comparison, all sellers, except the last seller, $\hat{v}_S$ (or $(2-\alpha)/2$) make offers *above* their valuation. However, as α increases his offer curve gains a greater slope *albeit* with a smaller intercept. Thus, at v_S below a critical level his extent of overstatement falls while above the critical level it rises.

12.6.2 Sequential one-sided-offer bargaining

We now study a one-sided-offer bargaining game with two periods developed by Fudenberg and Tirole (1983). Specifically, the seller makes an offer, and the buyer accepts or rejects. There are at most two chances to strike a deal over the sale of an indivisible object. Both sides know their own valuation but not their counterpart's. To keep matters simple, we consider the buyer of two types $v \in \{1, b\}$ (clearly, $b > 1$) and the seller also of two types $s \in \{s_f, s_t\}$. By seller's type, we mean what the seller can earn, in the event of a 'no trade'. The seller's production cost is assumed to be zero. The seller announces p_1 in the first period. If the buyer rejects, he announces p_2 in the second period. The buyer accepts or rejects, and the game ends. If trade takes place, the seller gets a pay-off of $p_i\ (i = 1, 2)$, and the buyer gets $v - p_i$. If the game ends in disagreement, the seller gets s (either s_f or s_t) by selling the good elsewhere. The buyer gets nothing. Let the buyer's and seller's discount factors be δ_B and δ_S, respectively. We denote the buyer's strategy of accepting a first period offer by probability α.

12.6.2.1 The seller's type is known

We first consider a simpler version of the model with only one type of seller and two types of buyer. This means that the buyer knows the seller's type. Let us assume $s < 1$ and that it is known to the buyer.[18] Here, the seller's offer has no information value, but the buyer's response can signal her true valuation and, in turn, allow the seller to update his belief should the game proceed to the second stage.

- *Seller's belief* Let us begin with the seller's belief about the buyer's type:

$$\text{Prob.}(v = 1) = \begin{cases} 1/2 & \text{in period 1} \\ \beta & \text{in period 2} \end{cases}.$$

Period 1 belief is the prior of the seller and period 2 belief is the updated belief following a rejection of p_1. Following Bayes' rule, β is

$$\beta \equiv \text{prob.}(v = 1 \mid \text{reject}) = \frac{\text{prob.}(v = 1) \cdot \text{prob}(\text{reject} \mid v = 1)}{\text{prob.(reject)}}$$
$$= \frac{\frac{1}{2} \cdot \text{prob}(\text{reject} \mid v = 1)}{\frac{1}{2} \cdot \text{prob.}(\text{reject} \mid v = 1) + \frac{1}{2} \cdot \text{prob.}(\text{reject} \mid v = b)}.$$

In the second period, the seller would charge b (which is accepted with probability $1 - \beta$) instead of charging 1 (which guarantees trade). With probability β, there is no trade, and he gets s from outside. Thus, he charges b if $(1 - \beta)b + \beta s > 1$ or $\beta < (b - 1)/(b - s) \equiv \hat{\beta}$. Alternatively, he would charge 1 if $\beta > \hat{\beta}$ and randomise between b and 1 if $\beta = \hat{\beta}$.

But note that β depends on the strategies of the buyer of type $v = 1$ and $v = b$. Since if $p_1 \leq 1$, both types of buyers will accept and, if $p_1 > b$, neither will accept, the seller will not announce $p_1 < 1$ or $> b$. So, for the low-type buyer, the strategy is simple: accept if $p_1 = 1$, otherwise reject.

- *High-type buyer's strategy* The strategy of the high-type buyer is non-trivial. Suppose she expects the seller to charge $p_2 = 1$ with probability σ. Then she is going to accept p_1 if $b - p_1 > \delta_B[\sigma(b-1)]$ or $p_1 < \delta_B\sigma + b(1-\delta_B\sigma) \equiv v(\sigma)$. She will reject p_1 if $p_1 > v(\sigma)$ and will be indifferent if $p_1 = v(\sigma)$.

To play a mixed strategy, she must be indifferent. Thus, from $p_1 = v(\sigma)$, we derive $\sigma(p_1) = (b - p_1)/[\delta_B(b-1)]$. Also, note that when $\sigma = 0, v(\sigma) = b$ and that when $\sigma = 1$ $v(\sigma) = \delta_B + b(1-\delta_B)$. Let us denote $v(\sigma = 1)$ by $\tilde{v}$. If $p_1 \le \tilde{v}$, the high-type buyer always accepts.

If $\tilde{v} < p_1 < b$, the high-type buyer will randomise between acceptance and rejection if she expects the seller to set 1 with probability σ and b with probability $1-\sigma$ (in the event his randomised play leads to rejection of p_1). Suppose $\tilde{\alpha}$ is the probability of accepting p_1 which makes the seller update his belief and announce $p_2 = 1$ with probability σ. Then, his updated belief about the buyer being $v = 1$ is

$$\beta = \frac{\frac{1}{2}}{\frac{1}{2} + \frac{1}{2}(1-\tilde{\alpha})} = \frac{1}{2-\tilde{\alpha}},$$

and from the indifference condition of the seller's second-period profit, we get

$$\beta = \frac{b-1}{b-s} \quad \Rightarrow \quad \frac{1}{2-\tilde{\alpha}} = \frac{b-1}{b-s} \quad \Rightarrow \quad \tilde{\alpha} = \frac{b+s-2}{b-1}.$$

Of course, we must have $\tilde{\alpha} > 0$ which requires $(b+s)/2 > 1$. That is, the average of the seller's valuation and the high-type buyer's valuation should exceed the valuation of the low-type buyer. If not, the buyer will never randomise. For the sake of discussion, let us call the case of $(b+s)/2 > 1$ a case of a 'tough seller'. Here, s is such that on the basis of his prior beliefs the seller prefers to charge b instead of 1; that is, $(b+s)/2 > 1$, or $s > 2-b$. If $s < 2-b$ the seller can be called a 'soft seller' who charges 1 (on the basis of priors). Facing a soft seller, the high-type buyer never randomises.

We now summarise the buyer's and the seller's strategies in the following two lemmas.

Lemma 5. *(The high-type buyer's strategy) In the one-sided-(seller-side-)offer game with the seller's type known as described earlier, the buyer's optimal strategies are as follows:*

1. *The low-type buyer rejects any $p_1 > 1$, and accepts any $p_1 \le 1$.*
2. *The high-type buyer accepts*

   a. *any $p_1 \le \tilde{v}$.*
   b. *any $p_1 \in (\tilde{v}, b]$ with probability $\tilde{\alpha}$ in anticipation that the seller will set $p_2 = 1$ with probability $\sigma(p_1)$ and $p_2 = b$ with probability $1-\sigma(p_1)$ should the game proceed to the second stage, where $\tilde{v} = \delta_B + b(1-\delta_B)$, $\tilde{\alpha} = \frac{b+s-2}{b-1}$ and $\sigma(p_1) = \frac{b-p_1}{\delta_B(b-1)}$.*

Lemma 6. *(The seller's strategy) When the first-period price p_1 is rejected, the seller's second-period pricing strategy will be as follows:*

1. *If he is a 'soft seller' (i.e., $s \le 2-b$), he will set $p_2 = 1$.*
2. *If he is a 'tough seller' (i.e., $s > 2-b$), he will set $p_2 = 1$ with probability $\sigma(p_1)$ and $p_2 = b$ with probability $1-\sigma(p_1)$.*

- *Seller's profit* The seller's profit from two periods can be computed separately.

1. First, consider the seller's second-period profit, if p_1 was turned down. Here we have two cases to consider:
   a. $p_1 \le \tilde{v}$, and therefore, it was definitely rejected by the low-type buyer, in which case he would set $p_2 = 1$ and earn profit $\pi_2 = 1$.
   b. $\tilde{v} < p_1 \le b$. Therefore, it could be rejected by the low-type buyer or by the high-type buyer because of her randomisation. If the seller sets $p_2 = 1$, he gets 1 with certainty. If he randomises between b and 1 with probabilities $(1-\sigma(p_1))$ and $\sigma(p_1)$, respectively, as he was expected to do by the high-type buyer (when she randomised in period 1), the seller's expected profit is $\pi_2 = (1-\sigma(p_1))(1-\beta)b + \sigma(p_1)b$. But he must also be indifferent between charging b and 1; otherwise, the high-type buyer would not have randomised in the first place. That means the seller's second-period profit must be 1 from either option.
2. Now consider the combined profit of the two periods: $\pi = \pi_1 + \delta_S \pi_2$. For any $p_1 \in (s, b]$, the seller's total profit is

$$\pi = \begin{cases} p_1 & \text{if } s < p_1 \le 1 \\ \frac{1}{2} p_1 + \frac{1}{2}\delta_S & \text{if } 1 < p_1 \le \tilde{v} \\ \frac{1}{2}\left[\tilde{\alpha} p_1 + \delta_S (1-\tilde{\alpha})\right] + \frac{1}{2}\delta_S & \text{if } \tilde{v} < p_1 \le b. \end{cases} \tag{12.42}$$

The last expression takes into account that with a low-type buyer, trade can occur only if $p_2 = 1$ (through randomisation), while with a high-type buyer trade can occur at p_1 with probability $\tilde{\alpha}$ or with probability $(1-\tilde{\alpha})$ in period 2.

Note in all cases, the seller's pay-off is increasing in p_1. Therefore, the seller's highest profit in each interval of the price is given by the highest price. That is, $p_1 \in \{1, \tilde{v}, b\}$, and p_2 is either 1 (if the seller is a soft seller) or 1 with probability σ and b with probability $1-\sigma$ (if the seller is a tough seller). Thus, we write the seller's equilibrium profit levels as

$$\pi = \begin{cases} 1 & \text{if } \; p_1 = 1 \\ \frac{1}{2}\tilde{v} + \frac{1}{2}\delta_S & \text{if } \; p_1 = \tilde{v} \\ \frac{1}{2}\tilde{\alpha} b + \delta_S \left(\frac{2-\tilde{\alpha}}{2}\right) & \text{if } \; p_1 = b. \end{cases} \tag{12.43}$$

Here, it is noteworthy that when the tough seller sets $p_1 = b$, his probability of setting $p_2 = 1$; that is, $\sigma(b)$ goes to zero. He will set $p_2 = b$. Thus, in equilibrium the tough seller sets $p_1 = p_2 = b$.

A comparison between three profit levels proves to be cumbersome, as anyone can dominate the others depending on parameter values. It shows that a tough seller can play soft or tough depending on how impatient or patient he is. However, with some restrictions on the parameters, the following can be said.

Proposition 31.

1. *Suppose*

$$\delta_B < \frac{1}{2} + \frac{bs-1}{2(b-1)^2}.$$

   a. *Then a 'soft' seller announces* $p_1 = 1$ *if* $\delta_S < \delta_S^0$, *and* $p_1 = \tilde{v}$ *if* $\delta_S \geq \delta_S^0$.

   b. *A 'tough' seller announces (provided* $\delta_S^0 < \delta_S^1$ *as shown in panel* a *of Figure 12.8)*

$$p_1 = \begin{cases} 1 & \text{if} \quad \delta_S < \delta_S^0 \\ \tilde{v} & \textit{if} \quad \delta_S \in [\delta_S^0, \delta_S^1] \\ p_2 = b & \textit{if} \quad \delta_S > \delta_S^1 \end{cases}$$

2. *If the buyer becomes more impatient (i.e.,* δ_B *falls leading to an increase in* $\tilde{v}$*), the region of the optimality of* $\tilde{v}$ *increases.*
3. *If* s *increases (indicating an increase in toughness)* $\tilde{\alpha}$ *increases (leading to an increase in* $\pi(b)$*) the region of the optimality of* b *increases. With sufficiently large* s*, the tough seller never charges* $\tilde{v}$*; he would charge either* 1 *or* b.

The seller's profit and the associated optimal first-period prices are illustrated in panel *a* of Figure 12.8. It depicts only one possibility, but other cases can be drawn by shifting the profit curves around. One idea that is conveyed by this simple model is that the seller's bargaining strength is constituted by his so-called disagreement pay-off s and degree of patience. The higher the magnitude of s or δ_S, the greater the likelihood of charging b along with a greater probability of trade ($\tilde{\alpha}/2$).

Similarly, the buyer's bargaining strength, which applies only to the high-type buyer, is driven by her degree of patience. If she becomes more 'impatient' then the likelihood of $\tilde{v}$ increases and the probability of trade increases, vis-à-vis the price regime of b. A buyer's impatience means she is better off making a deal earlier than later. This encourages the seller to offer $\tilde{v}$ instead of b. However, if the buyer's patience increases, a tough seller's incentive to hold out with the highest price increases. In the extreme case, where both sides are very patient, we will see holding out from both sides; the seller will announce b, and the buyer will reject with high probability. Even in the second period, trade is not guaranteed, either because the buyer is a low type or because the high-type buyer is indifferent between accepting or rejecting b.

12.6.2.2 *Two-sided asymmetric information*

Let us now turn to the case where the seller's type is also unknown. Suppose the seller is either s_f or $s_t, s_f < s_t < 1$, which he knows but the buyer does not. Depending on the value of s_f and

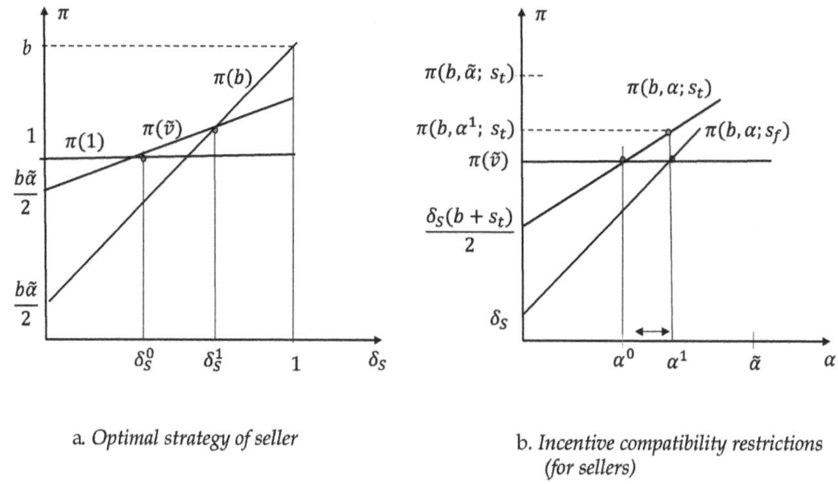

a. *Optimal strategy of seller*

b. *Incentive compatibility restrictions (for sellers)*

Figure 12.8 Seller's pay-off

s_t a variety of possibilities opens up. However, we restrict our attention to a specific case, where $s_f < 2-b < s_t$. As in the previous section, here too a soft seller will set $p_2 = 1$ and a tough seller will set $p_2 = b$ or randomise between b and 1.

Now, a key difference to the one-sided information case is that the seller's offer transmits some information about his type and the buyer will try to update her belief (if possible) about the seller's type, and this updating is important in determining what the second-period price she might face, should she turn down the first-period offer. Let us assume that the buyer's prior belief about the seller being s_f is ½, and her updated belief is γ.

As explained in the (job market) signalling model of the last chapter, there are two types of equilibrium that are of great interest—pooling and separating.[19] See Fudenberg and Tirole (1983) for an analysis of the full range of equilibrium. Here, we just focus on the separating equilibrium.

Intuitively, a tough seller who wants to charge b faces a problem from the soft seller who wants to imitate him. The tough seller, therefore, has to sacrifice a bit of profit to signal that he is truly the tough seller by accepting a lower probability of trade than $\tilde{\alpha}/2$ while charging b. For the soft seller then, impersonation is not worth the risk. This is our separating equilibrium.

By definition, a separating equilibrium is information-revealing, and it generally mimics the full information outcome. We consider the following path of play as an equilibrium path. Suppose the s_f seller charges 1 or $\tilde{v}$ in the first period (depending on whichever gives the higher profit) and 1 in the second period, while the s_t seller charges b in both periods. Seeing these offers the high-type buyer correctly figures out the identity of the seller. If $p_1 = \tilde{v}$ or 1, she accepts. If $p_1 = b$, she accepts it with probability α and rejects with probability $1-\alpha$. Upon rejection, she will accept any offer $p_2 \le b$ in period 2.

Now let us establish the preceding as an equilibrium. We start with the soft seller's profit from $\tilde{v}$ as $\pi(\tilde{v};s_f) = \frac{1}{2}\tilde{v} + \frac{\delta_s}{2}$ and from $p_1 = 1$ as $\pi(1;s_f) = 1$. Suppose $\pi(\tilde{v};s_f) > \pi(1;s_f)$ so that the s_f seller sets $p_1 = \tilde{v}$ and $p_2 = 1$.

The s_t seller announces $p_1 = b$ which the buyer accepts with probability α and rejects with probability $1-\alpha$. Following the rejection of p_1 the high-type seller sets $p_2 = b$ again, which the high-type buyer accepts (as she is indifferent). The tough seller's profit from strategy $p_1 = b$ is $\pi(b,\alpha;s_t) = \frac{1}{2}\{\alpha b + (1-\alpha)b\delta_S\} + \frac{1}{2}\delta_S s_t$.

Now, let us also consider the pay-off of the seller s_f if he sets $p_1 = b$ and then $p_2 = 1$. His profit is $\pi(b,\alpha;s_f) = \frac{1}{2}\{\alpha b + (1-\alpha)\delta_S\} + \frac{1}{2}\delta_S = \frac{1}{2}\alpha b + \frac{1}{2}(2-\alpha)\delta_S$. Similarly, the pay-off of the seller s_t from charging $\tilde{v}$ is $\pi(\tilde{v};s_t) = \frac{1}{2}\tilde{v} + \frac{1}{2}\delta_S$, which is same as $\pi(\tilde{v};s_f)$.

For a separating equilibrium, we require two incentive compatibility conditions to be satisfied simultaneously:

$$IC_{s_f} : \pi(\tilde{v};s_f) \geq \pi(b,\alpha;s_f) \Rightarrow \frac{1}{2}\tilde{v} + \frac{1}{2}\delta_s \geq \frac{1}{2}\alpha b + \frac{1}{2}(2-\alpha)\delta_S \tag{12.44}$$

$$IC_{s_t} : \pi(b,\alpha;s_t) \geq \pi(\tilde{v};s_t) \Rightarrow \frac{1}{2}\{\alpha + (1-\alpha)\delta_S\}b + \frac{1}{2}\delta_S s_t \geq \frac{1}{2}\tilde{v} + \frac{1}{2}\delta_S. \tag{12.45}$$

Any probability of acceptance by the high-type buyer, α, must satisfy both Eqs. (12.44) and (12.45). The incentive-compatible region of α is shown in panel b of Figure 12.8. Note that the equilibrium pay-off of the soft seller and the deviation (from truth-telling) pay-off of the tough seller are same, $\pi(\tilde{v})$. The equilibrium pay-off of the tough seller and the deviation pay-off of the soft seller increases in α and meet at $\tilde{\alpha}$. $\pi(b,\alpha;s_t) = \pi(\tilde{v})$ at α^0 while $\pi(b,\alpha;s_f) = \pi(\tilde{v})$ at $\alpha = \alpha^1$; clearly, $\alpha^0 < \alpha^1$. Furthermore, since for assuming $s_t > 2-b$, the intercept of the $\pi(b;s_t)$ curve is greater than the intercept of the $\pi(b;s_f)$ curve, which allows separation of the two types in the interval $[\alpha^0, \alpha^1]$. Note that as $\tilde{\alpha}$ is outside this interval, it is not incentive-compatible. Therefore, the highest acceptance probability of a high-type buyer (which we take as her equilibrium strategy) is α^1. In the separating equilibrium, the soft seller earns $\pi(\tilde{v})$, while the tough seller gets $\pi(b,\alpha^1;s_t) < \pi(b,\tilde{\alpha};s_t)$.

But how is the buyer's strategy formed, and how is it rationalised in the minds of the sellers? The buyer's probability to accept an offer above $\tilde{v}$ must be supported by a belief about the seller. Here, she is unsure whether she is facing a soft seller or a tough seller. Therefore, she remains indifferent between acceptance and rejection and assigns γ as her updated belief about the seller being a soft seller. Then by rejecting p_1, she expects a pay-off $\delta_B[\gamma(b-1) + (1-\gamma)(b-b)]$. Then her indifference condition is $(b-p_1) = \delta_B\gamma(b-1)$, from which we can derive her belief γ to support her strategy.

Now we state the equilibrium.

Proposition 32. *The separating equilibrium of the two-sided asymmetric information game is described as follows.*

- *A soft seller announces $p_1 = \tilde{v}$ and $p_2 = 1$ (in sequence), and the high-type buyer responds by accepting it in the first period. The low-type buyer rejects p_1 and waits for the next period.*
- *A tough seller announces $p_1 = p_2 = b$, and the high-type buyer accepts it with probability α^1, where α^1 solves $\pi(b,\alpha;s_f) = \pi(\tilde{v})$, and while rejecting it, she holds the following belief about the seller being a soft seller:*

$$\gamma = \begin{cases} 1 & \text{if } p_1 \leq \tilde{v} \\ \dfrac{b-p_1}{\delta_B(b-1)} & \text{if } \tilde{v} < p_1 \leq b. \\ 0 & \text{if } b < p_1 \end{cases}$$

An important observation is that this specified buyer's belief also works as a threat of punishment against the seller for deviating from the equilibrium strategy. However, a perfect Bayesian equilibrium allows other types of beliefs as well to support the equilibrium actions.[20]

12.7 Conclusion

In this chapter, we studied both cooperative (axiomatic) and non-cooperative bargaining. As the literature on bargaining is vast, we have focused on a few selected topics. In particular, we highlighted the natural applicability of the Nash bargaining solution, especially in the context of firms and workers. The incomplete information literature is very long, and most of the developments are to be regarded as advanced and should be the subject matter of a specialised course on bargaining. For Nash bargaining and non-cooperative bargaining theory, see the excellent textbook by Muthoo (1999). Some of the articles listed at the end of the chapter also provide further guidance.

Summary

In this chapter, we have learnt about the following:

1. A number of axioms underpin the Nash bargaining solution.
2. The Kalai-Smorodinski solution is an alternative to the Nash bargaining solution.
3. The Rubinstein (full information) game of offers and counter-offers provides a non-cooperative game theoretic approach to the bargaining problem.
4. A number of simultaneous and sequential bargaining games over wage and employment were also studied, including bargaining within a public-sector firm.
5. The role of delegation in wage bargaining is examined. Delegation is individually beneficial but can be collectively harmful.
6. We then studied two asymmetric information games, the sealed-bid-offer game and the one-sided-offer game with two periods. The equilibrium in each of these models was derived and analysed in detail.

12.8 Appendix

12.8.1 Proof of Property 3

Let the mass of sellers whose offer is $s \leq b$ according to the strategy $\sigma(v_S)$ be denoted by a cumulative probability function $G_B(s \mid s \leq b)$ with density function $g_B(s)$. That is, $G_B(.)$ is the probability of finding an s that is less than b. Similarly, the seller's ask s generates a mass of buyers whose bids are $b \geq s$ according to the strategy $\beta(v_B)$. Let this distribution be $G_S(b \mid b \geq s)$ with density $g_S(b)$. $G_S(.)$ is the probability of finding a buyer whose offer is greater than s. Note that $G_B(s \mid s \leq b)$ is the probability of trade from the buyer's perspective when he bids b and $G_S(b \mid b \geq s)$ is the same from the seller's perspective when he asks s. These probabilities are to be derived from the distributions of v_S and v_B in combination with the proposed strategies.

Because of the uniform distribution assumption on v_B, we can write $G_B(s \mid s \leq b) = \dfrac{b-\sigma(0)}{1-\sigma(0)}$ and $g_B(s) = \dfrac{1}{1-\sigma(0)}$. Likewise, the uniform distribution of v_S implies $G_S(b \mid b \geq s) = \dfrac{\beta(1)-s}{\beta(1)}$

and $g_S(b)=\frac{1}{\beta(1)}$. From panel *a* of Figure 12.7, it is clear that for $G_B(.)>0$, we must have $b>\sigma(0)$, and for $G_S(.)>0$, we must have $s<\beta(1)$.

Therefore, the expected profit of a buyer from his offer b (conditional on $b>\sigma(0)$) and the expected profit of a seller from his offer s (conditional on $s<\beta(1)$) are

$$\pi_B(b;v_B)=\int_{\sigma(0)}^{b}\left[v_B-\alpha b-(1-\alpha)s\right]\frac{1}{1-\sigma(0)}ds \tag{12.46}$$

$$\pi_S(s;v_S)=\int_{s}^{\beta(1)}\left[\alpha b+(1-\alpha)s-v_S\right]\frac{1}{\beta(1)}db. \tag{12.47}$$

We want to restrict our attention to the offers that reveal the buyer's and the seller's true valuations. Therefore, consider the incentive compatibility conditions.

Suppose b is optimal for the v_B buyer and b' is optimal for the v_B' buyer. Then the buyer's truthful offers must satisfy

$$\begin{aligned}
&\pi_B(b';v_B')-\pi_B(b;v_B')\geq 0, \quad \text{and} \quad \pi_B(b;v_B)-\pi_B(b';v_B)\geq 0\\
\text{or}\quad &[\pi_B(b';v_B')-\pi_B(b;v_B')]+[\pi_B(b;v_B)-\pi_B(b';v_B)]\geq 0\\
\text{or,}\quad &[\pi_B(b';v_B')-\pi_B(b';v_B)]\geq[\pi_B(b;v_B')-\pi_B(b;v_B)].
\end{aligned} \tag{12.48}$$

Using Eq. (12.46), we write the inequality (12.48) as

$$\left[\pi_B(b';v_B')-\pi_B(b';v_B)\right]=\frac{(v_B'-v_B)\left[b'-\sigma(0)\right]}{1-\sigma(0)}>$$

$$\left[\pi_B(b;v_B')-\pi_B(b;v_B)\right]=\frac{(v_B'-v_B)\left[b-\sigma(0)\right]}{1-\sigma(0)}.$$

If we assume $v_B'>v_B$, then the above inequality implies $b'>b$, or $\beta(v_B')>\beta(v_B)$.

Similarly, consider s' and s being optimal for v_S' and v_S sellers, respectively. Assume $v_S'>v_S$. Imposing incentive compatibility in the same way as stated earlier, we write

$$\begin{aligned}
&\pi_S(s';v_S')-\pi_S(s;v_S')\geq 0, \quad \text{and} \quad \pi_S(s;v_S)-\pi_S(s';v_S)\geq 0\\
\text{or}\quad &[\pi_S(s';v_S')-\pi_S(s;v_S')]+[\pi_S(s;v_S)-\pi_S(s';v_S)]\geq 0\\
\text{or}\quad &[\pi_S(s';v_S')-\pi_S(s';v_S)]\geq[\pi_S(s;v_S')-\pi_S(s;v_S)].
\end{aligned} \tag{12.49}$$

Using Eq. (12.47) we write inequality (12.49) as

$$\left[\pi_S(s';v_S')-\pi_S(s';v_S)\right]=-\frac{(v_S'-v_S)\left[\beta(1)-s'\right]}{\beta(1)}>$$

$$\left[\pi_S(s;v_S')-\pi_S(s;v_S)\right]=-\frac{(v_S'-v_S)\left[\beta(1)-s\right]}{\beta(1)},$$

which will be true if $s'>s$ or, equivalently, $\sigma(v_S')>\sigma(v_S)$.

12.9 Exercises

1. Suppose a competitive firm sells q at a price p and its production function is $q = Al - \frac{l^2}{2}$. A worker supplies l following the (inverse) labour supply curve $w(l) = \bar{\omega} + \frac{\omega}{2}l$, and his utility function is $u = w(l)l$. Derive the monopsony employment and wage.
2. Assume the same labour supply curve as in question 1. But let the firm be a monopolist in the product market, and assume the production function is CRS $q = l$ while the market demand curve is linear $p = A - q$. Again derive the monoposony equilibrium.
3. Consider a firm's production function $q = l$ and its market demand $p = A - q$. There is a union that supplies labour l. The union's objective is to maximise $U = (w - \underline{w})l$, where $\underline{w}$ is the minimum wage and w is negotiated with the union. Both sides' disagreement pay-offs are zero. The bargaining power of the union is α. Derive the Nash bargaining solution for wage and employment for two scenarios: (a) wage and employment are bargained simultaneously, and (b) wage is negotiated first and then employment is chosen unilaterally by the firm.
4. Consider the sàme set-up of question 3. But assume that the firm is fully publicly owned. The firm's objective is to maximise social welfare $W = \pi + CS$. Again derive the Nash bargaining solution for wage and employment for two scenarios: (a) efficient bargaining and (b) right-to-manage bargaining.
5. Suppose a firm uses two inputs l and k, both essential to produce a positive level of output. Suppose the production function is $q = f(k) + l$ if $k > 0, l > 0, f'(k) > 0, f''(k) < 0$ and $q = 0$ if k or $l = 0$. A fixed unit of labour is needed, say, 1 unit, the cost of which is w, but the wage cost is negotiated. Let the firm's bargaining power be 1/2. The cost of capital is rk, and the price of the good is p. The minimum wage is $\underline{w}$. The firm buys capital at the beginning and then engages in bargaining over wage (assuming 1 unit of labour will be used). If there is disagreement, then labour cannot be used, and the firm cannot produce any output. It can resell the capital but still loses βrk. Derive the negotiated wage and the firm's optimal capital.
6. Consider the set-up of question 3. But assume that the firm hires a manager and asks him to maximise $z = \pi + \beta q$. The union members hire a union leader who is then asked to maximise $v = \gamma(w - \underline{w})l + (1 - \gamma)wl$. Assume the bargaining power of the union leader is α. Wage and employment are both (or at least wage) are determined through bargaining between the manager and the union leader.

   a. First assume that bargaining takes place over both wage and employment together. Solve this problem. Show how γ and β affect the wage and employment. Also how does the union's pay-off $U = (w - \underline{w})l$ change with an increase in α?
   b. Next assume that wage is negotiated first and then employment is left to the manager's choice. How does your answer change?

7. Consider a one-sided-offer game with two types of buyer and one type of seller. The buyer's type is $v_B \in \{1, b\}$ with equal probability. The seller's cost is $c < 1$. There is only one unit to sell, and there are two periods. In the first period, the seller quotes p_1, and the buyer says yes or no. Following a no, the seller quotes p_2 in the second period. The buyer says yes or no. The game ends with or without trade. Let the buyer's and the seller's common discount factor be δ. Derive the equilibrium prices of the seller.

Notes

1 It is essentially marginal cost of hiring labour. But we do not use the term MC here because MC is defined in reference to output.

2 We ignore the case of $u_1(0) > \underline{u_1}$ and $u_2(0) > \underline{u_2}$. Both players are terribly worse off in the event of a disagreement. But the Nash maximand $B = [u_1(s) - u_1(0)]^{\alpha} [u_2(1-s) - u_2(0)]^{1-\alpha}$ does not change, although the solution should be interpreted carefully.

3 We are not insisting that $d \in \omega$.

4 There are several variations of this game. For instance, when $s_1 + s_2 > 1$, the players may be awarded a strictly positive amount say d. If $1/2 < d < 1$, the range of equilibrium s_1 and s_2 will be shortened. However, the economic interpretation of such a large d is problematic. Nevertheless, the Nash demand game has remained a game of significant interest to behavioural economists because it combines a coordination problem and a fair allocation problem in a single framework.

5 If the last-period disagreement rule is different, we may end up with a very different equilibrium.

6 Note $\delta = 1$ gives the same solution, but the logic is not the same as people being perfectly patient. It is the time lapse between offers that is important.

7 If the two items are negotiated sequentially with one item at a time and neither party takes any action in the intervening period, then the sequential bargaining reduces to efficient bargaining.

8 In reality, there are various practices for laying off, such as last-in-first-out—most juniors go first.

9 Surprisingly (or not so surprisingly), if the sequence of choice involves employment first and wage next (via bargaining), the outcome will be the same as that of efficient bargaining.

10 Note that we are not explicitly considering the salary of the manager or the union leader. Implicitly it is assumed that the manager's salary is linked to z, just as the leader's salary to y.

11 Szymanski (1994) was the first to explore delegation in bargaining, but his analysis was confined only to the firm side, the bargaining protocol was right-to-manage and the market environment was duopoly.

12 It is important that the two valuation sets must have an overlap; otherwise, the problem is trivial. The common knowledge assumption, you should recall, refers to the premise that the seller knows what the buyer believes and the buyer knows that the seller knows what the buyer believes, that the seller knows that the buyer knows what the seller knows about the buyer's beliefs and so on so forth. The same logic applies to the buyer's knowledge about the seller's beliefs and the seller's knowledge about the buyer knowing about what the seller believes and so on.

13 Let us remind ourselves of the Leibniz integration rule that is applicable to differentiation under integration, which is the case here. By this rule,

$$\frac{d}{dx}\int_{l(x)}^{h(x)} f(x,y)dy = f(x,h(x))h'(x) - f(x,l(x))l'(x) + \int_{l(x)}^{h(x)} \frac{\partial f(x,y)}{\partial x}dy.$$

14 If a function is continuous, monotonic and differentiable, then the inverse of its slope is equal to the slope of its inverse function.

15 Note that by construction, m and n will only be functions of α.

16 These are independent first-order differential equations, but with variable coefficient and term. The solution is a bit complex. However, for linear offer functions, the solution is straightforward.

17 You can check that from $\beta(v_B = 1) = \frac{2+(1-\alpha)\alpha}{2(1+\alpha)} = \frac{2(1+\alpha)-\alpha(1+\alpha)}{2(1+\alpha)} = \frac{2-\alpha}{2}$.

18 The case of $s > 1$ is trivial. Since setting $p = 1$ is ruled out, the seller will always set $p = b$ and hope that the buyer is high type.

19 There is also a hybrid equilibrium, called semi-separating, where one type randomises between a pooling and a separating strategy.

20 For example, if the buyer believes that $\tilde{v} < p_1 < b$, the seller is soft with probability 1, which means she is going to accept $p_2 = 1$ with certainty, then she is not going to accept any offer above $\tilde{v}$. This will deter the soft seller from going above $\tilde{v}$ and the tough seller from going below b.

References and further readings

Chatterjee, I. & Saha, B. (2013). Bilateral delegation in wage and employment bargaining in monopoly. *Economics Letters*, 120, 280–283. DOI: 10.1016/j.econlet.2013.04.009 [available under the terms of the Creative Commons Attribution License (CC BY) https://creativecommons.org/licenses/by/4.0/].

Chatterjee, K. & Samuelson, W. (1983). Bargaining under incomplete information. *Operations Research*, 5, 835–851.

Fershtman, C. & Judd, K. (1987). Equilibrium incentives in oligopoly. *American Economic Review*, 77, 927–940.

Fudenberg, D. & Tirole, J. (1983). Sequential bargaining with incomplete information. *The Review of Economic Studies*, 50, 221–247.

Kalai, E. & Smorodinsky, M. (1975). Other solutions to Nash's bargaining problem. *Econometrica*, 43, 513–518.

McDonald, I. & Solow, R. (1981). Wage bargaining and employment. *American Economic Review*, 71, 896–908.

Mukherjee, A. & Saha, B. (2024). Bilateral delegation, wage bargaining and innovation. *Journal of Institutional and Theoretical Economics*. Forthcoming.

Muthoo, A. (1999). *Bargaining Theory with Applications*. Cambridge: Cambridge University Press.

Myerson, R. & Satterthwaite, M. (1983). Efficient mechanism for bilateral trading. *Journal of Economic Theory*, 29, 265–281.

Nash, J. (1950). The bargaining problem. *Econometrica*, 18, 155–162.

Nash, J. (1953). Two-person cooperative games. *Econometrica*, 21, 128–140.

Rubinstein, A. (1982). Perfect equilibrium in a bargaining model. *Econometrica*, 50, 97–110.

Saha, B. (1995). Side choice and bargaining under asymmetric information. *Economica*, 62, 521–539.

Shaked, A. & Sutton, J. (1984). Involuntary unemployment as a perfect equilibrium in a bargaining model. *Econometrica*, 52, 1351–1364.

Szymanski, S. (1994). Strategic delegation with endogenous costs: A duopoly with wage bargaining. *International Journal of Industrial Organization*, 12, 105–106.

Chapter 13

Oligopoly

Abstract

Oligopoly is the most common form of market in modern economies. With fewer producers trying to woo their customers with different brands, varieties and attractive prices, oligopoly presents a very rich model of strategic interactions between firms. We first study Cournot, Bertrand and Stackelberg models of competition. We also study scope for limit pricing that may or may not deter entry. The basic analysis of Cournot duopoly is then extended to public-sector firms and wage bargaining with workers via managers and union leaders. Product variety models, such as differentiated goods and the Hotelling model of spatial competition, are presented as well. We end the chapter by studying a model of mixed duopoly with foreign trade/investment.

Keywords: Cournot duopoly, Bertrand competition, Stackelberg leadership, Limit pricing, Capacity, The Hotelling model, Strategic delegation, Privatisation

13.1 Introduction

In 1838, when Leon Walras was merely a toddler the French mathematician-cum-philosopher Antoine Augustin Cournot published his book *Researches on Mathematical Principles of the Theory of Wealth* that later became an object of great interest to Walras himself but otherwise remained unappreciated until more than a century later when game theorists discovered how pioneering Cournot's contribution was. There is a wide spectrum of markets that fall between perfect competition and monopoly, where firms' decisions are interdependent and the decisions may concern not just output or price but also many other critical aspects of businesses, such as product quality, location of the firm, research and development and more. Cournot was the first to consider a model of output competition between two firms who are trying to sell spring water collected from a local mountain. He asked: How many buckets of water should each bring to the village market so that neither of them would want to change their supply? We now know, thanks to game theory, that this was a problem of finding a Nash equilibrium.

Clearly, there are other types of interaction between firms possible besides the output. Price for instance is an obvious one, as was later pointed out by another French mathematician named Joseph Louis François Bertrand in 1883. Besides price and quantity, firms seem to compete in terms of variety, whether in the market for clothing, in the restaurant industry, in supermarkets, television programming and so on. Competition in such markets is conceptually different to what we have seen in the context of perfect competition. Here, each firm is always mindful of, at least at the level of introspection, what other firms are doing, whereas under perfect competition, firms just stay focused on their own activities.

DOI: 10.4324/9781003226994-13

In this chapter, we will study classic Cournot, Bertrand and Stackelberg duopolies and the models of product differentiation along with issues of entry deterrence, strategic delegation and public ownership of firms. Any type of market that is not perfectly competitive or a monopoly or a bilateral monopoly falls in this large group of markets which we call oligopoly (or imperfectly competitive markets). While *oligopoly* refers to a market having two or more firms, we restrict our attention mostly to two firms, that is, duopolies, unless we are considering free entry or issues that are specific to three or more firms.

13.2 Cournot duopoly

The key feature of a Cournot model is simultaneous output setting by firms, where goods are fairly homogeneous. Markets for bottled water, carbonated beverages, supermarkets and generic food are some of the examples of Cournot competition.

Suppose there are two firms, indexed 1 and 2, selling a good whose demand curve is given by $p = p(q_1 + q_2;\alpha)$, where α is a demand-shifting parameter and $p'(.) < 0$. Assume $p''(.) < 0$ and $p(\bar{Q}) = 0$, where $\bar{Q} < \infty$. In other words, the demand function is concave, and there is a finite level of output at which the consumers' willingness to pay becomes zero.[1] Each firm wants to maximise profit $\pi_i = q_i p(q_1 + q_2;\alpha) - C_i(q_i;k_i)$, $i = 1,2$, where k_i is a firm-specific cost-shifting parameter and $C_i'(.) \geq 0, C_i''(.) \geq 0$. Production technology is convex. Increasing returns can be accommodated, but keep in mind that that with strong increasing returns, the industry is better served by a single firm, so we avoid that issue.

Each firm simultaneously announces q_i. The market price is determined from the demand curve by simply adding the quantities that two firms have announced to supply. Implicitly we are assuming that the firms will honour their announcement, or equivalently, if the firms have already supplied the output, an invisible auctioneer will set the price from the aggregate supply. *Firms cannot adjust the output they have already supplied; they must sell it all.*

The preceding restriction on output revision implies that the firms must do some *introspection* before making their announcement or bringing the output physically to the market. Suppose firm 1 expects firm 2 to announce q_2^0. Then it would choose q_1 by setting its first-order condition of profit maximisation to zero:

$$\partial \pi_1 / \partial q_1 \equiv p(q_1 + q_2^0;\alpha) + q_1 p'(q_1 + q_2^0) - C_1'(q_1;k_1) = 0, \tag{13.1}$$

with the second-order condition $2p'(.) + q_1 p''(.) - C_i''(.) < 0$ being met. Eq. (13.1) gives the optimal response of firm 1 when it anticipates q_2^0 from its rival. Note that the firm's output choice will be the same if its response was to an *actual* choice of q_2^0. But in that case, we need to assume that in search of its optimal q_1 firm 1 must believe that firm 2 *will not change* its output from q_2^0 in response to firm 1's output choice. Such an assumption, often referred to as *Cournot conjecture* in the literature, may appear as a violation of the assumption of simultaneity of output setting and interdependence of their strategy. This is why we will place such output revisions only in the realm of introspection. Once the output is chosen, it cannot be changed.

While introspecting about firm 2's possible output choice, firm 1 must consider all possible $q_2 \in [0,\bar{Q}]$. Thus, from Eq. (13.1) we get (by varying q_2) firm 1's best response function as $q_1 = \beta_1(q_2)$. From continuity and differentiability of the profit function, we get $\beta_1(q_2)$ to be continuous and single-valued. Profit then becomes a function of q_2 via $\beta_1(.)$ as $\pi_1 = \pi_1(\beta_1(q_2), q_2)$, and so does $\partial\pi_1 / \partial q_1$. Furthermore, differentiating first-order condition $\partial\pi_1 / \partial q_1 = 0$ with respect to q_2, we derive the slope of $\beta_1(q_2)$ as follows:

$$\frac{\partial^2 \pi_1}{\partial q_1 \partial q_2} = \frac{\partial^2 \pi_1}{\partial q_1^2} \times \frac{\partial q_1}{\partial q_2} + \frac{\partial^2 \pi_1}{\partial q_1 \partial q_2} = 0$$

or, $$\frac{\partial q_1}{\partial q_2} = -\frac{\partial^2 \pi_1}{\partial q_1 \partial q_2} \times \underbrace{\frac{1}{\partial^2 \pi_1 / \partial q_1^2}}_{(<0 \text{ by S.O.C.})}. \tag{13.2}$$

In Eq. (13.2), the sign of $\partial q_1 / \partial q_2$ is crucially dependent on the sign of $\frac{\partial^2 \pi_1}{\partial q_1 \partial q_2}$. If the latter is negative, $\partial q_1 / \partial q_2$ (or $\beta_1'(q_2)$) is negative.

Definition 17. *Firm* j*'s strategy x_j is called strategic substitute for x_i, the strategy of firm* i, *if* $\frac{\partial^2 \pi_i}{\partial x_i \partial x_j} < 0$ *and strategic complement if* $\frac{\partial^2 \pi_i}{\partial x_i \partial x_j} > 0$.

Note the qualifier 'strategic' before substitute. A good/strategy x_j is ordinary substitute for x_i if the total profit of firm i (π_i) falls inx_j. But it is called strategic substitute if the marginal profit ($\partial\pi_i / \partial x_i$) falls with x_j. Strategic complements are similarly defined for a positive impact of x_j on firm i's marginal profit. The concepts of strategic substitutes and complements were proposed by Bulow et al. (1985).

Let us note that $\frac{\partial^2 \pi_1}{\partial q_1 \partial q_2} = p'(.) + q_1 p''(.) < 0$, because of our assumption of concavity of the demand function.[2] Thus, q_2 is strategic substitute for q_1. Similarly, from the first-order condition for profit maximisation of firm 2, $\partial\pi_2 / \partial q_2 \equiv p(q_1 + q_2; \alpha) + q_2 p'(q_1 + q_2) - C_2'(q_2; k_2) = 0$, we derive firm 2's best response function $q_2 = \beta_2(q_1)$. q_1 is also a strategic substitute for q_2. Let us now identify two more levels of output.

Definition 18. *The monopoly output of firm* i *is* $q_i^M = \beta_i(0)$, *and the limit output of firm* i *is* $\beta_j(\bar{q}_i) = 0$, *where* $\bar{q}_i \le \bar{Q}$.

Firm 1's monopoly output is its best response to the zero output of firm 2, when firm 1 gets to serve the whole market. However, if there is a high level of output of firm 1 against which firm 2's best response is to shut down then that output is firm 1's limit output. That is to say, firm 1's limit output forces firm 2 to leave the market. Firm 2's monopoly and limit outputs have the same interpretations vis-à-vis firm 1.

Proposition 33. *Suppose* $q_1^M < \bar{q}_1$ and $q_2^M < \bar{q}_2$. *Then there exist a pair of outputs* (q_1^*, q_2^*), $q_1^* < q_1^M, q_2^* < q_2^M$, *such that* $q_1^* = \beta_1(q_2^*)$ *and* $q_2^* = \beta_2(q_1^*)$, *and they constitute a Cournot-Nash equilibrium. Furthermore, the following holds for* (q_1^*, q_2^*).

1. $q_1^* \ge q_2^*$ *if and only if* $C_1'(q_1^*; k_1) \le C_2'(q_2^*; k_2)$, *and* $q_1^* < q_2^*$ *if and only if* $C_1'(q_1^*; k_1) > C_2'(q_2^*; k_2)$.
2. $\partial q_i^* / \partial k_i < 0$, $\partial q_j^* / \partial k_i > 0$ $(i \ne j)$.
3. *When* α *is the demand intercept,* $\partial q_i^* / \partial \alpha > 0$, *and when* α *is the demand slope,* $\partial q_i^* / \partial \alpha < 0$, *for* i = *1, 2 in both cases.*

Proof of Proposition 33. The informal proof of existence is as follows: Each player's strategy set is $Q_i = [0, \bar{Q}]$, which is convex and compact. The game's strategy space is $Q_1 \times Q_2$, which is also convex and compact. The best response functions are continuous, and thus the best response correspondence, which essentially becomes a vector of functions, is upper hemi-continuous (because its constitutent functions are all continuous). Therefore, by the Kakutani fixed-point theorem, we have a Nash equilibrium. The condition $q_i^M < \bar{q}_i$ says that there is room for both firms. Otherwise, one of the equilibrium outputs will be zero. The rest of the proposition concerns the characterisation of the equilibrium outputs.

1. Write the two first-order conditions:

$$p(.) + q_1^* p'(.) - C_1'(q_1^*) = 0 \qquad \text{and} \qquad p(.) + q_2^* p'(.) - C_2'(q_2^*) = 0.$$

Substituting one into the other and rearranging terms, we can write

$$p'(q_1^* + q_2^*)[q_2^* - q_1^*] = C_2'(q_2^*) - C_1'(q_1^*).$$

Given $p'(.) < 0$, $q_1^* \geq q_2^*$ must imply (and is implied by) $C_2'(q_2^*) \geq C_1'(q_1^*)$, and $q_1^* < q_2^*$ implies (and is implied by) $C_2'(q_2^*) < C_1'(q_1^*)$.

2. Now we study the effects of an increase in k_1 and k_2 on q_1^* and q_2^* by differentiating the two first-order conditions with respect to k_1 and then k_2.

$$\frac{\partial^2 \pi_1(q_1^*, q_2^*)}{\partial q_1^2}\frac{\partial q_1^*}{\partial k_1} + \frac{\partial^2 \pi_1(q_1^*, q_2^*)}{\partial q_1 \partial q_2}\frac{\partial q_2^*}{\partial k_1} = \frac{\partial C_1'(q_1^*; k_1)}{\partial k_1}$$

$$\frac{\partial^2 \pi_2(q_1^*, q_2^*)}{\partial q_2 \partial q_1}\frac{\partial q_1^*}{\partial k_1} + \frac{\partial^2 \pi_2(q_1^*, q_2^*)}{\partial q_2^2}\frac{\partial q_2^*}{\partial k_1} = 0.$$

Applying Cramer's rule, we derive

$$\frac{\partial q_1^*}{\partial k_1} = \left[\frac{\partial C_1'(q_1^*; k_1)}{\partial k_1}\frac{\partial^2 \pi_2(q_1^*, q_2^*)}{\partial q_2^2}\right]\frac{1}{\Delta_N}$$

and $$\frac{\partial q_2^*}{\partial k_1} = -\left[\frac{\partial C_1'(q_1^*; k_1)}{\partial k_1}\frac{\partial^2 \pi_2(q_1^*, q_2^*)}{\partial q_2 \partial q_1}\right]\frac{1}{\Delta_N},$$

where

$$\Delta_N = \frac{\partial^2 \pi_1(q_1^*, q_2^*)}{\partial q_1^2}\frac{\partial^2 \pi_2(q_1^*, q_2^*)}{\partial q_2^2} - \frac{\partial^2 \pi_1(q_1^*, q_2^*)}{\partial q_1 \partial q_2}\frac{\partial^2 \pi_2(q_1^*, q_2^*)}{\partial q_2 \partial q_1} > 0,$$

by the stability condition of the Nash equilibrium. In addition, $\partial C_1'(q_1^*; k_1) / \partial k_1 > 0$ by assumption, $\partial^2 \pi_2(q_1^*, q_2^*) / \partial q_2^2 < 0$ by the second-order correlation, and $\partial^2 \pi_2(q_1^*, q_2^*) / \partial q_2 \partial q_1 < 0$ by the strategic substituteness property of the two goods. Therefore, $\partial q_1^* / \partial k_1 < 0$ and $\partial q_2^* / \partial k_1 > 0$.

Similarly, for a change in k_2, we derive

$$\frac{\partial q_1^*}{\partial k_2} = -\left[\frac{\partial C_2'(q_2^*;k_2)}{\partial k_2}\frac{\partial^2 \pi_1(q_1^*,q_2^*)}{\partial q_1 \partial q_2}\right]\frac{1}{\Delta_N} > 0$$

and $$\frac{\partial q_2^*}{\partial k_2} = \left[\frac{\partial C_2'(q_1^*;k_2)}{\partial k_2}\frac{\partial^2 \pi_1(q_1^*,q_2^*)}{\partial q_1^2}\right]\frac{1}{\Delta_N} < 0.$$

3. Now consider a change in α, the demand parameter.

$$\frac{\partial^2 \pi_1(q_1^*,q_2^*)}{\partial q_1^2}\frac{\partial q_1^*}{\partial \alpha} + \frac{\partial^2 \pi_1(q_1^*,q_2^*)}{\partial q_1 \partial q_2}\frac{\partial q_2^*}{\partial \alpha} = -\frac{\partial^2 \pi_1(q_1^*;q_2^*)}{\partial q_1 \partial \alpha}$$

$$\frac{\partial^2 \pi_2(q_1^*,q_2^*)}{\partial q_2 \partial q_1}\frac{\partial q_1^*}{\partial k_1} + \frac{\partial^2 \pi_2(q_1^*,q_2^*)}{\partial q_2^2}\frac{\partial q_2^*}{\partial \alpha} = -\frac{\partial^2 \pi_2(q_1^*,q_2^*)}{\partial q_2 \partial \alpha}.$$

Let us note that there are two possible cases with α: either it affects the demand intercept or it affects the slope. When α affects the intercept only, we have $\frac{\partial^2 \pi_1}{\partial q_1 \partial \alpha} = \frac{\partial^2 \pi_2}{\partial q_2 \partial \alpha} = \frac{\partial p(.)}{\partial \alpha} > 0$. Following the same procedure as earlier, we derive

$$\frac{\partial q_1^*}{\partial \alpha} = \frac{\partial p(.)}{\partial \alpha}\cdot\frac{1}{\Delta_N}\left[-\frac{\partial^2 \pi_2(.)}{\partial q_2^2} + \frac{\partial^2 \pi_1(.)}{\partial q_1 \partial q_2}\right], \frac{\partial q_2^*}{\partial \alpha} = \frac{\partial p(.)}{\partial \alpha}\cdot\frac{1}{\Delta_N}\left[-\frac{\partial^2 \pi_1(.)}{\partial q_1^2} + \frac{\partial^2 \pi_2(.)}{\partial q_2 \partial q_1}\right].$$

The term inside the bracket should be positive on regularity grounds because the magnitude of own output change on a firm's marginal profit must be larger than the effect induced by change in the rival firm's output. Thus, $\frac{\partial q_1^*}{\partial \alpha} > 0$ and $\frac{\partial q_2^*}{\partial \alpha} > 0$.

However, if α is the slope of the demand curve then both $\frac{\partial p}{\partial \alpha} < 0$ and $\frac{\partial p'(.)}{\partial \alpha} < 0$. Therefore, both $\frac{\partial^2 \pi_1}{\partial q_1 \partial \alpha} = \frac{\partial p(.)}{\partial \alpha} + q_1^* \frac{\partial p'(.)}{\partial \alpha} < 0$ and $\frac{\partial^2 \pi_2}{\partial q_2 \partial \alpha} = \frac{\partial p(.)}{\partial \alpha} + q_2^* \frac{\partial p'(.)}{\partial \alpha} < 0$. Again applying Cramer's rule, we derive for a change in the slope of the demand:

$$\frac{\partial q_1^*}{\partial \alpha} = \frac{\partial^2 \pi_1(.)}{\partial q_1 \partial \alpha}\cdot\frac{1}{\Delta_N}\left[-\frac{\partial^2 \pi_2(.)}{\partial q_2^2} + \frac{\partial^2 \pi_1(.)}{\partial q_1 \partial q_2}\right] < 0$$

$$\frac{\partial q_2^*}{\partial \alpha} = \frac{\partial^2 \pi_2(.)}{\partial q_2 \partial \alpha}\cdot\frac{1}{\Delta_N}\left[-\frac{\partial^2 \pi_1(.)}{\partial q_1^2} + \frac{\partial^2 \pi_2(.)}{\partial q_2 \partial q_1}\right] < 0.$$

Thus, our proof is completed.

13.2.1 Linear demand and constant marginal cost

The previous discussion is further elaborated with an example of linear demand and constant marginal cost. Suppose the marginal costs of the two firms are c_1 and c_2, and there are no fixed costs (for the time being). The market demand curve is $p = A - b(q_1 + q_2)$.

At the level of introspection, firm 1 maximises its profit: $\pi_1 = pq_1 - c_1q_1 = (A - c_1 - bq_2)q_1 - bq_1^2$ by taking the output of firm 2 as *given*. The first-order condition $\frac{\partial \pi_1}{\partial q_1} = (A - c_1 - bq_2) - 2bq_1 = 0$ yields the best response function (or the reaction function) of firm 1 as

$$RF_1 : q_1 = \frac{(A - c_1)}{2b} - \frac{q_2}{2}.$$

Similarly, the best response function of firm 2 is obtained by maximising its profit with respect to q_2 as

$$RF_2 : q_2 = \frac{(A - c_2)}{2b} - \frac{q_1}{2}.$$

For each firm, the following can be said:

1. By setting $q_2 = 0$ in RF_1, we get $q_1^M = \frac{A - c_1}{2b}$, and by setting $q_2 = 0$ in RF_2, we get $\overline{q}_1 = (A - c_2)/b$. Similarly, $q_2^M = \frac{A - c_2}{2b}$ and $\overline{q}_2 = (A - c_1)/b$.
2. When firm i enjoys a monopoly, its profit is $\pi_i^M = \frac{(A - c_i)^2}{4b}$. But if firm i produces its limit output and drives firm j out of the market (or, equivalently, deter its entry), firm i's profit will be $\pi_i(\overline{q}_i) = (c_j - c_i)(A - c_j)/b$, which is positive only if $c_j > c_i$.

The reaction functions we derived earlier is actually a locus of all the highest points of the firm's own iso-profit curves. To see this, let firm 1's profit be held constant at $\overline{\pi}_1$. Then we can write the implicit equation for firm 1's iso-profit curve as

$$(A - c_1 - bq_2)q_1 - bq_1^2 - \overline{\pi}_1 = 0.$$

Allowing changes in both q_1 and q_2 while holding π_1 fixed at $\overline{\pi}_1$, we derive

$$\frac{dq_2}{dq_1} = \frac{A - c_1 - bq_2 - 2bq_1}{bq_1}.$$

In other words, the slope of firm 1's iso-profit curve is

$$\left.\frac{dq_2}{dq_1}\right|_{\pi_1 = \overline{\pi}_1} \begin{cases} > 0 & \text{if}(A - c_1 - bq_2) > 2bq_1 \\ = 0 & \text{if}(A - c_1 - bq_2) = 2bq_1 \\ < 0 & \text{if}(A - c_1 - bq_2) < 2bq_1 \end{cases}.$$

Thus, the iso-profit curve of firm 1 is inverted U-shaped against the axis of q_1. Note that by collecting the (q_1, q_2) combinations corresponding to $dq_2 / dq_1 = 0$ from each and every iso-profit curve that gives non-negative profit, we get the reaction function $q_1 = \frac{A - c_1 - bq_2}{2b}$.

Similarly, from firm 2's iso-profit curve (when drawn on the (q_1, q_2) plane),

$$(A - c_2 - bq_1)q_2 - bq_2^2 - \overline{\pi}_2 = 0,$$

we derive its slope as

$$\frac{dq_2}{dq_1} = \frac{q_2}{2\left[\frac{A-c_2-bq_1}{2b} - q_2\right]}.$$

Clearly,

$$\left.\frac{dq_2}{dq_1}\right|_{\pi_2=\bar{\pi}_2} \begin{cases} >0 & \text{if}(A-c_2-bq_1) > 2bq_2 \\ \to\infty & \text{if}(A-c_2-bq_1) = 2bq_2 . \\ <0 & \text{if}(A-c_2-bq_1) < 2bq_2 \end{cases}$$

Figure 13.1 panel *a* shows the iso-profit curves of firms 1 and 2. The highest iso-profit curve corresponds to zero profit and the lowest iso-profit curve to the highest (monopoly) profit. For each firm, the peak of the iso-profit curves gives the firm's best response. Thus, firm 2's iso-profit curves have an infinitely large slope along its reaction function, while firm 1's iso-profit curves have zero slope along its reaction function. Panel *b* shows the two reaction functions and their intersection point *N*, which is the Nash equilibrium.

There are a few things to note: (a) The profit of firm *i* increases with its own output q_i as it travels along its own reaction function. (b) When firm *i* travels along firm *j*'s reaction function, its profit increases with q_i but only up to a point, after which it declines. This point is well beyond the Cournot equilibrium point. (c) The slopes of the reaction functions, $\partial q_1 / \partial q_2$ for firm 1 and $\partial q_2 / \partial q_1$ for firm 2, are strictly less than unity (in fact they are exactly 1/2 in this example).

From the two (linear) reaction functions, we can easily compute the Cournot–Nash equilibrium outputs as

$$q_1^* = \frac{A-2c_1+c_2}{3b} \qquad q_2^* = \frac{A-2c_2+c_1}{3b}.$$

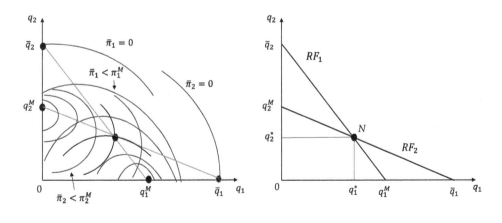

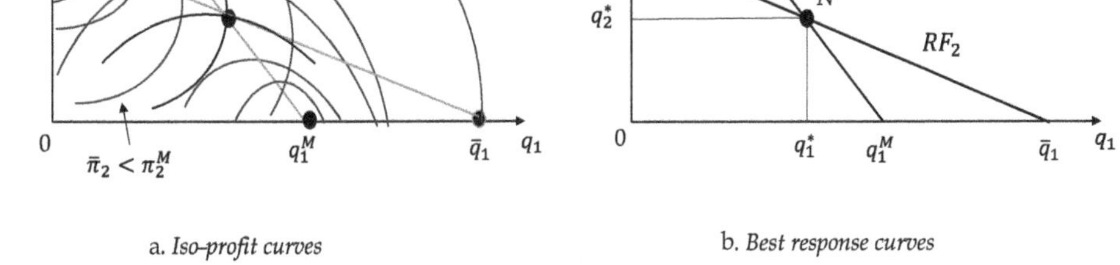

Figure 13.1 Iso-profit curves and reaction functions

Furthermore, the aggregate output and market price are

$$Q^* = \frac{2A - c_1 - c_2}{3b}, \quad p^* = \frac{A + c_1 + c_2}{3},$$

and firm profits are

$$\pi_1^* = \frac{(A - 2c_1 + c_2)^2}{9b} = bq_1^{*2}, \quad \pi_2^* = \frac{(A - 2c_2 + c_1)^2}{9b} = bq_2^{*2}.$$

As expected, each firm's equilibrium output is increasing in the other firm's marginal cost. Also note that (1) each firm produces less than its monopoly output. (2) The industry (or, aggregate) output is greater than monopoly but falls short of the competitive output $q = [A - \min\{c_1, c_2\}]/b$. (3) Consequently, price is below the monopoly level but still above the marginal cost, indicating that the firms have 'market power'. (4) Firms earn positive profits. (5) Social welfare (industry profit plus consumer surplus) in Cournot is greater than that in monopoly but again less than the competitive level.

13.2.1.1 *Fixed cost*

So far, we have not considered any fixed cost. Now let us introduce fixed cost for one firm, say, firm 2. Suppose firm 2 has a fixed cost F_2. The size of the fixed cost matters for the limit output, but not for the Nash equilibrium outputs. From Figure 13.1 panel *a*, we can see that firm 2's reaction curve will not run all the way to zero profit; it will have to be truncated when $\bar{\pi}_2 = F_2$ as shown by point *L* on panel *a* of Figure 13.2. The size of the fixed cost becomes important. If the fixed cost is F_2', then $\bar{q}_1$ gets larger, but the equilibrium does not change. By comparison, if F_2 is such that $q_1^* < \bar{q}_1(F_2) < q_1^M$, then we have an interesting situation. There are two Nash equilibria: (q_1^*, q_2^*) and $(q_1^M, 0)$. The second equilibrium corresponds to an intersection of the two reaction curves just as the first one. The reaction curves intersect twice at *N* and *M*.

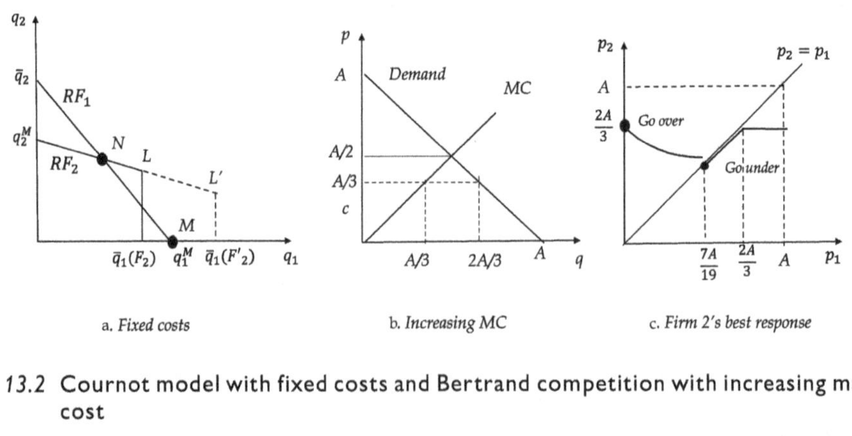

a. *Fixed costs* b. *Increasing MC* c. *Firm 2's best response*

Figure 13.2 Cournot model with fixed costs and Bertrand competition with increasing marginal cost

13.3 Bertrand duopoly

Now continuing with the assumption of constant marginal cost (MC), consider a similar set-up of two firms but a different price rule. Instead of relying on an invisible auctioneer, each firm directly quotes a price and they do it simultaneously. Assume production is carried out concurrently with price announcement. Seeing the prices consumers choose which firm to buy from. If the firms charge the same price, consumers choose randomly, and we assume that the two firms share the market equally. Otherwise, the lower price firm captures the whole market. This pricing rule was proposed by Joseph Luis François Bertrand in 1883.

To adapt to the price competition environment, let us invert the demand function and write it as $q = q(p)$. At (p_1, p_2) the firms' profits are

$$\pi_1 = \begin{cases} 0 & \text{if} \quad p_1 > p_2 \\ \dfrac{(p_1 - c_1)q(p_1)}{2} & \text{if} \quad p_1 = p_2, \\ (p_1 - c_1)q(p_1) & \text{if} \quad p_1 < p_2 \end{cases}$$

and

$$\pi_2 = \begin{cases} 0 & \text{if} \quad p_2 > p_1 \\ \dfrac{(p_2 - c_2)q(p_1)}{2} & \text{if} \quad p_2 = p_1. \\ (p_2 - c_2)q(p_2) & \text{if} \quad p_2 < p_1 \end{cases}$$

Remarkably, the unique Nash equilibrium of this one-shot price game is $p^* = \max\{c_1, c_2\}$, with the lowest cost firm capturing the whole market. The proof is fairly simple. Suppose $p^* > \max\{c_1, c_2\} = c_2$ (without loss of generality), in which both firms share the market equally and firm i earns a profit of $\pi_i = (p^* - c_i)q(p^*)/2$. Then any firm can deviate by quoting $p^* - \epsilon$ (ϵ being arbitrarily small) and sell $q(p^* - \epsilon)$ instead of $q(p^*)/2$, which yields profit $(p^* - \epsilon - c_i)q(p^* - \epsilon)$. For a sufficiently small ϵ, $(p^* - \epsilon - c_i)q(p^* - \epsilon) > (p^* - c_i)q(p^*)/2$. Thus, $p^* > c_2$ cannot be equilibrium.

Can $p^* < c_2$ be an equilibrium? Clearly, any $p < c_2$ allows firm 1 to steal the market from firm 2. But firm 1 can increase its profit by raising p^* up to $\min\{p_M, c_2\}$. If c_2 is so large that it exceeds the monopoly price, then, of course, firm 1 will simply stop at p_M. But $p_M < c_2$ is not an interesting case. When $p_M > c_2$, firm 1 can simply charge arbitrarily close to c_2 and capture the whole market.

In the special case, when $c_1 = c_2 = c$, both firms earn zero profit, share the market equally and the equilibrium price is c.

Proposition 34. *Suppose marginal costs are constant:* c_1 *and* c_2 *and* $p_M > \max\{c_1, c_2\}$. *Then the unique Nash equilibrium is* $p^* = \max\{c_1, c_2\}$, *and the lower cost firm captures the whole market and earns positive profit. If* $c_1 = c_2 = c$, *then* $p^* = c$ *and firms earn zero profit.*

13.3.1 Increasing marginal costs

That Bertrand competition produces a competitive outcome (price = MC) even without the structural characteristics of perfect competition is interesting. But at the same time, the result is paradoxical, because it does not conform to empirical observations in general. More worryingly, the zero-profit outcome is very special; it occurs only when firms have constant (and identical) MC. If firms have an increasing MC (or, equivalently, capacity constraint), then the possibility of positive profit emerges, but it turns out that a pure strategy solution will not generally exist. In the absence of capacity constraint (constant MC), undercutting becomes attractive. But with capacity constraint, a firm can supply only up to its MC and not necessarily up to the market demand. Thus, a residual market remains for a higher price–charging firm, which allows for positive profit for both firms. But the downside is that such price cuts will be endless, making a pure-strategy equilibrium unviable.

Remark 2

If firms are identical and have increasing marginal costs, there is no pure-strategy equilibrium. But a mixed-strategy equilibrium exists.

Let us illustrate the problem of the non-existence of a pure-strategy equilibrium with the help of an example, where $q = A - p$ and $C = q^2/2$ for each firm so that the (identical) marginal cost is $MC = q$. Panel *b* of Figure 13.2 depicts this case. The core logic of the non-existence of equilibrium can be easily adapted to a more general model of increasing marginal costs.

At $p = A/3$, each firm can supply $A/3$ units of q exactly up to its marginal cost, and their combined supply meets the market demand exactly ($p = MC$ for each firm). This is competitive equilibrium. At $p = A/2$, each firm can alone serve the whole market and produce up to its capacity. Let us now make the following key observations:

1. At $p \geq A/2$, neither firm can ever sell up to their capacity (i.e., what the marginal cost curve permits). If the firms set different prices in this range, the lower price firm will sell up to the demand (and capture the whole market).
2. At $A/3 < p < A/2$, each firm's individual capacity is less than the market demand, but their combined capacity exceeds the market demand. If the firms charge different prices, the lower price firm will sell up to its capacity and leave a residual demand for the higher price firm.
3. At $p = A/3$, the combined capacity of the two firms exactly matches the market demand.
4. At $p < A/3$, the market demand is too large. Each firm will sell up to its own capacity, and some buyers will remain unserved.

Following these observations, let us make an assumption about the rationing rule, which is relevant when firms are not able to collectively meet the demand (at $p < A/3$). We invoke an *efficient rationing rule* by which the customers are served in order of their willingness to pay, starting with the highest. In particular, when one firm has announced a lower price, say, p_1, and could sell p_1 units of q but not serve all customers, the other firm faces a residual demand $q = A - p_1 - p$ (with the restriction $p > p_1$). Relative to the residual demand, the firm will be able to both serve the whole (residual) market and produce up to its capacity if it sets $p = (A - p_1)/2$. If it sets $p < (A - p_1)/2$, it will sell only up to its capacity but not meet the market demand, and if it sets $p > (A - p_1)/2$, it will sell below capacity but meet the demand.

Now let us examine a firm's best response strategy. Without loss of generality let us assume that firm 2 is contemplating how to respond to firm 1's price p_1. It can *match, go under* or *go over*. If it matches, it earns a duopoly profit.

1. **Duopoly** If prices are **matched** each firm earns

$$\pi_D = \begin{cases} p^2 - \frac{p^2}{2} = p^2/2 & \text{if } \; p \le \frac{A}{3} \\ \frac{(A-p)}{2}\left[p - \frac{(A-p)}{4}\right] = \frac{(A-p)}{8}(5p-A) & \text{if } \; p > A/3 \end{cases}.$$

2. If firm 2 chooses to **go under**, it will undercut firm 1 by ϵ (which is arbitrarily close to zero), unless p_1 exceeds the monopoly price 2*A*/3. Thus, its price and profit (from the 'go under' strategy) are

$$p_2^-(p_1)\begin{cases} p_1 - \epsilon & \text{if } \; p_1 \le \frac{2A}{3} \\ \frac{2A}{3} & \text{if } \; p_1 > \frac{2A}{3} \end{cases}, \qquad \pi_2^-(p_1) \approx \begin{cases} \frac{p_1^2}{2} & \text{if } \; p_1 \le \frac{A}{2} \\ \frac{(A-p_1)}{2}(3p_1 - A) & \text{if } \; \frac{A}{2} < p_1 \le \frac{2A}{3} \\ \frac{A^2}{6} & \text{if } \; p_1 > \frac{2A}{3} \end{cases}.$$

3. But if it wants to **go over**, then its optimal price response should be examined considering three intervals of p_1

Case 1 ($p_1 < \frac{A}{3}$) Here, firm 2 has two options: set (1) either $p_2 \le \frac{A-p_1}{2}$ and sell up to capacity or (2) $p_2 > \frac{A-p_1}{2}$. Under the first option, it will get $\pi_2 = \frac{p_2^2}{2}$. Since this must observe a constraint $p_2 \le \frac{A-p_1}{2}$ optimal $p_2 = \frac{A-p_1}{2}$. Thus, firm 2 will earn $\pi_2 = \frac{(A-p_1)^2}{8}$. Under the second option, it will try to maximise $\pi_2 = \frac{(A-p_1-p_2)}{2}(3p_2 - A + p_1)$. Here, the optimal price is $p_2 = \frac{2(A-p_1)}{3}$, resulting in a profit of $\pi_2^+ = \frac{(A-p_1)^2}{6}$. Clearly, the second option dominates. Firm 2 will set a high price and serve up to the market demand.

Case 2 ($\frac{A}{3} \le p_1 < \frac{A}{2}$) Here, firm 2 has only one option: set $p_2 \ge \frac{(A-p_1)}{2}$ and serve the full residual market. The optimal price is then $p_2 = \frac{2(A-p_1)}{3}$, which results in $\pi_2^+ = \frac{(A-p_1)^2}{6}$. But note this pricing must observe a constraint $p_2 > p_1$ or $\frac{2(A-p_1)}{3} > p_1$, which is met only if $p_1 < \frac{2A}{5}$. Thus, at $\frac{2A}{5} \le p_1 < \frac{A}{2}$, such a strategy of going over implies setting $p_2 = p_1 + \epsilon$.

Case 3 ($\frac{A}{2} \le p_1 \le A$) Firm 2 cannot sell anything by charging in excess of p_1.

Combining these three cases, we now summarise the price and profit under the going-over strategy:

$$p_2^{+}(p_1)\begin{cases} \dfrac{2(A-p_1)}{3} & \text{if} \quad p_1 \le \dfrac{2A}{5} \\ p_1+\epsilon & \text{if} \quad p_1 > \dfrac{2A}{3} \end{cases}, \quad \pi_2^{+}(p_1) \approx \begin{cases} \dfrac{(A-p_1)^2}{6} & \text{if} \quad p_1 \le \dfrac{2A}{5} \\ \dfrac{(A-2p_1)}{2}(4p_1-A) & \text{if} \quad \dfrac{2A}{3} < p_1 \le \dfrac{A}{2} \\ 0 & \text{if} \quad p_1 > \dfrac{A}{2} \end{cases}$$

Comparing three profit levels, namely, $\pi_D, \pi_2^{-}(p_1)$ and $\pi_2^{+}(p_1)$, we determine firm 2's best response in the following lemma.

Lemma 7. *Firm 2's best response to firm 1's price announcement* p_1 *is*

$$p_2(p_1) = \begin{cases} \dfrac{2(A-p_1)}{3} & \text{if} \quad p_1 < \dfrac{7A}{19} \\ p_1-\epsilon & \text{if} \quad \dfrac{7A}{19} \le p_1 \le \dfrac{2A}{3} \\ \dfrac{2A}{3} & \text{if} \quad p_1 > \dfrac{2A}{3} \end{cases}.$$

Firm 1's best response to firm 2's price p_2 *is analogously defined.*

Figure 13.2 panel *c* shows the best response function of firm 2. It is discontinuous, and it either exceeds p_1 (at $p_1 < \frac{7A}{19}$) or remains below it. You can check that up to $p_1 < \frac{A}{3}$, $\pi_2^{+} > \pi_D > \pi_2^{-}$; then in the interval $\frac{A}{3} \le p_1 < \frac{7A}{19}$, we have $\pi_2^{+} > \pi_2^{-} > \pi_D$, and from $p_1 = \frac{7A}{19}$, onward $\pi_2^{-} > \pi_D > \pi_2^{+}$. Then it is clear that there is no mutually best response price $p_1 = p_2$.

Proposition 35. *If two firms selling an identical product also have identical and increasing marginal costs, a pure strategy Nash equilibrium does not exist, but a mixed-strategy equilibrium exists.*

The fact that a pure-strategy equilibrium does not exist in Bertrand oligopoly is troublesome. A mixed strategy offers a way out. But playing a mixed strategy in the context of real-world price competition may not be simple. From a theoretical point of view, there is another solution. If the firms are required to sell up to the market demand, then an undercutting incentive will be severely restricted. In this case, a deviating firm (undercutting or overcharging) will have to produce at a level far beyond (or less than) its MC curve, which may wipe out additional profit. Here, a pure-strategy equilibrium is possible. Dastidar (1995) has explored this avenue. Finally, the assumption of a homogeneous good can be relaxed to allow for product differentiation. We explore this next.

13.4 Differentiated products

If we look around, we may feel that price competition is more common than quantity competition. Low-cost airlines fiercely compete over budget tourists. Supermarkets aggressively offer discounts on household essentials and food. Internet-based movie channels lower their subscription rates every now and then. There are many such examples, which suggest that price is a major instrument of competition, probably more than quantity. One probable reason can be that price is more salient than quantity. But it is also the case that where price wars are frequent goods don't seem to be perfect substitutes. Supermarkets do offer competitive discounts but not necessarily on the same items; low-cost airlines vary in terms of services and destinations. Stores avoid being located in the same part of a city. These patterns suggest that even though price is a common device of competition firms do take care to reduce the intensity of it by differentiating their products or services. Product differentiation reduces the mobility of consumers between rival brands or close substitutes as some customers remain loyal to certain brands or varieties and respond less to competitively priced alternatives. We now consider one such set-up and show that both quantity and price competitions can be studied in a single model.

Suppose two firms are selling two differentiated good, which are described by the following *direct demand* curves:

$$q_1 = A - bp_1 + kp_2$$
$$q_2 = A + kp_1 - bp_2.$$

We assume $k < b$ to indicate that demand for good 1 is more sensitive to its own price changes than to a price change of its substitute good. Furthermore, $k > 0$ reflects the fact that two goods are substitutes. The firms have constant marginal costs, c_1 and c_2. For this model, we can study both price and quantity competition.

13.4.1 Price competition

First consider price competition. Here, the price rule is that each firm announces its price simultaneously, and since each has an effective monopoly, the consumers in each marketplace their demand and the firms serve them. The firms' objective is then to maximise π_1 and π_2 with respect to p_1 and p_2:

$$\pi_1 = (p_1 - c_1)q_1 = (p_1 - c_1)[A - bp_1 + kp_2]$$
$$\pi_2 = (p_2 - c_2)q_2 = (p_2 - c_2)[A + kp_1 - bp_2].$$

We can draw the iso-profit curves on the (p_1, p_2) plane from these profit functions, by holding the profits fixed as $\pi_1 = \bar{\pi}_1$ and $\pi_2 = \bar{\pi}_2$. For instance, the equation for an iso-profit curve of firm 1 is

$$p_2 = \frac{\bar{\pi}_1}{k(p_1 - c_1)} - \frac{A - bp_1}{k}.$$

Similarly, the equation for an iso-profit curve of firm 2 can be derived. Note that at a given p_1 if $\bar{\pi}_1$ increases, p_2 must increase. This means that on the price plane, the *higher* the iso-profit curve, the *higher* the level of profit. This is opposite to the iso-profit curves on the output plane.

The slopes of the iso-profit curves are

$$\left.\frac{dp_2}{dp_1}\right|_{\pi_1=\bar{\pi}_1} = \frac{2b}{(p_1 - c_1)k}\left[p_1 - \frac{A + kp_2 + bc_1}{2b}\right]$$

and

$$\left.\frac{dp_2}{dp_1}\right|_{\pi_2=\bar{\pi}_2} = \frac{(p_2 - c_2)k}{2b}\left[\frac{-1}{\frac{A + kp_1 + bc_2}{2b} - p_2}\right].$$

Figure 13.3 panel *a* shows the iso-profit curves of the two firms. The price reaction function of firm 1 is the locus of all the points where the iso-profit curves of firm 1 have zero slope, while the reaction function of firm 2 is the locus of all the points where the firm 2's iso-profit curves have infinitely large slope. Importantly, $\bar{\pi}_1^1 < \bar{\pi}_1^2 < \bar{\pi}_1^3$ and $\bar{\pi}_2^1 < \bar{\pi}_2^2 < \bar{\pi}_2^3$. In panel *b* of Figure 13.3, we have the two price reaction curves.

Note that the price reaction curves are upward-sloping. As we have explained in Section 13.2 in the context of Cournot duopoly, strategic substitutes give rise to downward-sloping reaction curves, and strategic complements give rise to upward-sloping reaction curves. Prices are strategic complements.

A word of caution is warranted about the intercepts of the price reaction curves. The intercepts, namely, $\frac{A + bc_1}{2b}$ of RF_1 and $\frac{A + bc_2}{2b}$ of RF_2, correspond to the prices that are best responses to the rival firm's zero prices. These are also the monopoly prices when the two goods are unrelated, that is, the case of $k = 0$, but in that case, each firm's demand is also the smallest. In a differentiated framework, the market expands when the price of a related good rises. Therefore, at these intercepts, profits are the lowest.

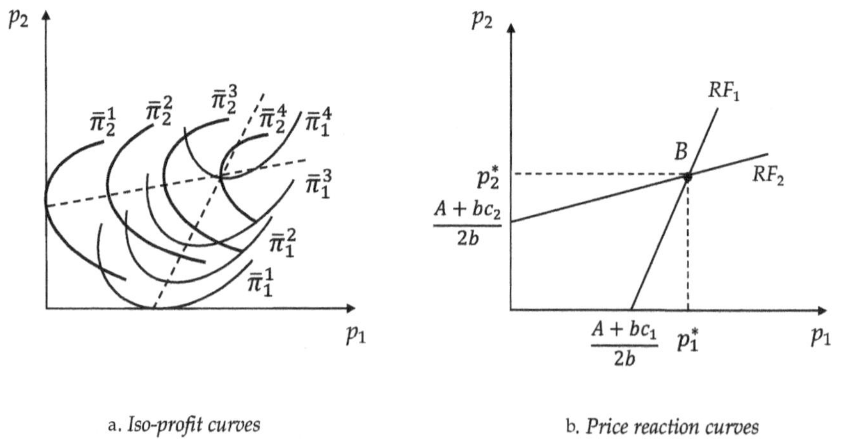

Figure 13.3 Bertrand competition

In order to directly derive the price reaction functions, differentiate π_1 and π_2 with respect to p_1 and p_2, respectively:

$$\frac{\partial \pi_1}{\partial p_1} = -b(p_1 - c_1) + [A - bp_1 + kp_2] = 0$$
$$\frac{\partial \pi_2}{\partial p_2} = -b(p_2 - c_2) + [A + kp_1 - bp_2] = 0.$$

The reaction functions are

$$RF_1 : p_1 = \frac{A + bc_1}{2b} + \frac{k}{2b} p_2 \tag{13.3}$$
$$RF_2 : p_2 = \frac{A + bc_2}{2b} + \frac{k}{2b} p_1. \tag{13.4}$$

The equilibrium Bertrand–Nash prices are

$$p_1^* = \frac{A + bc_1}{2b - k} + \frac{(c_2 - c_1)bk}{4b^2 - k^2}, \qquad p_2^* = \frac{A + bc_2}{2b - k} + \frac{(c_1 - c_2)bk}{4b^2 - k^2}.$$

An increase in c_1 increases p_1 and p_2 both, but p_2 increases less than p_1. This is evident from panel *b* of Figure 13.3, where an increase in c_1 induces a shift of RF_1 to the right and makes the equilibrium move north-east. This can also be verified from

$$\frac{\partial p_1^*}{\partial c_1} = \frac{2b^2}{4b^2 - k^2}, \qquad \frac{\partial p_2^*}{\partial c_1} = \frac{bk}{4b^2 - k^2}.$$

Clearly, the latter is smaller because of $k < b$.

Substituting the equilibrium prices into the demand functions, we calculate first $(p_1^* - c_1)$ as

$$\begin{aligned}(p_1^* - c_1) &= \frac{A + bc_1}{2b - k} + \frac{(c_2 - c_1)bk}{4b^2 - k^2} - c_1 \\ &= \frac{A + bc_1 - c_1(2b - k) + kc_2 - kc_2}{2b - k} + \frac{(c_2 - c_1)bk}{4b^2 - k^2} \\ &= \frac{A - bc_1 + kc_2}{2b - k} - k(c_2 - c_1)\frac{(b + k)}{4b^2 - k^2}.\end{aligned}$$

The price-cost mark-up has two components. The first one is the standard one whereby the own MC has a negative effect and the rival firm's MC has a positive effect (due to strategic complementarity). The second component is entirely due to asymmetry in the MCs that occurs through the degree of substitutability. Here, having a lower (own) cost means a lower price-cost mark-up.

The equilibrium quantity is calculated as

$$q_1^* = A - b\left[\frac{A+bc_1}{2b-k} + \frac{(c_2-c_1)bk}{4b^2-k^2}\right] + k\left[\frac{A+bc_2}{2b-k} + \frac{(c_1-c_2)bk}{4b^2-k^2}\right]$$

$$= \frac{A(2b-k) - Ab - b^2c_1 + kA + kbc_2}{2b-k} - bk(c_2-c_1)\frac{(b+k)}{4b^2-k^2}$$

$$= b\left[\frac{A-bc_1+kc_2}{2b-k} - k(c_2-c_1)\frac{(b+k)}{4b^2-k^2}\right] = b(p_1^* - c_1).$$

Thus, firm 1's equilibrium profit is

$$\pi_1^* = b(p_1^* - c_1)^2 = \frac{q_1^{*2}}{b} = b\left[\frac{A-bc_1+kc_2}{2b-k} - k(c_2-c_1)\frac{(b+k)}{4b^2-k^2}\right]^2.$$

Symmetrically, firm 2's equilibrium profit is

$$\pi_2^* = b(p_2^* - c_2)^2 = \frac{q_2^{*2}}{b} = b\left[\frac{A-bc_2+kc_1}{2b-k} - k(c_1-c_2)\frac{(b+k)}{4b^2-k^2}\right]^2.$$

In the case of symmetric MCs,

$$p^B = \frac{A+bc}{2b-k}, \quad \text{and} \quad \pi^B = b\frac{[A-(b-k)c]^2}{(2b-k)^2}. \tag{13.5}$$

13.4.2 *Quantity competition*

It is understood that price competition is more intense than quantity competition. Therefore, profit under Bertrand competition is likely to be less than that under quantity competition. This can be verified only when the same framework allows for both types of competition. The differentiated product framework allows that.

In order to study quantity competition, we invert the direct demand curve of good 2 as

$$p_2 = \frac{A}{b} + \frac{k}{b}p_1 - \frac{q_2}{b}$$

then substitute this into the direct demand function of q_1 and write it as

$$q_1 = A - bp_1 + k\left\{\frac{A}{b} + \frac{k}{b}p_1 - \frac{q_2}{b}\right\}.$$

Now rearranging terms and mulitplying both sides by $\frac{b}{b^2-k^2}$, we can write

$$p_1 = \frac{A}{b-k} - \frac{b}{b^2-k^2}q_1 - \frac{k}{b^2-k^2}q_2.$$

Now denote $\alpha = \frac{A}{b-k}$, $\beta = \frac{b}{b^2-k^2}$, $\delta = \frac{k}{b^2-k^2}$ for short-hand notations, and apply the same procedure to the direct demand function of q_2. We get the *inverse demand* functions as

$$p_1 = \alpha - \beta q_1 - \delta q_2$$
$$p_2 = \alpha - \beta q_2 - \delta q_1.$$

With the help of these demand curves, we write the profit functions:

$$\pi_1 = (p_1 - c_1)q_1 = (\alpha - \delta q_2 - c_1)q_1 - \beta q_1^2$$
$$\pi_2 = (p_2 - c_2)q_2 = (\alpha - \delta q_1 - c_2)q_2 - \beta q_2^2.$$

By differentiating π_1 with respect to q_1 and $\pi_2$with respect to q_2, we get the reaction functions as follows:

$$RF_1 : q_1 = \frac{\alpha - c_1}{2\beta} - \frac{\delta}{2\beta} q_2 \tag{13.6}$$

$$RF_2 : q_2 = \frac{\alpha - c_2}{2\beta} - \frac{\delta}{2\beta} q_1. \tag{13.7}$$

Solving these two equations we get the Cournot–Nash equilibrium quantities:

$$q_1^* = \frac{\alpha(2\beta - \delta) - 2\beta c_1 + \delta c_2}{4\beta^2 - \delta^2}, \qquad q_2^* = \frac{\alpha(2\beta - \delta) - 2\beta c_2 + \delta c_1}{4\beta^2 - \delta^2}.$$

We can calculate the price-cost mark-ups as

$$p_1^* - c_1 = \beta \frac{\alpha(2\beta - \delta) - 2\beta c_1 + \delta c_2}{4\beta^2 - \delta^2}, \qquad p_2^* - c_2 = \beta \frac{\alpha(2\beta - \delta) - 2\beta c_2 + \delta c_1}{4\beta^2 - \delta^2}.$$

The resultant Cournot profits are

$$\pi_1^C = \beta q_1^{*2} = \beta \left[\frac{\alpha(2\beta - \delta) - 2\beta c_1 + \delta c_2}{4\beta^2 - \delta^2} \right]^2$$
$$\pi_2^C = \beta q_2^{*2} = \beta \left[\frac{\alpha(2\beta - \delta) - 2\beta c_2 + \delta c_1}{4\beta^2 - \delta^2} \right]^2.$$

After we substitute the expressions for α, β and δ and rearrange terms, we write the profits as

$$\pi_1^C = \frac{b(b+k)}{(b-k)(2b+k)^2}\left[A - c_1(b-k) + k(c_2 - c_1)\frac{(b-k)}{2b-k}\right]^2$$

$$\pi_2^C = \frac{b(b+k)}{(b-k)(2b+k)^2}\left[A - c_2(b-k) + k(c_1 - c_2)\frac{(b-k)}{2b-k}\right]^2.$$

In the special case of $c_1 = c_2 = c$, we have

$$\pi^C = \frac{[A - c(b-k)]^2 b(b+k)}{(b-k)(2b+k)^2}. \tag{13.8}$$

13.4.3 Profit comparison

In order to compare the firm profits between the Bertrand and Cournot equilibria, we restrict our attention only to the symmetric marginal costs. Comparing Eqs. (13.5) and (13.8), we show that Cournot gives higher profit than Bertrand:

$$\pi_1^C > \pi_1^B \quad \text{if and only if} \quad \frac{[A-c(b-k)]^2 b(b+k)}{(b-k)(2b+k)^2} > \frac{[A-c(b-k)]^2 b}{(2b-k)^2}$$

$$\text{or} \quad \frac{b+k}{(b-k)(2b+k)^2} > \frac{1}{(2b-k)^2}$$

$$\text{or} \quad (b+k)(2b-k)^2 > (b-k)(2b+k)^2$$

$$\text{or} \quad (b+k)[4b^2 + k^2 - 4bk] > (b-k)[4b^2 + k^2 + 4bk]$$

$$\text{or} \quad 2k^3 > 0 \text{ which is true.}$$

This shows that Cournot competition is softer than price competition. When marginal costs are asymmetric, comparing Cournot and Bertrand profits is a bit complex. If $c_2 > c_1$, it is easy to establish that $\pi_1^C > \pi_1^B$. However, if $c_1 < c_2$, then $\pi_1^C > \pi_1^B$ may depend on certain conditions.

Proposition 36. *Suppose goods are differentiated and firms have identical technology. Then they are better off under output competition than under price competition.*

13.5 The leader–follower model

Now let us get back to the quantity setting game of the Cournot model, but assume that firm 1 moves first (leads), and firm 2 moves second (follows). This is a sequential output-choice game and it is called the Stackelberg model. The appropriate solution concept is the subgame perfect Nash equilibrium, which is ensured through backward induction.

Returning to the general set-up of a homogeneous good with $p = p(q_1 + q_2)$, we start from the last stage of the game. At this stage, the leader firm has already chosen its output at some q_1. The follower firm responds to it by producing $q_2 = \beta_2(q_1)$, its best response output, where $\beta_2'(q_1) < 0$.

Firm 1 then maximises its profit by perfectly anticipating firm 2's future response. Thus, firm 1 maximises $\pi_1 = p(q_1 + \beta_2(q_1))q_1 - C_1(q_1)$ with respect to q_1. The first-order condition is

$$p(.) + p'(.)q_1 + p'(.)\beta_2'(q_1)q_1 - C_1'(q_1) = 0. \tag{13.9}$$

Note the third term, which is due to the sequential output choice, which was absent in the Cournot case. Since $p'(.)\beta_2'(q_1) > 0$, the marginal revenue of the leader is higher than that under simultaneous output choice. Therefore, the Stackelberg leader's output must be greater than the Cournot output. The leader firm must be earning a greater profit too. If not, it could always set the Cournot output.

13.5.1 The linear demand case

Let us take the demand curve as $p = A - b(q_1 + q_2)$ with constant MCs, c_1 and c_2. The follower firm, firm 2, chooses q_2 from its reaction function $q_2 = \dfrac{A - c_2 - bq_1}{2b}$. In the first stage, the leader, firm 1, substitutes firm 2's reaction function into its profit function and solves the following problem:

$$\text{Max} \quad \pi_1 = (A - c_1 - bq_1)q_1 - bq_1\left[\frac{A - c_2 - bq_1}{2b}\right].$$

This yields the leader's and the follower's outputs and market price as

$$q_1^S = \frac{A - 2c_1 + c_2}{2b}, \qquad q_2^F = \frac{A - 3c_2 + 2c_1}{4b}, \qquad p = \frac{A + 2c_1 + c_2}{4}.$$

The leader's and the follower's profits are

$$\pi_1^S = \frac{(A - 2c_1 + c_2)^2}{8b}, \qquad \pi_2^F = \frac{(A - 3c_2 + 2c_1)^2}{16b}.$$

The leader chooses its output from the follower's reaction function where the leader's iso-profit curve is tangent to it. Leadership is generally advantageous. The leader earns higher profit than in the Cournot case. Being the first mover, the leader firm can assure itself at least of the Cournot profit and generally can do better than the follower firm. However, the intuition of the leader earning a higher profit than the follower does not hold in price leadership games. However, to study price leadership and compare it with output leadership, we need to consider a differentiated goods framework, which we do next.

13.5.2 Differentiated goods

13.5.2.1 Output leadership

Let us now recall the quantity competition case of Section 13.4, but assume for simplicity that $c_1 = c_2$. Suppose firm 2 is the follower and firm 1 is the leader. Substituting the follower's reaction function (as given in Eq. (13.7)) into the leader's profit function, we write

$$\pi_1^S = (p_1 - c)q_1 = \left[\alpha - \beta q_1 - \delta\left(\frac{\alpha - c}{2\beta} - \frac{\delta}{2\beta}q_1\right) - c\right]q_1$$
$$= (\alpha - c)\left[1 - \frac{\delta}{2\beta}\right]q_1 - \left[\beta - \frac{\delta^2}{2\beta}\right]q_1^2$$
$$= \frac{1}{2\beta}\left[(\alpha - c)(2\beta - \delta)q_1 - (2\beta^2 - \delta^2)q_1^2\right].$$

Maximising the preceding, we get q_1 and in turn q_2 as

$$q_1^S = \frac{(2\beta - \delta)}{2(2\beta^2 - \delta^2)}(\alpha - c), \qquad q_2^F = \frac{(4\beta^2 - \delta^2 - 2\delta\beta)}{4\beta(2\beta^2 - \delta^2)}(\alpha - c). \tag{13.10}$$

Here, we take note of an interesting fact.

REMARK 3

Under product differentiation and identical MC, the Stackelberg leader's output is smaller than the monopoly output. That is, $q^S < q^M$.

When goods are homogeneous $q^S = q^M$ (for identical MC), but that changes under differentiated goods, because the absence of competition from the differentiated good does not boost the demand as much as it does under homogeneous goods. In Figure 13.4 panel *a*, we record this fact.

Now we turn our attention to profits. However, because of the lengthy nature of the derivation of profits, we first report the profit and then show the derivation of it separately in the notes section.[3]

$$\pi_1^S = \frac{(2\beta - \delta)^2}{8\beta(2\beta^2 - \delta^2)}(\alpha - c)^2, \qquad \pi_2^F = \frac{(4\beta^2 - \delta^2 - 2\beta\delta)^2}{16\beta(2\beta^2 - \delta^2)^2}(\alpha - c)^2. \tag{13.11}$$

Just to compare these profits with the benchmark case of Cournot, let us recall that under Cournot

$$q^C = \frac{2\beta - \delta}{4\beta^2 - \delta^2}(\alpha - c), \qquad \pi^C = \frac{\beta(2\beta - \delta)^2}{(4\beta^2 - \delta^2)^2}(\alpha - c)^2 = \frac{\beta}{(2\beta + \delta)^2}(\alpha - c)^2. \tag{13.12}$$

It is easy to check that $q_1^S > q^C$ because clearly $\frac{2\beta - \delta}{2(2\beta^2 - \delta^2)} > \frac{2\beta - \delta}{4\beta^2 - \delta^2}$. For $q^C > q_2^F$, we need

$$\frac{2\beta - \delta}{4\beta^2 - \delta^2} > \frac{4\beta^2 - \delta^2 - 2\delta\beta}{4\beta(2\beta^2 - \delta^2)} \Rightarrow \delta^3 > 0,$$

which is true because $\delta > 0$. As for profits, the same condition ensures that $\pi^C > \pi_2^F$ and $\pi_1^S > \pi^C$, if $(4\beta^2 - \delta^2)^2 > 8\beta^2(2\beta^2 - \delta^2)$ which is also true. This ordering of outputs and profit applies to all duopolies (and oligopolies) under fairly general conditions with identical firms, although we demonstrated them with an example of linear demand and constant MC. When firms have different cost conditions, a higher cost firm can earn less than a follower firm if the follower firm's marginal cost is sufficiently small. But cost asymmetry obscures the strategic advantage

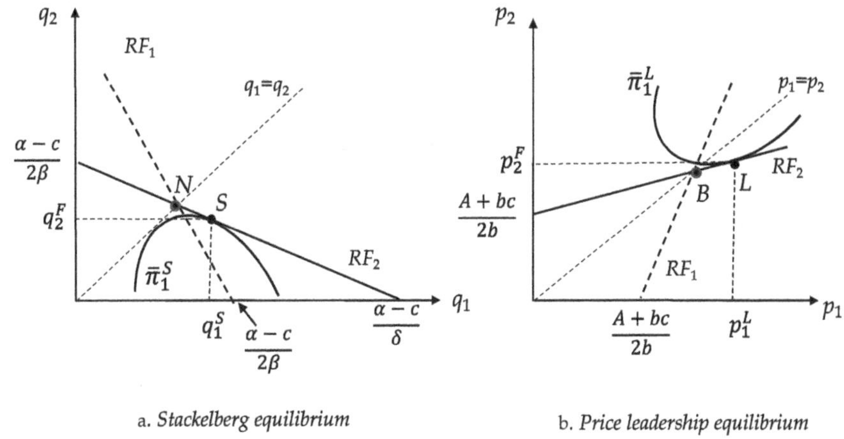

Figure 13.4 The leader–follower model for differentiated goods

of moving first. The Stackelberg case is demonstrated in panel *a* of Figure 13.4, assuming that$c_1 = c_2 = c$. Point *S* is the equilibrium point where firm 1's iso-proift curve is tangent to the output reaction curve of firm 2.[4]

Proposition 37. *Under identical cost conditions, a Stackelberg (output) leader produces more than a Cournot duopolist who produces more than a Stackelberg follower, and their profits also follow the same order.*

13.5.2.2 Price leadership

Now we consider the sequential price-setting game. Firm 1 announces p_1 first, and then firm 2 announces p_2. Consumers then make their decision about how much to buy. Substitute the follower's price reaction function as given in Eq. (13.4) in the leader firm's profit function:

$$\pi_1 = (p_1 - c)\left[A - bp_1 + k\left(\frac{A+bc}{2b} + \frac{k}{2b}p_1\right)\right].$$

Maximising this function with respect to p_1, we get the leader firm's price as

$$p_1^L = \frac{(A+bc)(2b+k) - k^2c}{2(2b^2 - k^2)}. \tag{13.13}$$

Firm 2's price is determined from its reaction function as

$$\begin{aligned} p_2^F &= \frac{A+bc}{2b} + \frac{k}{2b}\left[\frac{(A+bc)(2b+k) - k^2c}{2(2b^2 - k^2)}\right] \\ &= \frac{(A+bc)[4b^2 - k^2 + 2bk]}{4b(2b^2 - k^2)} - \frac{k^3c}{4b(2b^2 - k^2)}. \end{aligned} \tag{13.14}$$

Let us also recall that the Bertrand equilibrium price is $p^B = \frac{A+bc}{2b-k}$.

Now we compare these prices. Note that $p_2^F < p_1^L$ if

$$\frac{(A+bc)[4b^2-k^2+2bk]-k^3c}{4b(2b^2-k^2)} < \frac{(A+bc)(2b+k)-k^2c}{2(2b^2-k^2)}$$

$$\text{or,} \quad (A+bc)[4b^2-k^2+2bk]-k^3c < (A+bc)(2b+k)-2k^2bc$$

$$\text{or,} \quad (A+bc)k^2 > k^2c(2b-k) \Rightarrow A-(b-k)c > 0,$$

and $p^B < p_2^F$ if

$$\frac{A+bc}{2b-k} < \frac{(A+bc)[4b^2-k^2+2bk]-k^3c}{4b(2b^2-k^2)}$$

$$\text{or,} \quad (A+bc)\left[\frac{(4b^2-k^2+2bk)(2b-k)-4b(2b^2-k^2)}{4b(2b^2-k^2)(2b-k)}\right] > \frac{k^3c}{4b(2b^2-k^2)}$$

$$\text{or,} \quad \frac{(A+bc)k^3}{2b-k} > k^3c \Rightarrow A-(b-k)c > 0.$$

Thus, we see that both the leader and the follower set a higher price than the Bertrand level, and more importantly, the follower sets a lower price than the leader.

The price leadership case is depicted in panel *b* of Figure 13.4. The equilibrium point is *L*, where the iso-profit curve of firm 1 is tangent to firm 2's price reaction function.

Now we turn our attention to profits. These derivations are too lengthy and therefore have been placed in the notes section.[5] We have the leader's and follower's profit as

$$\pi_1^L = \frac{(2b+k)^2}{8b(2b^2-k^2)}[A-c(b-k)]^2. \tag{13.15}$$

$$\pi_2^F = \frac{[4b^2-k^2+2bk]^2}{16b(2b^2-k^2)^2}[A-c(b-k)]^2. \tag{13.16}$$

Comparing these two profit levels and the Bertrand profit, we see that

$$\pi_2^F > \pi_1^L \quad \text{if} \quad [4b^2-k^2+2bk]^2 > 2(2b+k)^2(2b^2-k^2).$$

Rewriting the left-hand-side term of the preceding inequality, we write

$$(4b^2-k^2)^2 + 4b^2k^2 + 4bk(4b^2-k^2) > 2(2b+k)^2(2b^2-k^2).$$

If we expand the terms on either side, this inequality reduces to $k^3(3k+4b) > 0$, which is true.

Next, compare the (price) leader's profit with the Bertrand profit as given in Eq. (13.5). See that

$$\pi_1^L > \pi^B \quad \text{if} \quad \frac{(2b+k)^2}{8b(2b^2-k^2)} > \frac{b}{(2b-k)^2}.$$

This inequality becomes $(2b+k)^2(2b-k)^2 > 8b^2(2b^2-k^2)$. Expanding both sides,

$$(4b^2-k^2)^2 > 16b^4-8b^2k^2 \quad \Rightarrow \quad 16b^4+k^4-8b^2k^2 > 16b^4-8b^2k^2 \quad \Rightarrow \quad k^4 > 0.$$

We summarise the profit comparison in the next proposition.

Proposition 38. *Under price leadership, the follower makes a higher profit than the leader. However, both will make higher profits than under Bertrand competition.*

Under quantity competition, leadership is always advantageous. The leader earns more profit than the follower. But under price competition, the follower earns more profit than the leader, because the follower gets an opportunity to undercut and steal a bit of the market from the leader.

13.5.2.3 Endogenous leadership

A natural question is how the leadership is determined. From an empirical point of view, the question may be settled by the history of the industry. A firm that has been around for a long time is most likely to be followed by firms that are of recent vintage. Market leadership can also be determined by a prior innovation race—a race to come up with a new process or new product. Keeping aside these additional considerations, we may ask: What if the firms are given the option to lead or follow, what will they choose?

Suppose both firms have to simultaneously choose one of the two options: lead or follow. Assume symmetry; that is, $c_1 = c_2$. If they both choose 'Follow', they play Cournot under quantity competition and Bertrand under price competition. If one chooses 'Lead' and the other chooses 'Follow', they play the leader–follower game. But if both choose 'Lead', they are required to take the action of the leader, that is, set p^L under price competition and q^S under quantity competition. For the case of both playing the 'Lead', you can compute the profit for each firm. However, we can demonstrate graphically that under output competition, both firms badly suffer from overproduction; they will earn a profit below the Cournot level. See panel *a* of Figure 13.5. At (q^S, q^S), which corresponds to the point S', profit is given by the curve $\bar{\pi}_1^{S'}$ and $\bar{\pi}_2^{S'}$ (which are equal due to symmetry). Both curves are farther from the profit curves passing through the Stackelberg point S and the Counrot point N. Thus, this is the worst outcome for both firms.

In contrast, panel *b* of Figure 13.5, where we capture price competition, shows that if both firms charge the leader's price p^L (at point L'), then their profit is strictly greater than the Bertrand profit (do not forget that here a further iso-profit represents a higher profit). But the leader's profit rises, if the follower moves from following to leading, and interestingly, the follower's profit falls from such a move; note $\pi_2^{L'} < \pi_2^F$, while$\pi_1^{L'} > \pi_1^L$. Thus, we conclude that (assuming symmetry)

$$\pi(q^S, q^S) < \pi^F < \pi^C < \pi^S \text{ under output competition}$$

$$\text{and } \pi^B < \pi^L < \pi(p^L, p^L) < \pi^F \text{ under price competition.}$$

Under output competition, $\pi(q^L, q^L) < \pi^F < \pi^C < \pi^L$, and under price competition, $\pi^B < \pi^L < \pi(p^L, p^L) < \pi^F$.

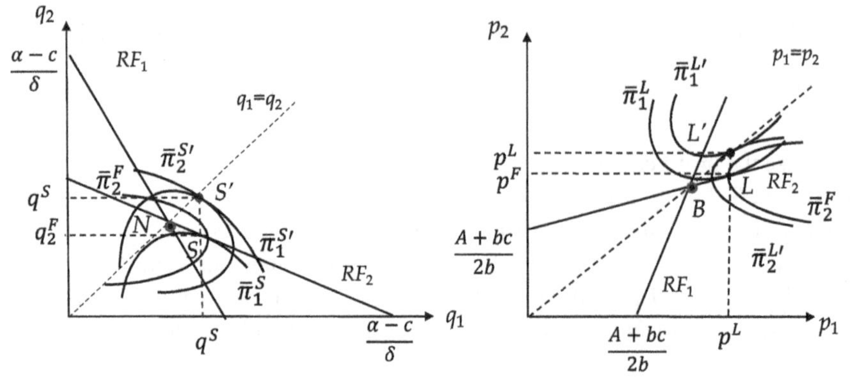

a. *Output competition*   b. *Price competition*

Figure 13.5 Endogenous leadership

With the preceding profit comparison, it is easy to see that under both types of competition there are two asymmetric Nash equilibria: (Lead, Follow) and (Follow, Lead). Even though leadership is disadvantageous under price competition, leading is still better than following, when the other player plays 'follow'. Thus, we conclude that leadership may emerge from these interactions among the firms, when they are nearly identical. Of course, this is a static environment. In a dynamic environment, it is more plausible to expect that firms may take a turn to lead, as an act of coordination over the two equilibria. The same argument can be made by invoking a mixed strategy.

13.6 Anti-competitive behaviours

While oligopoly produces market outcomes that are closer to perfect competition than to monopoly, it is also vulnerable to many activities that undermine competition. Collusion, open or tacit, is a big problem. Two firms in a duopoly might talk to each other to avoid competition. Together they can form a *cartel* and charge monopoly prices from the consumers. Fortunately, colluding openly, or forming a cartel, is illegal in most countries.[6] It is not just open collusion but also implicit attempts to coordinate price or output decisions that are likely to be judged illegal under US or European laws. This is a separate area of study in the field of industrial economics.

Here, we consider three types of anti-competitive efforts. The first one is the attempt to collude through repeated interactions. Two other efforts that we consider in some detail are entry deterrence activities.

13.6.1 *Collusion*

In the game theory chapter, we discussed how an infinite repetition of the prisoner's dilemma can induce cooperation among the prisoners to not confess. Can we extend the same logic to a duopoly? If two firms play Cournot or Bertrand games over and over again, will they be able to collude? Mind that even if colluding is not prohibited, firms may have incentive to cheat on the collusion agreement.

Table 13.1 Endogenous leadership

	(a) Output competition			*(b) Price competition*	
	Lead	*Follow*		*Lead*	*Follow*
Lead	$\pi(q^S,q^S),\ \pi(q^S,q^S)$	π^S,π^F	Lead	$\pi(p^L,p^L),\pi(p^L,p^L)$	π^L,π^F
Follow	π^F,π^S	π^C,π^C	Follow	π^F,π^L	π^B,π^B

Now, unlike the prisoner's dilemma game, Cournot or Bertrand games do not have any dominant strategy. Still the main intuition goes through. Any finite repetition of a Cournot or a Bertrand game produces the one-shot outcome of the Nash equilibrium, because in the last period, no matter what has happened in the past, both firms would selfishly compete and arrive at the Nash equilibrium. Thereby, by the logic of backward induction, the only equilibrium credible is to play the Nash equilibrium in every period. However, with infinite repetition, cooperation is sustainable. Let us now examine the prospect of cooperation/collusion.

Suppose that the firms agree to produce a cartel output q^* and that they each earn π^* as a result, every period. With a common discount factor δ, each earns a present value pay-off of $\frac{\pi^*}{1-\delta}$. If a firm deviates from q^*, it earns $\tilde{\pi}$ in the deviating period, but from the next period onwards, they must all play a punishment strategy by producing the one-shot (i.e., the stage-game) Nash equilibrium output forever. The stage-game Nash equilibrium is profit π^N. The deviating firm then earns $\tilde{\pi}+\frac{\delta}{1-\delta}\pi^N$. Deviation is unprofitable if

$$\tilde{\pi}+\frac{\delta}{1-\delta}\pi^N<\frac{\pi^*}{1-\delta} \quad\Rightarrow\quad \delta>\frac{\tilde{\pi}-\pi^*}{\tilde{\pi}-\pi^N}\equiv\hat{\delta}$$

If the firms' discount factor exceeds $\hat{\delta}$, then they will be able to sustain collusion. The exact value of $\hat{\delta}$ depends on whether the firms are trying to collude in an environment of output or price competition and on the cartel agreement, which may not necessarily be the monopoly output but some output in between the duopoly and the monopoly output.

For the sake of concreteness, assume the market demand curve to be $p=A-bq$ and symmetric firms with $c_1=c_2=c$. Under Cournot competition firms, each produce $q^c=(A-c)/3b$ and earn $\pi^C=(A-c)^2/9b$, while under Bertrand competition, they will produce $q^B=(A-c)/2b$ each and earn zero profit. A cartel counterpart of this market is that the two firms together produce $q_1+q_2=(A-c)/2b$ and earn a combined profit of$(A-c)^2/4b$. The firms may agree to share the cartel output and profit equally. Then $\pi^*=(A-c)^2/8b$. Let us examine if the cartel agreement to supply $q=(A-c)/4b$ by each firm can be made sustainable. Suppose the punishment strategy is that if a firm deviates from $q=(A-c)/4b$, then both firms must produce the Cournot–Nash output $q=(A-c)/3b$.

If a firm sticks to the collusive agreement, then $\pi=(A-c)^2/8b$ it earns. But if it wants to deviate, it should produce $q=\frac{A-c}{2b}-\frac{A-c}{8b}=\frac{3(A-c)}{8b}$, which is its best response to the other firm's collusive output. This will give it profit $\pi = \left[A - c - b\left(\frac{A-c}{4b} + \frac{3(A-c)}{8b}\right)\right]\frac{3(A-c)}{8b}$, which becomes $\tilde{\pi} = \frac{9(A-c)^2}{64b}$. This is clearly greater than its share of the cartel profit of $\frac{(A-c)^2}{8b}$.

Thus, $\hat{\delta} = \dfrac{\frac{9}{64} - \frac{1}{8}}{\frac{9}{64} - \frac{1}{9}} = \frac{9}{17}$.

If the firms were to engage in price competition, then $\pi^N = 0$ and the collusive profit is $\tilde{\pi} = \pi^M$. Therefore, $\hat{\delta} = 1/2$.

Note that the critical value of δ under Bertrand is smaller than the critical value of δ under Cournot. The reason is under Bertrand punishment is severe; there is a lot to lose. Therefore, the incentive to cooperate is also stronger. Hence, collusion is more sustainable when non-cooperation entails engaging in fierce price competition.

13.6.2 Entry deterrence

Now we will discuss the possibility of undertaking a predatory level of production by an incumbent firm in order to prevent future competition, specifically by discouraging entry. This has been a long-standing theme of industrial economics, first raised by Bain (1956). Since then, for two decades, it was widely thought that an existing firm consolidates its strategic advantage by extending production beyond its normal (i.e., ordinarily optimal) level that would enable it to quickly retaliate any entry, and as long as this overproduction is a public knowledge, the entrant would spare itself of the pains of an unsuccessful entry.

This conventional wisdom of the last century was in apparent contradiction to another wisdom (which is, however, still valid) that a monopolist produces 'too little'. Bain (1956) argued that the monopolist does not *actually* overproduce but holds on to excess capacity so that it can fight off entry efficiently if needed. This idea known as the excess capacity hypothesis has been examined both theoretically and empirically. It is not hard to see that when there is sufficient uncertainty about market demand or when the market is expected to grow, an existing firm would like to build up more capacity, which then also helps thwart entry. But the idea of holding excess capacity solely for the purpose of deterring entry has been found to be generally inconsistent with the idea of subgame perfect Nash equilibrium. In this section, we review the seminal work of Dixit (1980) on excess capacity. But first, we recast the Stackelberg model in the context of entry to get a first glimpse of the argument.

Without loss of generality assume that firm 1 is the incumbent firm, and it is a Stackelberg leader, while firm 2 is the entrant. Also, the two firms are identical in terms of production cost, that is, $c_1 = c_2 = c$, but the entrant must incur a set-up cost or entry cost F, which is now sunk for the incumbent and has no bearing on its own actions. Furthermore, the demand curve is linear $p = A - bq$. If entry occurs, we assume that the firms will compete in output.

We ask: Will the incumbent produce at the standard Stackelberg level and accommodate entry or produce more and deter entry? The answer to this question depends on the size of the entry cost and its impact on the entrant's profit, $\pi_2 = (A - b(q_1^L + q_2) - c)q_2 - F$. If entry occurs, in the Stackelberg equilibrium (recall from Section 13.5), the entrant would earn as a follower $\pi_2 = \frac{(A-c)^2}{16b} - F$. If this is negative, the entrant will not enter, and the Stackelberg output, which is also same as the monopoly output, becomes an entry-deterring output. This is, in the parlance of Bain, called *entry-blockaded*.

However, if $\pi_2 = \frac{(A-c)^2}{16b} - F > 0$, then the incumbent is in a dilemma. Should he produce more than the Stackelberg output and deter entry or accommodate entry and still enjoy a higher profit as the leader?

Let $\bar{q}$ be the limit output that makes $\left[A - b\left(\bar{q} + \frac{A-c-b\bar{q}}{2b}\right) - c\right]\frac{A-c-b\bar{q}}{2b} - F = 0$. You can calculate $\bar{q} = \frac{A-c}{b} - 2\frac{\sqrt{F}}{\sqrt{b}}$. Now consider firm 1's iso-profit curve, $\bar{\pi}_1 = \left[A - b(q_1 + q_2) - c\right]q_1$. The lowest profit the incumbent is assured of is the Stackelberg (leader) profit $\pi = (A-c)^2/8b$. So let us see where the iso-profit curve that passes through the Stackelberg equilibrium point hits the q_1 axis. Suppose this q_1 is denoted as $\tilde{q}_1$. Setting $q_2 = 0$ and $\bar{\pi}_1 = (A-c)^2/8b$, we solve for $\tilde{q}_1$ from the equation $\frac{(A-c)^2}{8b} - (A - c - b\tilde{q}_1)\tilde{q}_1 = 0$ as

$$\tilde{q}_1 = \frac{A-c}{2b} + \frac{A-c}{2\sqrt{2}b}, \qquad \text{whereas } \bar{q} = \frac{A-c}{b} - 2\frac{\sqrt{F}}{\sqrt{b}}.$$

If $\bar{q} > \tilde{q}_1$, which will be true if $F < \frac{(A-c)^2(\sqrt{2}-1)^2}{32b}$, then the incumbent finds that stretching its output to $\bar{q}$ is too costly; hence, it is better off accommodating entry. This scenario is called *ineffectively impeded entry*, in the language of Bain. Alternatively, if $\bar{q} < \tilde{q}$ but still $q_S < \bar{q}$, then producing that extra output from $q_S = (A-c)/2b$ to $\bar{q}$ is indeed profitable, and the incumbent will *effectively impede entry*. That is, in order to deter entry, the incumbent will be willing to overproduce a little bit but not too much. But this 'overproduction' is possible only because the set-up cost is high and not because of any inherently strategic action of the incumbent.

13.6.2.1 A model of capacity choice

While the preceding argument is very clear-cut, there are two grounds for dissatisfaction. First, it does not address the excess capacity hypothesis, and second, it (unjustifiably) assigns first-mover advantage to the incumbent.[7] Dixit (1980) addressed both concerns, which we present briefly.

Suppose there are two stages of the game. Production requires investing in capacity, which can be done concurrently with production or at a pre-production stage. The incumbent has the option of building capacity first, while the entrant does not. Although capacity is a long-lasting investment, in our world it just lasts for two periods and depreciates immediately after the output is produced.[8] In the first stage, the incumbent has the option of building capacity, while in the second stage, entry occurs and outputs are chosen simultaneously.

In addition, the following assumptions on capacity are crucial.

Assumption 9.

1. *Capacity, once chosen, cannot be reduced, but it can be increased.*
2. *Output can be produced at a lower cost up to the capacity constraint, but to produce beyond the existing capacity, both the capacity cost and the production cost are to be incurred.*

The first assumption captures the core idea of commitment. If the incumbent builds capacity prior to the entrant's entry, it clearly sends a message that he would produce at least that much output because capacity cannot be reduced. Thus, capacity takes the role of *costly commitment.* The second assumption underscores asymmetry between the two firms endogenously created through an asymmetry in cost and sequential output choice.

Let the capacity cost be $C_k = rk$ and the subsequent production cost be $C_q = cq$ with the restriction $q \leq k$. To expand production beyond *k*, the firm must incur an additional cost of $(c+r)(q-k)$. Thus, the incumbent's production cost structure from the sequential choice of capacity, and output is

$$C_q = \begin{cases} rk + cq & \text{if} \quad q \leq k \\ (r+c)q & \text{if} \quad q > k \end{cases}.$$

If q and k are chosen at the same time, the cost becomes $C_q = (r+c)q$. For the entrant, there is an additional cost, which is the entry cost *F*. Two things are clear. First, if the incumbent does not choose capacity beforehand, there is no difference between the two firms in the post-entry game as they have to choose outputs simultaneously. Second, if capacity has been chosen earlier, then it must be used in the post-entry game. Holding idle capacity is *ex ante* not optimal. This is, however, far from obvious. We now present a graphical analysis of this argument and see what the optimal choice of capacity is.

Assuming the market demand to be $p = A - b(q_1 + q_2)$, we demonstrate the implication of capacity choice for the incumbent. Its reaction function is going to be

$$q_1 = \begin{cases} \dfrac{A-c-q_2}{2b} & \text{if} \quad q_1 \leq k \\ \dfrac{A-c-r-q_2}{2b} & \text{if} \quad q_1 > k \end{cases}.$$

Panel *a* of Figure 13.6 depicts the reaction curves of firm 1 and firm 2. Having chosen capacity *k*, firm 1 is able to respond to firm 2's output more aggressively as its marginal cost of production will be just *c*. But the aggressive response will not extend beyond *k*, when the firm has to switch to the reaction curve $RF_1(c+r)$ as production can be continued only at a higher cost, just like firm 2 would have to do throughout.

We here note that the incumbent will not choose a capacity below $\underline{k}$ or above $\bar{k}$. The reason is that if no capacity is chosen, the resultant Cournot equilibrium is given by point *N*, which then corresponds to a capacity of $\underline{k} = \dfrac{A-c-r}{3b}$. However, if the incumbent has chosen a large capacity, such as $\bar{k}$ or more, the equilibrium will be given by point N', which is also the farthest point the duopoly equilibrium can be moved to. Therefore, it is pointless to choose capacity beyond $\bar{k} = \dfrac{A-c+r}{3b}$, as long as the intention is to accommodate entry. Thus, we can be certain that in any *post-entry duopoly*, the incumbent's output must lie in the interval $\left[\dfrac{A-c-r}{3b}, \dfrac{A-c+r}{3b}\right]$. The lower limit of the interval is given by the standard duopoly of two firms with identical marginal cost of production as $c+r$. The upper limit is given by the duopoly output between two firms with asymmetric production costs, with firm 1 having MC as *c*, while firm 2 has MC as $c+r$.

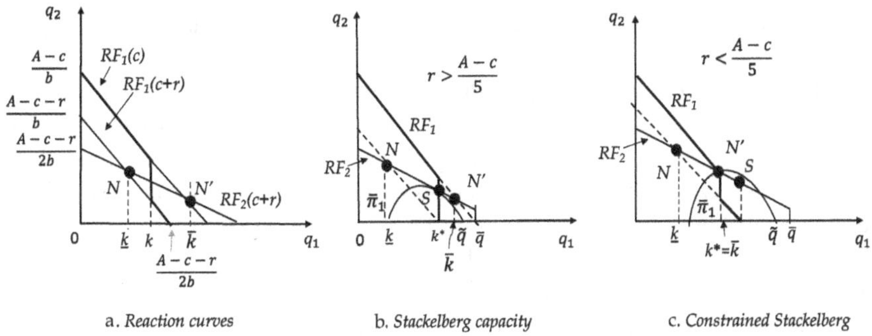

Figure 13.6 Capacity choice and duopoly equilibrium

Panels b and c of Figure 13.6 show how the equilibrium would look like, when entry is accommodated. Two figures correspond to two alternative assumptions about the marginal capacity cost r. When $r > (A-c)/5$, the Stackelberg output is less than $\bar{k}$, which is shown in panel b. But when $r < (A-c)/5$, the Stackelberg output is greater than $\bar{k}$, which is shown in panel c. The equilibrium in the first case occurs at point S, as the Stackelberg output is most profitable, given that entry is inevitable, while in the second case, the equilibrium will be at point N'.

Now the question is, Will the incumbent choose capacity exactly equal to the output to be chonsen later in the post-entry equilibrium? The answer is yes, because idle capacity is costly and has no strategic value. Intuitively, choosing capacity beforehand is akin to choosing output like a Stackelberg leader, provided the Stackelberg leader's output is feasible in a post-entry Cournot game, where firm 1 has a marginal cost c and the firm 2 has a marginal cost $c+r$. If the Stackelberg output is not feasible (i.e., beyond $\bar{k}$), then $\bar{k}$ is the second-best thing the incumbent can do.

Mathematically, since in all entry-accommodating equilibrium firm 1's output is k, its *ex ante* profit in the first stage is $\pi_1 = [A - b\left(k + \frac{A-bk-c-r}{2b}\right) - (c+r)]k$. Firm 1 will try to maximise π_1 subject to the restriction $\frac{A-c-r}{3b} < k < \frac{A-c+r}{3b}$. The unconstrained solution is $k^* = \frac{A-c-r}{2b}$, which is the Stackelberg output at the symmetric MC of $c+r$. If $\frac{A-c-r}{3b} < k^* < \frac{A-c+r}{3b}$, then the optimal solution is the Stackelberg capacity. For this to be true, the marginal cost of capacity must be sufficiently large; that is, $r > (A-c)/5$ (as shown in panel b). This can be obtained by checking $k^* < \frac{A-c+r}{3b}$. Alternatively, if $r < (A-c)/5$ the Stackelberg output is beyond $\bar{k}$, and therefore, the firm will choose the constrained optimal capacity $\bar{k} = \frac{A-c+r}{3b}$ (as shown in panel c).

13.6.2.2.1 ENTRY DETERRENCE

In the previous discussion, we focused on entry accommodation. Now, let us consider the scope of entry deterrence. The incumbent in the preceding discussion chooses $\bar{k}$ or the Stackelberg capacity, if the entry cost is such that entry is profitable at $\bar{k}$. Recall that the limit output to deter entry is $\bar{q}$, at which the entrant gross profit just covers the entry cost F, while $\tilde{q}$ is the maximum output that the incumbent is willing to produce, where $\tilde{q}$ gives exactly the same profit as the duopoly profit, denoted by $\bar{\pi}_1$ (that occurs at the duopoly equilibrium S or N'). If $\bar{q} \leq \tilde{q}$ entry will be deterred by extending capacity up to $\bar{q}$, because then at $\bar{q}$ the incumbent will make more profit than at $\tilde{q}$. But note that then production is to be carried up to the chosen capacity $\bar{q}$. The firm will never hold idle capacity in this environment. Alternatively, if $\tilde{q} < \bar{q}$, producing capacity at $\bar{q}$ to fight entry is not credible. Hence, optimal k is either at the Stackelberg output level or the constrained Stackelberg level as shown in the graph.

In sum, when $\tilde{q} < \bar{q}$, optimal capacity is

$$k^* = \begin{cases} \dfrac{A-c-r}{2b} & \text{if} \quad r > \dfrac{A-c}{5} \\ \dfrac{A-c+r}{3b} & \text{if} \quad r < \dfrac{A-c}{5} \end{cases},$$

and entry is accommodated. Alternatively, if $\tilde{q} > \bar{q}$ then the incumbent chooses

$$k^* = \max\left\{\bar{q}, \frac{A-c-r}{2b}\right\}, \text{ and entry is deterred.}$$

If $k^* = \bar{q}$, then entry is effectively impeded and if $k^* = \dfrac{A-c-r}{2b}$ entry is blockaded.

13.6.3 *Limit pricing*

While the capacity choice model of Dixit (1980) shows that holding excess capacity to deter entry is generally not optimal, there are plenty of other means to discourage entry. Holding idle patents in the context of industrial products, creating excessive varieties in markets for breakfast cereals and light consumer goods, and writing exclusive dealings contracts with input suppliers or even consumers are some of the well-known practices that tend to restrict entry. Such practices are not necessarily illegal because they often entail some benefits, such as greater variety for consumers and greater earnings for workers and input suppliers in exclusive dealing contracts.

A classic well-known strategy of entry deterrence is to do limit pricing or, in the parlance of anti-trust economics, predatory pricing. It had been long thought that an existing firm (or a small group of firms) can charge extremely low prices to make it impossible for a newcomer firm to match. Obviously, consumer benefits of such price reductions are only temporary, because once the competitors are driven out of the market the existing firm(s) can return to their (near) monopoly prices.

However, while price wars are not uncommon their implications for entry deterrence are questionable. From the insights of game theory, we know that charging a low price today does not create incentives for charging a low price tomorrow, unless today's low price is a result of an irreversible investment, signifying a credible commitment to do the same in future. The capacity choice model has clearly established that. In the absence of such investments, setting a low price at a pre-entry stage will be clearly seen as a bluff or an empty threat of price war in the post-entry game, and therefore, it is a futile exercise.

There is a caveat, however. This argument presupposes that firms, both existing and incoming, know what everything they need to know, such as each other's costs and the size of the market. If the entrant firm is unsure about the costs of the incumbent firm and, in particular, if entry against a vastly superior incumbent would turn out to be a fatal mistake, then the incumbent is in a position to exploit the informational uncertainty and can benefit by strategically charging a very low price. In a seminal paper, Milgrom and Roberts (1982) examined the scope and benefits of limit pricing in such an environment of incomplete information.

In the Milgrom–Roberts model, there are two firms: one incumbent (firm 1) and one entrant (firm 2). The entrant does not know for sure whether the incumbent's marginal cost is c_1 or c_2. His belief is that it is c_2 with probability α and c_1 with probability $1-\alpha$. Let the market demand be $p = A - b(q_1 + q_2)$ as before. The entrant has a fixed cost of entry *F*, and its marginal cost of production is *r*, which is known to the incumbent. There are two periods to the game. In the first period, the incumbent is alone in the market. The entrant observes the price charged by the incumbent and tries to update his belief about what type of opponent he is up to. Based on the updated beliefs (or priors, if beliefs could not be updated), he enters or stays away in the second period. If he enters, a Cournot duopoly emerges, if he does not the incumbent will enjoy his uncontested monopoly.

As we saw in Chapter 11 in the context of job market signalling and Chapter 12 for sequential bargaining, any action taken by an informed party is likely to have some signal value that an uninformed party does not want to miss. Aware of the entrant's crucial incentive to update his beliefs, the incumbent can pursue one of the two well-known strategies: reveal the cost information through a **separating equilibrium** or keep the cost uncertainty alive through a **pooling equilibrium**. There is also a third strategy of partial information revelation, but that would not apply here. Which equilibrium is in the best interest of the incumbent and what implications it has for entry are analysed next.

First, let us sort out some notation issues. We are going to denote the entrant's profit as $R(r \mid c_i)$, which can take two values, depending on the type of the incumbent. In a post-entry Cournot duopoly (you can easily derive the following profit expressions),

$$R_1 \equiv R(r \mid c_1) = \frac{(A-2r+c_1)^2}{9b} - F \quad \text{and} \quad R_2 \equiv R(r \mid c_2) = \frac{(A-2r+c_2)^2}{9b} - F.$$

For the entry game we are interested in, the following assumptions are important.

Assumption 10.

1. *The entrant is superior or equal to the high-cost incumbent but inferior to the low-cost one. That is,* $c_1 < r \leq c_2$.
2. *Entry is unprofitable against the low-cost incumbent:* $R_1 < 0 < R_2$.
3. *If the entrant is not able to update his belief and decides to enter, he will learn about the incumbent's MC immediately upon entry.*

If the entrant was inferior to both types, entry is ruled out straight away, and if he was outright superior, entry is inevitable (except in the trivial case of an extremely high entry cost). The second assumption captures the entrant's dilemma, which also creates some problems as well as opportunities for the incumbent as we shall see shortly.

Returning to notations, we denote the incumbent's profit by π. Since the incumbent's second-period price and output are trivial, we just denote his standard profits corresponding to monopoly and duopoly as π_i^M and π_i^D, respectively, each of which can take two values depending on his MC $i = 1,2$. It is easy to check that

$$\pi_i^M(c_i) = \frac{(A-c_i)^2}{4b} \quad \text{and} \quad \pi_i^D(c_i) = \frac{(A-2c_i+r)^2}{9b}, \quad \text{where} \quad i = 1,2.$$

As for the first-period profits (when duopoly does not apply), we use π_i^M for standard monopoly profit from cost c_i when $p^M(c_i)$ is charged. But to permit potential deviation of p from $p^M(c_i)$, we denote the price and profit as $\tilde{p}$ and $\pi(\tilde{p};c_i)$, respectively. You can easily check that $\pi(\tilde{p};c_i) = (\tilde{p}-c_i)q_i(\tilde{p}) = (\tilde{p}-c_i)\left[\frac{A-\tilde{p}}{b}\right]$. Finally, the notation for the equilibrium price of the incumbent of type c_i is $p^*(c_i)$.

The incumbent's objective is to maximise the present value of his total profit, where the second-period profit is discounted by a factor of δ. He sets $p^*(c_i)$ (in the first period) depending on whether he wants to reveal or hide information, which we determine next.

13.6.3.1 SEPARATING EQUILIBRIUM

Whether the incumbent prefers to reveal information or not depends on what the entrant might do based on his prior beliefs. Suppose the following condition holds:

$$\alpha R(r \mid c_2) + (1-\alpha)R(r \mid c_1) > 0. \tag{13.17}$$

This means that if no information is revealed, the expected profit of the entrant is large enough to cover the cost of entry. Knowing this the low-cost incumbent will be keen to reveal that he is a low type and make the entrant stay away because entry is truly unprofitable. But the high-cost incumbent will also have incentive to pretend that he is low type. Therefore, the low-cost incumbent will have to set the price in an incentive-compatible manner.

Given the condition in Eq. (13.17), prices$(p^*(c_1), p^*(c_2))$, where $p^*(c_2) = (A+c_2)/2$ and $p^*(c_1) = \tilde{p}$, form a separating equilibrium if the following incentive compatibility conditions are satisfied:

$$IC_1 : \pi(\tilde{p};c_1) + \delta\pi^M(c_1) \geq \pi(p^M(c_1)) + \delta\pi^D(c_1) \tag{13.18}$$

$$IC_2 : \pi^M(c_2) + \delta\pi^D(c_2) \geq \pi(\tilde{p};c_2) + \delta\pi^M(c_2). \tag{13.19}$$

These inequalities can be rewritten as follows:

$$IC_1 : \delta\Delta\pi(c_1) \equiv \underbrace{\delta[\pi^M(c_1) - \pi^D(c_1)]}_{\text{Future gain}} \geq \underbrace{\pi^M(c_1) - \pi(\tilde{p};c_1)}_{\text{Present loss}} \equiv \phi(\tilde{p}, c_1) \tag{13.20}$$

$$IC_2 : \phi(\tilde{p};c_2) \equiv \underbrace{\pi^M(c_2) - \pi(\tilde{p};c_2)}_{\text{Present gain}} \geq \underbrace{\delta[\pi^M(c_2) - \pi^D(c_2)]}_{\text{Future loss}} \equiv \delta\Delta\pi(c_2). \tag{13.21}$$

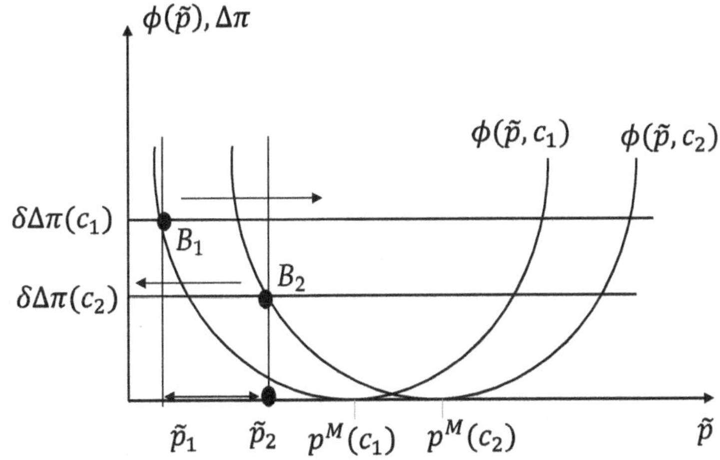

Figure 13.7 Signalling cost through limit pricing

The inequality in Eq. (13.18) states that the low-cost incumbent should distort the price from $p^M(c_1)$ to $\tilde{p}(c_1)$ and convince the entrant that he is facing the low-cost incumbent and hence should not enter, which then results in monopoly in the second period. By following this strategy, the low-cost incumbent gets a higher profit than by charging the standard monopoly price and inducing entry (because without updating his beliefs the entrant will enter). This translates into a comparison between future gain by protecting monopoly and the present loss of profit from a price distortion, which is shown by inequality (13.20).

The inequality in Eq. (13.19) states that the high-cost incumbent should set the standard monopoly price and allow entry instead of setting $\tilde{p}_1(c_1)$ and fooling the entrant to stay out of the market. Equivalently, as shown in the inequality in Eq. (13.21), the high-cost incumbent's present gain from charging the monopoly price (and thereby revealing his type) should be greater than the future loss of the profit from monopoly to duopoly.

Figure 13.7 demonstrates the two incentive compatibility constraints. The present value of the future gain for type c_1 is a flat line $\delta\Delta\pi(c_1)$, while its loss is a U-shaped curve $\phi(\tilde{p};c_1)$. The loss is zero if $\tilde{p} = p^M(c_1)$. For the gain to exceed the loss, $\tilde{p}$ must be at least $\tilde{p}_1$. That is, all prices in the interval $[\tilde{p}_1, p^M(c_1)]$ satisfy the incentive constraint (Eq. (13.20)). Notably, $p^M(c_1)$, the standard monopoly price is not believable, because the high-cost type can also set this price and be better off. Therefore, the low-cost incumbent must lower his price sufficiently below $p^M(c_1)$.[9]

Similarly, for type c_2, the present value of future loss is given by the flat line $\delta\Delta\pi(c_2)$, and the present gain is U-shaped as shown by the curve $\phi(\tilde{p};c_2)$. This gain is zero if $\tilde{p} = p^M(c_2)$. For the present gain to exceed the present value of the future loss, $\tilde{p}$ must be less than $\tilde{p}_2$.

Thus, both incentive constraints are satisfied only in the region between B_1 and B_2. Any price selected from the interval $[\tilde{p}_1, \tilde{p}_2]$ credibly conveys that it must have been set by the low-cost incumbent; the high-cost incumbent would find such a low price too costly for him. As expected, there are too many perfect Bayesian equilibria. However, from the set of the infinite prices from this interval, we select as a refinement the best Pareto-dominating price, that is, the highest price $\tilde{p}_2$.

Setting the inequality constraint (Eq. (13.21)) to equality, we write

$$\tilde{p}^2 - (A + c_2)\tilde{p} + Ac_2 + b\pi_a = 0,$$

where $\pi_a = (1-\delta)\pi^M(c_2) + \delta\pi^D(c_2)$. The solution to this equation gives $\tilde{p}_2$ as

$$\tilde{p}_2 = \frac{1}{2}\left[(A + c_2) - \sqrt{(A + c_2)^2 - 4(Ac_2 + b\pi_a)}\right]. \tag{13.22}$$

Under the assumption $r = c_2$ (i.e., when the entrant's MC is same as that of the high-cost incumbent), the above solution simplifies to

$$\tilde{p}_2 = \frac{1}{2}\left[A + c_2 - \frac{(A - c_2)}{3}\sqrt{5\delta}\right].$$

As long as δ is not too small (which is necessary to make signalling worthwhile), $\tilde{p}_2$ will be strictly less than $p^M(c_1)$.[10]

Now let us also discuss the entrant's beliefs that underpin his entry strategy and, in turn, the incumbent's expectation of the entrant's play. In the incentive constraints (Eq. (13.18)), it is assumed that the entrant will not enter if $\tilde{p}$ is played and the entrant will enter if $p^M(c_1)$ is played. In Eq. (13.19), almost the same is assumed except that $p^M(c_2)$ replaced $p^M(c_1)$. Here, the entrant is updating his belief about the incumbent's type, which we write as

$$\beta(c_2 \mid \tilde{p}) = \frac{\text{Prob.}(\tilde{p} \mid c_2) \times \text{Prob.}(c_2)}{\text{Prob.}(\tilde{p})}.$$

In the posterior $\beta(.)$, the probability of c_2 is α, and the probability of playing $\tilde{p}$ is part of the incumbent's strategy. In equilibrium, as we have ascertained earlier the incumbent will play $\tilde{p}_2$ if he is type c_1 and $p^M(c_2)$ if he is type c_2. Therefore, in equilibrium,

$$\beta(c_2 \mid \tilde{p}_2) = \frac{\text{Prob.}(\tilde{p}_2 \mid c_2) \times \text{Prob.}(c_2)}{\text{Prob.}(\tilde{p}_2)} = \frac{0 \cdot \alpha}{1 - \alpha} = 0 \quad \text{and} \quad \beta(c_1 \mid \tilde{p}_2) = 1 - \beta(c_2 \mid \tilde{p}_2) = 1.$$

In addition to the equilibrium beliefs, we also need to specify the entrant's beliefs for off-the-equilibrium path of play. That is, if he observes some price other than $\tilde{p}_2$ and $p^M(c_2)$ he must need to form a belief about the incumbent's type.[11] We are going to assume that if $p \neq \tilde{p}_2$, the entrant will assume that the incumbent is type c_2 with probability 1. Given this out-of-equilibrium belief of the entrant, the incumbent of type c_1 will not deviate from $\tilde{p}_2$.

Now we state our equilibrium in the following proposition.

Proposition 39. *Suppose the condition in Eq. (13.17) holds. The following first-period prices*

$$p^*(c_1) = \tilde{p}_2 \quad \text{and} \quad p^*(c_2) = \frac{A + c_2}{2},$$

along with the entrant's updated beliefs $\beta(c_2 \mid \tilde{p}_2) = 0$ *and* $\beta(c_2 \mid p \neq \tilde{p}_2) = 1$, *form the information revealing the perfect Bayesian equilibrium of the entry game. In particular,* $\tilde{p}_2$ *is the limit price that deters entry by perfectly signalling the low-cost incumbent's type.*

13.6.3.2 POOLING EQUILIBRIUM

What if the entrant's priors are such that the condition in Eq. (13.17) is reversed? That is, he is generally pessimistic about the profitability of entry. That is, $\alpha R(r \mid c_2) + (1-\alpha)R(r \mid c_1) < 0$. Unless his priors are updated, he will stay away. In this case, the low-cost incumbent has no incentive to signal his type, while the high-cost incumbent has the incentive to hide his type. In simple terms, inequality in Eq. (13.19) (or equivalently, Eq. (13.21)) needs to be reversed, while the incentive constraint in Eq. (13.18) (or equivalently, Eq. (13.20)) becomes irrelevant.

There are many prices in the interval $[\tilde{p}_2, p^M(c_2)]$ that can be seen as non-revealing price. The most interesting one and Pareto-dominant (for type c_1) is $p^M(c_1)$. If both types set $p = p^M(c_1)$, the entrant cannot make out whether it is played by the low-cost type or the high-cost type, and therefore, going by his priors, he will stay away. Note in Figure 13.7 $p^M(c_1)$, which gives the highest profit to the low-cost-type incumbent (as his loss becomes zero), allows the high-cost-type incumbent to pretend that he is low type.

Once again, we need to specify the out-of-equilibrium beliefs. If we say that any price strictly less than $p^M(c_1)$ will induce the entrant to believe that he is facing a low-cost incumbent and that any price strictly above $p^M(c_1)$ will make him believe that he is facing a high-cost incumbent, then the pooling equilibrium holds.

Proposition 40. *Suppose* $\alpha R(r \mid c_2) + (1-\alpha)R(r \mid c_1) < 0$. *Then* $p^*(c_1) = p^*(c_2) = p^M(c_1)$ *is information non-revealing perfect Bayesian equilibrium, provided the entrant holds the following beliefs:*

$$\beta(c_2 \mid p) = \begin{cases} 1 & \text{if} \quad p > p^M(c_1) \\ \alpha & \text{if} \quad p = p^M(c_1) \\ 0 & \text{if} \quad p < p^M(c_1) \end{cases}.$$

Considering the welfare implications of the two different equilibria, separating and pooling, we see that in both cases entry is deterred, *albeit* for different reasons. Under separating equilibrium, the outcome is the same as that under full information: entry is restricted only when entry should not occur. Thus, the separating equilibrium restores the full information welfare. Under pooling equilibrium entry is restricted when it would not have been under full information. Thus, the pooling equilibrium is welfare-reducing. The high-cost incumbent is able to protect his informational advantage and secures rent by restricting entry.

13.7 Strategic delegation

That a duopolist firm produces more than its rival despite being otherwise identical is a theme that goes beyond the Stackelberg model. Economist William Baumol observed that for corporate firms, sales were more important than profit, and therefore, he proposed a *sales maximisation hypothesis* to capture the behaviours of modern corporations. As these organisations are run by professional managers and not the shareholders directly, a different type of firm behaviour emerges. While in managerial economics a number of reasons have been proposed to explain why managers are given strong incentives to increase sales, in oligopoly theory, a particular line of argument gained ground after the writings of Vickers (1985), Fershtman and Judd (1987) and Sklivas (1987). These authors argued that there is a distinction between the shareholders' goal and the firm's behaviour. While shareholders still want to achieve maximum profit, they try to achieve this goal by instructing the manager to maximise sales. This seemingly contradictory instruction actually induces the manager to steal market from the rival firms and help raise profits for the shareholders. Of course, you can expect that when all firms try to do the same, there will be overproduction and incentivising the manager to maximise sales can be self-defeating. While broadly this is true, there are some nuances to this argument. A lot depends on whether the firms are playing Cournot or Bertrand and whether their input suppliers are also incentivising their managers or not. In the following, we present a generalised version of the Fershtman and Judd (1987) model based on Chatterjee and Saha (2017), which is an extension of the delegation model presented in Chapter 12.

13.7.1 A model of bilateral delegation and duopoly

Two identical firms, indexed 1 and 2, use labour as the only input and produce an identical good through a concave production function $q = q(l)$. Assume that their sales revenues satisfy the following restrictions for $i \neq j, i, j = 1,2$.

Assumption 11.

(1) Two goods are substitutes: $\frac{\partial R_i}{\partial l_j} < 0$. *(2) The revenue functions are concave:* $\frac{\partial^2 R_i}{\partial l_i^2} < 0$. *(3) The second-order cross partial derivatives are negative, that is,* $\frac{\partial^2 R_i}{\partial l_i \partial l_j} < 0$, *to ensure that employments are strategic substitutes.*

Workers of firm i come from a union of size N_i. If the employment level is l_i, then l_i workers are randomly drawn for employment, who then receive a wage of w_i each, while the remaining workers receive a reservation wage $\underline{w}$. Union i's objective is to maximise the net wage bill of an average worker $u_i = (w_i - \underline{w})l_i$. Furthermore, union i appoints a union leader and instructs him to maximise:

$$y_i = \rho_i u_i(.) + (1-\rho_i)w_i l_i = w_i l_i - \rho_i \underline{w} l_i. \tag{13.23}$$

As in Chapter 12, delegation is captured by $\rho_i \neq 1$. Deviation from $\rho_i = 1$ represents orientation to net or gross wage bill maximisation.

On the firm side, there is a similar delegation effort. Shareholders in each firm who care for profit $R_i - w_i l_i$ hire a manager and instruct him to maximise a linear combination of sales R_i and profit π_i as shown by the following function:

$$z_i = \mu_i \pi_i + (1-\mu_i)R_i(.) = R_i(.) - \mu_i w_i l_i. \tag{13.24}$$

Here, too, delegation refers to the case when μ_i deviates from 1. *Downward deviation* refers to sales maximisation, while *upward deviation* means profit maximisation.

Wage and employment or output are determined through 'efficient bargaining' in both firms. The bargaining power of the union leader is α, $0 \leq \alpha \leq 1$, and that of the manager is$(1-\alpha)$. The reservation pay-offs of all parties are zero. Note that this bargaining power configuration is the same across firms. This is justified when bargaining power is largely derived from labour institutions, such as labour laws, rules and regulations. One can allow for different $\alpha - s$ in different firms when the firms are located far apart, or they operate in different sectors while producing the same good as often seen in developing countries. But analysis becomes more complex, although qualitatively, the results should not change much.

As can be seen, this is a model of duopoly with endogenous wage choice via two-sided delegation. Each firm–union pair holds a shared Cournot conjecture about their rival pair's wage and employment; that is, pair i assumes that pair j holds a combination of w_j and l_j as given while choosing their own combination. The game is a two-stage game, in which stage 1 involves simultaneously hiring delegates and setting ρ_i and μ_i by the unions and shareholders, respectively. In stage 2, bargaining takes place between the delegates, and all pay-offs are determined. Managers receive a fixed salary, which is normalised to zero.[12]

13.7.1.1 *Optimal wages and outputs*

As we solve the game by backward induction, the stage 2 game of efficient bargaining is solved first when the incentive schemes (ρ_i, μ_i) are given from stage 1. We maximise $B_i = y_i(w_i, l_i)^{\alpha} z_i(w_i, l_i)^{(1-\alpha)}$ with respect to(w_i, l_i). The implicit solution is given by the following two pairs of equations:[13]

$$\frac{\partial R_i(l_i, l_j)}{\partial l_i} = \mu_i \rho_i \underline{w}, \qquad i = 1,2 \tag{13.25}$$

$$w_i = (1-\alpha)\rho_i \underline{w} + \alpha \frac{R_i}{\mu_i l_i}, \quad i = 1,2. \tag{13.26}$$

Note that due to efficient bargaining employment is solved independently of wages. Furthermore, the employment Eq. (13.25) involves the product of $\mu_i \rho_i$. Therefore, our employment solution, and thereby, the outputs are

$$l_i = l_i(\mu_1 \rho_1, \mu_2 \rho_2), \qquad q_i = q_i(\mu_1 \rho_1, \mu_2 \rho_2) \quad \text{for} \qquad i = 1,2.$$

It is easy to check that $\frac{\partial l_i}{\partial \mu_i} < 0$, $\frac{\partial l_i}{\partial \rho_i} < 0$ and$\frac{\partial l_i}{\partial \mu_j} > 0 \frac{\partial l_i}{\partial \rho_j} > 0, i \neq j$. As for wages, Eq. (13.26) shows that they are a weighted average of 'incentive adjusted' reservation wage and average revenue product.

13.7.1.2 Optimal incentives

Before we solve the optimal incentive problem of stage 1, it is instructive to see how incentives of either side contribute to the profit and wage variations when wage and employment are bargained over. For that, we rewrite profit and the union's utility in the following way:

$$\begin{aligned}\pi_i &= R_i\left(1-\frac{\alpha}{\mu_i}\right)-(1-\alpha)\underline{w}\rho_i l_i \\ &= (R_i-\underline{w}l_i)-\underbrace{\alpha\left(\frac{R_i}{\mu_i}-\underline{w}\rho_i l_i\right)}_{\text{due to bargaining}}-\underbrace{(\rho_i-1)\underline{w}l_i}_{\text{due to union delegation}}\end{aligned} \tag{13.27}$$

$$\begin{aligned}u_i &= \left(R_i\frac{\alpha}{\mu_i}+(1-\alpha)\underline{w}\rho_i l_i\right)-\underline{w}l_i \\ &= \underbrace{\alpha\left(\frac{R_i}{\mu_i}-\underline{w}\rho_i l_i\right)}_{\text{due to bargaining}}+\underbrace{(\rho_i-1)\underline{w}l_i}_{\text{due to union delegation}}.\end{aligned} \tag{13.28}$$

Eq. (13.27) can be seen as a profit decomposition. The standard case of no delegation and no bargaining is captured by the first term. This is the first-best profit or surplus, and this is why it is also the bargaining pie. The second term shows to what extent the first-best profit is reduced due to wage bargaining (when negotiations take place between delegates). The third term shows how a union-side delegation further reduces profit. Eq. (13.28) decomposes the union's pay-off. The base pay-off is zero, which occurs if there was no delegation and no bargaining. The first term of Eq. (13.28) shows the contribution of bargaining (between delegates), and the second term shows the specific contribution of hiring a delegate. The two equations show what the firm's loses becomes the union's gain:

$$\pi_i + u_i = (R_i - \underline{w}l_i).$$

Now the following observations can be made about optimal incentives:

1. Since in equilibrium profit must be non-negative, we must have

$$\mu_i \geq \frac{\alpha R_i}{R_i-(1-\alpha)\underline{w}\rho_i l_i} > \alpha.$$

   That is, the firm-side optimal incentive μ_i must be bounded below. In particular, when $\alpha = 1$, that is, the union has all the bargaining power, μ_i must exceed 1, suggesting that the firm must resort to 'profit orientation'. However, if $\alpha = 0$, that is, when the firm has all the bargaining power, μ_i has no role to play in wage bargaining. Therefore, when $\alpha = 0$, the only purpose of hiring managers is strategic, that is, to capture the market from the rival firm.

2. When seeking advantage in wage bargaining is the sole objective of delegation, the shareholders should set $\mu_i > 1$, and the union should set $\rho_i > 1$. These objectives are to be read from the instances of $\alpha = 0$ for the union and $\alpha = 1$ for the firm. Each side would then try to 'produce less', which runs against the strategic motive of duopoly. Conversely, if the firm or the union wants to exert strategic motive, they have to sacrifice a bit on the wage-bargaining front. The two motives, bargaining (internal to the firm) and strategic (stealing the rival's market), inherently contradict each other.
3. When a side is at its zero bargaining power, it can guarantee a strictly positive profit by resorting to delegation: $\pi_i(\alpha = 1) > 0$ if $\mu_i > 1$, and $u_i(\alpha = 0) > 0$ if $\rho_i > 1$. Thus, delegation also acts as a substitute for low bargaining power.

Now let us derive the optimal incentives by considering the stage 1 problem. Given (ρ_i, μ_j, ρ_j), the shareholders of firm i maximise Eq. (13.27). The first-order condition for profit maximisation can be written (utilising Eq. (13.25)) for $i = 1,2$ and $i \neq j$ as

$$\frac{\partial \pi_i}{\partial \mu_i} = \frac{1}{\mu_i^2}\underbrace{\left[\left\{\mu_i^2(\mu_i - 1)\rho_i \underline{w}\right\}\frac{\partial l_i}{\partial \mu_i} + \alpha R_i\right]}_{\text{Bargaining effect }(>0)} + \underbrace{\left(1 - \frac{\alpha}{\mu_i}\right)\frac{\partial R_i}{\partial l_j}\frac{\partial l_j}{\partial \mu_i}}_{\text{Strategic effect }(<0)} = 0, \tag{13.29}$$

Just as profit can be decomposed, the marginal effect of incentive on profit can also be decomposed in two distinct parts. The first terms in Eq. (13.29) shows the direct distributional effect, which we call the bargaining effect of delegation, and the second term shows the indirect effect that occurs through the employment choice of the rival firm and then transmitted back via duopoly competition. The second effect is negative, as an increase in μ_i leads to an increase in l_j, which, in turn, reduces marginal profit. But the first effect, which is entirely a distributional/ bargaining effect, must be positive. Although an increase in μ_i reduces l_i and thus creates some ambiguity about the bargaining effect, the optimal incentive μ must rise above or fall below 1 in accordance with high or low values of α.

The union of firm 1 designs incentives for its union leader by maximising its utility as given in Eq. (13.28) by taking (μ_i, μ_j, ρ_j) as given. Their first-order condition for optimal incentive, as shown in the following, can also be broken into two effects, namely, the bargaining effect and the strategic effect, which are very similar to the firm's marginal incentive effects, except for their interaction with the bargaining power:

$$\frac{\partial u_i}{\partial \rho_i} = \underline{w}\underbrace{\left[(\rho_i - 1)\frac{\partial l_i}{\partial \rho_i} + (1-\alpha)l_i\right]}_{\text{Bargaining effect}(>0)} + \underbrace{\frac{\alpha}{\mu_i}\frac{\partial R_i}{\partial l_j}\frac{\partial l_j}{\partial \rho_i}}_{\text{Strategic effect}(<0)} = 0. \tag{13.30}$$

Note that in the extreme case, where the unions have no bargaining power, the strategic effect of their incentive disappears. Their decision to delegate will then be entirely motivated by rent sharing. In contrast, the strategic effect of the firm-side incentive never disappears.

Next, we analyse the equilibrium incentives and their implications for duopoly for three cases.

Case 1: Only the shareholders delegate; unions don't

Let us assume that $\rho_1 = \rho_2 = 1$ is given exogenously, while μ is chosen by the shareholders in both firms. This is the standard case of strategic delegation proposed by Fershtman and Judd (1987). Our version also includes bargaining, as was the case in Szymanski (1994).[14] From Eq. (13.29) we determine the symmetric equilibrium incentive $\mu^*(\alpha)$. It can be shown that $\partial\mu^* / \partial\alpha > 0$. When α is sufficiently small, that is, the bargaining effect is insignificant, the shareholders will instruct the managers to maximise sales. This is the case where Baumol's hypothesis about corporations holds. The following proposition also tells us that the tendency to encourage sales maximisation is the strongest when the shareholders can keep the entire amount of rent with itself.

Proposition 41. *There exists a critical* α, *say* $\hat{\alpha}$ *such that at* $\alpha > \hat{\alpha}$, *a firm's optimal incentive is* $\mu^*(\alpha) > 1$ *(profit orientation) and at* $\alpha < \hat{\alpha}$, *it sets* $\mu^*(\alpha) < 1$ *(sales orientation).*

From Eq. (13.29), it is clear that when $\alpha = 0$, the only way the bargaining effect can be positive (and thus the equation can be satisfied) only if $\mu^* < 1$. Alternatively, when $\alpha = 1$, we must have $\mu^* > 1$ as has been noted earlier that the equilibrium μ always exceeds α. Then, by continuity and monotonicity of μ^*, the critical value of α, namely, $\hat{\mu}$, must exist and that it is generically unique.

Case 2: Only the unions delegate; shareholders don't

What about the polar opposite case of only union delegating? Let us set $\mu = 1$ in Eq. (13.30) and solve for the symmetric equilibrium incentive $\rho^*(\alpha)$. Here, too, it can be verified that $\rho^*(\alpha)$ is monotonic and continuous, but it will be a strictly declining function of α. Although the union delegation is largely motivated for rent sharing, unions are not entirely shy of playing a strategic role vis-à-vis the rival firm–union pair. In particular, when the union is sufficiently powerful and assured of capturing most of the rents, it will push for wage-bill maximisation, which is equivalent to sales maximisation.

Proposition 42. *If the unions' bargaining power is above a critical level, say,* $\tilde{\alpha}$, *then the unions will set* $\rho^*(\alpha) < 1$ *and if* $\alpha < \tilde{\alpha}$ *they choose* $\rho^*(\alpha) > 1$. *Furthermore,* $\rho^*(\alpha = 1) = \mu^*(\alpha = 0)$.

By examining Eqs. (13.29) and (13.30), we see that if we set $\alpha = 0$ in Eq. (13.29) and $\alpha = 1$ in Eq. (13.30), we get exactly identical equations:

$$(\alpha = 0; \rho_i = 1): \ \underline{w}(\mu_i - 1)\frac{\partial l_i}{\partial \mu_i} + \frac{\partial R_i}{\partial l_j}\frac{\partial l_j}{\partial \mu_i} = 0,$$

$$(\alpha = 1; \mu_i = 1): \ \underline{w}(\rho_i - 1)\frac{\partial l_i}{\partial \rho_i} + \frac{\partial R_i}{\partial l_j}\frac{\partial l_j}{\partial \rho_i} = 0.$$

Case 3: Bilateral delegation

The combined case of both parties engaging in delegation unsurprisingly reflects a tension between within-firm rent sharing and outward-looking market-stealing strategy. Roughly speaking, the stronger of the two parties will go for market stealing, and the weaker party will go for rent capturing. Therefore, there is a check on the scale of market stealing that a firm or union can do. We should expect to see the employment and output of a firm expand beyond the standard duopoly level when α is either very high or very low and contract when α has an intermediate value. The contraction can potentially reach the collusive level.

Proposition 43. *When all firms and unions delegate, the symmetric incentive equilibrium is such that at a sufficiently small* α*, we have* $\mu^*(\alpha) < 1$ *and* $\rho^*(\alpha) > 1$*, and exactly the opposite holds at a sufficiently large* α*. At some intermediate value of* α*, the output can contract, and the total rent can rise to the collusive level.*

Example

From Chatterjee and Saha (2017), we can quote an example: $p = 2 - q_1 - q_2$, $q = l$ and $\underline{w} = 1$. Here, the collusive industry profit is 0.25, of which each firm gets 0.125. Each firm's non-collusive standard Cournot profit is 0.111. These two benchmarks are invariant to α because they do not involve delegation. It can be computed that with bilateral delegation each firm's surplus remains above the Cournot level of 0.111 at all α and even rises to the collusive level of 0.125 at $\alpha = 0.42$.

The bottom line of strategic delegation is that even though in a quantity setting game firms become aggressive to their rivals and tend to overproduce, such aggression can turn into implicitly collusive gestures when the firms face internal rent-sharing threats. In a price-setting game, Fershtman and Judd (1987) showed that delegation leads to implicit collusion even without any unions or threats of rent sharing.

Therefore, the two incentive terms in these two polar opposite cases are mirror images of each other. Therefore, one can argue that in duopolies, the market stealing incentives are strong for both firms and unions. Whoever is assured of retaining a large part of the rent will engage in market-stealing activities like sales maximisation.

13.8 The Hotelling model of spatial competition

Although most of our discussion has centred on homogeneous goods, we did allow for product differentiation, which enabled us to directly compare price competition with quantity competition. However, there, product differentiation is given exogenously, mainly through the segregation of demands. Hotelling (1929) proposed a model of spatial competition where consumers reside on a straight line and two stores are located on the same line. Consumers travel to one of the stores at their own cost. If prices are the same, travelling to a nearer store gives a lower cost of consumption. In turn, stores have an incentive to locate near the biggest concentration of consumers.

The linear city of Hotelling can be seen as an analogy of product differentiation. The distance between the stores reflects the extent of their product differentiation. Since the location choice is endogenous, product differentiation is also endogenous. Furthermore, a consumer's distance from her nearest store also reflects how much compromise the consumer has to make from her most preferred variety. Two key questions are of interest here: First, what are the equilibrium locations of the two firms? Will they locate next to each other or far apart? Second, what is the socially optimal location and how can it be achieved?

We consider a standard linear city of length of 1 mile, along which consumers are uniformly distributed. The total mass of consumers is 1. Each consumer demands exactly 1 unit of the good. There are two identical firms, 1 and 2, producing a good at marginal cost c. Let us call the left-located firm, firm 1, and the right-located firm, firm 2. We will denote the location of firm 1 by l and the location of firm 2 by $1 - r$; by definition, $l < 1 - r$. Thus, $l = 1/3$ and $r = 2/5$ refer to the configuration where firm 1 is located a third of a mile away from the left corner and firm 2 is two-fifths of a mile away from the right corner. When $l = r = 1/2$, both firms are at the midpoint.

As consumer's utility from buying 1 unit of the good is independent of the stores it is bought from the travel cost matters. Let us assume that their travel cost is quadratic in distance between their residence location, $x \in [0,1]$, and the store location $y_i, y_i = \{l, 1-r\}$. That is, the travel cost of a consumer located at x is $T(x) = t(y_i - x)^2$ where t is exogenously given. Here, it is worth pointing out that the symmetry assumed in the quadratic cost function can be imposed also by a linear modulus function, such as $t \mid y_i - x \mid$, but the linear cost function has some technical issues concerning the existence of a pure-strategy equilibrium. Hence, we just restrict ourselves to the quadratic cost function. A relatively minor issue is that we need to assume that all consumers get sufficiently large utility to make a trip to the farthest store worthwhile. This is known as the full market-coverage assumption. This assumption along with the uniform distribution assumption implies that the total market demand and the combined total sales of the two stores are both 1 unit. This means that each firm's sale is just equal to its market share.

The game is as follows: In the first stage, two firms simultaneously decide where to locate subject to the constraint $l \leq 1-r$. In the second stage, they simultaneously announce their prices p_1 and p_2. Consumers learn about the prices at zero cost, and they select the store/firm they want to go to. All demands are met instantly.

13.8.1 Demand

We will solve the game by backward induction. Therefore, assuming a given configuration of the firm locations (l, r), we first derive each firm's demand. It is easy to see that if both firms are located in the same place, then whoever charges the lower price will get the full market; otherwise, the market will be divided equally between them. But if they are at different locations and they announce the same price, then all consumers to the left of firm 1 will buy from firm 1 and all consumers located to the right of firm 2 will buy from firm 2, and the consumers located in between will be split equally. Thus, there is a consumer at the midpoint of the two store locations who will be indifferent. But note that the point of indifference is sensitive to the prices the stores announce. So we need to define the indifferent consumer for any arbitrary price pairs.

Suppose the price pair announced is (p_1, p_2) and $\hat{x}$ is the location of the indifferent consumer. Then $\hat{x}$ must be such that the total cost, that is, the travel cost and the price paid, must be the same between the two stores:

$$p_1 + t(l - \hat{x})^2 = p_2 + t(1 - r - \hat{x})^2$$

or $$t\left[l^2 - (1-r)^2 - 2\hat{x}(l - 1 + r)\right] = p_2 - p_1$$

or $$t(1 - r - l)\left[2\hat{x} - l + (1-r)\right] = p_2 - p_1$$

or $$\hat{x} = \frac{1 - r + l}{2} + \frac{p_2 - p_1}{2t(1 - r - l)}$$

All consumers located to the left of $\hat{x}$ will buy from firm 1 and all others will buy from firm 2. Since we have assumed a uniform distribution of the consumers and each of them buying 1 unit of the good, firm 1's aggregate demand is just $\hat{x}$, and firm 2's aggregate demand is $1-\hat{x}$. So, we write

$$
\begin{aligned}
q_1 &= \frac{(l+1-r)}{2} + \frac{(p_2 - p_1)}{2t(1-l-r)} \\
q_2 &= \frac{(1-l+r)}{2} + \frac{(p_1 - p_2)}{2t(1-l-r)}.
\end{aligned}
\tag{13.31}
$$

If the firms charge an identical price, they split the market at their midpoint. But the position of the indifferent consumer will move to right (of the midpoint) if $p_2 > p_1$ and to the left if $p_1 > p_2$. In the first case, firm 1's market share increases, and the opposite happens in the second case. Since q_1 and q_2 are market shares, they must obey the natural restrictions $0 \le q_1 \le 1$ and $0 \le q_2 \le 1$. These restrictions imply the following:

1. If $p_2 < p_1 + t[(1-l)^2 - r^2]$, $q_1 < 1$ and $q_2 > 0$.
2. If $p_2 > p_1 - t[(1-r)^2 - l^2]$, $q_2 < 1$ and $q_1 > 0$.
3. If $p_1 - t[(1-r)^2 - l^2] < p_2 < p_1 + t[(1-l)^2 - r^2]$, $0 < q_1, q_2 < 1$.

We would assume that price competition between the two firms results in the two prices falling in the preceding interval.[15]

13.8.2 Price competition

The firms simultaneously maximise their profits $\pi_i = (p_i - c)q_i(p_i)$ and announce p_i. Their first-order conditions are (assuming $l < 1-r$):

$$
\begin{aligned}
\frac{\partial \pi_1}{\partial p_1} &= -\frac{p_1 - c}{2t(1-l-r)} + \frac{(l+1-r)}{2} + \frac{(p_2 - p_1)}{2t(1-l-r)} = 0 \\
\frac{\partial \pi_2}{\partial p_2} &= -\frac{p_2 - c}{2t(1-l-r)} + \frac{(1-l+r)}{2} + \frac{(p_1 - p_2)}{2t(1-l-r)} = 0.
\end{aligned}
$$

Denoting $a \equiv (1-l)^2 - r^2$ and $b \equiv (1-r)^2 - l^2$, we write the price reaction curves of the two firms as

$$
p_1 = \frac{c}{2} + \frac{tb}{2} + \frac{p_2}{2} \tag{13.32}
$$

$$
p_2 = \frac{c}{2} + \frac{ta}{2} + \frac{p_1}{2}. \tag{13.33}
$$

Note that the price reaction curves shift upward as the firms' individual locations move inside, that is, when l or r increases, respectively, for firm 1 and 2 maintaining the inequality $l < 1-r$. When the locations of the two firms are identical, that is, $l = 1-r$, the price reaction curve of the ith firm is $p_j - \epsilon$, provided $p_j - \epsilon \ge c$.

Proposition 44. *In the price setting stage, if the firms are located at the same position, that is,* $l = 1 - r$, *the equilibrium price is* $p_1^* = p_2^* = c$. *If the firms are located at different positions, that is,* $l < 1 - r$ *then their equilibrium prices are*

$$p_1^* = c + \frac{t}{3}[a + 2b], \quad \text{and} \quad p_2^* = c + \frac{t}{3}[2a + b]. \tag{13.34}$$

The equilibrium prices are obtained by solving Eqs. (13.32) and (13.33) assuming $l < 1 - r$. Of course, if they are located at the same position, the usual Bertrand argument holds and firms end up charging their marginal cost. These equilibrium prices correspond to the case in which both firms have a strictly positive market share. Here, too, there is a possibility of limit pricing, but we do not go into the questions of entry or exit.

To derive the firms' equilibrium outputs and profits, we first note that

$$p_2^* - p_1^* = \frac{2}{3}t\left[(1-r)r - l(1-l)\right].$$

The equilibrium outputs are then

$$\begin{aligned} q_1^* &= \frac{l+1-r}{2} + \frac{p_2^* - p_1^*}{2t(1-l-r)} \\ &= \frac{1-r+l}{2} + \frac{(1-r)r-(1-l)l}{3(1-l-r)} \\ &= \frac{1}{6(1-l-r)}\left[3(1-r)^2 - 3l^2 + 2(1-r)r - 2(1-l)l\right] \\ &= \frac{1}{6(1-l-r)}\left[(3-r)(1-r) - l(2+l)\right] \\ &= \frac{1}{6(1-l-r)}\left[a+2b\right] \text{ and} \end{aligned}$$

$$\begin{aligned} q_2^* &= \frac{1-l+r}{2} + \frac{p_1^* - p_2^*}{2t(1-r-l} \\ &= \frac{1-l+r}{2} + \frac{l(1-l)-(1-r)r}{3(1-l-r)} \\ &= \frac{1}{6(1-l-r)}\left[(3-l)(1-l) - r(2+r)\right] \\ &= \frac{1}{6(1-l-r)}\left[2a+b\right]. \end{aligned}$$

Consequently, the equilibrium profits are

$$\pi_1^* = \frac{t\left[a+2b\right]^2}{18(1-l-r)}, \quad \text{and} \quad \pi_2^* = \frac{t\left[2a+b\right]^2}{18(1-l-r)}. \tag{13.35}$$

Moving on to the first stage of the game, firms maximise their profits as given in Eq. (13.35) with respect to l and r, respectively. It is clear that

$$\frac{\partial \pi_1^*}{\partial l} = \frac{t[a+2b]}{18(1-l-r)^2} \times [-4(1+l)(1-l-r)+(3-r)(1-r)-l(2+l)]$$
$$= \frac{t[a+2b]}{18(1-l-r)^2} \times \left[\underbrace{-1-2l\{(1-r)-l\}+(l+r)^2}_{<0 \ \ (\text{since } \ l+r \le 1)} \right] < 0.$$

Symmetrically,

$$\frac{\partial \pi_2^*}{\partial r} = \frac{t[2a+b]}{18(1-l-r)^2} \times \left[-1-2r\{(1-l)-r\}+(l+r)^2 \right] < 0.$$

Therefore, the optimal choice of location is 0 for firm 1 and 1 for firm 2 (recall that its location is $1-r$).

Proposition 45. *In the location-choice stage, firms will locate themselves at the two ends of the linear city (as $l^* = r^* = 0$). Following their location choice, the firms set $p_1^* = p_2^* = c+t$, earn profit $\pi_1 = \pi_2 = t/2$ and share the market equally.*

The intuition behind the preceding equilibrium is that when firms are going to compete in terms of prices, they know that their profit will be significantly diminished if they locate close to each other. Therefore, by locating far apart the firms manage to reduce the intensity of (price) competition. Put differently, by differentiating their products to the maximal extent, the firms are able to make the competition less damaging.

13.8.3 Socially optimal locations

Is the maximal differentiation achieved in a duopoly equilibrium the right one from society's point of view? As the aggregate welfare depends only on the travel cost, the socially optimal locations of the firms must be such that the aggregate travel cost is reduced to a minimum.

To determine the socially optimal locations, we introduce a social planner who directs the firms to the travel cost–minimising locations. Firms, once located in those places, compete with the prices as modelled earlier. We begin with the aggregate travel cost as

$$TC = t\left[\int_0^{\hat{x}} (l-x)^2 dx + \int_{\hat{x}}^1 (1-r-x)^2 dx \right],$$
$$= -\frac{t}{3}\left[(l-\hat{x})^3 - l^3 - r^3 - (1-r-\hat{x})^3 \right] \tag{13.36}$$

where $\hat{x}$ is a function of l and r from the second-stage competition (as already derived):

$$\hat{x}(l,r) = q_1^* = \frac{a+2b}{6(1-l-r)}.$$

If we minimise TC with respect to l and r, respectively, we get the following first-order conditions:

$$\frac{\partial TC}{\partial l}=-t\left[\frac{\partial \hat{x}}{\partial l}\left\{(1-r-\hat{x})^2-(l-\hat{x})^2\right\}-\left\{l^2-(l-\hat{x})^2\right\}\right]=0$$

$$\frac{\partial TC}{\partial r}=-t\left[\frac{\partial \hat{x}}{\partial r}\left\{(1-r-\hat{x})^2-(l-\hat{x})^2\right\}-\left\{r^2-(1-r-\hat{x})^2\right\}\right]=0.$$

Note that the indifferent consumer $\hat{x}$ finds the travel cost to either firm to be same. Since $(1-r-\hat{x})^2=(l-\hat{x})^2$, in both of these equations, we must have

$$l^2=(l-\hat{x})^2 \Rightarrow l=\hat{x}-l, \Rightarrow \hat{x}=2l,$$

$$\text{and } r^2=(1-r-\hat{x})^2, \Rightarrow \hat{x}=1-2r.$$

$\hat{x}=2l$ and $\hat{x}=1-2r$ are both simultaneously possible if and only if $l=r=1/4$.

Under the socially optimal locations $l=r=1/4$, no consumer will have to travel more than a quarter of the length of the city, so the total transportation cost is minimised at $t/48$. The equilibrium locations, however, give a total transportation cost of $t/12$ (you can easily check this). Thus, the oligopoly equilibrium creates too much differentiation and creates a welfare loss.

13.8.3.1 *Mixed duopoly*

Given the observation that a market equilibrium fails to produce socially optimal product differentiation, one wonders how to achieve it. One solution is to have public ownership in one firm. As the public firm cares about social welfare and thus will choose the socially optimum location, the other firm (which is fully private) will respond to it by distancing itself to the most profitable extent, which also turns out to be 'socially right'. This is the intuition. We formally present this argument following Kumar and Saha (2008).

Suppose firm 2 has θ proportion of its ownership in private hands and $1-\theta$ proportion vested with the government. Its objective function is then a weighted average of social welfare and profit, where social welfare is just the negative of the travel cost:

$$W_2=\theta\pi_2-(1-\theta)TC.$$

The objective function of firm 1 is as before given by profit. The price reaction function of firm 1 remains unchanged from Eq. (13.32), while that of the public firm significantly changes. To see how firm 2's reaction function changes, let us derive it by separately differentiating TC and then combining it with the derivative of π_2 (which we derived earlier).

Let us recall $\hat{x}=\dfrac{1-r+l}{2}+\dfrac{p_2-p_1}{2t(1-r-l)}$ and

$$TC=-\frac{t}{3}\left[(l-\hat{x})^3-l^3-r^3-(1-r-\hat{x})^3\right].$$

Differentiating TC with respect to p_2, we obtain

$$\frac{\partial TC}{\partial p_2} = -t\left[-(l-\hat{x})^2 + (1-r-\hat{x})^2\right]\frac{\partial \hat{x}}{\partial p_2}$$
$$= -\frac{1}{2(1-l-r)}\left[-(l-\hat{x})^2 + (1-r-\hat{x})^2\right].$$

Furthermore, substituting the expression for $\hat{x}$, we get

$$(1-r-\hat{x})^2 - (l-\hat{x})^2$$
$$= \left(\frac{1-r-l}{2} - \frac{p_2-p_1}{2t(1-l-r)}\right)^2 - \left(\frac{l-1+r}{2} - \frac{p_2-p_1}{2t(1-l-r)}\right)^2$$
$$= \frac{(1-r-l)^2}{4} - \frac{(l-1+r)^2}{4} - \frac{p_2-p_1}{t} = -\frac{p_2-p_1}{t}.$$

Thus,

$$\frac{\partial TC}{\partial p_2} = \frac{p_2-p_1}{2t(1-l-r)}.$$

By setting the preceding expression equal to zero, we see that a fully public firm's price reaction function is $p_2 = p_1$[16] For a partially public firm, $0 < \theta < 1$, the price reaction function is obtained from

$$\frac{\partial W_2}{\partial p_2} = \theta\frac{\partial \pi_2}{\partial p_2} - (1-\theta)\frac{\partial TC}{\partial p_2} = 0.$$

If we write out this derivative, then

$$\frac{\partial W_2}{\partial p_2} = \frac{1}{t(1-l-r)}\left[\theta\left\{-p_2 + \frac{c}{2} + \frac{p_1}{2} + \frac{ta}{2}\right\} - \frac{(1-\theta)}{2}(p_2-p_1)\right] = 0,$$

where, let us recall, $a \equiv (1-l)^2 - r^2$. From this, we derive the price reaction function of the (partially) public firm as

$$p_2 = \frac{\theta c}{1+\theta} + \frac{p_1}{1+\theta} + \frac{\theta ta}{1+\theta}. \tag{13.37}$$

Combining Eq. (13.37) and Eq. (13.32), we get the (second-stage) equilibrium prices in the presence of public firms as

$$p_1^*(\theta) = c + \frac{t}{1+2\theta}[\theta(a+b)+b] \quad \text{and} \quad p_2^*(\theta) = c + \frac{t}{1+2\theta}[2\theta a + b], \tag{13.38}$$

where (recall) $b \equiv (1-r)^2 - l^2$ and $a+b \equiv 2(1-l-r)$. Also note that $a-b \equiv 2[r(1-r)-l(1-l)]$.
Alternatively,

$$p_1^* = c + t\frac{(1-l-r)[1-r+l+2\theta]}{1+2\theta} \tag{13.39}$$

$$p_2^* = c + t\frac{(1-l-r)[1+l-r+2\theta(1-l+r)]}{1+2\theta}. \tag{13.40}$$

Furthermore,

$$p_2^*(\theta) - p_1^*(\theta) = \frac{t}{1+2\theta}2\theta(r-l)(1-l-r) = \frac{t}{1+2\theta}(r-l)(a+b)\theta.$$

Consequently,

$$\hat{x} = q_1^*(\theta) = \frac{1-r+l}{2} + \frac{\theta(r-l)}{1+2\theta} = \frac{1-r+l+2\theta}{2(1+2\theta)} \tag{13.41}$$

$$\text{and } q_2^*(\theta) = \frac{1+r-l}{2} + \frac{\theta(l-r)}{1+2\theta} = \frac{1+r-l+2\theta}{2(1+2\theta)}. \tag{13.42}$$

13.8.3.2 *Location choice*

Now let us turn to location choice. Using Eqs. (13.39) and (13.41), we write the profit of firm 1 as

$$\pi_1^*(\theta) = \frac{t}{2(1+2\theta)^2}(1-l-r)[1-r+l+2\theta]^2.$$

Maximising the preceding with respect to l, we get

$$\frac{\partial \pi_1}{\partial l} = 2(1-l-r) - (1-r+l+2\theta) = 0,$$

which gives the private firm's best-response location function as

$$l = \max\left\{\frac{1-r-2\theta}{3}, 0\right\}. \tag{13.43}$$

Now consider the public firm's location choice problem. It chooses r to maximise $W_2 = \theta\pi_2 - (1-\theta)TC$, where TC is given by Eq. (13.36) and $\pi_2^*(\theta) = (p_2^* - c)q_2^*(\theta)$.[17] The first-order condition turns out to be

$$\frac{\partial W_2}{\partial r} = \frac{t}{4(1+2\theta)^2}\left[(1+2\theta-l+r)(1+\theta)(1-2\theta-l-3r)\right] = 0.$$

Since only the third term inside the bracket can be zero, the partially public firm's best-response location function is given by

$$r = \max\left\{\frac{1-l-2\theta}{3}, 0\right\}. \tag{13.44}$$

The equilibrium locations then are

$$l^* = r^* = \begin{cases} \dfrac{1-2\theta}{4} & \text{for } \theta < 1/2 \\ 0 & \text{for } \theta \geq 1/2 \end{cases}.$$

It is noteworthy that a fully public-sector firm, that is, $\theta = 0$, always sets $p_2 = p_1$ regardless of its location and serves exactly the half of the market. The reason for the invariant market shares of the firms is that if the public firm follows a strategy of price matching, then the indifferent consumer will always be at the midpoint of the locations of the two firms. Given this fixed nature of the indifferent consumer, the private firm tries to move farther inside, as close as possible to $1-r$. Since a fully public firm only cares only about lowering the transportation cost, it will always choose $r = 1/4$ from the right end, and in response, the private firm will choose 1/4 from the left end.

It has been shown by Kumar and Saha (2008) that to achieve socially optimal locations via market competition, one of the firms has to be fully public, and crucially starting from the full private ownership of both firms, if one of the firm's ownership is gradually transferred to the government, the privately optimal locations do not change instantly. They stubbornly stay at the two extreme corners and begin to move inward only after the public ownership reaches a critical threshold. For a similar analysis, see also Lu and Poddar (2007).

13.9 Foreign trade and mixed duopoly with differentiated products

Continuing with the theme of competition between a public and a private firm, we now consider foreign trade. Before we do that, let us take note of a key feature of any mixed duopoly (or oligopoly in general) that the social welfare–minded public firm, even if it is partially public, adjusts its output to accommodate the interest of its rival firms. To appreciate this point, let us do some thought experiments. Suppose a social planner decides how much output should be produced in the economy and by how many firms so that the social welfare (sum of consumer surplus and profit) is maximised. We know that if the marginal cost is constant, production should be consolidated in a single firm and that output should be extended to the point where price equals marginal cost. But if the marginal cost is increasing, then production needs to be distributed among several firms while still ensuring that, at the end, price equals marginal cost across all (operative) firms.

In a mixed oligopoly, the public firm tries to mimic the role of a social planner *albeit* with a restriction that private firms should be allowed to make a profit, because from the social welfare point of view, private firms' profit is just a transfer from the consumers. Therefore, regardless of whether the marginal cost is constant or increasing and goods are homogeneous or not, the public firm sets its output at a level that holds price above the marginal cost and guarantees the solvency of private firms.[18] In short, while public ownership induces a firm to be little aggressive and produce more, its social welfare concern restrains the aggression. It ends up being accommodating to its private competitors by holding the price above the marginal cost. The end result is only second best; social welfare is greater than a private oligopoly but falls short of the maximum.

The introduction of a foreign firm changes this story considerably. Now the profit earned by the foreign firm is a leakage from the national economy, while the output supplied by it directly benefits the consumers. A natural response of the public firm would be to produce more and substitute the foreign supply by a domestic one. To what extent this substitution occurs and how this substitution depends on the degree of public ownership are not obvious. We address these questions with two firms and two differentiated products. The following is a mixed-duopoly model adapted from Ghosh et al. (2015).

Suppose firm 1 is a (partially) public firm with θ proportion of its ownership in private hands, while firm 2 is a private joint venture, which is domestically owned by λ fraction and foreign owned by $1-\lambda$ fraction. We will loosely call it the foreign firm. The case of $\lambda = 0$ can be seen as the foreign import.[19] Two goods are imperfect substitutes, although in a special case, they can be treated as perfect substitutes. Consumers derive utility from both goods, and a representative consumer's utility function is $U = u(q_1, q_2) + y$, where y is a numeraire good. Given her income M and the quasi-linearity of preference, her utility maximisation boils down to maximising her consumer surplus $CS = u(q_1, q_2) + M - p_1 q_1 - p_2 q_2$.[20]

We assume that $u(q_1, q_2)$ is continuous and monotonic in both q_1 and q_2 and differentiable at least up to second order. Furthermore, for $i = 1, 2$ and $i \neq j$, (1) $u_{ii}(.) < 0$, (2) $u_{ij}(.) < 0$ and (3) $|u_{ii}(.)| > |u_{ij}(.)|$ so that the utility function is strictly concave. The first assumption ensures concavity of $u(.)$ and in turn $U(.)$. The second assumption tells us that the two goods are net substitutes, and the third assumption is standard. Many utility functions can satisfy the assumptions we have specified. A common example can be the linear quadratic utility function $u = a(q_1 + q_2) - (q_1^2 + q_2^2) - bq_1 q_2$, with $0 < b \leq 1$. When $b = 1$, two goods become perfect substitutes.

From the first-order condition of the utility maximisation, we get $\frac{CS}{\partial q_i} = u_i(.) - p_i = 0$, which gives rise to the market demand for good $i, p_i(q_i; q_j)$. From our utility function, it follows $\frac{\partial p_i(.)}{\partial q_j} = \frac{\partial p_j(.)}{\partial q_i} < 0$ for $i \neq j$.

The production cost is given by an identical cost function $C(q)$, which is increasing and weakly convex in q. The two firms' profit are $\pi_i = p_i(.)q_i - C(q_i)$. They play a Cournot game. While the objective function of the second firm is profit maximisation, the first firm maximises a weighted sum of social welfare and profit, where social welfare is the usual sum of consumer surplus and the domestic firm's profit, $W = CS + \pi_1 + \lambda \pi_2$. As the mass of consumers is 1 by assumption, we need to consider only one consumer's utility to calculate the consumer surplus. Since the second firm is foreign-owned the portion of its profit remitted abroad is excluded from social welfare. The public firm maximises

$$\begin{aligned} V(\theta) &= \theta \pi_1(.) + (1-\theta)W \\ &= \theta[p_1 q_1 - C(q_1)] + (1-\theta)[u(.) + M - (1-\lambda)p_2 q_2 - C(q_1) - \lambda C(q_2)]. \end{aligned}$$

We note that

$$\frac{\partial V}{\partial q_1} = \theta\left\{q_1 \frac{\partial p_1(.)}{\partial q_1} + p_1(.) - C'(q_1)\right\} + (1-\theta)\left\{u_1(.) - C'(q_1) - (1-\lambda)q_2 \frac{\partial p_2}{\partial q_1}\right\}.$$

Since $u_1(.) - p_1 = 0$ from utility maximisation, we rewrite the preceding as

$$\frac{\partial V}{\partial q_1} = (p_1(q_1, q_2) - C'(q_1)) + \theta q_1 \frac{\partial p_1(.)}{\partial q_1} - (1-\theta)(1-\lambda)q_2 \frac{\partial p_2}{\partial q_1}.$$

Now let us look at the Cournot equilibrium, which is given by the following two implicit reaction functions arising from $\frac{\partial V}{\partial q_1} = 0$ and $\frac{\partial \pi_2}{\partial q_2} = 0$:

$$(p_1(q_1, q_2) - C'(q_1)) + \theta q_1 \frac{\partial p_1(.)}{\partial q_1} - (1-\theta)(1-\lambda)q_2 \frac{\partial p_2}{\partial q_1} = 0 \tag{13.45}$$

$$(p_2(q_1, q_2) - C'(q_2)) + q_2 \frac{\partial p_2(.)}{\partial q_2} = 0. \tag{13.46}$$

Suppose $(q_1(\theta), q_2(\theta))$ is the Cournot–Nash outputs. It can be shown that $q_1'(\theta) < 0$ and $q_2'(\theta) > 0$. To see this let us differentiate Eqs. (13.45) and (13.46) with respect to θ as follows:

$$\begin{bmatrix} \frac{\partial^2 V}{\partial q_1^2} & \frac{\partial^2 V}{\partial q_1 \partial q_2} \\ \frac{\partial^2 \pi_2}{\partial q_1 \partial q_2} & \frac{\partial^2 \pi_2}{\partial q_2^2} \end{bmatrix} \times \begin{bmatrix} \frac{\partial q_1}{\partial \theta} \\ \frac{\partial q_2}{\partial \theta} \end{bmatrix} = -\begin{bmatrix} q_1 \frac{\partial p_1}{\partial q_1} + (1-\lambda)q_2 \frac{\partial p_2}{\partial q_1} \\ 0 \end{bmatrix}$$

In the preceding equation, by the concavity of $V(.)$ and $\pi_2(.)$ and by the strategic substituteness of the two goods, we have

$$\frac{\partial^2 V}{\partial q_1^2} < 0, \quad \frac{\partial^2 \pi_2}{\partial q_2^2} < 0, \quad \text{and} \quad \frac{\partial^2 V}{\partial q_1 q_2} < 0, \quad \frac{\partial^2 \pi_2}{\partial q_2 \partial q_1} < 0.$$

Then by applying Cramer's rule, we obtain

$$q_1'(\theta) = -a \frac{\partial^2 \pi_2 / \partial q_2^2}{\Delta} < 0 \quad \text{and} \quad q_2'(\theta) = a \frac{\partial^2 \pi_2 / \partial q_1 \partial q_2}{\Delta} > 0, \tag{13.47}$$

where

$$a = q_1 \frac{\partial p_1}{\partial q_1} + (1-\lambda)q_2 \frac{\partial p_2}{\partial q_1} < 0,$$

$$\Delta = \frac{\partial^2 V}{\partial q_1^2}\frac{\partial^2 \pi_2}{\partial q_2^2} - \frac{\partial^2 V}{\partial q_1 \partial q_2}\frac{\partial^2 \pi_2}{\partial q_1 \partial q_2} > 0.$$

That $\Delta > 0$ is a requirement for the stability of the Cournot equilibrium. The public firm's output must decline with the degree of privatisation, and the foreign firm's output must increase simultaneously. This is as expected.

13.9.1 Characterisation

Now we further explore Eqs. (13.45) and (13.46) for the characterisation of the mixed-duopoly equilibrium.

1. The private firm always sets a price above its marginal cost and thus is assured of positive profit. This will be true even if the private firm is not foreign. That is, $p_2 > C'(q_2)$ regardless of the values of θ and λ. This is evident from Eq. (13.46) as $\partial p_2 / \partial q_2 < 0$.
2. Consider Eq. (13.45). If firm 1 is fully public ($\theta = 0$), then it sets a price below its marginal cost ($p_1 < C'(q_1^*)$) if its rival private firm has some foreign ownership and thus can potentially make losses.[21] If $C''(q_1) = 0$, then surely the public firm makes losses. Intuitively, in response to a loss in the national economy in the form of profit going to the foreign partner of the joint venture, the fully public firm expands its output far beyond its marginal cost. If the rival firm is entirely domestically owned, that is, $\lambda = 1$ then the fully public firm sets a price equal to its marginal cost ($p_1 = C'(q_1)$).
3. If the public firm is fully privatised ($\theta = 1$), then regardless of λ, firm 1 sets the price above its marginal cost.
4. Given the previous two observations, it then follows from the continuity and monotonicity of $q_1(\theta)$ and $q_2(\theta)$ that there exists a critical θ, say, $\hat{\theta}(\lambda)$, such that at all $\theta < \hat{\theta}(\lambda)$, the public firm sets the price below its marginal cost and that at all $\theta > \hat{\theta}(\lambda)$, it sets the price above the marginal cost.
   The greater the value of λ, the lower the value of $\hat{\theta}$.
5. In the special case of q_1 and q_2 being undifferentiated (homogeneous) goods, $p_i(q_1, q_2) = p(q_1 + q_2)$ for $i = 1, 2, \partial p / \partial q_1 = \partial p / \partial q_2$. So, Eq. (13.45) becomes

$$C'(q_1) - C'(q_2) = \frac{\partial p}{\partial q_1}[\theta q_1 - \{1 + (1-\theta)(1-\lambda)\}q_2]. \tag{13.48}$$

   If the demand curve is linear of the form $p = A - b(q_1 + q_2)$ and, say, the marginal cost is of the form $C'(q_i) = c + kq_i$, then the previous relation simplifies to

$$(k + b\theta)q_1 = [k + b\{1 + (1-\theta)(1-\lambda)\}]q_2 \quad \Rightarrow \quad \frac{q_2}{q_1} = \frac{k + b\theta}{k + b\{1 + (1-\theta)(1-\lambda)\}}.$$

   Here, certain results become obvious:

   a. If $\theta = 1$, we must have $q_1 = q_2$. If the two firms are entirely private, then they must have identical output because they are technologically identical. This is true regardless of λ.
   b. If firm 1 is partially public, then $\frac{q_2}{q_1} = \frac{k + b\theta}{k + b} < 1$ if firm 2 is entirely domestically owned. But if it is entirely foreign-owned ($\lambda = 0$), then $\frac{q_2}{q_1} = \frac{k + b\theta}{k + b(2-\theta)}$; this would be lowest

q_2/q_1 ratio for any given θ. The (partially) public firm's output response is most aggressive when the private firm is entirely foreign-owned.

c. Firm 2's output is positive if $k > 0$, regardless of θ and λ. But if $k = \theta = 0$, then the private firm ceases to operate. This is the case of constant marginal cost. A fully public firm becomes the sole supplier to the market.

d. Finally, for the case of $p = a - b(q_1 + q_2)$ and $C'(q_i) = c + kq_i$, we can calculate $q_1(\theta)$ and $q_2(\theta)$ and verify if the two equilibrium outputs indeed satisfy Eq. (13.48). In this case, the output reaction functions are

$$q_1 = \frac{a-c}{k+b(1+\theta)} - \frac{b\theta_\lambda}{k+b(1+\theta)} q_2$$

$$q_2 = \frac{a-c}{k+2b} - \frac{b}{k+2b} q_1,$$

where $\theta_\lambda \equiv \theta + (1-\theta)\lambda$. The Cournot equilibrium outputs are

$$q_1(\theta) = \frac{(a-c)[k+2b-b\theta_\lambda]}{(k+2b)[k+b(1+\theta)]-b^2\theta_\lambda},$$

$$q_2(\theta) = \frac{(a-c)(k+b\theta)}{(k+2b)[k+b(1+\theta)]-b^2\theta_\lambda}.$$

Clearly, as claimed,

$$\frac{q_2(\theta)}{q_1(\theta)} = \frac{k+b\theta}{k+2b-b\theta_\lambda} = \frac{k+b\theta}{k+b\{1+(1-\theta)(1-\lambda)}.$$

e. We can also check that $p(q_1(\theta)+q_2(\theta)) > c + kq_1(\theta)$ if and only if

$$\theta > \frac{k(1-\lambda)}{b+k(2-\lambda)} \equiv \hat{\theta}(\lambda).$$

If $\lambda = 1$ or $k = 0$, the public firm does not sell below its marginal cost. It is easy to check that $\hat{\theta}(\lambda)$ is declining in λ, with the highest value taken as $k/(b+2k) < 1$ at $\lambda = 0$.

13.9.2 *Optimal privatisation*

In reality, public-sector enterprises very often make losses. It can be because of its cost inefficiency, but it can also be, as shown here, due to the presence of a foreign firm or unrestricted import. The public firm then deliberately overproduces. Not only does it overproduce compared to the private sector, but it overporduces above the benchmark set by the 'no foreign competition' case. One question is, Does the problem of overproduction go away, if the government chooses the degree of privatisation that maximises social welfare? The answer is that optimal privatisation does not guarantee profitability of the public-sector enterprises. But one thing we can say for sure is that some privatisation is always welfare improving. In fact, neither complete public ownership nor full privatisation is ever optimal if there is foreign competition.

To see the preceding point, let us assume that the Cournot game discussed earlier is preceded by a stage of privatisation. The government maximises $W(q_1(\theta), q_2(\theta))$ with respect to θ before the firms choose their outputs:

$$\frac{\partial W(.)}{\partial \theta} = \frac{\partial W}{\partial q_1}\frac{\partial q_1}{\partial \theta} + \frac{\partial W}{\partial q_2}\frac{\partial q_2}{\partial \theta} = 0.$$

In the second stage, the public firm maximises $V = \theta\Pi_1 + (1-\theta)W$, from which we obtain $\frac{\partial W}{\partial q_1} = -\frac{\theta}{(1-\theta)}\frac{\partial \pi_1}{\partial q_1} > 0$, which implies $\partial\pi_1/\partial q_1 < 0$. Substituting this expression, we rewrite the preceding first-order condition as

$$\frac{\partial W(.)}{\partial \theta} = -\frac{\theta}{(1-\theta)}\frac{\partial \pi_1}{\partial q_1}\frac{\partial q_1}{\partial \theta} + \left[\underbrace{\lambda(p_2 - C'(q_2)) - q_2(1-\lambda)\frac{\partial p_2}{\partial q_2}}_{=\partial W/\partial q_2}\right]\frac{\partial q_2}{\partial \theta} = 0.$$

In this equation, the first term is negative while the second term is positive, because $q_1'(\theta) < 0$ and $q_2'(\theta) > 0$. We can see that

$$\left.\frac{\partial W(.)}{\partial \theta}\right|_{\theta=0} > 0, \quad \text{and} \quad \left.\frac{\partial W(.)}{\partial \theta}\right|_{\theta=1} \to -\infty.$$

At $\theta = 0$, the public firm suffers too much of loss, and at $\theta = 1$, it suffers too much leakage of national income. Optimal privatisation is somewhere in between. However, at optimal privatisation, overproduction relative to a private firm's output must be maintained. That is, $\frac{\partial \pi_1}{\partial q_1} < 0$ must hold.

The public firm overproduces relative to the private benchmark, and consequently, its profit is below the privately optimal level. This does not necessarily mean that the public firm is making losses.

One final observation is that the result of 'underpricing' (pricing below MC) by the public firm does not survive in the long run. Ghosh et al. (2015) have shown that in the long run, as more private firms (domestic or foreign) enter, they bring new varieties to the benefit of the consumers, as well as lower the price. In addition, profit is eventually driven down to zero for all (private) firms, which means the national economy does not experience any leakage to foreign firms. These gains from entry offset the adverse (i.e., higher price) effect of privatisation. Therefore, optimal privatisation will be greater and will eventually eliminate losses (if any) from the public firm.

13.10 Conclusion

Oligopoly is now a vast literature. We have been very selective in providing a compressed version of the literature. Our main focus has been on Cournot and Bertrand models for both private and public firms with or without product differentiation. We also studied the scope for limit pricing and entry deterrence. We extended a standard duopoly model of delegation with or without wage negotiation. Such an extension presents an array of outcomes from overproduction to implicit collusion. However, one big omission is platform competition. Vertical quality choice models also have been ignored for reasons of space. Students are advised to read Tirole (1989) for advanced topics in this area.

Summary

In this chapter we have learnt the following:

1. Quantity competition is softer than price competition ensuring positive higher profit.
2. Profit in quantity competition models increases even further with leadership.
3. Under price competition, following is more advantageous than leading.
4. Bertrand competition is more interesting and meaningful when products are differentiated.
5. Capacity choice under full information and limit pricing under asymmetric information can both lead to monopolisation of a market through strategic entry deterrence.
6. Even when firms move simultaneously, an advantage of leadership type can be generated through strategic delegation. However, if both the union and the firm take recourse to delegation, there can be an opposite effect, whereby the market output can approach the collusive level.
7. Public ownership of a firm also helps improve social welfare, both in homogeneous goods markets and in a linear city model.

13.11 Exercises

1. Suppose there are two firms producing a homogeneous good. Their outputs are denoted as q_1 and q_2. They have an identical cost function $C = cq_i + (kq_i^2/2)$, $(i = 1,2)$. The market demand curve is $p = A - q_1 - q_2$. They choose output in the Cournot fashion.

   a. Derive the output reaction functions. Determine the Nash equilibrium outputs and profits.
   b. Also solve the Stackelberg case with firm 1 as the leader.

2. Consider a market for two differentiated products served by two firms whose identical marginal cost of production is c. The direct demand curves for the two products are

   $$q_1 = 1 - p_1 + \delta p_2 \qquad \text{and} \qquad q_2 = 1 - p_2 + \delta p_1.$$

   Assume $c, \delta < 1$. Two firms simultaneously announce prices.

   a. Derive the Bertrand–Nash equilibrium prices. Calculate profits.
   b. Present your answer graphically.
   c. What if the firms were competing in quantity? Derive the Cournot–Nash equilibrium quantities of this game.

3. Two firms compete in terms of quantities q_1 and q_2 for a homogeneous good. The inverse demand curve is $p = A - q_1 - q_2$. For both firms, the marginal cost of production is c.

   a. Derive the Cournot–Nash equilibrium of this game. Derive equilibrium profits.
   b. Show the equilibrium on a graph.

c. Now let firm 1 choose the output first and firm 2 next. Derive the equilibrium outputs of this game. Show it on a graph.
d. Compare the firms' profit between this game and the simultaneous-move game.

4. Consider a duopoly with the inverse demand curve $p = A - x_1 - x_2$ and the two firms' marginal costs are c_1 and c_2. Assume $A > c_1, A > c_2$. There is no fixed cost. Suppose that initially, the firms play Cournot. But if they are asked to play the Stackelberg leader–follower game whereby the leader's role is chosen by tossing a coin (Head for leader), would they both agree to the proposal?
5. Consider a duopoly with two imperfectly substitute goods and two firms with identical marginal cost c. The firms simultaneously choose their outputs.

$$p_1 = A - x_1 - \beta x_2\,, \qquad p_2 = A + k - x_2 - \beta x_1.$$

Assume $k > 0$, $A > c$ and $\beta < 1$.

a. Derive the Cournot–Nash equilibrium outputs of the two firms.
b. Derive their equilibrium profits and determine which firm earns greater profit.
c. Now set $k = 0$, and consider a scenario in which firm 2 offers to collude with firm 1 and suggests that firm 1 should move first to choose its output. Would firm 1 agree to collude and move first?

6. Suppose the inverse market demand curve of a duopoly is $p = A - q_1 - q_2$. The firms' marginal cost is c. Shareholders of firm i hire a manager and ask him to maximise $z_i = \beta_i \pi_i + (1-\beta_i)R_i$, where R_i is revenue of firm i. Derive the Cournot–Nash outputs and the optimal incentives β_i.
7. Again consider the duopoly with the demand curve $p = A - q_1 - q_2$. Each firm's total cost is $C_i = cq_i + \dfrac{kq_i^2}{2}$. Assume firm 1 is partly government-owned. Its θ proportion is owned by a private firm and $1-\theta$ proportion is owned by the government. Firm 2 is entirely private. Firm 1's objective is to maximise $Y = \theta\pi_1 + (1-\theta)SW$, where $SW = CS + \pi_1 + \pi_2$.

a. Derive the Cournot–Nash outputs, profit and social welfare for any given θ. If the government wishes to have an optimal extent of privatisation in firm 1, what θ would it choose?
b. Suppose firm 2 is a joint venture with a foreign partner which takes away λ proportion of the profit. Derive the Cournot–Nash outputs again. What will be the market price in relation to the marginal cost of firm 1?
c. Show how your answer is sensitive to $k = 0$ in the cases in parts (a) and (b).

8. Consider an entry game with two firms. Firm 1 is an incumbent, and firm 2 is an entrant considering entry to the market currently monopolised by firm 1. The market demand curve is $p = 24 - q_1 - q_2$. The entrant's marginal cost is $MC_2 = 8$, and it is known to the incumbent.
The incumbent's true marginal cost is his private information. The entrant knows that $MC_1 = 4$, with a probability of 0.40, and $MC_1 = 8$, with a probability of 0.60. The incumbent's marginal cost is revealed automatically after entry, but there is an entry cost of 20. After entry, the firms will play a Cournot game.
There are two periods to the firms' interactions. In the first period, the incumbent sets a price, which is observed by the entrant. Based on the price observed, the entrant decides on entry in the second period.

a. Derive the post-entry Cournot profits for each type of incumbent.
b. Determine if it is optimal for the incumbent to enter the market without receiving any new information.
c. What would be the first-period pricing strategy of the incumbent? Explain the perfect Bayesian equilibrium of this game.

Notes

1 Allowing convex demand curve and $\bar{Q}$ to go to infinity requires making some additional assumptions down the line purely for technical reasons.
2 Note that if the demand function were convex, the two goods may not necessarily always be strategic substitutes.
3 **Derivation of Stackelberg profits** We first derive the price-cost mark-ups as

$$p_1^S - c = \left[\alpha - \beta\left\{\frac{2\beta-\delta}{2(2\beta^2-\delta^2)}\right\}(\alpha-c) - \delta\left\{\frac{4\beta^2-\delta^2-2\delta\beta}{4\beta(2\beta^2-\delta^2)}\right\}(\alpha-c)\right] - c$$

$$= \frac{\alpha-c}{4\beta(2\beta^2-\delta^2)}\left\{2\beta^2(2\beta-\delta)-\delta^2(2\beta-\delta)\right\} = \frac{(2\beta-\delta)}{4\beta}(\alpha-c)$$

and

$$p_2^F - c = \left[\alpha - \beta\left\{\frac{4\beta^2-\delta^2-2\delta\beta}{4\beta(2\beta^2-\delta^2)}(\alpha-c) - \delta\left\{\frac{2\beta-\delta}{2(2\beta^2-\delta^2)}\right\}\right\}(\alpha-c)\right] - c$$

$$= \frac{\alpha-c}{4\beta(2\beta^2-\delta^2)}\left\{4\beta^3-\beta\delta^2-2\beta^2\delta\right\}$$

$$= \frac{(4\beta^2-\delta^2-2\beta\delta)}{4(2\beta^2-\delta^2)}(\alpha-c).$$

This gives Eq. (13.11).

4 Note that the Stackelberg leader's output is smaller than the output which is firm 1's best response to firm 2's zero output. This can be verified easily.
5 **Derivation of profits under price leadership** Using the expression of p_1^L, we write the leader's mark-up as

$$p_1^L - c = \frac{(A+bc)(2b+k)-k^2c-2(2b^2-k^2)c}{2(2b^2-k^2)}$$

$$= \frac{(A+bc)(2b+k)-c(4b^2-k^2)}{2(2b^2-k^2)} = \frac{(2b+k)[(A+bc)-c(2b-k)]}{2(2b^2-k^2)}$$

$$= \frac{(2b+k)}{2(2b^2-k^2)}[A-c(b-k)]$$

and

$$q_1^L = A - bp_1^L + kp_2^F$$
$$= A - b\left[\frac{(A+bc)(2b+k)-k^2c}{2(2b^2-k^2)}\right] + k\left[\frac{(A+bc)[4b^2-k^2+2bk]-k^3}{4b(2b^2-k^2)}\right]$$
$$= \frac{A[4b(2b^2-k^2)+(A+bc)[4b^2k-k^3+2bk^2-4b^3]+k^2c(2b^2-k^2))}{4b(2b^2-k^2)}$$
$$= \frac{A(2b^2-k^2)(2b+k)+k^2c(2b^2-k^2)-bc(2b^2-k^2)(2b-k)}{4b(2b^2-k^2)}$$
$$= (2b^2-k^2)\left[\frac{A(2b+k)+k^2c-bc(2b-k)}{4b(2b^2-k^2)}\right]$$
$$= \frac{A(2b+k)-c(2b+k)(b-k)}{4b} = \frac{(2b+k)}{4b}[A-c(b-k)].$$

Using the expressions of $p_1^L - c$ and q_1^L, we get the expression shown in Eq. (13.15)

Similarly, using Eq. 13.14 we write the mark-up of the follower as

$$p_2^F - c = \frac{1}{4b(2b^2-k^2)}\left[(A+bc)[4b^2-k^2+2bk]-ck^3-4bc(2b^2-k^2)\right]$$
$$= \frac{1}{4b(2b^2-k^2)}\left[A(4b^2-k^2+2bk)+bc(4b^2-k^2+2bk-8b^2+4k^2)-ck^3\right]$$
$$= \frac{1}{4b(2b^2-k^2)}\left[(A-bc)(4b^2-k^2+2bk)+ck(4b^2-k^2+2bk)\right]$$
$$= \frac{(4b^2-k^2-2bk)}{4b(2b^2-k^2)}\left[A-c(b-k)\right]$$

and its output as

$$q_2^F = A - b\left[\frac{(A+bc)[4b^2-k^2+2bk]-k^3c}{4b(2b^2-k^2)}\right] + k\left[\frac{(A+bc)(2b+k)-k^2c}{2(2b^2-k^2)}\right]$$
$$= \frac{1}{4b(2b^2-k^2)}\left[A4b(2b^2-k^2)-(A+bc)\{b(4b^2-k^2+2bk)-2bk(2b+k)\}-k^3bc\right]$$
$$= \frac{1}{4b(2b^2-k^2)}\left[A(4b^3-bk^2+2b^2k)-bc(4b^3-bk^2-2b^2k)+bck(2bk-k^2)\right]$$
$$= \frac{1}{4b(2b^2-k^2)}\left[Ab(4b^2-k^2+2bk)-b^2c(4b^2-k^2+2bk)+bck(4b^2-k^2+2bk)\right]$$
$$= \frac{(4b^2-k^2+2bk)}{4(2b^2-k^2)}\left[A-c(b-k)\right].$$

These expressions give us Eq. (13.16).

6 Of course, there are some exceptions. The international cartel OPEC is legal.

7 We can extend the same analysis to simultaneous output choice. But then entry deterrence (of the 'effectively impeded' variety) will be one of two Nash equilibria. See panel *a* graph in Figure 13.2.

8 This static version can be thought of as a steady state of a dynamic process.

9 Technically, prices to the right of $p^M(c_1)$ also meet the constraint. But any price above $p^M(c_1)$ will never be chosen, nor will it have any information value.

10 If δ is too small, $p^M(c_1)$ falls below $\tilde{p}_2$, and $p^M(c_1)$ itself will be incentive compatible.

11 Note that in the Bayes' rule, the denominator then takes a value of zero because it is not expected to be played. Thereby, Bayesian updating becomes ineffective. Perfect Bayesian equilibrium allows players to form beliefs off-the-equilibrium path in any manner they want.

12 If F_i is taken as the manager's salary, then the shareholders maximise net profit. Our analysis does not change.

13 You can look up Chapter 12 to see the output choice in the monopoly case of bilateral delegation. The solution follows a similar method.

14 However, Szymanski (1994) considered right-to-manage bargaining.

15 See Kumar and Saha (2008) for a detailed treatment of these boundary constraint.

16 Note that the second-order condition for travel cost minimisation is easily met.

17 You can check that

$$\frac{\partial \pi_2}{\partial r} = t[(1-r)^2 - l^2 + 2\theta\{(1-l)^2 - r^2\}] - t[1+r-l+2\theta]\{2(1-r)+4r\theta\}$$

$$\frac{\partial TC}{\partial r} = t\left[(1-r-\hat{x})^2 - r^2 - \left((l-\hat{x})^2 - (1-r-\hat{x})^2\frac{1}{2(1+2\theta)}\right)\right].$$

In the special case of $\theta = 0$, that is, when firm 2 is fully public, $p_2 = p_1$ and $(l-\hat{x})^2 = (1-r-\hat{x})^2$, we have

$$\frac{\partial W_2}{\partial r} = \frac{\partial TC}{\partial r} = (1-r-\hat{x})^2 - r^2 = 0, \qquad \Rightarrow 2r = 1-\hat{x}.$$

Since $\hat{x} = \dfrac{l+1-r}{2}$ (because of $p_2 = p_1$), the public firm's best-response function becomes $r = (1-l)/3$. Combine this with the private firm's best response function as given in Eq. (13.43) under the assumption $\theta = 0$, we have the solution $l = r = 1/4$, the socially optimal location.

18 Remember that $p > MC$ ensures positive profit because $MC \geq AC$.

19 It does not matter where the joint venture organises its production. It would if we introduce tariff/subsidy into the model.

20 We restrict our attention to $M > p_1q_1 + p_2q_2$.

21 Remember that $MC > AC$ if $C''(q_1) > 0$, and thus, $p_1 < MC$ may not necessarily imply $p_1 < AC$. The converse is true, however. $p_1 \geq MC$ implies non-negative profit when $C''(q_1) \geq 0$.

References and further readings

Anderson, S. P., de Palma, A. & Thisse, J.-F. (1997). Privatization and efficiency in a differentiated industry. *European Economic Review*, 41(7), 1635–1654.

Bain, J. (1956). *Barriers to New Competition*. Cambridge, MA: Cambridge University Press.

Baumol, W. (1958). On the theory of oligopoly. *Economica*, 25(99), 187–198.

Bennett, J. & Maw, J. (2003). Privatization, partial state ownership, and competition. *Journal of Comparative Economics*, 31(1), 58–74.

Bertrand, J. (1883). Book review of theorie mathematique de la richesse sociale and of recherches sur les principles mathematiques de la theoric des richesses. *Journal de Savants*, 67, 499–508.

Bulow, J., Geanakoplos, J. & Klemperer, P. (1985). Multimarket oligopoly: Strategic substitutes and complements. *Journal of Political Economy*, 93, 488–511.

Chatterjee, I. & Saha, B. (2017). Bilateral delegation in duopoly wage and employment bargaining. *Managerial & Decision Economics*, 38(4), 607–621.

Cournot, A. (1838). *Recherches sur les Principes Math'ematiques de la Th'eorie des Richesses [Researches into the Mathematical Principles of the Theory of Wealth]*, trans. Nathaniel T. Bacon. New York: The Macmillan Company.

Dastidar, K. G. (1995). On the existence of pure strategy Bertrand equilibrium. *Economic Theory*, 5(1), 19–35.

De Fraja, G. & Delbono, G. (1989). Alternative strategies of a public enterprise in oligopoly. *Oxford Economic Papers*, 41, 302–311.

Dixit, A. (1980). The role of investment in entry deterrence. *Economic Journal*, 94, S1–S16.

Espinosa, M. P. (1992). Delivered pricing, FOB pricing, and collusion in spatial markets. *Rand Journal of Economics*, 23(1), 64–85.

Fershtman, C. (1990). The interdependence between ownership status and market structure: The case of privatization. *Economica*, 57, 319–327.

Fershtman, C. & Judd, K. 1987. Equilibrium incentives in oligopoly. *American Economic Review*, 77, 927–940.

Fjell, K. & Pal, D. (1996). A mixed oligopoly in the presence of foreign private firms. *Canadian Journal of Economics*, 29(3), 737–743.

Ghosh, A., Mitra, M. & Saha, B. (2015). Privatization, underpricing, and welfare in the presence of foreign competition. *Journal of Public Economic Theory*, 17(3), 433–460 [available under the terms of the Creative Commons Attribution License (CC BY)].

Hotelling, H. (1929). Stability in competition. *Economic Journal*, 39, 41–57.

Kumar, A. & Saha, B. (2008). Spatial competition in a mixed duopoly with one partially privatized firm. *Journal of Comparative Economics*, 36(2), 326–341.

Lu, Y. & Poddar, S. (2007). Firm ownership, product differentiation and welfare. *Manchester School*, 75(2), 210–217.

Matsumura, T. (1998). Partial privatization in mixed duopoly. *Journal of Public Economics*, 70(3), 473–483.

Milgrom, P. & Roberts, J. (1982). Limit pricing and entry under incomplete information: An equilibrium analysis. *Econometrica*, 50, 443–460.

Pal, D. & White, M. (1998). Mixed oligopoly, privatization, and strategic trade policy. *Southern Economic Journal*, 65, 264–281.

Saha, B. & Sensarma, R. (2004). Divestment and bank competition. *Journal of Economics*, 81(3), 223–247.

Sklivas, S. D. (1987). The strategic choice of managerial incentives. *RAND Journal of Economics*, 18(3), 452–458.

Szymanski, S. (1994). Strategic delegation with endogenous costs: A duopoly with wage bargaining. *International Journal of Industrial Organization*, 12, 105–106.

Tirole, J. (1989). *The Theory of Industrial Organization*. Cambridge, MA: The MIT Press.
Vickers, J. (1985). Delegation and the theory of the firm. *Economic Journal (Supplement)*, 95, 138–147.
White, M. (1997). Mixed oligopoly, privatization and subsidization. *Economics Letters*, 53(2), 189–195.
Zhang, M. & Sexton R. J. (2001). FOB or uniform delivered prices: Strategic choice and welfare effects. *Journal of Industrial Economics*, 49(2), 197–221.

Chapter 14

The principal–agent problem

Abstract

When an employer is uninformed about a worker's productivity whom he is about to hire, there is risk of adverse selection. A somewhat similar problem arises when the employer knows his worker's productivity but cannot observe her work or effort. In this case, there is a risk of moral hazard. In the framework of two individuals engaging in a potentially beneficial transaction, we study the problems of adverse selection and moral hazard. Assuming that the un-informed party has the power to write a take-it-or-leave-it offer, we study how the optimal contracts can be designed to elicit correct information or to induce best effort. Generally, the contract needs to be distorted from the first-best level to avoid adverse selection by causing inefficiency and yielding information rent. To mitigate moral hazard, an incentive has to be given to induce correct effort, which, in turn, requires not providing complete insurance.

Keywords: Adverse selection, Moral hazard, Optimal incentive, Separating contracts, Incentive compatibility, Countervailing incentives

14.1 Introduction

In firm theory, when we analysed a firm's input choice, including the choice of labour, we made an implicit assumption that the firm knows the worker's innate productivity and is also able to observe the worker's effort (or labour). In addition, we also assumed that the worker's effort is observable directly or via a supervisor or that if the worker is working away from the firm's premise, then her effort is verifiable by a third party (such as the court of law) so that the terms of the employment contract can be perfectly enforced. But this assumption may not be easily met in many contexts. A worker's productivity is better known to herself than to anybody else. An employer can learn her productivity at some cost. A similar problem arises when a firm deals with another firm for supplying an input or for outsourcing a part of its output. One of the parties may hold private information regarding its cost, which can put the other firm at a disadvantage. And it should be obvious by now that working from home is also problematic for employers as far as the supervision of the effort goes. Outside the firm–worker context, the problem can occur between a consumer and a seller, whereby the buyer is uncertain about the quality of the product she is buying.

Several variants of the problem of asymmetric information have already been discussed in previous chapters. In Chapter 10, we analysed the case of second-degree price discrimination in which a monopolist seller does not know the consumers' willingness to pay and therefore resorts to bulk discounting that is both profit maximising (under the informational constraint)

DOI: 10.4324/9781003226994-14

and truth-revealing. In Chapter 11, we discussed Spence's model of job market signalling, and in Chapter 13, we presented a model of limit pricing whereby the entrant is uninformed about the incumbent's marginal cost. These two models of signalling concern a case in which the informed party takes an action. Also in Chapter 12, we presented two models of bargaining whereby both seller and buyer are uninformed about each other's valuations.

In this chapter, we look at again a context of two economic actors, one of whom has private information or has taken a private action. The other actor, who is uninformed, writes a contract which would be mutually beneficial under the informational or observability constraint. The class of models that deal with these problems are called principal–agent models, and this is what contract theory is all about. Here, the principal is the uninformed party, and the agent is the informed party. There are two broad classes of problems. One is that of **hidden information**, and the other is that of **hidden action**. Hidden information gives rise to *adverse selection*, and hidden action gives rise to *moral hazard*. The principal writes a contract to mitigate the problems that arise from the informational or observability constraint. We study both problems in the following discussion.

14.2 Hidden information

Under asymmetric information, the principal can resort to a number of contracts, or a number of mechanisms, so to speak. Although looking for the optimal contract from the set of all feasible contracts is a complex task, there is a general result that the optimal contract can be found from the set of **direct mechanisms** that rely on the agent's **truth-telling** and conditioning the contract on her announced type.

The idea is that the agent can be asked to announce her type, and the principal can offer a contract based on that announcement. Though the agent can lie about her type, in the optimal contract, she would find that lying is unprofitable. Another way to think about the optimal contract is to think about a **menu contract** that contains several options from which the agent self-selects from it (based on her private information).

14.2.1 *Example 1*

Let us assume that our principal is a garment seller who outsources his product, denoted q, from an overseas supplier whose marginal cost is her private information. But the principal knows (and it is common knowledge) that the agent's marginal cost (MC) is c_1 with probability p_1 or c_2 with probability $p_2\left(=1-p_1\right);c_1<c_2$. We may refer to the agent of c_1 type as the 'low cost' type and the agent of c_2 type as the 'high cost' type. The agent, of course, knows her true MC. She receives revenue $T\left(q\right)$ from the principal for supplying q. So, her profit is $u_i=T\left(q\right)-c_iq$. The principal's revenue function is $R\left(q\right)$, which is increasing and strictly concave $\left(R'\left(q\right)>0, R''\left(q\right)<0\right)$, resulting in profit $\pi=R\left(q\right)-T\left(q\right)$.

We assume that the reservation pay-off of both parties is zero. Zero-reservation pay-off is a simplification. The problem does not change much if it is changed to a positive (but small) number. However, what is important is that *both types of the agent have the same reservation pay-off.*

Note that in this story, the lower MC type is more desirable to deal with from the principal's point of view, because for a given amount of q, less is to be paid than to the higher MC type, if all information was public. Of course, all information is not public, and this is why the principal's problem is not trivial.

14.2.1.1 The full information case

First, we look at the first-best scenario, where the principal knows whether the agent is truly c_1 or c_2. Then he can choose (q,T) in such a way that the agent gets her reservation pay-off (and no more) and his own profit will be maximum. That is to say, he solves the following problem:

$$\text{Max} \quad \pi = R(q) - T, \qquad \text{subject to} \qquad u_i = T - c_i q \geq 0,\ i = 1,2.$$

You can easily see that the principal must set $u_i = T - c_i q = 0$, because setting T above its minimum (i.e., equal to $c_i q$) is like wasting a bit of profit. Any contract that gives at least zero utility to the agent is a feasible contract. Let us denote the set of feasible contracts for type i agent as

$$S_i^A = \{(q_i, T_i) \mid u(q_i, T_i) \geq 0\},$$

and the set of feasible contracts for the principal as

$$S^P = \{(q_i, T_i) \mid \pi(q_i, T_i) \geq 0\}.$$

For a solution to exist, the set S^P must overlap with each S_1^A, i =1, 2. Let us assume that is the case. The following claim is important.

Claim 1

If $(q,T) \in S_2^A$ *then* (q, T) *must be in* S_1^A. *That is,* $S_2^A \subset S_1^A$. *The converse is not true.*

Proof Contrary to the claim, assume that $S_1^A \subset S_2^A$. If $(q,T) \in S_1^A$, then $T - c_1 q \geq 0$. Without loss of generality take $T = (c_1 + c_2)q/2$. The agent's utility is $u_1 = \frac{(c_1 + c_2)q}{2} - c_1 q = (c_2 - c_1)q/2 > 0$, which confirms that $\left(q, \frac{(c_2 + c_1)q}{2}\right) \in S_1^A$. Now check if it also belongs to $S_2^A \cdot u_2 = \left(\frac{c_2 + c_1}{2} - c_2\right)q = -(c_2 - c_1)q < 0$, which means $\left(q, \frac{(c_2 + c_1)q}{2}\right) \notin S_2^A$. That is a contradiction.

The first-best solution is straightforward.

Proposition 46. *Under full information, the optimal contract is*

$\{(q_1^*, T_1^*), (q_2^*, T_2^*)\}$, *where* q_i^* *solves* $R'(q_i^*) - c_i = 0$, *and* $T_i^* = c_i q_i^*$. *Notably,* $q_1^* > q_2^*$ *and* $\pi_1^* > \pi_2^*$.

When all information is public, the principal can identify the agent by her type, and therefore, his best option is to maximise the surplus $R(q) - c_i q$ by choosing q_i^* and pay $T_i^* = c_i q_i^*$ to cover the agent's cost. Dealing with agent c_1 gives a higher profit than dealing with agent c_2. If not, the principal could choose (q_2^*, T_2^*) for agent c_1 and that would be acceptable to her, because whatever is acceptable to agent c_2 is also acceptable to agent c_1 (Claim 1).

In Figure 14.1, we illustrate the first-best contracts on panel *a*. Point *A* corresponds to the contract for type c_1 and *B* for type c_2. The straight lines are the indifference curves of the agent, where her utility is set to be zero; for agent c_2, the indifference curve would be a steeper line,

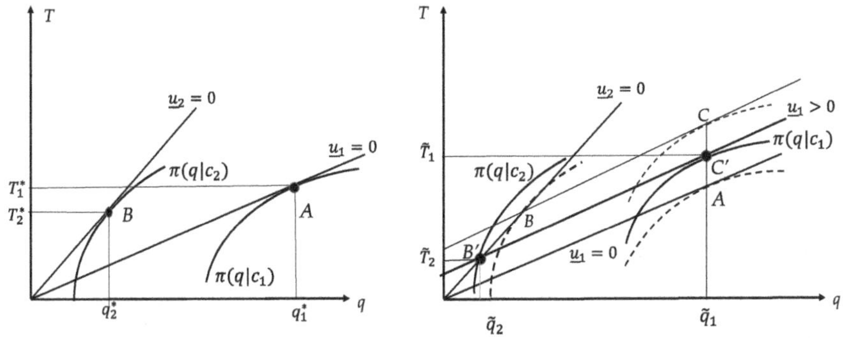

a. *Full-information contracts*

b. *Asymmetric-information contracts*

Figure 14.1 Optimal contracts

because $c_2 > c_1$. For each type, the area including and above their respective indifference curve representing $\bar{u}_i = 0$ corresponds to the feasible set of contracts. The higher the indifference curve, the higher the agent's utility.

On the same diagram, we have also drawn the principal's iso-profit curves, which are concave and upward-sloping. Since the vertical axis represents the principal's cost, a higher iso-profit curve represents a lower level of profit. The optimal contract is given by the tangency point between an iso-profit curve and the indifference curve for the reservation utility level for type i. Notably, point A is outside the feasible set of type c_2, but point B is in the feasible set of type c_1.

14.2.1.2 Asymmetric information

When the principal is uninformed about the agent's type, he may first want to know whether the agent is type c_1 or type c_2. If he asks the agent about her type, she may not necessarily be truthful without knowing what contract she would get in return. To see this point, suppose she knows that the principal is going to offer (q_1^*, T_1^*) if she says, "I am type c_1," and (q_2^*, T_2^*) if she says, "I am type c_2.". Then she is always going to say, "I am type c_2." Why? Because by saying so the c_1-type agent will get higher utility, while the c_2-type agent cannot do any better. Type c_1 agent's utility from lying is $u(q_2^*, T_2^*; c_1) = T_2^* - c_1 q_2^* = c_2 q_2^* - c_1 q_2^* = (c_2 - c_1) q_2^* > 0$, whereas by being truthful, she only gets $u(q_1^*, T_1^*; c_1) = 0$. In Figure 14.1 panel a, we see that a higher indifference curve for the c_1 type passes through point B. Therefore, truth-telling is not optimal for her. In fact, because of the point made in Claim 1, type c_1 will not tell the truth unless she expects a pay-off at least as large as what she can get by lying to be c_2. For type c_2, there is not much of a choice. She cannot say, "I am type c_1," because that will lead to an offer that gives utility below her reservation pay-off.

Finding the optimal contract for the principal requires explicitly imposing two incentive compatibility (IC) constraints alongside two individual rationality (IR) constraints. The solution will be a menu contract, $\{(q_1, T_1), (q_2, T_2)\}$, that can be presented before the agent, and she will select (q_1, T_1) if she is c_1 type and (q_2, T_2) if she is c_2 type.

To explore the IC constraints, let us write the utility of agent i when she selects the offer intended for type j as $u(c_j; c_i) = T_j - c_i q_j$. If $i = j$ then it is her truth-telling pay-off, $u(c_i, c_i) = T_i - c_i q_i$.

The IC constraint of type c_1 is

$$u(c_1;c_1) \geq u(c_2;c_1).$$

Subtracting $u(c_2;c_2)$ from both sides, we write

$$u(c_1;c_1) - u(c_2;c_2) \geq u(c_2;c_1) - u(c_2;c_2).$$

Now use the IC constraint for $c_2, u(c_2;c_2) \geq u(c_1;c_2)$ to write

$$u(c_1;c_1) - u(c_2;c_2) \leq u(c_1;c_1) - u(c_1;c_2).$$

Note that the change in the inequality sign. This is due to the fact that we are subtracting a smaller term. Combining two IC constraints, we then get

$$u(c_1;c_1) - u(c_1;c_2) \geq u(c_1;c_1) - u(c_2;c_2) \geq u(c_2;c_1) - u(c_2;c_2).$$

Next, substituting the expressions of $u(c_j;c_i) = T_j - c_i q_j \; (i, j = 1, 2)$, we can write the preceding relation as

$$(c_2 - c_1) q_1 \geq u(c_1;c_1) - u(c_2;c_2) \geq (c_2 - c_1) q_2$$

or

$$q_2 \leq -\left[\frac{u(c_2;c_2) - u(c_1;c_1)}{c_2 - c_1}\right] \leq q_1. \tag{14.1}$$

Note that $\frac{u(c_2;c_2) - u(c_1;c_1)}{c_2 - c_1}$ is nothing but the slope of the utility function $\left(\frac{\Delta u}{\Delta c}\right)$ of the agent when she tells the truth. Therefore, IC implies that the agent's pay-off under truthful revelation must decrease as her marginal cost increases. We note this and some additional observations in the following lemma.

Lemma 8.

1. *In an incentive-compatible contract, (1)* $q_1 > q_2$; *(2)* $-q_1 \leq \frac{\Delta u}{\Delta c} \leq -q_2$, *where* $\Delta u = u(c_2;c_2) - u(c_1;c_1)$; *and (3)* $u(c_1;c_1) \geq u(c_2;c_2) + q_2 \Delta c$.
2. *The individual rationality constraint of type* c_l *cannot bind in an incentive-compatible contract.*
3. *The IC constraints of both types of agents cannot bind at the same time.*
4. *It is never optimal for the principal to make the IC and the IR constraints of a given type bind at the same time.*

Proof.

1. This follows from inequality (14.1), which is given by the IC constraint for type c_1.
2. From inequality (14.1), it directly follows that $u(c_1;c_1) > 0$; hence, the IR constraint for type c_1 cannot bind.
3. To prove this part, let us assume that the contrary is true. That is, $u(c_2;c_2) = u(c_1;c_2)$ along with $u(c_1;c_1) = u(c_2;c_1)$. From the first inequality, we get $T_1 - T_2 = c_2(q_1 - q_2)$, and from the second inequality, we get $T_1 - T_2 = c_1(q_1 - q_2)$. Since $c_1 < c_2$, both cannot be true at the same time.
4. For type c_1, we have already shown that if IR binds, then IC cannot bind. For type c_2, consider the following. Suppose it is optimal to make both IC and IR constraints bind for c_2. Then we must have $T_2 = c_2 q_2$ and $T_1 - T_2 = c_2(q_1 - q_2)$, which implies that $T_1 = c_2 q_1$. Now substitute $T_1 = c_2 q_1$ into the IC constraint of type c_1, we have $c_2 q_1 - c_1 q_1 \geq c_2 q_2 - c_1 q_2$ or $(c_2 - c_1) q_1 \geq (c_2 - c_1) q_2$, which would imply $q_1 \geq q_2$. Now consider another contract that reduces T_1 by ϵ to $c_2 q_1 - \epsilon$, and ϵ is so small that the IC constraint for type c_1 still remains non-binding. Such a revised contract will make the IC constraint for type 2 strictly non-binding while holding her IR constraint at equality. So she will accept it. This contract clearly increases the expected profit of the principal. Hence, the contract that makes both IC and IR constraints for type c_2 bind cannot be optimal.

This lemma not only characterises the agent's utility function under an incentive-compatible contract but also explains which constraints will bind. Of the two IC and IR constraints, the IC constraint for type c_2, and the IR constraint for type c_1 will not bind; the remaining two constraints should bind to allow for maximum profit. Thus, the principal's optimisation problem is as follows:

$$\text{Max} \quad E\pi = p_1[R(q_1) - T_1] + p_2[R(q_2) - T_2]$$

subject to

$$\text{IC}_1: \; u(c_1;c_1) = u(c_2;c_2) + q_2 \Delta c \quad \Rightarrow \quad T_1 - c_1 q_1 = T_2 - c_2 q_2 + q_2 \Delta c$$

$$\text{IR}_2: \; u(c_2;c_2) = 0 \quad \Rightarrow \quad T_2 = c_2 q_2.$$

Substituting $T_2 = c_2 q_2$ in the IC_1 constraint, we write $T_1 = c_1 q_1 + q_2 \Delta c$. Substituting both expressions in the objective function, we then write the principal's problem as to maximise the following with respect to q_1 and q_2:

$$E\pi = p_1\left[R(q_1) - c_1 q_1 - q_2 \Delta c\right] + p_2\left[R(q_2) - c_2 q_2\right].$$

Two first-order conditions are

$$R'(q_1) = c_1 \text{ and } R'(q_2) = c_2 + \frac{p_1}{p_2}\Delta c. \tag{14.2}$$

Proposition 47. *The optimal contract under asymmetric information is a menu contract of the following kind:* $\{(\tilde{q}_1, \tilde{T}_1), (\tilde{q}_2, \tilde{T}_2)\}$, *where* $(\tilde{q}_1, \tilde{q}_2)$ *are implicitly given by Eq.* (14.2) *and* $\tilde{T}_2 = c_2 \tilde{q}_2$ *and* $\tilde{T}_1 = c_1 \tilde{q}_1 + \tilde{q}_2 \Delta c$. *Importantly,* $\tilde{q}_1 = q_1^*$ and $\tilde{q}_2 < q_2^*$. *Agent* c_1 *receives an information rent* $\tilde{q}_2 \Delta c$.

It is noteworthy that the output of type c_1 is chosen at the first-best level and that the output of type c_2 is reduced below the first-best level. Alongside this, type c_1 is given an additional payment of $\tilde{q}_2 \Delta c$, which increases her utility above the reservation level by the same amount. This is entirely due to the informational advantage she has, and therefore, it is called 'information rent'. By 'informational advantage', we mean that she can always take the contract of type c_2 because the feasible set of contracts for type c_2 is a subset of her feasible set of contracts (recall Claim 1). Hence, an additional payment has to be made to her to make her supply q_1, which brings a much greater profit than q_2.

The asymmetric information contracts are shown on panel *b* of Figure 14.1. If the principal were to offer points *A* and *B* (the full information contracts), type c_1 would select point *B* (type c_2's contract). Therefore, to induce her to produce $q_1 > q_2$, which is more profitable from the principal's perspective, an offer like point *C* needs to be offered if point *B* is on the menu. Type c_1 is indifferent between points *B* and *C*. However, while point *C* solves the incentive compatibility problem, it is not optimal for the principal. He is paying too much for c_1, and he can reduce the payment by some amount. But as he does that, he needs to maintain the incentive compatibility constraint for type c_1, which, in turn, requires moving leftward from point *B* along the indifference curve $\underline{u}_2 = 0$. This way, he is sacrificing a bit of profit on type c_2 and gains from type c_1. Since type c_1 is more profitable, the gain from the type c_1 exceeds the loss from the type c_2 until point B' is reached. Note that lowering the output from q_2^* and $\tilde{q}_2$ allows the principal to reduce T_1 from point *C* to point C' while maintaining q_1^*. But clearly, C' is above point *A*. Therefore, it should be said that to maintain the first-best output from type c_1, the principal must give her some rent, that is, pay in excess of the full information payment T_1^*, but it need not be as high as what is needed to retain the first-best output from type c_2. By distorting q_2, rent on the type c_1 can be optimally reduced.

We conclude the discussion of this example with a comment. In Proposition 47, we have said that the derived menu contract is the optimal contract, but we did not consider any other type of contract than those that rely on truth-telling. How do we know that this is the best that the principal can do? The answer lies in a well-known result called the **revelation principle**, which says that if we restrict our attention to *direct revelation mechanisms* that induce truth-telling on the part of the economic actors, then we need not look further. See chapter 23 of Mas-Colell et al. (1995) and Dasgupta et al. (1979). The basic idea is that we can view many economic activities as implementation of some mechanism that help distribute scarce resources. Examples include assignment of school admissions, public goods contribution, voting, auctions, employment contracts, bargaining between a buyer and a seller and so on. Even impersonal markets can be viewed as a mechanism to distribute resources widely. In many situations, individuals' own preferences may not be observable to others, as in the problem of public goods provision. We all would enjoy a nice park, but if asked to contribute for it, we may understate the true extent of our enjoyment. A good mechanism should try to induce people to reveal their preferences so that the public good is provided for the collective benefit. Similarly, in some situations, as in our example of hidden information, some individuals may hold private information that would affect the welfare of all parties. An optimal contract or agreement has to be a direct mechanism that encourages everybody to reveal their private information as a dominant strategy (regardless of others revealing their private information or not). This result is called the revelation principle, and with this insight, we can be assured that the menu contract we have derived is the best contract under informational constraint.

14.2.2 Example 2 (three types of agents)

Suppose we extend our story to three types of agents, c_1, c_2 and c_3. The principal knows only the probability of the types, p_1, p_2 and p_3, respectively $(p_1 + p_2 + p_3 = 1)$. The agent knows her type. As before, we assume that c_1 is the best type from the principal's perspective; $c_1 < c_2 < c_3$.

The first-best or the full information solution does not change from the optimality condition $R'(q_i^*) - c_i = 0$ and $T_i^* = c_i q_i^*$ for $i = 1,2,3$. For the asymmetric information case, we now have three IC conditions and three IR conditions. The menu of contracts would now involve three pairs of quantity and payment, $\{(q_1, T_1), (q_2, T_2), (q_3, T_3)\}$. IC requires that type c_1 should choose (q_1, T_1) over (q_2, T_2) and (q_3, T_3). The same logic applies to types c_2 and c_3 as well. However, due to a single crossing property of the agent's utility function, that is, if a type c_1's indifference curve crosses an indifference curve of type c_2 or c_3, it will cross only once (you can check Figure 14.1), the incentive compatibility restriction needs to be imposed only two successive types (in the direction of incentives).

Formally, the IC constraints are

$$
\begin{aligned}
u(c_1;c_1) &\geq \max\{u(c_2;c_1), u(c_3;c_1)\} \\
u(c_2;c_2) &\geq \max\{u(c_1;c_2), u(c_3;c_2)\} \\
\text{and} \quad u(c_3;c_3) &\geq \max\{u(c_1;c_3), u(c_2;c_3)\}.
\end{aligned}
$$

You can check that the set of feasible contracts that guarantee IR for each type, namely, S_1^A, S_2^A and S_3^A are such that $S_3^A \subset S_2^A \subset S_1^A$. It turns out that the principal's optimal strategy will be (as you have seen in the two-type case) to select (q_1, T_1) from the region of S_1^A that falls outside S_2^A (and thus outside S_3^A too). Similarly, he will select (q_2, T_2) from S_2^A that falls outside S_3^A. Therefore, IC for type c_3 will be non-binding. For type c_2, we just need to consider $u(c_2;c_2) \geq u(c_3;c_2)$ (as $u(c_1;c_2) < 0$). This yields $T_2 - T_3 \geq c_2(q_2 - q_3)$, which also means $T_2 - T_3 > c_1(q_2 - q_3)$. But from the inequality $T_2 - T_3 > c_1(q_2 - q_3)$, we arrive at $T_2 - c_1 q_2 \equiv u(c_2;c_1) > u(c_3;c_1) = T_3 - c_1 q_3$. Therefore, we can just restrict our attention to $u(c_1;c_1) \geq u(c_2;c_1)$.

To state the implications of incentive compatibility, let us define $\Delta u_1 = u(c_2;c_2) - u(c_1,c_1)$, $\Delta u_2 = u(c_3;c_3) - u(c_2,c_2), \Delta c_1 \equiv c_2 - c_1$ and $\Delta c_2 = c_3 - c_2$.

Lemma 9. *The IC conditions imply that*

$$
q_1 \geq -\frac{u(c_2;c_2) - u(c_1,c_1)}{c_2 - c_1}\left(\equiv -\frac{\Delta u_1}{\Delta c_1}\right) \geq q_2 \tag{14.3}
$$

$$
q_2 \geq -\frac{u(c_3;c_3) - u(c_2,c_2)}{c_3 - c_2}\left(\equiv -\frac{\Delta u_2}{\Delta c_2}\right) \geq q_3. \tag{14.4}
$$

Clearly, $q_1 > q_2 > q_3$ *and* $u(c_1;c_1) > u(c_2;c_2) > u(c_3;c_3)$

The proof of the lemma has been omitted. You can derive the preceding inequalities by following the steps previously used to derive inequality (14.1) (in the two-type case).

In the optimal contract, the principal will set $u(c_3;c_3) = 0$. because there is no need to concede any surplus to the least preferred type and will make the IC constraints of the other two types bind. Thus, the principal's problem becomes

$$
\text{Max} \quad E\pi = p_1[R(q_1) - T_1] + p_2[R(q_2) - T_2] + p_3[R(q_3) - T_3]
$$

subject to

$$\begin{array}{lll} \mathrm{IC}_1: & u(c_1;c_1)=u(c_2;c_2)+q_2\Delta c_1 & \Rightarrow \; T_1-c_1q_1=T_2-c_2q_2+q_2\Delta c_1 \\ \mathrm{IC}_2: & u(c_2;c_2)=u(c_3;c_3)+q_3\Delta c_2 & \Rightarrow \; T_2-c_2q_2=T_3-c_3q_3+q_3\Delta c_2 \\ \mathrm{IR}_3: & u(c_3;c_3)=0 & \Rightarrow \; T_3-c_3q_3=0. \end{array}$$

In the objective function, we substitute $T_3=c_3q_3, T_2=c_2q_2+q_3\Delta c_2$ and $T_1=c_1q_1+q_3\Delta c_2+q_2\Delta c_1$ and differentiate $E\pi$ with respect to q_1, q_2 and q_3. The first-order conditions are implicitly solved for q_1, q_2 and q_3:

$$R'(\tilde{q}_1)=c_1, \qquad R'(\tilde{q}_2)=c_2+\frac{p_1}{p_2}\Delta c_1, \tag{14.5}$$

$$R'(\tilde{q}_3)=c_3+\frac{\Delta c_2(p_1+p_2)}{p_3}. \tag{14.6}$$

Proposition 48. *The optimal menu contract under asymmetric information over three types of agents is* $\{(\tilde{q}_1,\tilde{T}_1),(\tilde{q}_2,\tilde{T}_2),(q_3;\tilde{T}_3)\}$, *where* $\tilde{q}_1=q_1^*$, $\tilde{q}_2(<q_2^*)$ *and* $\tilde{q}_3(<q_3^*)$ *are given by Eqs* (14.5), (14.6) *and, correspondingly,*

$$\tilde{T}_1=c_1q_1^*+\tilde{q}_3\Delta c_2+\tilde{q}_2\Delta c_1 \tag{14.7}$$

$$\tilde{T}_2=c_2\tilde{q}_2+\tilde{q}_3\Delta c_2 \tag{14.8}$$

$$\tilde{T}_3=c_3\tilde{q}_3. \tag{14.9}$$

Types c_1 *and* c_2 *receive information rents of* $\tilde{q}_3\Delta c_2+\tilde{q}_2\Delta c_1$ and $\tilde{q}_3\Delta c_2$, *respectively.*

Figure 14.2 shows both the full information (panel *a*) and the asymmetric information contracts (panel *b*). As in the two-type case, the most preferred type c_1 produces efficient output,

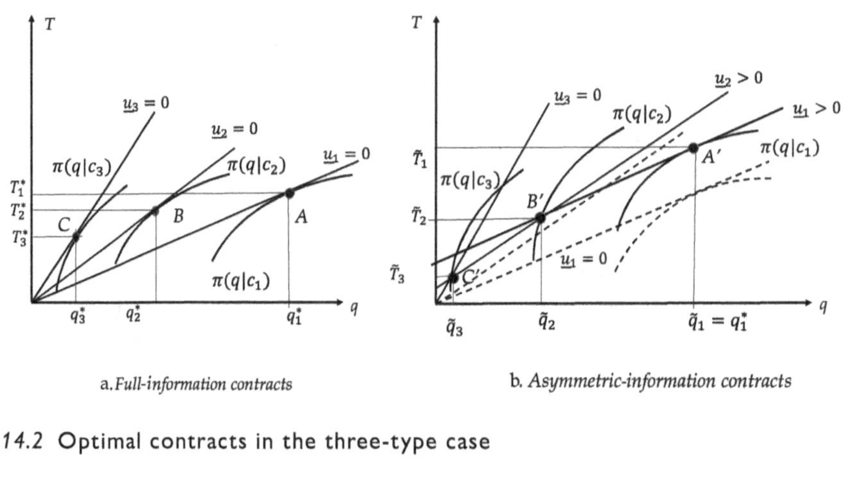

a. *Full-information contracts* b. *Asymmetric-information contracts*

Figure 14.2 Optimal contracts in the three-type case

while all other types produce inefficient outputs, and amongst them, the inefficiency is maximum for the least preferred type c_3. Points A', B' and C' correspond to the contracts of c_1, c_2 and c_3, respectively. Type c_1 is made indifferent between the contract intended for herself (at point A') and the contract for type c_2 (given by point B'). Type c_2 is made indifferent between the contract for herself (given by point B') and the contract for type c_3 (given by point C'). Type c_1 gets the highest information rent, type c_2 also gets some rent but type c_3 gets no rent.

14.2.3 *Continuous types*

The intuition of the three-type case of treating the best type efficiently and the worst type most inefficiently is easily extended to continuous types. Suppose the agent's type c is continuously distributed over an interval $[\underline{c},\overline{c}]$ according to a non-atomic cumulative probability distribution function $F(c)$ with density $f(c)>0$. The principal knows the distribution but not the actual draw of c. The IR constraint is still $u(c)=T-cq\geq 0$ for every c.

Now let us turn our attention to the incentive compatibility condition for an arbitrary type c. Let the agent's utility from truthful revelation be $u(c;c)$, while her utility from misrepresenting herself as c' is $u(c';c)$. IC requires $u(c;c)\geq u(c';c)$. Proceeding in the same way as in the two-type case, we derive the following:[1]

$$q(c')\leq -\left[\frac{u(c';c')-u(c;c)}{c'-c}\right]\leq q(c) \quad \text{for } c'>c.$$

By letting $c'\to c$, we can write the above relation as

$$u'(c)=-q(c) \text{ and } q'(c)<0.$$

This implies that under truthful revelation an agent's utility is a decreasing and concave function of c, and it is given by

$$u(c)=u(\overline{c})+\int_c^{\overline{c}}q(x)dx.$$

Substituting the definition of $u(c)$ in Eq. (14.10), we write

$$T(c)-cq(c)=u(\overline{c})+\int_c^{\overline{c}}q(x)dx, \text{ or } T(c)=u(\overline{c})+cq(c)+\int_c^{\overline{c}}q(x)dx.$$

The principal's problem is to maximise

$$E\pi=\int_{\underline{c}}^{\overline{c}}[R(q(c))-T(c)]f(c)dc,$$

subject to

$$T(c)=cq(c)+u(\overline{c})+\int_c^{\overline{c}}q(x)dx,\ u(\overline{c})\geq 0 \text{ and } q'(c)<0.$$

It is always optimal to set $u(\bar{c})=0$. Then by substituting the expression of $T(c)$ into $E\pi$ while temporarily ignoring the condition $q'(c)<0$, we write $E\pi$ as

$$E\pi=\int_{\underline{c}}^{\bar{c}}[R(q(c))-cq(c)]f(c)dc-\int_{\underline{c}}^{\bar{c}}\left[\int_{c}^{\bar{c}}q(x)dx\right]f(c)dc.$$

Now let us consider the second term separately. Using the integration by parts rule, we write

$$\int_{\underline{c}}^{\bar{c}}\left[\int_{c}^{\bar{c}}q(x)dx\right]f(c)dc=\left[\int_{c}^{\bar{c}}q(x)dx\cdot F(c)\right]_{\underline{c}}^{\bar{c}}-\int_{\underline{c}}^{\bar{c}}F(c)\frac{d}{dc}\left[\int_{c}^{\bar{c}}q(x)dx\right]dc$$
$$=\left[\int_{\bar{c}}^{\bar{c}}q(x)dx\cdot F(\bar{c})\right]-\left[\int_{\underline{c}}^{\bar{c}}q(x)dx\cdot F(\underline{c})\right]-\int_{\underline{c}}^{\bar{c}}F(c)\frac{d}{dc}\left[\int_{c}^{\bar{c}}q(x)dx\right]dc$$
$$=0-0-\int_{\underline{c}}^{\bar{c}}F(c)\frac{d}{dc}\left[\int_{c}^{\bar{c}}q(x)dx\right]dc.$$

By the Leibniz rule of differentiation under integration (see Chapter 12, note 16),

$$\frac{d}{dc}\left[\int_{\underline{c}}^{\bar{c}}q(x)dx\right]=-q(c).$$

Therefore,

$$\int_{\underline{c}}^{\bar{c}}\left[\int_{c}^{\bar{c}}q(x)dx\right]f(c)dc=\int_{\underline{c}}^{\bar{c}}q(c)F(c)dc=\int_{\underline{c}}^{\bar{c}}q(c)\frac{F(c)}{f(c)}\cdot f(c)dc,$$

where $F(c)/f(c)$ is the inverse of the hazard rate function. Using the preceding expression, we can write the principal's expected profit as

$$E\pi=\int_{\underline{c}}^{\bar{c}}\left[R(q(c))-cq(c)-q(c)\frac{F(c)}{f(c)}\right]f(c)dc. \tag{14.10}$$

The maximisation of $E\pi$ requires maximising profit with respect to q at every c of the support of the distribution. The first-order condition for $q(c)$ is

$$R'(q(c))-c-\frac{F(c)}{f(c)}=0,\ \text{for all}\ c\in[\underline{c},\bar{c}]. \tag{14.11}$$

We note that $R'(q(\underline{c}))-\underline{c}=0$ because $F(\underline{c})=0$ implying $q(\underline{c})=q^{*}(\underline{c})$, and for $c>\underline{c}$, we have $R'(q(c))>c$, or $q(c)<q^{*}(c)$. Suppose $\tilde{q}(c)$ implicitly solves Eq. (14.11). We need to check that $\tilde{q}(c)$ is strictly decreasing in c. Differentiating $\tilde{q}(c)$ with respect to c in Eq. (14.11), we get

$$R''(q(c))q'(c)-1-\frac{d}{dc}\left(\frac{F(c)}{f(c)}\right)=0,\Rightarrow q'(c)=\frac{1+\frac{d}{dc}\left(\frac{F(c)}{f(c)}\right)}{R''(q(c))}. \tag{14.12}$$

If $\frac{F(c)}{f(c)}$ is increasing in c, then $q'(c)<0$ (because $R''(q(c))<0$). The following can be said about the optimal contract.

Proposition 49. *Suppose* $\frac{d}{dc}\left(\frac{F(c)}{f(c)}\right)>0$. *Then the asymmetric information contract for continuous types of agent is* $\{(\tilde{q}(c),\tilde{T}(c))\}$, *where* $\tilde{q}(c)$ *is given by Eq. (14.11), and it is strictly decreasing in c so that information is fully revealing. Notably,* $\tilde{q}(\underline{c})=q^*(\underline{c})$ *and* $\tilde{q}(c)<q^*(c)$ *for* $c>\underline{c}$. *The payment received by agent c is*

$$\tilde{T}(c)=c\tilde{q}(c)+\int_{c}^{\overline{c}}\tilde{q}(x)dx,$$

where $\int_{\underline{c}}^{c}\tilde{q}(x)dx$ is the information rent of type c. For type $\underline{c}$ the information rent is maximum and for type $\bar{c}$ there is no information rent.

The condition on the inverse hazard function, which is only a sufficient condition, is important. Without it, $\tilde{q}(c)$ may not necessarily be strictly decreasing. If that is the case and $q(c)$ is not even weakly monotonic, then the incentive compatibility condition will not hold over the non-monotonic interval of c. To enforce truth-telling, $q(c)$ needs to be held constant over this interval. The contract then becomes a pooling contract, where over an interval of c, the same output is chosen and the truth is not fully revealed. However, our interest is in the fully revealing equilibrium, which is also called complete sorting equilibrium.

14.2.4 Countervailing incentives

So far, we have assumed that the reservation utility of all workers is same, and we have set it to be zero for simplicity. This assumption meant that the feasible set of contracts of a less desirable type (from the principal's perspective) is a proper subset of the feasible set of contracts of a more desirable type. In the example we have considered so far, a higher marginal cost agent's feasible contracts cannot be made unavailable to a lower marginal cost agent. Therefore, to induce truthful revelation, the principal needs to incentivise the lower cost types much more than a higher cost type. In other words, the agent's incentive to misrepresent her type (or be untruthful) runs only in one direction—upward in the example we considered.[2]

In many instances, the agent's reservation utility does depend on her type. The firm's alternative opportunity may lie in a different sector, where a low-cost firm is expected to earn a higher profit than a high-cost firm. This alternative opportunity affects contract negotiations. A hard-working worker (i.e., who suffers less disutility from work) is also more likely to be self-employed if out of work than someone who suffers more disutility from work. In general, an agent's access to alternative income opportunities can depend on her type. Here, we present a model of bureaucratic corruption and red tape adapted from Saha (2001), whereby the agent's reservation pay-off depends on her type in a natural way. In such models, the agent's incentive to misrepresent can run in either direction—upward or downward, a case referred to as *countervailing incentives* in the literature.

14.2.4.1 *A model of red tape and bribery*

Consider a bureaucratic setting where a small business owner is entitled to receive a subsidy s from the government. This can be cheaper credit, lower electricity tariff, a sales tax concession, or a permit for free parking for its customers on a busy street, and any such thing. This subsidy translates into a profit of π^g for the firm. But availing subsidy is not entirely cost free. An entitled firm has to apply for it with appropriate documents, which are then scrutinised by an official to ensure that the subsidy is not going to any ineligible firm. Time taken by the official is exogenously set at T by the higher authority, and this delay has a cost of θT. One can broadly define T as red tape that can also apply to the volume of paperwork and not necessarily the time taken to get the subsidy.

The cost of bearing the red tape varies between firms. Suppose there are only two types of firms in terms of the cost, θ_1 and $\theta_2, \theta_1 < \theta_2$. The firm's cost θ is its private information. Thus, the firm is the agent in our story, and in keeping with the convention of this chapter, we refer to the agent as 'she'.

The agent has the option of not availing the subsidy, and instead, she can pay the market price on the input that is otherwise entitled for subsidy. Her profit from relying entirely on market is π^m. We can set $\pi^m + s = \pi^g$ Thus, her reservation pay-off is

$$\bar{\pi}_i = Max\left\{\pi^g - \theta_i T, \pi^m\right\}, \quad \text{for } i = 1,2.$$

If $T > \left[\pi^g - \pi^m\right]/\theta_i = s/\theta_i$, then agent i's reservation pay-off is simply π^m. Let us denote the critical value of T as $\hat{T}_i$ Clearly, $\hat{T}_1 = s/\theta_1 > \hat{T}_2 = s/\theta_2$. If $T > \hat{T}_1$, then the reservation pay-off of either type is same, π^m; similarly, if $T = 0$ then also their reservation pay-offs are identical, but it is then much higher, π^g.

In general, the reservation utility of the agent takes the following values:

$$\bar{\pi}_1 = \begin{cases} \pi^m & \text{if } \ T \geq \hat{T}_1 \\ \pi^g - \theta_1 T & \text{if } \ T < \hat{T}_1 \end{cases} \tag{14.13}$$

$$\bar{\pi}_2 = \begin{cases} \pi^m & \text{if } \ T \geq \hat{T}_2 \\ \pi^g - \theta_2 T & \text{if } \ T < \hat{T}_2. \end{cases} \tag{14.14}$$

The agent's reservation pay-off differs depending on her type. We shall see that this has implications for the bribe game we are going to consider now.

The official, our principal, has some discretion to reduce the red tape or skip some paper checks, but in so doing, he faces some risk of being investigated by the higher authority and even being reprimanded. If t is the actual extent of red tape chosen by the official, then $T - t$ is the 'reduction in the pre-specified red tape' or a measure of his discretion. The greater the discretion used, the greater the risk of investigation. The maximum discretion he can use is T, where the actual red tape imposed is zero $(t = 0)$. In the other extreme, he may choose $t = T$, the default red tape, so no discretion is used at all, and no red tape is reduced. His potential cost of using discretion is given by an increasing and convex disutility function $\phi(T - t), \phi'(.) > 0, \phi''(.) > 0$.

Of course, the official is willing to undergo this disutility only if he receives bribe, b. Thus, we write his utility function as $u = b - \phi(T - t)$. Agent i can benefit from the reduced red tape in exchange for a bribe, as her profit from paying the bribe is $\pi_i(b) = \pi^g - b - \theta_i t$. She will pay bribe only when $\pi_i(b) \geq \bar{\pi}_i$.

The interaction between the agent and the official is a type of principal–agent relationship, as the official is uninformed about the agent's type (or her marginal cost of bearing red tape) but has to make decisions that will affect both his and the agent's pay-offs. We begin by noting the full-information offers.

Proposition 50. *The full -nformation offer for type* i *is given by* (t_i^*, b_i^*), *where* t_i^* *solves*

$$\phi'(T - t_i^*) - \theta_i = 0, \text{ and } b_i^* = \pi^g - \bar{\pi}_i - \theta_i t_i^*. \tag{14.15}$$

The official's red tape t_i^* *deceases with* θ. *That is to say, more discretion (or less actual red tape) is used for a higher cost agent. An increase in* T *(the exogenous red tape) increases* t_i^* *by the same amount.*

In the first-best case, the principal equates his marginal disutility from discretion (or reduction in red tape) with the agent's marginal cost of red tape. Their common goal is to reduce the joint cost of disutility from discretion and the cost of red tape. The surplus that the agent is able to realise is then taken away by the principal through bribe leaving the agent just enough to get her reservation utility.

While the results stated in Proposition 50 are straightforward, it may be more instructive to consider a graphical illustration of it, which we have presented in Figure 14.3 for three possible scenarios. In all cases, the agent's net reservation profit curve v_1 or v_2 gives higher profit in the downward direction (as such a movement indicates a lower bribe), while the official's utility u increases in the upward direction.

If T is very small, say, $T < \hat{T}_2$, both agents' reservation pay-offs are $\bar{\pi}_i = \pi^g - \theta_i T$. Note that this reservation pay-off is sensitive to the type. The agent's net pay-off is $v_i = \pi_i - \bar{\pi}_i = \theta_i(T - t) - b$. The principal maximises his pay-off $u = b_i - \phi(T - t_i)$ subject to $v_i = 0$. Panel a of Figure 14.3 shows this case. Agent's indifference curves are drawn for $v_i = 0$ for each type, which are shown to be tangent to the principal's indifference curve u. The optimal offers are given by point A for type θ_1 and by point B for type θ_2. Note that in this case, the feasible contract set for type θ_1 is a subset of the feasible contract set of type θ_2.

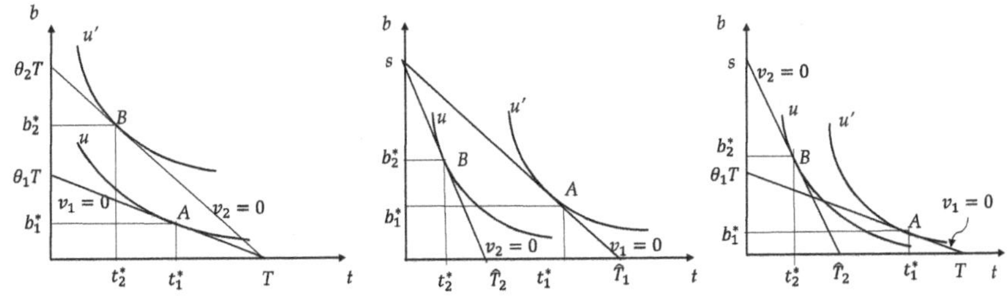

a. $T < \hat{T}_2$ b. $T > \hat{T}_1$ c. $\hat{T}_2 < T < \hat{T}_1$

Figure 14.3 Full-information offers

Panel *b* shows the case of a very high *T*, namely, $T > \widehat{T}_1$, when both agents' reservation pay-off is π^m. Net pay-off of type *i* is $v_i = \pi^g - b - \theta_i t - \pi^m = s - b - \theta_i t$. This case is similar to the case we have considered in the previous sections in which the participation constraints are type-independent. The optimal red tapes are still given by the same conditions, and thus, they are t_1^* and t_2^*. But note the reversal of the position of the indifference curves $v_1 = 0$ and $v_2 = 0$. Now the feasible contract set of θ_2 is a subset of the feasible contract set of θ_1. The principal's utility from type 1 is now higher than the utility he receives from θ_2, quite in contrast to panel *a*. However, keep in mind that u' of panel *b* does not correspond to the same level of utility as u' of panel *a*.

A completely different picture emerges when *T* is at an intermediate value, namely, $\widehat{T}_2 < T < \widehat{T}_1$. Agent θ_1's reservation pay-off is $\bar{\pi}_1 = \pi^g - \theta_1 T$, and agent θ_2's reservation pay-off is π^m. In this case, two net reservation pay-off curves ($v_i = 0$) cross each other sharing a common part, but neither is a subset of the other. Again, point *A* corresponds to the optimal offer for θ_1, and point *B* does the same for θ_2. The principal's pay-off can be greater from either type, although we have shown the case where θ_1 yields greater profit.

14.2.4.1.1 ASYMMETRIC INFORMATION

The official cannot identify the agent by her type, but he knows that the likelihood of the agent being θ_1 is p_1 or θ_2 is probability $p_2, p_1 + p_2 = 1$. From Figure 14.3, it should be clear that the most preferred type of agent is not fixed here; nor has one type a uniform incentive to misrepresent. In panel *a*, type θ_2 has the incentive to misrepresent herself, while in panel *b*, type θ_1 has, and in panel *c*, neither type does. It all depends on the magnitude of the exogenous parameter *T*.

It is the case of the intermediate values of *T* that is of greater interest to us, as it brings about the most important implications of countervailing incentives. But for the sake of completeness, let us take note of the optimal offers when $T < \widehat{T}_2$ or $T > \widehat{T}_1$ These two cases are straightforward.

The official's problem in the general case is

$$Max\ Eu = p_1\left(b_1 - \phi(T - t_1)\right) + p_2\left(b_2 - \phi(T - t_2)\right)$$

subject to

$$\text{IC}_1: \quad \pi(\theta_1;\theta_1) \ge \pi(\theta_2;\theta_1) \quad \Rightarrow \quad \pi^g - b_1 - \theta_1 t_1 \ge \pi^g - b_2 - \theta_1 t_2 \tag{14.16}$$

$$\text{IC}_2: \quad \pi(\theta_2;\theta_2) \ge \pi(\theta_1;\theta_2) \quad \Rightarrow \quad \pi^g - b_2 - \theta_2 t_2 \ge \pi^g - b_1 - \theta_2 t_1 \tag{14.17}$$

$$\text{IR}_1: \quad \pi(\theta_1;\theta_1) \ge \bar{\pi}_1 \quad \Rightarrow \quad \pi^g - b_1 - \theta_1 t_1 \ge \bar{\pi}_1 \tag{14.18}$$

$$\text{IR}_2: \quad \pi(\theta_2;\theta_2) \ge \bar{\pi}_2 \quad \Rightarrow \quad \pi^g - b_2 - \theta_2 t_2 \ge \bar{\pi}_2, \tag{14.19}$$

where $\bar{\pi}_1$ and $\bar{\pi}_2$ are given in Eqs. (14.13) and (14.14). You can simplify the IC and IR constraints simply by writing the agent's pay-off in terms of net profit: $v_i = \pi - \bar{\pi}$. The IC constraints for two types, $v_1(\theta_1;\theta_1) \ge v_1(\theta_2;\theta_1)$ and $v_2(\theta_2;\theta_2) \ge v_2(\theta_1;\theta_2)$ together imply

$$\theta_1(t_1 - t_2) \le b_2 - b_1 \le \theta_2(t_1 - t_2). \tag{14.20}$$

As you have seen before, two constraints cannot bind together (because $\theta_2 > \theta_1$). Which one will bind depends on which IR constraint binds. We know that when $T < \hat{T}_2$ agent θ_2's feasible contract set includes the feasible contract set of agent θ_1 (recall our Claim 1), and therefore, agent θ_2 has incentive to misrepresent her type as θ_1, but θ_1 cannot misrepresent (relative to the first-best contract). Therefore, IR_1 and IC_2 will bind. Conversely, when $T > \hat{T}_1$, the feasible set of contracts of θ_1 includes the feasible set of contracts for θ_2. Therefore, IR_2 and IC_1 will bind. The proof of these claims follows the same argument given earlier.

Therefore, in the optimal offers the four constraints lead to

$$b_1 = \theta_1(T - t_1) \quad \text{and} \quad b_2 = \theta_2(T - t_2) - \Delta\theta(T - t_1), \quad \text{if} \quad T < \hat{T}_2 \tag{14.21}$$

$$b_2 = s - \theta_2 t_2 \quad \text{and} \quad b_1 = s - \theta_1 t_1 - \Delta\theta t_2, \quad \text{if} \quad T > \hat{T}_1, \tag{14.22}$$

where $\Delta\theta = \theta_2 - \theta_1$. Substituting the above in the official's objective function we can determine his optimal red tape t. The following proposition summarises the key results.

Proposition 51.

1. *If $T < \hat{T}_2$ the optimal offers are $\{(\tilde{t}_1, \tilde{b}_1), (t_2^*, \tilde{b}_2)\}$ where $\tilde{b}_1$ and $\tilde{b}_2$ are given by Eq. (14.21), t_2^* is the full-information offer for θ_2* and *$\tilde{t}_1$ is given by the following equation*:

$$\phi'(T - \tilde{t}_1) = \theta_1 - \Delta\theta \frac{p_2}{p_1}. \tag{14.23}$$

Furthermore, $\tilde{t}_1 > t_1^*$ and the information rent for θ_2 agent is $v_2 = b_2^* - \tilde{b}_2 = \Delta\theta(T - \tilde{t}_1)$.

2. *If $T > \hat{T}_1$ the optimal offers are $\{(t_1^*, \tilde{b}_1), (\tilde{t}_2, \tilde{b}_2)\}$, where $\tilde{b}_1$ and $\tilde{b}_2$ are given by Eq. (14.22), t_1^* is the full-information offer for θ_1* and *$\tilde{t}_2$ is given by*

$$\phi'(T - \tilde{t}_2) = \theta_2 + \Delta\theta \frac{p_1}{p_2}. \tag{14.24}$$

Notably $\tilde{t}_2 < t_2^*$ and the information rent for θ_1 agent is $v_1 = b_1^* - \tilde{b}_1 = \Delta\theta\tilde{t}_2$.

The results of Proposition 51 are illustrated in Figure 14.4. Panel *a* shows the low–red tape (*T*) case, while panel *b* shows the high–red tape case. In the first case, the official chooses a red tape for θ_1 above the full information level, and in the second case, his chosen red tape is below the full information level. Truthful revelation in either case requires distorting the red tape for the least preferred type. When the exogenous red tape *T* is low, θ_1 is the least preferred type, and since this type suffers lower cost the subsidy is given to her with an 'excess' delay. However, when *T* is high, θ_2 is the least preferred type, and since to her the delay cost is higher, she is offered a 'much lower' delay.

14.2.4.1.2 THE CASE OF MODERATE RED TAPE

When *T* has an intermediate value, $\hat{T}_2 \le T \le \hat{T}_1$ the reservation profit changes to $\bar{\pi}_1 = \pi^g - \theta_1 T$ and $\bar{\pi}_2 = \pi^m$. Consequently, the net profit changes to $v_1 = \pi_1 - \bar{\pi}_1 = \theta_1(T - t_1) - b_1$ and $v_2 = \pi_2 - \bar{\pi}_2 = s - \theta_2 t_2 - b_2$. The feasible set of contracts of each type includes a region that falls

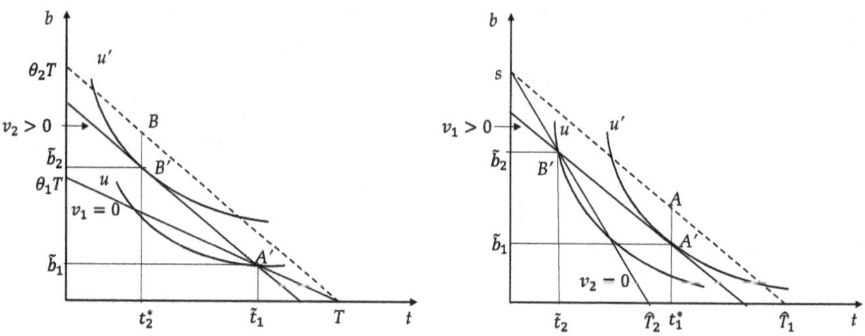

a. $T < \hat{T}_2$ b. $T > \hat{T}_1$

Figure 14.4 Asymmetric information offers under low and high *T*

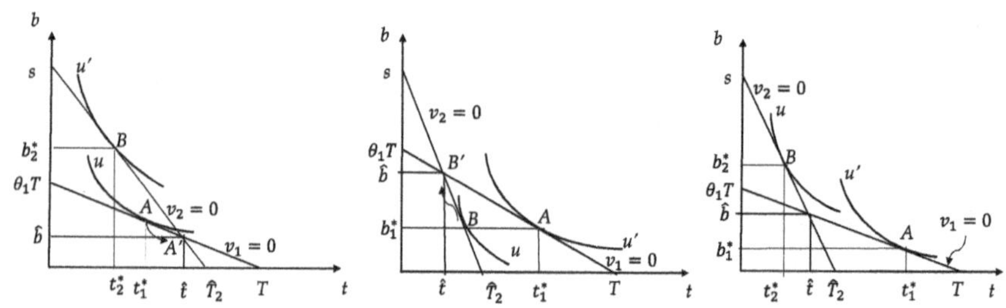

a. *Optimal* $t_1 = \hat{t}$ b. *Optimal* $t_2 = \hat{t}$ c. *Optimal* $t_i = t_i^*$

Figure 14.5 Moderate red tape and elimination of information rent

outside the feasible set of the other type. In other words, the indifference curves representing zero net pay-off, namely, $v_1 = 0$ and $v_2 = 0$ intersect each other, as shown in Figure 14.5, which describes three possible scenarios corresponding to different levels of *T*. The intersection point of the two reservation (net) pay-off curves is given by $(\hat{t}, \hat{b})$, where

$$\hat{t} = \frac{s - \theta_1 T}{\Delta\theta} \quad \text{and} \quad \hat{b} = s - \theta_2 \hat{t}. \tag{14.25}$$

It is also easy to check that

$$\hat{t} = T, \hat{b} = 0, \quad \text{if } T = \hat{T}_2 (= s/\theta_2)$$
$$\hat{t} = 0, \hat{b} = s, \quad \text{if } T = \hat{T}_1 (= s/\theta_1).$$

The incentive regime in this case depends on whether the first-best offers lie on one side of the point $(\hat{t}, \hat{b})$ or on either side of it. On panel *a* of Figure 14.4, it is shown that $\hat{t}$ is not too far from t_1^*, and both of the first-best offers are to the left of $(\hat{t}, \hat{b})$. Under asymmetric information,

θ_2 type would pick up the offer for θ_1 unless she is given information rent and made indifferent between the two offers. Hence, t_1 is distorted upwardly, but note that t_1 cannot be increased beyond $\hat{t}$. Thus, the asymmetric information solution or the second-best solution sets $\tilde{t}_1 = \hat{t}$, which, in turn, helps *eliminate the information rent* for type θ_2. Such a situation would be optimal when

$$\tilde{t}_1 > \hat{t} \quad \Rightarrow \quad \phi'(T-\hat{t}) > \theta_1 - \Delta\theta p_2 / p_1.$$

Panel *b* shows a similar case that occurs to the right of $(\hat{t},\hat{b})$ Here, the optimal red tape for type θ_2 needs to be distorted downward, but if

$$\tilde{t}_2 < \hat{t} \quad \Rightarrow \quad \phi'(T-\hat{t}) < \theta_2 + \Delta\theta p_1 / p_2,$$

the optimal red tape for θ_2 is then restricted at $\hat{t}$, which, in turn, eliminates the information rent for θ_1. Thus, in both panel *a* and panel *b*, information rent from the preferred type has been eliminated, and the agent has been pushed down to her reservation profit. However, this has also involved some distortion of the least preferred type's red tape. Here, the IR constraint binds for either type along with the incentive constraint for the preferred type.

On panel *c*, we show that there is a range of *T*, when the first-best offers straddle on both sides of the intersection point $(\hat{t},\hat{b})$. Here, not only is the information rent eliminated from the preferred type, but no distortion is also needed to eliminate the rent. The first-best offers are incentive compatible and truthful revelation occurs at no cost. The principal is able to offer a menu of $\{(t_1^*,b_1^*),(t_2^*,b_2^*)\}$, agent θ_1 will accept (t_1^*,b_1^*) and agent θ_2 will accept (t_2^*,b_2^*). Their IC constraints are strictly non-binding while their IR constraints bind, as evident from the graph. The proofs are trivial, but you can see Saha (2001) for a more formal argument.

Proposition 52. *Assume* $\hat{T}_2 \le T \le \hat{T}_1$ *and consider* $\tilde{t}_1$, $\tilde{t}_2$ *and* $\hat{t}$ *as given in Eqs. (14.23), (14.24) and (14.25), respectively. Then at any given* T, *the asymmetric information offers are as follows:*

1. *If* $t_1^* < \hat{t} < \tilde{t}_1$, *the menu contract is* $\{(\hat{t},\hat{b}),(t_2^*,b_2^*)\}$, *and no type receives information rent.*
2. *If* $\tilde{t}_2 < \hat{t} < t_2^*$, *the menu contract is* $\{(t_1^*,b_1^*),(\hat{t},\hat{b})\}$, *and no type receives information rent.*
3. *If* $t_2^* < \hat{t} < t_1^*$, *the menu contract is* $(t_1^*,b_1^*),(t_2^*,b_2^*)$, *and no type receives information rent.*

The key point of countervailing incentives that they are disadvantageous to the agent. The principal can not only achieve truthful revelation at lower costs (both less information rent and less distortion in quantity) but also implement the first best in some instances. However, even when the first-best offers are incentive-compatible, he still needs to offer a menu contract, because he cannot identify the type.

Countervailing incentives emerge in many contexts when the reservation pay-off of the agent is type-dependent. In the regulation context, this problem has been studied by Lewis and Sappington (1989), and Maggi and Rodriguez-Clare (1995) with continuous types, where the agent's incentive to misrepresent can switch from understating her type to overstating it. In these models, the source of the countervailing incentives is not a variation in some exogenous parameter as in Saha (2001), but these incentives are embedded within the reservation utility function of the agent. The classic work of regulation is due to Baron and Myerson (1982), where a regulator stipulates a payment and a quantity based on the truthful revelation of the privately known marginal cost of the agent. The problem is similar to the garment procurer's problem studied here in Section 14.2.3.

14.3 Hidden actions

A principal engages an agent to supply effort or labour, which the principal cannot observe (or verify and prove in a court of law), nor can he deduce the agent's effort from the output/revenue he receives at the end. The most common example of this kind is a situation in which the agent works out of sight of the principal and mother nature interferes between the agent's exertion of effort and the realisation of output. So, if the output turns out to be low, the principal cannot determine whether Mother Nature was unkind or the agent did not give the right effort. An absentee landowner hires a farmer to work on his land unsupervised. Two months later, if the harvest is found to be poor, the principal may doubt the farmer's honesty but cannot be certain about it, because the outcome could also be due to some unexpected bouts of rain. Equally, a good harvest cannot be attributed to the hard work of the farmer if Mother Nature did not play a spoilsport. For an energy company that has appointed a door-to-door sales campaigner to steal its rival's business, a sudden surge in new subscriptions could be attributed to the efforts of the campaigner, but it could also be due to poor customer service of the rival company, which is not observable to outsiders.

The moot point of these examples is that the principal confronts a problem of *hidden action* on the part of the agent. Knowing that her action is not observable, deducible and verifiable in the court of law the agent has the incentive to give low effort, despite promising to do otherwise. This is called the problem of **moral hazard**. As the principal typically prefers the agent to give high effort, the agent's preference runs into a conflict with the principal's. This conflict defines the core of any agency problem.

The question is, Can the principal design a compensation scheme so that the agent, though left unsupervised, will still exert the desired level of effort? The answer is 'yes'. Before we delve into the details, the short answer is that the compensation scheme cannot be made conditional on the effort (because it is unobservable) but on output or revenue provided it is observable to both parties. Mind that the compensation scheme is meant only to ensure high effort, but by no means does it guarantee high output/revenue, because Mother Nature still can upset everything.

14.3.1 Discrete effort and discrete output

We consider two effort levels: e_h (high) and e_l (low); $e \in \{e_l, e_h\}$. High effort gives higher disutility to the agent and low effort gives low disutility. The principal cannot observe the effort. After the effort is given, the outcome of the effort, say, a harvest or sales revenue, q, is realised randomly. Suppose there are two possible realisations of q: either q_h or $q_l, q_h > q_l$. The probability of q_h being drawn is p and that of q_l is $1 - p$. The value of p depends on what effort the agent has given. Crucially, p increases in effort as follows:

$$p = \begin{cases} p_h & \text{if } e = e_h \\ p_l & \text{if } e = e_l \end{cases}.$$

Consider a contracting arrangement between the (risk-neutral) principal and the (risk-averse) agent. The principal stipulates w_h and w_l, which are contingent on the realisation of q_h and q_l, respectively. Assume that the price of the good is fixed at 1. The state contingent profit of the principal is $\pi_i = q_i - w_i$ and utility of the agent is $u_i(w_i \mid e_h) = v(w_i) - z(e_h)$ if she has given high effort and $u(w_i \mid e_l) = v(w_i) - z(e_l)$ if she has given low effort. We assume $v'() > 0$, $v''(.) < 0$ and $z'(.) > 0, z''(.) > 0$. The contract is signed before the agent gives effort. Therefore, she will agree to it only if her expected utility is not less than her reservation utility, which we set to be zero.

If the agent is expected to give low effort, her IR constraint is then

$$Eu(e_l) = p_l v(w_h) + (1 - p_l)v(w_l) - z(e_l) \geqslant 0,$$

and similarly, if she is expected to give high effort, her IR constraint will be

$$Eu(e_h) = p_h v(w_h) + (1 - p_h)v(w_l) - z(e_h) \geqslant 0. \tag{14.26}$$

Along with these two IR constraints, there is also an (effort) incentive compatibility constraint which ensures that the agent finds it optimal to give high effort. That is,

$$p_h v(w_h) + (1 - p_h)v(w_l) - z(e_h) \geqslant p_l v(w_h) + (1 - p_l)v(w_l) - z(e_l). \tag{14.27}$$

Note that this incentive compatibility condition is different from the hidden information case. Here, there are no types, and the incentive issue does not apply to the low effort.

The principal's problem is to induce his most preferred effort level, which is generally e_h by offering a contract that maximises

$$E\pi = p_h(q_h - w_h) + (1 - p_h)(q_l - w_l)$$

subject to the IR and IC constraints given in Eqs. (14.26) and (14.27).

14.3.1.1 *The first-best contract*

We first take note of the case where the agent's effort is observable, as if the agent is working under direct supervision of the principal. Wage then can be made directly conditional on the observed effort. If high effort is given, from the IR condition the wage is determined $v(w_h^*) = z(e_h)$ or $w_h^* = v^{-1}(z(e_h))$. The principal's expected profit is then $E\pi^*(e_h) = p_h q_h + (1 - p_h)q_l - w_h^*$. For low effort, the wage is $w_l^* = v^{-1}(z(e_l))$, and we assume $E\pi(e_l) = p_l q_h + (1 - p_l)q_l - w_l^* < E\pi^*(e_h)$ so that the principal strictly prefers the high effort.

On panel *a* of Figure 14.6, the first-best case is illustrated. For the purpose of graphical illustration, we take effort e as a continuous variable. The agent's utility is independent of the state of nature (or realisation of *q*). Her indifference curve $u = v(w) - z(e)$ is upward-sloping and convex, due to the assumption $v''(.) < 0$ and $z''(.) > 0$.[3]

The principal, by comparison, is concerned about her expected profit, $E\pi = p(e)q_h + (1 - p(e))q_l - w$. Note that for the case of continuous *e*, it is more appropriate to think of the probability *p* of getting a high output increases with effort. That is, $p'(e) > 0$ and $p''(e) < 0$ so that this probability becomes an increasing but concave function. The iso-expected profit curve is also upward-sloping but concave and lower the position of the curve higher the profit level.[4] We assume that e_h is the optimal effort for the principal, which is shown by the tangency point A between the expected profit curve and the indifference curve. In contrast, point B, which is a low-effort point, is not a tangency point. Therefore, it is natural that the principal would try to implement e_h. But without observability of effort implementation of e_h requires providing incentive to the agent so that she would refrain from giving low effort.

14.3.1.2 The second-best case

When effort cannot be observed, the contract can specify wages that are conditional on the realisation of the output. Suppose it takes the form of $\{w_h, w_l\}$. That is, if q_h is realised, w_h is given, and if q_l is realised, w_l is given. Note in this case, a key difference from the first-best contract is that the agent is not paid before the realisation of q, a point that deserves some comment, which we will make later on.

The contract must be incentive compatible, and from the profit maximisation point of view, the principal should make the constraint bind. That is, from condition (14.27), we must have (after forcing equality)

$$v(w_h) = v(w_l) + \frac{\Delta z}{\Delta p}, \tag{14.28}$$

where $\Delta z = z(e_h) - z(e_l)$ and $\Delta p = p_h - p_l$ Eq. (14.28) is critical to the optimal contract. As $\Delta z(.)$ is strictly positive $v(w_h)$ must exceed $v(w_l)$ That means, two output-contingent wages must differ, and w_h must exceed w_l.

On panel b of Figure 14.6, we draw the expected utility curve of the agent and the IC constraint (14.28). Here, for the sake of convenience we use $v(w_l)$ and $v(w_h)$ on the two axes instead of w_l and w_h directly. The expected utility indifference curves are linear and downward-sloping. To see this, write $Eu = p_h v(w_h) + (1 - p_h) v(w_l) - z(e_h)$, from which we get $dv(w_h)/dv(w_l) = -(1 - p_h)/p_h$, This is shown by the straight line $Eu(e_h) = 0$ passing through points A and C. This is the reservation utility curve of the agent when she gives high effort.

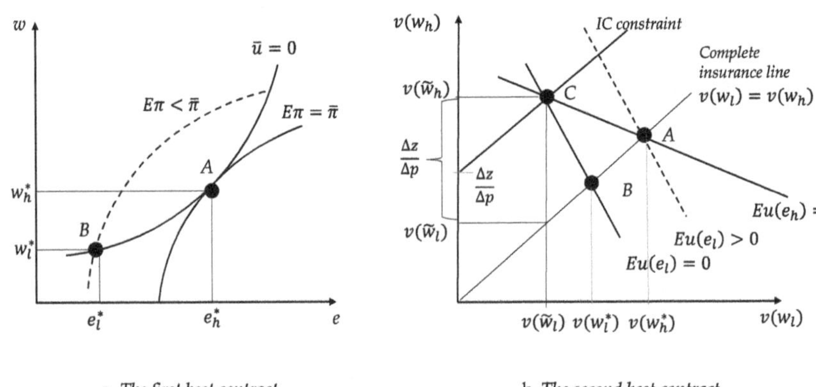

Figure 14.6 Optimal contracts under hidden actions

Every point on this line is a contract as it promises a pair of wages. Point A corresponds to the first-best contract, where w_h is conditioned on high effort, which is equivalent to saying that $w_h = w_l$. Any indifference curve parallel to this line and lying above induces high effort and yields strictly positive utility to the agent (in excess of her reservation utility).

The 45-degree line corresponds to the complete insurance line, as the agent's utility is held fixed across the states of nature. The area below the 45-degree line is irrelevant because any combination of a low wage in the high-output state and a high wage in the low-output state is ruled out.

For reference, the agent's indifference curve representing the reservation utility and resulting from low effort is also drawn. It is a steeper line and passes through points C and B. Check that its slope is $(1-p_l)/p_l$. Point B corresponds to the first-best contract for giving low effort. Any line parallel to and above this line represents higher utility than the reservation level when the low effort is given. For instance, the dashed line passing through point A is one such indifference curve. Here, we take note of an important fact in the following lemma.

Lemma 10. *Any fixed wage contract that specifies* $w_h = w_l \geq w_l^*$ *always induces the low effort* e_l.

It is obvious from the graph that if the wages are selected from the complete insurance line, say, w_h^*, the agent will give e_l and attain a strictly positive expected utility level given by the dashed line passing through point A. Therefore, it is never in the interest of the principal to offer a fixed wage contract when he cannot monitor the effort. He needs to make the contract incentive compatible.

The IC condition (14.28) is shown by the upward-sloping line that passes through point C. Clearly, it is parallel to the 45-degree line. Point C is the unique point where both the IR and IC constraints for giving e_h bind simultaneously. Note that the size of $\Delta z / \Delta p$ uniquely determines the difference between $v(w_h)$ and $v(w_l)$. The intersection of the two constraints (which is point C) gives the optimal second-best contract. It is important to note that the optimal wage for the low output state is strictly less than w_l^*, giving her *ex post* utility $v(w_l)$ below the effort cost $z(e_h)$.

Proposition 53. *In the second-best contract, if the principal wishes to induce effort* e_h, *he specifies* $\{\tilde{w}_h, \tilde{w}_l\}$ *where these two wages simultaneously satisfy the IC and IR constraints for high effort. In contrast, if the principal wishes to induce low effort he will offer a fixed wage contract* $w_h = w_l = w_l^*$.

Several points are worth emphasising here:

1. The wage schedule mimics a pattern of *reward and punishment*. If the high output is observed, the agent is rewarded a higher wage (higher than w_h^*), while if the low output is observed, she is punished with a lower wage (lower than w_l^*). But this reward and punishment should not be seen as the principal's response to the agent's possible shirking. The moral hazard contract is not about detecting shirking. Rather, it is about providing an incentive to induce higher effort, based on the promise of giving a very high wage in the good state and a low wage in the low state. The *ex post* payment is just honouring the promise. All contracts presuppose commitment on the part of signatories.
2. The agent's individual rationality constraint applies to the 'expected utility' to be zero (or some reservation level). That means the agent's *ex post* pay-off will be below the reservation level in the bad state. In some cases, the agent can be even asked to make a payment to the principal. The contract presupposes that the agent is capable of making this transfer.

That means she is not facing a wealth or credit constraint to make this transfer to the principal or support her minimum consumption in the bad state. In short, there is no *limited liability* constraint. Her income can be reduced as far as needed to make the contract incentive compatible for the agent and optimal for the principal. But if there is a limited liability constraint or a minimum wage constraint, then the agent's low-state wage cannot be reduced below a level. The incentive contract then will be different. We address this issue later.

3. Incentive contracts are costly from the principal's point of view. He makes less expected profit by providing incentives. To see this note that in the optimal contract, the agent's reservation utility binds. That means $Ev(w) = p_h v(\tilde{w}_h) + (1-p_h)v(\tilde{w}_l) = z(e_h)$. Since $v(w)$ is a concave function, by the standard logic of risk aversion, $Ev(w) < v(Ew)$. As $Ev(w) = z(e_h)$ means $z(e_h) = v(w_h^*)$, the first-best wage is the *certainty equivalent* of the risky income stream that the agent is inevitably exposed to under moral hazard. As the certainty equivalent is always less than the expected income, we have $w_h^* < Ew \equiv p_h\tilde{w}_h + (1-p_h)\tilde{w}_l$.
4. Finally, the contract presupposes that the agent will be paid *ex post*. When the time gap between the exertion of effort and the realisation of output is significant, as in many agricultural production contexts, it may not be practical (or even fair) to ask a worker to wait a few more months to receive her wage. A more practical solution is employing a supervisor to alleviate the problem of moral hazard. Another solution is to pay a small fixed wage and then ask the worker to wait for the harvest to receive the variable component of her wage. In many developing countries, especially in South and South-East Asia, agricultural production is organised under share tenancy where the tenant receives a share of the output, which is akin to a variable wage. Although the tenant will employ less than the efficient level of input (including her labour) due to the fact that she will not be given the full marginal product of her work, the overall arrangement can be seen as a risk-sharing incentive contract that addresses a moral hazard problem. However, we should also keep in mind that hiring a supervisor shifts the moral hazard problem elsewhere; the principal needs to write a moral hazard contract with the supervisor.

14.3.1.4.3 LIMITED LIABILITY

What if the agent has a wealth/credit constraint so that she cannot be made to suffer a significant drop in her low state wage? Clearly, the optimal contract is then constrained by a compensation floor. In Figure 14.7 we show how the limited liability protection will affect the optimal contract. Suppose wage cannot fall below $\underline{w}$, which can be the minimum wage of the economy. By the incentive constraint, which must bind for the inducement of high effort, the agent will then receive a very high wage $\overline{w}_h$ in the good state. But then her IR constraint will not bind. Her expected utility from giving high effort must be strictly positive.

Thus, in the presence of a limited liability constraint inducing high effort can be significantly costlier. One possibility is that the principal may find it too costly and may prefer to just settle for low effort. Formally, if

$$p_h(q_h - \overline{w}_h) + (1-p_h)(q_l - \underline{w}) < p_l q_h + (1-p_l)q_l - w_l^*$$

or $$\Delta p \Delta q < p_h \overline{w}_h + (1-p_h)\underline{w} - w_l^*,$$

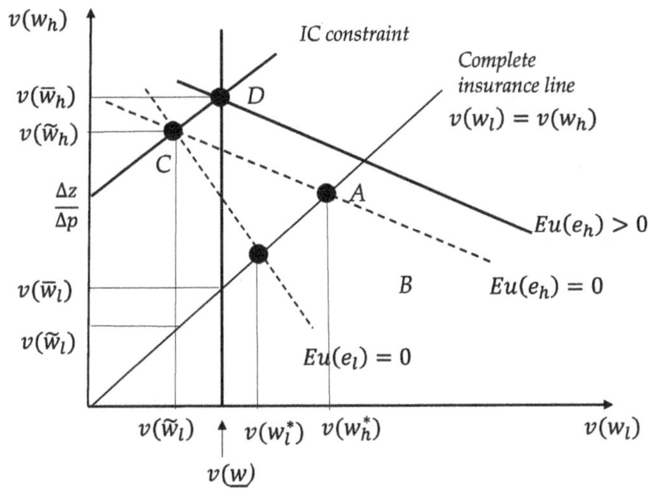

Figure 14.7 Optimal contracts under limited liability

the principal will prefer the agent to give low effort. The expected gain from inducing higher effort is less than the expected wage loss above the low-effort wage w_l^*. He then simply settles for low effort.

14.3.2 Discrete effort but continuous output

So far, we have assumed that there are only two possible realisations of the output. But there could be many, and in principle, the incentive contract can be generalised to infinitely many realisations of the output. Suppose $q \in \left[\underline{q}, \overline{q}\right]$ and it is drawn by Mother Nature with a cumulative distribution function $F(q)$ with its probability density function being $f(q) > 0$. We assume that $F(q)$ is a function of effort e. We assume that the distribution of q conditional on e_h first-order stochastically dominates the distribution of q conditional on e_l. That is, $F(q \mid e_h) \leq F(q \mid e_l)$, meaning that the probability of getting an output level q or less is lower when the effort level is high. It also means that the expected output is greater under higher effort $\int_{\underline{q}}^{\overline{q}} qf(q \mid e_h)dq > \int_{\underline{q}}^{\overline{q}} qf(q \mid e_l)dq$.

Assuming that e_h is more preferable than e_l, the principal wants to maximise $E\pi = \int_{\underline{q}}^{\overline{q}} \left[q - w(q)\right] f(q \mid e_h)dq$, with respect to $w(q)$ subject to the IC and IR constraints, which are

$$\text{IC}: \quad \int_{\underline{q}}^{\overline{q}} v(w(q)) f(q \mid e_h)dq - z(e_h) \geq \int_{\underline{q}}^{\overline{q}} v(w(q)) f(q \mid e_l)dq - z(e_l)$$

$$\text{or,} \quad \int_{\underline{q}}^{\overline{q}} v(w(q)) \{f(q \mid e_h) - f(q \mid e_l)\} \geq \Delta z \tag{14.29}$$

$$\text{IR}: \quad \int_{\underline{q}}^{\overline{q}} v(w(q)) f(q \mid e_h)dq - z(e_h) \geq 0. \tag{14.30}$$

We assume that there is no limited liability constraint.

14.3.2.1 The first-best contract

In the first-best case, when the agent's effort is observable, the principal needs to satisfy just the IR constraint. His problem is to maximise the following Lagrangian with respect to $w(q)$:

$$\mathcal{L} = \int_{\underline{q}}^{\overline{q}} \left[q - w(q)\right] f(q \mid e_h) dq + \lambda_1 \left[\int_{\underline{q}}^{\overline{q}} v(w(q)) f(q \mid e_h) dq - z(e_h)\right]$$

The first-order condition is

$$f(q \mid e_h)\left[-1 + \lambda_1 v'(w(q))\right] = 0 \text{ for all } q \in \left[\underline{q}, \overline{q}\right].$$

The optimal state-contingent wage $w(q)$ is given by $v'(w(q)) = 1/\lambda_1$. Clearly, the IR constraint must be binding so that $\lambda_1 > 0$; otherwise, this first-order condition will not be met with equality. Since $v'(w(q))$ is invariant, $w(q)$ must be invariant to the realisation of q. Let this wage be equal to w_h^* so that $v(w_h^*) = z(e_h)$. As expected, the agent is offered complete insurance.

14.3.2.2 The second-best contract

When the effort is not observable, the IC constraint is to be taken into account. Then the principal's problem is to maximise

$$\mathcal{L} = \int_{\underline{q}}^{\overline{q}} \left[q - w(q)\right] f(q \mid e_h) dq + \lambda_1 \left[\int_{\underline{q}}^{\overline{q}} v(w(q)) f(q \mid e_h) dq - z(e_h)\right]$$
$$+ \lambda_2 \left[\int_{\underline{q}}^{\overline{q}} v(w(q)) \{f(q \mid e_h) - f(q \mid e_l)\} dq - \Delta z\right].$$

The first-order condition is

$$f(q \mid e_h)\left[-1 + v'(w(q))\left\{\lambda_1 + \lambda_2\left(1 - \frac{f(q \mid e_l)}{f(q \mid e_h)}\right)\right\}\right] = 0 \text{ for all } q \in \left[\underline{q}, \overline{q}\right].$$

Given $f(q \mid e_h) > 0$ the preceding equation can be rewritten as

$$v'(w(q)) = \frac{1}{\lambda_1 + \lambda_2\left(1 - \dfrac{f(q \mid e_l)}{f(q \mid e_h)}\right)}. \tag{14.31}$$

Eq. (14.31) is critical for the optimal wage/compensation scheme, regarding which we make the following observations:

1. If the agent were risk-neutral, that is, $v''(w(q)) = 0$, any fixed wage contract would be optimal as risk sharing is not an issue. In this case, the principal can offer w_h^* for all realisations of q.
2. The IC and IR constraints will both bind. If one of them did not bind, we would have either $\lambda_1 = 0$ or $\lambda_2 = 0$. If $\lambda_1 = 0$, the principal can always find a wage scheme $w(q) - \epsilon$ that would

satisfy both IC and IR constraints and improve the principal's profit. Therefore, λ_1 must be positive. λ_2 must also be positive; otherwise, again by a similar argument, profit can be improved by offering $w(q)-\epsilon$. Besides, if IC is non-binding, then Eq. (14.31) would hold only if complete insurance is offered, which, in turn, will encourage the agent to give e_l.

3. There exists a critical q, say, $\hat{q}$, at which $f(q\,|\,e_l)=f(q\,|\,e_h)$ and $w(q)=w_h^*$. This follows from the fact that the distribution function $F(q\,|\,e_h)$ first-order stochastically dominates $F(q\,|\,e_l)$. First-order stochastic dominance implies that their associated probability density functions cross only once. In this case, $f(q\,|\,e_l)$ crosses $f(q\,|\,e_h)$ from left. Thus, there is a unique $\hat{q}$. See panel *b* of Figure 14.8. The likelihood ratio of lower q is below 1 at $q>\hat{q}$ and is above 1 at $q<\hat{q}$. Eq. (14.31) then implies that $w(q)$ will exceed w_h^* at $q<\hat{q}$ and will be less than w_h^* at $q<\hat{q}$. This is shown on panel *a* of Figure 14.8.
4. The optimal wage scheme will be strictly increasing in q due to the incentive compatibility constraint. It can also be verified from Eq. (14.31) that

$$w'(q)=\frac{1}{v''(w(q))}\times\frac{\lambda_2\dfrac{d}{dq}\left(\dfrac{f(q\,|\,e_l)}{f(q\,|\,e_h)}\right)}{\left[\lambda_1+\lambda_2\left(1-\dfrac{f(q\,|\,e_l)}{f(q\,|\,e_h)}\right)\right]^2}>0$$

if and only if

$$\frac{d}{dq}\left(\frac{f(q\,|\,e_l)}{f(q\,|\,e_h)}\right)<0. \tag{14.32}$$

Condition (14.32) is called the monotone likelihood ratio condition. If the agent gives lower effort, the relative likelihood of getting a higher output should fall; conversely, the relative probability of getting a higher output should monotonically increase if the agent has given higher effort. In essence, the monotone likelihood ratio property makes higher output a credible signal of higher effort, and that is why wage is also conditioned to rise with output.

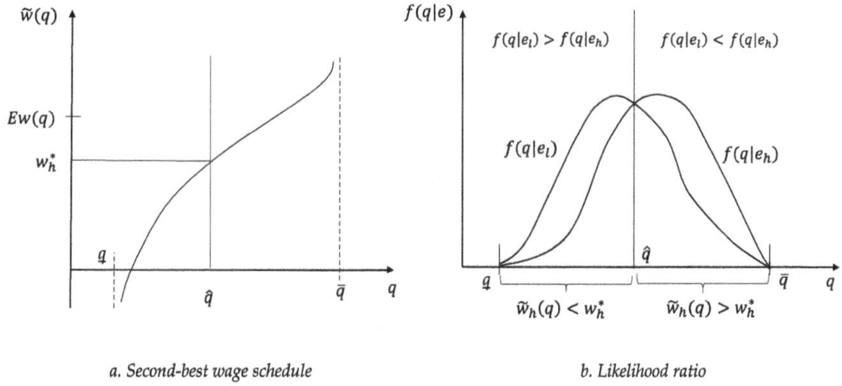

Figure 14.8 The continuous output case

5. The expected wage cost $\left(\int_{q}^{\bar{q}} wf\left(q \mid e_h\right)dq\right)$ will be greater than w_h^*. The argument is risk aversion, and it is same as given before in the case of discrete outputs. w_h^* is the certainty equivalent for the agent, and therefore, it is strictly less than Ew.
6. Figure 14.8 is drawn under the assumption that there is no limited liability constraint, preventing the principal to push the wage down as far as needed, including negative values. If the wage is not permitted to be negative, then the optimal wage scheme will be truncated at some q, say, $\hat{q}_l$. At all $q \leq \hat{q}_l$, we will have $w(q) = 0$, and at all $q > \hat{q}_l$, the optimal wage scheme should be such that the following holds (i.e., the IC constraint binds):

$$\int_{\hat{q}_l}^{\bar{q}} v(w(q))\left[f\left(q \mid e_h\right) - f\left(q \mid e_l\right)\right]dq = dz. \tag{14.33}$$

Proposition 54. *When* q *is continuous and effort is discrete, the following holds:*

1. *In the absence of limited liability, the optimal wage/compensation scheme $\tilde{w}(q)$ satisfies Eq. (14.31), such that there exists a critical* q*, namely, $\hat{q}$, $\tilde{w}(q) \geq w_h^*$ and $q \geq \hat{q}$ at $\tilde{w}(q) < w_h^*$ at $q < \hat{q}$. The agent's expected utility is held zero.*
2. *If there is a limited liability constraint such that $\tilde{w}(q) \geq 0$, then there may be a cutoff* q*, say, $\hat{q}_l$ (if $\tilde{w}(q) < 0$ at $q < \hat{q}_l$). The optimal $w(q)$ will then be given by Eq. (14.33), and the agent's expected utility will be strictly positive.*

We conclude this section by noting that a further generalisation is making effort continuous. In this case, the principal needs to recognise that given any wage scheme, the agent will choose an effort level that is optimal for her. This is essentially an incentive compatibility condition similar to the one applied here. The first-order condition for the optimal effort then replaces the discrete version of the IC constraint in the principal's optimisation. But here, too, the monotone likelihood ratio becomes important in determining the shape of the wage scheme. Readers are directed to Laffont (1989, Chapter 11) for this topic. In many contexts, such as in a sales campaign, the principal can appoint two agents and rely on their competition to induce higher effort. Mookherjee (1984) made a seminal contribution regarding this problem in which the efforts are a Nash equilibrium while the optimal wage scheme still retains incentives.

Moral hazard can arise even when there is no uncertainty in production. An important example is the case of team production. When multiple agents participate in production and all need to work cooperatively but if their individual contribution is unobservable to the principal, a moral hazard problem arises. Holmstrom (1982) studied this problem, and his solution was a collective punishment for the group if production does not cross a threshold. Essentially, the principal creates an incentive for the agents to monitor one another. That said, the principle of collective punishment gives rise to another moral hazard problem, on the part of the principal if the principal's profit rises from confiscating the output in the punishment states. Besides team production, bilateral moral hazard is another advanced topic that you may want to learn in future.

14.4 Conclusion

We have provided a basic discussion of hidden information and hidden action that may arise in a principal–agent setting. In both cases, the agent is able to derive some concession from the principal, in spite of the fact that the principal is writing a take-it-or-leave-it offer (meaning the principal has all the bargaining power). When the information is hidden, the principal faces a problem of adverse selection. A menu contract is optimal here, but he has to sacrifice production efficiency to one type of agent and concede information rent to another type of agent. However, if the agent's outside opportunity depends on her type, then countervailing incentives arise, which take away the agent's advantage from private information and often the principal may be able to get his first-best outcome.

When actions are hidden, the principal faces a moral hazard problem. Under moral hazard, the agent's wage needs to be conditioned on the state of nature. As higher effort makes the favourable states of nature more likely than a lower effort, wage must rise in favourable states and fall in unfavourable states to make the agent self-select higher effort. This inevitably eliminates efficient risk sharing that would be otherwise optimal under full observability of the agent's action.

Summary

In this chapter, we learnt the following:

1. Optimal contract between a principal and agent when the agent has private information on her 'type' is analysed.
2. Such contracts are typically menu contract, and they exhibit non-linear pricing.
3. The most preferred type is efficiently employed but is conceded information rent, while the less preferred types are inefficiently employed, with information rent progressively reduced down to zero for the least preferred type.
4. We studied the preceding problem for both finite and infinite types.
5. We also studied optimal contract under moral hazard, which arises when the agent's actions are not observable. Optimal contract here involves paying a higher wage/compensation in states of nature that are favourable from the principal's point of view.
6. Moral hazard contracts typically do not provide complete insurance to the agent in order to induce her to give high effort.
7. We studied the moral hazard problem with two types of effort and both finite and infinite possible realisations of output or principal's revenue.

14.5 Exercises

1. A computer company is hiring a software engineer whose skill θ is unknown to them. It is common knowledge that $\theta \in \{\theta_L, \theta_H\}, \theta_L < \theta_H$ with probability $(p, 1-p)$, respectively. The engineer knows her own skill θ. Her utility function is increasing in her skill, $u = W - \frac{l^2}{2\theta}$, where l is the hours worked and W is the total wage bill. The company's profit is $\pi = Al - W$. Assume both parties have their reservation pay-off as zero.

   a. Derive the company's optimal contract that induces truthful revelation by the engineer. Compare this contract with the full-information contract.
   b. Graphically illustrate your answer.
   c. Calculate the information rent that may be conceded to the engineer.

2. Staying on the same computer company's problem, now assume that the engineer's reservation pay-off depends on her skill in the following way:

$$\bar{u} = \begin{cases} 0 & \text{if } \theta = \theta_L \\ v^H & \text{if } \theta = \theta_H \end{cases},$$

where $v^H = \text{Max}\, bl - \dfrac{l^2}{2\theta_H}$ is her pay-off from self-employment. Assume $b < A$.

   a. First find the value of v^H.
   b. How does the optimal contract change now?
   c. Identify the values of b such that the first-best contracts become incentive compatible.
   d. Comment on the case $b > A$.

3. Consider a worker's problem, in which the worker wants to make an offer to an employer about how many hours he wants to work at what wage. The employer must be guaranteed of a minimum profit $\bar{\pi}$ and the firm's technology is $2k\sqrt{l}$, where $k \in \{k_1, k_2\}$, with probability (p_1, p_2) The employer knows his true k; the worker does not. There is no other input needed. The firm's profit is $\pi = 2k\sqrt{l} - w$, while w is the wage bill. The worker's utility function is $u = w - bl$. His reservation utility is 0.

   a. Derive the worker's optimal contract with the firm.
   b. Compare it with the full information contract.
   c. Graphically illustrate your answer.
   d. If we add a fixed cost to the firm, does your answer change?

4. Consider the same problem as in question 3. But assume that k is a continuous variable and k is uniformly distributed over the interval $[k_1, k_2]$.

   a. Derive the optimal contract in this case.
   b. Specify what assumptions you may need on b and/or k to ensure that the worker receives non-negative utility for every $k \in [k_1, k_2]$.
   c. Suppose b is such that below some k, say, $\hat{k} > k_1$, the worker's reservation utility may not be guaranteed. Then how is the optimal contract modified?

5. Suppose the principal's pay-off is $\pi = \ln x - r$ while the agent's pay-off is $u = r - \dfrac{x}{t}$, where t is her private type, and it is common knowledge that $t \in \{t_1, t_2\}$ with probability (p_1, p_2). Reservation pay-offs are zero for both parties.

   a. Derive the optimal contract under asymmetric information.
   b. Graphically compare these contracts with the full information contract.
   c. Now extend the agent's type to three types: $t \in \{t_1, t_2, t_3\}$ with probabilities (p_1, p_2, p_3). How do the optimal contracts change?

6. Continuing with the three types of agent as in question 5, assume that the agent's reservation utility is $\bar{u} > 0$ if $t = t_3$, while it is still zero if $t = t_1$ or $t = t_2$. Construct a scenario (graphically or mathematically) where the principal implements the first best for type t_3 but may not be able to do so for t_2 or t_1.
7. Mr Homer has opted to work from home, so his effort is not observable to his employer Mr Hazard. Mr Homer can exert effort $e = 1$ or $e = 0$. His effort affects Mr Hazard's revenue $R(e) = a(e)\left[1 + \sqrt{e}\right]$. The wage given to Mr Homer is w. More importantly, $a(e)$ is random in the following way:

$$a(1) = \begin{cases} 2 & \text{with prob.} 0.7 \\ 1/2 & \text{with prob.} 0.3 \end{cases} \quad \text{and} \quad a(0) = \begin{cases} 4 & \text{with prob.} 0.3 \\ 1 & \text{with prob.} 0.7 \end{cases}.$$

Homer's preference is given by $u = w - ce$ where c is disutility per unit of effort. The reservation utility of Homer is zero.

a. If Homer were working in the office under the direct supervision of Mr. Hazard, what contract would he get?
b. Derive the optimal work-from-home contract and compare it with the work-on-site contract. Does Mr Hazard have a preference between the two modes of working? How about Mr Homer? Explain your answer.
c. Now suppose the labour law grants limited liability protection to workers. How does your answer to part (b) change?
d. Consider an alternative scenario where Homer's utility function is $u = bw^{1/3} - ce$, $(b > 0)$. Discuss what difficulty Mr Hazard might face in designing the optimal work-from-home contract and how it might affect Mr Hazard's preference between the two modes of working.

8. A salesman may give effort e_h or e_l, $e_h > e_l = 0$, which is unobservable to his employer. Based on his effort, he receives a stochastic revenue $R(e) = 2b(e)$, where

$$b(e_h) = \begin{cases} 4 & \text{with prob.} 0.6 \\ 1 & \text{with prob.} 0.4 \end{cases} \quad \text{and} \quad b(0) = \begin{cases} 4 & \text{with prob.} 0.3 \\ 1 & \text{with prob.} 0.7 \end{cases}$$

The salesman's preference is given by $u = w - e$, and his reservation utility is $\bar{u}$. The employer's ex post profit is $\pi = 2b(e) - w$.

a. Derive the first-best and second-best contracts assuming $\bar{u} = 0$.
b. Does the employer prefer to induce to high effort of the salesman under the second-best contract?
c. How does your answer change if there is limited liability protection?
d. What if the employer has a reservation profit 4?

9. Consider question 8. Suppose b is a continuous variable uniformly distributed over its support $\left[\underline{b}, \bar{b}\right]$. However, the support depends on the salesman's effort level. If $e = e_l$, the support is $[0,1]$, and if $e = e_h$, the support is $[0.5, 1.5]$. What would be the optimal second-best contract now?

Notes

1 Note that incentive compatibility means that for any c and c', we must have $u(c;c) \geq u(c';c)$ and $u(c';c') \geq u(c;c')$. By subtracting $u(c;c)$ from both sides, the second inequality can be written as $u(c';c') - u(c;c) \geq u(c;c') - u(c;c)$. Then using the first inequality, on both sides, we can write $u(c';c') - u(c';c) \geq u(c';c') - u(c;c) \geq u(c;c') - u(c;c)$. Next substituting the expression for $u(c';c) = T(c') - cq(c')$ and $u(c;c') = T(c) - cq(c')$, we get the desired expression.

2 There can be cases where the incentive runs downward; for instance, in a price discrimination problem (recall second-degree price discrimination from Chapter 10) a high-value consumer has an incentive to misrepresent as a low-value consumer. The common theme between that and the present example is that incentives are unidirectional.

3 Check $\frac{dw}{de} = \frac{z'(e)}{v'(w)} > 0,$ and $\frac{d^2w}{de^2} = \frac{v'(w)z''(e) - z'(e)v''(w)[dw/de]}{v'(w)^2}$

$= \frac{v'(w)^2 z''(e) - z'(e)^2 v''(w)}{v'(w)^3} > 0$ because $v''(w) < 0$.

4 Check for the iso-expected profit curve, $\frac{dw}{de} = p'(e)(q_h - q_l) > 0$, and $\frac{d^2w}{de^2} = p''(e)(q_h - q_l) < 0$.

References and further readings

Baron, D. P. & Myerson., R. B. (1982). Regulating a monopolist with unknown cost. *Econometrica*, 50, 911–930.

Dasgupta, P., Hammond, P. & Maskin. E. (1979). The implementation of social choice rules: Some general results on incentive compatibility. *Review of Economics Studies*, 46, 185–216.

Holmstrom, B. (1979). Moral hazard and observability. *Bell Journal of Economics*, 10, 74–91.

Holmstrom, B. (1982). Moral hazard in teams. *Bell Journal of Economics*, 13, 324–340.

Laffont, J.-J. (1989). *The Economics of Uncertainty and Information*. Cambridge, MA: The MIT Press.

Laffont, J.-J. & Martimort, D. (2002). *The Theory of Incentives: The Principal-Agent Model*. Princeton, NJ: Princeton University Press.

Lewis, T. R. & Sappington, D. E. (1989). Countervailing incentives in agency problems. *Journal of Economic Theory*, 49, 294–313.

Maggi, G. & Rodriguez-Clare, A. (1995). On countervailing incentives. *Journal of Economic Theory*, 66, 238–263.

Mishra, A. (2002). Hierarchies, incentives and collusion in a model of enforcement. *Journal of Economic Behavior and Organization*, 47, 165–178.

Mookherjee, D. (1984). Optimal incentive schemes in multi-agent situations. *Review of Economic Studies*, 51, 433–446.

Myerson, R. B. & Satterthwaite, M. A. (1983). Efficient mechanisms for bilateral trading. *Journal of Economic Theory*, 29, 265–281.

Mas-Colell, A., Whinston, M. D., & Green, J. R. (1995). *Microeconomic Theory*. New York: Oxford University Press.

Saha, B. (2001). Red tape, incentive bribe and the provision of subsidy. *Journal of Development Economics*, 65, 113–133.

Saha, B. & Thampy, T. (2006). Extractive bribe and default in subsidized credit programs. *Journal of Economic Behavior and Organization*, 60, 182–204.

Spulber, D. F. (1988). Bargaining and regulation with asymmetric information about demand and supply. *Journal of Economic Theory*, 44, 251–268.

Chapter 15

Public goods

Abstract

Public goods cannot be provided through market because they are non-excludable and non-rivalrous in their use or consumption. We study several methods, such as the Groves–Clarke mechanism, the Lindahl tax, voluntary contributions and voting, to explore how a public good can be provided at its socially optimal level. We then address the problem of pollution, which is a type of public 'bad'. The Coase theorem is discussed with an example. Finally, a duopoly model with both pollution and abatement is studied to examine how the socially optimum level of production, pollution and abatement can be implemented. A negative result is that a standard pollution tax may fail to achieve the social optimum.

Keywords: Groves–Clarke mechanism, Lindahl solution, Voluntary contributions, Coase theorem, Abatement, Pollution tax

15.1 Introduction

What is a public good? Goods that are **non-excludable** and **non-rival** in consumption (or use) are public goods. Non-excludability means that other people cannot be excluded from a good's consumption when one is consuming it. For example, a road can be simultaneously used by many people, all having equal access and user rights. *Non-rivalry* means that one's consumption of a good does not deplete the amount available to others. Again, one's use of a footpath does not reduce its size available to others. Other examples are emission reduction, defence services, policing, education, patio or balcony gardens, Christmas (or Indian Diwali) lighting, charitable contributions and so on so forth. All of these examples share non-excludability and non-rivalry.

Private goods, by comparison, either exclude others from their consumption or are rivalrous, or both. One's back garden is a restricted area, and even though a beautiful garden view is non-rivalrous, typically it is exclusive. A private consumption good like a Big Mac is both exclusive and rivalrous. If one has it, others cannot have it. The right to exclude others is obtained by paying for it. This is nothing but a *private property right*. Therefore, a good's publicness is closely connected to the property right over it. The absence of private property rights makes a good public.

From these examples, it should be clear that not all public goods have equal 'publicness'. For instance, a college education provides largely private benefits. In contrast, a primary education has a strong positive externality benefitting the whole society much more than an individual. Christmas lighting of one's house is a privately provided public good. Blood

DOI: 10.4324/9781003226994-15

donation is a free service to society, but by the very nature of the good, one person's blood can save only one other person's life. This is a publicly provided private good. Thus, there is a whole range of goods between pure private goods like bread and butter and pure public goods like roads and bridges; these goods are called *impure* public goods. There is yet another category of goods—club goods, where only the members of the club enjoy equal access. These are public goods with restricted access. Club goods are public goods exclusively for club members.

Public goods are provided in many ways. General public goods like roads, defence and policing are provided by the government, while many community-level public goods, such as places of worship, cultural festivals and the like are provided through private initiatives. In the extreme cases of patio flower gardens and Christmas lighting, the cost of providing a public good is borne by a single individual. However, in this case the public good is a positive externality of private consumption.

Government finances public goods by taxation, which is generally non-discriminatory (it is different from income tax) and coercive. A toll bridge charges the same toll from every vehicle of the same size regardless of the motorist's ability or willingness to pay. But generally, people derive different marginal benefits from the consumption of the same public good. The widening of a village road will bring much greater benefits to those who commute to work than those who do not. To finance the road widening work, if a uniform levy is imposed on all village residents, it is likely to be met with strong opposition. Therefore, an important question is how to price a public good.

We discuss several models of public good provision, such as Lindahl pricing, voluntary contributions and democratic decision-making. Lindahl pricing is a scheme of differential pricing depending on individuals' willingness to pay, while voluntary contribution is more applicable to charitable donations. Democratic decision-making involves getting majority support for a proposal. Then we explore some of the issues of environmental economics for the obvious reason that negative externality is a public 'bad'.

15.2 Providing an indivisible public good

Let us first consider an indivisible public good like a road, a school or a bridge. There are n citizens who value this good not necessarily in an identical way. Let their true willingness to pay for the public good be v_i and let the cost of the public good be k. If the aggregate willingness to pay exceeds k, that is, $\sum_i^n v_i > k$, then efficiency dictates that the public good should be provided. However, how the cost of k is to be allocated between n individuals is not straightforward. If people are asked to state their true willingness to pay very likely people will understate v_i in the fear of being asked to pay an amount proportional to v_i.

Can we find a mechanism that would induce people to reveal their true willingness to pay? The answer is yes. One such mechanism is the **Groves–Clarke mechanism.** Suppose individual i's share of the cost is $s_i k$, where $0 < s_i < 1$, $\sum_i^1 s_i = 1$. An individual's net utility from paying $s_i k$ and seeing the public good provided $u_i = v_i - s_i k$.

The Groves-Clarke mechanism proceeds in three steps:

- Step 1: Every citizen is asked to place a bid b_i (not necessarily equal to v_i).
- Step 2: The public good is provided if the sum of the bids is non-negative, $\sum_{i}^{n} b_i \geq 0$.
- Step 3: If the public good is provided then citizen i receives a side payment equal to the sum of the other citizens' bids $\sum_{j \neq i}^{n} b_j$. That also means that if $\sum_{j \neq i}^{n} b_i < 0$ citizen i will have to pay that amount. If the public good is not provided, then no side payment is applied.

The strength of this mechanism is that everybody will bid $b_i = v_i$ (you should see some similarity with the English auction).[1] If the good is provided, citizen i's pay-off does not depend on what her bid is. Therefore, she is indifferent between lying and truth-telling, so truth-telling is her weakly dominant strategy. Similarly, when the good is not provided, she is again indifferent between truth-telling and lying, and she would just reveal her willingness to pay v_i. While the Groves–Clarke mechanism is a *demand-revealing mechanism* it suffers from a serious budget balancing issue. If everybody has stated $b_i > 0$, then the aggregate side payment can be potentially very large.

We can modify the Groves–Clarke mechanism to resolve the budget balancing issue, by changing the side-payment rule specified in Step 3. The modified Step 3 is

- Step 3′: *Receiving rule:* If the public good is provided, receive $\sum_{j \neq i}^{n} b_j$ even if $\sum_{j \neq i}^{n} b_j < 0$ (which means paying). If the public good is not provided, then receive nothing. *Paying rule:* Regardless of the public good is provided or not, if $\sum_{j \neq i}^{n} b_j > 0$ pay $\sum_{j \neq i}^{n} b_j$, and if $\sum_{j \neq i}^{n} b_j < 0$, pay nothing. See Table 15.1.

Table 15.1 Modified Groves–Clarke mechanism

	$\sum_{j \neq i}^{n} b_j > 0$	$\sum_{j \neq i}^{n} b_j < 0$
$\sum_{j}^{n} b_j > 0$ (Public good is provided)	Receive $\sum_{j \neq i}^{n} b_j$ Pay $\sum_{j \neq i}^{n} b_j$	Receive $\sum_{j \neq i}^{n} b_j$ Pay 0
$\sum_{j}^{n} b_j < 0$ (Public good is not provided)	Receive 0 Pay $\sum_{j \neq i}^{n} b_j$	Receive 0 Pay 0

As a result of this mechanism a citizen's pay-off becomes

$$u_i = \begin{cases} v_i - s_i k & \text{if } b_i > 0 \text{ and } \sum_{j \neq i}^{n} b_j > 0 \\ v_i - s_i k + \sum_{j \neq i}^{n} b_j & \text{if } b_i > 0 \text{ and } \sum_{j \neq i}^{n} b_j < 0 \\ -\sum_{j \neq i}^{n} b_j & \text{if } b_i < 0 \text{ and } \sum_{j \neq i}^{n} b_j > 0 \\ 0 & \text{if } b_i < 0 \text{ and } \sum_{j \neq i}^{n} b_j < 0. \end{cases}$$

The first row of the pay-off applies to the case in which the ith citizen's bid is positive and the sum of all other citizen's bid is also positive, so the public good is provided. Here, the receipt and the payment cancel out. The second row refers to the case in which the public good is provided solely because of the ith citizen's bid (despite $\sum_{j \neq i}^{n} b_j < 0$ a high $b_i > 0$ makes $\sum_{j}^{n} b_j > 0$). Citizen i is a pivotal bidder. However, she receives a negative sum (meaning she actually pays). In the third row, she is again a pivotal bidder, but this time, her bid is so significantly negative that the public good is not provided despite all other citizens collectively posting a positive bid. Here, she has to make a payment. Finally, in the fourth row, the public good is not provided, and the sum of all other bids is negative. Hence, she receives nothing and pays nothing. Her pay-off is zero.

Note that only on two occasions, in the second and the third row, citizen i pays a net positive tax for being a pivotal bidder on both occasions. However, on one occasion, she makes the public good provision possible and hence pays an extra tax (above her share of the cost $s_i k$), and on the other occasion, she pays a tax for preventing the provision of the public good. This tax is called the *Clarke tax*, and the modified mechanism is called the **pivotal mechanism.**

15.3 Divisible or continuous public goods

Many goods are available in divisible units. A park can be small or large. A flower garden can be of different shapes and sizes. A firework display can be short or long. What would be the optimal size of a public good when it is of a continuous type, and how do we provide it? To develop our intuition for a price system similar to private goods, we start with a simple example.

15.3.1 *Lindahl price: a simple example*

Imagine a small housing society of five households. They share a communal garden, which they want to beautify by planting flower beds. One idea is to allow households to bring as many flower plants as they want. Let us denote a flower plant by g and its market price by p_g. The aggregate public good is $G = \sum_{i=1}^{5} g_i$. Household i's utility depends on the public good G and a private good x as follows:

$$u_i = x_i - \frac{(\theta_i - G)^2}{2}.$$

The quadratic utility function has a unique peak at a value θ_i for the preference over the public good. Households vary in their most preferred G (ranging from θ_1 to θ_5) and income Y_i.

If households are left to decide for themselves how many flower plants they will buy, each will decide by maximising their utility functions subject to their own budget constraint, which is

$$Y_i = x_i + p_g g_i, i = 1, 2, ..., 5.$$

Substitute the budget equation of i into their utility function and maximise the following:

$$u_i = Y_i - p_g g_i - \frac{(\theta_i - G)^2}{2}.$$

Private demands are obtained by equating the marginal benefit with price: $\theta_i - G - p_g = 0$, or $G = \theta_i - p_g$. Clearly, a positive amount of public good is demanded by household i only if $\theta_i > p_g$. Only those individuals whose willingness to pay exceeds the price p_g will contribute $g_i = G - G_{-i}$, where G_{-i} refers to contributions of all other households. If G_{-i} is already large enough to equal $\theta_i - p_g$, then individual i will not contribute.

To illustrate the individual decision problem, let us take some values for p_g and θ_i. Suppose $p_g = \$35$, and $\theta_1 = 40, \theta_2 = 35, \theta_3 = 32, \theta_4 = 30, \theta_5 = 28$. If left to themselves, only household 1 will contribute 5 units of the public good. Others will contribute none. The end result is a patchy garden. See panel *a* of Figure 15.1.

Now consider the **Pareto optimal** problem, the socially optimal flower bed for the housing society.

$$\text{Max} \sum_{i=1}^{5} u_i = \sum_{i=1}^{5} \left[Y_i - \frac{(\theta_i - G)^2}{2} \right] - p_g G.$$

The first-order condition for G is

$$(\theta_1 - G) + (\theta_2 - G) + ... + (\theta_5 - G) - p_g = 0$$

$$\text{or,} \qquad \theta_1 + \theta_2 + \theta_3 + \theta_4 + \theta_5 - 5G = p_g.$$

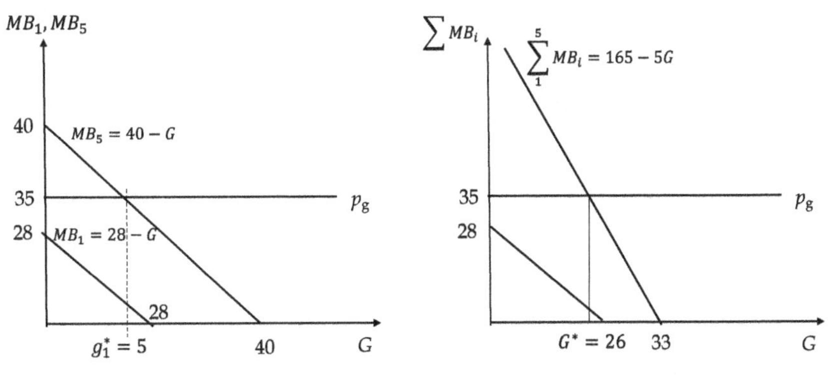

a. *Private demand for public good*

b. *Socially optimal quantity of public good*

Figure 15.1 Private demand versus socially optimal public good

Note that Pareto optimality requires that the sum of the marginal benefit of all households must be equal to the marginal cost of the public good. This is the well-known Samuelson condition for the efficient provision of a public good. See panel *b* of Figure 15.1. In the present example, substituting the relevant numbers for θ_i and p_g, we arrive at $40+35+32+30+28-5G=35$. The socially optimal solution is $G = 26$, which costs \$910.

Now the question is how to allocate the total cost of \$910 among five individuals. As we have seen, only one household wants to voluntarily contribute. If the total cost is distributed equally many will object. Swedish economist Erik Lindahl proposed a 'pricing' solution based on individual willingness to pay so that no individual will be reluctant to pay.

For our example, let us substitute the Pareto optimal solution $G = 26$ into each household's public good demand equation: $\theta_i - G - p_g = 0$. But replace p_g with a household-specific price p^i_g, which is essentially the amount of money the ith household is willing to pay per flower plant if 26 flower plants are supplied. For household 1, this amount is 40 − 26 = 14 per unit, and it should pay \$364. Likewise, households 2–5 should pay 9, 6, 4 and 2, respectively, per unit of the 26 units. You can check that the per unit price adds up to \$35.

This is the Lindahl cost allocation rule. Note that the price or contribution varies between households because of their different willingness to pay. But under such a scheme, everybody will be happy to pay their per unit price p^i_g. The Lindahl prices have the virtue of being **unanimously agreed on.** It is essentially a **tax subsidy scheme** that implements the Pareto optimal amount of a public good with unanimous agreement. The end result is an efficient provision of the public good.

One caveat is that Lindahl prices do require the knowledge of everybody's willingness to pay. If not, a separate demand revelation mechanism like the Groves–Clarke mechanism is needed. But we will keep this issue aside.

15.3.2 The Lindahl rule of cost sharing

The idea of Lindahl prices is very general and applicable to any public good as long as we know the preferences of all the users of the public good. Consider a situation where there is no reference market price for the public good. Suppose a public good of size G costs exactly \$$G$ and our problem is to decide how to divide \$$G$ between two individuals, 1 and 2, who are the only consumers in the economy. Suppose the cost is to be shared as tG for individual 1 and $(1 - t)G$ for individual 2.

To simplify further and for ease of exposition, we assume that individuals have identical Cobb–Douglas preference: $u = x^{\alpha} G^{1-\alpha}$, where x is a private good with price p_x, which we set equal to 1 for simplicity. But the individuals vary in terms of their incomes, which are Y_1 and Y_2, respectively. We need to determine the Pareto optimal G and the Lindahl tax t.

Let us first see what individual 1's demand for G would be if he is asked to pay tG. Substituting his budget equation into the utility function to replace x, we reduce his problem as

$$\text{Max} \ \ u_1 = (Y_1 - tG)^{\alpha} G^{1-\alpha}.$$

The first-order condition for utility maximisation yields

$$-\alpha(Y_1 - tG)^{\alpha-1} tG^{1-\alpha} + (1-\alpha)(Y_1 - tG)^{\alpha} G^{-\alpha} = 0$$

$$\text{or,} \quad (Y_1 - tG)^{\alpha-1} G^{-\alpha}\left[-\alpha tG + (1-\alpha)(Y_1 - tG)\right] = 0$$

$$\text{or,} \quad \frac{(1-\alpha)}{\alpha}\frac{(Y_1 - tG)}{G} = t \tag{15.1}$$

$$\text{or,} \quad t = \frac{(1-\alpha)Y_1}{G}.$$

Panel a of Figure 15.2 depicts the inverse demand curve (D_1) for G of individual 1 as given by Eq. (15.1). Clearly, $\frac{\partial t}{\partial G} = -\frac{(1-\alpha)Y_1}{G^2} < 0$. The demand curve is truncated at $t = 1$.

Likewise, for individual 2 the problem is

$$\text{Max} \quad u_2 = [Y_2 - (1-t)G]^{\alpha} G^{1-\alpha}.$$

The first-order condition gives

$$-\alpha[Y_2 - (1-t)G]^{\alpha-1}(1-t)G^{1-\alpha} + (1-\alpha)[Y_2 - (1-t)G]^{\alpha} G^{-\alpha} = 0$$

$$\text{or,} \quad [Y_2 - (1-t)G]^{\alpha-1} G^{-\alpha} \{-\alpha(1-t)G + (1-\alpha)[Y_2 - (1-t)G]\} = 0$$

$$\text{or,} \quad \frac{(1-\alpha)}{\alpha}\frac{(Y_2 - (1-t)G)}{G} = (1-t) \tag{15.2}$$

$$\text{or,} \quad 1 - t = \frac{(1-\alpha)Y_2}{G}.$$

Eq. (15.2) is the inverse demand for G of individual 2. To compare this demand with that of individual 1, we rewrite the demand for the public good of individual 2 as given in Eq. (15.2) as

$$t = 1 - \frac{(1-\alpha)Y_2}{G}. \tag{15.3}$$

Note that individual 2's demand curve is upward-sloping: $\frac{\partial t}{\partial G} = \frac{(1-\alpha)Y_2}{G^2} > 0$. Panel b of Figure 15.2 depicts this curve.

Now we turn our attention to the determination of a Pareto optimal level of public good. Any Pareto optimal provision of public good must be given by tangency of two indifferent curves. For this purpose, we first derive the indifference curves of individual 1 (on the (G, t) plane). Set $[Y_1 - tG]^{\alpha} G^{1-\alpha} = \bar{u}_1$ and take the total differential with respect to t and G to write

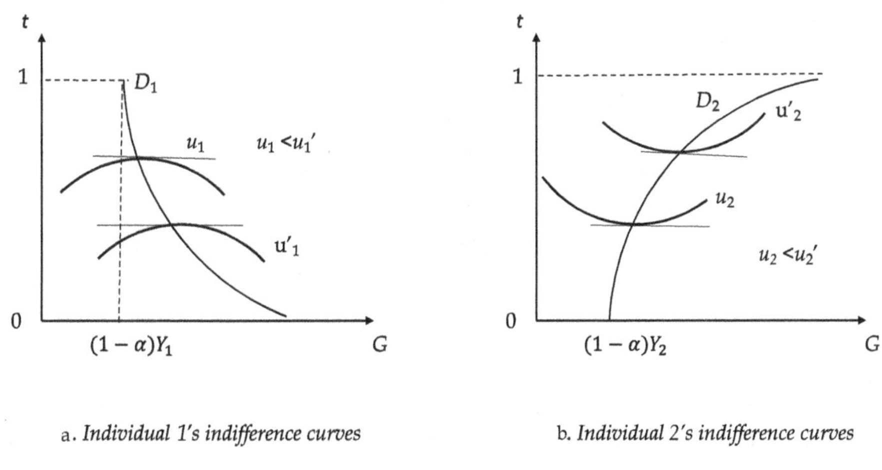

Figure 15.2 Indifference curves and tax-induced demand

$$du_1 = 0 = \alpha(Y_1 - tG)^{\alpha-1}G^{1-\alpha}[-t\cdot dG - G\cdot dt] + (1-\alpha)(Y_1 - tG)^{\alpha}G^{-\alpha}\cdot dG$$

$$\text{or, } 0 = \left[\underbrace{(Y_1 - tG)^{\alpha-1}G^{-\alpha}}_{>0}\right]\times\left[\underbrace{\alpha G\{-t\cdot dG - G\cdot dt\} + (1-\alpha)(Y_1 - tG)\cdot dG}_{=0}\right].$$

From the second term, which must be zero when the utility is held constant, we derive the slope of an indifference curve of individual 1 as

$$\left.\frac{dt}{dG}\right|_{\bar{u}_1} = \frac{-tG + (1-\alpha)Y_1}{\alpha G^2} = \frac{1}{\alpha G}\left[-t + \frac{(1-\alpha)Y_1}{G}\right]. \tag{15.4}$$

The indifference curve of 1 is inverted U-shaped with its peak reached at $t = (1-\alpha)Y_1 / G$, which you must recognise as a point on individual 1's demand curve D_1. The inverted U-shape is verified by the (negative) second-order derivative d^2t/dG^2. Also note that the higher the position of an indifference curve (of individual 1), the lower the utility level it corresponds to. This is shown in panel *a* of Figure 15.2.

Similarly, for individual 2, set $[Y_2 - (1-t)G]^{\alpha}G^{1-\alpha} = \bar{u}_2$, and taking the total differential with respect to t and G, write (as $du_2 = 0$)

$$0 = \alpha(Y_2 - (1-t)G)^{\alpha-1}G^{1-\alpha}[-(1-t)\cdot dG + G\cdot dt] + (1-\alpha)(Y_2 - (1-t)G)^{\alpha}G^{-\alpha}\cdot dG$$

$$\text{or, } 0 = \left[(Y_2 - (1-t)G)^{\alpha-1}G^{-\alpha}\right]\times\left[\underbrace{\alpha G\{-(1-t)\cdot dG + G\cdot dt\} + (1-\alpha)(Y_2 - (1-t)G)\cdot dG}_{=0}\right].$$

The slope of an indifference curve of individual 2 is

$$\left.\frac{dt}{dG}\right|_{\bar{u}_2} = \frac{(1-t)G - (1-\alpha)Y_2}{\alpha G^2} = \frac{1}{\alpha G}\left[1 - \frac{(1-\alpha)Y_2}{G} - t\right]. \tag{15.5}$$

The indifference curve of 2 is U-shaped, with its minimum point is reached at $t = 1 - \dfrac{(1-\alpha)Y_2}{G}$; this is a point on the demand curve D_2, shown in panel *b* of Figure 15.2. The higher the position of the curve (of individual 2), the higher the utility level that corresponds to the indifference curve (of individual 2), and the higher the utility level it corresponds to.

Setting the two slopes as given in Eqs. (15.4) and (15.5) equal, we get the Pareto optimal public good as

$$G^* = (1-\alpha)(Y_1 + Y_2). \tag{15.6}$$

We can call it a *contract curve for public good*. Clearly, it is vertical (due to the Cobb-Douglas preferences). There is a unique level of Pareto optimal public good, but the Pareto optimal t can be anywhere between 0 and 1. But only one point will be the Lindahl price/tax, the one at

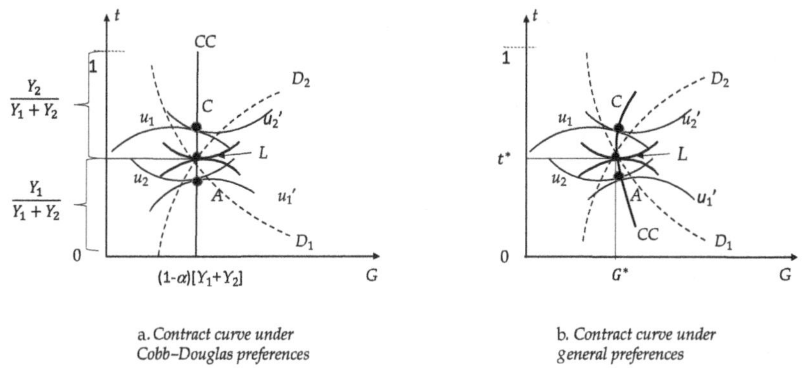

Figure 15.3 Lindahl equilibrium

which both individuals' demand curves meet, and that point is given by L in Figure 15.3 (in both panels). Substituting $G^* = (1-\alpha)(Y_1+Y_2)$ into the demand equations (15.1) and (15.2), we get $t^* = Y_1/(Y_1+Y_2)$ (individual 1's cost share) and $1-t^* = Y_2/(Y_1+Y_2)$ (individual 2's cost share). Panel *a* of Figure 15.3 shows a vertical contract curve and efficient cost allocation.

On the contract curve of Figure 15.3 (panel *a*), we depict three situations:

- **Point *A*:** Given *t*, individual 1 demands more *G* than individual 2: Here, $D_1 > D_2$, and both indifference curves (ICs) have *positive* slopes. A positive slope of IC_1 means $\frac{(1-\alpha)Y_1}{G} > t$. A positive slope of IC_2 means $1-\frac{(1-\alpha)Y_2}{G} > t$
- **Point *C*:** Given *t*, individual 1 demands less *G* than individual 1: Here, $D_1 < D_2$, and both ICs have *negative* slopes. A negative slope of IC_1 means $\frac{(1-\alpha)Y_1}{G} < t$. A negative slope of IC_2 means $1-\frac{(1-\alpha)Y_2}{G} < t$.
- **Point *L*:** At this point, we have $D_1 = D_2$ given the corresponding *t*. Both IC_1 and IC_2 have zero slopes: $\frac{(1-\alpha)Y_1}{G} = 1-\frac{(1-\alpha)Y_2}{G} = t$. This is our Lindahl allocation. If the consumers have equal income, they will pay equally; otherwise, the *richer* individual will *pay more*. But for the size of the public good, income inequality does not matter.
- Finally, how do we relate our Lindahl t^* to the marginal willingness to pay? To understand that, we need to go back to the utility function and put back *x* into the budget equation. Recall p_g is *t* for individual 1, and 1 − *t* for individual 2, while $p_x = 1$. So the first-order conditions for utility maximisation give

$$MRS^1_{G,x} = t \text{ for individual 1 and } MRS^2_{G,x} = 1-t.$$

Equivalently, the marginal rate of substitution (MRS) for the public good and the private good for individual *i* is equal to p^i_g / p_x. We can also check that in our Cobb–Douglas example, as $G^* = (1-\alpha)(Y_1+Y_2)$, the demand for the *private* good is $x_1^* = \alpha Y_1$ for individual 1 and $x_2^* = \alpha Y_2$ for individual 2.

15.3.2.1 General utility function

The argument holds equally well for a general utility function $u_i = u_i(x_i, G)$. From the budget equation of individual 1, we substitute $x_1 = Y_1 - tG$ and $x_2 = Y_2 - (1-t)G$ into their respective utility functions and derive the slope of the indifference curves as

$$\left.\frac{dt}{dG}\right|_{\bar{u}_1} = \frac{\frac{\partial u_1}{\partial G} - \frac{\partial u_1}{\partial x}t}{\frac{\partial u_1}{\partial x}G} = \frac{MRS^1_{G,x} - t}{G},$$

and

$$\left.\frac{dt}{dG}\right|_{\bar{u}_2} = -\frac{\frac{\partial u_2}{\partial G} - \frac{\partial u_2}{\partial x}(1-t)}{\frac{\partial u_2}{\partial x}G} = -\frac{MRS^2_{G,x} - (1-t)}{G}.$$

The equation for the contract curve is obtained by equating these two slopes:

$$MRS^1_{G,x} - t = -MRS^2_{G,x} + (1-t) \Rightarrow MRS^1_{G,x} + MRS^2_{G,x} = 1.$$

This is nothing but the Pareto efficiency condition for public goods (assuming $p_G = 1$). This equation does not necessarily give rise to a vertical contract curve. Panel *b* of Figure 15.3 shows a contract curve where G varies with t. The Lindahl allocation is the one where the two slopes are zero and, given t and $(1-t)$, the individuals demand exactly the efficient level of G. The overall insight of the above analysis is summarised in the following proposition.

Proposition 55. *A Lindahl allocation $(x_1^*, x_2^*, \ldots, x_n^*, G^*)$ of private and public goods is Pareto-efficient. In particular, G^* is such that $\sum_{i=1}^{n} MRS^i_{G,x}(G^*, x_i^*) = p_g$. Furthermore, given the Lindahl tax on individual i, $t_i^* G^*$, his demands for x_i^* and G^* will be exactly the same as in the Lindahl allocation.*

15.4 Voluntary contributions to public goods

Many public goods, like supporting an environmental cause or animal welfare, are provided entirely through private contributions. Lindahl prices are then not the most useful idea, because the state may not be an active intermediary to enforce the Lindahl prices. Three issues arise in the context of voluntary contributions: (1) free riding (contributing nothing or very little in response to others' contributions), (2) under-provision (aggregate voluntary contributions being less than Pareto optimal), and (3) neutrality (the size of the public good is neutral to small redistribution of incomes among the contributors).

15.4.1 Possibility of free riding

Before we consider a formal model in the next section, it is important to look at the basic condition for contribution. Imagine there are two individuals, 1 and 2, who may contribute g_1 and g_2 (simultaneously), while they will consume $G = g_1 + g_2$ along with a private good x. Their

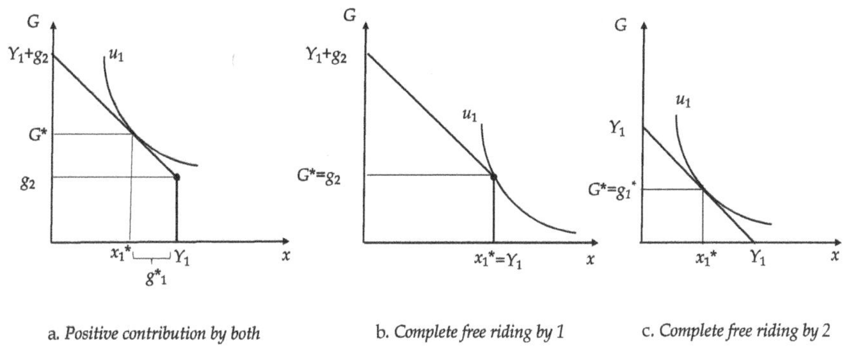

Figure 15.4 Private contributions

preferences are given by the utility function $u = (x, G)$. Assume their incomes are Y_1 and Y_2. Prices of the two goods are set to 1 for simplicity.

Individual 1 maximises $u = u(x_1, g_1 + g_2)$ with respect to x_1 and g_1 subject to the budget constraint $x_1 + g_1 = Y_1$, assuming that individual 2's contribution g_2 is given. Figure 15.4 gives three scenarios to demonstrate how individual 1's decision is affected by the contribution of individual 2. Panel *a* depicts a scenario where both individuals contribute, $g_1, g_2 > 0$. Individual 1's consumption of the private good cannot exceed his income Y_1; hence, the budget line is truncated at $x = Y_1$, where the size of the public good falls to its minimum g_2. However, individual 1's preference can also be such that he may not contribute at all. If his highest indifference curve hits the right corner of the budget set, then he completely free rides (panel *b*). However, if $g_2 = 0$, then individual 1's budget line falls all the way to the *x*-axis. This case is shown in panel *c*. Note that in general (when preference is not quasi-linear or two goods are not perfect substitutes), the case of neither individual contributing is impossible. If one does not, then the other will.

These graphs should also convince you that one's contribution to the public good depends on whether and how much others are contributing. Since there is an obvious benefit from free riding, it is expected that one's contribution is likely to be a decreasing function of others' contributions. Thus, while complete free riding is an extreme case, under-provisioning of public good is a common problem. We illustrate this with a simple model of voluntary contributions.

Suppose there are *n* identical individuals, each having income *Y* and preference $u_i = Ax_i^{\alpha} G^{1-\alpha}$. Individual *i* wishes to 'buy' g_i amount of the public good.[2] Let the price of *g* be p_g and the price of the private good be 1 for simplicity.

Privately optimal allocation: Let us now set the individual optimisation problem for a representative consumer:

$$\text{Max } u_i = Ax_i^{\alpha} G^{1-\alpha}$$

subject to

$$x_i + p_g g_i = Y \quad \text{and} \quad G = g_1 + g_2 + g_3 + \ldots + g_n.$$

Forming the Lagrangian

$$L = Ax_i^{\alpha} (g_1 + g_2 + \ldots + g_n)^{1-\alpha} - \lambda_i [x_i + p_g g_i - Y]$$

and maximising it with respect to x_i, g_i and λ_i, we get (for every i)

$$\frac{\partial L}{\partial g_i} = (1-\alpha)Ax_i^{\alpha}(g_1+g_2+...+g_n)^{-\alpha} - \lambda_i p_g = 0 \tag{15.7}$$

$$\frac{\partial L}{\partial x_i} = \alpha Ax_i^{\alpha-1}(g_1+g_2+...+g_n)^{1-\alpha} - \lambda_i = 0. \tag{15.8}$$

$$\frac{\partial L}{\partial \lambda_i} = -[x_i + p_g g_i - Y] = 0. \tag{15.9}$$

Dividing Eq. (15.7) by Eq. (15.8), we get

$$\frac{(1-\alpha)x_i}{\alpha G} = p_g. \tag{15.10}$$

In place of x_i, substitute the budget constraint $x_i = Y - p_g g_i$ and write

$$\frac{(1-\alpha)(Y-p_g g_i)}{\alpha(g_1+g_2+...+g_n)} = p_g.$$

Now, since all individuals are identical, their consumption g_i and x_i must be identical. Thus, $g_1+g_2+...+g_n = ng = G$. Then rearranging terms, we get the *privately optimal individual contribution* to the public good:

$$g = \frac{(1-\alpha)Y}{p_g[\alpha n+(1-\alpha)]}, \tag{15.11}$$

which leads to an aggregate level of public good

$$G = \frac{n(1-\alpha)Y}{p_g[n\alpha+(1-\alpha)]}. \tag{15.12}$$

Individually optimal consumption of the private good is

$$x = Y - p_g g = Y - p_g\left[\frac{(1-\alpha)Y}{p_g[n\alpha+(1-\alpha)]}\right] = \frac{n\alpha Y}{n\alpha+(1-\alpha)}. \tag{15.13}$$

Pareto optimal allocation: To establish under-provisioning, we need to compare the above solution with the Pareto-efficient allocation. For Pareto optimality, the problem is

$$\text{Max} \sum_i u_i = \sum_i Ax_i^{\alpha}G^{1-\alpha} \quad \text{subject to} \quad \sum x_i + p_g G = nY.$$

Forming the Lagrangian and differentiating it with respect to x_i, G and λ, we get

$$\text{Max } L = \sum_i A x_i^{\alpha} G^{1-\alpha} - \lambda\left[\sum_i x_i + p_g G - nY\right]$$

$$\frac{\partial L}{\partial G} = (1-\alpha)\sum_i A x_i^{\alpha} G^{-\alpha} - \lambda p_g = 0 \tag{15.14}$$

$$\frac{\partial L}{\partial x_i} = \alpha A x_i^{\alpha-1} G^{1-\alpha} - \lambda = 0, \quad i = 1,2,\ldots,n. \tag{15.15}$$

$$\frac{\partial L}{\partial \lambda} = -\left[\sum_i x_i + p_g G - nY\right] = 0. \tag{15.16}$$

Dividing Eq. (15.14) by Eq. (15.15) for any i, we get (assuming symmetry)

$$\sum_i \frac{(1-\alpha)x_i}{\alpha G} = p_g, \quad p_g G = \frac{(1-\alpha)}{\alpha}\sum_i^n x_i. \tag{15.17}$$

Using symmetry $\sum_i^n x_i = nx$ and substituting Eq. (15.17) in the aggregate budget constraint $nY = \sum_i x_i + p_g G$, we derive the **Pareto optimal solution** as

$$G^* = \frac{n(1-\alpha)Y}{p_g}, \quad x^* = \alpha Y. \tag{15.18}$$

Compare G in Eq. (15.18) with that in Eq. (15.12). Since $n\alpha + (1-\alpha) > 1$, the privately provided level of the aggregate public good is smaller. The voluntarily contributed public good is under-provided. The argument can be easily extended to a general utility function.

15.4.2 Cournot interactions in voluntary contributions

When the number of public good users is small, we can think of their contributions as an outcome of a game. Each individual holds a Cournot-type conjecture about other individuals' contributions and decides on their own contribution. Thus, the solution to the private contribution problem that we have derived in Eqs. (15.7) and (15.8) constitutes a Cournot–Nash equilibrium.

Assuming $n = 2$ and $Y_1 \neq Y_2$ we can easily formulate a game of contributions. Assume that both contribute to the public good. Their utility function is $u = x^{\alpha} G^{1-\alpha}$. Assume, for simplicity, $p_x = p_g = 1$. Their budget equations are $Y_1 = x_1 + g_1$ and $Y_2 = x_2 + g_2$.

Set up the Lagrangian for individual 1, and maximising it with respect to g_1, x_1, we arrive at the reaction function of individual 1:[3]

$$\frac{(1-\alpha)(Y_1 - g_1)}{\alpha(g_1 + g_2)} = 1 \quad \Rightarrow \quad g_1 = (1-\alpha)Y_1 - \alpha g_2. \tag{15.19}$$

Similarly, the reaction function of individual 2 is

$$g_2 = (1-\alpha)Y_2 - \alpha g_1. \tag{15.20}$$

The reaction functions (15.19) and (15.20) and the resultant Nash equilibrium (point E) are shown in Figure 15.5. The Nash equilibrium contributions are

$$g_1 = \frac{Y_1 - \alpha Y_2}{1+\alpha}, \qquad g_2 = \frac{Y_2 - \alpha Y_1}{1+\alpha} \qquad \text{and} \qquad G = \frac{(Y_1 + Y_2)(1-\alpha)}{1+\alpha}. \tag{15.21}$$

The equilibrium consumption of the private good is

$$x_1 = x_2 = \frac{\alpha}{(1-\alpha)} G = \frac{\alpha(Y_1 + Y_2)}{1+\alpha}. \tag{15.22}$$

15.4.2.1 *Conditions for positive contribution*

While we have assumed so far that both individuals contribute to the public good, that need not always be the case. In the example considered, for positive contributions in equilibrium, we must have $Y_1 > \alpha Y_2$ and $Y_2 > \alpha Y_1$. That is, the income difference between the two individuals must not be too large. You may look at Figure 15.4. On panel *a* suppose g_2 increases (exogenously following an increase in Y_2). Individual 1's budget line will shift upward as a greater amount of a public good is available at the same Y_1. With successive increase in Y_2, g_2 can reach the level of G^*, where individual 1 stops contributing. Panel *b* of Figure 15.4 shows a situation like this, but we attributed it to preference rather than income difference. This discussion also suggests that if an individual shares the same preference with others but does not contribute, then his income must be very low.

An additional observation from Eq. (15.22) is that despite income differences, the private consumption is identical for the two individuals. This is however not due to the Cobb–Douglas

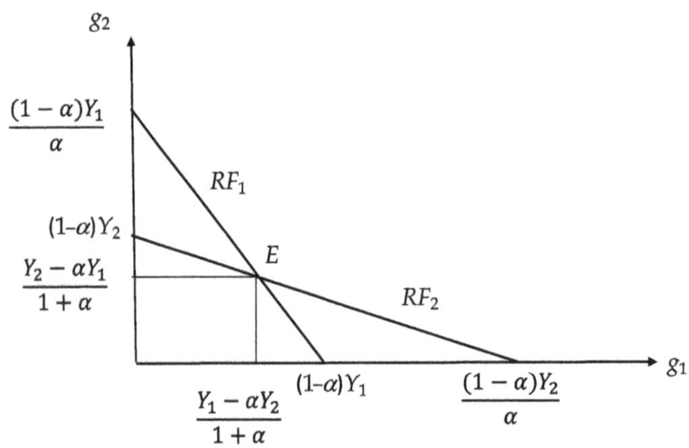

Figure 15.5 Contribution reaction functions

preferences. As long as we have identical preferences, the income difference between individuals will reflect in their different contributions, allowing them to have identical consumption of the private good. This is a *positive spillover* effect of public good.

How does the preceding solution compare to the Pareto optimal provision of the public good? Predictably it will be less. Substituting $p_g = 1$, $n = 2$ and $nY = Y_1 + Y_2$ in Eq. (15.18) we obtain

$$G = (1-\alpha)(Y_1 + Y_2) \qquad \text{and} \qquad x_1 = x_2 = \frac{\alpha(Y_1 + Y_2)}{2}. \tag{15.23}$$

The Pareto-efficient allocation shows that the social planner is pooling the individuals' income and then recommending a split of it in two proportions, $\alpha(Y_1 + Y_2)$ and $(1-\alpha)(Y_1 + Y_2)$, of which the first part goes to private consumption and is further equally divided between the two individuals. The remaining part is spent on the public good. As private consumption is decided through the market, the social planner's recommendation inevitably involves 'contribute according to your ability' principle. Thus, a public good has a strong egalitarian implication even for private goods.

Proposition 56. *Suppose there are n individuals who have identical preferences over one public good and one private good, but they may differ in income. Let the equilibrium arrived at through a voluntary contribution game be denoted by* $(x_1^c, x_2^c, ..., x_n^c, G^c)$. *Compared to the Pareto optimal allocations, the public good is under-provided, and the private good is over-consumed. However, everybody will consume the private good in equal amount, despite their income differences.*

15.4.3 Income inequality

Given that low-income people may fail to contribute to public goods, it is important to explore the role of income inequality in determining the size of a public good. To compare the result of this section with our previous analysis of the identical income and preference scenario, we assume that while the aggregate income is still nY, there are two income groups of sizes n_r and n_p, rich and poor, respectively, so that $n_r Y_r + n_p Y_p = nY$. Furthermore, we assume that it is only the rich who contribute to the public good and we continue with Cobb–Douglas preferences. There are two relevant questions: (1) Does individual contribution go up when only a subset of the population contributes? The answer to this question is, yes. (2) Does the size of the public good get smaller? The answer to the second question is somewhat ambiguous.

Based on our understanding of non-contribution, we can say that if n_r people's contributions add up to G^* then each of the n_p individuals must find their demand for G less than or equal to G^*.

They spend their entire income on the private good. We then need to consider only the demands of the rich individuals.

The problem of a rich person is

$$\text{Max } L = A x_i^{\alpha} (g_1 + g_2 + .. + g_{n_r})^{1-\alpha} - \lambda_i [x_i + p_g g_i - Y_r].$$

From the first-order conditions

$$\frac{\partial L}{\partial g_i} = (1-\alpha)Ax_i^{\alpha}(g_1+g_2+...+g_{n_r})^{-\alpha} - \lambda_i p_g = 0$$

$$\frac{\partial L}{\partial x_i} = \alpha Ax_i^{\alpha-1}(g_1+g_2+...+g_{n_r})^{1-\alpha} - \lambda_i = 0,$$

we arrive at the voluntary contribution solution

$$g^c = \frac{(1-\alpha)Y_r}{p_g[\alpha n_r + (1-\alpha)]}, \quad G^c = n_r g^c \tag{15.24}$$

$$\text{and} \quad x_r = Y_r - \frac{(1-\alpha)Y_r}{n_r\alpha + (1-\alpha)}. \tag{15.25}$$

Now let us compare the privately optimal contributions in the presence and absence of income inequality. Comparing Eq. (15.24) with Eq. (15.11), we see that under income inequality, *private contribution goes up*. This is evident from the fact that $n_r < n$ and $Y_r > Y$.

But there is an **ambiguity** with respect to the aggregate contribution. Comparing Eq. (15.24) with Eq. (15.12), we see that G is smaller under income inequality if

$$n_r Y_r[n\alpha + (1-\alpha)] < nY[n_r\alpha + (1-\alpha)]$$

$$\frac{n_r Y_r}{nY} < \frac{n_r\alpha + (1-\alpha)}{n\alpha + (1-\alpha)} (<1).$$

That is, if the total income of the rich as the proportion of the aggregate income is less than a critical level, a privately provided public good will be smaller than that in an egalitarian society.

15.4.4 A neutrality theorem

We now state a neutrality theorem, proposed by Warr (1983) and developed by Bergstrom et al. (1986), which says that any **small** redistribution of income does not alter the size of the public good. By 'small', it is meant that the redistribution does not alter the contribution incentive of the agents and the number of contributing members does not change. If so, then one's reduction in contribution will be made up by others' increased contribution. In the post-redistribution equilibrium, the public good remains unchanged and so will everybody's private consumption.

Theorem 11. *(Bergstrom et al., 1986, p. 29) Consider an economy with n individuals each having income Y_i and strictly convex preferences $u_i = u_i(x_i, G)$, where x is a private good and $G = g_1 + g_2 + ... + g_n$ is a public good, with both being normal goods to all consumers.*[4] *Then starting from a Cournot–Nash equilibrium, where $g_i > 0$ for all $i = 1,2,...,n$, any redistribution of incomes within m consumers, $1 < m \leq n$ that leaves the aggregate income unchanged and renders no $g_i = 0$, will also leave the equilibrium G unchanged. Furthermore, for every individual, $\Delta g_i = \frac{\Delta Y_i}{p_g}$, where ΔY_i refers to any changes in income due to the redistribution.*

Proof. Given the prices of the two goods p_g and p_x, individual utility maximisation yields

$$x_i = \frac{Y_i - p_g g_i}{p_x}, \quad \text{and} \quad \frac{\partial u_i(G, x_i)) / \partial g_i}{\partial u_i / \partial x_i} = \frac{p_g}{p_x}, \quad \text{for} \quad i = 1, 2, ..., n. \tag{15.26}$$

Due to the strict convexity of preferences, g_i^* and x_i^* are uniquely determined as the Cournot–Nash equilibrium, where g_i^* is best response to G_{-i}^*, the sum of all other individuals' contributions. Furthermore, as both goods are normal goods, along the income expansion path, optimal x_i must be a monotonically increasing function of optimal G^*:

$$x_i^* = f_i(G^*) \times \frac{p_g}{p_x}, \text{where} \quad f_i'(G^*) > 0 \quad \text{for} \quad i = 1, 2, .., n. \tag{15.27}$$

Substituting Eq. (15.27) into the budget equation of consumer *I*, we can write

$$p_g g_i^* + p_g f_i(G^*) = Y_i, \text{ for } i = 1, 2, ..., n. \tag{15.28}$$

Summing g_i^* over *n* consumers, we arrive at

$$p_g G^* + p_g [f_1(G^*) + f_2(G^*) + ... + f_n(G^*)] = Y_1 + Y_2 + ... + Y_n. \tag{15.29}$$

Now consider a redistribution of income, without loss of generality, between individuals 1 and 2. Suppose $\Delta Y_1 (< g_1^*)$ is transferred from individual 1 to individual 2. The right-hand side of Eq. (15.29) does not change, which means that the left-hand side of it must not change or, equivalently, G^* must remain unchanged.

Finally, we need to show that $\Delta g_1 = -\Delta Y_1 / p_g, \Delta g_2 = \Delta Y_1 / p_g$ and $\Delta g_i = 0$ for $i = 3, 4, ..., n$. To show these, let us evaluate the budget equation of the consumers after income redistribution:

$$p_g (g_1^* + \Delta g_1) + p_g f_1(G^*) = Y_i - \Delta Y_1$$
$$p_g (g_2^* + \Delta g_2) + p_g f_2(G^*) = Y_2 + \Delta Y_1$$
$$p_g (g_i^* + \Delta g_i) + p_g f_i(G^*) = Y_i, \text{for } i = 3, 4, ..., n.$$

Subtracting Eq. (15.28) from these equations for respective *I*, we get $\Delta g_1 = -\frac{\Delta Y_1}{p_g}$, $\Delta g_2 = \frac{\Delta Y_1}{p_g}$ and $\Delta g_i = 0$ for $i = 3, 4, ...n$.

15.4.4.3 Example

We demonstrate the theorem with a simple example of three individuals, whose incomes are Y_1, Y_2 and Y_3. Each consumes a private good and a public good. Suppose their preference is given by the utility function $u_i = \sqrt{x_i} + \sqrt{g_1 + g_2 + g_3}$. Although the preference need not be identical, we assume so for convenience, and for simplicity (once again), we set $p_g = 1$. From the individual utility maximisation, we get the following three equations for the private contributions to the public good:

$$x_i = \frac{(g_1 + g_2 + g_3)}{p_x^2} = \frac{G}{p_x^2}, \quad i = 1, 2, 3.$$

Substitute the budget equation $x_i = (Y_i - g_i)/p_x$ for each individual in the preceding and write

$$Y_1 - \frac{g_2 + g_3}{p_x} = g_1 \frac{(1+p_x)}{p_x} \quad \Rightarrow \quad g_1 = Y_1 - \frac{G}{p_x}$$
$$Y_2 - \frac{g_1 + g_3}{p_x} = g_2 \frac{(1+p_x)}{p_x} \quad \Rightarrow \quad g_2 = Y_2 - \frac{G}{p_x}$$
$$Y_3 - \frac{g_1 + g_2}{p_x} = g_3 \frac{(1+p_x)}{p_x} \quad \Rightarrow \quad g_3 = Y_3 - \frac{G}{p_x}.$$

Summing over incomes, we obtain

$$Y_1 + Y_2 + Y_3 - \frac{2G}{p_x} = \frac{G(1+p_x)}{p_x} \quad \Rightarrow \quad G^* = \frac{p_x(Y_1 + Y_2 + Y_3)}{3 + p_x}.$$

Thus, G^* depends only on the aggregate income, and not on its distribution. If an individual's contribution falls, because his income has fallen, there will be a compensating increase in the contribution of the individual whose income has increased. To see this, suppose individual 1's income is reduced by $\Delta Y_1 (< g_1^*)$ and individual 2's income is increased by ΔY_2. Then their individual contributions will change to

$$g_1^* + \Delta g_1^* = Y_1 - \Delta Y_1 - \frac{G^*}{p_x} \quad \text{and} \quad g_2^* + \Delta g_2^* = Y_2 + \Delta Y_1 - \frac{G}{p_x}.$$

Clearly, $\Delta g_1^* = -\Delta Y_1$ and $\Delta g_2^* = \Delta Y_1$. Obviously, $\Delta g_3^* = 0$ as Y_3 did not change.

Figure 15.6 illustrates the neutrality theorem and proves that the key insight is fairly simple. As long as the redistribution of income between two individuals is small (meaning a contributor is not turned into a non-contributor) the changes in the optimal contributions of these two individuals exactly offset each other. In the graph, individual 1's contribution is reduced by ΔY_1, and individual 2's contribution increases by ΔY_1.

15.5 Voting

In the last two sections, we discussed that a (divisible) public good can be provided through voluntary contribution or by 'unanimous' agreement (via Lindahl prices). Very often governments decide on public goods by holding a referendum. Two alternative proposals can be placed before the people, and they are asked to vote. If a majority voting rule is followed, then the proposal that gets more than 50% votes wins and is implemented. The same idea is used in committees, local-level governments and even in households. This is also called direct democracy, where the will of the majority is honoured and the minority has to accept the outcome even if they are not to their liking.

Consider an economy with a continuum of individuals who differ in their preference for a public good, say the size of a local park. Let s be the size of the park, which can be at most 1 (say, 1 square kilometer). The minimum is 0, that is, no park at all. Thus, people have the whole range of possibilities $s \in [0,1]$. Some people like smaller park, because with a larger park, less

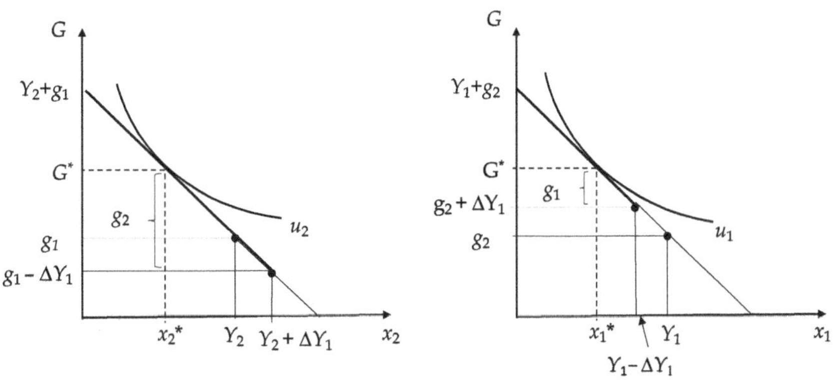

a. *Individual 2 receives* $\Delta Y_1 > 0$

b. ΔY_1 *taken away from Individual 1*

Figure 15.6 Neutrality of aggregate contribution

area will be left for cars and roads. Similarly, there are people who like a bigger park. Their preference is described by a common utility function $u = -(G-s)^2$, where s can be seen as an individual's most preferred size of the park. We can describe an individual's type as s. The utility function of type s attains its maximum height 0 if $G = s$; otherwise, the individual suffers a disutility. The farther the position of G from s, the greater the disutility of type s. We can describe the diversity in people's preferences by assuming that the distribution of type s is given by a cumulative probability distribution function $F(s)$, with density $f(s) > 0$ and median s_m; clearly, $F(0) = 0$, $F(1) = 1$ and $F(s_m) = 1/2$. Since the individual's type exactly corresponds to the support of s, the total mass of population is also 1.

There are two key features of this economy: (1) All individuals have single-peaked preference, and (2) the proposal under consideration is only one-dimensional, the size of the park. Given these two features, there is a simple prediction about the park of what size will be chosen. The unbeatable size of the park is s_m.

To see that, consider any alternative $s' > s_m$. Given the preference function, any individual to the right of s' will vote for s' and any individual to the left of s_m will vote for s_m, because these two proposals are, respectively, closer to their ideal points. Now all the individuals whose s is between s_m and s' will be divided. Those to the left of the midpoint of s' and s_m (i.e., $(s'+s_m)/2$) will vote for s_m, and the individuals to the right of the midpoint will vote for s'. But as $F(s_m) = 1/2$ the proposal s_m will easily win. A symmetric argument rules out any $s' < s_m$ beating s_m either. Therefore, the only proposal that wins for sure is s_m. This is a simple and yet very powerful result known as the *median voter theorem* (MVT).

Median voter theorem: *If the policy/proposal under consideration is one-dimensional and all voters have single-peaked preferences, then the median voter is decisive (in the sense that her preferred policy will win).*

We demonstrate this on panel *a* of Figure 15.7 by assuming three types of voters, who are ordered in terms of their preferred size of the park as s_1, s_2 and s_3. Clearly, s_2 is the median voter. As all voters have a unique bliss point, the only equilibrium is s_2.

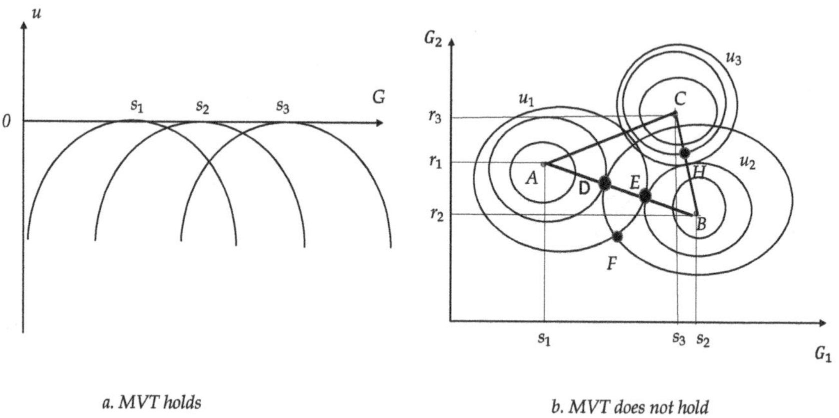

Figure 15.7 Median voter theorem

However, the two conditions critical for MVT may be violated in many circumstances. For example, the voters may care not only about the size of the park but also about the facilities in it. Whether there will be a flower garden, a public swimming pool, a children's playground, a picnic area and so on all may enter into the voters' consideration. Suppose we represent the voters' preferences as $u = -(G_1 - s)^2 - (G_2 - r)^2$, where effectively there are two public goods G_1 and G_2, and the voters' preferences vary on both dimensions. On panel *b* of Figure 15.7, we extend our three-voter example to two public goods, where *r* represents another dimension of the public good about which the voters' type varies (along with *s*). The voters' preferences are described by circular indifference curves. Individual 1's bliss point is (s_1, r_1), individual 2's (s_2, r_2) and individual 3's (s_3, r_3). Such indifference curves reflect lower utility when they are farther away from the bliss point. We can also draw a contract curve (or Pareto-efficient allocations) between any two voters.

Note that the notion of the median voter does not exist, unless all the bliss points fall on a single line. The proposals that lie on the contract curves, *AB*, *BC* or *AC*, are of special interest, because any proposal lying outside the contract curves can be beaten by a proposal on at least one of the contract curves. For instance, *F* is beaten by both *D* and *E*. A similar argument can be made for any proposal lying inside the area bounded by the three contract curves. Now consider proposal *D* against proposal *H*. Proposal *D* will receive one vote (from voter 1), and proposal *H* will get two votes (from voters 2 and 3). But then consider proposal *E* against *H*. Proposal *E* will get two votes (from 1 and 2) and beat *H*. Voter 1 will switch because *E* falls on a higher indifference curve. Thus, it can be seen that there is no clear winner here. Although individual voters have a clear preference, the economy's aggregate preference does not produce a winner. The MVT fails in this case. But it can also be seen that if points *A*, *B* and *C* fall on a line with *B* being the intermediate point, then *B* will be the winner. In that case, a median voter exists, and the MVT holds. The bottom line is that when policies are multidimensional the median voter theorem *may not* hold.

15.6 Negative externality

So far, we talked about positive externality as a public good (such as Christmas lighting). But negative externalities like air pollution, industrial emissions and effluents are public 'bad', as no one wants them. But as these bad goods are not owned by anybody, they share the same problem of public goods in the sense that private actions do not lead to their provision at the socially optimal level. However, a negative externality problem may not necessarily be resolved in the same way as for a positive externality problem.

15.6.1 A two-firm story of pollution

Consider two firms, enjoying a monopoly in two markets. Firm A produces x at a constant marginal cost (MC), c, and its market demand curve is $p = a - x$. However, x creates pollution that affects the profit of another firm B in a nearby area, which is selling a product y. Firm B's market demand curve is $q = b - y$, and its MC is also c. Its profit is reduced by σx. In the absence of any environmental regulation, firm A produces its monopoly output, and so does firm B. Firm A maximises $\pi_A = [a - x - c]x$ with respect to x. The privately optimal output, profit and pollution (let us denote it as z) as follows:

$$x = \frac{a-c}{2} \qquad \pi_A = \frac{(a-c)^2}{4} \qquad z = \sigma\frac{(a-c)}{2}.$$

Firm B maximises $\pi_B = [b - y - c]y - \sigma x$. Note that the loss in its profit due to pollution is like a fixed cost and will not influence its output choice; hence whether the two firms choose output simultaneously or sequentially does not matter. Firm B's output and profit are as follows:

$$y = \frac{b-c}{2} \qquad \pi_B = \frac{(b-c)^2}{4} - \sigma\frac{(a-c)}{2}.$$

The total profit of the two firms in the so-called private equilibrium is

$$\Pi = \pi_A + \pi_B = \frac{(a-c)^2}{4} + \frac{(b-c)^2}{4} - \sigma\frac{(a-c)}{2}. \tag{15.30}$$

Now consider the **Pareto optimal** solution that maximises joint profit. Here, we use the term *Pareto optimality* in a restricted sense because the consumer surpluses of the two markets are not taken into account. When we do that, we maximise the 'social surplus'; as such we have market imperfection due to monopoly. Full efficiency requires achieving both the competitive outputs of the two markets and reducing pollution to its socially efficient level.

Maximising $W = [a - x - c]x + [b - y - c]y - \sigma x$ with respect to x and y, we get

$$x^* = \frac{a-c-\sigma}{2}, y^* = \frac{b-c}{2}, z^* = \sigma\frac{(a-c-\sigma)}{2} \tag{15.31}$$

$$\begin{aligned}\Pi^* &= \frac{(a-c-\sigma)^2}{4} + \frac{(b-c)^2}{4} \\ &= \left[\frac{(a-c)^2}{4} + \frac{(b-c)^2}{4} - \sigma\frac{(a-c)}{2}\right] + \frac{\sigma^2}{4} = \Pi + \frac{\sigma^2}{4}.\end{aligned} \tag{15.32}$$

Let us note that the total profit under the Pareto optimal solution (Eq. (15.31)) is indeed higher than the total profit under the private equilibrium; it is greater by $\sigma^2/4$.

Now the question is, How do we implement the Pareto optimal solution? There are several options:

1. **Merger** If the two firms are merged, we achieve the Pareto optimum. The merged firm will then maximise joint profit, which is precisely Π. The polluting firm is then forced to internalise the harm it inflicts on the other firm.
   However, a merger is not very practical when there are multiple firms involved. Even in the case of two firms, there might be issues with competition policy. As the Pareto optimal solution restricts the output of the polluting firm, consumers will pay a higher price, and any merger is likely to be unpopular among consumers.
2. **Pollution tax** Firm A can be levied with a tax t per unit of x. Since a per unit tax would raise firm A's marginal cost to $c+t$, and if $t=\sigma$, the marginal damage, indeed the optimal x to be chosen by firm A will be $x^* = \frac{a-c-\sigma}{2}$. The Pareto-efficient outputs and pollution are implemented. Furthermore, if the tax revenue σx^* is transferred to firm B, then firm B's profit also reaches the pollution-free level.
   Under the tax-transfer scheme, the profits of the two firms are

$$\pi_A = \frac{(a-c-\sigma)^2}{4}, \pi_B = \frac{(b-c)^2}{4}, \pi_A + \pi_B = \Pi = \Pi^*. \tag{15.33}$$

   Note that the distribution of profit between the two firms is of secondary importance. Our key concerns should be output and pollution.
3. **Regulation** The government can also take recourse to regulation and ask firm A to just restrict its output to the Pareto optimal level, without imposing any tax. Then the Pareto optimal pollution outcome is achieved, and the resultant aggregate profit will also reach the Pareto optimal level. However, the distribution of profit between the two firms will be different. Firm B is clearly worse off than under the tax-transfer scheme.

$$\pi_A = [a-c-\frac{(a-c-\sigma)}{2}]\frac{(a-c-\sigma)}{2} = \frac{(a-c)^2}{4} - \frac{\sigma^2}{4}$$

$$\pi_B = \frac{(b-c)^2}{4} - \sigma\frac{(a-c-\sigma)}{2}$$

$$\Pi = \left[\frac{(a-c)^2}{4}\frac{(b-c)^2}{4} - \sigma\frac{(a-c)}{2}\right] + \frac{\sigma^2}{4} = \Pi^*.$$

4. **Property rights assignment** Ronald Coase (1960) argued that when two parties, like the two firms in our model, are in a situation in which one's actions cause harm to the other as a by-product then a property right over the 'harm' (or social bad) can be assigned to any one of them and as long as the two parties can negotiate at no cost over the use of the property right, the Pareto-efficient outcome will be achieved.

   At first glance, this is a remarkable claim. Contrary to popular perceptions, the government does not need to actively engage with industries. Just create ownership of the 'social bad' which nobody owns, then private incentives will take over the process of arriving at the

Pareto optimal outcome. Though originally proposed as a conjecture, Coase's idea came to be known as the *Coase theorem*. The basic intuition is fairly simple: whoever values the bad good will find his way to optimally use it. If the pollutees value it more than the polluter, then the pollutees will pay to the polluter to stop or charge a price for it (depending on whether they have the property rights or not). Similarly, if the polluter values it more, then they will pay the pollutees to be able to pollute. Who gets the property right is not important for the efficient outcome.

The Coase theorem offers a solution to another problem, *the tragedy of the commons*, originally discussed by Hardin (1968).[5] The tragedy of the commons problem is best described by the story of a village pasture where the villagers bring their cows for grazing at free of cost. Since rearing an additional cow does not inflict any cost, the villagers will continue to add more cows until the land is so overgrazed that no cows can be fed anymore. Every additional cow exerts a negative externality to all other cows that were already grazing there. But in the absence of property right, this cost is not internalised. Coase's idea suggests that charging an entry fee would remedy the problem.

Subsequent investigation of the Coase conjecture, however, reveals that when the problem involves consumers, their preferences should be quasi-linear for the theorem to hold. In our example, firms maximise profit so that assumption is met. Moreover, the theorem is applicable to multiple firms or individuals, as long as they can negotiate at no cost over the price at which they can buy and sell the right to pollute or the right to be unaffected by pollution. Let us see how this idea can work in our example.

a. First, consider giving property rights to the polluter, firm A. Under this assignment, firm A is free to pollute as much as it wants, and it can secure a profit of $\pi_A = \frac{(a-c)^2}{4}$. However, it can do better by restricting its output to the Pareto optimal level and demanding payment from firm B. Consider the following scheme. Suppose A says that B must pay $\sigma^2/2$ to have the pollution restricted to $\sigma(a-c-\sigma)/2$ or else A can pollute as much as it wants. If B agrees, their profits will be

$$\pi_A = \frac{(a-c-\sigma)}{2}\left(a-c-\frac{(a-c-\sigma)}{2}\right)+\frac{\sigma^2}{2} = \frac{(a-c)^2}{4}+\frac{\sigma^2}{4}$$

$$\pi_B = \frac{(b-c)^2}{4}-\sigma\frac{(a-c-\sigma)}{2}-\frac{\sigma^2}{2}=\frac{(b-c)^2}{4}-\sigma\frac{(a-c)}{2}$$

$$\pi_A+\pi_B = \Pi+\frac{\sigma^2}{4} = \Pi^*.$$

This is the 'victim pays' principle. Either way, the joint surplus is maximised and shared, and the Pareto optimal pollution is implemented.

In Figure 15.8 we represent the property right assignment solutions. Point M indicates the baseline case with no property assignment. Firms produce privately optimal outputs, and the aggregate profit is Π. After the property right assignment, the outcome should lie anywhere between points P_A and P_D on the enlarged aggregate profit frontier Π^*.

At point P_A, firm A restricts its production to the Pareto optimal level and demands a payment of $\sigma^2/2$ from firm B (the victim-pays principle). However, firm A can also be

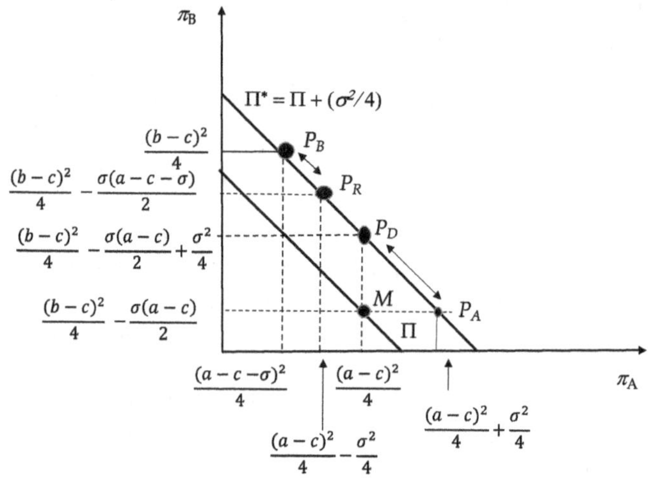

Figure 15.8 Profits of the polluter and the affected firm

generous and ask for $\sigma^2/4$ (half the amount at P_A) to restrict its output, in which case they will earn

$$\pi_A = \frac{(a-c)^2}{4}$$

$$\pi_B = \frac{(b-c)^2}{4} - \sigma\frac{(a-c-\sigma)}{2} - \frac{\sigma^2}{4} = \frac{(b-c)^2}{4} - \sigma\frac{(a-c)}{2} + \frac{\sigma^2}{4}$$

$$\pi_A + \pi_B = \Pi + \frac{\sigma^2}{4} = \Pi^*.$$

This is shown at point P_D, the best B can hope for. In fact, any point between P_D and P_A can be implemented by A by charging a fee between $\frac{\sigma^2}{4}$ and $\frac{\sigma^2}{2}$. With right to pollute granted firm A will not move to a point left of P_D along the aggregate profit curve.

b. Now suppose firm B is given the property right over water/air (through which the pollution is carried over to firm B). Firm B then can impose a tax at the rate of σ on every unit of x, just as we discussed earlier in the tax regime. Firm A's profit falls to $(a-c-\sigma)^2/4$, and firm B's profit rises to $(b-c)^2/4$. Pollution is reduced to $\sigma(a-c-\sigma)/2$. This outcome is given by point P_B. Here, the 'polluter pays' principle is implemented. Of course, B can be little generous and might say, "Produce $x = \frac{a-c-\sigma}{2}$, but give me a fee $F = \lambda\sigma\left[\frac{(a-c-\sigma)}{2}\right]$," where $\lambda \in [0,1]$. If $\lambda = 1$, we have the tax-regime pay-offs; that is, $\pi_B = \frac{(b-c)^2}{4}$ and $\pi_A = \frac{(a-c-\sigma)^2}{4}$. On the other extreme, if $\lambda = 0$, we have

$\pi_A = \frac{(a-c)^2}{4} - \frac{\sigma^2}{4}$, $\pi_B = \frac{(b-c)^2}{4} - \sigma\frac{(a-c-\sigma)}{2}$. This is shown by point P_R, which is also the regulation-regime pay-off. By varying λ between 0 and 1, we can capture any point between P_B and P_R. One word of caution is in order here. Under the proposed scheme, x should be specified at the Pareto optimal level rather than specifying a lower tax rate and letting A choose its optimal x. If not, firm A would choose a larger x, and the Pareto frontier cannot be achieved.

In principle, the whole frontier can be achieved by agreeing on some (potentially complicated) payment mechanism. For example, to go to the right of P_R, firm B must pay something to A even when B has the property right. Likewise, to go to the left of P_D firm A must pay something to B even if it has the property right.

To sum up, who gets the property right affects the distribution of profit but not the aggregate profit or the Pareto optimal outputs and pollution.

15.6.1.1 *Tradable emissions permit*

Ronald Coase's idea of the assignment of property rights can be applied to other contexts, such as the one where all parties are polluters. If an industry has n firms all polluting in different intensities and if they vary in their technologies, then an aggregate emission target can be achieved by distributing among those n firms emission quotas, which are essentially property rights up to a specific quantity. If the aggregate emission is at some unaccepted level, say, $\bar{E}$, and if it needs to be restricted at $\hat{E}$, then n firms can be given individual quota (or permit to pollute) up to a certain level, say, $\hat{e}_i$, so that $\hat{e}_1 + \hat{e}_2 + ... + \hat{e}_n = \hat{E}$. It must be that some firms were over-polluting and some were under-polluting, given that they differ in technology. With the distribution of quotas, the firms are allowed to trade among themselves any unused quotas. The expected end result is that the most efficient firm (which has the least polluting technology) will be able to buy more quotas from others, while the least efficient firm (which has the most polluting technology) will sell most of its quota. The resulting distribution of output and pollution will be socially efficient. Of course, the initial distribution of quotas affects the distribution of gains from trading but leaves the efficient implementation of the emission target unaffected. European Union's Emissions Trading System is a prime example of this, which has remained its key policy tool to reduce greenhouse gas emissions. The Environmental Protection Agency of the United States also has a large emissions-trading programme.

15.6.2 A broader notion of efficiency

In our two-firm story, we focused on the joint profit while ignoring any concern for the consumers. At a broader level, however, efficiency needs to be judged taking account of the consumer surplus as well. The assumption of monopoly was for convenience, but it is also true that a competitive market is bad when the product it sells is a polluting product. Therefore, we may focus on an intermediate form of market like oligopoly and explicitly consider both pollution and abatement. In addition, we allow one firm to be under public ownership so that we can directly incorporate the social planner's objective of meeting environmental goals and maximising market-specific social welfare. The following model is based on Pal and Saha (2014).

15.6.2.1 *A mixed-duopoly model of environment*

Suppose a public firm competes with a private firm. Let the production cost of firm i be given by an increasing function $C_i = C_i(q_i), C_i'(.) > 0, C_i''(.) \geq 0$, where q_i refers to firm i's output. Production inevitably results in pollution. But firms undertake abatement measures (denoted a_i) at the time of production. Examples may include treatment of effluents at source by paper mills, tanneries and others. The abatement cost function is also a convex function: $g_i(a_i), g_i'(.) > 0, g_i''(.) \geq 0$. Pollution of firm i is expressed as a linear function of output, and for simplicity, it is written as $h_i = q_i - a_i$. Social damage due to pollution is given by $E = E(Q - A)$, where $Q = q_1 + q_2$ and $A = a_1 + a_2$, $E' > 0, E''(.) \geq 0$.

The inverse market demand for the good is given by $p = p(Q), p'(.) < 0$, and for ease of exposition, we assume $p''(Q) \leq 0$. We want to permit both an output tax t and abatement subsidy s, both per unit of q_i. When $t = s$ our tax subsidy scheme would turn into a simple pollution tax. The profit for firm i is

$$\pi_i = p(Q)q_i - C_i(q_i) - g_i(a_i) - tq_i + sa_i, i = 1,2.$$

The social welfare of this economy is a sum of industry profit and consumer surplus minus the social damage due to pollution:

$$W = \int_0^Q p(x)dx - C_1(q_1) - C_2(q_2) - g_1(a_1) - g_2(a_2) - E(Q - A). \tag{15.34}$$

By the assumptions on $p(Q)$, $C_i(q_i)$ and $g_i(a_i)$ the welfare function $W(.)$ is a strictly concave function in (q_1, q_2, a_1, a_2) and so are $\pi_1(q_1, a_1)$ and $\pi_2(q_2, a_2)$

15.6.2.1.1 SOCIAL OPTIMUM

We want to see what the social optimum is for this economy, and then we will see if a combination of t and s can achieve it. By maximising social welfare as given by Eq. (15.34) with respect to q_i and a_i, we get

$$p(q_1 + q_2) - C_i'(q_i) - E'(q_1 + q_2 - a_1 - a_2) = 0, i = 1,2, \tag{15.35}$$

$$-g_i'(a_i) + E'(q_1 + q_2 - a_1 - a_2) = 0, \ i = 1,2. \tag{15.36}$$

Suppose (q_i^S, a_i^S), $i = 1,2$ solve Eqs. (15.35) and (15.36), and thus, they are the socially optimal output and abatement of firm i. The solution is well defined for the properties of the $W(.)$ function. In the social optimum the price of the polluting product is set equal to the true social marginal cost of production, and abatement in each firm is so chosen that its marginal cost equals the marginal environmental damage.[6]

15.6.2.2 *A privatisation and tax subsidy scheme*

It is a widely shared view that public firms are major polluters. This is because often large power plants and resource-intensive industries are under public ownership in many countries and because the government may go soft on itself in enforcing the environmental rules and regulations. Nevertheless, it is an interesting question to ask whether public ownership *per se* is detrimental to achieving environmental objectives.

Without loss of generality let us assume that firm 1 is (partially) publicly owned, and the extent of private ownership is θ. While firm 2 maximises profit, firm 1 maximises $O = \theta\pi_1 + (1-\theta)W$. The government's scheme of privatisation and tax subsidy is announced in the first stage of the game, and firms then choose their outputs and abatements.[7]

In the second stage, the equilibrium outputs and abatement must satisfy the following first-order conditions for optimisation:

$$\frac{\partial O}{\partial q_1} = p(.) - C_1'(q_1) - (1-\theta)E'(.) + \theta q_1 p'(.) - \theta t = 0 \tag{15.37}$$

$$\frac{\partial O}{\partial a_1} = -g_1'(a_1) + (1-\theta)E'(.) + \theta s = 0 \tag{15.38}$$

$$\frac{\partial \pi_2}{\partial q_2} = p(.) + q_2 p'(.) - C_2'(q_2) - t = 0 \tag{15.39}$$

$$\frac{\partial \pi_2}{\partial a_2} = -g_2'(a_2) + s = 0. \tag{15.40}$$

Now let us take note of two important observations about abatement.

Lemma 11. *If firms have identical production and abatement technologies, unless* $C''(q_i) = 0$ *and* $g''(a_i) = 0$ *for* $i = 1,2$, *the optimal tax and subsidy would be such that the private firm produces a strictly positive output at all* $\theta \in [0,1]$.

Usually, when both firms have constant returns to scale technology, it is socially optimal to concentrate all production in one firm. That will not be true anymore because of abatement. Zero output means zero pollution and zero abatement. Unless the other firm is vastly superior in its abatement technology, such a specialisation would be inefficient.

Now we consider a tax subsidy scheme and privatisation. The following result holds.

Proposition 57. *When the two firms have asymmetric technologies, the government will choose zero privatisation (i.e.,*$\theta = 0$*) and set* $t^* = E'(q_1^S + q_2^S - a_1^2 - a_2^S) + q_2^S p'(q_1^S + q_2^S)$ *and* $s^* = E'(q_1^S + q_2^S - a_1^2 - a_2^S)$ *in order to implement the social optimum. If the firms have symmetric technologies, then the degree of privatisation does not matter.*

Proof. Substitute $s = E'(q_1^S + q_2^S - a_1^2 - a_2^S)$ in Eq. (15.40) and solve for a_2. This solution must be a_2^S given by Eq. (15.36) for $i = 2$. Next, set $\theta = 0$ and $s = E'(q_1^S + q_2^S - a_1^2 - a_2^S)$ in (15.38). This gives a_1^S as Eq. (15.36) did for $i = 1$. Now set $\theta = 0$ in Eq. (15.37) and substitute $t = E'(q_1^S + q_2^S - a_1^2 - a_2^S) + q_2^S p'(q_1^S + q_2^S)$ in (15.39). The resultant two equations are two output reaction functions given a_1^S and a_2^S. Under the assumptions made, these two reaction functions will have a unique intersection point (q_1^S, q_2^S). Hence, the stated policy implements the social optimum.

Next, to see that optimal $\theta = 0$ when firms have asymmetric technologies, note that $q_1^S \neq q_2^S$ and/or $a_1^S \neq a_2^S$. It suffices to show that with $\theta > 0$, the social optimum is not achievable. To see this set $\theta > 0$, but substitute $t = E'(q_1^S + q_2^S - a_1^S - a_2^S) + q_2^S p'(q_1^S + q_2^S)$ in Eq. (15.37) and then evaluate it at $(q_1^S, q_2^S, a_1^S, a_2^S)$. We get (15.37) as

$$\frac{\partial O}{\partial q_1} = \underbrace{p(q_1^S + q_2^S) - C_1'(q_1^S) - E'(q_1^S + q_2^S - a_1^S - a_2^S)}_{=0 \text{(by Eq. (15.35))}} + \underbrace{\theta p'(q_1^S + q_2^S)[q_1^S - q_2^S]}_{\neq 0 \text{(as } q_1^S \neq q_2^S\text{)}} \neq 0.$$

Hence, when firms are not identical a tax subsidy scheme without full nationalisation cannot implement the social optimum. When firms are identical social optimality demands $q_1^S = q_2^S$ and $a_1^S = a_2^S$. Then regardless of θ, Eq. (15.37) will coincide with Eq. (15.35) for $i = 1$ under the stated tax subsidy scheme.

The key idea is fairly simple. With one firm under full public ownership, it is directly guided to social welfare maximisation, while the tax subsidy scheme guides the private firm to social optimality. Note that in the tax subsidy scheme, the subsidy is above the tax rate. In particular, the tax rate is below the marginal social damage. This is done to induce the private firm to produce *more* than the private duopoly level (to correct for market imperfection). This takes us to our final observation that a standard pollution tax (i.e.,$t = s$), which penalises pollution and rewards abatement at the same rate cannot implement the social optimum.

REMARK 4

A pollution tax cannot implement the social optimum in this economy even at $\theta = 0$.

To sum up, public ownership is often regarded as a burden for society for its technological backwardness. However, it provides a regulatory tool to the government in the context of environmental problems. Public ownership helps overcome both the environmental problems and market power issues. With this additional tool, private firms can be guided to the social optimum by rewarding abatement *more* than by penalising output.

15.7 Conclusion

The literature on public good is vast. We have tried to give a brief overview of some key issues. But there are some major omissions. To name a few, these are impure public goods, motives for voluntary contribution and sequential models of contribution. Do people make charitable contributions out of altruism, to signal their wealth or to get some private benefit from doing some social service (halo effect)? Many authors have examined this question both within theoretical models and by using experimental methods. Does sequential contribution improve efficiency? Some papers have shown that early contributors tend to free ride more and late contributors try to compensate for that, but still the overall contributions may be less than the simultaneous contribution case (see Bag and Roy (2011)). In the context of environmental economics, there is a big literature on multilateral negotiations climate agreement. Such topics are extremely important, but they are beyond the scope of the present book.

Summary

In this chapter, we have learnt the following:

1. The Groves–Clarke mechanism is a demand-revealing mechanism to finance the provision of a discrete public good.

2. The Lindahl rule is for allocating the cost of a divisible public good and providing it at an efficient level.
3. Voluntary contributions can make a (divisible) public good possible.
4. There exists a neutrality theorem of voluntary contributions.
5. The Coase theorem shows how to efficiently solve environmental problems, such as pollution.
6. Mergers, regulation, and property rights assignment can help achieve the social optimum.
7. We also studied a duopoly model to analyse the (combined) efficient provisions of a polluting product and pollution.

15.8 Exercises

1. Suppose there are two individuals, 1 and 2 whose preferences over a private good x and a public good G are given by $u_i = \sqrt{x_1} + \sqrt{G}$. Their incomes are Y_1 and Y_2. Furthermore, the cost of providing G is \$$G$, and it is allocated between 1 and 2 as tG and $(1-t)G$, respectively. Assume a price of x is p.

   a. Derive the Lindahl equilibrium tax t^* for this economy.
   b. Show the Lindahl equilibrium on a contract curve diagram.

2. Consider the voluntary contribution game of Section 15.4.1. What would be the equilibrium outcome if individual 1 contributes first and individual 2 next?
3. Consider the pollution problem studied in Section 15.6.1. Suppose that in the downstream market (which is affected by pollution) there are two firms and that the loss in profit is still σx, which is shared by the two downstream firms.

   a. Recalculate the free-market solution and the Pareto optimal outputs.
   b. If the upstream firm is merged with one of the downstream firms, what will be an equilibrium outcome? Does it attain the social optimum?

4. Staying on the same pollution problem, suppose that the downstream demand is affected by the upstream pollution in the following way: $q = b - \alpha x - y$ (assume a relatively small). There are two firms in the downstream market (affected by pollution).

   a Again, calculate the free-market and Pareto optimal solutions.
   b. How would the merger of the upstream firm with one of the downstream firm work? Will it improve efficiency?

5. Consider a duopoly producing a homogeneous good, whose demand curve is $p = B - (q_1 + q_2)$. Production causes pollution, part of which can be remedied through abatement. Two firms differ in their production and abatement technologies. The production cost of firm i is $C_i^q = c_i q_i^2 / 2$. Each unit of q_i generates a pollution of z_i by a linear function $z_i = \sigma q_i$. The aggregate social harm is a linear function of aggregate pollution, $H = h[z_1 + z_2 - a_1 - a_2]$. The abatement cost of firm i is $C_i^a = \alpha_i a_i^2$. Each firm's profit is $\pi_i = pq_i - C_i^q - C_i^a$. Assume $c_1 > c_2$ and $\alpha_1 < \alpha_2$.

   a. What are the duopoly equilibrium outputs for pollution and abatement.
   b. Derive the socially optimal level of outputs and abatement.
   c. Can a pollution tax achieve the social optimum?
   d. Can you think of a tradable pollution permit programme here?

Notes

1 See the appendix to Chapter 10 (Section 10.6). In the ascending bid open auctions, also known as the English auction, the winning bid approximately equal to the second-highest bid. This auction encourages people to bid up to their true valuation with the objective of winning. The process reveals everybody's valuation, like the Groves–Clarke mechanism.

2 'Buying' in this context means contributing to the public good. It can be a charitable contribution or buying a private good that has a public good externality. For example, firecrackers or Christmas lighting. Such private consumption contributes to the collective pool $G = \sum_i g_i$.

3 Solve the following problem:

$$\text{Max } L = x_1^{\alpha} (g_1 + g_2)^{1-\alpha} - \lambda_1 [x_1 + g_1 - Y_1]$$

$$\frac{\partial L}{\partial g_1} = (1-\alpha) x_1^{\alpha} (g_1 + g_2)^{-\alpha} - \lambda_1 = 0$$

$$\frac{\partial L}{\partial x_1} = \alpha x_1^{\alpha-1} (g_1 + g_2)^{1-\alpha} - \lambda_1 = 0$$

$$\frac{\partial L}{\partial \lambda_1} = -[x_1 + g_1 - Y_1] = 0.$$

Dividing the first equation by the second equation, we get $\frac{(1-\alpha)x_1}{\alpha(g_1 + g_2)} = 1$. Then substitute the budget equation $x_1 = Y_1 - g_1$ to derive the demand for g_1.

4 A strictly convex preference is assumed for expositional convenience. The theorem holds also under weak convexity.

5 Hardin (1968) wrote, "Picture a pasture open to all. It is to be expected that each herdsman will try to keep as many cattle as possible on the commons. Such an arrangement may work reasonably satisfactorily for centuries because tribal wars, poaching and disease keep the numbers of both man and beast well below the carrying capacity of the land. Finally, however, comes the day of reckoning, that is, the day when the long-desired goal of social stability becomes a reality. At this point, the inherent logic of the commons remorselessly generates tragedy" (p. 1243).

6 We implicitly assume that $q_1^S > 0$, $q_2^S > 0$, which requires assuming that the cost asymmetry between firms (if any) is not too large. More formally, we need, at $q_1 = 0$, $p(q_2^S) > C_1'(0) + E'(q_2^S - a_2^S)$ and, at $q_2 = 0$, $p(q_1^S) > C_2'(0) + E'(q_1^S - a_1^S)$.

7 It is natural to expect that firms will not abate beyond their individual pollution level (unless abatement is tradable). However, this constraint is not explicitly imposed for simplicity.

References

Bag, P. K. & Mondal, D. (2014). Group size paradox and public goods. *Economics Letters*, 144(1), 215–218.

Bag, P. K. & Roy, S. (2011). On sequential and simultaneous contributions under incomplete information. *International Journal of Game Theory*, 40, 119–145.

Bergstrom, T., Blume, L. & Varian, H. R. (1986). On the private provision of public goods. *Journal of Public Economics*, 29, 25–49.

Coase, R. (1960). The problem of social cost. *The Journal of Law & Economics*, 3, 1–44.

Comes, R. & Sandier, T. (1985). The simple analytics of pure public good provision. *Economica*, 52, 103–116.

Cornes, R. & Sandler, T. (1984). Easy riders, joint production, and public goods. *Economic Journal*, 94, 580–598.

Hardin, G. (1968). The tragedy of the commons. *Science, New Series*, 162, 1243–1248.
Lindahl, E. (1958 [1919]). Just taxation – a positive solution. In R. A. Musgrave & A. T. Peacock (Eds.), *Classics in the Theory of Public Finance*. London: Macmillan.
Mueller, D. C. (2003). *Public Choice III*. Cambridge: Cambridge University Press.
Pal, R. & Saha, B. (2014). Mixed duopoly and environment. *Journal of Public Economic Theory*, 16, 96–118.
Samuelson, P. A. (1954). The theory of public expenditure. *Review of Economics and Statistics*, 36, 386–389.
Warr, P. (1982). Pareto optimal redistribution and private charity. *Journal of Public Economics*, 19, 131–138.
Warr, P. (1983). The private provision of a public good is independent of the distribution of income. *Economic Letters*, 13, 207–211.
Young, D. (1982). Voluntary purchase of public goods. *Public Choice*, 38, 73–86.

Chapter 16

Mathematical appendix

16.1 Sets

We briefly review some of the essential mathematical concepts. We begin with the notion of sets. A collection of numbers or vectors bearing a common property is a set. Examples are

- The set of all integers from 5 to 10: $A_1 = \{5,6,7,8,9,10\}$.
- The set of all real numbers from 5 to 10: $A_2 = \{x \mid 5 \le x \le 10\}$.
- The set of all real numbers strictly between 5 and 10: $A_3 = \{x \mid 5 < x < 10\}$.

A Cartesian product of two sets is also a set. Suppose $A = \{x_1 \mid 1 \le x_1 \le 2\}$ and $B = \{x_2 \mid 2 \le x_2 \le 3\}$, then the Cartesian product of A and B is $A \times B = \{(x_1, x_2) \mid 1 \le x_1 \le 2, 2 \le x_2 \le 3\}$. Moreover, $A \subset R^1, B \subset R^1$, and $A \times B \subset R^2$, where R^1 is the set of all real numbers and R^2 is the set of all vectors of real numbers (x_1, x_2). R^2 is also called the two-dimensional Euclidean space of real numbers. The notation $\subset$ means subset.

You can visualise the set $A \times B$ as a 1 × 1 box on a two-dimensional graph of with x_1 on the horizontal axis and x_2 on the vertical axis. A similar Cartesian set of $A \times B \times C$ can be arrived at by 'multiplying' $C = \{x_3 \mid 0 \le x_3 \le 1\}$ to $A \times B$. The set $A \times B \times C \subset R^3$.

A consumption bundle consisting of two goods is typically an element of the positive orthant of R^2. A bundle of n goods is an element of R^n.

A set is *closed* if its boundary is included. In the previous examples, A_1, A_2 and $A \times B$ are closed, but A_3 is not because the boundaries 5 and 10 are not included. Formally, the boundary of a set consists of points x such that a small ball around x will contain points that are not in the set. The complement of a closed set is open.

Distance between any two numbers x and y in R^n is given by its Euclidean distance function $\| x - y \| = \sqrt{\Sigma_i^n (y_i - x_i)^2}$.

A set is bounded if for every x in the set one can draw a sufficiently large ball that includes the whole set. In other words, if all members of the set are above a lower bound and below an upper bound, then the set is bounded. Typically, consumption and production sets are bounded. A set that is both closed and bounded is called *compact*.

A set is *convex* if every weighted average of any two elements of the set is also contained in the set. Take set A_1 from the preceding examples. The set does not include any fractions and thus excludes all weighted averages of any two consecutive integers. So A_1 is not a convex set. But A_2 and A_3 are; they include by definition all weighted averages between any two numbers of the set.

DOI: 10.4324/9781003226994-16

A set $X = \{(x_1, x_2, \ldots, x_n) \geq 0\}$ is convex if for any $0 \leq \lambda \leq 1$, and for every $x \neq x' \in X$, we have $\lambda x + (1-\lambda)x' \in X$, where $x = (x_1, x_2, \ldots, x_n)$, $x' = (x'_1, x'_2, \ldots, x'_n)$ and $\lambda x + (1-\lambda)x'$ $(\lambda x_1 + (1-\lambda)x_1, \lambda x_2 + (1-\lambda)x'_2, \ldots, \lambda x_n + (1-\lambda)x'_n)$.

If a set is not convex, it is called non-convex. The convexity of a set refers to solidity as well as the shape of an object. A cube is a convex set, as it includes not just the outer surface area but also all the inside points. But a set consisting only edges is not convex, because the points between two opposite edges are not included in the set. A ball is convex, but a set consisting only the circumference of the ball is not convex. Caution: The convexity of a set should not be confused with the convexity of a function.

16.2 Matrices

A system of linear equations like the following

$$a_{11}x_1 + a_{12}x_2 + a_{13}x_3 = b_1$$

$$a_{21}x_1 + a_{22}x_2 + a_{23}x_3 = b_2$$

$$a_{31}x_1 + a_{32}x_2 + a_{33}x_3 = b_3$$

can be written concisely in the matrix form as follows.

$$\begin{bmatrix} a_{11} & a_{12} & a_{13} \\ a_{21} & a_{22} & a_{23} \\ a_{31} & a_{32} & a_{33} \end{bmatrix} + \begin{bmatrix} x_1 \\ x_2 \\ x_3 \end{bmatrix} = \begin{bmatrix} b_1 \\ b_2 \\ b_3 \end{bmatrix}$$

In short form, $Ax = b$, where A is the earlier 3 × 3 matrix and $x = (x_1, x_2, x_3)$ and $b = (b_1, b_2, b_3)$. The solution to the equation system is $x = A^{-1}b$, provided A^{-1} exists. A matrix is invertible if its determinant, denoted $|A|$, is not equal to zero. The determinant of matrix A is given by

$$|A| = a_{11}\begin{vmatrix} a_{22} & a_{23} \\ a_{32} & a_{33} \end{vmatrix} - a_{12}\begin{vmatrix} a_{21} & a_{23} \\ a_{31} & a_{33} \end{vmatrix} + a_{13}\begin{vmatrix} a_{21} & a_{22} \\ a_{31} & a_{32} \end{vmatrix},$$

where

$$\begin{vmatrix} a_{22} & a_{23} \\ a_{32} & a_{33} \end{vmatrix} = a_{22}a_{33} - a_{23}a_{32}, \quad \begin{vmatrix} a_{21} & a_{23} \\ a_{31} & a_{33} \end{vmatrix} = a_{21}a_{33} - a_{23}a_{31}, \quad \begin{vmatrix} a_{21} & a_{22} \\ a_{31} & a_{32} \end{vmatrix} = a_{21}a_{32} - a_{22}a_{31}.$$

The first determinant refers to a submatrix called the *minor* of a_{11} formed by replacing the first row and the first column of the matrix A. Often, the determinant itself is referred to as the minor. In general, the minor of a_{ij} is the determinant of the submatrix after replacing the ith row and the jth column of A. If D_{ij} is the determinant of the minor of a_{ij}, then

$$\text{Cofactor of } a_{ij} = C_{ij} = (-1)^{i+j} D_{ij}.$$

Let the matrix of all cofactors be $C = \left[C_{ij}\right]$ and its transpose be denoted as C'. Then the inverse of matrix A is

$$A^{-1} = \frac{|C'|}{|A|} = \frac{1}{|A|}\begin{bmatrix} C_{11} & C_{21} & C_{31} \\ C_{12} & C_{22} & C_{32} \\ C_{13} & C_{23} & C_{33} \end{bmatrix}.$$

Therefore, the solution to the simultaneous equation system is

$$x_1 = \frac{C_{11}b_1 + C_{21}b_2 + C_{31}b_3}{|A|}$$

$$x_2 = \frac{C_{12}b_1 + C_{22}b_2 + C_{32}b_3}{|A|}$$

$$x_3 = \frac{C_{13}b_1 + C_{23}b_2 + C_{33}b_3}{|A|}.$$

These definitions can be applied to any $n \times n$ matrix. The determinants of the principal minors of a $n \times n$ matrix are

$$a_{11}, \begin{vmatrix} a_{11} & a_{12} \\ a_{21} & a_{22} \end{vmatrix}, \begin{vmatrix} a_{11} & a_{12} & a_{13} \\ a_{21} & a_{22} & a_{23} \\ a_{31} & a_{32} & a_{33} \end{vmatrix}, \ldots \begin{vmatrix} a_{11} & a_{12} & a_{13} & \ldots & a_{1n} \\ a_{21} & a_{22} & a_{23} & \ldots & a_{2n} \\ a_{31} & a_{32} & a_{33} & \ldots & a_{3n} \\ \ldots & \ldots & \ldots & \ldots & \ldots \\ a_{n1} & a_{n2} & a_{n3} & \ldots & a_{nn} \end{vmatrix}.$$

16.2.1 Cramer's rule

An alternative way of solving a system of linear equations is Cramer's rule. For the three-equation system given earlier,

$$x_1 = \frac{\begin{vmatrix} b_1 & a_{12} & a_{13} \\ b_2 & a_{22} & a_{23} \\ b_3 & a_{32} & a_{33} \end{vmatrix}}{|A|}, \qquad x_2 = \frac{\begin{vmatrix} a_{11} & b_1 & a_{13} \\ a_{21} & b_2 & a_{23} \\ a_{31} & b_3 & a_{33} \end{vmatrix}}{|A|}, \qquad x_3 = \frac{\begin{vmatrix} a_{11} & a_{12} & b_1 \\ a_{21} & a_{22} & b_2 \\ a_{31} & a_{32} & b_3 \end{vmatrix}}{|A|}.$$

Because of its simplicity, we have used Cramer's rule extensively in this book.

16.2.1.1 Definiteness of a matrix

In many economic applications, usually as the second-order conditions for maximisation or minimisation, quadratic equations of the following kind appear:

$$y = a_{11}x_1^2 + 2a_{12}x_1x_2 + a_{22}x_2^2 < 0 \text{(or} > 0\text{)}.$$

This equation can be written as (for x_1, x_2 both not being 0)

$$y = [x_1, x_2] \begin{bmatrix} a_{11} & a_{12} \\ a_{12} & a_{22} \end{bmatrix} \begin{bmatrix} x_1 \\ x_2 \end{bmatrix}.$$

That is, $y = x'Ax$. The symmetry of A is not necessary. Then the sign of y can be assigned by the definiteness of the matrix A.

1. $y > 0$ if A is positive definite for $x \neq 0$. A is a positive definite matrix if

$$a_{11} > 0, \quad \begin{vmatrix} a_{11} & a_{12} \\ a_{12} & a_{22} \end{vmatrix} > 0.$$

2. $y < 0$ if A is negative definite for $x \neq 0$. A is negative definite if

$$a_{11} < 0, \quad \begin{vmatrix} a_{11} & a_{12} \\ a_{12} & a_{22} \end{vmatrix} > 0.$$

3. In the general case of n variables and A being a square matrix $(n \times n)$ but not necessarily symmetric,
   a. A is positive definite if the determinants of its principal minors are all positive.
   b. A is negative definite if the determinants of its principal minors alternate in sign starting from negative.
4. Sometimes we may not insist on strictly positive or negative y. Instead $y \geq 0$ or ≤ 0 may suffice. In this case, we use the idea of semi-definite matrices.
   a. $y \geq 0$ if $x'Ax \geq 0$ for all x. Matrix A positive semi-definite if the determinants of its principal minors are all non-negative.
   b. $y \leq 0$ if $x'Ax \leq 0$ for all x. Matrix A negative semi-definite if the determinants of its principal minors alternate in sign from non-positive to non-negative starting from non-positive.
5. Sometimes there is an additional constraint on vector x in the form of $w_1 x_1 + w_2 x_2 = 0$ for $y > 0$ or $y < 0$. This is usually the case for constrained minimisation or maximisation, where w_1 and w_2 appear as the prices of x_1 and x_2. In this case, we write the following:
   a. $y = x'Ax > 0$ subject to $wx = 0$ for $x \neq 0$. This will be true if the following bordered matrix

$$B = \begin{bmatrix} 0 & w_1 & w_2 \\ w_1 & a_{11} & a_{12} \\ w_2 & a_{21} & a_{22} \end{bmatrix}$$

   is positive definite. In terms of the determinant condition, we must have $|B|$ negative. The condition for the general case with n variables is that all border-preserving principal minors must have *negative* determinants. Note the difference here from the case without the border.

$$\begin{vmatrix} 0 & w_1 & w_2 \\ w_1 & a_{11} & a_{12} \\ w_2 & a_{21} & a_{22} \end{vmatrix} < 0, \quad \begin{vmatrix} 0 & w_1 & w_2 & w_3 \\ w_1 & a_{11} & a_{12} & a_{13} \\ w_2 & a_{21} & a_{22} & a_{23} \\ w_3 & a_{31} & a_{32} & a_{33} \end{vmatrix} < 0 \ldots \begin{vmatrix} 0 & w_1 & \cdots & w_n \\ w_1 & a_{11} & \cdots & a_{1n} \\ w_2 & a_{21} & \cdots & a_{2n} \\ \cdots & \cdots & \cdots & \cdots \\ w_n & a_{n1} & \cdots & a_{nn} \end{vmatrix} < 0.$$

b. $y = x'Ax < 0$ subject to $wx = 0$ for $x \neq 0$. This requires $|B|$ to be negative definite. The determinant condition for the bordered matrix B being negative definite in the general case is the following:

$$\begin{vmatrix} 0 & w_1 & w_2 \\ w_1 & a_{11} & a_{12} \\ w_2 & a_{21} & a_{22} \end{vmatrix} > 0, \quad \begin{vmatrix} 0 & w_1 & w_2 & w_3 \\ w_1 & a_{11} & a_{12} & a_{13} \\ w_2 & a_{21} & a_{22} & a_{23} \\ w_3 & a_{31} & a_{32} & a_{33} \end{vmatrix} < 0 \ldots \text{alternate in sign.}$$

16.3 Functions

A function is a statement of a relationship between members of two sets. Consider two sets $X \subset R^2$ and $Y \subset R^1$. $y = f(x_1, x_2)$ is a mapping $f: X \to Y$. That is, for every (x_1, x_2) in X, we associate an element of the set Y, which is only a real number. Then $f(x_1, x_2)$ is a *function*. For example, $y = (x_1 x_2)^2$ assigns a single number to a pair of numbers (x_1, x_2). When $f(x_1, x_2)$ takes more than one value, it becomes a *correspondence*.

16.3.1 Continuity

Let us denote $x = (x_1, x_2)$ and $a = (a_1, a_2)$. A function $f(x)$ is continuous at $x = a$ if $f(x) \to f(a)$ as $x \to a$, or $\lim_{x \to a} f(x) = f(a)$. $f(.)$ is continuous if it is continuous at all $x \in X$. In other words, a continuous function should not have a break or jump.

An alternative way of defining continuity is to use a weaker notion of continuity that allows some discontinuity or jump. $f(x)$ is right-continuous at $x = a$ if $f(x) \to f(a)$ when x approaches a from right (i.e., from values higher than a). Similarly, $f(x)$ is left-continuous at $x = a$ if $f(x) \to f(a)$ when x approaches a from left (i.e., from values lower than a). In the following example, y_1 is left-continuous and y_2 is right-continuous:

$$y_1 = \begin{cases} x & \text{if } x \in [0,1] \\ 2x & \text{if } x \in (1,2] \end{cases}, \qquad y_2 = \begin{cases} x & \text{if } x \in [0,1) \\ 2x & \text{if } x \in [1,2] \end{cases}.$$

On the left, $y_1 = x$ when $x \to 1$ from the left (note the closed interval of x), and on the right, $y_2 = 2x$ when $x \to 1$ from the right. A function is continuous at $x = a$ if it is both left- and right-continuous.

A similar idea is *lower and upper semi-continuity*, which allows a drop or jump in addition to retaining the left- and right-continuity. Lower semi-continuity allows a sudden drop, while upper semi-continuity allows a sudden jump. A left-continuous function is also lower semi-continuous and a right-continuous function is upper semicontinuous. Here are two examples. The left one is lower semi-continuous (y_3), and the right one is upper semi-continuous.

$$y_3 = \begin{cases} x & \text{if } x \in [0,1) \\ 1/2 & \text{if } x = 1 \\ 2x & \text{if } x \in (1,2] \end{cases}, \qquad y_4 = \begin{cases} x & \text{if } x \in [0,1) \\ 3 & \text{if } x = 1 \\ 2x & \text{if } x \in (1,2] \end{cases}.$$

A function is *monotonic* if it is decreasing or increasing. If $f(x)$ is also continuous and differentiable, then monotonicity of $f(x)$ implies $f'(x) > 0$ or $f'(x) < 0$ at all x. If $x = (x_1, x_2)$ and the first derivative of $f(x_1, x_2)$ with respect to x_i is positive, that is, $\partial f(x_1, x_2)/\partial x_i \equiv f_i(.) > 0$, $i = 1, 2$, then $f(x_1, x_2)$ is said to be monotonically increasing in x_i. While monotonicity tells us about the effect of a change in one variable (when there are many variables), it does not tell us the effect of changing all variables at the same time. We then need to look at the homogeneity property of the function.

16.3.2 Homogeneous functions

Function $f(x_1, x_2)$ is a homogeneous function if for a scalar $\lambda > 0$ we have $f(\lambda x_1, \lambda x_2) = \lambda^r f(x_1, x_2)$, where r is the degree of homogeneity. For example, $f(x_1, x_2) = x_1 x_2$ is homogeneous of degree 2. Check $f(\lambda x_1, \lambda x_2) = \lambda^2 x_1 x_2$. $f(x_1, x_2) = \sqrt{x_1 x_2}$ is homogeneous of degree 1. However, $f(x_1, x_2) = x_1 x_2 + c$ is not a homogeneous function.

In economics, homogeneous functions recur frequently, and they are very useful for having some interesting properties:

1. If $f(x_1, x_2)$ is homogeneous of degree r, then its first derivatives are homogeneous of degree $r-1$, and by corollary, the second derivatives are homogeneous of degree $r-2$.
2. If $f(x_1, x_2)$ is homogeneous, then the ratio of its two first derivatives, $\frac{f_1(.)}{f_2(.)}$, is homogeneous of degree 0, which means $\frac{f_1(.)}{f_2(.)}$ is a function of the ratio $\frac{x_1}{x_2}$ only.
3. If $f(x_1, x_2)$ is homogeneous of degree r_1 and $g(x_1, x_2)$ is homogeneous of degree r_2, then $f(.)g(.)$ is homogeneous of degree $r_1 + r_2$, and $f(.)/g(.)$ is homogeneous of degree $r_1 - r_2$. But $f(.) + g(.)$ or $f(.) - g(.)$ is not a homogeneous function unless $r_1 = r_2$.
4. **(Euler's theorem)** If $f(x_1, x_2)$ is homogeneous of degree r, then $f_1(.)x_1 + f_2(.)x_2 = rf(x_1, x_2)$. To see this, let us write

   $$f(\lambda x_1, \lambda x_2) = \lambda^r f(x_1, x_2).$$

   Differentiate the preceding on both sides with respect to λ and obtain

   $$f_1(\lambda x_1, \lambda x_2)\frac{\partial \lambda x_1}{\partial \lambda} + f_2(\lambda x_1, \lambda x_2)\frac{\partial \lambda x_2}{\partial \lambda} = r\lambda^{r-1} f(x_1, x_2)$$

   or $$f_1(\lambda x_1, \lambda x_2)x_1 + f_2(\lambda x_1, \lambda x_2)x_2 = r\lambda^{r-1} f(x_1, x_2).$$

   Since $f_1(.)$ and $f_2(.)$ are homogeneous of degree $r-1$, we can substitute in the earlier $f_1(\lambda x_1, \lambda x_2) = \lambda^{r-1} f_1(x_1, x_2)$ and $f_2(\lambda x_1, \lambda x_2) = \lambda^{r-1} f_2(x_1, x_2)$ and then cancel out λ^{r-1} from both sides to get $f_1(.)x_1 + f_2(.)x_2 = rf(x_1, x_2)$.

16.3.3 Homothetic functions

If function $g(x_1,x_2)$ is a positive monotonic (i.e., order preserving) transformation of a homogeneous function $f(x_1,x_2)$, then $g(x_1,x_2)$ is called a homothetic function. For example, $g(x_1,x_2)=c+f(x_1,x_2)$ is homothetic but not homogeneous. $g(x_1,x_2)$ shares the same derivative properties as $f(x_1,x_2)$; specifically, $g_1(.)/g_2(.)$ is a function of only x_1/x_2 ratio.

16.3.4 Implicit function theorem

Consider an implicit function $f(x;a)=0$. Can we write x as a function of a? The answer is yes, if the implicit function theorem is satisfied. Suppose there is a function $x(a)$ such that $f(x(a);a)\equiv 0$. Then we can write $\frac{\partial f(.)}{\partial x}x'(a)+\frac{\partial f(.)}{\partial a}=0$, from which $x'(a)=-\frac{\partial f(.)/\partial a}{\partial f(.)/\partial x}$ holds.

Clearly, $x'(a)$ exists only if $\partial f(.)/\partial x\neq 0$. Then we can find $x(a)$ by integrating over $x'(a)$. But note that while the condition $\partial f/\partial x\neq 0$ is necessary for the existence of $x'(a)$, it is not necessary for the existence of $x(a)$. The function $x(a)$ does not have to be differentiable. Therefore, we can treat $\partial f/\partial x\neq 0$ as a sufficient condition. An example of sufficiency is $f(x;a)=(x-a)^2$, where $f_x=2(x-a)=0$ at $x=a$, yet we can obtain a function $x=a$.

Consider the following system of implicit equations:

$$f_1(x_1,x_2;a_1)=0 \quad f_2(x_1,x_2;a_2)=0,$$

where $f_1(.)$ and $f_2(.)$ are continuous and differentiable. Then if

$$\begin{vmatrix} f_{11} & f_{12} \\ f_{21} & f_{22} \end{vmatrix}\neq 0,$$

there exists a neighbourhood $(x_1^0,x_2^0;a_1^0,a_2^0)$ such that in that neighbourhood for every (a_1,a_2), there is a unique (x_1,x_2), and we can write $x_1=x_1(a_1,a_2)$ and $x_2=x_2(a_1;a_2)$, satisfying

$$f_1(x_1(a_1,a_2),x_2(a_1,a_2);a_1)\equiv 0 \text{ and } f_2(x_1(a_1,a_2),x_2(a_1,a_2);a_2)\equiv 0.$$

The condition is easily generalised to n variables and n equations.

16.3.5 Concave, convex, quasi-concave and quasi-convex functions

Concavity and convexity of functions relate to their curvatures or second-order derivatives. We consider four such functions: concave, convex, quasi-concave and quasi-convex. Each gives rise to two types of definitions—global and local.

16.3.5.1 Global definitions

We begin with the global definition of concavity:

1. A function $f(x)$ is globally **concave** if for any x, x' and $0\leq\lambda\leq 1$

$$f(\lambda x+(1-\lambda)x')\geq\lambda f(x)+(1-\lambda)f(x'). \tag{16.1}$$

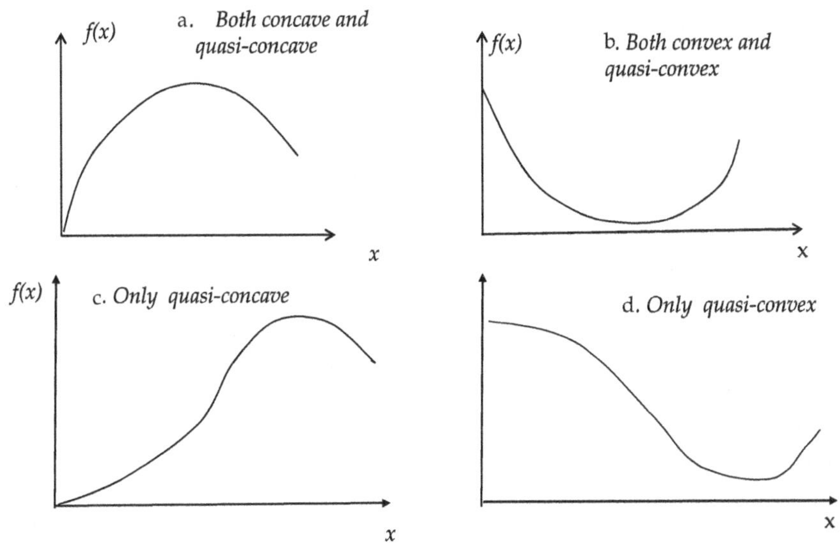

Figure 16.1 One-variable case

For **strict concavity**, we have

$$f\left(\lambda x+(1-\lambda)x'\right) > \lambda f(x)+(1-\lambda)f(x') \text{ for } 0<\lambda<1.$$

Panel *a* of Figure 16.1 shows a concave function, which is also quasi-concave (see the later discussion about quasi-concavity). For the two-variable case, the function $f(x_1,x_2)$ is (globally) concave if for any (x_1,x_2), (x_1',x_2') and $0\le\lambda\le1$,

$$f\left(\lambda x_1+(1-\lambda)x_1', \lambda x_2+(1-\lambda)x_2'\right)\ge \lambda f(x_1,x_2)+(1-\lambda)f(x_1',x_2').$$

Examples of a concave function are $f(.)=\sqrt{x}$, $f(.)=\ln x$, $f(.)=x_1^{\frac{1}{4}}x_2^{\frac{1}{2}}$.

2. A function $f(x)$ is globally **convex** if for any x, x' and $0\le\lambda\le1$

$$f\left(\lambda x+(1-\lambda)x'\right)\le \lambda f(x)+(1-\lambda)f(x'). \tag{16.2}$$

Panel *b* of Figure 16.1 shows a convex function. For the two-variable case, the function $f(x_1,x_2)$ is convex if for any (x_1,x_2), (x_1',x_2') and $0\le\lambda\le1$,

$$f\left(\lambda x_1+(1-\lambda)x_1', \lambda x_2+(1-\lambda)x_2'\right)\le \lambda f(x_1,x_2)+(1-\lambda)f(x_1',x_2')$$

Examples of a convex function are $f(.)=x^2$, $f(.)=1-\ln x$, $f(.)=x_1^{\frac{3}{4}}x_2^{\frac{1}{2}}$.

3. Sometimes we have functions that are, in part, concave and, in part, convex in the manner shown in Figure 16.1 panel *c*. Such functions are called quasi-concave functions. A function $f(x)$ is globally **quasi-concave** if for any x, x' and $0\le\lambda\le1$

$$f\left(\lambda x+(1-\lambda)x'\right)\ge \min\left[f(x), f(x')\right]. \tag{16.3}$$

For strict quasi-concavity the inequality in Eq. (16.3) will be strict. For the two-variable case, the definition of quasi-concavity is modified accordingly as

$$f\left(\lambda x_1+(1-\lambda)x_1',\lambda x_2+(1-\lambda)x_2'\right)\geq \min\left[f(x_1,x_2),f(x_1',x_2')\right].$$

Quasi-concave functions assume greater relevance in the two-variable case (or the n-variable case in general). They are very important for utility and (sometimes) production functions. Note that the function in part looks like a dome, which tells us something more.

Imagine you are standing inside a round-shaped dome. The height of the dome can be thought of as a quasi-concave function of the breadth and width of the floor. If you were to engage in an imaginary act of horizontally slicing off this dome from the top as thinly as possible, you will get many thin concentric circles. The smallest circle will come from the peak of the dome and the largest circle from the base of the dome. Each of these circles is nothing but an **upper contour set**. Pick a circle that gives height a. Then that circle contains all points that give height a on the circumference and greater than a at all interior points. Note that the circle is a convex set. Thus, what we just learnt is that for a quasi-concave function, *its upper contour sets are convex*. You have seen graphs of quasi-concave functions in Chapter 2.

From the example of the dome, it is clear that the same thought experiment can be applied to pyramids, oval-shaped objects, tower blocks and the like. Their height and shape can be described by a quasi-concave function.

4. A function $f(x)$ is **quasi-convex** if $-f(x)$ is quasi-concave. That is to say, $f(x)$ is quasi-convex if for x, x' and $0\leq\lambda\leq 1$

$$f\left(\lambda x+(1-\lambda)x'\right)\leq \max\left[f(x),f(x')\right]. \tag{16.4}$$

For the two-variable case, the definition of quasi-convexity is

$$f\left(\lambda x_1+(1-\lambda)x_1',\lambda x_2+(1-\lambda)x_2'\right)\leq \max\left[f(x_1,x_2),f(x_1',x_2')\right].$$

In Figures 16.2 and 16.3, we have drawn two quasi-convex functions, one for a downward-sloping and the other for an upward-sloping function. In both cases, the lower contour set is convex. Remember that if $f(x)$ is quasi-convex, then $-f(x)$ is quasi-concave. Then the upper contour set of $-f(x)$ is convex, which means the lower contour set of $f(x)$ is convex.

5. It is to be noted when $f(x)$ is a one-variable function and monotonic then it is both quasi-concave and quasi-convex. If $f(x)$ is a function of more than one variable, then they cannot be both at the same time (except in the special case of weak quasi-concavity). However, a function can be neither.

Some relationships between concavity and quasi-concavity and between convexity and quasiconvexity are worth noting. A concave function is also a quasi-concave function. Similarly, a convex function is also a quasi-convex function, but the converse is not true.

$$f\left(\lambda x+(1-\lambda)x'\right)\geq \lambda f(x)+(1-\lambda)f(x')\geq \min\left[f(x),f(x')\right],$$

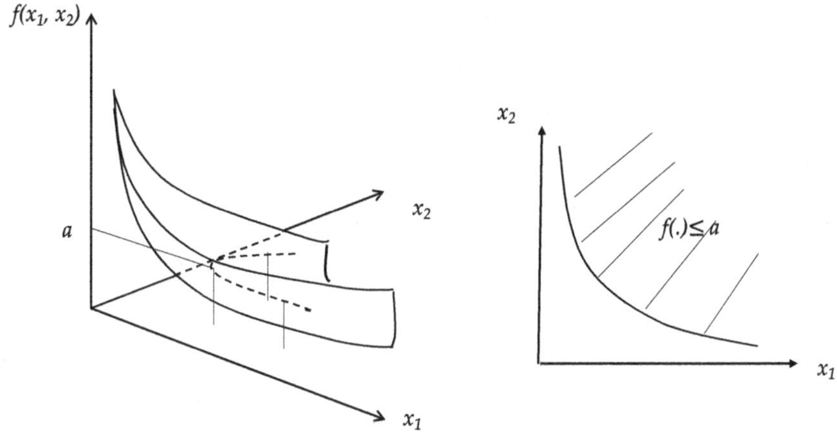

a. *Quasi-convex function* b. *Convex lower contour set*

Figure 16.2 Downward-sloping quasi-convex function of two variables

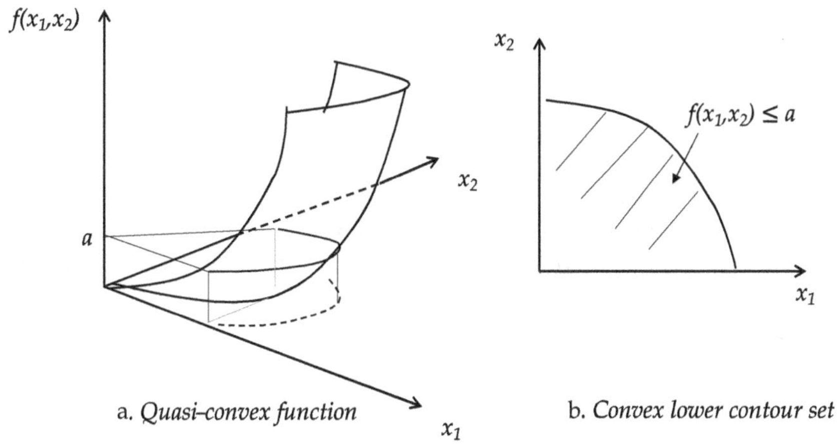

a. *Quasi-convex function* b. *Convex lower contour set*

Figure 16.3 Upward-sloping quasi-convex function of two variables

and

$$f\left(\lambda x+(1-\lambda)x'\right)\leq\lambda f(x)+(1-\lambda)f(x')\leq\max\left[f(x),f(x')\right].$$

16.3.5.2 *Local definitions of concavity and convexity*

When a function is not concave or quasi-concave everywhere, we need to check if it is locally concave or quasi-concave. That also means that the condition needs to be stated in terms of second derivatives.

If $f(x)$ is (locally) **concave** (at some point x^0), then $f''(x^0) \leq 0$. For strict concavity, $f''(x^0) < 0$. Alternatively, $f(x)$ is **convex** at point x^0 if $f''(x^0) \geq 0$. That is to say, for a concave function, the value of $f(.)$ *increases at a decreasing rate* (or decreases at an increasing rate). For a convex function, the value of $f(.)$ *increases at an increasing rate* (or decreases at a decreasing rate). See Figure 16.1 panels a and b.

The preceding conditions can be generalised to n variables. For a function $f(x_1, x_2, \ldots, x_n)$, consider the following matrix consisting of all second-order own- and cross-partial derivatives obtained at some vector $(x_1^0, x_2^0, \ldots, x_n^0)$. This is called the Hessian matrix of $f(.)$.

$$H = \begin{bmatrix} f_{11} & f_{12} & \cdots & f_{1n} \\ f_{21} & f_{22} & \cdots & f_{2n} \\ \cdot & \cdot & \cdots & \cdot \\ f_{n1} & f_{n2} & \cdots & f_{nn} \end{bmatrix}$$

1. **Strict concavity:** The function $f(.)$is **strictly concave** if the determinants of the principal minors of the matrix H alternate in sign starting from negative. In other words, H must be a negative definite matrix. Applying the negative definiteness of H we state the condition for $n = 2$ as

$$f_{11} < 0, \quad \begin{vmatrix} f_{11} & f_{12} \\ f_{21} & f_{22} \end{vmatrix} > 0.$$

   For **concavity,** the signs will be modified as weak inequalities.
2. **Strict convexity:** The function $f(.)$ is **strictly convex** if the determinants of the principal minors of the matrix H are all **positive**. That is to say, H should be a positive definite matrix. In the two-variable case,

$$f_{11} > 0, \quad \begin{vmatrix} f_{11} & f_{12} \\ f_{21} & f_{22} \end{vmatrix} > 0.$$

3. **Strict quasi-concavity:** For quasi-concave and quasi-convex functions, the conditions need to be stated in terms of the bordered Hessian matrix H_B. It does not matter where we place the border at the beginning or at the end.

$$H_B = \begin{bmatrix} f_{11} & f_{12} & \cdots & f_{1n} & f_1 \\ f_{21} & f_{22} & \cdots & f_{2n} & f_2 \\ \cdot & \cdot & \cdots & \cdot & \cdot \\ f_{n1} & f_{n2} & \cdots & f_{nn} & f_n \\ f_1 & f_2 & \cdots & f_n & 0 \end{bmatrix}$$

   The matrix H_B should be negative definite. Now consider border-preserving principal minors starting from the top-left corner of the big matrix and then adding one row and one column at a time (while extending the border as well). Determinants of the border-preserving principal minors should alternate in sign starting from positive. In the n-variable case, the last sign should be positive if n is even and negative if n is odd.

$$\begin{vmatrix} f_{11} & f_{12} & f_1 \\ f_{21} & f_{22} & f_2 \\ f_1 & f_2 & 0 \end{vmatrix} > 0, \begin{vmatrix} f_{11} & f_{12} & f_{13} & f_1 \\ f_{21} & f_{22} & f_{23} & f_2 \\ f_{31} & f_{32} & f_{33} & f_3 \\ f_1 & f_2 & f_3 & 0 \end{vmatrix} < 0, \ldots\ldots$$

4. **Strict quasi-convexity:** For strictly quasi-convex functions, H_B is required to be positive definite. The signs of the preceding determinants should be all negative.

16.4 Maximum and minimum

In economics, we solve unconstrained, as well as constrained, maximisation problems. If $F(x_1, x_2)$ is to be maximised (without constraint), then in addition to the first-order conditions

$$F_1(x_1, x_2) = 0, F_2(x_1; x_2) = 0,$$

we need to ensure the second-order condition $x'\left[F_{ij}\right]x < 0$ for $x \neq 0$, which means that the matrix Hessian matrix $\left[F_{ij}\right]$ must be negative definite, where

$$\left[F_{ij}\right] = \begin{bmatrix} F_{11} & F_{12} \\ F_{21} & F_{22} \end{bmatrix}.$$

For unconstrained minimisation, $\left[F_{ij}\right]$ should be a positive definite matrix. When there is a constraint in the form of $w_1x_1 + w_2x_2 = k$ to the maximisation or minimisation problem of $F(x_1, x_2)$, the second-order condition reduces to verifying that the following bordered Hessian matrix

$$\begin{bmatrix} F_{11} & F_{12} & \cdots & F_{1n} & F_1 \\ F_{21} & F_{22} & \cdots & F_{2n} & F_2 \\ \cdots & \cdots & \cdots & \cdots & \cdots \\ F_{n1} & F_{n2} & \cdots & F_{nn} & F_n \\ F_1 & F_2 & \cdots & F_n & 0 \end{bmatrix}$$

is negative definite for constrained maximisation and positive definite for constrained minimisation. Then the conditions for negative and positive definiteness of a bordered Hessian matrix will apply.

16.4.1 *Envelope theorem*

Suppose $F = F(x; a)$ is maximised (or minimised) at $x = x^*$. Then $x^* = x(a)$ is a (local) maximum, and $F^*(a) = F(x^*(a); a)$ is the maximal value of the function, which continuously varies with a. Note that continuity of $F^*(a)$ does not depend on the continuity of $x^*(a)$; rather, it is a result of optimisation. $F^*(a)$ is the minimal value of F when $F(.)$ is minimised.

We want to know how $F^*(a)$ varies if a changes. The envelope theorem says that regardless of $F^*(a)$ being a maximal or minimal value,

$$F^{*\prime}(a) = \frac{\partial F(.)}{\partial a} + \frac{\partial F(.)}{\partial x}\frac{\partial x^*(.)}{\partial a} = \frac{\partial F(.)}{\partial a},$$

since by the first-order condition of maximisation (or minimisation) $\partial F(.)/\partial x = 0$. This remarkably powerful result follows from the fact that the other effect of changing a that occurs through x is washed away because of optimisation. The only effect that remains is the direct effect of a on the function F. Note that the envelope theorem predicts not only the direction of change in $F^*(.)$ but also the magnitude of the change. We have used and proved the envelope theorem for Roy's identity and Shephard's lemma. You may refer to the relevant chapters.

16.4.2 Curvature of the value function

We can easily ascertain the curvature of the value function (or the second-derivative property) of the value function under both constrained and unconstrained optimisation. See Table 16.1.

First, consider the unconstrained case. Suppose $F(x;a)$ is being maximised. The value function is $F^*(x(a);a)$ and consider two values of it at a and a'. Take a convex combination of a and a', and call it $a^* = \lambda a + (1-\lambda)a'$. Then, by definition, $F^*\left(x\left(a^*\right);a^*\right) = \max F\left(x;a^*\right)$. But this must be less than $\lambda\left[\max F(x;a)\right] + (1-\lambda)\left[\max F(x;a')\right] = \lambda F^*\left(x(a) + (1-\lambda)F^*(a'\right)$, because the latter is a weighted average of two maxima, whereas the former is a maximum for a weighted average. Therefore, $F^*(x(a);a)$ is a convex function of a.

A similar argument running in the opposite direction proves that $F^*(x(a);a)$ is a concave function when $F(x;a)$ is minimised without a constraint.

16.4.2.1 Constrained maximisation

For the constrained case, we provide a graphical proof. First, take constrained maximisation, and let us specify the problem as

$$\max\ F(x_1, x_2), \text{subject to } a_1x_1 + a_2x_2 = m.$$

The problem resembles utility maximisation. See Figure 16.4 panel a. Here, at $a = (a_1, a_2)$, the constraint is denoted by the line $C(a_1, a_2)$; that is, $C(a_1, a_2) = a_1x_1 + a_2x_2 - m = 0$. Suppose the optimal choice occurs at point A. Similarly, at $a' = (a_1', a_2')$ when the constraint is $C(a_1', a_2')$ the choice is at point B. Thus, $x(a)$ gives rise to $F^*(x(a);a)$ and $x(a')$ gives rise to $F^*(x(a');a')$.

Table 16.1 Value function $F^*(a_1, a_2)$

	Unconstrained	*Constrained*
Maximisation	Convex	Quasi-convex
Minimisation	Concave	Concave

Now let us take a convex combination of a and a', namely $a^* = \lambda a + (1-\lambda)a'$, for some $0 < \lambda < 1$. Then the constraint line $C(a_1^*, a_2^*)$ must be between the two constraint lines and pass through their intersection point as shown in the graph. The optimal solution must be either at a point like C, in which case $F^*\left(x\left(a^*\right);a^*\right) < F^*\left(x(a);a\right)$, or at a point like C', in which case $F^*\left(x\left(a^*\right);a^*\right) < F^*\left(x(a');a'\right)$.

Combining the two relations, we get $F^*\left(x\left(a^*\right);a^*\right) < \max\left\{F^*\left(x(a);a\right), F^*\left(x(a');a'\right)\right\}$. This means that $F\left(x(a);a\right)$ is a quasi-convex function.

16.4.2.2 Constrained minimisation

For constrained minimisation, consider the problem (like cost minimisation):

$$\min C = a_1 x_1 + a_2 x_2, \text{ subject to } f(x_1, x_2) = k.$$

Consider panel *b* of Figure 16.4. Given the constraint, solution at a occurs at point A giving rise to the value function $C(a) = C(a_1, a_2)$, which is a straight line. Similarly, at a', the solution is at point B, where the value function is $C(a_1', a_2')$. By construction, $a_1 > a_1', a_2 < a_2'$ and $C(a) < C(a')$.

Now consider a convex combination of a and a'. Take $a^* = \lambda a + (1-\lambda)a' = (\lambda a_1 + (1-\lambda)a_2, \lambda a_2 + (1-\lambda)a_2')$. Consider a convex combination of the two value lines $C(a)$ and $C(a')$, which must travel through their intersection point. We call it $\tilde{C} = \lambda C(a) + (1-\lambda)C(a')$, which corresponds to a^* but may not be optimal. In fact, it is not. It is clear that $\tilde{C}$ cannot meet the constraint $f(x_1, x_2) = k$. Therefore, C must be raised to reach the optimal point D as shown in the graph. Since the solution D corresponds to a^*, the value function at D is $C\left(a^*\right)$. Therefore, we have $C\left(\lambda a + (1-\lambda)a'\right) > \lambda C(a) + (1-\lambda)C(a')$; that is, $C(a)$ is concave. □

16.5 Fixed-point theorems

Previously we have defined what a function is. A distinctive feature of a function is that for every $x \in X$, $f(x)$ takes a unique value. But sometimes $f(x)$ may take more than one value. For example, the following is a correspondence, because $f(x) = \{1, 2\}$ at $x = 1$:

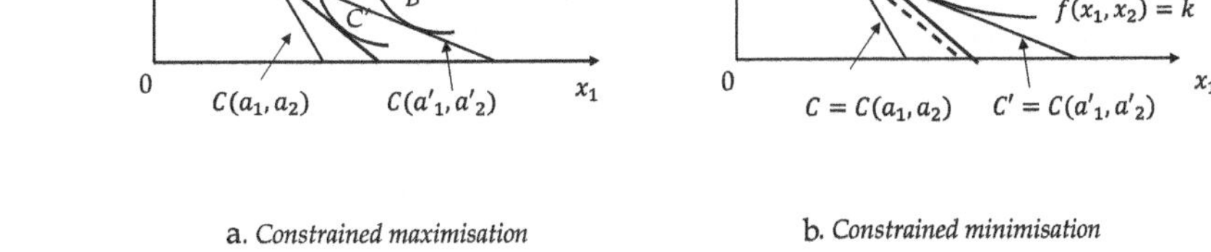

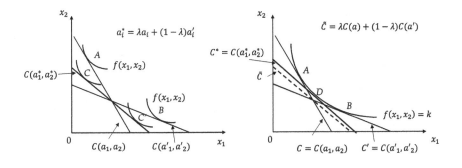

a. *Constrained maximisation*

b. *Constrained minimisation*

Figure 16.4 Constrained maximisation and minimisation

$$f(x)=\begin{cases} x & \text{if} \quad x\in[0,1] \\ 2x & \text{if} \quad x\in[1,2] \end{cases}.$$

In general, a correspondence is itself a set, as is the case when $X \subset R^2, Y \subset R^2$ and $f(x): X \to Y$. The notion of continuity here is based on the notion of lower and upper hemi-continuity. Upper hemi-conitunity means that the set $f(x)$ should be closed at every x, which is equivalent to saying that $f(x)$ should have a closed graph. In the previous example, $f(x)$ is closed everywhere including at $x = 1$.

Lower hemi-continuity, by comparison, insists on the following. Consider a sequence $x^n \in X$ that converges to $x \in X$. Find the set $f(x)$, and for every $y \in f(x)$, find a sequence y^n that converges to y such that $y^n \in f(x^n)$ for n greater than some integer K. If this holds for every convergent sequence x^n, then $f(x)$ is lower hemi-continuous. Roughly speaking, if x^n converges to x, then every element of the set $f(x)$ must be a limit of some sequence in the set Y. As discontinuity in the environment of correspondence appears in the form of a sudden expansion or contraction of the image set (i.e., $f(x)$), upper hemi-continuity permits sudden expansion, while lower hemi-continuity permits sudden contraction.

Our example given earlier is also lower hemi-continuous. A correspondence is continuous if it is both upper hemi-continuous and lower hemi-continuous.

For the existence of equilibrium such as in game theory or general equilibrium, the notion of correspondence may be very relevant. There are two fixed-point theorems that are commonly used, one relies on function and the other on correspondence.

16.5.1 Brouwer's fixed-point theorem

Suppose $f: X \to X \subset R^n$ is a continuous function from X onto itself, and X is a non-empty, compact and convex set. Then there exists a fixed point such that $f(x) = x$. Note we are calling $f(.)$ a function despite $f(.) \in R^n$ because in this case, $f(x)$ is a vector of single-valued functions. Therefore, it can be called a function. We do not need to use correspondence here.

Proving the theorem is complex for $n \geq 2$. For $n = 1$, the theorem is simple. Suppose $X = [0,1]$, which is compact and convex. Since $f(x)$ is continuous and the range of $f(x)$ is also $[0,1]$, then $f(x) \geq 0$ and $f(x) \leq 1$. Therefore, by the intermediate value theorem, there exists a x^* such that $f(x^*) = x^*$.

16.5.2 The Kakutani fixed-point theorem

Suppose $X \subset R^n$ is non-empty, compact and convex, and $f: X \to X$ is an upper hemi-continuous correspondence, such that $f(x) \subset X, f(x)$ is non-empty and convex for every $x \in X$. Then there exists an $x \in X$ such that $x \in f(x)$.

Intuitively, $x \in f(x)$ is the set equivalent of $x = f(x)$. Here, the convexity of $f(x)$ is important. If $f(x)$ is not convex everywhere, then $x \in f(x)$ is not guaranteed, because $f(x)$ may contain values greater or smaller than x but not x; convexity rules it out.

Further readings

Chiang, A. C. (1984). *Fundamental Methods of Mathematical Economics*, 3rd ed. New York: McGraw-Hill.

Dixit, A. (1990). *Optimization in Economic Theory*, 2nd ed. New York: Oxford University Press.

Henderson, J. H. & Quandt, R. E. (1980). *Microeconomic Theory: A Mathematical Approach*. Singapore: McGraw-Hill.

Index

Note: Page numbers in *italics* indicate a figure on the corresponding page.